AN INTRODUCTION TO FINANCIAL MANAGEMENT

Second Edition

Ezra Solomon

Dean Witter Professor of Finance
Stanford University

John J. Pringle

Professor of Finance
University of North Carolina at Chapel Hill

Goodyear Publishing Company, Inc.
Santa Monica, California

To our children

Library of Congress Cataloging in Publication Data

Solomon, Ezra.
   An introduction to financial management.

   Includes bibliographies and index.
   1. Business enterprises—Finance.   2. Corporations—
Finance.   I. Pringle, John J., joint author.
II. Title.
HG4026.s66   1980   658.1′5   79-26623
ISBN 0-87620-475-2

Copyright 1980 © by Goodyear Publishing Company, Inc.
Santa Monica, California

Library of Congress Catalog Card Number: 79-26623
ISBN: 0-87620-475-2
Y-4752-2
Current Printing (last number):   10 9 8 7 6 5 4 3 2 1
Printed in the United States of America

Acquisitions editor: Robert "Chip" Price
Production manager: Suzanne Knott
Production coordination: Jean Varven
Composition: Interactive Composition Corp. and Typothetae

Contents

III TIME, RISK, AND VALUE

IV ANALYZING INVESTMENT OPPORTUNITIES

VI   SPECIAL TOPICS IN FINANCIAL MANAGEMENT

Preface

The theme and basic objective of this book remain the same. We continue to view financial management as applied microeconomics in a business policy context. The firm's goals give rise to its commercial strategy, which prescribes the appropriate investment policy. Financing policies then are tailored to fit. The student is encouraged to view financial management decisions as part of a broader management process. Throughout, the viewpoint is managerial rather than technical.

As was the first edition, this edition is addressed specifically to beginning students of financial management. Our major objective is to provide a sound conceptual framework within which a wide variety of financial management decisions can be analyzed. Emphasis is placed on concepts and understanding as well as on techniques and skills and on the limitations of theories and models along with their uses.

Those familiar with our first edition will note that this is a very substantial revision. New material has been added to reflect major recent developments in theory and empirical work. We have also tried, as much as possible, to incorporate the many helpful suggestions of users and reviewers of the first edition. The most important changes in this edition are described below.

In the first edition, we departed from the tradition of using the firm's weighted average cost of capital as the central organizing concept for investment and financing decisions. Instead of *cost of capital*, we used the label *required rate of return* and developed an approach to capital budgeting around the capital asset pricing model. We have continued that approach in this edition but have included (by popular demand!) a full discussion of the weighted average cost of capital in a new Chapter 15. In addition, the material on setting return targets (Chapter 14) has been completely rewritten and simplified. Those who want a more technical treatment can turn to the material on the capital asset pricing model and the impact of financing mix on capital investment covered in Chapter 15.

Several other chapters also have been substantially revised and new chapters added. The chapter on discounted cash flow (9) has been completely rewritten and expanded. A new chapter (10) on valuation and the capital asset pricing model has been added. Parts of Chapter 18 have been rewritten to include recent theory and empirical work on capital structure. A new part, Part VI, has been added that includes chapters on international financial management and on mergers and acquisitions.

We have added material throughout the book to provide more help for students and instructors. Sample problems, with solutions and narrative, are provided at the ends of chapters that require problem work. In addition, the number of end-of-chapter problems has been substantially increased. Many parts of the book have been rewritten to simplify and improve it, and a large number of real-life examples have been added to the textual material. The entire book has been updated throughout to include changes that have occurred since 1976 in the field of financial management.

There are many ways to teach financial management and hence a number of alternative sequences for using this book. Our own preference is to take material in the order presented in the table of contents. An alternative sequence that may be preferred by some instructors is to proceed from Part I directly to Part III, taking up valuation early in the course. A special introduction to Part III is provided to facilitate this sequencing. Instructors following this sequence then would have the option of returning to Part II (current operations), or proceeding through Parts IV and V (investment and financing decisions) and then returning to Part II. The four principal parts of the book, II, III, IV, V, are arranged so that they can be taken in any one of several sequences. Part VI, special topics, normally would be taken up last.

A good grounding in basic financial accounting is an essential prerequisite. A course in basic microeconomics would be helpful but is not essential. Except for Chapter 15, the second edition does not require a background in probability theory. For those who cover Chapter 15, a brief appendix on probability concepts is included at the end of the book.

Our package of supplementary materials has been expanded and improved. An instructor's manual is available to adopters of the book. It includes our commentary on each chapter, answers to questions, and solutions to end-of-chapter problems. Transparencies can be prepared directly from the problem solutions. In addition, transparency masters of selected charts and tables from the book are included. Also in the instructor's manual are test questions for each chapter prepared by Russell P. Biosjoly and Severin C. Carlson of the University of Maryland.

Available for student use is a very helpful study guide by John A. Halloran and Howard P. Lanser of the University of Notre Dame. For instructors wishing to assign cases, a companion casebook is available, *Cases in Introductory Finance,* by Michael Rice and John J. Pringle.

Although many improvements have been made in this edition, opportunities for still further improvements undoubtedly exist. As before, we will be grateful to users for bringing these to our attention.

Ezra Solomon
John J. Pringle

Acknowledgments

In the preface to the first edition, we asked users to give us their suggestions for improving the book. Many did so, and we have revised the book extensively in order to incorporate the many thoughtful suggestions we received. We would like to thank especially the following people who read and reviewed the manuscript for the first and second editions: Gordon R. Bonner, University of Delaware; Severin C. Carlson, University of Maryland; Richard F. Demong, University of Virginia; M. Chapman Findlay, University of Southern California; Roger A. Formisano, University of Wisconsin; David W. Glenn, University of Utah; Irwin Harvey, University of Georgia; Hugh Hobson, Loyola University in New Orleans; Ron E. Hutchins, Eastern Michigan University; James Kehr, Miami University, John H. Lewis, Stephen F. Austin State University; Surendra K. Mansinghka, San Francisco State University; Sheldon Novack, Widener University; William L. Sartoris, Indiana University; Herbert T. Spiro, California State University at Northridge; Charles E. Wade, Texas Technical University; Robert Wood, Pennsylvania State University; and Kent Zumwalt, University of Illinois.

The many responses to a survey conducted by the publisher were a great help in planning the new edition. In particular we would like to thank the following individuals: Sheldon Balbirer, University of North Carolina at Greensboro; Stuart Bancroft, Pacific Lutheran University; Stanley Bodalski, St. Joseph's College; Carl Chen, University of Dayton; James Clay, Slippery Rock State College; Maclyn Clouse, University of

Denver; Rust Gray, Wright State University; John Harbell, San Francisco State University; Dale Johnson, University of South Florida; William Lane, Louisiana State University; Andrew McCollough, University of Florida; Vince Mercurio, San Diego State University; George Moody, West Virginia University; Peter Rosko, University of Minnesota; Fred Scherr, West Virginia University; and Daniel Vellenga, University of Denver.

As do all authors of textbooks, we owe an intellectual debt to those who have contributed to the rapid developments in the theory of financial management over the past 20 years. Any attempt to acknowledge specific contributions would leave us at a loss as to where to draw the line. Specific works are cited in the text where doing so seemed useful to instructors and students and key references are provided at the end of each chapter.

We are grateful also to our colleagues at Stanford, The University of North Carolina, and elsewhere who have contributed ideas and influenced our thinking on the subject of financial management.

Finally, we wish to thank those who contributed directly to the preparation and production of the book. Maria DiMenna, Christina Benson, and David Peterson assisted with end-of-chapter problems and Pamela Peterson with the instructor's manual. Chip Price of Goodyear provided valuable advice in preparation of the manuscript and supplementary materials, and Suzanne Knott took the project from manuscript to finished product.

THE SCOPE AND SETTING OF FINANCIAL MANAGEMENT

I

What Is Financial Management?

1

The Scope of Financial Management
The Role of Firms in a Market Economy
Applying the Profit-Maximization Criterion
Value-Maximization
Financial Management and Larger Goals
Applicability of Financial Management Concepts
A Normative Framework

Financial management is two things: It is an extensive body of professional practice; it is also an academic discipline that spans nearly a century of writing and teaching devoted to what financial management does or should do. Practice and theory have each undergone a process of continuous change and development. Since the late 1950s this process has been an especially lively one, with significant interaction between the two facets of the field.

The Scope of Financial Management

One way we can approach the problem of defining the *scope* of financial management is to examine what practicing "financial managers" do. But we will soon find that this "grass-roots" approach, in itself, will not get us very far. The reason is that in most business organizations there is no single individual who is designated as *the* "financial manager" and who has all the responsibilities of "financial management."

Firms have corporate treasurers and controllers, vice-presidents of finance and chairmen of finance committees, and sometimes all four titles are found within a single enterprise. On the other hand, we may find only one and sometimes none of these titles in the organizational structure of other firms. Yet, in some more fundamental sense, there is always a financial manager, title or no.

Although what we have dubbed a grass-roots approach to the task of defining the scope of the field cannot, in itself, produce a final answer, it does provide two valuable insights:

1. *Responsibility for "financial management" is often highly diffused within a business corporation.* Thus, operating managers frequently have a considerable say in proposing and analyzing investment opportunities that lead to the commitment of corporate funds in plant, equipment, inventory, or acquisitions; central staff groups, sometimes under the treasurer, but just as frequently under the controller or an executive in charge of planning, play a large role in analyzing investment and financing ideas; investment and financing decisions often involve committees of senior officers of the firm and in the case of most major decisions, the board of directors itself.

2. *In addition to being diffused, finance involves a large diversity of actions.* Some of these are better classified as administrative functions incidental to finance rather than as finan-

cial management proper: for example, the receipt, disbursement, and custody of funds and securities; the preparation of confidential payrolls; the supervision of how securities are registered or transferred; the management and payment of various taxes; the negotiation and placement of a myriad of insurance policies. Other functions are more major: for example, the preparation and review of cash budgets, the investment of temporarily idle funds, the hedging of foreign exchange risks, the arrangement of bank credit, supervision of the company's pension funds, the decision to change the company's dividend rate or to float new securities, the task of explaining the company's performance and prospects to groups of financial analysts.

One way to deal with the diversity of actions and decisions would be to examine them, one at a time, and cover each item separately in a handbook. This has been done. But such a compilation is unsuitable to an academic discipline for one simple reason: It produces a subject of bits and pieces and thus obscures the underlying thread of continuity that comprises the very core of what is now an intellectually exciting, difficult, and important field.

An Alternative Approach

An alternative approach to the problem of defining the *scope* of financial management is to isolate the thread of continuity that unites the diffused and diverse set of actions and decisions in which operating financial managers engage (whoever they are and however they are titled). This is what the academic treatment of the field has tried to do. With the passage of time, academic emphasis on what comprises the real core of the finance function has undergone large shifts, driven as much by practitioners as by professors. During this century three major themes have been put forward:

1. From its inception as a separate field of study to around World War II, the unifying theme of finance, as an academic field, was that it should be concerned with the relationships between a corporation and its sources of funds. This concentration on the procurement of funds shaped the content of the field. It covered the financing instruments, institutions, and practices through which a corporation obtained funds in the capital markets and the

accounting and legal relationships between a firm and its sources of financing.[1]

2. After World War II both practitioners and academics came to believe that the "classic" treatment of finance was deficient in several respects. It spent too much of its effort "on the outside looking in" (the viewpoint of the investment banker) rather than "on the inside looking out" (the viewpoint of a financial manager).[2] It gave too much of its attention to the liabilities side of the balance sheet and too little to the asset side. It focused too much on those episodic, but infrequent, phases in the life cycle of a corporation in which external relations are dominant (such as promotion, incorporation, merger, consolidation, recapitalization, and bankruptcy) and far too little on the problems of a normal ongoing company. As a result, the emphasis of the field (and of the practitioner) shifted to what is now called *working capital management*.

3. The third major shift in emphasis and content, which is still going on, began in the late 1950s. This "modern" view that both practitioners and theorists endorse today can be summarized as follows:

   a. Financial management is essentially an extension of the microeconomic theory of the firm. As such, it should deal with the optimal use of resources, especially the financial resources available to a firm.

   b. As an *applied* rather than a *pure* field of study, it should extend the more abstract concepts used in microeconomics into operationally measurable and usable categories. Specifically, it should explicitly incorporate the two key dimensions that distinguish the real world from the world of basic microeconomics, that is, *uncertainty* and *time.*

   c. The proper central theme of the field is the *wise usage* of funds, that is, the mutual determination of the major variables of financial policy: level and type of funds

---

1. The classic work that dominated practice and teaching between the two world wars was Arthur S. Dewing, *The Financial Policy of Corporations* (New York: Ronald Press, successive editions, 1926, 1934, 1941).
2. See Pearson Hunt's review of the 1941 edition of Dewing's book, *Quarterly Journal of Economics* **58**, pp. 303–313.

raised, the level and type of investments made, and the
rate and quality of the growth of a firm.

d. Finally, with the modern redefinition of financial management, the subject has come to be considered an integral part of top management rather than a staff specialty
concerned with administering a company's *sources*
of funds.[3]

To lay the groundwork for a discussion of financial management in
more depth, let us first consider the role of firms in a market economy.

The Role of Firms in a Market Economy

A market economy is one in which goods and services are bought and
sold at prices determined in free and competitive markets. In a market
economy, business firms are the principal agents for the production of
goods and services. In a broad social sense, firms are the stewards of
society's stock of productive resources and are charged with producing
as efficiently as possible the goods and services society desires.

In producing goods and services, firms employ scarce resources,
namely, land, labor, and capital assets. Production and investment requires that society forego consumption opportunities in the present in
order to generate greater consumption opportunities in the future. Resources are employed to produce outputs of greater value, and new value
is created, thereby leading to a steady improvement in average living
standards.

How do firms know what goods and services to produce? What signals do managers use to guide the allocation of scarce resources? Leaving
aside services produced by the government, the answer is that consumers
themselves make the decisions and communicate their wishes to producers via the *price system*. Goods and services valued highly by consumers command higher prices, which in turn result in higher profits for
producers. Other producers are attracted by profit opportunities, and
supplies of the valued goods and services increase. In principle, a point
of equilibrium is reached at which price and profit opportunities are just
sufficient to bring forth the quantity demanded by consumers at that
price. In the jargon of the economist, the equilibrium price is that which
clears the market, or equates supply and demand.

3. For a more comprehensive discussion of the evolution of financial management, see
Ezra Solomon, *The Theory of Financial Management* (New York: Columbia University
Press, 1963). See also J. F. Weston, *The Scope and Methodology of Finance* (Englewood
Cliffs, N.J.: Prentice-Hall, 1966).

In the case of goods and services not highly valued or in oversupply, the process works in reverse. Prices and profits fall, producers drop out to search for better opportunities, and supply decreases.

Managers of firms direct their efforts toward areas of attractive profit potential, using prices as their signals. Those prices are determined in the marketplace by the actions of consumers and firms competing against one another. By means of their buying decisions, consumers send signals that ultimately determine the allocation of scarce resources.

Thus, in a market economy, decisions to produce and consume are guided by prices set in free and competitive markets by the actions of the producers and consumers themselves. A central feature of a market economy is decentralization of decision-making. Decisions with respect to production and consumption are made by millions of economic units acting individually. There is no master plan.

What assurance is there that the outcome of the market process will serve the interests of society as a whole? Two hundred years ago, Adam Smith described the process in these words:

> [The businessman,] by directing . . . industry in such a manner
> as its produce may be of greatest value . . . intends only his own
> gain, and he is in this, as in many other cases, led by an invisible
> hand to promote an end which was not a part of his intention.
> . . . pursuing his own interest he frequently promotes that of
> Society more effectually than when he really intends to pro-
> mote it.[4]

Smith's great insight was that under the proper conditions, mainly free competition, the decisions of entrepreneurs in pursuit of their own individual self-interests lead to an outcome that serves society's interests as well. Smith's "invisible hand" thus provides the rationale for the decentralized market economies of North America, Western Europe, and Japan. Economists who came after Smith have demonstrated that profit-maximizing behavior by individual firms does indeed lead to the efficient use of scarce resources.

Profit-Maximization

Modern microeconomic theory on how the private firm should and does behave is based on profit-maximization as a decision criterion. Actions that increase the firm's profit are undertaken and those that decrease profit are avoided. To maximize profit, the firm must maximize output

---

4. Adam Smith, *The Wealth of Nations,* Cannan ed. (New York: Modern Library, 1937), p. 423. *The Wealth of Nations* was first published in 1776.

for a given set of scarce inputs or, equivalently, minimize the cost of producing a given output. In short, the firm must be *efficient* in its use of resources. Thus, from the perspective of economic theory, profit-maximization is simply a criterion for economic efficiency. When markets are reasonably competitive, profits provide a yardstick by which economic performance can be judged. There is also broad agreement that under idealized conditions (generally referred to as *perfect* competition), where all prices accurately reflect true values and consumers are well informed, profit-maximizing behavior by firms leads to an efficient allocation of resources and maximum social welfare. The goods and services desired by society are produced in the greatest quantity possible given the available stock of productive resources.

Under actual conditions, a system based on profit-maximization has been questioned and criticized on several grounds.

Objections to the Profit-Maximization Criterion

One objection, which is essentially ethical rather than economic, is that a system based on private ownership and profit-maximization might be efficient, but it leads to a serious inequality of income and wealth among different groups. The counterargument is that society as a whole is clearly better off if its production of goods and services is as efficient as possible, that is, if its limited resources are used in ways that provide the level and mix of output that has the highest value to the public. Given this output, society can and does shift the distribution of income and hence of output among different groups through taxes and other forms of policy. For any given set of policies, everyone is better off if the level of output produced is higher rather than lower.

A second form of criticism, associated with Karl Marx's writings, is that a system of private ownership and profit-maximization simply will not work; that is, it will inevitably break down. The counterargument is that it has worked, and although imperfect, it has produced average living standards far higher than those produced by any alternative system that has ever been tried, now or in the past.

A third criticism is that as market economies mature, they begin to produce goods and services that are frivolous, unnecessary, and wasteful. The counterargument is that a market economy is based on the notion of *consumer sovereignty,* and if consumers want frivolous goods and services, the market economy will produce them. Those who judge certain goods and services to be frivolous may be right, but they are suggesting that the wishes and judgments of consumers be countermanded and replaced by their own—a subtle form of dictatorship by a self-appointed elite.

It is difficult to imagine an economic system other than the market economy that is compatible with a political system based on the principles of democracy. Just as all citizens do not agree with all acts of all democratically elected politicians, we cannot expect all to agree with the economic priorities set in a market economy. In both cases, the rule of the majority prevails.

A fourth, and more serious, avenue of criticism is that market prices may not in fact reflect true values. In practice, price competition is perfect in only a few industries and far from perfect in some. Certain cost structures give rise to oligopolies, characterized by small numbers of large firms, or even to monopolies. Barriers to entry exist because of costs, technology, and capital requirements. Trade unions restrict entry to labor markets, and minimum wage legislation distorts the functioning of those markets. Regulation, price controls, and subsidies produce other distortions. Certain "costs," such as that of pollution, have not been included in the prices of goods and services, and therefore have to be borne by society as a whole rather than by users. Managers and employees do not always behave legally and ethically. In pursuing maximum profit, firms may take advantage of opportunities they should not. Under such conditions, price competition is imperfect and profit-maximizing behavior does not lead automatically to the social welfare optimum. In general, production is lower and prices and profits are higher than would be the case under perfect competition.

The counterargument is that these difficulties are real enough, but the remedy for such difficulties does not lie in abandoning the market economy and profit-maximization as a criterion. Instead, the market's deficiencies should be corrected by legislation. Antitrust legislation and regulation of natural monopolies such as utilities are steps in this direction. Legislation regarding pollution is another. Ethical standards are getting increasing attention in practice as well as in the curricula of schools of business administration. The objective of such efforts should be to promote maximum price competition among producers of goods and services. A market economy characterized by a high degree of competition remains the best guarantee of efficient production of the goods and services desired by consumers.

To some, the word *profit* may connote exploitation and may be a symbol of ill-gotten gains. Where profits are excessive because of imperfect competition or illegal or unethical behavior, such labels may be justified. However, in this book, profit is an economic concept and profit-maximization is nothing more nor less than a criterion for economic efficiency.

Applying the Profit-Maximization Criterion to Financial Management

Financial management is concerned with the efficient use of an important economic resource, namely, capital funds. Indeed, a good case can be made for the idea that capital is the most important scarce resource in modern societies. It would therefore follow that profit-maximization should also serve as the basic criterion for the decisions made by the financial managers of privately owned and controlled firms. In a broad sense, it does. But first it has to be transformed in order to provide the financial manager with an operationally useful guideline.

The reason for such a transformation is that the simple, shorthand phrase *profit-maximization* does not take account of several real-world problems we encounter when we seek to make actual decisions about the efficient use of capital funds. Without these transformations, we cannot implement the basic idea that underlies the rationale of Adam Smith's "invisible hand." Let us see why.

Uncertainty

The microeconomic theory of the firm was developed around simplified models that assumed away the problems of uncertainty and time. In the simple model, managers are assumed to know with certainty the outcomes of decisions, and cash flows take place in a single time period. Under these conditions, the simple guideline of profit-maximization is unambiguous and sufficient.

In reality, the problems of uncertainty and time render profit-maximization unsuitable as an operational criterion for investment and financing decisions. When future profits are uncertain, the criterion profit-maximization loses meaning, for it is no longer clear what is to be maximized. Suppose profits can vary over a wide range. Some choices affect the upper end of the range more than the lower, and vice versa. Should actions be chosen to maximize the likelihood of favorable outcomes, or to minimize the likelihood of unfavorable outcomes?

One way to resolve such tradeoffs is to maximize the *expected value* of profits, that is, the weighted average outcome, which, in many cases is approximately equal to the most likely outcome. However, maximizing expected value gives no weight to the *degree of uncertainty* regarding an outcome. For example, two alternative courses of action might have the same expected (most likely) outcome, but one might be far more risky than the other.

Consider two investment opportunities, *A* and *B,* whose profits depend on the state of the economy as indicated in Table 1-1. If a normal economy is the most likely prospect, then the most likely profit from alternatives *A* and *B* is the same, $100. However, profit from *A* will lie between $90 and $110, whereas that from *B* can vary from 0 to $200, a much wider range. The most likely outcome is the same, but *B* is far more risky.

Table 1-1 Uncertainty About Outcomes

State of Economy	Profit (dollars)	
	A	*B*
Recession	90	0
Normal	100	100
Boom	110	200

A criterion that considers only expected or most likely outcomes provides no basis for choosing between alternatives *A* and *B,* whereas few investors would be indifferent between the two. The expected value criterion gives no weight to differences in the degree of uncertainty of outcomes. As we will see later, nearly all investors who provide capital funds to firms are *risk-averse,* meaning that, other things being equal, they prefer less uncertainty to more. Such preferences are reflected in the financial markets and must be taken into account by firms when they make decisions. Therefore, we must reject expected value as a decision criterion, because it does not take account of risk.[5]

Timing

Another major shortcoming of the simple profit-maximization criterion is that it cannot take account of the fact that the timing of benefits expected from investments varies widely. Consider the choice given in Table 1-2. Alternative *X* provides higher profit in period 1, but alternative *Y* provides higher profit in period 2. Which should we select? In

5. Daniel Bernoulli demonstrated the inadequacy of expected value as a decision criterion in 1738 in a classic paper entitled "Exposition of a New Theory on the Measurement of Risk." Bernoulli's paper, originally published in Latin, is as relevant today as it was 200 years ago. For those of us who cannot read Latin, an English translation can be found in S. H. Archer and C. D'Ambrosio, eds., *The Theory of Business Finance,* 2d ed. (New York: Macmillan, 1976).

Table 1-2 Timing of Anticipated Profit

	Period 1	Period 2
Alternative X	100	75
Alternative Y	75	100

practice, most investment and financing decisions involve complex patterns of cash flows over many periods. Simply adding the cash flows over time and picking the alternative with the highest total does not solve the problem, because money has *time value*. Money can be put to work to earn a return, so savers and investors are not indifferent to the timing of cash receipts. Cash flows in early years are valued more highly than equivalent cash flows in later years. The profit-maximization criterion thus must be abandoned for a second reason: It does not take account of differences in timing of cash flows and the time value of money.

A third difficulty with profit-maximization concerns ambiguity. Measuring profits is not easy, and profit figures can vary widely depending on the accounting conventions employed.

As a decision criterion for practical use, profit-maximization thus has three shortcomings: It does not take account of risk, it does not take account of the time value of money, and it is ambiguous. For these reasons, *value-maximization* has replaced profit-maximization as the operational criterion for financial management decisions. By measuring benefits in terms of *cash flows,* we can avoid much of the ambiguity of profits. By *discounting* those cash flows over time, using the concepts of compound interest, we can take account of both risk and the time value of money. Let us examine value-maximization in more depth.

Value-Maximization

The value of an asset is best viewed not in terms of its cost, but in terms of the benefits it can produce. Similarly, the worth of a course of action can be judged in terms of the value of the benefits it produces less the cost of undertaking it. The benefits of an investment or financing decision can be measured in terms of the stream of future expected cash flows generated by the decision.

The value of a stream of future cash flows must take account not only of the magnitude (expected value) of the flows, but also their degree of uncertainty. When other factors are equal, less uncertain flows are valued more highly than more uncertain flows. The value of a stream of cash flows can be calculated by discounting its elements back to the present at an interest rate that reflects both time and risk.

The value-maximization decision criterion involves a comparison of value to cost. An action that has a discounted value, reflecting both time and risk, that exceeds its cost can be said to create value. Such actions increase the value of the firm and should be undertaken. Conversely, actions with value less than cost reduce the value of the firm and should be rejected. In the case of mutually exclusive alternatives, when only one is to be chosen, the alternative with the greatest net present value should be selected. In short, the objective of financial management is to maximize the value of the firm. It is important to note that value-maximization is simply the extension of profit-maximization to a world that is uncertain and multiperiod in nature. Where the time period is short and the degree of uncertainty is not great, value-maximization and profit-maximization amount to essentially the same thing.

Value to Whom?

The value of a course of action must be viewed in terms of its worth to those providing the resources necessary for its undertaking. In applying the value-maximization criterion, value is defined as value to the investors who supply the necessary capital funds. Value therefore must be calculated in a way that takes account of the time and risk preferences of the suppliers of funds.

The theory of financial management, with value-maximization as the criterion, is based on the same general principle as is the classical theory of the firm under profit-maximization: *optimization with respect to owner interests.* As before, we rely on Adam Smith's "invisible hand" to ensure that the interests of owners and society coincide. In professionally managed firms, as distinct from owner-managed firms, management acts as the agent of the owners and in the owners' behalf.

Let us summarize our conclusions to this point. Throughout this book, we adopt valuation as the unifying theoretical and conceptual framework, and value-maximization as the criterion for financial management decisions. Management acts as the agent of owners and optimizes with respect to owner interests, seeking out actions that increase the value of the firm and avoiding actions that decrease it.

In Part IV, we extend the general value-maximization criterion to develop operational criteria for investment decisions. In Part V, we do the same for financing decisions. As we will see later, consistently applied over the long run, value-maximization provides greater returns to owners than would any alternative criterion. We will examine value-maximization from a broader perspective shortly.

Value versus Current Market Price

Is the value of a firm equal to the market price of its stock quoted in the financial pages of the daily newspaper? The extent to which market prices fairly reflect true value is a complex and difficult issue and one to which we will return later.

In the short run, stock market prices are influenced by many factors beyond the control of management, such as general economic conditions, government actions, and the emotions of investors. Over the long run, market prices are a function of underlying economic variables—earning power and cash flows—which management can control. Using valuation as a conceptual framework does not require that we consider every change in stock price as an indicator of the wisdom of our policies.

Even though external factors may cause short-run fluctuations, in the long run, wise managerial decisions will be recognized and reflected in market prices. In other words, in the long run, "true value will out."

Financial Management and the Larger Goals of the Firm and Society

Is value-maximization the goal of the firm, that is, its reason for being? Do firms exist for the primary purpose of making owners as rich as possible? The answer clearly is no. Here it is useful to distinguish between *goals* and *decision criteria*. We concluded earlier that the primary function of firms in a market economy is to produce goods and services. Society's economic goals are to have the desired goods and services produced in maximum quantity given the available stock of resources, while at the same time maintaining full employment and reasonably stable prices.

Given their function, firms should conceive their highest-level policy goals in qualitative, mission-oriented terms. A firm might conceive of itself as a builder of commercial aircraft, a provider of financial services, or a provider of equipment and technology for processing information. Around such a basic statement of purpose is built the firm's commercial strategy, which defines its markets, products, and production technology. From these follow supporting policies in operations, marketing, accounting, personnel, financial management, and so on.

Profit-maximization and value-maximization are best viewed as decision criteria, not goals. The theory of financial management provides the analytical framework for evaluating courses of action that already have passed a higher-level policy screen and have been judged consistent with the firm's commercial strategy. Value-maximization constitutes a second-level criterion for ensuring that actions constitute wise and efficient uses of funds and meet minimum standards of economic performance. Value-maximization can also be used for choosing the best among several available alternatives.

In discharging its responsibilities, it is argued by many that a modern-day firm serves many constituencies, with management acting as trustee not only for the owners, but for all others connected with the enterprise, including employees, customers, suppliers, creditors, the government, and the general public. Management must concern itself with social responsibility, ethics, quality, safety, and a constellation of factors that are difficult to quantify. A firm can pursue all these objectives and still use profit-maximization and its counterpart, value-maximization, as criteria for making efficient economic choices. Indeed, it is precisely these criteria that society should wish firms to apply to economic choices in order to ensure an efficient allocation of scarce resources.

We will return to a discussion of financial management and these larger goals later in this book.

Broader Applicability of Financial Management Concepts

Business firms are not the only organizations that produce services needed by society. Other important producers of services include individuals such as lawyers, doctors, accountants, and engineers; federal, state, and local governments and government-owned enterprises; nonprofit organizations such as churches, educational institutions, and hospitals; and mutual associations owned by their customers, such as farm cooperatives and mutual insurance companies, savings banks, and savings and loan associations.

All these organizations must make economic choices, and all have an obligation to use scarce resources efficiently, just as profit-making enterprises do. Most make investment decisions or financing decisions or both, and all can benefit from financial planning. A church, for example, must balance receipts and expenditures and can do so effectively by preparing a projected cash budget and balance sheet. Universities and government-owned enterprises commit large sums to projects that incur costs and generate benefits over long time periods. Individuals make investment and financing decisions and can benefit from financial planning.

The criterion for financial management decisions in nonprofit organizations requires careful consideration. Benefits often are difficult to quantify—sometimes impossible. Dollar values cannot be attached to the output of churches or schools, for example. Where both benefits and costs of a course of action can be quantified, value-maximization is the appropriate criterion. Where only costs can be quantified, a cost/benefit approach still is useful, with cost estimates compared to benefits in qualitative terms. Where mutually exclusive alternatives are under consideration, cost-minimization is the appropriate criterion. Where cash flows occur over long time periods, the techniques of financial management such as discounted cash flow are useful to discount future costs and benefits to present values. Discount rates must reflect the time and risk preferences of those who bear the costs and receive the benefits.

The concepts and analytical framework of financial management are applicable to investment decisions involving the use of economic resources and to financing decisions involving the acquisition of funds, no matter who makes those decisions. Financial management techniques therefore are applicable to decisions of individuals and nonprofit organizations as well as to those of business firms. Much of the discussion in this book will center around business firms, for it is around firms that the concepts of financial management have developed, but broader applicability will be emphasized throughout.

A Normative Framework

This is a *normative* book. The focus is on what firms and other organizations *should* do and on policies that *should* be followed if certain objectives are to be achieved.

In all such discussions, the question inevitably arises of what firms and managers actually do in practice. In principle, the interests of owners and managers should coincide, and the greatest rewards should come to managers who most ably represent the interests of those for whom they are trustees.

In practice, situations undoubtedly arise in which the interests of owners and managers diverge. It is undoubtedly true that managers do not always act in the interests of owners. Sometimes the managerial reward structure may induce behavior that is inconsistent with value-maximization. Executive compensation, for example, may be perceived as being more closely related to the size of the firm than to profitability. Certain events, such as bankruptcy, may be far more costly to managers than to owners holding well-diversified portfolios of assets. In other cases, managers may select courses of action on the basis of their own personal comfort or peace of mind rather than owner interests.

When managers fail to act in behalf of those whose interests they represent, we would expect those managers ultimately to be replaced. Just how well the system of managerial selection works in practice is an important question, but it is not addressed in this book. We will assume throughout this book that a manager's job is to act in the interests of those for whom he or she is trustee, recognizing the interests of other parties as well. We will discuss analytical techniques, concepts, and policies that are useful to managers in discharging this responsibility.

Summary

Financial management deals with the efficient use of capital funds by firms and other organizations. Financial management decisions can be grouped into three broad categories: (1) financing ongoing operations and management of working capital; (2) investment in long-lived assets; and (3) alternative methods of financing assets. Financial decisions are interdependent and must be coordinated over time as part of the process of financial planning.

Any approach to the financial management of business firms must begin with the role of firms in a market economy, which is to produce goods and services. Via the price system, consumers in a market economy send signals to firms indicating the goods and services they wish to have produced. A major feature of a market economy is decentralization, with decisions regarding production and consumption being made by millions of consumers and firms acting individually. Under idealized conditions, especially a high degree of price competition, profit-maximizing behavior by individual firms leads to efficient use of economic resources in producing those goods and services. Profit-maximization, therefore, has become the generally accepted theoretical criterion for making efficient economic decisions. In practice, this criterion can be criticized on grounds that it does not lead to equality in the distribution of economic benefits and that competition in many industries is insufficient to ensure efficient decisions. Although these criticisms are valid, the remedies for such difficulties lie not in abandoning the market economy and the profit-maximization criterion but in correcting specific deficiencies in the system via legislation. In this book, profit is an economic concept and profit-maximization is a criterion for economic efficiency.

For application to financial management decisions, the profit-maximization criterion must be modified. In its pure form, profit-maximization has three shortcomings as a decision criterion: (1) it does not take account of uncertainty, or risk; (2) it ignores the time value of money; and (3) it is ambiguous in its computation.

Because of these shortcomings, *value-maximization* has replaced profit-maximization as the operational criterion for financial management decisions. The technique of discounted cash flow, based on the principles of compound interest, provides a way to deal with all three shortcomings of pure profit-maximization. Value is defined as value to owners, and society relies on a high degree of competition and Adam Smith's "invisible hand" to ensure efficient decisions.

As is true of profit-maximization, value-maximization is a decision criterion, not a goal. The goal of the firm is properly conceived in qualitative, mission-oriented terms. Value-maximization constitutes a second-level criterion that is applied to actions that already have been judged consistent with the firm's overall commercial strategy.

Although the theory and practice of financial management have developed around business firms, many of the concepts are applicable to the decisions of nonprofit organizations and individuals as well.

Questions

1. What is the role of business firms in a market economy? *PRODUCE GOODS + SERVICE*
2. What are the major types of financial management decisions that business firms make? Describe each. *PROFIT + VALUE MAXIMIZATION*
3. If business firms attempt to maximize profits, are society's economic goals met? Under what circumstances does profit-maximization lead to efficient use of economic resources?
4. Contrast profit-maximization and value-maximization as criteria for financial management decisions in practice.

References

R. N. Anthony, "The Trouble with Profit Maximization." *Harvard Business Review* **38**, 126–134 (November–December, 1960).

B. Branch, "Corporate Objectives and Market Performance," *Financial Management*, **2**, 24–29 (Summer 1973).

G. Donaldson, "Financial Goals: Management versus Stockholders," *Harvard Business Review* **41**, 116–129 (May–June, 1963).

W. G. Lewellen, "Management and Ownership in the Large Firm," *Journal of Finance* **24**, 299–322 (May 1969).

D. Norr, "Management and the Investor," *Financial Analysts Journal*, 45–48 (March–April 1979).

E. Solomon, *The Theory of Financial Management* (New York: Columbia University Press, 1963), Chaps. 1 and 2.

J. F. Weston, *The Scope and Methodology of Finance* (Englewood Cliffs, N.J.: Prentice-Hall, 1966).

The Firm
and Its
Environment

2

Forms of Business Organization
Taxes
Regulation
The Financial Environment
Function of Financial Markets
Principal Participants in Financial Markets
Types of Financial Claims
The Money Market and the Capital Market

The preceding chapter on the scope and objectives of financial management suggests, quite deliberately, that the subject contains a large component of theory. It does. A large part of this theoretical component has been developed over the past 20 years. Interestingly enough, the questions addressed owe their origin, if not their development, to practicing financial managers.

But the subject of financial management also contains a large component of practicality. The decisions about which it theorizes must be made within the real world of laws, regulations, taxes, and hard-headed financial markets. These factors are also relevant. This chapter introduces some of the facts that shape the operating environment of financial managers.

Forms of Business Organization

In the United States, there are three basic forms of business organizations: proprietorships, partnerships, and corporations. The form of organization has important implications for the ability of the firm to obtain financing, for the degree of risk borne by owners, and for the payment of earnings to owners. Organizational form also has important tax implications.

Over 12 million firms operate in the United States. In terms of numbers of firms, proprietorships are the most prevalent organizational form. In terms of income, output, and the control of society's stock of productive resources, corporations are by far the dominant form. The degree of dominance varies widely by line of business. In agriculture, for example, proprietorships account for the majority in terms of both numbers and sales. In manufacturing, communications, and transportation, on the other hand, corporations account for over 90 percent of sales. In retail trade and services, proprietorships account for more in numbers but corporations account for more in sales. In all these fields, partnerships are less often found than either proprietorships or corporations, but partnerships do find wide use in professions such as law and architecture.

Even among corporations, small firms outnumber large ones, but the large firms dominate in sales and output. *Fortune's* list of the 500 largest industrial corporations in the United States in 1979[1] represented only a small fraction of the 200,000 active manufacturing corporations but accounted for over 80 percent of the sales of all industrial corporations.

---

1. "*Fortune's* Directory of the 500 Largest U.S. Industrial Corporations," *Fortune Magazine,* 268–295 (May 1979).

Sole Proprietorship

In a sole proprietorship, one individual owns all the assets of the firm and is responsible for all its liabilities. The proprietor is entitled to all profits and must stand all losses. He is responsible for all actions of the firm and is personally liable in the event of civil damage suits against the firm. With respect to such suits and debts of the firm, the proprietor's liability is *unlimited;* that is, it is not limited to investment in the firm. Creditors or plaintiffs may proceed against the personal assets of the proprietor. The principal virtue of the proprietorship is its simplicity; in most cases, it is necessary only to set up shop and begin operations.

A proprietorship itself is not subject to taxation of income. Rather, the income or loss derived from the proprietorship is included and taxed in the personal tax return of the proprietor.

Partnership

Partnerships are similar to proprietorships in all essential respects except one: Partnerships involve two or more owners. In a *general* partnership, all partners have unlimited liability for the debts and acts of the firm. Normally, a partnership agreement is made that specifies the capital contribution of the partners, the share of each partner both in the assets and in the profits of the firm, and provisions for the withdrawal or death of a partner. Aside from the need for an agreement, partnerships are about as easy to form as are proprietorships. As in the case of proprietorships, income of a partnership is included in the personal tax returns of the partners.

Some states permit *limited* partnerships, which consist of at least one general partner and one or more limited partners. The general partner(s) manages the firm and has responsibilities as described above. including unlimited liability. The limited partners' main function is to contribute capital; they share in the profits, but have no voice in directing the operations of the firm, and their liability is limited to their investment.

Corporation

A *corporation* is an entity created by law that is empowered to own assets, to incur liabilities, and to engage in certain specified activities. The corporate form differs from the proprietorship and partnership forms in several important respects. First, and probably most important, the liability of owners for debts and actions of the firm is limited to their investment in the firm. Creditors and plaintiffs in damage suits can proceed against the assets of the corporation but not against the personal assets of the owners. Second, ownership in a corporation is easily transferable, which is not true for a partnership. The corporation is an ongoing entity, and its owners may sell their shares without affecting the operation of the firm. Third, because the corporation itself may incur liabilities, the corporate form provides better access to external sources of capital. We noted earlier that the corporation is the dominant form of organization in the United States in terms of total output of goods and services. This dominance is due to the advantages of limited liability, transferability of ownership, continuous long-term existence, and access to capital. A disadvantage of the corporate form is that, because it is a legal entity, the corporation itself pays taxes on its income.

Corporations are formed under the laws of the various states. A charter is issued by the state establishing the corporation as a legal entity and setting forth its purpose and its relationship to the state. Corporate *bylaws* then are established governing the internal management of the firm. A board of directors is elected by the owners to set policy and oversee the affairs of the firm in the owners' behalf. The directors appoint the executive officers of the firm, often referred to as the management, who are full-time employees charged with executing the policies established by the directors and administering the operations of the firm. Selecting the firm's top management personnel and evaluating their performance is a major function of the board of directors.

Subchapter S Corporations

Under a provision of the tax law (known as subchapter S) certain small business corporations may elect to be treated in a manner similar to partnerships for income tax purposes. Although such a corporation enjoys limited liability, the corporation's income is taxed directly at the shareholder level and not at the corporate level. This form of organization is widely used in the professional service sector of the economy. Under the Revenue Act of 1978, the maximum number of shareholders allowed under the subchapter S rule was expanded to 15 persons.

Taxes

We mentioned above that the different organizational forms are taxed in different ways. Now we will go into a bit more detail. Taxes deserve special mention because of their importance and influence on business decision-making. In fact, tax considerations affect nearly every decision a firm makes and are especially important in financial management decisions. Tax considerations affect many decisions of individuals also. Most nonprofit organizations, on the other hand, are exempt from many of the taxes to which firms and individuals are subject.

We will deal with the relevant aspects of taxation throughout this book, and here we will mention only some general considerations. Let us note also that the tax laws are so complex and their impact is so important that nearly all firms and many individuals require expert tax advice that goes far beyond the discussion in this book.

Business Taxes

The income of all firms is taxed by the federal government and by most state governments. As we noted above, the income of proprietorships and partnerships is included in the return of the owners, and the tax is paid by the owners. Corporations, on the other hand, pay specific corporate taxes on their income. The rate at which the income of proprietorships and partnerships is taxed depends on the personal tax status of the owners. Corporate income is taxed by the federal government at specified rates.

In order to spur business growth, the Revenue Act of 1978 lowered corporate tax rates and installed a graduated rate structure that favors smaller corporations. Table 2-1 compares the regular tax rates under the new act with rates for prior periods. Thus, for small corporations, the tax payable on the first $100,000 of corporate income has been significantly reduced to $26,750 (an average rate of 26.75 percent) from $41,500 (an average rate of 41.5 percent), which prevailed prior to 1975.[2] For large corporations, the major change is the reduction in the *marginal* tax rate from 48 percent to 46 percent.

For purposes of simplicity, all of the examples in the present book assume that the pre-1975 tax rates prevail, that is, 22 percent on the first $25,000 and 48 percent on income above that amount.

Table 2-1 Tax Rates

Taxable Income	Tax Rate (Percent)		
	Since 1 January 1979	1975–1979	Before 1975
$ 0 to $25,000	17	20	22
$25,001 to $50,000	20	22	48
$50,001 to $75,000	30	48	48
$75,001 to $100,000	40	48	48
$100,001 and over	46	48	48

Source: U.S. Department of the Treasury, Internal Revenue Service, *Tax Guides* (various annual issues).

---

2. The new rates put into effect in 1975 were on a temporary basis.

The income tax is applicable to *net* income, that is, revenues less expenses. This means that where the applicable tax rate is T, of each \$1 of revenue, the government gets T and the firm keeps $1 - T$. Likewise, \$1 of expense costs the firm only $1 - T$. To illustrate, if $T = 0.48$, out of \$100 of revenue, the government gets \$48 and the owners get \$52. A \$100 expense item reduces taxes by \$48, so the net outlay by the owners is only \$52. Ultimately, it is cash flow *after taxes* that concerns owners. As we will see later, tax considerations loom large in firms' and individuals' investment decisions.

Interest and dividends deserve special mention. Interest paid on the debt obligations of a firm is deductible for income tax purposes, whereas dividends paid on common and preferred stock are not. We will discuss these matters in more depth later in this book, because the differential tax treatment has very important implications for financing decisions of firms. With respect to dividend income, present federal tax law exempts from taxation 85 percent of dividends received by a corporation on its holdings of preferred or common stock of other firms. This 85 percent exclusion is intended to reduce the effect of multiple taxation of the same income, since it already has been taxed once when earned.

Business firms are subject to a variety of taxes other than income tax. One of the most important of these is the *capital gains* tax, which is lower than the tax on income[3] and is applied to gain or loss on the sale of assets that are not used or bought and sold in the ordinary course of the firm's business. For example, consider a manufacturing firm that acquires some land for a proposed plant site and later sells it because it decides not to construct the plant. Any proceeds of the sale in excess of the original cost would be subject to capital gains tax. The firm's primary business is presumed to be manufacturing, not buying and selling land, so the gain on the sale is taxed as a capital gain and not as ordinary income. In the case of a firm dealing in land, on the other hand, the difference between selling price and cost of goods purchased for resale is taxed as income. In this latter case, purchase and sale of the goods in question, i.e., land, represents the firm's principal business. The capital gains tax is important in many decisions involving investment in capital assets where an existing asset is to be disposed of. Besides the tax on capital gains, certain business assets, such as real estate, usually are subject to state and local property taxes.

The *investment tax credit* is a special provision in the tax laws that permits a firm to subtract from its tax liability a specified percentage of the purchase price of new capital assets of certain types and a limited

---

3. Capital gains taxes are extremely complex. Roughly speaking, the Revenue Act of 1978 reduced the maximum rate of tax on capital gains to 28 percent.

amount (generally $100,000 a year) of used property. The tax credit was first instituted in 1962, eliminated in 1966, reinstituted in 1971, and significantly liberalized in 1978. The allowable percentage initially was 7 percent and presently is 10 percent on assets held for 7 years or more. The tax credit has the effect of lowering the purchase price of the asset and is a relevant consideration in many investment decisions. From a public policy viewpoint, the tax credit represents a subsidy of business investment for the purpose of stimulating economic growth.

Personal Taxes

Income of individuals is subject to taxation by the federal government and by many states. The provisions of the various tax codes are complex, and we will discuss here only several points especially relevant to financial management decisions. We noted earlier that the income of proprietorships and partnerships is taxed on the personal returns of their owners. The tax is levied regardless of whether any part of the earnings is paid out to the owners. If all the earnings are retained, the tax still is paid. In the case of a corporation, income tax is paid by the corporation when income is earned, and dividends are taxed if and when they are paid to individual shareholders. If no dividends are paid, shareholders pay no income tax, although the income tax paid by the firm remains unchanged. The taxation of both corporate income and dividends in a sense represents double taxation of the same income. To reduce somewhat the impact of such double taxation, present federal tax law exempts from taxation the first $100 of dividends received by an individual or $200 for married couples filing jointly. As we will see later, the taxation of dividends is an important consideration in setting a firm's dividend policy.

Regulation

Business firms are affected by the actions of a wide and growing range of federal and state regulatory agencies. As former President Ford put it in May 1976: "In the last 15 years, 236 departments, agencies, bureaus, and commissions have been created while only 21 have been eliminated. Today we have more than a thousand different federal programs, more than 80 regulatory agencies, and more than 100,000 government workers whose primary responsibility is to regulate some aspect of our lives." For many top managers, especially of larger companies, dealing with governmental regulation has become the single most attention-consuming function.

Of course, we cannot begin to cover such a vast and complex component of the business environment. We will, therefore, confine what follows to a brief classified review of those aspects of current regulation that have direct implications for financial decisions.

Antitrust Regulation

One of the oldest forms of economic regulation in the United States is designed to prevent the development of monopoly power and to promote procompetitive behavior. This responsibility is shared between the Department of Justice and the Federal Trade Commission. Many of the issues involved are structural ones concerning the concentration of market power within one or more firms in an industry. However, financial factors such as rates of return on investment are frequently critical issues. Many of our larger corporations are now under investigation, in part because their rates of return are alleged to be "abnormally" high, among them IBM, the eight largest integrated oil companies, and the four largest breakfast cereal manufacturers.

Franchised Monopolies

The financial performance of public utilities, which are granted franchises to operate in specific service areas, are closely controlled by state and federal commissions and agencies. These controls cover the rates (prices) utilities may charge, their accounting practices, and their dividend and financing policies and practices. Many of the regulatory issues are *financial* issues. Most rate cases (in which a company or an industry appeals for a change in rates) draw heavily on financial theory and on the expertise of the financial officer involved.

Electric and gas utilities, which provide power or gas for cities, telephone and telegraph companies, which provide communications services, and pipelines, which transport natural gas, are subject to detailed regulation by state utility commissions and where *interstate* commerce is involved by the Federal Power Commission (now part of the Federal Energy Regulatory Commission) and the Federal Communications Commission.

Transportation companies have also been heavily regulated, although starting with airlines in 1977, there is now an ongoing effort to reduce the level of regulation imposed on the industry. Railroads and trucking are regulated by the Interstate Commerce Commission (ICC), airlines by the Civil Aeronautics Board (CAB), and interstate petroleum pipelines (which previously had been regulated by the ICC) by the Federal Energy Regulatory Commission (FERC).

Financial Institutions

All major types of financial institutions are subject to close controls by a large number of regulatory agencies. Commercial banks are regulated by state banking commissions, the Federal Reserve Board, the Comptroller of the Currency in the case of national banks, and the Federal Deposit Insurance Corporation. Federal savings and loan associations are regulated by the Federal Home Loan Bank Board, and mutual savings banks and insurance companies by state authorities. In the case of most of these institutions, regulation extends to rates that may be charged and paid, capital positions that must be maintained, activities in which the institutions may engage, and credit standards. Regulatory agencies in many cases act also as the *lender of last resort* in the event of serious difficulties. The purpose of the regulation generally is to protect the customers of financial institutions and to guarantee public confidence in a sound financial system.

Social Regulatory Agencies

Starting in the late 1960s and with accelerated speed in the 1970s, the scope of regulation was widened significantly to embrace previously uncovered areas. Unlike most of the older agencies, which had jurisdiction over specific industries, the newer legislation cuts across all businesses and industries. To mention just three major agencies, the passage of the Equal Employment Opportunity Act led to the Equal Employment Opportunity Commission (EEOC), the Clean Air and Clean Water Acts to the Environmental Protection Agency (EPA), and the Occupational Safety and Health Act to the Occupational Safety and Health Administration (OSHA), all of which have major powers of control over almost everything *any* corporation does. All of these agencies have such profound effects on the future course of corporate investment and financing needs that any modern financial manager must take them into account in developing financial plans for the future.

Another major piece of social legislation passed in the 1970s that intimately affects future financial planning for most corporations is the Employee Retirement Income Security Act (ERISA). Contributions to pension funds have become a major addition to annual labor costs, and the continuing responsibility for seeing that the funds themselves are invested prudently and profitably has emerged as a major responsibility for the chief financial officer of many of our larger corporations.

The Securities and Exchange Commission

Of all the agencies that regulate business activity, the one that lies closest to the financial manager is the Securities and Exchange Commission

(SEC). The commission directly regulates all the securities markets in which corporate stocks and bonds are traded, all major new issues of securities, mergers between existing firms or acquisitions of one firm by another. In addition, it indirectly regulates communications between a firm and its bondholders and shareholders, including financial and other statements released to the public. In recent years, the SEC has been active in influencing accounting practices underlying financial statements as well as practices related to the internal control of a company's financial flows, including the composition and function of audit committees of a firm's board of directors.

Although the SEC has the power to lay down accounting standards, it has thus far delegated this task to "self-regulation" by the private sector. Private bodies such as the American Institute of Certified Public Accountants (AICPA), the Financial Accounting Standards Board (FASB), and the New York Stock Exchange (NYSE) now share responsibility for seeing that disclosure of a firm's financial affairs is as full and complete as the SEC deems sufficient. Nonetheless, almost nothing a financial officer says or does that might be related to the value placed on a company's securities is outside the potential purview of the commission.

The Financial Environment

Of all the many environments within which the firm operates, the one closest to the financial manager is the financial market. Here the firm raises the funds required for its ongoing operations and for its capital expenditures. Here also the firm temporarily *places* or invests[4] its surplus funds pending their more final disposition. Finally, and most important of all, it is the financial market that ultimately determines whether the firm's policies are a success or failure. In a fundamental sense, financial management is nothing more or less than a continuing two-way interaction between the firm and its financial environment.

Because of its pervasive importance for both the theory and practice of financial management, some consideration of the financial environment is spread throughout most of this book.[5] What follows in the re-

---

4. The word *invest* is used in many different senses. In economics, investment refers to the act of capital formation, that is, the use of funds to acquire tangible capital assets. In finance, it is used to denote any commitment of funds for the purpose of getting future returns. Among laymen, it is used (in contradistinction to *speculation*) to refer to the careful or prudent use of funds for the purpose of getting future gain or income. *Place* is a less technical term: It refers to the act of putting funds to use in order to earn income or capital gains.

5. In particular, the short-term money markets are discussed in Chapter 7 and the long-term markets in Chapters 17 and 21.

mainder of this chapter is a brief descriptive introduction to the domestic financial market itself. International markets are discussed in Chapter 23.

The financial market is not a single, physical place. It comprises thousands, indeed millions, of participants and offices linked by a vast telecommunication network that brings buyers and sellers together and sets prices in the process of doing so. In order to understand the complex institutions, instruments, and submarkets that collectively comprise the financial market, it is useful to classify them into smaller components. There are many ways of doing this; one way is to address the following questions:

1. What functions does the financial market perform?
2. Who are the principal participants?
3. What major types of claims or instruments are traded in the financial market?
4. What are the major submarkets with which the financial manager deals?

Function of Financial Markets

Like any market, the financial market is where buyers and sellers meet in order to exchange things for money and vice versa. The things exchanged in financial markets are *claims.* Individuals, companies, or government bodies who have excess funds (we will call them *surplus* spending units) exchange these funds in return for claims to future sums of money. On the other side of the equation, individuals, companies, or government bodies who need funds (we will call them *deficit* spending units) sell claims, that is, promises to pay money in the future, in exchange for present funds.

We can see right away that the market performs several functions essential to a modern industrial society based on free enterprise principles:

1. It allows those who wish to defer consumption (i.e., to save) a convenient way of doing so. Imagine a society without any financial markets or instruments, including money, which, incidentally, was one of the earliest financial instruments. How could an individual in such a society conveniently defer the use of current income to a later date? There is no easy way.
2. It allows those who wish to accelerate consumption (i.e., to dissave) to do so conveniently. Consumer credit, credit cards, and mortgage loans allow millions of individuals to enjoy clothing, cars, and homes now rather than later.

3. More importantly, the financial market provides a channel through which new saving can flow into capital formation (*investment* in the terminology of economics). It therefore allows some groups, such as corporations, to specialize in capital formation. In order for living standards to rise, an economy has to add to its stock of tangible capital, that is, residences, roads, plants, equipment, and inventory. The resources required for these purposes must come from current saving—that part of current output (gross national product) not immediately consumed. A major purpose of the financial market is to gather the current savings of millions of surplus spending units and channel them to the millions of deficit spending units that engage in capital formation.

4. With well-developed financial markets, those who save do not have to make an irrevocable decision to defer consumption for any particular length of time. They sell their savings (i.e., current funds) for claims on future funds. But in a modern economy, the claims themselves can be resold at any time and thus reconverted into current funds. Thus, another major function of modern financial markets is to provide a market for existing claims. The better the *secondary* market, as it is called, the more likely it is that people will be willing to save and transfer their current saving to those who can use it.

While the primary function of modern financial markets is to facilitate saving, on the one hand, and capital formation or investment, on the other, by making things more convenient for both parties, the market also performs another major function. It sets prices. In this case, prices are *interest rates*, the rates of exchange between money now and claims to future money. For financial management, this may well be the most important function of the financial market, and we will devote a full section to it later.

Excluding its important price-setting function, the financial market can be divided functionally into two connected parts. One is the *new issues* market through which society's annual saving eventually flows from the surplus spending units in society to the deficit spending units in exchange for newly issued claims. The other is the *secondary* market, in which units that hold previously issued claims can exchange them for money.

The size of the new issues market is small relative to the secondary market, because the latter includes all past issues still outstanding. In

Table 2-2, the first column shows the major types of financial claims outstanding as of the end of 1978. The second column shows the net new issues of each type of claim during 1978.

Table 2-2   Major Financial Claims (billions of dollars)

	Outstanding, December 31, 1978	Net New Issues During 1978
(1) Corporate equities	1,086	7
(2) Corporate bonds	422	30
(3) United States government securities (bonds, notes, bills)	625	69
(4) United States government agencies	200	29
(5) State and local government securities	291	28
(6) Residential mortgages	884	111
(7) Business and farm mortgages	289	33
(8) Commercial bank loans	358	50

Source: Column 1 from Board of Governors, Federal Reserve System, *Flow of Funds: Assets and Liabilities Outstanding, September 1979;* Column 2 from Salomon Brothers, *Prospects for the American Financial Markets in 1979* (New York: Salomon Brothers, 1978).

Several lines in Table 2-2 require some explanation. Unlike all the other items, the volume of corporate equities outstanding shown in line 1 is measured in terms of market value. The figure shown *excludes* the value of shares held in open-end investment companies, that is, in mutual funds. The low volume of new equity financing through the issuance of new claims is a fairly typical phenomenon. It can be explained by the fact that corporations derive the largest part of their new equity financing internally, that is, from the plowback of retained earnings rather than from new issues.

The high level of new financing by the federal government in 1978 (relative to the level outstanding) is due, in part, to fact that *outstanding* debt excludes substantial amounts held by the Federal Reserve System and by United States Government Trust Funds, whereas the figure for net new issues during 1978 includes sales to all holders. The large change in conventional bank loans to business (the figure excludes mortgage loans and consumer credit loans by banks) reflects the high level of business demand for short-term loans typical during the latter stages of a business cycle expansion.

Principal Participants in Financial Markets

Who are the participants in the financial markets? The answer is almost everybody. But it is convenient to distinguish three categories within the participating population: operating sectors, financial intermediaries, and specialized institutions.

Operating Sectors

The first group consists of the ultimate providers and users of society's flow of saving, namely, households (or individuals), businesses (including corporations), and governments. To complete the picture, we add a fourth operating sector classified in the accounts as the "rest of the world," which lumps together our net transactions with entities outside the United States. In general, the household sector, which collects the largest part of income generated by economic activity, is a net saver and hence a net provider of funds to the other three sectors. However, while these other sectors are net users of funds on balance, they also participate on an individual basis as providers of funds to the market. For example, a corporation with a temporary excess of funds will typically lend those funds to the market rather than use them to reduce its net indebtedness to the rest of society. Likewise, although households as a group are net providers of funds to the market, many individual households borrow from the market in order to purchase homes and cars.

Financial Intermediaries

The transfer of funds from surplus units (mainly households) to deficit units (mainly business, government, and some households) can take place directly, but *direct finance*, as the process is called, is inconvenient both for the ultimate provider of funds and the ultimate user of funds. Although the aggregate flow of annual saving in the United States is very large, individual households save in relatively small amounts—usually a few hundred or a few thousand dollars a year. Imagine a firm or a government attempting to borrow millions of dollars. The financial officer would be busy indeed, for he would have to knock on hundreds or thousands of doors in order to obtain the total amount. To each lender would be issued an IOU. The cost to the firm for search and acquisition obviously would be quite high, significantly increasing the cost of borrowing. The higher the cost of obtaining funds, the smaller the number of investment opportunities that can be undertaken, and the lower the level of investment by the firm.

There is also a problem from the saver's standpoint. Suppose a household has $1,000 saved that it wishes to lend. Lending the entire amount to one borrower exposes the lender to considerable risk. To get reasonable diversification, the saver must lend to a number of firms rather than only one, analyzing the credit and evaluating the risk of each, and making a separate contract with each. The costs to the saver in terms of time and effort would be quite large in relation to the amount of interest that could be earned. Also, the claims held by the saver would be highly *illiquid,* meaning that they could not be turned back into cash quickly at low cost.

Direct finance between savers and investors thus involves very significant transaction costs of search, acquisition, analysis, and diversification. Such costs are directly analogous to friction in physical systems. The net return to savers would be so small (perhaps negative) that lending simply would not be worth the effort. Borrowing costs to firms would be so high that investment would be very low. In short, the losses due to *financial friction* would be so great that very little saving and investment would take place. As always, saving would equal real investment after the fact, but at a very low level of each. Economic growth would be very slow indeed, for few capital assets would be accumulated. That is why financial intermediaries came into being: to collect funds from savers and to transfer them to ultimate users. Today the largest part of saving flows into investment via financial intermediaries such as commercial banks, mutual savings banks, savings and loan associations, and life insurance companies.

With intermediation, savers lend to intermediaries, who in turn lend to firms and other fund-using units. The saver holds a claim against the intermediary, in the form of a deposit, rather than against the firm. The financial officer who wishes to borrow a large sum of money now makes a single trip to the bank or insurance company and negotiates with only one lender, or at most a few. The cost of search and acquisition is far lower than before, so the net cost of borrowed funds is much lower. Many investment opportunities that before were uneconomic now can be undertaken.

The lender also need make only one trip. The saver with $100 deposits it in a bank or savings and loan association and thereby acquires a claim against a *portfolio* of hundreds or even thousands of loans, for that individual now indirectly holds a claim against all the units to which the intermediary lends. The claim thus is far more diversified than under direct finance, and at the same time far more liquid, because it can be turned into cash on short notice at negligible cost. For a given degree of risk and liquidity, the saver's costs are far lower, and the net return is far higher, than under direct finance.

The financial intermediary thus performs many of the tasks formerly performed by lender and borrower—tasks of gathering funds, credit analysis, evaluation of risk, and handling of administrative and legal details. These tasks involve real costs, and the intermediary can perform them much more efficiently and at much lower total cost than can individual lenders and borrowers. In the jargon of the economist, financial intermediaries exhibit "economies of scale" with respect to costs of search, acquisition, analysis, and diversification.

By their actions, financial intermediaries provide a higher return to lenders for a given degree of risk and liquidity and a lower cost to borrowers than would be possible with direct finance. Higher savings rates encourage saving, and lower borrowing costs permit greater investment. Saving and investment are equated at a much higher level, capital assets are accumulated more rapidly, and economic growth is faster. Thus, financial intermediaries in conjunction with well-developed financial markets have a great influence on economic growth and development.

Types of Financial Intermediaries. Table 2-3 shows the relative importance of the various types of intermediaries that have evolved to serve the needs of society, classified by broad types. It also indicates the relative change in the position of each type over the past decade.

Table 2-3 Total Assets of Financial Intermediaries, Year-End, 1965 and 1978

	1965		1978	
	$(billions)	(Percent)	$(billions)	(Percent)
Depository Types				
Commercial banks	336	38.6	1,226	42.2
Savings and loan associations	130	14.9	524	18.0
Mutual savings banks	58	6.6	158	5.4
Credit unions	9	1.0	58	1.5
Contractual Types				
Life insurance companies	154	17.6	376	13.0
Pension and retirement funds[a,b]	106	12.1	356	12.3
Other				
Mutual funds[b]	35	4.0	54[c]	1.9
Finance companies	45	5.2	146	5.0
Real estate investment trusts	0	0	7	0.2
Total	873	100.0	2,905	100.0

Source: Board of Governors, Federal Reserve System, *Flow of Funds: Assets and Liabilities Outstanding,* 1978.

[a]Includes private as well as state and local retirement funds, but excludes Social Security and other federal retirement funds.
[b]Influenced by level of equity prices.
[c]Includes money market funds.

Commercial banks are the oldest and the single most important type of intermediary both in terms of volume and diversity of investment. Their importance is even larger than the figures in Table 2-3 indicate—many pension and retirement funds are administered by banks. Banks acquire the savings of individuals and firms and lend to other individuals and firms. Banks are also the most important supplier of short-term and intermediate-term credit to businesses; they are active as suppliers of consumer installment credit and do considerable mortgage lending.

Savings and loan associations and mutual savings banks acquire savings from individuals and engage heavily in real estate mortgage lending. These two types of intermediaries are the principal suppliers of credit to the residential mortgage market. Finance companies lend to both individuals and firms, usually on an installment basis. Insurance companies, pension and retirement funds, mutual funds, and trust funds supply credit primarily to firms by purchasing stocks and bonds. Business firms themselves act as financial intermediaries by supplying trade credit to other business firms.

Specialized Institutions

The financial intermediaries just discussed channel the flow of saving from surplus to deficit units. In this section, we discuss a third tier of specialized institution in the financial market whose purpose it is to facilitate the flow of funds among the intermediaries themselves as well as to and from the ultimate operating sectors. These include institutions such as investment bankers, security dealers and brokers, the organized security exchanges, and mortgage bankers, to name just a few of the many highly specialized functions within the market.

Investment Bankers. When a corporation or a municipality issues a new security, it generally sells that issue through a syndicate of investment bankers. In effect, the bankers buy the issue and then wholesale and retail it to financial intermediaries and individuals. Commercial banks are allowed to act as investment bankers for general obligation state and municipal bond issues but not for private corporate issues. The corporate business is dominated by investment banking houses such as Morgan Stanley, Salomon Brothers, Goldman Sachs, and Merrill, Lynch.

Brokers and Dealers. The major investment banking houses (referred to in England as merchant banks) resell new issues through their own branches or through the branch network of hundreds of brokers and dealers in securities. The same group of brokers and dealers provide the marketplace in which individuals and institutions can sell or buy stocks and bonds.

Government Bond Dealers. The federal government does not use investment bankers in order to raise the funds it needs to finance its operations. It sells directly to the public through the Federal Reserve System. However, many houses specialize in the federal government bond market (which includes not just long-term bonds, but intermediate-term notes and short-term bills and certificates). They buy the bulk of each new government issue and eventually retail it to institutions and individuals. This market is dominated by the major investment banking houses and by the larger commerical banks.

Organized Exchanges. The organized exchanges, such as the New York Stock Exchange, provide the venue through which the public can buy and sell existing stocks and bonds *listed* on those exchanges.

Over-the-Counter Market. Most bonds and all stocks not listed on the major exchanges are bought and resold on what is called the *over-the-counter* market. The participants here are the same brokers, dealers, and investment banking houses mentioned earlier.

Mortgage Bankers. The mortgage market is large and complex, and it has its own set of specialized institutions. Among them is the mortgage banker who serves as an intermediary between institutions that want to place some of their funds in mortgages rather than securities and individuals and institutions who wish to borrow mortgage funds.

Specialized Dealers. Finally, there are several groups of specialized dealers in the financial markets—dealers in commercial paper, federal funds, foreign exchange—virtually every function and subfunction that can be specialized has been specialized. Today, thanks to specialization, the United States has not only the largest but the most efficient set of financial markets ever known in the history of finance.

Types of Financial Claims

We have said that the financial market is where the operating units in society—the households, firms (or businesses), and government units—exchange money for *claims* to future money, and vice versa.

Why did we not say, more simply, that the financial market is where lenders and borrowers meet to transact business? The reason is that lending and borrowing refer to a very specific type of claim—one in which the borrower agrees to return the funds at specified times and at a specified rate of interest. These are known as *debt* claims. But there is another very important type of claim, generally known as *equity* claims, of which ordinary or common stock is a major example. The party providing the funds does not receive a contract from the party receiving the funds but gets a different kind of claim, namely, a share in the ownership of the entity to which the funds are provided. This, in turn, entitles the claim holder to a specified *share* in the future profits or value of the entity. The word *equity* refers to the fact that the claimant gets a fair or pro rata share in the business he or she helps to finance; that share is proportionate to the relative contribution.

This requires us to distinguish between debt claims and equity claims. There are also other distinctions worth noting.

Types of Equity

Although equity is distinct from debt, it is not a homogeneous category. Within the broad class of equity claims, there are many subclasses. Ordinary, or common, stock is the claim held by the true *residual* owner of a business. Holders of common stock get what is left after everybody else who has contributed capital to the firm has been paid what is due to them. Since most of the other payments are fixed, common stock holders gain enormously when receipts exceed payments due to others and can lose their stake when the reverse occurs.

Preferred stock represents a claim that is a senior claim to common, or ordinary, stock. Holders of preferred stock get paid their share before holders of common stock. Furthermore, there can be several degrees of preference, even with respect to a single corporation. Whatever the degree of preference the claim has, the maximum is always fixed or stated. The true residual, positive or negative, belongs to the holder of common stock, who is the ultimate risk taker.

Types of Debt

A debt obligation takes priority over any form of equity, preferred or common. But there are many levels of priority within the debt group as a whole. Some forms of debt (e.g., mortgages) have a specific lien on particular assets; others (such as debentures) have a general lien on all the borrower's assets after specific obligations have been settled.

Loans versus Securities.   Debt claims can take either of two basic forms—loans or securities. A loan is negotiated directly between a lender and a borrower; that is, there is personal contact between the two parties to the transaction. In contrast, the securities market is impersonal. The borrower sells securities through a middle person—generally, an investment banker, or in the case of government securities, a group of dealers.

As is true of most distinctions in the financial markets, the division between loans and securities is not watertight. In practice, the two methods of transferring funds from lender to borrower tend to overlap. For example, a bond issue may be *privately placed,* that is, sold to one or more insurance companies after a face-to-face meeting. Is it a loan or a security? Alternatively, an interest-bearing, short-term loan by a company to a commercial bank (known as a negotiable certificate of deposit) may be sold in the secondary market just as if it were a security. Was it a loan or a security? It could be called either.

Maturity of Claims

Claims vary with respect to their maturity, that is, the date when they must be repaid to the holder. At one extreme, a type of claim known as *federal funds* may have a 1 day maturity; the borrower of federal funds agrees to repay the amount borrowed plus interest 1 day after the loan is obtained. This instrument is used chiefly by commercial banks that are short of funds for meeting reserve requirements. At the other extreme, claims represented by common stock have no maturity date—they run until the corporation against which the claim exists is dissolved. In between, there is a continuous gradation of maturities, each of which has a special name in the jargon of "the street," as the financial market is frequently called. Thus, we have

3–9 months	Bills or certificates
1–10 years	Notes
10–50 years	Bonds
Perpetual	Stocks or consols

The real significance of the different maturities for the financial manager is the fact that interest rates payable or receivable vary by maturity and the additional fact that the way they vary changes sharply over the business cycle.

The Money Market and the Capital Market

One widely used classification divides the financial market as a whole into the *money market* and the *capital market*. Defined this way, the first category refers to open-market transactions in highly marketable short-term debt instruments; *capital market* is reserved for transactions in longer-term debt issues and stocks.

The Money Market

The principal participants in the money market are commercial banks (especially the large money center banks located in New York, Chicago, and San Francisco), the United States government, and nonfinancial corporations.

Commercial Banks. Although commercial banks are active in both the money market and the capital market, the very nature of their highly liquid liabilities requires that they hold a significant part of these assets in the form of short-term easily marketable claims that can be sold quickly and in large volume.

In recent years, commercial banks have also become major borrowers in the money market through the sale of negotiable *certificates of deposit* (CDs). The CDs issued by the larger banks are now actively traded and have emerged as a major money market instrument. By the end of 1978, the volume of CDs outstanding reached $100 billion.

Banks are also the principal participants in a highly specialized submarket known as the *federal funds market.* Member banks of the Federal Reserve System are required by law to hold legal reserves, that is, deposits at the Federal Reserve Bank. Although each bank's reserve position is computed on the basis of average reserves held over a 7 day period (a 14 day period in the case of smaller banks), most banks attempt to meet their reserve requirement on a daily basis. Given the large ebb and flow of payments into and out of each bank, an active market has developed through which banks with excess reserves on a given day lend these funds to banks with deficient reserves. Such day-to-day transactions among banks are known as *federal funds transactions* (hence, the term *federal funds market*), because the transfer of funds is effected through an immediate debit or credit of the bank's reserve account at the Federal Reserve Bank (as opposed to an ordinary transaction for which the debit and credit entries take place 1 or 2 days later). Through this market and the extensive network of correspondent banking relationships, the major money market banks funnel the temporarily idle funds of smaller banks throughout the country into the money market.

The interest rate on federal funds and the rates banks are willing to pay to borrow funds through the issuance of CDs are key rates in the financial market. They are the focal points through which Federal Reserve policies designed to tighten or ease monetary conditions get transmitted to the financial market as a whole, and vice versa.

United States Government.   The United States government is a major demander of funds in the money market. A large part of the federal debt has been financed by the issuance of short-term marketable securities. For example, at the end of 1978, there were over $160 billion of short-term, 3 month or 6 month United States Treasury Bills outstanding plus an additional $68 billion of other Treasury issues maturing in less than 12 months. In sheer volume, these represented the largest single form of claim traded in the money market. A large volume of this government short-term paper matures every week and has to be refinanced, which the Treasury does through its weekly auction of new short-term bills or certificates. The rates set in these auctions, especially the 3 month Treasury Bill (TB) rate, is another key rate in the money market.

Short-term United States government obligations are widely held by banks, other financial intermediaries, and business corporations as a highly liquid vehicle for holding their temporary excess funds. They are also widely held by foreign governments and foreign central banks. Thus, the TB rate has also become a major factor in determining international flows of funds and therefore plays a key role in determining exchange rates in the now active market for foreign currencies.

Nonfinancial Corporations. Business corporations have become important participants in the money market both as borrowers and lenders. Two types of commercial borrower use the open market as a continuing source of short-term funds. Well-known business firms, especially some of the large mail-order houses, issue short-term notes of 4–6 months' maturity (known as *commercial paper*) to finance their highly seasonal needs for inventory.

A second, and even more important, form of commercial paper is issued by the large finance companies (such as General Motors Acceptance Corporation), either directly or through commercial paper dealers. The borrowing firms use the funds to finance the installment sales of automobiles and major appliances. This form of commercial paper is frequently called *finance paper.* At year-end 1978, the total volume of commercial paper outstanding was around $84 billion.

Business corporations have also become active as suppliers of funds to the money market. Corporations have to hold large sums of liquid assets for the purpose of paying tax, wage, and dividend accruals, as well as for intended capital expenditures. They earn interest on these funds by placing them in the money market without incurring any serious risk of capital loss, because the short-term, highly liquid claims in which they invest can be sold easily should the need arise. For example, at the end of 1978 nonfinancial corporations as a group held $133 billion in liquid assets. Of this amount, some $55 billion was in the form of cash (demand deposits and currency), $29 billion was in the form of interest-bearing CDs, $13 billion was in short-term United States government securities, and $25 billion was in the form of commercial or finance paper of other corporations. The remainder was held in short-term obligations of state and local governments (which offer interest income that is exempt from federal taxes) and in security repurchase agreements (known as *Repos* or RPs). The last item mentioned refers to a process by which a firm lends money to another party in the market. The loan is secured by a security that the borrower sells to the lender with a firm agreement to repurchase the security on a specified date at a specified price.

Other Participants in the Money Market. In addition to the major money market participants discussed above, there are several other sectors that use the market regularly. Security brokers and dealers, who have to hold inventories of securities in the course of their businesses, finance themselves through money market borrowing. Brokers also need funds to relend to customers who wish to purchase securities on margin (i.e., with a cash down payment less than the market value of the purchase). As of year-end 1978, brokers' loans to customers amounted to some $16 billion.

Exporters and importers require short-term funds to finance goods in transit or in warehouses. The principal instrument used to finance such loans is the short-term *bill* or *acceptance*. In the case of bills, the exporter–importer is the debtor. In the case of acceptances, a commercial bank lends its name and credit to the instrument by *accepting* the obligation to repay the loan when it falls due. Bankers' acceptances are another important money market instrument, because they can be resold on the market at a discount before their maturity date.

State and local governments borrow in the money market when they need current funds for brief periods pending the expected arrival of large, periodic tax receipts. The instrument used for such purposes is a *tax anticipation* bill or note. State and local governments also lend to the money market during periods when they have a temporary excess of cash over and above their current need for cash outlays.

Money Market Rates

Short-term money market rates are extremely sensitive to cyclical changes in the economy and to monetary policy. They move up and down far more sharply than long-term rates (but note that the prices of long-term instruments move up and down more sharply than the prices of short-term claims).

Three key rates that reflect the influence of Federal Reserve policies in the money market are the federal funds rate, the 3 month United States Treasury bill rate, and the discount rate the Federal Reserve banks charge commercial banks who need to borrow to meet their legal requirements.

These rates are shown in Figure 2-1. Figure 2-2 shows that other major rates are scaled-up from the federal funds rate and the United States Treasury Bill rate. For example, the rates on commercial paper and CDs move closely in line with the bill rate. But divergencies do occur, and these influence the proportions in which the financial manager of a corporation places liquid funds.

Unlike these open market rates, the prime bank loan rate (the rate charged by banks on loans to their prime customers) is not a market rate that moves up or down daily. Rather, it is a rate posted by each bank. However, in recent years, many large banks (notably Citibank) have been setting their prime rate on a formula basis tied to the open market rate on

Figure 2-1 Selected Short-Term Interest Rates; Averages of Daily Rates Ended Friday

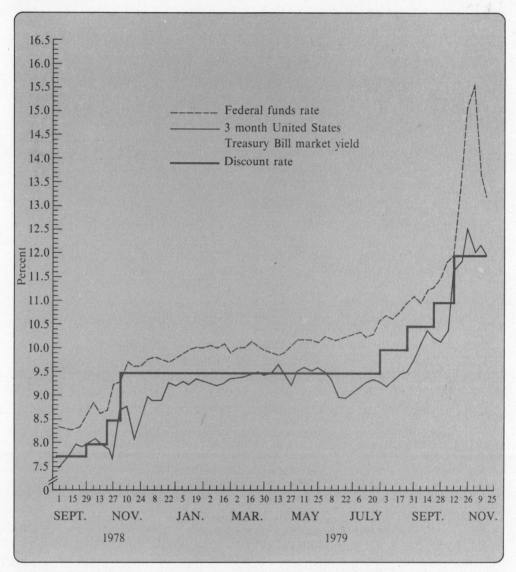

Source: "U.S. Financial Data," Federal Reserve Bank of St. Louis, Nov. 14, 1979.

commercial paper. Finally, the rates on long-term municipal and corporate bonds (depicted in Figure 2-2) fluctuate less than short-term rates.

Short-term rates as *quoted* on the "street" and in the financial press tend to show larger differences among the various instruments than actually prevail. Part of the reason for this is that rates are not quoted on a

Figure 2-2 Yields on Selected Securities; Averages of Daily Rates Ended Friday

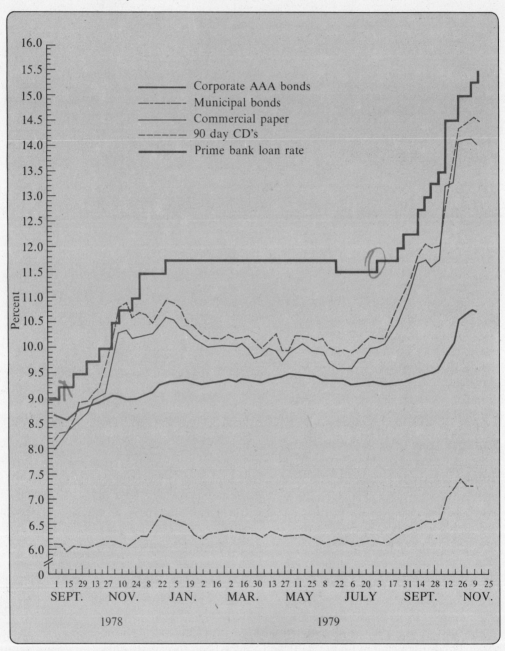

Source: "U.S. Financial Data," Federal Reserve Bank of St. Louis, Nov. 14, 1979.

standard basis. Rates on bills, acceptances, and commercial paper are quoted on a *discount* basis, whereas rates on short-term bonds or federal agency issues and bank CDs are generally quoted on a *coupon* basis just like the rates on long-term bonds.

The coupon basis is the true yield or yield to maturity of an instrument. For example, a 90 day bill purchased for $98 per $100 of maturity value actually offers a true yield of

$$\frac{2}{98} \times \frac{365}{90} = 8.276 \text{ percent per annum}$$

On the discount basis on which this rate is traditionally quoted, the yield is calculated by using the face value in the denominator instead of the purchase price and a convention of 360 days for the year instead of 365 days. Thus, the rate on the discount basis would be 8 percent, calculated as follows:

$$\frac{2}{100} \times \frac{360}{90} = 8.0 \text{ percent}$$

Likewise, the yield on tax-exempt notes issued by state and local governments cannot be directly compared with the taxable yield on fully taxable instruments and hence has to be adjusted by the tax bracket of the purchaser. Since banks and corporations have a marginal tax rate of 48 percent, this is the conventional rate normally used to make the tax adjustment.

The Capital Market

The capital market provides for the flow of the long-term financing required to finance society's long-term investments for purposes such as business plant and equipment, housing, municipal capital projects, and portions of the debt of the United States government. It also provides a place where investors who hold long-term instruments can sell them expeditiously to other groups, and thus it gives long-term instruments a degree of liquidity. However, long-term instruments, by their very nature, are less liquid than the short-term money market instruments we have just discussed. Because prices of long-term instruments such as bonds and stocks fluctuate more than the prices of short-term instruments such as CDs and United States Treasury Bills, there is a greater exposure to the risk of capital loss when these instruments are sold prior to their more distant maturity dates. There is also a greater risk that the borrower will default on the periodic payment of interest or the ultimate repayment of the loan.

The Money Market and the Capital Market

The major borrowers are business corporations, who issue bonds, debentures, mortgages, preferred stock, and common stock; federal, state, and local governments (or their agencies), who issue bonds and notes; and apartment and home buyers, who issue mortgages.

The major suppliers of long-term funds are the financial intermediaries discussed earlier in this chapter.

The instruments themselves will be discussed more fully in Chapter 17, which deals with long-term financing instruments.

Summary

Business firms may be organized as sole proprietorships, partnerships, or corporations. Proprietorships are the simplest and most prevalent in terms of numbers of firms. Corporations, though fewer in number, are much larger, on the average, and produce by far the largest part of the nation's output of goods and services.

The major distinctions between the three forms have to do with taxes and the liability of owners for debts of the firm. Proprietorships and partnerships pay no taxes themselves; taxes on income earned by such firms are paid by the owners personally. Corporations pay taxes on income earned, and, under present law, any profits distributed as dividends are taxed again as income to owners. Proprietors and general partners have unlimited liability for the debts and acts of the firm. The liability of shareholders of corporations, on the other hand, is limited to their investment in the firm. The corporate form provides other advantages in terms of transferability of ownership and access to capital markets.

Taxes on income and capital gains are an important factor in business decisions. Ultimately, it is cash flow *after taxes* in which owners are interested. Tax laws are so complex that treatment of tax effects constitutes an important aspect of financial analysis. Government regulation also is important in the financial management decisions of certain specialized types of firms, such as public utilities, railroads, airlines, and financial institutions. All firms whose securities are publicly owned are subject to regulation by the Securities and Exchange Commission.

An appreciation of the financial environment in which the firm operates is important to the financial manager. The financial system transmits the savings of surplus spending units (mainly households) to investing units (mainly firms and government). Financial markets provide the meeting place for suppliers and users of funds to make their transactions. Suppliers of funds receive claims against the assets and future income of borrowers.

The participants in the financial markets include the operating sectors, the financial intermediaries, and the specialized institutions. The operating sectors comprise the ultimate suppliers and users of funds. Financial intermediaries act as conduits to channel funds from suppliers to users. Financial intermediaries play a key role in the economy by reducing the costs to lenders and borrowers of search, acquisition, analysis, and diversification. By their actions, financial intermediaries provide higher interest returns to lenders and lower interest costs to borrowers. The third category of participants, the specialized institutions, act to facilitate the flow of funds.

Types of financial claims include debt (contractual claims) and equity (residual, or ownership, claims). Some, though not all, financial claims are publicly traded in markets that can be classified under two general headings, the money market and the capital market. The money market refers to transactions involving short-term, highly marketable debt instruments. The capital market refers to longer-term debt issues and stocks.

Questions

1. What are the three basic forms of business organization in the United States? In what essential respects do they differ?
2. How does a *limited* partnership differ from a general partnership?
3. Why is it said that income earned by corporations is subject to "double taxation"?
4. In terms of numbers of firms, sole proprietorships represent the dominant form of business organization in the United States. Can you think of reasons why this is so?
5. Economists sometimes argue that a reduction in the marginal tax rate on income leads to more efficient decisions by individuals and firms (leaving aside the effect on government revenues). Why might this be so?
6. What are the principal functions of financial markets?
7. What economic units are, in the aggregate, the net providers of funds in the United States economy? The net users?
8. What is the function of financial intermediaries in the financial system?
9. What are the major types of financial intermediaries in the United States?

References

W. J. Baumol, *The Stock Market and Economic Efficiency* (New York: Fordham University Press, 1965).

Board of Governors, Federal Reserve System. *Flow of Funds Accounts* (Quarterly Bulletins).

R. M. Davies and M. H. Lawrence, *Choosing a Form of Business Organization* (Durham, N.C.: Duke University, School of Law, 1963).

H. E. Dougall and J. E. Gaumnitz, *Capital Markets and Institutions,* 3d ed. (Englewood Cliffs, N.J.: Prentice-Hall, 1975).

C. N. Henning, W. Pigott, and R. H. Scott, *Financial Markets and the Economy* (Englewood Cliffs, N.J.: Prentice-Hall, 1975).

R. S. Holzman, *Tax Basis for Managerial Decisions* (New York: Holt, Rinehart and Winston, 1965).

J. O. Light and W. White, *The Financial System* (Homewood, Ill.: Richard D. Irwin, 1979).

M. Polakoff *et al., Financial Institutions and Markets* (Boston: Houghton Mifflin, 1970).

L. S. Ritter, *The Flow of Funds Accounts: A Framework for Financial Analysis* (New York: Graduate School of Business, New York University, 1968).

Salomon Brothers, *Prospects for the American Financial Markets in 1979* (New York: Salomon Brothers, 1979).

D. T. Smith, *Effects of Taxation: Corporate Financial Policy* (Boston, Mass.: Graduate School of Business Administration, Harvard University, 1952).

MANAGING ONGOING OPERATIONS II

Revenues, Costs, Profits, and Cash Flows

3

Financial Variables
Cost/Volume/Profit Relationships

We have discussed the scope and objectives of financial management and the environment in which financial management decisions are made. Now we are ready to get to work.

The six chapters of Part II examine the problems of managing a firm's current assets and current liabilities—the top half of its balance sheet. The term *working capital* often is used to refer to the firm's current assets (primarily cash, marketable securities, accounts receivable, and inventories). *Net* working capital usually refers to current assets minus current liabilities (primarily, accounts payable, accruals of various types, and short-term borrowing). *Working* capital refers to the fact that most of its components vary closely with the level of the firm's operations, that is, with the level of production and sales. Most decisions with respect to working capital and its components have their impact over weeks and months rather than years. For this reason, working capital management often is referred to as *short-term finance.*

The topics covered in Part II are important to the management of any firm. Short-term finance is especially important to the small or new firm, where survival and growth are matters of continuous concern. In any growing firm, we will find that financing a growing working capital requirement is a major problem. Short-term finance is especially important in retail and wholesale businesses and in many service businesses where the major investment is in short-term rather than long-term assets.

Although the emphasis is on business firms, that is, profit-making enterprises, many of the techniques of analysis and planning are applicable to nonprofit enterprises as well. Churches, hospitals, schools, and charitable organizations all have problems of financial planning and management of short-term assets and liabilities. So, too, do individuals. Some of the techniques discussed here, for example, cash budgets and pro forma analysis, are useful in individual and family financial planning.

We should note at the outset that some of the material in Part II has a heavy accounting flavor. Accounting provides much of the basic information for financial analysis, planning, and decision-making. Any discussion of these functions must begin with the key numbers generated by the financial accounting process.

Financial Variables

Financial Statements

The two basic financial statements of a firm, the income statement and the balance sheet, define many of the financial variables that concern us. These two statements provide the starting point for both the analysis of past performance and for planning ahead.[1] Consider the statements given in Tables 3-1 and 3-2 for the Beta Manufacturing Company. a manufacturer of paints and varnishes. The income statement and balance sheet constitute a financial model of the firm. The income statement rep-

Table 3-1 Beta Manufacturing Company: Income Statement, Calendar Year 1979

Sales	$1,140,000
Cost of goods sold	(730,000)
Gross profit	410,000
Depreciation	(15,000)
Selling, general, and administrative expense	(340,100)
Operating profit	54,900
Interest	(12,900)
Profit before taxes	42,000
Income taxes	(13,600)
Profit after taxes	$ 28,400

Table 3-2 Beta Manufacturing Company: Balance Sheet, December 31, 1979

Cash	$ 2,500
Accounts receivable	152,500
Inventory	420,000
Total current assets	575,000
Fixed assets, net of depreciation	112,500
Other assets	35,000
Total assets	$722,500
Note payable–bank	$160,450
Accounts payable	122,500
Taxes payable	18,000
Miscellaneous accruals	50,000
Total current liabilities	350,950
Mortgage payable	26,000
Total liabilities	376,950
Common stock	155,000
Retained earnings	190,550
Total liabilities and net worth	$722,500

---

1. Many companies now routinely provide a third statement known as "sources and uses of funds" (sometimes as "sources and applications of funds"). This will be discussed in the next chapter.

resents a record of events between two points in time, in this case December 31, 1978, to December 31, 1979. The balance sheet represents a "snapshot" of the firm's position at a single point in time, December 31, 1979. The income statement measures flows of dollars per unit of time. In technical terms, income is referred to as a *flow* number. In contrast, the items in the balance sheet are *stock* numbers; that is, they represent dollar values at a given point of time.

Accounting ground rules govern the construction of financial statements. Essentially, all transactions that affect the firm's net worth, with one exception to be noted below, appear in the income statement. For example, sales revenue increases net worth, and salary expense reduces net worth. Both are recorded in the income statement.

Transactions that do not affect net worth are recorded in the balance sheet but not in the income statement. Thus, when an account receivable is collected, cash is increased and accounts receivable are reduced. The accounting entries will affect these balance sheet items but will not show in the income statement. One asset (an account receivable) has been exchanged for another asset (cash), and therefore the firm's net worth is unaffected. Similarly, when the firm pays an account payable, cash and accounts payable both decline, with net worth again unaffected. Except for payment of dividends, the converse of the above also is true: Any transaction that changes net worth appears in the income statement. A dividend payment does affect the net worth of the firm but is not included in the income statement.

The distinction between income statement and balance sheet transactions gives rise to some accounting terminology that deserves a quick review. All cash outflows are *expenditures*, but only those that affect net worth and therefore appear in the income statement are labeled *expenses*. All cash inflows are *receipts*, but only those appearing in the income statement are *revenues*.

Working Capital

Within the balance sheet total it is useful to distinguish between current or circulating assets and fixed assets. Current assets include the firm's holdings of cash, accounts receivable, and the inventory of raw materials, goods in process, and finished goods. The term *working capital* often is used to refer to the firm's current assets, and *net* working capital to refer to current assets less current liabilities. Using these definitions, we can see from Table 3-2 that Beta Manufacturing Company had $575,000 of working capital as of December 31, 1979. Table 3-2 also tells us that the company's current liabilities on that date amounted to $350,950. Subtracting this figure from total current assets of $575,000 gives us net work-

1

Financial Variables

ing capital of $224,050. If we wish, we can restate Beta's balance sheet as in Table 3-3.

The balance sheet format in Table 3-3 makes clear the fact that *net* working capital—that portion of current assets not financed by current liabilities—must of necessity be financed by long-term funds. If the firm is a growing one, both the net working capital and its attendant financing requirement also increase.

Table 3-3 Beta Manufacturing Company: Balance Sheet, December 31, 1979

Assets		Liabilities and Net Worth	
Net working capital	$224,050	Mortgage payable	$ 26,000
Fixed assets, net	112,500	Common stock	155,000
Other assets	35,000	Retained earnings	190,550
Total	$371,550	Total	$371,550

It is also useful to separate the current liabilities that arise directly out of the firm's operations from those that do not. To support sales, the firm needs inventories and working cash balances. But sales also generate cash and accounts receivable. These working assets normally are partially financed by accounts payable and various other accruals, such as taxes payable, wages payable, and certain other expenses that at any point in time are owed but not yet paid. We will refer to current assets less these operating liabilities as net *operating* capital. For Beta Manufacturing Company, we can rearrange the balance sheet shown in Table 3-2 to indicate the required level of financing from nonoperating sources. For Beta, the operating liabilities are $190,500, consisting of the sum of accounts payable ($122,500), taxes payable ($18,000), and miscellaneous accruals ($50,000). In short, $190,500 of total current assets ($575,000) were financed spontaneously by operations, leaving $384,500 ($575,000 *less* $190,500) of net operating capital to be financed from other sources.

Such spontaneous sources of financing operations can be temporarily increased or decreased by slowing down or speeding up the punctuality with which bills due are paid. But generally, the remaining $384,500 must be financed by other means. In effect, as Table 3-4 shows, Beta has a total capital requirement (including net operating capital and fixed capital) of $532,000. Of this, $371,550 is financed by long-term sources and $160,450 by bank loans.[2]

---

2. Some firms hold liquid assets (frequently referred to as cash-equivalents) far above their actual requirements. Such assets (Beta has none) should be excluded from net operating capital and shown as a separate item on the balance sheet.

Table 3-4 Beta Manufacturing Company: Balance Sheet, December 31, 1979

Assets		Liabilities and Net Worth	
Net operating capital	$384,500	Notes payable—bank	$160,450
Fixed assets, net	112,500	Mortgage payable	26,000
Other assets	35,000	Common stock	155,000
		Retained earnings	190,550
Total	$532,000	Total	$532,000

The concept of net operating capital is useful in planning or making projections. If a firm's operations are managed consistently and it remains in more-or-less the same line of business, the relationship between its net operating capital and its sales should remain fairly stable, perhaps declining somewhat with growth. To generate $1,140,000 in sales during 1979, Beta Manufacturing Company required $384,500 in net operating capital as of year-end 1979 or approximately $0.34 per $1 of sales. Given a projection of future sales, we can quickly generate an estimate of the requirement for net operating capital. We will discuss financial projections in more depth in Chapter 5.

Income Measurement

A basic concern of accounting is *measurement*. One of the most difficult problems facing the accountant is the measurement of income. In economic terms, income equals change in net worth. The income to an economic unit, an individual or a firm, during any period of time is the change in that unit's net worth during the period. Our financial statements tell us that Beta Manufacturing Company earned $28,400 after taxes in 1979.

We must draw a distinction between *accounting* income and *economic* income.[3] Accounting income refers to the income figure resulting from the application of generally accepted accounting principles, for example, $28,400 for Beta during 1979. This figure, however, is the product of a number of essentially arbitrary judgments. A basic problem is that of *recognition*, the allocation of receipts and expenditures to particular time periods as revenue and expense. As goods are sold, when is the revenue earned? When the order is placed by the customer? When the goods are shipped? When the invoice is mailed? When the customer's check is received? Most firms keep their books on an *accrual* basis; that is, they

---

3. For a further discussion of this distinction, see R. K. Jaedicke and R. T. Sprouse, *Accounting Flows: Income, Funds, and Cash* (Englewood Cliffs, N.J.: Prentice-Hall, 1965).

recognize the sale as a transaction and record the revenue as earned in the accounting period during which the goods are shipped. Some smaller firms keep books on a *cash* basis, that is, they recognize the sale only when the customer's check is received.

When a firm purchases materials, similar questions arise with respect to allocating the expenditure to a particular time period as an expense. Is the expense incurred when the materials are ordered, received, consumed, or paid for? Again, the answer depends on whether the firm is on a cash or accrual basis of accounting. Further questions arise with respect to whether the outlay is to be treated as a *product* cost and recognized when the product is sold, or a *period* cost.

To produce financial statements, many other judgments are required that affect the allocation of revenue and expense to particular time periods. A number of options usually are open with respect to the treatment of depreciation, for example, straight-line versus declining balance. Research and development expenditures generally are expensed as they occur, but in some cases they are capitalized and amortized over several accounting periods. Likewise, the acquisition of patents and goodwill may be capitalized and subsequently amortized over several accounting periods. Taxes may be treated one way for reporting to the Internal Revenue Service (IRS) and another for financial reporting to investors. In all these cases, the question is not the total amount involved over the life of a transaction, but the time period to which the receipt or expenditure is to be allocated as revenue or expense.

Other difficulties in measurement have to do with changes in market value. If a firm owns securities and those securities rise in value during a particular period, should the increase be treated as income? In an economic sense, the increase does constitute income, and a decline in market value would constitute a real economic loss. For accounting purposes, however, such gains and losses usually are not recognized until the securities are sold.

A problem of major proportions in income measurement is the treatment of inflation. Inflation affects the market value of all the firm's assets. "Profits" are earned on inventories while held by the firm. Fixed assets rise in value. Replacement costs of new fixed assets to maintain the firm's earning power exceed depreciation allowances, since the latter are based on historical cost. When price levels are rising, the use of historical-cost depreciation and the emergence of inventory profits will tend to *overstate* earnings. On the other hand, if a firm has debt outstanding, the real value of this debt declines during inflation because the firm will eventually repay the debt in "cheaper" dollars. Because historical-cost accounting conventions do not recognize this effect, the firm's reported earnings will tend to *understate* its economic income when price levels rise. The net effect of the several forces of overstatement and understatement will depend, of course, on the particular mix of assets and liabilities in the individual balance sheet under consideration. To determine the *true* change in the firm's net worth during any period under such circumstances is a difficult problem indeed.

An objective of accounting should be to measure the true economic income of the firm. However, the state of the art at present is not adequate to deal with all the problems involved, especially during inflationary periods. With imperfect measurement techniques, determining true changes in value often gives rise to ambiguities. To avoid ambiguity, we often must retreat to measures we know to be less accurate. When faced with a choice between accuracy and objectivity in constructing financial statements, we have usually opted in favor of the latter. (objectivity)

While on the subject of income, let us note that income to a corporate firm is not the same as income to the firm's shareholders. Income to shareholders consists of dividends paid on the shares plus capital gains (or losses) due to changes in market value of the shares. In theory, in the case of a firm with shares that are publicly traded, the market value of the firm's shares should reflect all elements of value, those not measured directly by traditional financial statements as well as those that are. Market value often deviates substantially from the figure for book net worth given in a financial statement.

To compute market value, all the firm's outstanding shares are valued at the market quotation of the shares on the stock exchange where they are traded. If market value at any point in time is a good estimate of the firm's "true" value (technically referred to as an unbiased estimate), then the change in market value between two points in time along with dividends paid should represent a good, or unbiased, estimate of the firm's economic income for the period. Whether market price changes are useful as estimates of economic income is a subject of vigorous debate in accounting and finance circles. We will have more to say about stock prices as unbiased estimates of true value in a later chapter.

Over long time periods, economic income and accounting income converge, because problems of allocation to particular time periods disappear. Over short periods, the differences between the two can be substantial.

Operating Cash Flow

It is important also to distinguish between *profit* as reported and *cash flow*. Let us first consider cash flow generated by the firm's operations. In general, cash flow from operations during any period will exceed profit after tax by two factors: (1) the amount of noncash expenses charged during the period, mainly depreciation, but also possibly amortization of goodwill, patents, or research and development expenditures previously capitalized; and (2) investment outlays that are not capitalized but expensed against current revenues. In the case of Beta Manufacturing Company, we have only depreciation to consider. Depreciation is the process of allocating the cost of a long-lived asset to the time periods during which it is "used up." Cash changes hands at the time the machine is purchased, but subsequent depreciation charges represent *noncash* expenses. To determine the cash flow generated by a firm's operations during any period, we must adjust the profit figure by *adding back* depreciation. Consider Beta Manufacturing's income statement for 1979, as given in Table 3-5.

Table 3-5 Beta Manufacturing Company, 1979 *from operations*

	Profit and Loss	Cash Flow
Sales	$1,140,000	$1,140,000
Less cost of goods sold	(730,000)	(730,000)
Less depreciation	(15,000)	—
Less selling, general, and administrative expense	(340,100)	(340,100)
Less interest	(12,900)	(12,900)
Less taxes	(13,600)	(13,600)
Profit after taxes	28,400	
Add depreciation	15,000	
Cash flow from operations, after taxes	$ 43,400	$ 43,400

Adding back depreciation to profit after tax is a handy way to arrive at an approximate measure of cash flow from operations. In some cases, for example, when a capital asset is sold, correctly identifying all the noncash charges can be confusing. We can always arrive at the right answer simply by starting with cash revenues and subtracting all cash expenses (including taxes), required to generate those revenues.

Profit versus Cash Flow

Let us examine more closely the distinction between operating cash flow and profit. In principle, the profit figure is intended to measure change in value, albeit imperfectly. The operating cash flow figure measures funds generated by the firm's operations and available for expenditure. The funds might be used to expand the investment in fixed assets, to pay dividends, to expand working capital, to retire debt, or for a variety of other purposes.

Taking a long view, however, there are claims against operating cash flow that must be met. To sustain its earning power, the firm must reinvest to replace assets that wear out. Let us suppose that a particular firm reinvests exactly enough to sustain its real earning power, that is, its earning power adjusted for inflation. If we subtract the reinvestment requirement from operating cash flow, the remainder over the long run should approximately equal the firm's earnings. To generate a growing earnings stream (again, in real terms, adjusted for inflation), the firm must reinvest an amount over and above replacement requirements.

Our interpretation of operating cash flow and its uses thus depends on our time frame, whether we take a short or long view. In the short run, operating cash flow can be used for any purpose. In the long run, a large part must be earmarked for reinvestment if the cash flow itself is to be sustained.

Table 3-6 Beta Manufacturing Company: Balance Sheet Data

Assets	December 31, 1978	December 31, 1979
Cash	$ 10,000	$ 2,500
Accounts receivable	147,500	152,500
Inventories	410,000	420,000
Total current assets	567,500	575,000
Fixed assets, net of depreciation	55,000	112,500
Other assets	15,000	35,000
Total assets	$637,500	$722,500
Note payable—bank	$ 96,350	$160,450
Accounts payable	117,500	122,500
Taxes payable	21,000	18,000
Miscellaneous accruals	57,500	50,000
Total current liabilities	292,350	350,950
Mortgage payable	28,000	26,000
Total liabilities	320,350	376,950
Common stock	155,000	155,000
Retained earnings	162,150	190,550
Total liabilities and net worth	$637,500	$722,500

Total Cash Flow versus Operating Cash Flow

The firm's *total* cash flow during a period, as distinct from operating cash flow, is affected by balance sheet changes. Here we define total cash flow as the total change in the firm's cash account. Let us examine the balance sheet data for Beta Manufacturing Company for two successive years, as given in Table 3-6. In Table 3-5, we calculate Beta's cash flow from *operations* during 1979 as $43,400. Yet Table 3-6 shows that the cash balance *declined* by $7,500. Why the difference? Because cash flow from operations is only part of the picture. The firm's cash balance is affected also by other changes taking place in the balance sheet. We will examine balance sheet changes in more depth in Chapter 4 when we discuss sources and uses of funds.

Cost/Volume/Profit Relationships

Of all measures of firm performance, profit is one of the most important. Microeconomic theory tells us that in a market economy, profit is a signal for the allocation of resources and a yardstick for judging managerial efficiency. For planning and decision-making, an understanding of the effects of various actions on profit is clearly important. Such an understanding requires techniques for analyzing the response of revenues, costs, and profits to changes in sales volume. We will begin with costs.

Fixed versus Variable Costs

How do costs respond to changes in volume? Some costs, known as variable costs, vary directly with, and roughly proportionately to, changes in production volume. For example, every passenger car that General Motors builds needs five tires; thus, the *cost* of this component of the final product rises either in proportion or almost in proportion to the total number of cars built in a period. In contrast, the total cost of tools and dies used for stamping the body parts for a new model does *not* change with the volume of bodies produced but remains *fixed* over a very wide range of production. In a wholesale or retail business, variable costs would include the cost of goods purchased for resale and commissions paid to salespersons. In a manufacturing firm, variable costs include materials used in the manufacturing process, direct labor, supplies, energy costs, packaging, freight, and sales commissions.

What costs are fixed with respect to sales volume? Here we must be cautious. We might begin by identifying such costs as executive salaries, depreciation, rent, property taxes, insurance, and interest. We will have more to say shortly about what the term *fixed cost* really means.

Accepting for the moment that some costs vary with sales volume and some do not, we can define the concept of *contribution*. Suppose a manufacturing firm makes a product that is priced at $10 per unit. If variable cost per unit is $6, then each unit sold contributes $4 toward payment of fixed costs. If enough units are sold, total fixed costs will be covered. Sales above that *break-even* point contribute to profits. We will pursue the concept of break-even analysis shortly.

What Does *Fixed* Really Mean?

Let us return to our discussion of fixed costs. Suppose a pencil manufacturing firm operates a plant that has the capacity to produce 50,000 pencils per year. Suppose further that adequate managerial and supervisory personnel are available to produce at full plant capacity and that the accounting department, sales department, and company cafeteria also are staffed to support that level of operations. At any production level below 50,000 pencils per year, all these support or overhead costs remain fixed in total dollars per unit of time.

Suppose production is to be expanded above 50,000 units. New plant capacity is needed and possibly an additional foreman to supervise the additional production personnel. Additional personnel may be needed in the accounting department, and the cafeteria may have to be expanded. When we say that a particular element of cost is fixed, we mean that it is fixed over some *range* of sales volume. In the long run, all costs are variable! It is necessary, therefore, when speaking of fixed costs, to specify the relevant range of output. When output goes beyond the relevant range, fixed costs increase, often as a step function, as shown in Figure 3-1.

Figure 3-1 Behavior of Fixed Costs

Even over the relevant range of output, our classification of costs as either fixed or variable often is an oversimplification of reality. Some costs are semifixed and some are semivariable, meaning that they contain both fixed and variable components. A part of the electric power bill, for example, may be fixed, but part may vary with the level of output. Where the classification of costs as fixed or variable is an acceptable approximation, such classification provides a useful analytical technique. We must apply the technique with caution, however, recognizing its limitations.

Break-Even Analysis

The proportion of fixed costs to total costs is an important factor in the relationship between revenue and profit. A useful technique for analyzing this relationship is called *break-even* analysis. The first step in break-even analysis is separation of costs into fixed and variable components. Then we determine the point at which revenues exceed total costs and profits begin. At this point, let us restrict our attention to *operating* profit, often referred to as earnings before interest and taxes, or EBIT. In this way, we can separate the effects of operating and financial leverage, both of which we will discuss shortly. Graphically, we can construct a break-even chart as shown in Figure 3-2. This chart is constructed for a product with a selling price of $3.00 and variable costs of $1.20 per unit. Fixed operating costs are $180,000 per year. To construct the chart, we first plot fixed costs as a horizontal line at $180,000. Next we plot the total revenue line. With a $3.00 selling price, total revenue at any level of output Q is 3Q$. With variable cost of $1.20 per unit, total variable cost is 1.20Q$ at Q units of output. We add variable cost to fixed costs to get the total

Figure 3-2 A Typical Break-Even Chart

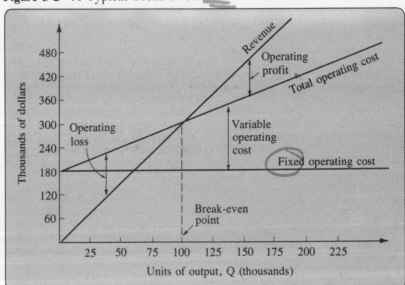

cost line. Since total cost is a linear function of output, we need plot only two points. If useful, we can construct a break-even chart with sales dollars or percent of production capacity, rather than units of output, on the horizontal axis.

The break-even point in this case is at 100,000 units. At that point, sales revenue is $300,000, variable costs are $120,000, fixed costs are $180,000, and operating profit is zero.

We can calculate the break-even point algebraically. The contribution of each unit sold is $3.00 − 1.20 = $1.80. We know that at the break-even point, total fixed costs are covered. If V is break-even volume, $1.80V$ must equal fixed costs (FC) of $180,000. Algebraically,

$$V = \frac{FC}{P - VC} \tag{1}$$

$$= \frac{180,000}{3.00 - 1.20} = \frac{180,000}{1.80}$$

$$= 100,000 \text{ units per year}$$

where P is unit selling price and VC is unit variable cost.

Some Limitations of Break-Even Analysis

Break-even analysis is a very useful tool, but we must keep its limitations firmly in mind. First, let us recall our earlier conclusion that fixed costs usually are fixed only over some relevant range of output. Our analysis therefore is valid only over that range. Also, we noted earlier an assumption that selling price is constant over the range of output analyzed. In practice, output and price may be related. Variable costs may not be absolutely constant per unit over the entire range. Where our previous assumptions do not hold, the cost and revenue lines in Figure 3-2 are not linear. Where refinement of the analysis is necessary and justified, nonlinear relationships can be approximated by a series of straight line segments.

Another limitation concerns multiple products. The analysis in Figure 3-2 is carried out for a single product. The fixed costs are those to be incurred because of a decision to market that product. In a multiproduct firm, break-even analysis can be applied to each product, but allocating expenses that are jointly attributable to all products, for example, a foreman's salary, may present problems. To perform break-even analysis for the firm as a whole, we must define output as the total for all products, assuming a stable product mix over the entire range of output. In some cases, such an assumption may not be realistic.

Finally, problems may be encountered in obtaining the data necessary for a break-even analysis. Some elements of cost may be uncertain. Cost relationships may change over time, and historical data may not always provide good estimates of future costs. Problems in using historical data are especially troublesome when rates of inflation are high.

Break-Even on a Cash Basis

Sometimes it may be useful to know the point at which a product will break-even on a cash basis. To perform the analysis on a cash basis, we subtract all noncash expenses, in most cases involving only depreciation, from operating costs. In the case of the product analyzed in Figure 3-2, let us assume that the fixed cost figure of $180,000 included $60,000 in depreciation. We construct a new fixed *cash* cost line at $120,000 and a new chart as in Figure 3-3.

Break-even volume on a cash basis (V_c) is

$$V_c = \frac{FC_c}{P - VC} \qquad (2)$$

$$= \frac{120,000}{3.00 - 1.20} = \frac{120,000}{1.80}$$

$$= 66,667 \text{ units per year}$$

where FC_c is fixed cash operating cost. To cover total cash expenses, the firm must sell only 66,667 units versus 100,000 to cover all costs.

Figure 3-3 Break-Even on a Cash Basis CHART

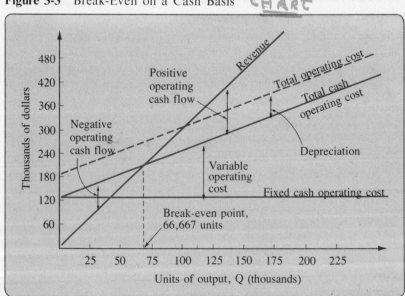

Operating Leverage

In Figure 3-2, we can see that above the break-even point, operating profits rise rapidly. A given change in volume of output produces a larger percentage change in operating profit. For example, a 10% change in volume from 125,000 units to 137,500 units produces a 10% change in sales revenue. Operating profit, however, increases by 50%, from $45,000 at 125,000 units to $67,500 at 137,500 units. Below break-even volume, we have the same relationship, but in the opposite direction.

The term *operating leverage* refers to the sensitivity of operating profit to changes in sales. The degree of operating leverage at any level of output is given by

$$\text{Degree of operating leverage} = \frac{\text{Change in operating profit, \%}}{\text{Change in sales, \%}} \qquad (3)$$

Operating leverage is a function of the firm's cost structure, specifically the ratio of fixed operating costs to total operating costs. If a firm had no fixed costs, it would have operating leverage equal to 1.0, and a given change in sales would produce the same percentage change in operating profit. Where fixed costs do exist, the firm has positive operating leverage greater than 1.0, and a given change in sales produces a larger percentage change in operating profit. The higher the ratio of fixed to total operating costs, the higher the operating leverage.

The concept of operating leverage is illustrated in Figure 3-4. In part B of the figure, we repeat the break-even chart presented earlier in Figure 3-2. This chart was constructed for a product with a selling price of $3.00, variable costs of $1.20 per unit, and fixed operating costs of $180,000 per year. Part A of Figure 3-4 constructed for a product with a selling price of $3.00, variable costs of $2.20 per unit, and fixed operating costs of $40,000 per year. Part A illustrates low operating leverage, and part B illustrates high operating leverage. Any given change in sales produces a much larger percentage change in B's operating profit than in A's. When sales are rising, high operating leverage is desirable; when sales are falling, high operating leverage is not desirable. The sword has two edges.

The degree of operating leverage (DOL) at any level of sales can be expressed directly in terms of the cost structure as follows:

$$\text{DOL} = \frac{S - VC}{S - VC - FC} \qquad (4)$$

where *S* is sales, *VC* is variable costs, and *FC* is fixed costs, all in dollars.

Figure 3-4 Operating Leverage

Units	Sales	Variable cost	Total cost	Operating profit
25	$ 75	$ 55	$ 95	−$ 20
50	150	110	150	0
75	225	165	205	20
100	300	220	260	40
125	375	275	315	60
150	450	330	370	80
175	525	385	425	100

Selling price $ 3.00
Variable cost 2.20
Fixed cost $40,000

(A) Low operating leverage

Units	Sales	Variable cost	Total cost	Operating profit
25	$ 75	$ 30	$ 210	−$ 135
50	150	60	240	− 90
75	225	90	270	− 45
100	300	120	300	0
125	375	150	330	45
150	450	180	360	90
175	525	210	390	135

Selling price $ 3.00
Variable cost 1.20
Fixed cost $180,000

(B) High operating leverage

Using data from Figure 3-4 as an example, at a sales level of $450,000, the DOL for A and B would be calculated as follows:

$$DOL(A) = \frac{450 - 330}{450 - 330 - 40} = 1.50$$

$$DOL(B) = \frac{450 - 180}{450 - 180 - 180} = 3.00$$

Expression (4) makes it clear that the DOL for a given firm is different at different levels of operations.

A good example of a firm with high operating leverage is an airline. Fixed operating costs are very high, primarily salaries, fuel, maintenance, and depreciation. All these costs are incurred no matter how many passengers are carried. Variable costs are minimal, perhaps involving not much more than the cost of in-flight meals and ticket blanks. Once above the break-even passenger load factor, each additional dollar of revenue is practically all operating profit. Operating profit is very sensitive to the number of passengers carried.

A typical retail business, on the other hand, has much lower operating leverage. Variable costs are high, primarily the cost of goods purchased for resale. A wholesaler might have even lower operating leverage, with fixed salaries a smaller proportion of total costs.

In an uncertain world, sales revenue is likely to vary over time, and to be uncertain for any period looking ahead. Variable sales result in variable operating profits. Variability of operating profits over time, and uncertainty as to what future operating profits will be, is referred to as *operating risk*. We can see from Figure 3-4 that operating leverage is an important determinant of operating risk. For any given variability of sales, the higher the operating leverage, the more variable is operating profit. We will find in later chapters that the degree of operating risk is an important consideration in formulating many financial policies.

Financial Leverage

Thus far, we have focused on operating costs and operating profits, with interest excluded. We did so to draw a distinction between *operating* leverage and *financial* leverage.

Operating leverage is determined by the firm's cost structure and therefore by the nature of the business. The firm's commercial strategy dictates the markets in which it operates and therefore the technology of its production and marketing operations and their resulting cost structures.

Financial leverage, on the other hand, is determined by the mix of debt and equity funds used to finance the firm's assets. We will defer a detailed discussion of financial leverage until later in the book and here make only a few brief observations. In our income statement in Table 3-1, we can see that interest is subtracted from operating profit to obtain net profit before taxes. The more debt a firm employs, the more interest it pays. Interest cost is fixed with respect to output and therefore is directly analogous to fixed operating costs. In the presence of financial leverage, a given change in operating profit produces a larger percentage change in net profit before taxes. The analogy with operating leverage is direct. The sensitivity of net profit before (and after) taxes to changes in sales thus depends on the combined effects of both operating and financial leverage.

Applications of Cost/Volume/Profit Analysis

Cost/volume/profit analysis has many applications. It is useful in making projections of cash flow and profits for the period ahead. It is also useful in analyzing decisions regarding new products and decisions to expand or contract or drop existing products. It sometimes is useful in make-or-buy decisions. Break-even analysis also may be useful in decisions involving equipment selection and replacement, especially where fixed costs are being substituted for variable costs via automation. It may find use also in marketing decisions involving pricing, promotion and advertising, and distribution channels.[4]

Summary

Short-term finance, or working capital management, deals with the management of current assets and liabilities. The income statement and balance sheet provide the starting point for financial analysis and planning. The income statement presents a record of events between two points in time, while the balance sheet presents a "snapshot" of the firm's position at a particular point in time. The firm's working capital is financed in part by current liabilities that arise naturally as a consequence of the firm's operations and in part by discretionary liabilities.

A basic concern of accounting is measurement. Measurement of income requires allocation of receipts and expenditures to particular time periods. Recognition of income and expense often involves arbitrary judgments. Inflation greatly complicates the measurement problem. For these and other reasons, accounting income often is an imperfect measure of economic income.

An important distinction in financial analysis is that between profit and cash flow. Operating cash flow is cash revenues less cash expenses. A shorthand way of calculating operating cash flow is by adding depreciation back to after-tax profits. Total cash flow during any period includes balance sheet changes in addition to operating cash flow.

Successful financial planning requires an understanding of the response of revenues, costs, profits, and cash flows to changes in sales volume. In the short run, some costs vary with sales volume and some

---

4. For an excellent discussion of cost/volume/profit analysis and its uses, see Richard I. Levin and Charles A. Kirkpatrick, *Quantitative Approaches to Management,* 3d ed. (New York: McGraw-Hill, 1975), Chap. 2.

do not. Some costs are fixed within a given range of sales volume and are variable outside that range. In the long run, over wide ranges of sales volume, all costs are variable.

Break-even analysis is a technique for examining the relationship between operating profit and sales volume. Its usefulness, however, sometimes is limited where costs cannot be separated into fixed and variable components or where joint costs are attributable to more than one product.

The term *operating leverage* refers to the sensitivity of a firm's operating profit to changes in sales. The degree of operating leverage of a firm is a function of its cost structure (the ratio of fixed to total operating costs) and hence is determined by the nature of its business. Financial leverage, the subject of Part V of this book, depends on the mix of debt and equity used to finance the firm's assets.

Sample Problem

Montana Lumber Company raises timber and manufactures lumber products and furniture components. Projected 1980 net sales are $530,000,000, with cost of goods sold 76 percent of sales. Selling, administrative, and research expenses should reach $50,000,000. Montana Lumber pays 8.5 percent interest on $5,000,000 of long-term bank debt. Annual depreciation on fixed assets is $8,000,000. The 1979 balance sheet reflected a $530,000,000 balance in the lumber and timber account. It is expected that 4 percent of this will be depleted in 1980. The company pays 48 percent corporate income taxes. What amount of funds generated by Montana Lumber's operations should management consider to be available for expenditure? (*Note:* Depletion of timber is a noncash charge analogous to depreciation of machinery or other fixed assets.)

Solution

This problem illustrates the difference between operating cash flow and accounting profit. After arranging the given revenue and expense information into profit and loss statement format, those figures that represent cash items are combined to find the operating cash flow. Depreciation and depletion are methods of allocating the cost of assets to the period in which they are used to generate revenue. Depreciation and depletion are noncash expenses. We can arrive at the cash flow figure in two ways: by adding noncash expenses to the profit after tax figure as in column 1 in the table on the following page or by starting with cash revenues and subtracting all cash expenses required to generate those revenues, as in column 2.

	(1) Profit and Loss (in thousands)	(2) Cash Flow (in thousands)
Sales	$530,000	$530,000
Cost of goods sold	(402,800)	(402,800)
Gross profit	127,200	127,200
Expenses		
Selling, administrative, research	(50,000)	(50,000)
Interest	(425)	(425)
Depreciation	(8,000)	—
Depletion	(21,200)	—
Pretax profit	47,575	
Less taxes (48 percent)	(22,836)	(22,836)
Profit after tax	24,739	
Add back noncash expense	29,200	
Cash flow from operations, after tax	$ 53,939	$ 53,939

Questions

1. What is the general rule for determining whether an accounting transaction appears in the income statement?
2. What is the difference between an *expenditure* and an *expense?* Between a *receipt* and *revenue?*
3. Define *working capital, net* working capital, and net *operating* capital.
4. Contrast *profit* with *operating cash flow.*
5. Define the terms *fixed* and *variable* costs. Does the term *fixed* imply that a particular element of costs is constant over all ranges of output?
6. What are some of the limitations of break-even analysis?
7. Why would a firm's break-even point for operating profit differ from its break-even point on a cash basis?
8. What is *operating leverage?* Give some examples of businesses with both high and low operating leverage.
9. How does *financial* leverage differ from *operating* leverage?

Problems

1. Calculate the amount of working capital, the amount of net working capital, and the amount of net operating capital for the Acme Manufacturing Corporation for each year 1976–1979 given the data in the tables on page 71.

Acme Manufacturing Corporation: Income Statement (Thousands)

	1976	1977	1978	1979
Sales	$48,200	$60,600	$72,500	$81,400
Cost of goods sold	35,600	46,000	56,200	63,100
Gross profit	12,600	14,600	16,300	18,300
Depreciation	2,200	2,400	2,400	2,900
Amortization of goodwill[a]	200	200	200	200
Selling, general, and administrative expense	4,100	5,500	7,100	7,700
Income from operations	6,100	6,500	6,600	7,500
Interest	1,525	1,650	1,530	1,686
Profit before taxes	4,575	4,850	5,070	5,814
Taxes	2,100	2,200	2,400	2,700
Profit after taxes	$ 2,475	$ 2,650	$ 2,670	$ 3,114

[a]Amortization of goodwill is not deducted in computing taxes.

Balance Sheet (Thousands)

	December 31, 1976	December 31, 1977	December 31, 1978	December 31, 1979
Cash	$ 1,900	$ 2,800	$ 4,600	$ 2,700
Accounts receivable	7,900	9,600	11,400	13,600
Inventory	5,000	6,600	7,200	8,900
Other	1,000	1,100	1,100	1,200
Current assets	15,800	20,100	24,300	26,400
Plant and equipment	42,000	45,500	45,500	54,500
Less: Accumulated depreciation	12,900	15,300	17,700	20,000
Net fixed assets	29,100	30,200	27,800	34,500
Goodwill	6,600	6,400	6,200	6,000
Total assets	$51,500	$56,700	$58,300	$66,900
Notes payable	$ 5,550	$ 5,700	$ 4,500	$ 5,600
Accounts payable	6,500	6,300	7,400	8,900
Accruals	2,600	2,900	3,000	3,200
Tax payable	900	1,200	1,000	1,800
Current liabilities	15,550	16,100	15,900	19,500
Senior debentures @ 7 percent	7,000	9,000	9,000	9,000
Subordinated debentures @ 9 percent	7,000	7,000	7,000	8,000
Common stock ($5 par)	7,000	7,000	7,000	8,000
Capital surplus	3,500	3,500	3,500	4,500
Retained earnings	11,450	14,100	15,900	17,900
Total liabilities and net worth	$51,500	$56,700	$58,300	$66,900

2. Acme's sales are expected to increase by 15 percent in 1980 over 1979. Assuming that the relationship between net operating capital and sales remains the same in 1980 as in 1979, how much additional net operating capital will Acme require in 1980?

3. Calculate the after-tax cash flow from operations for Acme for each year 1976–1979. Use both the long method of subtracting all cash expenses from revenues and the shortcut method of adding back noncash expenses to profit after tax.

4. Benchmark Corporation sells a single product for $30.00 with variable costs per unit of $18.00. If fixed costs are $3,000,000, calculate the break-even point in units. If fixed costs include $900,000 of noncash expenses (depreciation and amortization), what is the break-even point on a cash basis?

5. Using the data in Problem 4, prepare a break-even chart following the format of Figure 3-3 in the text.

6. If we assume that the information given in Problem 4 remains valid over all levels of output, would you expect the degree of operating leverage to remain constant over all levels of output? Calculate the degree of operating leverage at sales levels of 300,000 units and 400,000 units in order to answer the question.

7. Assume that Benchmark Corporation (Problem 4) decides to automate its production process by replacing some of the manual production tasks with a robot. If fixed costs increase to $3,300,000 because of the added depreciation while variable costs decrease to $17 per unit because of the lower labor expense, what is the effect on the break-even point? What would be the effect on operating profit at an output of 400,000 units?

8. The Lakeland Manufacturing Company is determining its budget for 1980. There is some concern about expected profits. Three alternatives that may improve profits are being considered. The proposed budget, in thousands, is given in the table.

Sales (14,000 units @ $1)		$14,000
Cost of goods sold		
Fixed	$5,325	
Variable	3,150	8,475
Gross margin		5,525
Selling and general expenses		
Fixed	$2,800	
Variable	2,500	5,300
Net income		$ 225

(a) Compute the break-even point using a break-even chart.

(b) Alternative 1 for improving profits requires a 5 percent increase in sales prices. Evaluate its effect on profits and the break-even point when the number of units sold is unchanged.

(c) Alternative 2 would reduce fixed costs by 5 percent. Evaluate the effect on profits and the break-even point (assuming alternative 1 is not put into effect).

(d) Alternative 3 would reduce variable costs by 5 percent. Evaluate the effect on profits and the break-even point (when neither 1 nor 2 is put into effect).

(e) Evaluate the effect on profits and the break-even point assuming all three alternatives are implemented simultaneously.

9. Competition in the small kitchen appliance industry has forced Home Products Company to consider two different product line strategies. Plan 1 involves the elimination of two of the four existing food processor models. This would result in decreased start-up and packaging costs. Plan 2 would retain all four models but would replace the current hand assembly of the three-piece body with a one-piece, injection-molded body. A large initial investment for the molds would pay off in the form of lower labor and material costs.

The current annual sales level is about 60,000 units. Half of these are sold at $40 each and half at $60 each. Plan 1 would eliminate one $40 and one $60 model. It is expected that unit sales would remain at 60,000 with the $40 model comprising 45 percent of unit sales. Management is primarily concerned with the relative riskiness of profits under each plan. The costs for the current sales volume and the projected costs under each plan are given in the table.

Estimated Costs	Currently	Plan 1	Plan 2
Raw materials	440,000	390,000	265,000
Factory labor	615,000	500,000	215,000
Depreciation on fixed assets	800,000	980,000	1,257,500
Salary expense	640,000	700,000	775,000
Variable selling expense	70,600	72,012	70,600
Property taxes	36,000	45,000	63,000
Other fixed expenses	52,000	75,000	103,000

(a) Compute the degree of operating leverage at current volume (60,000 units) for each of the three possibilities.

(b) What is the effect on profit of a 5 percent decrease in dollar sales?

(c) Rank the possibilities according to their degree of riskiness, as measured by operating leverage.

10. The income statement of Tarrytown Corporation for 1979 is given in the table.

Sales (12,200,000 units @ $1)		$12,200,000
Cost of sales		
Fixed	$3,910,000	
Variable	4,240,000	8,150,000
Gross margin		4,050,000
Selling and general expenses		
Fixed	1,500,000	
Variable	1,950,000	3,450,000
Income		$ 600,000

Projected sales of $20,000,000 (at $1 per unit) for 1980 are expected to increase expenses by the following amounts:

Advertising expense	$275,000
Depreciation and insurance on plant	450,000
Interest expense	120,000
Fixed factory overhead	150,000
Salaries expense	500,000

(a) Prepare a projected income statement for the expected (1980) sales and expenses.

(b) Compare break-even points at present and projected operating levels.

(c) Compare profits before and after expansion at present sales volume.

References

E. A. Helfert, *Techniques of Financial Analysis*, 3d ed. (Homewood, Ill.: Richard D. Irwin, 1972), Chap. 2.

R. K. Jaedicke and R. T. Sprouse, *Accounting Flows: Income, Funds, and Cash* (Englewood Cliffs, N.J.: Prentice-Hall, 1965).

R. I. Levin and C. A. Kirkpatrick, *Quantitative Approaches to Management*, 3d ed. (New York: McGraw-Hill, 1975). Chap. 2.

G. M. Von Furstenberg and B. G. Malkiel, "Financial Analysis in an Inflationary Environment," *Journal of Finance* **32**, 575–588 (May 1977).

$\dfrac{\$}{units}$ $\dfrac{.34}{\$}$ .VC

.3375

.35

.VC + units → New VC $ total.

.1598

.16

Analyzing
Financial Performance

4

Managers must measure performance if they are to manage effectively. Owners and directors must measure performance if they are to evaluate management. Investors and creditors must decide whether to supply funds. Suppliers who provide materials to a firm on other than a cash basis (known as trade credit) are also concerned with the firm's ability to pay. Each of these groups may have a different viewpoint and find different tools useful. Trade creditors, for example, are concerned mainly with liquidity and the ability of the borrower to pay in the short term. Bondholders more likely are concerned with the firm's long-run earning power. In this chapter, we discuss techniques useful in a variety of situations. More specialized techniques are covered in the references given at the end of the chapter.

For analyzing performance, we need benchmarks, or standards of comparison. If we know a firm's profits or its return on investment or its inventory turnover rate for a single year or quarter, we cannot say whether its performance is good or bad. If we have data for another similar firm, or perhaps industry averages, we can begin to make some judgments as to "better" or "not as good." If we have data on the firm in question over several years or several quarters, we can draw conclusions as to "getting better" or "getting worse." As we will see, performance measurement is relative.

For decision-makers, whether managers, investors, or creditors, the future usually is more of interest than the past. However, analysis of the future often begins with analysis of the past to examine trends. Then the question becomes " Will the trends continue?" In this chapter, we focus on history. In the next chapter, we will look ahead and develop a financial plan. The performance measurement techniques we develop here can be applied to a financial plan as well as to historical data.

Financial analysis is never a simple task. In order to understand fully a company either from the outside or from the inside, it is necessary to go through the motions of a financial "detective." The clues consist of various financial ratios for a company—at least 20 of them and in some cases more. The ratios are compared with the company's own past as well as against those of other companies in the same or similar industries.

Like any dissection of data, the purpose of financial analysis is to develop an underlying understanding of what is going on. Students frequently wonder if this effort is really necessary. Later, when they serve as security analysts, commercial bank loan officers, investment banking executives or assistants to corporate management, they invariably find that the effort is not only worth it but is essential.

Although the analysis of past events cannot, in itself, provide an accurate forecast of the future, it can provide an "alert" to difficulties that might lie ahead. The bankruptcy of the Penn-Central Railroad and

Table 4-1 Beta Manufacturing Company: Income Statements, 1974–1979

	1974	1975	1976	1977	1978	1979
Sales	$515,000	$557,500	$647,500	$930,000	$990,000	$1,140,000
Cost of goods sold						
Material	335,000	355,000	387,500	592,500	622,500	730,000
Labor	167,500	177,500	192,500	300,000	317,500	375,000
Overhead	77,500	80,000	90,000	147,500	157,500	205,000
	90,000	97,500	105,000	145,000	147,500	150,000
Gross profit	180,000	202,500	260,000	337,500	367,500	410,000
Depreciation	7,500	5,000	5,000	5,000	10,000	15,000
Selling, general, and administrative expense	149,400	181,100	190,600	282,400	307,900	340,100
Operating profit before taxes	23,100	16,400	64,400	50,100	49,600	54,900
Interest	8,100	3,900	4,400	5,100	9,600	12,900
Net profit before taxes	15,000	12,500	60,000	45,000	40,000	42,000
Taxes[a]	3,300	2,750	22,300	15,100	12,700	13,600
Profit after taxes	11,700	9,750	37,700	29,900	27,300	28,400

[a]Taxes are computed as 22 percent of the first $25,000 of income and 48 percent of all over $25,000. These were the tax rates actually in effect prior to 1975. The new tax rates legislated in 1975 and 1978 (see Chapter 2) are ignored in this table and in other calculations involving taxes in this chapter.

Table 4-2 Beta Manufacturing Company: Year-End Balance Sheets, 1974–1979

	1974	1975	1976	1977	1978	1979
Assets						
Cash	$ 1,000	$ 1,000	$ 2,500	$ 12,500	$ 10,000	$ 2,500
Accounts receivable	125,000	90,000	95,000	107,500	147,500	152,500
Inventory	187,500	180,000	250,000	325,000	410,000	420,000
Total current assets	313,500	271,000	347,500	445,000	567,500	575,000
Fixed assets, net of depreciation	55,000	50,000	45,000	52,500	55,000	112,500
Other assets	17,500	15,000	15,000	17,500	15,000	35,000
Total assets	$386,000	$336,000	$407,500	$515,000	$637,500	$722,500
Liabilities and net worth						
Notes payable—bank	$ 65,000	$ 15,750	$ 23,050	$ 34,150	$ 96,350	$160,450
Accounts payable, trade	52,500	42,500	42,500	110,000	117,500	122,500
Taxes payable	5,000	4,000	30,000	26,000	21,000	18,000
Miscellaneous accruals	15,000	17,500	20,000	25,000	57,500	50,000
Total current liabilities	137,500	79,750	115,550	195,150	292,350	350,950
Mortgage payable	36,000	34,000	32,000	30,000	28,000	26,000
Total liabilities	173,500	113,750	147,550	225,150	320,350	376,950
Common stock	155,000	155,000	155,000	155,000	155,000	155,000
Retained earnings	57,500	67,250	104,950	134,850	162,150	190,550
Total liabilities and net worth	$386,000	$336,000	$407,500	$515,000	$637,500	$722,500

of W. T. Grant and Co. were both amply foreshadowed by trends in their balance sheets and income statements.

Basic Data

The starting points for analyzing financial performance are the two basic financial statements of the firm, the income statement and the balance sheet. Tables 4-1 and 4-2 present 6 years of data for the Beta Manufacturing Company. We will use these data throughout this chapter.

In the material that follows, we begin with the analysis of sources and uses of funds. Sources-and-uses analysis is an essential starting point to identify specific areas that need further investigation. The performance measures that follow sources-and-uses analysis are grouped under five main headings: profits and profitability, return on investment, activity and turnover, liquidity, and indebtedness. Our discussion focuses on firms, but some of the techniques discussed, such as sources-and-uses analysis, are applicable to nonprofit organizations as well.

Sources and Uses of Funds

To produce goods and services, firms acquire assets and put these assets to work productively. Assets are paid for initially by using capital funds provided by owners or by issuing liabilities for cash and then using the cash to acquire assets. As the goods and services produced by the firm are sold, more assets are acquired, and a cycle is established. We can view the cyclical flow of cash in the simplified terms illustrated in Figure 4-1. A useful first step in analyzing a firm's performance often is to analyze the flow of cash through the income statement and balance sheet. This type of analysis is referred to as sources-and-uses-of-funds analysis. Here, we are defining *funds* to mean cash, although it is not always so defined.[1] By sources-and-uses analysis, we can determine over any period of time where a firm obtained its funds and what it did with them—what had been going on financially in a firm.

Balance Sheet Changes

Sources-and-uses analysis begins with an analysis of balance sheet changes over the period of time in which we are interested. Using data from Table 4-2, let us prepare a statement of balance sheet changes for

---

1. An alternative is to define *funds* as working capital. Our purposes here are better served by defining funds as cash.

Figure 4-1 The Flow of Cash

the Beta Manufacturing Company over the period December 31, 1974, to December 31, 1979, as in Table 4-3.

A Sources-and-Uses Table

Now let us reorganize Table 4-3 into a statement of sources and uses. In addition to acquisition of assets, funds may be used to reduce liabilities. Sources of funds include reductions in assets as well as increases in liabilities. So we define *sources of funds* as follows:

1. Increases in liabilities via additional bank borrowing or an increase in accounts payable.
2. Increases in net worth via retained earnings or additional capital contributions by owners.
3. Reductions in assets via the liquidation of inventory or the sale of plant.

And we define *uses of funds* as:

1. Reductions in liabilities; for example, the payment of debt.
2. Reductions in net worth via payment of dividends, retirement of stock, or operating losses (the latter perhaps better viewed as a negative source).
3. Increases in assets, such as the purchase of fixed assets, the extension of more credit to customers, or expansion of inventories.

Table 4-3 Beta Manufacturing Company: *SVRS*
Balance Sheet Changes, December 31, 1974–December 31, 1979

	1974	1979	Change
Assets			
Cash	$ 1,000	$ 2,500	+$ 1,500
Accounts receivable	125,000	152,500	+ 27,500 U
Inventory	187,500	420,000	+ 232,500 U
Total current assets	313,500	575,000	+ 261,500
Fixed assets, net of			
depreciation	55,000	112,500	+ 57,500 U
Other assets	17,500	35,000	+ 17,500 U
Total assets	$386,000	$722,500	+$336,500
Liabilities and Net Worth			
Notes payable—bank	$ 65,000	$160,450	+$ 95,450 S
Accounts payable, trade	52,500	122,500	+ 70,000 S
Taxes payable	5,000	18,000	+ 13,000 S
Miscellaneous accruals	15,000	50,000	+ 35,000 S
Total current liabilities	137,500	350,950	+ 213,450
Mortgage payable	36,000	26,000	− 10,000 U
Total liabilities	173,500	376,950	+ 203.450
Common stock	155,000	155,000	—
Retained earnings	57,500	190,550	+ 133,050 S
Total liabilities and			
net worth	$386,000	$722,500	+$336,500

— INCREASE IN ASSETS IS A USE
— DECREASE IS A SOURCE

— INCREASE IN LIABILITIES IS A SOURCE
— DECREASE IS A USE

Table 4-4 Beta Manufacturing Company: Sources and Uses of Funds,
December 31, 1974–December 31, 1979

Sources	
Bank borrowing	$ 95,450
Increase accounts payable	70,000
Increase taxes payable	13,000
Increase miscellaneous accruals	35,000
Retained earnings	133,050
Total sources	$346,500
Uses	
Increase accounts receivable	$ 27,500
Increase inventories	232,500
Increase fixed assets, net	57,500
Increase other assets	17,500
Reduce mortgage	10,000
Total uses	$345,000
Increase in Cash	$ 1,500

Reorganizing the changes in the balance sheet into this format gives us the sources-and-uses statement of Table 4-4. As an alternative to this format, we could interpret the change in cash as a use or a source, depending on whether it increases or decreases. Then total uses would equal total sources.

In Table 4-4, all of Beta's asset accounts increased over the period 1974–1979, so all of these changes represented *uses* of funds. This was not the case for the year 1975 viewed individually. Let us construct a sources-and-uses statement for the period December 31, 1974–December 31, 1975.

Table 4-5 Beta Manufacturing Company:
Sources and Uses of Funds, December 31, 1974–December 31, 1975

Sources	
Reduce accounts receivable	$35,000
Reduce inventory	7,500
Reduce fixed assets	5,000
Reduce other assets	2,500
Retained earnings	9,750
Total sources	$62,250
Uses	
Reduce bank borrowing	$49,250
Reduce accounts payable	10,000
Reduce mortgage	2,000
Reduce taxes payable	1,000
Total uses	$62,250
Change in Cash Balance	$ 0

Table 4-5 shows that changes in accounts receivable, inventories and fixed assets during 1975 represented *sources* of funds, rather than uses as in Table 4-4. When an asset account increases, it uses funds; when it decreases, it releases or *provides* funds and hence becomes a source.

Similarly, when a liability account increases, it provides funds (a source), like accounts payable in Table 4-4. But in Table 4-5, accounts payable is a *use* because $10,000 in funds had to be used to reduce the amount owed trade creditors. Likewise, bank debt was reduced by $49,250 (a use), and the mortgage was reduced by $2,000 (another use). When a liability account increases, it provides funds (a source); when it decreases, funds are required to make the reduction (a use).

Interpreting the Sources-and-Uses Statement

What do we learn from the sources-and-uses analysis? Let us examine the entire period 1974–1979 using the data in Table 4-4. First, we see that the largest use of funds by far was to expand inventories. Was the increase due to growth of the firm, or are inventories being managed ineffectively? We cannot tell from the data in Table 4-4, but we can put inventory management on our list for further investigation. We see also that the increase in cash was quite small relative to other asset categories. Has the firm's liquidity declined dangerously? Another question for our list. With respect to sources, we see retained earnings providing the largest single source, with bank borrowing and accounts payable also providing large amounts. Has Beta Manufacturing Company borrowed too heavily? Is trade credit being used to the point that relations with suppliers might be damaged? More questions for our list.

We can see that the sources-and-uses statement provides valuable insights into the firm's operations. In addition to the questions raised above, we can examine the expansion of accounts receivable and fixed assets, the mix of internal versus external financing, and the mix of short-term versus long-term financing relative to the kinds of assets being financed. If, for example, we were to find a large expansion in fixed assets financed primarily by short-term sources of funds, we would want to investigate further.

Over what time period should the sources-and-uses analysis be performed? The period in which we are interested. It may be any length, from a month or even a shorter period up to several years. The relevant period may be defined by events in the life of the firm, such as a period of growth or a period of decline. Sometimes it is useful to break the time period into two or more smaller periods to determine whether there were significant differences in fund flows. In addition to being useful for analyzing historical performance, sources-and-uses analysis may be useful in connection with planning for the future. We will discuss financial planning in Chapter 5.

Some Refinements

Some refinements of the sources-and-uses statement are often desirable. The payment of dividends, for example, is sometimes an important use of funds that we would not detect by examining only the changes in the retained earnings account on the balance sheet. If we cannot obtain data on dividend payments directly, we may be able to draw some inferences from the income statement and balance sheet data we have. We know that the transfer to retained earnings each year, in the absence of other complicating transactions, will equal profit after taxes for the year minus dividends paid. We examine the change in the retained earnings account for Beta Manufacturing Company from December 31, 1974, to December 31, 1975, and find it to be $9,750, exactly the amount of profit after taxes in 1975. Thus, we infer that Beta paid no dividends in 1975. Repeating this analysis over the remaining years indicates that no dividends were paid over the period 1974–1979.

We also may wish to look further into the fixed asset account. In our balance sheet for Beta, we have fixed assets, *net* of depreciation. Our sources-and-uses statement thus gives the expenditures on fixed assets, *net* of depreciation over the period. We know from the income statements in Table 4-1 that depreciation charges during 1975–1979 totaled $40,000. Thus, we can infer that Beta's total expenditures for fixed assets from December 31, 1974, to December 31, 1979, were $97,500, rather than $57,500, as indicated by the net figure in Table 4-4.

Let us now revise our sources-and-uses statement to take into account the refinement just discussed. In the sources category, we will show "Funds from operations" rather than the change in retained earnings. Funds from operations is equal to profit after taxes plus depreciation for the period. Under uses, we will show *gross* fixed asset expenditures and dividends (even though Beta paid none). The result is shown in Table 4-6.

In addition to taking account of dividends and expenditures for fixed assets, there are other refinements that sometimes may be appropriate. Included might be sales of stock, sales of fixed assets, and payment of stock dividends.[2]

Where longer-term changes in the balance sheet account are of primary importance, rather than changes in current assets and liabilities, we can prepare a statement of sources and uses of *working capital.* Recall the definition of working capital from the previous chapter. Net working capital is equal to current assets *less* current liabilities. By the same token, *changes* in net working capital (or sources and uses of net working capital) are obtained by taking *changes* in the current asset accounts and subtracting *changes* in the current liability accounts. With reference to Table 4-6, we can see that current assets (CA) increased by $261,500 as follows:

1. Cash increase	$ 1,500
2. Accounts receivable	$ 27,500
3. Inventories	$232,500
Total CA increase	$261,500

---

2. For a discussion of these and other refinements of the sources-and-uses statement, see Erich A. Helfert, *Techniques of Financial Analysis,* 3d ed. (Homewood, Ill.: Richard D. Irwin, 1972).

Over the same period, current liabilities (CL) increased by $213,450 as follows:

1. Bank borrowing	$ 95,450
2. Accounts payable	$ 70,000
3. Taxes payable	$ 13,000
4. Miscellaneous accruals	$ 35,000
Total CL increase	$213,450

Thus, net working capital increased by $261,500 *less* $213,450 or by $48,050.

We can therefore recast the data in Table 4-6 into the different format shown in Table 4-7. All Table 4-7 does is *net* out the working capital elements shown in detail in Table 4-6.

In addition to giving a financial picture of a firm's activities, sources-and-uses analysis identifies potential trouble spots that may need further investigation. The performance measures that follow provide some of the necessary tools for more detailed analysis.

Table 4-6 Beta Manufacturing Company: Revised Sources-and-Uses Statement, December 31, 1974–December 31, 1979

Sources		
Bank borrowing		$ 95,450
Increase accounts payable		70,000
Increase taxes payable		13,000
Increase miscellaneous accruals		35,000
Funds from operations		
Profit after taxes	133,050	
Depreciation	40,000	173,050
Total sources		$386,500
Uses		
Increase accounts receivable		$ 27,500
Increase inventories		232,500
Increase fixed assets, gross		97,500
Increase other assets		17,500
Reduce mortgage		10,000
Dividends		0
Total uses		$385,000
Increase in Cash		$ 1,500

Table 4-7 Beta Manufacturing Company:
Sources and Uses of Working Capital,
December 31, 1974–December 31, 1979

Sources of Working Capital	
Funds from operations	$173,050
Uses of Working Capital	
Increase fixed assets, gross	97,500
Increase other assets	17,500
Reduce mortgage	10,000
Dividends	0
Total uses	$125,000
Increase in Net Working Capital	$ 48,050

Measuring Profits and Profitability

In Chapter 3, we noted the importance of profits as a measure of performance. We noted also some of the difficulties of measuring profits. The longer the time period with which we are concerned, the less difficult the measurement problem and the smaller the divergence between true economic profit and measured accounting profit. Here we are using the terms *profit, income,* and *earnings* as synonyms.

Dollar Profits

Let us return now to the Beta Manufacturing Company. From Table 4-1, we see that Beta earned $28,400 after taxes in 1979. From this figure alone, we can draw few conclusions as to whether Beta's performance was good or bad. Dollar profit figures for another similar company or for the relevant industry grouping would be of little additional help. One way of evaluating the flow of profits is to compare the 1979 profit to corresponding figures from prior years. From such comparisons we can determine trends.

Several different measures of profits are available in Table 4-1. On the bottom line, we have *profit after taxes* (PAT), which takes account of all factors influencing earnings. We see that Beta's PAT increased rapidly from 1974 to 1976, then declined somewhat and remained essentially flat from 1977 to 1979. In the next section, when we measure *profitability*, profits in relation to sales, we will see a different picture.

Tax rates are beyond the control of management. To factor out the effects of taxes, we look at *profit before taxes* (PBT). In this case, PBT tells much the same story as does PAT, because tax rates remained unchanged over the period (see note *a*, Table 4-1).

Operating profit measures the performance of the firm's commercial activities without regard to financing. In 1975, operating profit declined by 29 percent relative to 1974, whereas PAT declined by only about 17 percent. In 1979, operating profit rose, whereas PAT remained essentially flat. Operating profit often is referred to as earnings before interest and taxes (EBIT).

Another widely used earnings measure is *earnings per share* (EPS), which is PAT divided by the number of shares of stock outstanding. Where the number of shares remains constant, EPS and PAT tell the same story.

Profitability—The Normalized Income Statement

We can learn still more about a firm's performance by measuring profits in relation to the sales necessary to generate these profits. Profits per dollar of sales gives us a measure of *profitability*. A convenient way to analyze profitability is to prepare a *normalized income statement* in which all items are expressed as percentages of sales. We then can examine the behavior of various elements of cost as well as that of profits. In Table 4-8, we prepare normalized income statements for Beta Manufacturing Company from the data in Table 4-1. What conclusions can we draw from the data in Table 4-8? As before, single figures mean little, and we need a standard of comparison.

Table 4-8   Beta Manufacturing Company: Normalized Income Statements

	1974	1975	1976	1977	1978	1979
Sales	100.0%	100.0%	100.0%	100.0%	100.0%	100.0%
Cost of goods sold	65.0	63.7	59.8	63.7	62.9	64.0
Materials	32.5	31.8	29.7	32.3	32.1	32.9
Labor	15.0	14.3	13.9	15.9	15.9	18.0
Overhead	17.5	17.5	16.2	15.6	14.9	13.2
Gross profit	35.0	36.3	40.2	36.3	37.1	36.0
Depreciation	1.5	0.9	0.8	0.5	1.0	1.3
Selling, general, and administrative expense	29.0	32.5	29.4	30.4	31.1	29.8
Operating profit	4.5	2.9	9.9	5.4	5.0	4.8
Interest	1.6	0.7	0.7	0.5	1.0	1.1
Profit before taxes	2.9	2.2	9.3	4.8	4.0	3.7
Taxes	0.6	0.5	3.4	1.6	1.3	1.2
Profit after taxes PAT	2.3	1.7	5.8	3.2	2.8	2.5

We can look at the figures over time to identify *trends.* Beta's profit after tax per dollar of sales declined during 1977–1979, whereas in absolute terms it remained flat. Materials costs have remained more or less a constant percentage of sales, labor has risen, and overhead has fallen. Gross profit and operating profit both rose during 1974–1976, then fell during 1977–1979. By looking at trends, we cannot tell whether a particular element is too high or too low, but we can tell whether it is getting better or worse. Trouble spots are identified, and management can determine causes. Normalized income statements can be prepared in any format and at any level of detail for which data are available.

To make a judgment as to whether an element of cost or profit in a given year is too high or too low, we must compare Beta with another firm with similar characteristics or with an industry average. Beta manufactures a wide variety of paints and varnishes, some of which are produced to specifications set forth by customers. We may have some difficulty finding comparable firms or groupings of firms. In the case of a department store or lumber wholesaler or electric utility, interfirm comparisons may be more meaningful.

Industry averages are available from at least two sources, Dun and Bradstreet and Robert Morris Associates (RMA), a national association of bank lending and credit officers. The RMA industry grouping that best fits Beta is the paint, varnish, and lacquer industry. RMA data for this industry indicate PBT/Sales of 4.0 percent, about in line with Beta's recent experience.[3] We must make such comparisons cautiously, however, because the firms in the RMA sample may not be exactly comparable to Beta.

Measuring Return on Investment

It is also useful to relate profits and sales to the investment required to generate these flows. Capital is one of society's scarce resources. A measure of the efficiency with which these resources are being utilized is return per dollar of investment, known as *return on investment* (ROI). Return on investment is widely used as a measure of financial performance.

Return on Investment (ROI)

Return on investment can be calculated in many ways. Some are based on standard accounting data and others on discounted cash flow tech-

---

3. For RMA data, see Table 4-21 at the end of this chapter.

niques, which we will discuss in Part III. The accounting-based measures of ROI involve some measure of profit or return divided by some measure of outlay or investment. The resulting ratio is usually expressed in percentage terms.

Let us consider an example. Suppose a bank advertises savings accounts that pay interest of 5 percent per year. A deposit, or investment, of $100 on February 1, 1980, would yield $105 in 1 year, of which $5 is interest and $100 is the original principal.

$$\text{ROI} = \frac{\text{Return}}{\text{Investment}} = \frac{\$5}{\$100} = 0.05 \tag{1}$$

$$= 5 \text{ percent per year}$$

In expression (1), the numerator, return, has a time dimension—dollars per unit of time—in this case, dollars per year. The denominator is in dollars. The quotient, ROI, therefore is a rate or percentage per unit of time—in this case, percent per year.

Calculating Return on Investment

Return on investment based on accounting data sometimes is referred to as the *accounting rate of return*. Both the numerator and the denominator can be calculated in a number of ways. These alternatives provide flexibility but result in ambiguity. Let us consider another example. Suppose an investment of $1,000 made at time 0 generates the earnings listed in Table 4-9 over its 4 year life.

Table 4-9 Return on an Investment Project

	Year 1	Year 2	Year 3	Year 4
Revenue	$670	$700	$730	$750
Cash expenses	200	200	200	200
Depreciation	250	250	250	250
Profit before taxes	220	250	280	300
Taxes @ 0.50	110	125	140	150
Profit after taxes	110	125	140	150

To calculate accounting ROI, we first must determine the return. We can choose profits either before tax or after tax. We also see that profit is different each year. Which profit figure do we pick? We can calculate an average over the 4 years, or we can calculate ROI for each year if we wish.

Now for the investment. Should we define it as the initial outlay, $1,000? Alternatively, we might argue that the funds actually devoted to the project decline as the outlay is "recovered" via depreciation. The book value of the investment, outlay minus accumulated depreciation, is $750 at the end of year 1, and $500, $250, and $0 at the ends of years 2, 3, and 4, respectively. We might define the *average* investment as $500.

Thus, we see that there are many ways to calculate accounting ROI. We can calculate it pretax or after tax. We can calculate ROI for each year or an average over the 4 years. If we calculate an average, we still have alternative ways to define the investment. Which method of calculating ROI is correct? All are correct—each answers a different question. There is no standard, generally agreed upon calculation. Therefore, when we use accounting ROI, in order to avoid confusion, we must specify exactly how it is calculated.

Return on Investment for a Firm

How do we measure a firm's overall ROI? Here, too, there are alternative ways to make the calculations. We might define investment as the total assets of the firm and calculate *return on assets*, that is,

$$\text{Return on assets} = \frac{\text{Profit after taxes}}{\text{Total assets}} \qquad (2)$$

Usually it is desirable to purge the total assets figure of intangible assets such as goodwill or patents. A variation on the calculation above would be to substitute operating profit before interest and taxes in the numerator to get *operating* return on assets, before taxes. We might also net out against assets all current liabilities that arise directly from operations, such as accounts payable, taxes payable, and various other accruals. We then have a balance sheet (Table 4-10) similar to that in Table 3-4. We then can calculate return on *net operating assets*, using either net profit or operating profit.

Table 4-10 Operating Assets

Net operating capital	Short-term borrowing
Fixed assets	Long-term debt
	Equity

Another variation is to calculate *return on equity*, that is,

$$\text{Return on equity} = \frac{\text{Profit after taxes}}{\text{Net worth}} \qquad (3)$$

Return on equity (ROE) explicitly takes account of the effects of financial leverage, whereas the various return on assets (ROA) measures described above do so only indirectly (when profit is measured after interest). By using a higher proportion of debt to finance its operating assets, a firm can increase its ROE via the effect of financial leverage. We will discuss financial leverage in depth in Part V, where we will find that, while an increase in leverage increases ROE, it also increases *risk*. For now, let us note that ROE must be used as a performance measure with great caution. Return on equity gives us a measure of return but ignores the riskiness or variability of that return.

The various measures of ROI are calculated for the Beta Manufacturing Company in Table 4-11, using data from Tables 4-1 and 4-2.

Each of the four ROI measures answers a different question, but all tell much the same story. Beta's ROI rose from 1974 to 1976 and then declined from 1977 to 1979.

Margin versus Turnover

The return generated by a firm's assets represents the difference between revenues and total expenses, including taxes. This difference often is referred to as *profit margin*. Over a period of time, say, a year, the total return depends not only on the profit margin per dollar of sales but also on the rate at which sales are generated. The rate of sales in relation to assets often is called the sales *turnover* rate. Thus, we can represent return on assets (ROA) as the product of two components:

$$\text{Margin} \times \text{Turnover} = \underline{\text{ROA}}$$

$$\frac{\text{Profit}}{\text{Sales}} \times \frac{\text{Sales}}{\text{Assets}} = \frac{\text{Profit}}{\text{Assets}} \tag{4}$$

By decomposing ROA into margin and turnover components, we can better analyze changes over time. If ROA is decreasing, for example, we can determine whether the decrease is due to declining profit margin or declining turnover rate. Such information is useful for planning corrective action. We also can compare data on margin and turnover with industry averages. Let us decompose ROA for Beta Manufacturing Company, as shown in Table 4-12. Note that line 3 is the product of lines 1 and 2, with differences due to rounding. Now some new conclusions emerge. The big increase in ROA in 1976 was due mainly to improved profit margins. The big drop in ROA in 1977 was due to a sharp decline in margins, offset somewhat by an increase in turnover. With the exception of 1977, turnover remained more or less constant from 1975 to 1979. Differences in ROA thus were attributable to variations in margin. Of particular signifi-

Table 4-11 Beta Manufacturing Company: Return on Investment

	1974	1975	1976	1977	1978	1979
1. Return on assets						
$ROA = \dfrac{PAT}{Total\ assets}$	3.0%	2.9%	9.3%	5.8%	4.3%	3.9%
2. Operating ROA, before taxes						
$OROA = \dfrac{Operating\ profit}{Total\ assets}$	6.0%	4.9%	15.8%	9.7%	7.8%	7.6%
3. Net-operating ROA, before taxes						
Net operating assets (thousands)[a]	$314	$272	$315	$354	$442	$532
$NOROA = \dfrac{Operating\ profit}{Net\ operating\ assets}$	7.4%	6.0%	20.4%	14.2%	11.2%	10.3%
4. Return on equity						
Net worth (thousands)[b]	$213	$222	$260	$290	$317	$346
$ROE = \dfrac{PAT}{Net\ worth}$	5.5%	4.4%	14.5%	10.3%	8.6%	8.2%

[a] Net operating assets equal total assets less accounts payable, taxes payable, and miscellaneous accruals.
[b] Net worth equals common stock plus retained earnings.

93

Table 4-12 Beta Manufacturing Company: Margin and Turnover

	1974	1975	1976	1977	1978	1979
1. Margin $\dfrac{\text{PAT}}{\text{Sales}}$	2.27%	1.75%	5.82%	3.22%	2.76%	2.49%
2. Turnover $\dfrac{\text{Sales}}{\text{Assets}}$	1.33	1.66	1.59	1.81	1.55	1.58
3. Return on Assets $\text{ROA} = \dfrac{\text{PAT}}{\text{Sales}} \times \dfrac{\text{Sales}}{\text{Assets}}$ $= \dfrac{\text{PAT}}{\text{Assets}}$	3.03%	2.90%	9.25%	5.81%	4.28%	3.93%

cance is the conclusion that the deterioration of ROA from 1976 to 1979 is due to a decline in profit margin, not sales turnover. Knowing this, Beta's management can focus its efforts to improve ROA.

The principal factors that determine the *margin* (the ratio of PAT to sales) and *turnover* (the ratio of sales to assets) can themselves be traced to more detailed changes in subfactors. A system of financial analysis and control designed to pinpoint the salient elements underlying the ROA achieved during any given period was developed by the DuPont Company many decades ago. It is a summary presentation that captures in one page (or one photographic slide) a concise picture of how and why ROA changes from one period to another. This system, adapted to suit the particular needs of individual companies, is widely used today to present results, both by major divisions and for the company as a whole, at periodic board meetings.

Figure 4-2 presents one adaptation of the DuPont system to report the results for Beta Manufacturing for the year 1979. Compared with a similar presentation for the preceding year or several preceding years, it indicates at a glance why ROA for Beta fell between 1976 and 1979.

Measuring Activity and Turnover

In this section, we explore some measures of turnover other than the Sales/Asset turnover rate discussed above. The measures discussed below pertain to three specific areas of managerial performance, namely, accounts receivable, inventory, and accounts payable.

Accounts Receivable Turnover

The majority of firms sell on credit. Credit terms often are viewed as a marketing tool to be used to increase the firm's profits. Sales transacted

Figure 4-2 DuPont System of Financial Control Applied to Beta Manufacturing Company

*Fixed assets plus other assets.

but not collected appear on the balance sheet as accounts receivable. Accounts receivable must be financed. A loose credit policy may increase sales and operating profits, but it also increases accounts receivable and therefore financing costs. The objective of credit policy should be to trade off costs and benefits and thus to maximize profits, or more precisely, to maximize the value of the firm.

In this section, we will limit our discussion to techniques for measuring the effectiveness with which receivables are being collected. We will measure collection experience against credit terms. We will not discuss how credit terms should be set; this topic, credit policy, will be discussed later in Chapter 8.

One useful measure of collection experience is the number of *days sales outstanding* (DSO) at any point in time:

$$DSO = \frac{\text{Accounts receivable}}{\text{Credit sales per day}} \qquad (5)$$

To calculate DSO, we consider only sales made on credit, excluding sales for cash. Sometimes accounts receivable will be reported net of a reserve for bad debts, and sometimes both the gross outstandings and the reserve will be given. When available, the gross receivables figure should be used to calculate DSO.

Selecting the period over which to calculate sales per day also is important. Usually it is best to use the shortest and most recent period for which data are available, say a quarter or even a month. We must be especially careful in selecting the averaging period when sales are seasonal or growing rapidly. Where a seasonal sales pattern exists, variations in the sales rate over the year will cause the DSO figure to vary even when there is no change in the underlying collection rate; the DSO figures computed at different points during the year therefore must be interpreted with caution. Where the firm is growing rapidly, we should select a short averaging period to reflect the most recent sales rate. We will discuss more refined techniques for monitoring accounts receivable in Chapter 8.

For Beta Manufacturing Company, we have only annual sales data, so we must use a year as our averaging period. Let us now calculate DSO figures for Beta Manufacturing Company. For December 31, 1979 we have

$$DSO = \frac{\$152,500}{\$1,140,000/365 \text{ days}} = \frac{\$152,500}{\$3,123/\text{day}}$$

$$= 49 \text{ days}$$

Assuming all sales were on credit, Beta's average daily sales rate during 1979 was $3,123 per day. Thus, the receivables balance of $152,500 on December 31, 1979, represented about 49 days of sales. Sometimes, the DSO figure is referred to as the *average collection period*.

As financial analysts, our principal objective in calculating DSO is to determine whether Beta is managing its receivables effectively. To answer this question, we must compare Beta's DSO with its terms of sale. Beta sells on two different terms, depending on competition and the bargaining power of customers. Some sales are on a *net 30* basis; that is, if bills are not paid within 30 days of the sale, the customer pays a higher price. Other sales are on a *net 60* basis.[4] If all sales were net 30, a DSO figure of 49 would indicate laxity in Beta's collection procedures. In this case, Beta's sales are approximately half net 30 and half net 60. We would therefore expect a DSO figure of about 45 if all customers were paying exactly on time. If data are available, we might compare Beta's DSO figure against an industry average.

It is useful also to examine the DSO figure over time to identify any trends in collection experience. Data are given in Table 4-13.

Table 4-13 Beta Manufacturing Company:
Year-End Days Sales Outstanding

Time	1974	1975	1976	1977	1978	1979
DSO	89	59	54	42	54	49

We find some variability but, excluding 1974, no clear trend. The variability might be due either to variations in the sales mix, changes in economic conditions, or some inconsistency on Beta's part in managing its receivables.

The DSO figure is useful in part because it can be compared to credit terms. To measure the relationship of accounts receivable to sales, the *Receivables/Sales ratio* can be calculated and expressed as a percentage. This ratio bears no intuitive relationship to credit terms, but for analyzing trends, it often serves as well as DSO. The reciprocal figure, Sales/Receivables, is referred to as the *receivables turnover rate*. We should note that the average collection period divided into 365 also gives us the turnover rate in annual terms.

Another technique for analyzing accounts receivable is to prepare an *aging schedule*. To do this, we categorize the receivables outstanding at any point in time according to the length of time outstanding. Suppose

---

4. A more detailed discussion of credit terms is provided in Chapter 6.

we examined Beta's receivables on December 31, 1979, and obtained the results given in Table 4-14. The aging schedule thus gives us considerably more information than does the DSO figure. The DSO figure of 49 days masks the fact that 30 percent of Beta's receivables on December 31, 1979, were more than 60 days old. The aging schedule tells management to look further at collection procedures.

Table 4-14 Beta Manufacturing Company: Accounts Receivable Aging Schedule. December 31, 1979

Month of Sale	Age of Account (Days)	Proportion of Total Receivables (Percent)
December	0–30	40
November	31–60	30
October	61–90	17
September	91–120	10
Prior	Over 120	3
		100

Inventory Turnover

An important aspect of managerial performance is the efficiency with which inventories are utilized. The basic function of inventories is to decouple the production process from purchases on the one hand and sales on the other. To reduce purchasing costs, firms buy raw materials in quantity and hold them until needed. Since sales and production seldom are exactly synchronized on a daily basis, inventories of finished goods are held to avoid lost sales due to lack of stocks. Inventory policy involves a tradeoff between the costs of purchasing and the cost of lost sales on the one hand, and inventory-carrying costs (primarily storage and financing) on the other. In Chapter 8, we will address the issue of how much to invest in inventory. Here, we are concerned only with measuring inventory utilization.

Inventory management must be judged relative to some overall measure of firm output. A widely used measure is the *inventory turnover ratio:*

$$\text{Inventory turnover} = \frac{\text{Cost of goods sold}}{\text{Average inventory}} \qquad (6)$$

Cost of goods sold, rather than sales, is the appropriate activity measure, because it contains elements of cost comparable to those included in the inventory figure. We can pick any period over which to measure turnover—a month, a quarter, or a year. Here again, we must be careful to take account of seasonal patterns. The inventory figure often must be calculated as simply the average of beginning and ending figures for the period in question. Sometimes, it is necessary to make do with only a beginning or an ending inventory figure.

We can compare turnover to industry averages or examine it over time. The inventory turnover figure for Beta Manufacturing for December 31, 1979 would be calculated as follows:

(A) Cost of goods sold   = $730,000   *INCOME STATEMENT*

(B) Average inventory   *BAL SHEET*

$$\frac{\$410,000 + \$420,000}{2} = \$415,000$$

     BEG. 2 END

(C) Inventory turnover (A/B) = 1.76 times

The inventory turnover figures for the period 1975–1979 are as shown in Table 4-15.

Table 4-15   Beta Manufacturing Company

TIME	1975	1976	1977	1978	1979
Inventory turnover	1.93	1.80	2.06	1.69	1.76

In our discussion of sources-and-uses analysis earlier in this chapter, we found inventories to be the largest single user of funds. Now we can see why. Beta is turning its inventory less than twice a year, far below the industry average, which we find from RMA data to be 4.9 times per year. Another interpretation is that on an average, materials are remaining in inventory for over 6 months. In addition, the data in Table 4-15 indicate a worsening trend. Inventory management seems to be a major problem area for Beta.

Payment Period

Creditors, especially trade creditors, are interested in how promptly a firm pays its bills. We can calculate the number of days purchases outstanding as follows:

$$\text{Days purchases outstanding} = \frac{\text{Accounts payable}}{\text{Purchases/day}} \qquad (7)$$

If we do not have data on purchases, we may have to improvise. In the case of Beta Manufacturing Company, we have (in Table 4-1) data on the materials component of cost of goods sold. If usage and purchasing rates were about the same, and if selling, general, and administrative expense does not include significant purchases (for office supplies, etc.), then we can use the cost of material as a proxy for purchases. The payment period for Beta for December 31, 1979 is calculated as follows:

$$\text{Days purchases outstanding} = \frac{\$122,500}{\$375,000/365}$$

COF Goods sold   MATERIAL   A/P

$$= \frac{\$122,500}{\$1,027/\text{day}}$$

$$= 119 \text{ days}$$

Calculating the payment period for each of the other years we obtain the data in Table 4-16.

Table 4-16 Beta Manufacturing Company: Year-End Days Purchases Outstanding (DPO)

Time	1974	1975	1976	1977	1978	1979
DPO	114	87	81	134	135	119

Days purchases outstanding also can be interpreted as the average payment period. Since Beta's terms of purchase are net 30 in most cases, we find Beta far overdue on its trade credit. Our earlier sources-and-uses analysis raised the question of whether Beta was relying too heavily on trade credit to finance its operations. Analysis of Beta's payment period confirms that this indeed is the case.

If we were Beta's management, we would immediately look further into the accounts payable situation to determine the reason for the slow payment and to plan corrective action. If we were a potential lender or supplier, we would look much more deeply into Beta's treatment of its trade creditors before advancing credit. One technique for looking further is the aging schedule, constructed in the same manner as that for accounts receivable in Table 4-14. As before, seasonal patterns and growth can seriously distort the calculation of the payment period. To avoid such distortion, it is best to use purchase data for the shortest and most recent period available.

Measuring Liquidity

The *liquidity* of a firm measures its ability to meet expected and unexpected cash requirements, expand its assets, reduce its liabilities, or cover any operating losses. In Part V, we will discuss policy decisions that determine how liquid the firm will be. Here, our objective is to measure liquidity.

Ratio Measures of Liquidity

One of the most widely used liquidity measures is the *current ratio,* defined as

$$\text{Current ratio} = \frac{\text{Current assets}}{\text{Current liabilities}} \qquad (8)$$

Current assets and current liabilities, according to standard accounting practice, have maturities shorter than 1 year. The ratio of the two thus gives a measure of the firm's ability to make ends meet in the short run. The current ratio for Beta for December 31, 1979 is calculated as follows:

(A) Current assets   = \$575,000

(B) Current liabilities = \$350,950

(C) Current ratio $= \dfrac{A}{B} = \dfrac{\$575,000}{\$350,950}$

$ = 1.64$

However, the current ratio is crude in that it does not take account of differences among categories of assets. Inventories, for example, may not be as quickly and readily turned into cash as are accounts receivable. The *acid test ratio,* or *quick ratio,* is a more stringent measure:

$$\text{Acid test ratio} = \frac{\text{Cash} + \text{Marketable securities} + \text{Receivables}}{\text{Current liabilities}} \qquad (9)$$

For Beta, the acid test ratio for December 31, 1979 is given by:

(A) Cash + Marketables + Receivables = \$155,000

(B) Current liabilities   = \$350,950

(C) Acid test ratio $= \dfrac{\$155,000}{\$350,950}$

$ = 0.44$

Dollar Measures of Liquidity

Sometimes it is useful to measure liquidity in dollar terms. One widely used dollar measure is simply *net working capital* (NWC), defined as current assets minus current liabilities. Dividing by sales gives *net working capital per dollar of sales*.

A much more stringent measure is *net liquid assets*, defined as short-term marketable securities minus discretionary debt maturing in less than 1 year. By "discretionary" we mean debt that excludes "operating" liabilities such as accounts payable and other accruals. The net liquid assets figure gives a measure of the firm's ability to respond to unexpected cash demands without reducing operating assets, such as cash, receivables, and inventories. By subtracting discretionary short-term debt, we obtain the net liquid assets available after repayment of current debt.

Let us now calculate the principal liquidity measures for the Beta Manufacturing Company and list the data in Table 4-17. We must omit the net liquid assets measure, since Beta holds no marketable securities. According to our ratio measures, Beta's liquidity has declined steadily since 1975. Net working capital increased moderately in dollar terms through 1978 but has declined steadily in relation to sales except in 1976. Overall, we see a picture of declining liquidity. Our analysis of liquidity thus confirms the suspicion raised earlier in our sources-and-uses analysis.

Liquidity may be declining, but is it too low? Perhaps Beta had excess liquidity during the mid-1970s. Small firms have excess liquidity so infrequently that we can dismiss this as a possibility. We may be able to get a better feel for Beta's liquidity by comparing its current and acid test ratios with industry standards, but we must take care that the industry data are from similar firms.

Table 4-17 Beta Manufacturing Company: Liquidity Measures

	1974	1975	1976	1977	1978	1979
Current ratio	2.28	3.40	3.01	2.28	1.94	1.64
Acid test ratio	0.92	1.14	0.84	0.61	0.54	0.44
Net working capital (thousands)	$176	$191	$232	$250	$275	$224
NWC / Sales	0.34	0.34	0.36	0.27	0.28	0.20

In measuring liquidity as well as other aspects of financial performance, we must avoid being too mechanical. We should be less concerned with standard labels and methods of calculation and more concerned with what we are trying to measure. Sometimes we may find that we can devise our own tailor-made measures in situations which standard measures do not fit.

Measuring Indebtedness

It is often of interest to creditors, investors, or management to measure a firm's indebtedness. There are two kinds of measures that can be used. *Debt ratios* are based on balance sheet relationships. These are of particular concern in the event of liquidation. The higher the level of debt relative to the liquidating or sale value of assets, the less likely it is that all creditors will receive all payments due them in the event of liquidation. *Coverage ratios* are based on income statement relationships. They measure the ability of an ongoing firm to meet periodic payments due on its debt obligations. The larger the annual debt burden (the sum of interest and partial return of capital due each year) relative to the size and stability of the annual income flow, the higher the probability that a *fall* in income might push the firm into default.

Debt Ratios

The ratio of *debt to total assets* measures the percentage of total assets financed by creditors. Debt includes all current liabilities plus long-term debt. A variation on the debt/assets ratio is the *debt/net worth* ratio, also known as the *debt/equity* ratio.

The debt/assets and debt/net worth ratios tell essentially the same story, since net worth is total assets less debt. Both ratios measure the protection afforded to creditors in the event of liquidation. A debt/assets ratio of 0.50 (debt/net worth of 1.0) indicates that assets need bring only 50¢ on the dollar in liquidation to fully protect creditors. We must take note, however, that the market value of assets in liquidation may be substantially less than book value. When using debt ratios to measure protection in liquidation, it is usually wise to eliminate from the balance sheet any intangible assets such as goodwill.

A third debt ratio that is sometimes useful is *long-term debt/total capital.* Total capital is the sum of long-term debt and net worth, where net worth includes common stock, retained earnings, and preferred stock if any. Long-term debt (LTD) includes both secured debt (mortgages) and unsecured debt (debentures). The LTD/capital ratio tells us the proportion of total long-term funds supplied by creditors as opposed to owners. For Beta, the debt ratios for December 31, 1979 are:

$$\frac{\text{Debt}}{\text{Total assets}} = \frac{\text{Total liabilities}}{\text{Total assets}} = \frac{\$376,950}{\$722,500}$$

$$= 0.52$$

$$\frac{\text{Debt}}{\text{Net worth}} = \frac{\text{Total liabilities}}{\text{Common stock} + \text{Retained earnings}} = \frac{\$376,950}{\$155,000 + \$190,550}$$

$$= \frac{\$376,950}{\$345,550}$$

$$= 1.09$$

$$\frac{\text{Long-term debt}}{\text{Capital}} = \frac{\text{Long-term debt}}{\text{Long-term debt} + \text{Net worth}} = \frac{\$26,000}{\$26,000 + \$345,550}$$

$$= \frac{\$26,000}{\$371,550}$$

$$= 0.07$$

In many situations, adjustments of the data are necessary to get an accurate picture of a firm's debt ratios. For example, firms using last-in, first-out (LIFO) inventory accounting will find their inventories, and therefore total assets and net worth, understated during periods of inflation. The value of plant and equipment may exceed its balance sheet cost. Leases and unfunded pension benefits are contractual liabilities that are not carried on the balance sheet. Adjustments such as these are too complex for us to take up here, but they can be quite important in some situations.[5]

We now compute these debt ratios for Beta Manufacturing Company for 1974–1979 and list them in Table 4-18. Beginning in 1975, Beta's total debt has been increasing relative to assets and net worth. The increase has been in short-term debt, with the long-term debt ratio declining as the mortgage was paid down. From the standpoint of creditors, the trends are in the wrong direction. Some additional conclusions might be drawn from a comparison of Beta's debt ratios against industry standards.

Coverage Ratios

Coverage ratios examine indebtedness in terms of *flows*, that is, using income statement relationships. In contrast to balance sheet debt ratios,

---

5. For an excellent discussion of these issues, see D. A. Lasman and R. L. Weil, "Adjusting the Debit/Equity Ratio," *Financial Analysts Journal*, 49–58 (Sept.–Oct. 1978).

Table 4-18 Beta Manufacturing Company: Year-End Debt Ratios

TIME	1974	1975	1976	1977	1978	1979
Debt / Total assets	0.45	0.34	0.36	0.44	0.50	0.52
Debt / Net worth	0.82	0.51	0.57	0.78	1.01	1.09
Long-term debt / Capital	0.14	0.13	0.11	0.09	0.08	0.07

which measure protection of creditors in the event of liquidation, coverage ratios examine the ability of the firm to meet its debt obligations as a going concern.

The *times interest earned* ratio measures the margin by which current earnings cover interest charges, and the extent to which earnings can decline before interest is threatened. The higher the ratio, the greater the margin of safety for creditors. One version of this ratio is calculated by dividing earnings before interest and taxes (EBIT) by interest charges on all debt, short-term and long-term. For Beta in 1979 we find

$$\text{Times interest earned} = \frac{\text{EBIT}}{\text{Interest}} \qquad (10)$$

$$= \frac{\$54,900}{\$12,900}$$

$$= 4.3 \text{ times}$$

When a firm has several debt issues outstanding and some are senior to others, we may wish to calculate coverage of each issue separately. Here we must proceed with care. Suppose a firm has outstanding two bond issues, *A* and *B; A* is senior to *B*, meaning that *A*'s interest is paid in full before any of *B*'s. We calculate the interest coverage for issue *A* using expression (10) with only the interest on *A* in the denominator. To get coverage on *B*, we include total interest (on both *A* and *B*) in the denominator. If we (mistakenly) calculated the coverage of *B* as earnings available after payment of interest on *A*, divided by interest on *B*, *B* would appear to have a higher coverage than *A*. The correct calculation gives *B*'s coverage as the same as overall coverage of both issues.

To illustrate, assume (quite hypothetically) that Beta's total interest payments of $12,900 in 1979 consist of a *senior* obligation of $8,000 that must be satisfied in full before any other interest payments may be made and a *junior* obligation of $4,900. The times interest earned for the first obligation would be $54,900/$8,000 or 6.9 times. For the junior obligation it is *not* ($54,900 − $8,000)/$4,900, which would give 9.6 times, and wrongly suggests that the junior obligation is *safer* than the senior; rather, it is given by $54,900/$12,900 or 4.3 times, exactly the same as the overall coverage of both issues together.

A variation on the times interest earned ratio is the ratio of interest to PAT plus interest. This ratio is the reciprocal of that in expression (10), with PAT plus interest substituted for EBIT. Profit after taxes plus interest constitutes the total payments going to creditors and owners together. The proportion of this figure going to interest gives a measure of financial leverage, the counterpart, in flow terms, of the debt/net worth ratio.

A more comprehensive coverage measure is *fixed-charge coverage,* which includes all contractual obligations rather than interest alone. Other contractual obligations include rent, lease payments, and principal repayments on long-term debt. The latter often are referred to as *sinking fund* payments about which we will have more to say in Part V. There are two complications involved in calculating the fixed-charge coverage number. Since lease payments and rent are *subtracted* before we arrive at EBIT, we have to add them back both to the numerator and to the denominator of the ratio. Also since principal repayments on fixed debt are not deductible for tax purposes, we have to convert this number to a before-tax basis when we include them in the calculation; we do so by dividing by the factor $(1 − T)$, where T is the marginal income tax rate, which is *assumed* to be 48 percent in all of the calculations in this section. With these two factors included, the fixed-charge coverage (FCC) for Beta for 1979 can be calculated as follows:

$$\text{FCC} = \frac{\text{EBIT} + \text{Lease} + \text{Rent}}{\text{Lease} + \text{Rent} + \text{Interest} + \text{Principal}/(1 − T)} \tag{11}$$

$$= \frac{\$54,900 + \$0 + \$0}{\$0 + \$0 + \$12,900 + (\$2,000/0.52)}$$

$$= \frac{\$54,900}{\$16,746}$$

$$= 3.3 \text{ times}$$

Note that Beta has neither lease payments nor rental payments.

A variation on the above is to add depreciation and other noncash charges to the numerator, thus providing a coverage measure in terms of operating cash flow rather than earnings. Over the long run, however, fixed charges must be covered by earnings.[6]

The concept of coverage can be extended to dividends on preferred and common stock. Although dividends are not contractual, as are interest and principal payments, dividends are an important obligation that should be covered except in times of serious financial difficulty. Coverage of dividends by earnings gives a measure of the likelihood of their being discontinued or reduced during hard times. The usual procedure in calculating dividend coverage is to add the before-tax equivalent of the dividend (dividend divided by $1 - T$) to the denominator of expression (11).

Let us now examine these coverage ratios for Beta Manufacturing Company (Table 4-19). Beta's principal payments on the outstanding mortgage amount to $2,000 per year. The tax rate during 1974–1979 is assumed to be 22 percent on the first $25,000 of income and 48 percent thereafter.[7] We see from Table 4-19 that Beta still is covering interest and fixed charges with some margin to spare, but a bad earnings year could put fixed charges in jeopardy. Also, the trend since 1976 is worrisome. Industry comparisons again might be helpful.

Table 4-19 Beta Manufacturing Company: Coverage Ratios

	1974	1975	1976	1977	1978	1979
Times interest earned	2.9	4.2	14.6	9.8	5.2	4.3
Fixed-charge coverage	2.2	2.5	7.8	5.6	3.7	3.3

Before leaving coverage ratios, let us note some limitations. First, coverage ratios consider only operating earnings and cash flows. During a financial emergency, fixed charges can be met from other sources of cash, such as a cut in planned capital expenditures or a reduction in working capital. Second, coverage ratios tell us nothing about the likelihood of a decline in earnings sufficient to put fixed charges in jeopardy. In Part V, we will consider all the firm's cash flows in analyzing debt capacity.

The various performance measures we have discussed thus far are outlined in Table 4-20, and summarized in Figure 4-3.

6. For a critique of alternative coverage ratios, see M. C. Findlay III and E. E. Williams, "Toward More Adequate Debt Service Coverage Ratios," *Financial Analysts Journal* **31**, 58–61 (Nov.–Dec., 1975).
7. For actual changes in rates in 1975 and again in 1979, see Chapter 2.

Table 4-20 Summary of Performance Measures.

Measure	Calculation
Profits	
1. Dollar profits	Profit after taxes (PAT); profit before taxes (PBT); operating profit
2. Earnings per share	$\dfrac{\text{PAT} - \text{Preferred dividends}}{\text{Average common shares outstanding}}$
3. Earnings per share (fully diluted)	$\dfrac{\text{PAT} - \text{Preferred dividends}}{\text{Potential shares outstanding}^{a}}$
Profitability	
4. Gross margin	$\dfrac{\text{Sales} - \text{Cost of goods sold}}{\text{Sales}}$
5. Operating expenses	$\dfrac{\text{Operating expenses}}{\text{Sales}}$
6. Net margin	$\dfrac{\text{PAT}}{\text{Sales}}$
7. Normalized income statement	$100 \times \dfrac{\text{Each item in income statement}}{\text{Sales}}$
Return on Investment (ROI)	
8. Accounting rate of return	$\dfrac{\text{PAT}}{\text{Average investment}}$ (typically)
9. Return on assets (ROA)	$\dfrac{\text{PAT}}{\text{Total assets}} = \dfrac{\text{PAT}}{\text{Sales}} \times \dfrac{\text{Sales}}{\text{Total assets}}$
10. Return on equity (ROE)	$\dfrac{\text{PAT}}{\text{Net worth}} = \dfrac{\text{PAT}}{\text{Sales}} \times \dfrac{\text{Sales}}{\text{Net worth}}$

[a] Assuming all convertible securities are converted.

Activity and Turnover

11. Days sales outstanding (DSO)
(also collection period)
$$\frac{\text{Accounts receivable}}{\text{Average credit sales per day}}$$

12. Inventory turnover rate
$$\frac{\text{Cost of goods sold}}{\text{Average inventory}}$$

13. Days purchases outstanding
(also payment period)
$$\frac{\text{Accounts payable}}{\text{Average purchases per day}}$$

Liquidity

14. Current ratio
$$\frac{\text{Current assets}}{\text{Current liabilities}}$$

15. Acid test ratio
$$\frac{\text{Cash} + \text{Marketable securities} + \text{Receivables}}{\text{Current liabilities}}$$

16. Net working capital to sales
$$\frac{\text{Current assets} - \text{Current liabilities}}{\text{Sales}}$$

17. Net liquid assets
$$\text{Short-term marketable securities} - \text{Discretionary short-term debt}$$

Indebtedness

18. Debt to total assets
$$\frac{\text{Total liabilities}}{\text{Total assets}}$$

19. Debt to net worth
$$\frac{\text{Total liabilities}}{\text{Net worth}}$$

20. Long-term debt to capital
$$\frac{\text{Long-term debt}}{\text{Long-term debt} + \text{Net worth}}$$

21. Times interest earned
$$\frac{\text{EBIT}}{\text{Interest}}$$

22. Fixed charge coverage
$$\frac{\text{EBIT} + \text{Lease} + \text{Rent}}{\text{Lease} + \text{Rent} + \text{Interest} + \text{Principal}/(1 - T)}$$

Figure 4-3 What to Look for on the Balance Sheet (all dollar figures in thousands) [Adapted from *Business Week* **58** (June 7, 1976)]

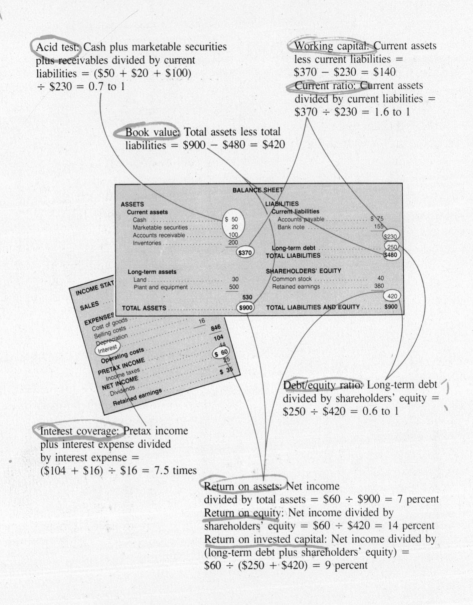

Acid test: Cash plus marketable securities plus receivables divided by current liabilities = ($50 + $20 + $100) ÷ $230 = 0.7 to 1

Working capital: Current assets less current liabilities = $370 − $230 = $140

Current ratio: Current assets divided by current liabilities = $370 ÷ $230 = 1.6 to 1

Book value: Total assets less total liabilities = $900 − $480 = $420

Debt/equity ratio: Long-term debt divided by shareholders' equity = $250 ÷ $420 = 0.6 to 1

Interest coverage: Pretax income plus interest expense divided by interest expense = ($104 + $16) ÷ $16 = 7.5 times

Return on assets: Net income divided by total assets = $60 ÷ $900 = 7 percent
Return on equity: Net income divided by shareholders' equity = $60 ÷ $420 = 14 percent
Return on invested capital: Net income divided by (long-term debt plus shareholders' equity) = $60 ÷ ($250 + $420) = 9 percent

Allowing for Inflation

Inflation causes serious distortions in financial reporting. Before the mid-1960s, when the rate of inflation was below 2 percent, the problem could be ignored without serious error. Today it cannot, because the effects of an inflation rate of 7, 8, or even 10 percent a year can be very significant.

How are financial reports affected? First, measurement of income is distorted in several ways. Increases in the prices of items held in inventory tend to overstate true earnings. Depreciation based on historical rather than replacement costs also overstates earnings. As a result of these distortions, firms pay taxes on "phantom" profits.

Offsetting these distortions is the impact of inflation on borrowed funds. During inflationary times, interest rates incorporate an "inflation premium" (discussed in detail in Chapter 14). This premium actually is not interest at all; rather, it is a repayment of principal to maintain the purchasing power of the lender's claim. Principal payments on debt should not be deducted from income, but the inflation premium included in the interest rate is so deducted under current accounting rules. So, unless some adjustment is made, taking the interest inflation premium through the income statement causes an understatement of earnings.

Distortions such as these affect many of the measures discussed in this chapter. Measurement of profits and profitability clearly are affected. So too are measures of ROI and debt coverage. Methods of dealing with these distortions are too complex for us to consider here, but financial analysts have to be aware of them.[8]

What about distortions of balance sheet data? Inflation causes problems here, too. Firms using LIFO inventory accounting find their inventories understated on their balance sheet relative to firms using the first-in, first-out (FIFO) method. Plant and equipment may have market values far above their balance sheet costs. Change in interest rates due to inflation affect the real value of previously incurred long-term indebtedness. All of these distortions add up to more headaches for the financial analyst. Both the accounting profession (through the Financial Accounting Standards Board) and the Securities and Exchange Commission (SEC) are in the process of developing reporting procedures that will provide financial data adjusted for changes in the price level. However, a final acceptable system has not yet been devised to replace the existing system of historical cost accounting for tax and reporting purposes.

Sources of Industry Data

Throughout this chapter we have emphasized the necessity for benchmarks, or standards of comparison, in analyzing performance. A single

---

8. For an excellent discussion of the problem of accounting for the cost of borrowed funds, see G. M. Von Furstenberg and B. G. Malkiel, "Financial Analysis in an Inflationary Environment," *Journal of Finance* **32,** 575–588 (May 1977).

Table 4-21 An Example of Data from Robert Morris Associates

MANUFACTURERS - PAINT, VARNISH & LACQUER
SIC# 2851

Current Data: 30(6/30-9/30/78) = columns 0-250M (4) and 250M-1MM (37); 99(10/1/78-3/31/79) = columns 1-10MM (74), 10-50MM (14), ALL (129)

Comparative Historical Data: 6/30/76-3/31/77 ALL (154); 6/30/77-3/31/78 ALL (147); 6/30/78-3/31/79 ALL (129)

0-250M (4)	250M-1MM (37)	1-10MM (74)	10-50MM (14)	ALL (129)	ASSET SIZE / NUMBER OF STATEMENTS			ALL (154)	ALL (147)	ALL (129)
%	%	%	%	%	**ASSETS**	%	%	%	%	%
	7.8	6.7	6.0	6.9	Cash & Equivalents			7.9	7.5	6.9
	32.2	28.5	29.9	30.0	Accts. & Notes Rec. - Trade(net)			27.6	28.3	30.0
	32.1	36.5	28.7	34.0	Inventory			33.3	33.7	34.0
	1.6	1.4	1.8	1.5	All Other Current			1.7	1.4	1.5
	73.7	73.1	66.5	72.4	Total Current			70.5	70.9	72.4
	20.2	19.3	26.4	20.7	Fixed Assets (net)			21.7	21.4	20.7
	.7	.6	1.4	.7	Intangibles (net)			.8	.7	.7
	5.5	7.0	5.8	6.3	All Other Non-Current			7.0	7.1	6.3
	100.0	100.0	100.0	100.0	Total			100.0	100.0	100.0
					LIABILITIES					
	8.0	6.1	5.1	7.2	Notes Payable-Short Term			7.8	7.2	7.2
	3.7	2.2	1.3	2.7	Cur. Mat.-L/T/D			2.2	2.5	2.7
	23.5	16.9	14.7	19.1	Accts. & Notes Payable - Trade			16.1	17.0	19.1
	6.2	7.1	8.1	6.9	Accrued Expenses			6.3	7.1	6.9
	1.6	2.9	2.6	2.6	All Other Current			3.8	3.0	2.6
	43.0	35.3	31.8	38.5	Total Current			36.2	36.8	38.5
	12.7	10.8	8.3	11.3	Long Term Debt			12.3	10.9	11.3
	2.3	1.0	2.3	1.5	All Other Non-Current			2.0	1.8	1.5
	42.0	52.9	57.7	48.7	Net Worth			49.5	50.5	48.7
	100.0	100.0	100.0	100.0	Total Liabilities & Net Worth			100.0	100.0	100.0
					INCOME DATA					
	100.0	100.0	100.0	100.0	Net Sales			100.0	100.0	100.0
	72.9	68.8	66.3	69.8	Cost Of Sales			69.5	69.0	69.8
	27.1	31.2	33.7	30.2	Gross Profit			30.5	31.0	30.2
	23.4	25.5	25.8	25.1	Operating Expenses			24.5	25.6	25.1
	3.7	5.7	7.9	5.1	Operating Profit			6.0	5.4	5.1
	1.0	1.1	.5	1.1	All Other Expenses (net)			1.5	.9	1.1
	2.6	4.6	7.4	4.0	Profit Before Taxes			4.5	4.5	4.0
					RATIOS					
	2.7	2.9	2.8	2.8				3.1	3.1	2.8
	2.0	2.1	2.2	2.0	Current			2.2	2.2	2.0
	1.4	1.6	1.8	1.5				1.6	1.6	1.5
	1.4	1.4	1.5	1.4				1.6	1.5	1.4
	1.0	1.1	1.2	1.1	Quick			1.1	1.1	1.1
	.7	.7	.9	.7				.8	.7	.7
	33 11.1	35 10.4	40 9.1	35 10.4				33 11.2	33 11.2	35 10.4
	43 8.5	46 8.0	45 8.1	45 8.1	Sales/Receivables			42 8.6	45 8.2	45 8.1
	51 7.1	59 6.2	59 6.2	57 6.4				56 6.5	54 6.8	57 6.4
	43 8.4	62 5.9	61 6.0	54 6.7				58 6.3	57 6.4	54 6.7
	59 6.2	87 4.2	74 4.9	74 4.9	Cost of Sales/Inventory			79 4.6	79 4.6	74 4.9
	87 4.2	122 3.0	89 4.1	107 3.4				99 3.7	104 3.5	107 3.4
	5.3	3.9	4.9	4.4				4.5	4.3	4.4
	8.2	6.2	7.0	7.1	Sales/Working Capital			6.4	6.4	7.1
	15.6	9.3	9.2	11.0				9.8	10.3	11.0
	9.4	14.8	11.5	11.5				9.8	17.6	11.5
	(26) 2.6	(55) 6.3	(11) 8.9	(95) 5.4	EBIT/Interest			(109) 4.9	(110) 5.5	(95) 5.4
	1.3	2.3	5.4	1.9				2.4	2.8	1.9
	5.2	8.2	16.0	9.5				7.0	8.8	9.5
	(21) 2.4	(50) 3.6	(11) 11.8	(85) 3.5	Cash Flow/Cur. Mat. L/T/D			(94) 3.4	(89) 3.9	(85) 3.5
	1.4	1.7	5.3	1.6				1.6	1.4	1.6
	.2	.2	.4	.2				.3	.2	.2
	.5	.3	.4	.4	Fixed/Worth			.4	.4	.4
	.8	.5	.6	.6				.7	.6	.6
	.8	.5	.6	.6				.5	.5	.6
	1.5	1.0	.7	1.1	Debt/Worth			1.0	.9	1.1
	3.2	1.7	.8	1.8				1.8	1.6	1.8
	32.0	29.9	38.6	30.8				28.3	28.6	30.8
	15.8	14.2	21.5	(128) 16.2	% Profit Before Taxes/Tangible Net Worth			(151) 18.2	(146) 18.4	(128) 16.2
	7.2	8.4	15.7	8.2				7.9	7.4	8.2
	11.7	16.1	17.1	13.4				14.4	14.7	13.4
	6.2	8.7	12.9	8.6	% Profit Before Taxes/Total Assets			8.4	8.2	8.6
	2.3	3.8	9.0	2.7				3.3	3.1	2.7
	31.5	22.4	11.3	22.2				20.7	22.0	22.2
	15.8	12.2	10.3	12.1	Sales/Net Fixed Assets			10.9	11.8	12.1
	10.2	7.6	5.6	8.0				7.1	7.2	8.0
	3.2	2.7	2.5	2.8				2.7	2.7	2.8
	2.6	2.2	2.2	2.3	Sales/Total Assets			2.3	2.3	2.3
	2.3	1.8	2.0	1.9				1.9	2.0	1.9
	.8	.7	1.1	.8				.9	.9	.8
	(34) 1.0	(70) 1.2	(12) 1.4	(119) 1.2	% Depr., Dep., Amort./Sales			(142) 1.2	(134) 1.2	(119) 1.2
	1.7	1.7	1.9	1.7				1.8	1.8	1.7
	.8	.5		.6				.6	.6	.6
	(19) 1.2	(38) .9		(64) 1.2	% Lease & Rental Exp/Sales			(71) 1.2	(62) 1.3	(64) 1.2
	2.0	1.7		1.8				1.8	2.1	1.8
	2.5	1.1		1.9				1.8	1.8	1.9
	(19) 4.7	(25) 2.9		(45) 3.4	% Officers' Comp/Sales			(61) 2.7	(52) 3.3	(45) 3.4
	6.7	3.8		5.2				4.7	5.6	5.2
1167M	59712M	489303M	740156M	1290338M	Net Sales ($)			1747704M	1790022M	1290338M
556M	21836M	230555M	364078M	617025M	Total Assets ($)			825533M	868475M	617025M

figure for a single period or point in time is of little use. We must compare that figure either to data for the same firm over time or to data for other similar firms. In this section, we discuss briefly sources of firm and industry data.

Firm Data

Publicly owned firms are required by regulations of the SEC to report financial data to investors on a regular basis. The *annual report* to stockholders is the primary reporting vehicle; this is often supplemented by quarterly reports. Even more detail is provided in the annual 10-K and quarterly 10-Q reports that must be filed with the SEC. Such reports contain the basic financial information that provides the starting point for financial analysis. Annual reports sometimes are collected by libraries and usually can be obtained directly from the firm.

Two important sources also obtainable in many libraries are the Moody's and Standard and Poor's services. Moody's publishes financial data on thousands of publicly owned firms organized by type of business. Moody's data go back many years and provide a valuable historical source. Standard and Poor's also publishes data on individual firms. In addition, the Standard and Poor's Compustat Tapes provide a machine-readable source of standard financial data on a large number of public companies over a 10 year period.

Industry Data

As noted earlier, Robert Morris Associates (RMA) compiles data for a large number of different industries. Included in RMA's data are basic balance sheet and income statement relationships and standard ratios of the type discussed in this chapter, broken down by size of firm. A sample of data available from RMA covering the paints, varnish, and lacquer segment of industry (in which Beta Manufacturing belongs) is reproduced in Table 4-21.

Dun and Bradstreet compile data on both individual firms and industries. They compile and publish 14 key financial ratios on 125 different lines of business, including manufacturing, wholesaling, and retailing.

The Federal Trade Commission (FTC) and the SEC jointly publish the *Quarterly Financial Report for Manufacturing Corporations*. The report includes balance sheet and income statement data broken down by industry groups and asset size.

Trade associations represent another source of industry data. Many industries maintain trade associations with a staff that collects data and makes it available on request.

---

categorize them by their *primary* product line, and be willing to tolerate any "impurity" thereby introduced.

In a word, don't automatically consider their figures as representative norms and don't attach any more or less significance to them than is indicated by the unique aspects of the data collection.

Fortune magazine, *Forbes* magazine, and *Business Week* also provide summary data on the largest corporations.

Summary

The income statement and balance sheet provide the basic data for analyzing financial performance. Sources-and-uses analysis identifies significant financial developments and points out areas for further investigation. A sources-and-uses statement is prepared by first recording all balance sheet changes over the period of time in question; then reorganizing the results into sources-and-uses format and refining the statement where necessary; and, finally, interpreting it.

Profits are measured in dollar terms by the income statement. Profitability (profit per dollar of sales) is measured by the normalized income statement. Such a statement also is useful for examining the behavior of costs over time in relation to sales. Return on investment (ROI) measures profit per dollar of investment. There are many different ways to calculate ROI, so care must be taken to avoid ambiguity. Often it is useful to decompose ROI into two components, margin and turnover. Margin and turnover themselves can be decomposed using the DuPont system of financial control.

The effectivenss of accounts receivable management can be measured by calculating how many days of sales are outstanding, also known as the average collection period. The accounts receivable aging schedule provides a second technique. Inventory management can be analyzed via the inventory turnover ratio. Accounts payable can be analyzed by calculating days of purchases outstanding. Activity and turnover measures must be interpreted very carefully where seasonal patterns and growth trends are present.

The ability of a firm to meet its obligations as these come due can be judged through the use of liquidity ratios. The current ratio (current assets divided by current liabilities) and the acid test ratio (current assets less inventories divided by current liabilities) are the most widely used. Dollar measures of liquidity are net working capital per dollar of sales and net liquid assets. Indebtedness can be measured both in stock terms, using various ratios of debt to other balance sheet items, and in flow terms, using coverage ratios calculated from income statement relationships. Two widely used coverage ratios are times interest earned and fixed charge coverage.

For analyzing financial performance, benchmarks, or standards of comparison, are necessary. Single figures for a single point in time are of little use by themselves and must be compared either to data for the same firm over time (to identify *trends*) or to data for other similar firms (*industry comparisons*).

Sample Problem

Alamance Corporation's balance sheet is shown here.

Assets	Dec. 31, 1978	Dec. 31, 1979
Cash	$ 435,000	$ 239,000
Marketable securities	648,000	378,000
Accounts receivable	1,079,000	1,459,000
Inventory	3,593,000	4,253,000
Other current assets	435,000	525,000
Total current assets	$ 6,190,000	$ 6,854,000
Fixed assets (net)	6,765,000	7,336,000
Total assets	$12,955,000	$14,190,000
Liabilities		
Accounts payable (trade)	$ 3,537,000	$ 3,932,000
Taxes payable	340,000	189,000
Other current liabilities	1,200,000	1,220,000
Total current liabilities	$ 5,077,000	$ 5,341,000
Long-term debt	3,012,000	3,000,000
Preferred stock	900,000	800,000
Common stock	1,500,000	1,700,000
Retained earnings	2,466,000	3,349,000
Total liabilities and owners' equity	$12,955,000	$14,190,000

1. Compute the balance sheet changes for Alamance Corporation from December 31, 1978 to December 31, 1979.
2. List the various sources and uses of funds for 1979.
3. Construct a sources-and-uses statement similar to Table 4-4.

Solution

1.

Assets	Change	Liabilities	Change
Cash	$− 196,000	Accounts payable	$+ 395,000
Marketable securities	− 270,000	Taxes payable	− 151,000
Accounts receivable	+ 380,000	Other current liabilities	+ 20,000
Inventory	+ 660,000	Long-term debt	− 12,000
Other current assets	+ 90,000	Preferred stock	− 100,000
Fixed assets	+ 571,000	Common stock	+ 200,000
		Retained earnings	+ 883,000
Total	$+ 1,235,000	Total	$+ 1,235,000

2. Sources	Uses
Changes in liabilities	Changes in liabilities
Increase in accounts payable	Decrease in taxes payable
Increase in other current liabilities	Decrease in long-term debt
Changes in assets	Changes in assets
Decrease in cash	Increase in accounts receivable
Decrease in marketable securities	Increase in inventory
	Increase in other current assets
	Increase in fixed assets
Changes in net worth	Changes in net worth
Increase in common stock	Decrease in preferred stock
Increase in retained earnings	

3. Sources

Increase in accounts payable	$ 395,000
Increase in other current liabilities	20,000
Decrease in marketable securities	270,000
Increase in common stock	200,000
Increase in retained earnings	883,000
Total sources	$1,768,000

Uses

Decrease in taxes payable	$ 151,000
Decrease in long-term debt	12,000
Increase in accounts receivable	380,000
Increase in inventory	660,000
Increase in other current assets	90,000
Increase in fixed assets	571,000
Decrease in preferred stock	100,000
Total uses	$1,964,000
Decrease in cash	$ 196,000

1. Thinking in terms of balance sheet changes, what are the principal sources of funds to a firm? What are the principal uses of funds?
2. Sometimes return on investment is ambiguous as a measure of performance. Why is this so?

3. Return on assets can be viewed as a product of two components. What are they?
4. What are the problems of measuring performance of accounts receivable and inventory management in a firm with a seasonal sales pattern?
5. What sources of information are available that provide data on firms? On industries?
6. Is it possible for a firm to earn a profit consistently and yet always be short of cash?
7. Can you imagine a firm having difficulty paying its bills when its current ratio is between two and three? Can you think of a firm that can operate successfully with an acid test ratio considerably lower than 1.0?

PROBLEMS

1. Below are year-end balance sheet data for Fuelish Motors, Inc. Arrange the data in a sources-and-uses format (following Table 4-4).

	1978	1979	Change	
Assets				
Cash	$ 434,400	$ 234,200	$ −200,200	S CASH
Marketable securities	647,800	371,700	−276,100	S
Accounts receivable	1,078,800	1,457,100	+378,300	u
Inventory	3,592,700	4,253,000	+660,300	u
Other current assets	435,800	525,200	+89,400	u
Total current assets	$ 6,189,500	$ 6,841,200	$ +651,700	
Buildings and equipment, net	5,192,700	5,684,000	+491,300	u
Other assets	1,571,800	1,648,400	+76,600	u
Total assets	$12,954,000	$14,173,600	$+1,219,600	
Liabilities				
Accounts payable	$ 3,537,100	$ 3,932,300	$ +395,200	S
Taxes payable	340,100	189,300	−150,800	u
Other current liabilities	651,800	1,219,300	+567,500	S
Total current liabilities	$ 4,529,000	$ 5,340,900	$ +811,900	
Accrued liabilities	921,300	1,087,500	+166,200	S
Deferred income tax	121,600	27,200	−94,400	u
Long-term debt	977,000	1,476,700	+499,700	S
Total liabilities	$ 6,548,900	$ 7,932,300	$ 1,383,400	
Owners' equity				
Common stock	$ 628,500	$ 595,900	$ −32,600	u
Retained earnings	5,776,600	5,645,400	−131,200	u
Liabilities and owners' equity	$12,954,000	$14,173,600	$+1,219,600	

2. A balance sheet for the Downtown Hardware Company is given here.

Balance Sheet

	Dec. 31, 1975	Dec. 31, 1976
Cash	$ 60	$ 1,420
Accounts receivable	60,290	118,826
Inventory	92,305	233,568
Total current assets	152,655	353,814
Fixed assets (net)	6,500	10,560
Total assets	$159,155	$364,374
Notes payable	$ 30,000	$ 51,000
Accounts payable	52,640	215,685
Accrued expense	1,500	2,110
Total current liabilities	84,140	268,795
Net worth	75,015	95,579
Total liabilities and net worth	$159,155	$364,374

(a) Prepare a statement of balance sheet changes.

(b) Organize the results of part a into sources-and-uses format (Table 4-4 of text).

(c) What further analysis does the sources-and-uses statement suggest?

3. A balance sheet for the Madison Company is shown at the top of the following page. Prepare a sources-and-uses statement for the Madison Company for the year 1979. Interpret the result.

4. Prepare a sources-and-uses statement for Beta Manufacturing Company for the year 1979 using data in Table 4-2.

5. Assume that Acme Manufacturing Corporation (Problem 1, Chapter 3) retired assets during 1979 that originally cost the company $600,000 and were carried at a zero book value. No new goodwill has been entered on the books since 1975.

(a) Prepare sources-and-uses-of-funds statements for Acme for each year 1977–1979.

(b) Prepare a single sources-and-uses-of-funds statement for the entire 3 year period.

(c) What areas of additional investigation are suggested by these sources-and-uses-of-funds statements?

6. Using the information given in Problem 5, prepare sources-and-uses-of-working-capital statements for Acme for each year 1977–1979. Prepare a single sources-and-uses-of-working-capital statement for the entire 3 year period.

The Madison Company

	Dec. 31, 1978	Dec. 31, 1979
Cash	$ 10,850	$ 431
Accounts receivable	41,614	68,313
Inventory	82,892	80,710
Miscellaneous current assets	7,681	6,413
Total current assets	$143,037	$155,867
Land	42,000	42,000
Plant and equipment	$217,575	$231,820
Less depreciation	36,816 180,759	42,015 189,805
Total assets	$365,796	$387,672
Accounts payable	$ 52,218	$ 50,946
Taxes payable	18,416	22,840
Accrued expenses	15,823	13,908
Total current liabilities	$ 86,457	$ 87,694
Mortgage payable	110,000	103,500
Paid-in capital	95,000	105,000
Retained earnings	74,339	91,478
Total liabilities and net worth	$365,796	$387,672

7. Prepare normalized income statements for Acme for each year 1976–1979. What questions are answered? What additional questions are raised?

8. Assume that all sales for Acme are on credit and that the company PROBLEM 1 ch 3 pg 71 averaged $58,000 per day in credit purchases from suppliers in 1976, $80,000 per day in 1977, $95,000 per day in 1978, and $108,000 per day in 1979.

   (a) Calculate the return on assets, the operating return on assets (before tax), the net operating return on assets (before tax), and the return on equity for each year 1976–1979. (*Note:* Exclude goodwill in this calculation.)

   (b) Calculate the following ratios for the December 31 balance sheet dates in each year 1976–1979: DSO, receivables turnover rate, inventory turnover, days purchases outstanding, current ratio, acid test ratio, net working capital per dollar of sales, debt to total assets, debt to net worth, and the times interest earned on both long-term debt issues. (Assume 1975 ending inventory of $3,900,000.)

   (c) Do these ratios answer any of the questions raised in Problem 5, part c?

9. The Beech Company has been suffering a severe decline in return on assets over the last 5 years, and management has asked you to recommend corrective action. Based on the preliminary information in the table, where would you begin your initial investigative efforts?

	1975	1976	1977	1978	1979
ROA (percent)	8.4	8.0	7.2	4.8	3.1
Sales (thousands)	$3,500	$4,600	$6,000	$9,200	$11,000
PAT (thousands)	$ 175	$ 225	$ 280	$ 415	$ 465

10. The ABC Company has enjoyed rapid growth in assets over the last 5 years although profits have been declining since 1977. Eight key ratios are shown in the table for the years 1977, 1978, and 1979. The median ratios for the industry are shown in a separate column.

Ratio	1977	1978	1979	Industry Norm
DSO	31	34	32	33
Inventory turnover	4.1×	3.6×	3.2×	4.0×
Days purchases outstanding	25	32	41	26
Current ratio	2.04	1.88	1.64	2.11
Acid test ratio	1.18	1.14	1.06	1.24
Debt/total assets	0.46	0.49	0.54	0.44
Debt/net worth	1.15	1.17	1.18	1.13
Times interest earned	11×	9×	7×	9×

(a) Evaluate the company's situation and suggest the most probable problem areas for further investigation.

(b) What problems do you see in relying on a strict comparison with median ratios for the industry?

11. Selected information from the Warm-Glow Light Company's financial records is summarized below. Using techniques discussed in this chapter, analyze the company's financial condition and performance. Does the analysis reveal any problems?

	1977	1978	1979
Sales	$10,385,000	$10,750,000	$9,495,000
Cost of goods sold	8,100,000	9,000,000	8,450,000
Net profit	750,000	500,000	250,000

11. (*Continued*)

	1977	1978	1979
Cash	$ 83,000	$ 50,000	$ 35,500
Accounts receivable	500,000	650,000	725,000
Inventory	1,000,000	1,200,000	1,500,000
Net fixed assets	2,000,000	2,000,000	2,000,000
Total assets	$ 3,583,000	$ 3,900,000	$4,260,500
Accounts payable	$ 583,000	$ 750,000	$ 973,000
Miscellaneous accruals	500,000	525,000	562,500
Bank loan, short-term	250,000	250,000	350,000
Long-term debt	750,000	750,000	750,000
Common stock	250,000	250,000	250,000
Retained earnings	1,250,000	1,375,000	1,375,000
Total liabilities and owners' equity	$ 3,583,000	$ 3,900,000	$4,260,500

12. The following summarized data were taken from the financial statements of two companies.

	(In Thousands)	
	Company *A*	Company *B*
Sales	$3,000	$9,000
Cost of goods sold	1,900	6,900
Operating expenses	400	1,600
Interest expense	10	110
Income taxes	240	300
Cash	1,000	4,000
Inventory	4,000	2,000
Fixed assets (net)	5,000	19,000
Long-term investments	400	100
Current liabilities	1,000	2,000
Long-term liabilities	100	1,800
Capital stock ($100 par value)	3,000	18,000
Retained earnings	6,300	3,300

(a) Which company has the better current position? Why?
(b) Which company has the greater working capital turnover?
(c) Which company has the better profit margin?
(d) Which company has the highest book value (net worth) per share?
(e) Which company is earning the better rate on resources available to the management?

13. During 1979 the Theta Company purchased a warehouse for $2 million cash. The company also acquired an office building for $3 million, giving a long-term note for that amount. In addition, the company issued common stock to retire a $4 million long-term note and retired other long-term notes totaling $3 million by paying cash. Net income during 1979 was $10 million. No assets were retired or sold during 1979. Balance sheets are given below.

	Dec. 31, 1978	Dec. 31, 1979
Cash	$ 4,000	$ 5,000
Accounts receivable	5,000	4,000
Inventory	10,000	14,000
Fixed assets (net)	25,000	28,000
Total assets	$44,000	$51,000
Accounts payable	$ 3,000	$ 5,000
Notes payable (short term)	4,000	3,000
Long-term notes payable	10,000	6,000
Common stock	15,000	19,000
Retained earnings	12,000	18,000
Total liabilities and owners' equity	$44,000	$51,000

(a) Determine the change in working capital during the year 1979.
(b) Construct a detailed sources-and-uses statement for 1979 similar to that in Table 4-5.

14. Selected data from three companies is provided below. Calculate the return on assets. Using the Dupont system, compare and contrast the three companies.

	A	B	C
Sales	$100,000	$375,000	$500,000
Profit after Taxes	1,500	3,000	4,500
Total Assets	$ 50,000	$100,000	$400,000

References

E. I. Altman, R. G. Haldeman, and P. Narayanan, "Zeta Analysis: A New Model to Identify Bankruptcy Risk of Corporations," *Journal of Banking and Finance* **1**, 29–54 (June 1977).

W. H. Beaver, "Financial Ratios as Predictors of Failure," *Empirical Research in Accounting, Selected Studies, 1966* (Institute of Professional Accounting, Jan. 1967), pp. 71–111.

R. O. Edmister, "An Empirical Test of Financial Ratio Analysis for Small Business Failure Prediction," *Journal of Financial and Quantitative Analysis* **7,** 1477–1493 (March 1973).

M. C. Findlay III and E. E. Williams, "Toward More Adequate Debt Service Coverage Ratios," *Financial Analysts Journal* **31,** 58–61 (November-December 1975).

M. J. Gordon, "Towards a Theory of Financial Distress," *Journal of Finance* **26,** 347–356 (May 1971).

E. A. Helfert, *Techniques of Financial Analysis,* 3d ed. (Homewood, Ill.: Richard D. Irwin, 1972), Chap. 2.

D. A. Lasman and R. L. Weil, "Adjusting the Debt/Equity Ratio," *Financial Analysts Journal,* 49–58 (September–October 1978).

B. Lev, *Financial Statement Analysis: A New Approach* (Englewood Cliffs, N.J.: Prentice-Hall, 1974).

R. F. Murray, "The Penn-Central Debacle: Lessons for Financial Analysis," *Journal of Finance* **26,** 327–332 (May 1971).

K. V. Smith and J. F. Weston, "Further Evaluation of Conglomerate Performance," *Journal of Business Research* **5,** 5–14 (March 1977).

G. M. Von Furstenberg and B. G. Malkiel, "Financial Analysis in an Inflationary Environment," *Journal of Finance* **32,** 575–588 (May 1977).

Developing the Financial Plan

5

In the last chapter, we were concerned primarily with analyzing past and ongoing performance. Our tools, such as sources-and-uses analysis and ratio analysis, were diagnostic in purpose, and our orientation was mainly historical, although we noted that the same analytical tools could be applied to plans for the future as well.

Another task of financial management is to look ahead—*to plan.* In simplest terms, a plan is a statement of what is to be done in some future period and effective ways of doing it. Why should a firm plan? Planning requires effort and therefore is not without cost. In an uncertain world, events are likely to deviate from even the most carefully formulated plan. Are the benefits of planning worth the cost? For most firms, planning of the type discussed in this chapter very definitely is worth the cost. A planning system improves coordination in an organization and encourages the kind of thinking that identifies difficulties before they occur. Many potential problems can be avoided and significant operating and financing economies achieved. A rather modest planning system usually will pay for itself many times over in terms of efficiency and lower costs.

Financial planning is one part of a larger planning process within an organization. A complete planning system begins at the highest level of policy with the firm's basic goal or purpose, usually stated in qualitative, mission-oriented, terms. From this is derived the firm's commercial strategy, defining the products or services it will produce and the markets it will serve. Supporting policies then are developed in production, marketing, research and development, accounting, finance, and personnel. The extent to which the system is formalized with detailed planning and budgeting systems in each area depends in part on the firm's size and the complexity of its operations. A planning system might be represented schematically as in Figure 5-1.

Broadly conceived, financial planning can be viewed as the representation of an overall plan for the firm in financial terms. Narrowly conceived, financial planning may refer only to the process of determining the financing requirements necessary to support a given set of plans in other areas. In this chapter, we will discuss techniques for accomplishing both of these purposes.

The basic elements of the financial plan are the projected income statement and balance sheet. Supporting elements may include a cash budget, personnel budget, production budget, purchasing budget, income and expense budget, and so on. These may be prepared by various organizational units within the firm and may be stated in terms of dollars, physical units, or people. These detailed budgets represent time-phased schedules of the expenditures, people, materials, and activities required to accomplish the objectives set forth in the overall financial plan.

Figure 5-1 A Planning System

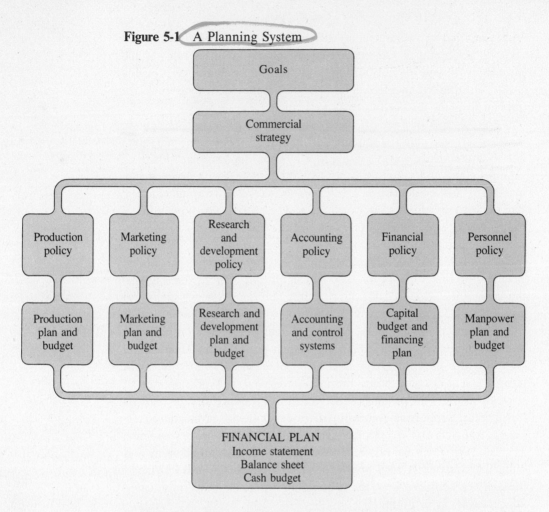

The starting point for the financial planning process is the firm's commercial strategy and the associated production, marketing, and research and development plans. We will refer to these plans collectively as the firm's *operating plan,* because they describe the activities in which the firm plans to engage. Initially, we will take the operating plan as given, although later we will see that operating plans sometimes must be modified in light of financing implications. In addition to the operating plan, we will also take as given the firm's long-term financial structure, its fixed assets and long-term liabilities. Decisions with respect to these areas are taken up later in this book.

Given the firm's long-term asset/liability structure and its operating plan, our objective is to represent its plans in financial terms and at the same time to determine financing requirements. We will focus our attention on financial planning over the near term, specifically the coming 12 months. We will discuss financial planning over longer periods later in the chapter.

The Neptune Company

As our vehicle for discussion and illustration, we will leave our old friend Beta, and use a new firm, the Neptune Company, a manufacturer of fishing and pleasure boats and electric outboard motors. Neptune was established in the 1950s and pursued innovative design and marketing policies coupled with conservative production and financing policies. It found this combination to be quite profitable. Financial statements for the year ending December 31, 1979, are given in Tables 5-1 and 5-2.

Neptune's sales pattern was highly seasonal, with nearly 50 percent of sales concentrated in the 4 months May–August. Over 90 percent of sales were in standard models, and Neptune followed a policy of level production throughout the year. The seasonal sales pattern coupled with level production resulted in a highly variable financing requirement

Table 5-1 Neptune Company: Income Statement, Year Ending December 31, 1979

	Thousands of Dollars
Sales	5,080
Cost of goods sold	
Materials and labor	3,150
Manufacturing overhead	290
Total	3,440
Gross profit	1,640
Depreciation	260
Selling and administrative expense	525
Profit before taxes	855
Income taxes @ 0.48	410
Profit after taxes	445
Dividends	240
To retained earnings	205

over the year. A firm with these particular characteristics will give us a good workout in financial planning. We also will see the flow of funds through the current section of the balance sheet as current assets expand and contract, and we will get a good illustration of the effect of operating policies on financial requirements.

Neptune normally begins its annual planning cycle each October and develops a financial plan for the 12 months January–December. To simplify matters for purposes of illustration, we will assume that the time is now early January 1980; the financial statements we need for 1979 appear in Tables 5-1 and 5-2. In the first section below, we will

Table 5-2 Neptune Company: Balance Sheet, December 31, 1979

	Thousands of Dollars
Assets	
Cash plus marketable securities	144
Accounts receivable	353
Inventories	1,080
Total current assets	1,577
Plant and equipment, gross	4,960
Less accumulated depreciation	1,850
Net	3,110
Total assets	4,687
Liabilities and Net Worth	
Note payable—bank	0
Accounts payable	148
Income taxes payable[a]	40
Other accruals	50
Total current liabilities	238
Mortgage payable[b]	960
Common stock	1,500
Retained earnings	1,989
Total liabilities and net worth	4,687

[a]Taxes payable of $40,000 is amount remaining to be paid on 1979 income taxes and is payable on April 15, 1980.
[b]Principal payments of $100,000 per year due in equal installments in June and December.

estimate financing requirements for each month during 1980. We then will discuss patterns of funds requirements, develop a cash budget, and discuss the uses of the financial plan. We will have something to say later about the applicability of our planning techniques to different types of organizations, including nonprofit organizations.

Estimating Requirements for Funds

Given Neptune's long-term asset/liability structure, what are the requirements to finance its operating plan over the next 12 months? Will outside bank financing be required? If so, how much? And when? When will it be repaid? The best way to answer such questions is to project the balance sheet to each date in question. If we leave the bank loan as the balancing or "plug" figure, the loan required to make the balance sheet balance is the answer to our question. The process requires painstaking work, but it is essential to good financial management.

The technique we will use often is referred to as *pro forma* analysis. As used in finance, the term *pro forma* can be translated to mean "as if." We project an income statement or balance sheet or cash budget ahead into the future to depict the firm's financial condition *as if* certain prospective events, namely, a given sales and production plan, had taken place. The term *pro forma* usually pertains to projections, but the concept is equally applicable to current or prior periods. A pro forma balance sheet could be constructed for some prior date depicting the state of affairs as if a prospective merger had taken place, or as if a particular division or subsidiary had been sold. Pro forma analysis is a very useful concept, with applications beyond those discussed in this chapter.

In constructing pro forma financial statements by the month for 1980 our starting point is the operating plan. In Neptune's case, the operating plan consists of sales and production plans and the expenditures for plant and equipment, materials, labor, overhead, marketing, and administration necessary to carry out those plans. The operating plan completely determines all items in Neptune's projected income statement except interest and taxes, and all items in the current section of the balance sheet except cash and the bank loan. In other words, the operating plan determines the short-term financing requirements. Our objective is to ascertain the amounts and timing of those financing requirements. To do so we will project, on the basis of the operating plan, the income statement and balance sheet, with cash and the bank loan as the balancing figures. Let us now describe Neptune's operating plan.

Operating Plan

Based on several economic forecasts, a knowledge of its markets, and the historical seasonal sales pattern, Neptune's marketing department estimated 1980 sales as listed in Table 5-3.

Table 5-3 Neptune Company: 1980 Sales Plan

	Thousands of Dollars		Thousands of Dollars
December 1979	250		
January 1980	220	July	715
February	275	August	605
March	385	September	495
April	495	October	385
May	605	November	275
June	770	December	275
		1980 total	$5,500

In order to minimize costs, production was scheduled at a level rate throughout the year. Neptune historically had followed a policy of maintaining a high inventory level, and in the past, inventory turnover had averaged only about 3.0 times per year. In an effort to improve turnover, management decided to reduce finished goods inventories gradually by holding production at the 1979 rate, even though a sales increase of about 8 percent was forecast. Accordingly, purchases were scheduled at $125,000 per month, and production was scheduled at a level rate of $285,000 per month ($125,000 in materials, $135,000 in labor, and $25,000 in manufacturing overhead).

Materials and labor historically had averaged 62 percent of sales. For 1980 as a whole, cost of goods sold should therefore total $3,411,000 for materials and labor (0.62 × $5,500,000) plus $300,000 for manufacturing overhead, or $3,711,000 in total. With production scheduled at $285,000 × 12 = $3,420,000, inventories should decline over the year.

Selling and administrative expenses, including interest, were expected to average approximately $45,000 per month. Work was expected to be completed in February on a $500,000 expansion and modernization program, with payments to be made in equal installments in January and February. No further capital expenditures were planned in 1980. Depreciation, with that for the new facilities and equipment included, was expected to average $25,000 per month.

All of Neptune's sales were made on credit, with approximately half on terms of net 30 and half net 60, the latter terms being made necessary by competitive pressures. Neptune's credit manager had determined that historically, essentially 100 percent of a month's sales remained outstanding at month end, about 50 percent were collected in the first month following, and about 50 percent were collected in the second month following. With respect to disbursements, accounts payable at the end of any month were settled in the following month. Payments for direct labor, manufacturing overhead, and selling and administrative expenses were generally made with a time lag of about 1 week, giving rise to accruals that remained constant at about $50,000 at the current rate of operations.

Internal Revenue Service regulations required that estimated taxes for any year be paid in four equal installments during the year in the months of April, June, September, and December. Mortgage principal payments of $50,000 were due in June and December. Dividend policy was to remain unchanged, with payments of $60,000 in March, June, September, and December.

Neptune followed a policy of maintaining a minimum cash balance of $50,000, borrowing where necessary to maintain that figure and investing all amounts over that figure in United States Treasury Bills. Holdings of bills amounted to $94,000 on December 31, 1979. Neptune historically had used bank credit to finance its seasonal buildup of receivables and inventories. Relations with a local bank were excellent, and Neptune currently had access to a seasonal line of credit of $1 million secured by a blanket lien on inventories and receivables. Under the agreement, Neptune could borrow up to $1 million at any time, provided only that inventories plus receivables exceeded the loan by 75 percent and the loan was off the books, that is, reduced to zero, for at least 2 months per year.

Pro Forma Income Statement

We now have the information necessary to construct pro forma financial statements for Neptune. It is necessary to begin with the income statement, because in order to do the balance sheet we need the transfer to retained earnings, and to get this figure we must know the profit after tax (PAT). We will use the same format as in Table 5-1. We have our sales projection in Table 5-3. Assuming no change in prices relative to costs, we can project cost of goods sold at the historical figure of 62 percent of sales for materials and labor plus $25,000 per month for manufacturing overhead. Subtracting depreciation and selling and administrative expenses gives profit before taxes (PBT). As in all the computations in this book, taxes are computed at 48 percent. The complete pro forma income statement for each month in 1980 is given in Table 5-4.

To get the transfer to retained earnings each month, we subtract dividends from PAT. Dividends often are not included in the income statement, because they are not expenses, but we have shown them in Table 5-4 for convenience. This transfer to retained earnings will become an input to our pro forma balance sheet.

Before leaving the pro forma income statement, let us note the critical importance of the sales plan. The sales plan forms the basis for planning production levels, marketing programs, and a variety of activities within the firm. In a firm with good management controls, particularly on expenses, most of the uncertainty about the profit plan results from uncertainty about the sales plan. As we will see shortly, the sales and production plans together determine a good part of the balance sheet. If actual sales deviate significantly from planned levels, the effects on the firm's financial condition are likely to be substantial.

Pro Forma Balance Sheet

Our objective is to determine the amounts and timing of financing required to carry out the operating plan over the next 12 months. Our procedure will be to project all items other than cash and the bank loan, leaving the latter two as our balancing figures. The items to be projected

Table 5-4 Neptune Company: Pro Forma Income Statements, 1980 (Thousands of Dollars)

	Actual 1979	Jan.	Feb.	Mar.	Apr.	May	June	July	Aug.	Sept.	Oct.	Nov.	Dec.	Total 1980
Sales	5,080	220	275	385	495	605	770	715	605	495	385	275	275	5,500
Cost of goods sold														
Materials and labor @ 0.62	3,150	136	171	239	307	375	477	443	375	307	239	171	171	3,411
Manufacturing overhead	290	25	25	25	25	25	25	25	25	25	25	25	25	300
Total	3,440	161	196	264	332	400	502	468	400	332	264	196	196	3,711
Gross profit	1,640	59	79	121	163	205	268	247	205	163	121	79	79	1,789
Depreciation	260	25	25	25	25	25	25	25	25	25	25	25	25	300
Selling and administrative expense[a]	525	45	45	45	45	45	45	45	45	45	45	45	45	540
Profit before taxes	855	(11)	9	51	93	135	198	177	135	93	51	9	9	949
Taxes @ 0.48	410	(5)	4	24	45	65	95	85	65	45	24	4	4	455
Profit after taxes	445	(6)	5	27	48	70	103	92	70	48	27	5	5	494
Dividends	240	—	—	60	—	—	60	—	—	60	—	—	60	240
To retained earnings	205	(6)	5	(33)	48	70	43	92	70	(12)	27	5	(55)	254

[a] Includes interest

are determined either directly or indirectly by the operating plan or by external commitment (taxes and mortgage payments). We will proceed item by item down the balance sheet, using the format in Table 5-2. We will give particular attention to accounts receivable and inventories, because we can expect these items to be highly variable where sales are seasonal and production is level.

In situations in which sales are not seasonal and the collection pattern is stable, we can project accounts receivable using historical relationships to sales. Perhaps the simplest method is to determine the historical receivables/sales ratio and multiply this figure by sales in each period of the projection. We get the same result by assuming that the number of days sales outstanding remains constant over time.

Where sales are highly seasonal, as in Neptune's case, neither of these methods is sufficiently accurate for projecting receivables balances during the year. In such cases, we must go more deeply into the relationship between sales and collections. In Neptune's case, we know that about 50 percent of any month's sales are collected in the first month following and the remainder in the second month following. Therefore, at the end of any month there will be outstanding that month's sales plus half of the prior month's sales. At the end of January, the receivables balance will include January's sales of $220,000 plus half of December's sales of $250,000, for a total of $345,000. At the end of February, we have February sales of $275,000 plus half of January's, and so on. The complete projection of receivables is given later in Table 5-6. When we discuss the cash budget, we will develop a schedule of collections that can be used as an alternative method of projecting receivables.

Inventories also require special attention. When production and sales follow approximately the same pattern, for example, both level or both seasonal, inventories can be projected using a simple inventory/sales ratio. In Neptune's case, production and sales are not in step, and we must take account of the relation between the two in each month in order to project inventories. At the end of any month, inventory will equal inventory at the beginning of the month, plus production for the month, less cost of goods sold during the month. We know that production each month is $285,000 at cost: $125,000 for materials, $135,000 for direct labor, and $25,000 for manufacturing overhead. We have the cost of goods sold in each month in Table 5-4. Using the months of January–March to illustrate, we can calculate inventory levels as shown in Table 5-5. The complete inventory projection is given in Table 5-6.

In Neptune's case, the problem is simplified somewhat by the fact that purchases are scheduled at $125,000 per month, exactly the rate at which raw materials are to be consumed. Were this not the case, it might

Table 5-5 Neptune Company:
Projection of Inventories

	Thousands of Dollars
Inventory, December 31, 1979	1,080
Add January production	+285
Subtract January cost of goods sold	−161
Inventory, January 31, 1980	1,204
Add February production	+285
Subtract February cost of goods sold	−196
Inventory, February 28, 1980	1,293
Add March production	+285
Subtract March cost of goods sold	−264
Inventory, March 31, 1980	1,314

be necessary to project raw materials, work in process, and finished goods inventories separately.

To project plant and equipment, we add the planned outlays of $250,000 in January and February to the gross plant and equipment figure for December. Depreciation accumulates at $25,000 per month.

Since payments for purchases are made in the month following, accounts payable at the end of each month will equal purchases made during the month. Other accruals should remain constant at $50,000.

Income taxes payable require a complete schedule. We know that 1980 estimated taxes of $455,000 must be paid in advance in equal installments in April, June, September, and December. Taxes payable at the end of any month equal the balance at the beginning of the month, plus taxes due on income for the month (Table 5-4), minus tax payments made during the month. In April, in addition to $114,000 on 1980 income (one-fourth of $455,000), Neptune also must pay the $40,000 still due as of December 31, 1979, on 1979 income.

The mortgage payable balance can be projected by subtracting the $50,000 payments due in June and December. Retained earnings are projected by adding to each month's beginning balance the amount retained during the month (from Table 5-4).

Common stock remains constant at $1,500,000, since no new issues are planned during 1980.

We now have projected all items except cash and the bank loan, with the final results given in Table 5-6. To complete the balance sheet for each month, we must determine whether Neptune must borrow that month. We know that Neptune maintains a minimum cash balance of

Table 5-6 Neptune Company: Pro Forma Balance Sheets, 1980 (Thousands of Dollars)

	Actual Dec. 31, 1979	Jan.	Feb.	Mar.	Apr.	May	June	July	Aug.	Sept.	Oct.	Nov.	Dec.
Assets													
Cash plus marketable securities	144	50	50	50	50	50	50	50	50	159	379	489	266
Accounts receivable	353	345	385	523	688	853	1,073	1,100	963	798	633	468	413
Inventories	1,080	1,204	1,293	1,314	1,267	1,152	935	752	637	590	611	700	789
Total current assets	1,577	1,599	1,728	1,887	2,005	2,055	2,058	1,902	1,650	1,547	1,623	1,657	1,468
Plant and equipment, gross	4,960	5,210	5,460	5,460	5,460	5,460	5,460	5,460	5,460	5,460	5,460	5,460	5,460
Less accumulated depreciation	1,850	1,875	1,900	1,925	1,950	1,975	2,000	2,025	2,050	2,075	2,100	2,125	2,150
Net	3,110	3,335	3,560	3,535	3,510	3,485	3,460	3,435	3,410	3,385	3,360	3,335	3,310
Total assets	4,687	4,934	5,288	5,422	5,515	5,540	5,518	5,337	5,060	4,932	4,983	4,992	4,778
Liabilities and Net Worth													
Note payable—bank	0	281	626	769	923	813	817	459	47	0	0	0	0
Accounts payable	148	125	125	125	125	125	125	125	125	125	125	125	125
Income taxes payable[a]	40	35	39	63	(46)	19	0	85	150	81	105	109	0
Other accruals	50	50	50	50	50	50	50	50	50	50	50	50	50
Total current liabilities	238	491	840	1,007	1,052	1,007	992	719	372	256	280	284	175
Mortgage payable[b]	960	960	960	960	960	960	910	910	910	910	910	910	860
Common stock	1,500	1,500	1,500	1,500	1,500	1,500	1,500	1,500	1,500	1,500	1,500	1,500	1,500
Retained earnings	1,989	1,983	1,988	1,955	2,003	2,073	2,116	2,208	2,278	2,266	2,293	2,298	2,243
Total liabilities and net worth	4,687	4,934	5,288	5,422	5,515	5,540	5,518	5,337	5,060	4,932	4,983	4,992	4,778

[a]The December 31, 1979 figure of $40,000 is the amount remaining on 1979 tax and is payable on April 15, 1980. The 1980 estimated tax is payable in equal installments in April, June, September, and December. The negative figure in April represents prepaid taxes.
[b]$100,000 per year payable in June and December.

$50,000 and borrows from the bank to prevent cash from falling below that figure. When cash rises above $50,000, the loan is paid down and any excess is invested in United States Treasury Bills. Thus, in any month in which Neptune borrows, cash will be at a level of $50,000. When cash plus marketable securities is above $50,000, the loan balance will be zero.

To determine the cash and loan balances in any month, we first assume a $50,000 cash figure and add it to other asset categories. If the resulting total asset figure exceeds total liabilities excluding the loan, then the loan makes up the difference. If less than total liabilities excluding the loan, marketable securities make up the difference. In January, for example, total assets including $50,000 cash are $4,934,000 (Table 5-6). Total liabilities excluding the loan are $4,653,000, so a loan of $281,000 is needed to balance. Proceeding this way, we can calculate the cash and loan balances for February through August. In September, total liabilities exceed total assets, so we know the loan will be zero. Cash of $159,000 is needed to balance. Cash figures for October–December are found in like manner. The complete balance sheet is shown in Table 5-6.

We see from Table 5-6 that Neptune must begin borrowing in January and borrow additional amounts each month through April, after which the loan declines to zero by the end of September. Neptune is "in the bank" for 8 months out of the year, and the loan reaches a maximum of $923,000. By increasing its long-term financing via common stock or mortgages or other long-term debt, Neptune could reduce both its level of short-term borrowing and the length of time each year during which it must borrow. Should Neptune rely more on long-term and less on short-term financing? Here we raise the important question of the appropriate *maturity structure* of Neptune's liabilities and the closely related question of *liquidity.* We will deal with these questions in Part V.

Let us note again the critical importance of the sales plan in constructing the pro forma balance sheet. To meet a given sales plan, we develop a production plan and programs of other kinds throughout the firm. The sales and production plans together determine much of the balance sheet.

Pro Forma Sources-and-Uses Statement

Because of seasonality, a sources-and-uses statement for a single month is not likely to be useful in Neptune's case. Over a full year, the effect of seasonality is eliminated. Following procedures discussed in Chapter 4, we can construct a sources-and-uses statement for the year 1980 (Table 5-7).

A sources-and-uses statement quickly reveals any changes in balance sheet relationships resulting from the financial plan. We see, for example,

Table 5-7 Neptune Company:
Sources and Uses of Funds,
December 31, 1979–December 31, 1980

		Thousands of Dollars
Sources		
Funds from operations		
Profit after taxes	494	
Depreciation	300	794
Reduce inventories		291
Total sources		1,085
Uses		
Increase accounts receivable		60
Expand plant and equipment		500
Reduce accounts payable		23
Reduce taxes payable		40
Reduce mortgage		100
Pay dividends		240
Total uses		963
Increase in Cash Balance		122

that Neptune is reducing inventories while receivables and other categories of assets are expanding. Although it is not always necessary in connection with a financial plan, a sources-and-uses analysis sometimes reveals aspects of the plan that are not otherwise apparent.

Shortcuts

Preparing financial plans is time-consuming and therefore costly. We must keep in mind costs as well as benefits and look for ways to streamline the procedure without sacrificing too much accuracy. In general, we should spend our time on items that are large and difficult to estimate—receivables and inventories, in Neptune's case. We should not spend excessive time on items that either are small or easily estimated with reasonably accuracy. It is important, however, to be *consistent,* to base all projected financial statements on a single consistent set of assumptions.

Monthly balance sheets were necessary in Neptune's case because of its highly seasonal sales pattern. Often, quarterly statements will do the job, and sometimes annual estimates are all that is required. Where we need only annual statements, seasonality is of no concern, because we are looking at the same point in each year.

Where seasonality is not a problem, we often can use simpler techniques than those used in Neptune's case. One such technique is the *percent of sales* approach. Since the sales plan is nearly always the critical element in a financial plan, when relationships remain fairly stable over time, we can project many items using historical percentage relationships to sales. Several of the major operating items in the income statement and balance sheet can be projected in this manner. For example, as a first approximation we can assume that the cost of materials and labor in 1980 will be in the same proportion to 1980 sales as they were in 1979. Thus, using the 1979 ratio of 62 percent of sales, we apply the 62 percent factor to projected sales of $5,500,000 expected in 1980 and get a figure of $3,410,000 as our estimate for cost of materials and labor in 1980 (see Table 5-4. The slight difference is due to rounding.)

Other items for which the percentage of sales method generally works well are (1) administrative and selling expenses, (2) accounts receivable, and (3) accounts payable. Of course, if there are specific reasons to believe that the ratio of these items to sales will change, the percentage factor can be adjusted up or down to get a better approximation.

Some items are not closely "sales-related." For example, items such as interest on debt, principal payments on debt, and depreciation can be projected more accurately on the basis of independent facts. In summary, the extent to which the simple percent-of-sales approach to projection is used depends on the characteristics of the firm itself and on the degree of accuracy required. As always we should note that the approach should be suited to the task and the available information.

Patterns of Funds Requirements

A firm's requirement for external financing depends on the nature of its business and the operating plan it adopts. Let us examine some of the more common patterns of financing.

Seasonal Requirements

Neptune's financing requirement is strongly seasonal, rising rapidly in the spring and falling to zero by September. *Seasonality* refers to changes that occur within a year in a regular pattern that recurs year after year. By definition, seasonal movements are predictable.

In Table 5-6, we see the flow of funds into and out of accounts receivable and inventory. The sales peak comes in June; the receivables peak in July. Because production is level, inventories rise when the sales rate (figured at cost) is below the production rate, as is the case during the period October–March. When cost of goods sold rises above production in April, inventories begin to decline from the March peak of

$1,314,000. Thus, the inventory peak comes before the sales peak, and the receivables peak after. The financing requirement is related to the sum of the receivables and inventory figures, and the peak occurs in April.

Any firm with a seasonal sales pattern is likely to exhibit a similar seasonal pattern in receivables, probably with a slight lag. If production and sales are not synchronized, inventories also will exhibit a seasonal pattern. The resulting financing requirement may be handled entirely by outside sources such as bank credit. Alternatively, as in Neptune's case, part may be handled via bank credit and part by expanding and contracting holdings of liquid assets. Where external financing is used, the requirement is said to be short term in nature, existing over only part of a year.

The Growing Firm

Neptune's 1980 sales are projected to increase about 8.3 percent over 1979. To generate sustained sales growth over long periods, additional assets normally are required, fixed assets as well as working capital. Where working capital is managed effectively, it should grow at approximately the same rate as sales, assuming the product mix and operating plan remain stable.

These increasing requirements must be financed. A portion of these requirements normally will be financed spontaneously by current liabilities that expand along with sales.

For example, as a firm expands its output, it will generally require larger inventories and it will make larger purchases of materials. As a result, its accounts payable will also increase, and this increase represents a source of funds. Also, if employment and profits rise along with increased output, then wages payable and taxes payable will rise automatically representing another source of funds. The remaining requirement must be financed by earnings retention or through outside sources.

To examine the financing requirement induced by growth, consider a firm with sales that are growing at a steady rate. Let us assume that a *steady-state* growth is attained and earnings retention is such that every item on the balance sheet grows at exactly the same percentage rate each year. The firm may require additional outside financing, but creditors are willing to supply the funds because balance sheet relationships and relative risk remain stable through time.

Now suppose that retained earnings grow more slowly than sales. Over the long run, with no outside equity financing, the rate of growth in equity (retained earnings plus common stock) will approximately equal the product of after-tax return on equity and the percentage of earnings retained, that is,

$$g = \frac{PAT}{Equity} \times \frac{Dollars\ retained}{PAT}$$

where g is the growth rate of equity. The rate of growth in equity thus depends on both *profitability* and *retention*. The higher the profitability, the higher the payout that still permits equity to grow at the same rate as sales. Where sales growth is especially high, or profitability low, even a zero dividend payout may not permit equity to grow as rapidly as sales. Such a situation often is encountered in small, rapidly growing firms.

When net worth grows less rapidly than sales and assets, balance sheet relationships change over time. Something other than net worth must grow at a faster rate. Often the deficit is made up for a time by bank credit or trade credit or some combination of the two. If bank credit is used and growth continues, the loan is a permanent one, growing larger each year. If trade credit is used, the lengthening of the firm's payment period is likely to have two undesirable consequences. First, relations with suppliers are likely to become strained; and second, the firm will be unable to take advantage of any prompt-payment discounts offered.

Current liabilities can expand more rapidly than other parts of the balance sheet for short periods—but not for long. At some point, suppliers and bankers will call a halt because of risk considerations. If the firm already has reduced its dividend payout and increased its profitability as much as possible, at that point it has two alternatives: obtain external long-term funds, or change commercial strategy and slow the rate of sales growth.

Thus, we see that growth must be financed, and that the financing requirement is *long term* in nature. The faster the growth in sales and assets, the more severe the financing problem is likely to become. Growth normally is desirable, but the financing requirements induced by growth must not be overlooked.

Financing Requirements that Cannot Be Predicted

Financing requirements induced by seasonality or growth usually can be anticipated. Some financing requirements, however, cannot. Most firms are subject to the swings of the business and monetary cycle that occur in the United States economy over periods of 3–5 years. In spite of advances in the state of the economic art, booms and recessions still cannot be anticipated with accuracy. Cyclical variations due to economic swings are common to all firms and may induce financing requirements in addition to those normally encountered.

Most firms are subject to other unpredictable events as well, some affecting an entire industry and some only individual firms. Strikes, product failure, changes in supply prices, sudden opportunities, or problems due to changes in technology or consumer tastes—all are events that may affect a firm's financing requirements. Where assets must be expanded suddenly, or profitability suddenly is reduced, outside financing at above-normal levels may be required.

Unexpected financing requirements may be short or intermediate in term. Requirements induced by the business cycle may persist for longer than a year, after which relationships return to normal. Unpredictable events due to temporary phenomena such as strikes may be short term in nature.

Operating Decisions and Financing Requirements

It is apparent that a firm's financing requirements are determined primarily by its commercial strategy and operating plan. Since firms exist to produce goods and services, commercial strategy normally comes first and financing is tailored to fit.

Though financing requirements are normally subordinate to the operating plan, they nevertheless must be considered when the operating plan is formulated. Changes in the operating plan must take account of effects they may have on financing requirements. Sometimes financing requirements themselves may become a constraint and require that the operating plan be modified. Some operating plans may be too risky to finance. For example, consider a plan calling for level production of a product with a seasonal sales pattern that is subject to fashion or fad risk, such as toys or women's fashion garments. The risk involved in accumulating large inventories of such products may be unacceptable to suppliers of funds.

Neptune provides a good example of the impact of production decisions on financing requirements. The decision to produce at a level rate lowers production costs and provides a better balance between people and equipment. But offsetting these benefits are the costs of storing and financing the large inventories and the added risk of obsolescence, which in Neptune's case was not excessive.

Marketing decisions also affect financing requirements. Advertising and selling efforts affect sales and accounts receivable and indirectly affect inventories and production schedules. Changes in credit terms likewise may affect sales and therefore receivables and inventories. Where receivables and inventories are affected, financing requirements will also be affected.

In theory, operating plans and financing requirements should be determined jointly. The optimal combination maximizes the value of the firm. In practice, it is often necessary first to formulate an operating plan, calculate its financing requirements, and then determine whether the financing is feasible. If not, the operating plan is modified and the process repeated. Such an iterative process can be greatly facilitated by the use of a computer to generate financial statements. By using a computer-based planning model, the financial implications of different operating plans can be analyzed quickly and inexpensively. A disadvantage of such models is the large initial expenditure usually required to develop and implement them.

From the financial plan we can determine the nature of the financing requirement. It is important to both the firm and its suppliers of funds that this determination be made so that the right kind of financing arrangement can be negotiated. If the situation is one of growth requiring long-term financing, it is best to recognize it as such at the outset. If the need is short-term financing, it can be tailored accordingly and unnecessary borrowing will be avoided.

Budgeting Cash Receipts and Disbursements

The Cash Budget

The *cash budget* is one of several specialized supporting components of the overall financial plan. Others include the advertising budget, materials budget, capital expenditures budget, income and expense budget by organizational unit, and so on. A *budget* is simply a time-phased schedule of activities or events or transactions, usually in dollar terms. A budget can be prepared for any activity of the firm to describe exactly what is to be done and when.

The cash budget is a time-phased schedule of cash receipts and disbursements. Its primary purpose is to provide control of cash at a level of detail not possible with the balance sheet alone. With a complete schedule of all planned receipts and disbursements, deviations from plan can be detected promptly and the reasons for the deviations can be ascertained. The balance sheet will tell us when cash is higher or lower than planned; the cash budget will pinpoint the reasons for the variance.

The cash budget is similar to the income statement in that it is in flow terms and describes activities that are to take place during some specified period of time. It differs from the income statement in two basic ways: It includes *cash* items only, and it is prepared on a cash basis, whereas the income statement is on an accrual basis. The criterion for deciding whether a particular item belongs in the cash budget is whether it affects the cash balance. If it goes in the cash drawer or is deposited to the checking account, or if a check is written for it, then it goes in. Depreciation has no place in a cash budget, nor do other noncash charges or accruals of any sort, revenue or expense. Only *cash received* or *disbursed* goes in.

Preparing the Cash Budget

Let us now prepare a cash budget for the Neptune Company for each month in 1980. We will concentrate first on cash *receipts*. In Neptune's case, the only receipts will come from collection of accounts receivable and increases in the bank loan. We will handle the bank loan as a balancing figure to maintain the cash balance at the appropriate figure. Using our knowledge of the patterns of payment by Neptune's customers, we can prepare the collection schedule given in Table 5-8. In this table, December sales of $250,000 are collected, half in January and half in February; January sales of $220,000 are collected, half in February and half in March, and so on.

Table 5-8 Neptune Company:
Collection of Accounts Receivable, 1980 (Thousands of Dollars)

Sales		Jan.	Feb.	Mar.	Apr.	May	June	July	Aug.
Nov.	206	103							
Dec.	250	125	125						
Jan.	220	0	110	110					
Feb.	275		0	137	138				
Mar.	385			0	192	193			
Apr.	495				0	247	248		
May	605					0	302	303	
June	770	—	—	—	—	—	0	385	385
Total collections		228	235	247	330	440	550	688	

		Aug.	Sept.	Oct.	Nov.	Dec.	Jan.
June	770	385					
July	715	357	358				
Aug.	605	0	302	303			
Sept.	495		0	247	248		
Oct.	385			0	192	193	
Nov.	275				0	137	138
Dec.	275	—	—	—	—	0	137
Total collections		742	660	550	440	330	275

The collections figures derived in Table 5-8 for the cash budget must be consistent with the sales and accounts receivable figures on the income statement and balance sheet. The relationship is

Accounts receivable, December 31, 1979	$353,000
Plus January sales	+ 220,000
Minus January collections	− 228,000
Accounts receivable, January 31, 1980	$345,000

If we know sales and receivables for each month, we can calculate collections. If we know sales and collections and the initial receivables balance, we can project receivables for each month.

Now let us focus on *cash disbursements*. Each month, checks will be written to settle accounts payable at the end of the prior month. In January, for example, payments to suppliers will be made totaling $148,000. Payments for direct labor, manufacturing overhead, and selling and administrative expense are made approximately 1 week after the expenses are incurred. Payment schedules for plant and equipment expenditures, taxes, mortgage principal, and dividends were given earlier.

Given the schedule of receipts and disbursements, we construct the cash budget as in Table 5-9, on the facing page. The line labeled "receipts less disbursements" gives us the gross change in the cash balance each month before increases or decreases in the bank loan. To this figure we add the beginning cash balance and then determine the loan increase or decrease required to maintain the ending cash balance at $50,000 or higher. The loan must be increased each month from January through April, is reduced in May, increased slightly in June, and then reduced each month until it reaches zero by the end of September. Note especially that the ending cash and loan balances match those in the pro forma balance sheet. If they did not, we would know that an error existed somewhere, either in the cash budget or the pro forma statements.

In Neptune's case, the only receipts were collections of accounts receivable and borrowings from the bank; the latter appear toward the end of Table 5-9 rather than under "receipts." In other situations, other types of receipts may be encountered. Some part of a firm's sales may be for cash. Fixed assets sometimes are sold, in which case the proceeds are treated as a receipt and any change in tax payments is treated as an increase or decrease in disbursements for taxes. Cash discounts received on purchases sometimes are treated as a separate item rather than netted against purchase prices. Dividends or interest on marketable securities, which we ignored in Neptune's case, should be treated as a receipt. Finally, proceeds of any issues of long-term securities by the firm, stock, or long-term debt, should be included as receipts.

Table 5-9 Neptune Company:
Cash Budget, 1980 (Thousands of Dollars)

	Jan.	Feb.	Mar.	Apr.	May	June	July	Aug.	Sept.	Oct.	Nov.	Dec.
Receipts												
Collection of accounts receivable	228	235	247	330	440	550	688	742	660	550	440	330
Disbursements												
Payment of accounts payable	148	125	125	125	125	125	125	125	125	125	125	125
Direct labor	135	135	135	135	135	135	135	135	135	135	135	135
Manufacturing overhead	25	25	25	25	25	25	25	25	25	25	25	25
Selling and administrative	45	45	45	45	45	45	45	45	45	45	45	45
Plant and equipment	250	250										
Taxes				154		114			114			113
Mortgage principal						50						50
Dividends			60			60			60			60
Total disbursements	603	580	390	484	330	554	330	330	504	330	330	553
Receipts less disbursements	(375)	(345)	(143)	(154)	110	(4)	358	412	156	220	110	(223)
Add beginning cash balance[a]	144	50	50	50	50	50	50	50	50	159	379	489
	(231)	(295)	(93)	(104)	160	46	408	462	206	379	489	266
Add loan increase (decrease)	281	345	143	154	(110)	4	(358)	(412)	(47)			
Ending cash balance[a]	50	50	50	50	50	50	50	50	159	379	489	266
Ending loan balance	281	626	769	923	813	817	459	47	0	0	0	0

[a]Cash plus marketable securities. All over $50,000 is marketable securities.

145

Relationships of Cash Budget to Pro Forma Statements

We noted above that the ending cash and loan figures in the cash budget must match those in the balance sheet, and that the collections figure must be consistent with the sales and receivables figures. Upon close inspection, we will see also that the payment of accounts payable in the cash budget is consistent with the accounts payable and inventory figures in the balance sheet and with the planned level of purchases and the cost of goods sold figure in the income statement. Disbursements for labor and overhead are consistent with cost of goods sold and inventory; disbursements for plant and equipment are consistent with fixed assets and depreciation; disbursements for taxes are consistent with taxes on the income statement and taxes payable on the balance sheet; and so on.

It is apparent that the cash budget and the pro forma income statement and balance sheet all are mutually interdependent. With consistent assumptions and accurate preparation, all the figures will mesh. If they do not, an error exists somewhere. Errors often become apparent when the ending cash and loan figures are calculated in the cash budget and the figures do not match those in the balance sheet. The cash and loan figures constitute our controls in preparing the statements.

A cash budget can be prepared to cover any time period. In the case of the Neptune Company, we prepared a monthly cash budget covering the entire year in order to demonstrate the interlocking character of the financial statements. In practice, Neptune might prepare a cash budget only for those months in which the loan is high and control of cash is most critical. At other times during the year, the pro forma balance sheet, coupled with an income and expense budget, might provide adequate control. Firms with especially acute cash shortages may find it useful to prepare a cash budget by week or even by day. Firms that employ detailed income and expense budgets by organizational units may find a cash budget unnecessary.

Using the Financial Plan

The pro forma income statement, balance sheet, and cash budget constitute the basic elements of the firm's financial plan. Some of the uses of the financial plan are apparent from the discussion thus far. Here we will elaborate a bit.

Planning

Planning essentially is making decisions in advance about what is to be done in the future. As a plan is developed, decisions are made. Hence the very process of developing the plan yields a major part of the overall benefits, regardless of what is done with the final product.

Development of a financial plan requires good coordination and communication throughout the firm. To support the sales plan, programs and budgets are developed in production, marketing, personnel, and finance. During the process, the feasibility of alternative operating plans can be examined. Performance measures such as those discussed in Chapter 4 can be applied and judgments made as to the plan's acceptability with respect to profitability, return on investment, inventory and receivables management, liquidity, and debt coverage. The feasibility of obtaining financing can be ascertained. Where necessary, the operating plan can be modified, and performance and feasibility tests can be applied again. Sometimes a firm may find it desirable to develop one or more alternative plans to allow for certain events. To deal with uncertainty, a firm might develop one set of plans representing the most favorable set of circumstances and another representing the least favorable.

The amounts, timing, and nature of the financing requirement can be determined from the financial plan. Appropriate sources of funds can be selected, and borrowing and repayment schedules can be prepared. We will discuss sources of short and intermediate financing in Chapter 6.

The final product of the financial planning process is a description in financial terms of what the firm intends to accomplish over the period of time in question. Besides providing a record of decisions made, the plan itself has other important uses.

Communications

One such use is in *communications* with outside parties, including investors and other suppliers of funds. After Neptune's management completes the financial plan, we can imagine the financial vice-president going to the bank to negotiate the loan arrangement for 1980. The plan contained in Tables 5-4, 5-6, and 5-9 is discussed in detail with the loan officer. The vice-president is able to tell the loan officer exactly how much money Neptune needs, when it is needed, how it will be used, and when and how the bank will be repaid.

Contrast the above bargaining session with one in which a potential borrower approaches a bank for a loan without a detailed financial plan. The borrower is unable to be specific with respect to how much, when and for what purpose the money is needed, and when and how it will be repaid.

By coming to the bargaining table equipped with a comprehensive financial plan, a firm's management sends an important message to the supplier of funds: "This management is in control of its business and knows what it is doing." Lenders and investors like to do business with such firms. The specific numbers are less important to the supplier of funds than the fact that a comprehensive plan has been developed.

By coming in with a plan, a firm's management is likely to gain a psychological advantage in the bargaining process. A feeling of confidence in the firm may lead the lender to assign a lower risk and therefore a lower interest rate to the loan. We can conclude that an important use of the financial plan is as a communications device.

Control

The financial plan also is useful for purposes of *control*, that is, seeing that the plans in fact are carried out. We should not allow the precise appearance of the numbers in Tables 5-4, 5-6, and 5-9 to lead us to forget about uncertainty. The elements of the plan that depend directly or indirectly on revenue and expense estimates are subject to uncertainty. Usually, the plan represents our best guess as to the most likely set of outcomes, or the outcomes that management hopes to achieve. Deviations above or below the plan are bound to occur and should be expected. When they do occur, we want to find out immediately and determine the reasons.

Most management control systems are based on comparisons of actual data versus plans. Such comparisons can be made at any level of detail and with any frequency. Expense control systems often compare actual versus plan data on a monthly basis. In decentralized firms, reporting systems using computers often are designed to provide information by organizational unit in a timely manner. Subordinate managers are able to identify problems quickly in their own areas of responsibility.

For the firm as a whole, progress against the operating plan can be monitored using the consolidated pro forma income statement and balance sheet. Each month, or each quarter, actual income statements and balance sheets are compared to the plan, item by item, and deviations are calculated. The effects of a deviation from the sales plan will be seen in accounts receivable, inventories, cash, the bank loan (if any), profits, tax accruals, and perhaps other areas. Sometimes it is useful to examine deviations in a sources-and-uses format, categorizing balance sheet changes as providing or using more or less funds than planned.

By comparing actual versus plan data at frequent intervals, deviations can be detected as events unfold, and corrective action can be taken in a timely manner. The control system tells management that things are off-track and identifies the problem areas. Production schedules can be modified, advertising budgets increased or decreased, collection efforts intensified, or expenses cut. As a control device, pro forma financial statements are very useful. Indeed, there is no way of achieving good control without them.

Applicability of Financial Planning Techniques

The financial planning techniques discussed in this chapter are applicable to any type of business firm, regardless of its line of business. Pro forma financial statements are always useful and usually necessary to the successful operation of any business, whether it is a manufacturer, retailer, wholesaler, service establishment, or financial institution. Any firm is likely to benefit from the process of developing a plan—from the improvement in internal communications, the requirement to think ahead and anticipate problems, the discipline of having to be specific, and the commitment to carry out the plan once formulated. The appropriate level of detail and sophistication will vary widely from one situation to another, as will procedures and the format for organizing and presenting information. The planning system appropriate for an appliance retailer will differ markedly from that appropriate for a manufacturer or a commercial bank. All, however, are likely to benefit from a financial planning system of some sort.

Is the usefulness of financial planning confined to profit-making enterprises? It is not. Nonprofit organizations also must plan and make decisions. Such organizations sometimes have no revenues, but nearly always have expenses and expenditures. An income statement may not be applicable, but a balance sheet and expense budget usually are. A cash budget often is very useful. Hospitals, schools, churches, and charitable organizations do not earn profits, but they do expend resources, handle large amounts of money, and invariably require financing. Although the procedures and details may differ, the basic techniques of financial planning and control are just as applicable to such organizations as to business firms.

Financial Planning Over Longer Time Periods

Thus far we have discussed financial planning over the relatively near term, 12 to perhaps 18 months. We took Neptune's commercial strategy and long-term asset/liability structure as given. Our emphasis was on the operating and financing necessary to support the longer-term strategy.

Commercial Strategy

Over the long run, the firm's commercial strategy is not fixed. A major purpose of long-range planning is to examine alternative commercial strategies and to select that most appropriate to the firm's overall goals. Should the Neptune Company begin manufacturing gasoline-powered outboard motors? Or commercial fishing vessels? Such questions have long-range strategic implications, and the answers determine the nature of the business. The firm's prosperity and survival depend on wise choices by management in these areas, and mistakes can be very costly.

The purposes of long-range planning thus differ from those of short-range planning. Emphasis is more on analysis of alternatives and decision-making and less on communications and control. To draw an analogy, the focus is on deciding what course the ship should steer and not on the tasks necessary to operate it.

Long-range financial planning plays the same role in formulating commercial strategy as does short-range financial planning in formulating the operating plan. The financing requirements of alternative commercial strategies are examined, performance measures applied, financing feasibility examined, sources of financing investigated, and the strategy modified if need be. The final product, as before, is a description in financial terms of what the firm intends to accomplish over the period in question.

Over the long run, the firm's long-term asset/liability structure is not given. An important part of the long-range planning process is to develop the long-term investment plan necessary to execute the firm's commercial strategy. What products is the firm to offer? What kind of manufacturing process is to be used? What facilities are needed? What equipment is appropriate? Decisions of this sort involve acquisition of assets with long lives. Alternatives often involve complex patterns of cash flows spread over many time periods. Techniques for analyzing such decisions will be our principal concern in Part IV.

The Long-Range Financial Plan

Given a commercial strategy and its associated long-term investment plan, the approach to financial planning is essentially the same as that used for the Neptune Company in the short run. The basic technique is pro forma analysis, with the income statement and balance sheet again used as the basic planning vehicles. As before, the sales plan is the critical element, and financing requirements are determined by the commercial strategy and operating plan.

Over long time periods, uncertainty usually is greater than in the short run. Some random elements may average out, but new elements of uncertainty enter. Consumer preferences change, new technologies develop, costs change, competition emerges, and entire industries rise and fall.

Given these greater uncertainties, different techniques are necessary for projecting sales and other uncertain elements of a long-range plan. Long-term trends and historical relationships between firm variables and general economic variables become more important. An economist may be better equipped to forecast sales over long periods than a sales manager. Sales of color television sets, for example, are likely to depend more on population and per capita income in the long run than on advertising and sales effort. Statistical techniques such as correlation and regression analysis may be useful in developing sales forecasting models. The economic technique of input/output analysis may be useful. Techniques of demand analysis, marketing research, and in-depth studies of markets may be appropriate in evaluating new products. Finally, computer-assisted planning models can be very useful in applying all of these approaches.[1]

Once the long-range sales and production plans and other elements of the operating plan are determined, financing requirements can be evaluated. Over the long run, financing choices are much wider than before and the decisions are more difficult. The appropriate mix of debt and equity must be determined, depending on the nature of the firm's business. The firm must choose between internal and external sources and thereby set its dividend policy. Once the appropriate debt policy is determined, a choice must be made with respect to maturity or the appropriate mix of short-term versus long-term debt. Where outside financing is necessary, a plan must be developed indicating the types and amounts of securities to be sold and the timing of the issues. These difficult questions of long-term financing policy will occupy us later.

Inflation and Financial Planning

Inflation has a pronounced impact on firms' financial planning. If revenues and expenses are affected equally, then each increases faster than it otherwise would have. Profits also increase more rapidly. If the effect on revenues and expenses is uneven, profit growth may be affected in either direction.

Balance sheets are also affected by inflation. To see the effects, let us consider an example. Suppose every item in a firm's balance sheet and income statement is growing at 6 percent per year. There is no inflation. The balance sheet projected ahead 3 years would look like Table 5-10. Note that everything grows at the same rate, 6 percent. Note especially that the ratio of debt to assets remains the same, and that debt provides

---

1. For an example of an operational planning model, see D. F. Rychel, "Capital Budgeting with Mixed Integer Linear Programming: An Application," *Financial Management* **6**, 11–19 (Winter 1977).

Table 5-10 Projected Balance Sheet, No Inflation

	Year End		
	1980	1981	1982
Cash	$100	$106	$112
Accounts receivable	300	318	337
Inventories	400	424	449
Fixed assets	300	318	337
Total assets	$1,100	$1,166	$1,235
Debt	600	636	674
Net worth	500	530	561
Debt/assets	0.55	0.55	0.55
△debt/△assets	—	0.55	0.55

55 percent of the total new financing required to expand assets from $1,100 to $1,235 (see the last line in Table 5-10).

Now suppose we have an inflation of 5 percent a year in 1981 and and 1982. The cash balance will have to grow by 11 percent in 1981, 6 percent to accommodate real growth in transactions and another 5 percent to accommodate inflation. So the cash balance will be $111 at the end of 1981, rather than $106 as it was originally. In 1982, cash grows another 11 percent to $123.

Similarly, receivables and inventory now grow at 11 percent per year rather than 6 percent. Fixed assets, however, are different. Only the *increment* to fixed assets is affected by inflation; with original-cost accounting, fixed assets already in place are not affected. Table 5-11 shows the complete balance sheet.

Look carefully at the net worth line; $532 in 1981 under inflation versus $530 with no inflation. Inflation hardly affected net worth at all, whereas assets were affected very significantly. Why? Because inflation acts only on the *increment* to net worth each year, that is, profits retained. Existing net worth, like existing fixed assets, is not affected at all.

So inflation has a much bigger impact on assets, specifically on current assets, than it does on net worth. With no inflation, net worth and assets grew at the same rate, 6 percent. Now, with inflation, net worth grows much more slowly than assets. The growth rate of total assets from 1980 to 1982 is 9.8 percent per year, of net worth only 6.5 percent.

Impact on Borrowing

The result of assets growing more rapidly than net worth is that debt must make up the difference. By 1982, debt is at $759, versus $674 in the no-

Table 5-11   Projected Balance Sheet, Inflation 5 Percent

	Year End		
	1980	1981	1982
Cash	$100	$111	$123
Accounts receivable	300	333	370
Inventories	400	444	493
Fixed assets	300	319	340
Total assets	$1,100	$1,207	$1,326
Debt	600	675	759
Net worth	500	532	567
Debt/assets	0.55	0.56	0.57
△debt/△assets	—	0.70	0.71

inflation case. Of the new financing required to expand assets, equity provides only 30 percent, so debt must provide 70 percent. The debt/asset ratio begins to rise.

Let us be clear about what is happening. Inflation affects fixed assets and net worth differently than it affects current assets. Why? Because they are *long-maturity* items. Cash, receivables, and inventory are quickly replaced by new items that reflect inflation. Not so with fixed assets and net worth. Existing fixed assets and net worth (in book value terms) are unaffected by inflation; only the *increments* are affected.

Policy Implications

In practice, the effects of inflation are more complex than those portrayed above. However, our simple example points up the major implications. In general, inflation increases the need for outside financing. To maintain a desired balance between debt and the book value of equity, equity growth must be accelerated. To do this requires either greater retention of profits or additional outside equity financing. Greater retention requires a cut in the dividend paid in the case of corporations or a cut in owner withdrawals in the case of proprietorships and partnerships.

All of these choices represent important policy changes. The problem can be especially acute for small firms that cannot sell stock publicly and must rely mainly on banks for their outside financing. A cut in withdrawals can be painful if owners need the money for living expenses. If withdrawals are not cut, debt rises to the point at which banks begin to become unhappy. The only alternative is to slow the firm's rate of growth.

Summary

Planning is a major function of management. Financial planning is a part of the larger planning process within an organization. The basic elements of the financial plan are the income statement and the balance sheet. The starting point is the operating plan, which describes the activities in which the firm intends to engage. In developing short-term financial plans that cover a 12-to-18 month horizon, the operating plan and the long-term asset/liability structure are taken as given. The objective of the planning process is to represent the operating plan in financial terms and to determine short-term financing requirements.

The pro forma (projected) balance sheet is the basic tool for estimating funds requirements. A standard approach is to project all items of the balance sheet except cash and the bank loan, which are left as plug or balancing figures. The figure that brings the balance sheet into balance is the required loan or, alternatively, the excess cash balance. To project the balance sheet, the income statement must be projected first in order to provide the transfer to retained earnings. The operating plan (sales plan, production plan, and expenditures for plant, equipment, materials, labor, overhead, marketing, research and development, and administration) provides the basis for the income projection. The operating plan also determines the levels of current operating assets and liabilities (working cash balance, accounts receivable, inventories, accounts payable, and various accruals). Projection of these items along with the addition to retained earnings and long-term assets and liabilities (taken as given) completes the balance sheet. Once the balance sheet has been projected, a pro forma sources-and-uses statement can be prepared if necessary. In general, the sales plan is of central importance in financial planning because of the effect of sales on many income statement and balance sheet items.

A firm's financing requirements depend on the nature of its business and the operating plan that it adopts. A seasonal sales and/or expense pattern usually will give rise to a seasonal financing requirement. Growth in sales gives rise to a growing financing requirement that is long-term in nature. The faster the growth, the larger the financing requirement in each period. Financing requirements also can be affected by general economic conditions and changes in technology, consumer tastes, and competitive factors. Normally, commercial strategy and the operating plan come first and the financing plan is tailored to fit. Nevertheless, financing requirements must be considered when the operating plan is formulated and the latter sometimes must be modified to take account of financing constraints.

The cash budget is one of several specialized supporting components of the financial plan and consists of a time-phased schedule of cash receipts and expenditures. Its purpose is to control cash at a level of detail not possible with the balance sheet alone. With consistent assumptions, all figures in the cash budget and pro forma income statement and balance sheet will mesh.

municating with outside parties, especially suppliers of funds. It is also useful as a control device for monitoring the firm's progress in executing the plan. Financial planning is essential not only for business firms but also for nonprofit organizations.

In the short run, the firm's commercial strategy and long-term asset/liability structure are taken as given. Over the long run, they are not. Long-term financial planning is useful for examining alternative commercial strategies and evaluating the investment and financing necessary to execute them.

A major benefit of financial planning is the process of preparing the plan itself, because once prepared, the plan also is very useful for com-

Inflation has a very pronounced impact on financial plans. More external financing is required. If equity growth is not increased via stock sales or higher retention of profits, firms can be forced to rely too heavily on debt.

Sample Problem A

Prepare a pro forma income statement for 1980 for Madison International using the following information:

1. Projected sales: $19,500,000
2. Cost of goods sold: 58 percent of sales
3. Selling and administrative expenses: $2,500,000/year
4. Depreciation: $80,000/month
5. Interest expense: $200,000/year
6. Tax rate: 48 percent

Solution

Sales		$19,500,000
Cost of goods sold		11,310,000
Gross margin		8,190,000
Selling and administrative expense	$2,500,000	
Depreciation ($80,000 × 12)	960,000	3,460,000
EBIT		4,730,000
Interest		200,000
PBT		4,530,000
Taxes		2,174,400
Net profit		$ 2,355,600

Sample Problem B

Madison International's balance sheet for December 31, 1979 is shown in the table. Use the information from Sample Problem A plus the December 31, 1979 balance sheet to construct a December 31, 1980 pro forma balance sheet (round off all numbers to nearest $1,000). Make the following assumptions.

1. Accounts receivable: The collection period is 61 days, and 61 days (all sales are on credit).
2. Inventory turnover is projected to be 6.5 times.
3. Dividends of $1,500,000 will be paid on December 31, 1980.
4. Accrued labor expense is expected to be $950,000, and taxes payable will be $800,000.
5. Purchases equal 75 percent of cost of goods sold, and the company's payment period is expected to be 36.5 days.
6. No changes are expected in the common stock account, plant and equipment account, and bonds.

Solution

We can go through the accounts on the balance sheet one item at a time and calculate each account balance.

1. Accounts receivable: The collection period is 61 days, and sales are $19,500,000. Therefore, the ending balance is

$$\frac{\$19,500,000}{6} = \$3,250,000 \quad (61 \text{ days} = 1/6 \text{ of a year})$$

2. Inventory: With turnover of 6.5 times, and cost of goods sold equaling $11,310,000, the average inventory during 1979 will be

$$\frac{\$11,310,000}{6.5} = \$1,740,000 = \text{Average inventory}$$

With beginning inventory equal to $1,900,000, ending inventory will be $1,740,000 × 2 − $1,900,000 = $1,580,000.

3. Plant and equipment: The gross amount will not change, but the net will be $960,000 less than in 1979 due to 1979 depreciation, that is, $2,540,000 − $960,000 = $1,580,000.

4. Accounts payable: Purchases equal 75 percent of cost of

Madison International: Balance Sheet
December 31, 1979

Assets		
Cash	$2,290,000	
Accounts receivable	2,850,000	
Inventory	1,900,000	
Total current assets		$7,040,000
Gross plant and equipment	$6,400,000	
Less: accumulated depreciation	3,860,000	
Net plant and equipment		2,540,000
Total assets		$9,580,000
Liabilities and net worth		
Accounts payable	$1,100,000	
Accrued labor	870,000	
Taxes payable	760,000	
Total current liabilities		$2,730,000
Bonds at 10 percent		2,000,000
Common stock		1,500,000
Retained earnings		3,350,000
Total liabilities and net worth		$9,580,000

goods sold, or $8,482,500. Ending accounts payable equals purchases per day times 36.5 days purchases outstanding. Accounts payable is

$$\frac{\$8,482,500}{365} \times 36.5 = \$848,000 \text{ (rounded)}$$

5. Accrued labor and taxes payable are given as $950,000 and $800,000.
6. Bonds will remain at $2,000,000.
7. Common stock will remain at $1,500,000.
8. Retained earnings will be $3,350,000 (beginning balance) + $2,356,000 (earnings) − $1,500,000 (dividends) = $4,206,000.
9. Cash can be calculated by finding the value that will balance the balance sheet.

The completed pro forma balance sheet is given on the following page.

Madison International: Pro Forma Balance Sheet
December 31, 1980

Assets		
Cash	$3,894,000	
Accounts receivable	3,250,000	
Inventory	1,580,000	
Total current assets		$ 8,724,000
Gross plant and equipment	6,400,000	
Less: accumulated depreciation	4,820,000	
Net plant and equipment		1,580,000
Total assets		$10,304,000
Liabilities and net worth		
Accounts payable	$ 848,000	
Accrued labor	950,000	
Taxes payable	800,000	
Total current liabilities		$ 2,598,000
Bonds @ 10 percent		2,000,000
Common stock		1,500,000
Retained earnings		4,206,000
Total liabilities and net worth		$10,304,000

Questions

1. How does financial planning fit into a larger planning process within a firm?
2. Why are the sales and production plans so important to financial planning?
3. What additional planning requirements does seasonality impose?
4. In a rapidly growing firm, sales and assets often grow more rapidly than net worth. What is the likely result?
5. What is the relationship between operating plans and financing requirements?
6. What is a cash budget? What is the criterion for determining what goes into a cash budget?
7. What is the relationship of the cash budget to the pro forma income statement and balance sheet?
8. What are the major uses of the financial plan?

Problems

1. Prepare a pro forma income statement for 1980 for Hi-Tech Manufacturing Company using the following information:
   (a) Projected sales: $2,025,000
   (b) Cost of goods sold: 65.9 percent of sales
   (c) Selling and administrative expense: $20,000 per month
   (d) Depreciation: $10,000 per month January–April; $12,000 per month May–December   4 (40000)   8 (96000) = (136000)
   (e) Interest expense: $40,000
   (f) Tax rate 48 percent

2. Utilize all the information from Problem 1 plus the balance sheet for December 31, 1979, and the following information to construct a pro forma balance sheet for Hi-Tech Manufacturing Company for December 31, 1980.
   (a) An addition to plant and equipment of $175,000 is due on April 15.
   (b) The company maintains an open line of credit with a local bank and was carrying an outstanding loan balance of $50,000 on December 31, 1979.

? PLUG

Hi-Tech Manufacturing Company: Balance Sheet, December 31, 1979

Assets		
Cash		$ 20,000
Accounts receivable		292,500
Inventory		118,000
Total current assets		430,500
Gross plant and equipment	$1,800,000	
Less: accumulated depreciation	963,000	
Net plant and equipment		837,000
Total assets		$1,267,500
Liabilities and net worth		
Bank loan		$ 50,000
Accounts payable		54,000
Accrued labor		54,000
Taxes payable		5,000
Accrued overhead		10,000
Total current liabilities		173,000
Debentures @ 7 percent		500,000
Common stock		300,000
Retained earinings		294,500
Total liabilities and net worth		$1,267,500

Pub

1.

(c) The minimum cash balance desired by the company is $20,000.

(d) Accounts receivable collection period (days sales outstanding) is projected to be 55 days (365 day year).

(e) Inventory turnover is projected to be 10.75 times.

(f) Purchases amount to 45.5 percent of cost of goods sold, and the company's payment period (days purchases outstanding) at year-end is expected to be 36 days.

(g) At December 31, 1980, accrued labor expense is expected to be $60,000, taxes payable zero, and accrued overhead expense $10,000.

(h) No change is expected in debentures or common stock.

3. Prepare pro forma income statements for Hi-Tech for each month of 1980 using the information given in Problem 1 above plus the following information:

(a) Monthly sales forecast for 1980 is as follows (in thousands):

(1979, actual)		June	$160
November	$190	July	175
December	230	August	200
(1980, forecasted)		September	180
January	180	October	160
February	150	November	200
March	130	December	240
April	120	(1981, forecasted)	
May	130	January	200

(b) A total of 90 percent of sales are on credit terms of net 45 and the remaining 10 percent are for cash. Credit sales have historically been collected on the basis of 50 percent in the month following sale and the remaining 50 percent in the second month after sale. Bad debt losses are negligible.

(c) Monthly production is scheduled at the level of forecasted sales for the following month. Materials expense and labor expense each average 30 percent of sales. Both expenses are payable in the month following production.

(d) Overhead expense of $10,000 per month is paid in the following month.

(e) Interest on bonds of $20,000 is due on June 5 and December 5.

(f) Selling and administrative expenses average $20,000 per month and are paid in the month incurred.

(g) Tax payments are due on April 15, June 15, September 15, and December 15, and are equal to the tax liability through the month of payment.

(h) No dividends will be paid.

4. Prepare monthly pro forma balance sheets for 1980 for Hi-Tech using all the information given in Problems 1, 2, and 3.

5. Prepare a monthly cash budget for Hi-Tech for 1980 using all the information given in Problems 1, 2, and 3.

6. Prepare an annual pro forma sources-and-uses-of-funds statement for Hi-Tech for 1980 using all the information given in Problems 1, 2, and 3.

7. Prepare a quarterly cash budget for the Chapel-on-the-Hill Church utilizing the following information and including any required borrowing. All annual receipts and disbursements are made in equal quarterly amounts unless otherwise noted.

(a) Annual expenditures are projected as follows:

Salary, allowances, and expenses (Rector)	$24,480.00
Salary, allowances, and expenses (Assistant Rector)	16,500.00
Clerical and janitorial expense	32,160.00
Building maintenance and taxes	12,800.00
Supplies and programs	11,600.00
Work outside the parish	25,000.00

(b) In addition to the above expenditures the church must make principal payments on the church mortgage of $2,000 in the second and fourth quarters, and interest payments of $700 per quarter.

(c) Receipts are projected as shown below, with plate collections evenly distributed throughout the year, and 40 percent of pledge payments to be received in quarter four and 20 percent in each of the other three quarters.

Plate collections	$ 7,800
Pledge payments	121,000

(d) The cash balance at the beginning of the year is $4,200.

8. Monthly sales of Bradley Home Furnishing for 1980 are projected as follows:

January	$26,500	July	$30,200
February	24,300	August	29,400
March	28,600	September	31,200
April	23,500	October	27,800
May	28,700	November	29,900
June	26,900	December	32,300

Accounts receivable are collected as follows:

(a) 25 percent within 10 days.

(b) 15 percent within 30 days.

(c) 40 percent in the month after the sale.

(d) 15 percent in the second month after the sale.

(e) 5 percent will never be collected.

How much cash will Bradley receive from sales during each month in 1980? The firm's first year in business is 1980, so there will be no cash receipts from prior years' sales. Bradley offers credit terms of a discount of 2 percent if the invoice is paid within 10 days, otherwise the net (full amount) is due within 30 days. Assume all sales take place on the first day of each month. (Round to the nearest $1.)

9. Compute the projected accounts receivable balance on December 31, 1980 for Futura Corporation from the following information (round to the nearest $10):

(a) December 31, 1979 accounts receivable balance: $83,210

(b) All sales are on credit, and are projected for 1980 as follows:

January	$36,300
February	39,850
March	45,700
April	51,540
May	48,390
June	54,400
July	52,230
August	57,230
September	53,710
October	47,930
November	44,260
December	41,000

(c) Accounts receivable are collected as follows:

35 percent in the month following the sale.

50 percent in the second month after the sale.

15 percent in the third month after the sale.

10. Michael's Fireplaces has projected sales as follows:

January 1980	$5,400	July	$2,200
February	4,800	August	2,300
March	4,100	September	3,900
April	4,300	October	4,500
May	3,600	November	6,600
June	3,700	December	8,200
		January 1981	6,000

The company's gross profit percentage is 40 percent. Seventy-five percent of cost of goods sold is materials that are purchased, and 25 percent is labor. Parts must be ordered 2 months before they are assembled and sold. They are received 1 month after being ordered. Michael's pays all of its bills 30 days after they are received, and bills arrive when the parts are delivered.

(a) Compute the accounts payable balance for each month in 1980.
(b) Compute the parts inventory for each month in 1980. The inventory balance on December 31, 1979 was $6,200.

References

W. T. Carleton, "An Analytical Model for Long-Range Financial Planning," *Journal of Finance* **25,** 291–315 (May 1970).

W. T. Carleton, C. L. Dick, and D. H. Downes, "Financial Policy Models: Theory and Practice," *Journal of Financial and Quantitative Analysis* **8,** 691–710 (Dec. 1973).

J. C. Chambers, S. K. Mullick, and D. D. Smith, "How to Choose the Right Forecasting Techniques," *Harvard Business Review* **49,** 45–74 (July–Aug. 1971).

G. Donaldson, *Strategy for Financial Mobility* (Homewood, Ill.: Richard D. Irwin, 1969).

J. C. Francis and D. R. Rowell, "A Simultaneous Equation Model of the Firm for Financial Analysis and Planning," *Financial Management* **7,** 29–44 (Spring 1978).

E. A. Helfert, *Techniques of Financial Analysis,* 3d ed. (Homewood, Ill.: Richard D. Irwin, 1972), Chaps. 1 and 3.

C. T. Horngren, *Accounting for Management Control,* 3d ed. (Englewood Cliffs, N.J.: Prentice-Hall, 1974).

R. D. Jaedicke and R. T. Sprouse, *Accounting Flows: Income, Funds, and Cash* (Englewood Cliffs, N.J.: Prentice-Hall, 1965), Chaps. 5 and 6.

J. L. Pappas and G. P. Huber, "Probabilistic Short-Term Financial Planning," *Financial Management* **2** (Autumn 1973).

G. G. C. Parker and E. L. Segura, "How to Get a Better Forecast," *Harvard Business Review* **49,** 99–109 (Mar.–Apr. 1971).

D. F. Rychel, "Capital Budgeting with Mixed Integer Linear Programming: An Application," *Financial Management* **6,** 11–19 (Winter 1977).

Sources of Short-Term and Intermediate-Term Funds

6

Having determined the amounts and timing of the firm's requirements for funds, we turn now to the question of where the funds can be obtained. To get funds, a firm issues *claims* against its income and assets—some are contractual claims (liabilities), others are ownership claims (equities). Liabilities are obligations, but they also represent sources of funds. Some liabilities, such as accounts payable and accruals of various kinds, arise naturally out of the firm's operations because of the lag between the time the liability is incurred and the time it is discharged. Other liabilities, such as loans, are incurred at management's discretion.

In this chapter, we discuss the major sources of short-term and intermediate-term funds. Long-term sources are discussed in Part V. The words *short* and *intermediate* refer to the *maturity* of the claim against the firm, that is, the time horizon over which the principal amount remains outstanding. *Short term* usually refers to periods of less than a year; *intermediate term* usually refers to periods between 1 and perhaps 8 or 10 years. These definitions are more or less arbitrary, and there often is no clear distinction between a short-term and an intermediate-term loan. A loan that begins as short term may become intermediate term if the borrower is unable to repay on schedule.

Perhaps more useful distinctions can be drawn with respect to the purpose of the loan and the means of repaying it. Short-term loans often are made to finance seasonal working capital requirements, such as the buildup of inventories and receivables each spring in the Neptune Company. Such seasonal loans are repaid during slow sales periods when inventories and receivables are low. Intermediate-term loans, on the other hand, usually are made to finance permanent additions to working capital or fixed assets. Funds to repay such loans usually come from profits or cash flows generated from operations over a period of several years, and not from liquidation of the assets being financed as in the case of a seasonal working capital loan. Short-term lenders thus are concerned mainly with the strength of the firm's balance sheet, the quality of assets, and other claims against the assets. Intermediate-term and long-term lenders are concerned more with the income statement, looking for their security to the firm's earning power over sustained periods of time.

Suppliers of Short-Term and Intermediate-Term Funds

Business firms obtain funds from a variety of sources—from other business firms, from banks, and from the money market. Nearly all firms rely to some extent on *trade credit* as a source of short-term funds. Trade credit is short-term credit extended by a supplier in connection with goods purchased for ultimate resale. The credit appears on the supplier's balance sheet as an account receivable. Thus, although the trade creditor is the direct supplier of funds, ultimately the funds come from those who finance the trade creditor.

Bank loans provide a major source of short-term and intermediate-term financing. Although *commercial banks* are the most important of the intermediaries that finance business firms, other financial institutions also supply short-term and intermediate-term funds. *Finance companies* make specialized loans to finance working capital and equipment, and *insurance companies* make intermediate-term and long-term loans to business firms.

Firms, especially the larger more credit-worthy corporations, also obtain funds by issuing interest-bearing unsecured promissory notes (known as *commercial paper*) in the open money market. Thus, the immediate suppliers of short- and intermediate-term funds to business firms are other business firms, commercial banks, finance companies, insurance companies, and pension funds. However, it is important to note that all these suppliers are themselves only intermediaries in the chain of finance, because they require financing also. Ultimately, the suppliers of all business funds are individuals, who, by consuming less than they earn, have excess funds to save and invest. These funds are channeled from savers to firms and other investors through the specialized financial markets and financial intermediaries in our system.

Some of the direct suppliers of funds make more than one type of loan. Business firms supply trade credit and are major purchasers of commercial paper. Commercial banks make both unsecured and secured short-term loans as well as *term* loans with maturities of up to 7–10 years. Finance companies make short-term working capital loans and intermediate-term loans to finance equipment. The discussion that follows is organized according to the type of financing instrument with respect to maturity and collateral, rather than by source.

From the borrower's point of view, the choice of which form of credit to use depends on the availability of funds and their effective costs, both of which can vary sharply over different phases of the business cycle.

Trade Credit

Earlier, we defined trade credit as credit extended in connection with goods purchased for resale. It is this qualification—goods purchased for resale—that distinguishes trade credit from other related forms. Machinery and equipment, for example, may be purchased on credit by means of an installment purchase contract of some sort. But if the equipment is used by the firm in its production process rather than resold to others, then the financing usually is not called "trade credit." Credit extended in connection with goods purchased for resale by a retailer or wholesaler, or raw materials used by a manufacturer in producing its products, is called "trade credit." Thus, we exclude also *consumer credit,* which is credit extended to individuals for purchase of goods for ultimate use rather than for resale.

Trade credit arises from the firm's normal operations, specifically from the time lag between receipt of goods and payment for them. The sum total of a firm's obligations to its trade creditors at any point in time normally is called "accounts payable" on the balance sheet. As we found in Chapter 4, an increase in accounts payable represents a source of funds to the firm; a decrease in accounts payable is a use of funds.

The extent to which trade credit is used as a source of funds varies widely among firms. In general, manufacturers, retailers, and wholesalers make extensive use of trade credit. Service firms purchase less and therefore rely less on trade credit. There is considerable variation also with respect to firm size; small firms generally use trade credit more extensively than large firms. When monetary policy is tight and credit is difficult to obtain, small firms tend to increase their reliance on trade credit. Large firms often have better access to financial markets and more bargaining power relative to commercial banks and other intermediaries than do small firms. During periods of *tight money,* small firms that are unable to obtain sufficient funds through normal channels may obtain financing indirectly from large suppliers by "stretching" their payment periods and expanding accounts payable. Large firms often are willing to finance their smaller customers in this manner in order to preserve their markets.

Within certain limits, a firm has discretion with respect to the extent to which it uses trade credit as a source of funds. By altering its payment period, a firm can expand or contract its accounts payable. In theory, a firm could reduce accounts payable to zero and use trade credit not at all simply by paying each invoice on the day received. However, since trade credit is noninterest-bearing, it represents a desirable source of financing. If used beyond certain limits, it is not without its costs. Let us now consider some of the factors pertinent to the decision regarding trade credit as a source of funds. Our concern here is with the use of trade credit extended by suppliers. In Chapter 8, we will discuss the other side of the coin, that is, the granting of trade credit to customers.

Forms of Trade Credit

Most trade credit is extended via the *open account.* Under this arrangement, goods are shipped and an invoice is sent to the purchaser, but the purchaser normally does not acknowledge the debt in writing. Payment is made later according to the terms of the agreement (discussed below). The major advantage of the open account is its simplicity and low administrative cost. Before granting credit via an open account, most suppliers perform a credit check.

A less common form of trade credit is the *promissory note*, usually called "note(s) payable, trade" on the balance sheet. The note is a written promise to pay that must be signed by the purchaser. Such notes usually bear interest and have specific maturity dates. They are used most often in situations in which the purchaser has failed to meet the terms of an open credit agreement and the supplier wishes a formal acknowledgment of the debt and a specific agreement regarding payment date. In exchange for lengthening the payment period, the purchaser usually pays interest. Thus, when we see "note(s) payable, trade" on a balance sheet, we usually can take it as an indication of some degree of financial difficulty. In a few industries, promissory notes are used as the standard vehicle for granting credit instead of the open account. In such cases, the presence of trade notes on the balance sheet does not indicate difficulty.

A third form of trade credit is the *trade acceptance*. Under this arrangement, the purchaser acknowledges the debt formally by accepting a draft drawn by the seller calling for payment on a specified date at a designated bank. After acceptance, the draft is returned to the seller and the goods are shipped. Trade acceptances of buyers with high credit ratings sometimes are marketable. On the due date, the holder of the acceptance, whether the original seller of the goods or another holder, presents the acceptance to the bank for collection from the purchaser. The trade acceptance is not widely used, mainly because of the rigidity and cost of the procedure.

Terms of Payment

Since the open account is by far the most common, we will restrict our discussion of payment terms to this form. The most restrictive terms are cash on delivery (COD) or cash before delivery (CBD). These terms are used to avoid credit risk entirely and represent no extension of credit at all.

A common arrangement is to specify a *net period* within which the invoice is to be paid. Terms of *net 30* indicate that payment is due within 30 days of the date of the invoice.

Suppliers often give *cash discounts* for payment within a specified period. Terms of *2/10, net 30* indicate that a discount of 2 percent may be taken if the invoice is paid within 10 days of the invoice date; otherwise the net (full) amount is due within 30 days. Such *prompt-payment* discounts are to be distinguished from *quantity* discounts given for purchase in large quantities, and also from *trade* discounts given at different points in the distribution chain (wholesale versus retail, etc.). Prompt-payment discounts are very common.

Seasonal datings sometimes are used in connection with goods that have seasonal sales patterns. By offering seasonal terms, the manufacturer is able to judge the size of the market more accurately and to maintain level production over the year. The buyer obtains the goods for sale but is not obligated to pay until the arrival of the peak selling season.

A specialized form of trade credit sometimes used is sale on *consignment*. Under this arrangement, the supplier retains title to the goods until sold, at which time the consignee remits to the supplier the proceeds of sale less the agreed upon discount. The consignee avoids the problem of financing the inventory, and the consignor reduces credit risk somewhat. The arrangement, however, is cumbersome and not widely used.

Trade Credit as a Source of Funds

In the final analysis, the principal consideration in the use of trade credit is cost. Trade credit on open account normally bears no interest, but its use does involve costs. If prompt-payment discounts are allowed by the supplier, a cost is incurred if the discount is not taken. For example, suppose a firm purchases goods on terms of 2/10, net 30. If the invoice is for $1,000, the firm can take a discount of $20 and pay only $980 if payment is made within 10 days. If the firm foregoes the discount, it pays $1,000 by day 30, assuming it maintains its accounts on a current basis, as it should. By foregoing the discount, the firm has the use of $980 for 20 days, for which it pays interest of $20. Annualized, the effective interest cost is

$$\frac{\$20}{\$980} \times \frac{365 \text{ days}}{20 \text{ days}} = 0.372 = 37.2 \text{ percent}$$

We find that in this case, not taking the discount is equivalent to borrowing at 37.2 percent per year, a rather expensive financing arrangement.

If there is no discount offered and the firm pays during the net period, trade credit still is not free. The supplier must operate a credit department to conduct credit analyses, maintain records, and proceed against overdue accounts. The accounts receivable on the supplier's books must be financed. These administrative and financing costs, like all costs of doing business, in the long run are borne by the buyers of the supplier's output. We should note, however, that the purchaser is bearing these costs whether the credit granted by the supplier is used or not.

Another element of cost is incurred if the firm delays payment beyond the net period. When a firm becomes overdue in its payments, its relations with suppliers are bound to suffer. Some suppliers can be "stretched" farther than others, and a given supplier may be more tolerant of late payment at some times than at others. Just how far a firm can push its suppliers depends on circumstances. A policy of late payment, however, is bad business practice, and in the long run is likely to be costly. At the least, late payment damages a firm's credit reputation, which is a valuable asset and, once lost, it is difficult to regain. At worst, late payment can cost a firm its sources of supply. During times of severe financial difficulty, a firm may be unable to avoid late payment. As a matter of long-run policy, however, obligations to suppliers should be discharged on schedule.

While late payment is dangerous and costly in the long run, early payment is uneconomic. Where prompt-payment discounts are offered, they should be taken if attractive, as they nearly always are. Otherwise, payment should be made within the net period. In either case, the full extent of the credit period should be utilized.

One further consideration involves furnishing information to suppliers and credit-rating agencies. Well-managed firms have no reason to balk at legitimate requests for information. If refused, suppliers and credit-rating agencies may conclude that difficulties exist and act accordingly.

Unsecured Short-Term Loans

An *unsecured* loan is one against which no specific assets are pledged as collateral. Secured loans will be discussed in a later section. Commercial banks are by far the largest suppliers of unsecured loans to business firms, so in this section we will restrict our discussion to bank loans.

Whereas nearly all firms use trade credit to some extent as a source of funds, not all firms use bank credit. Bank credit is, however, a very important source of credit for many businesses. At the end of 1978, aggregate trade credit outstanding was some $298 billion, whereas commercial and industrial loans by banks totaled $253 billion.[1] Firms that have a high proportion of current assets, such as those in retail and wholesale trade, use bank credit extensively. Manufacturing concerns also are heavy users. There is, however, considerable variation in the use of bank credit among different types of manufacturers.

Arranging Bank Financing

Most commercial banks view a relationship with a customer as involving more than just a loan. A loan is only one of a number of services that a bank normally will attempt to sell a business customer. Others are a checking account, time certificates of deposit, payroll and other accounting services, cash flow analysis, lock box services for speeding collections, investment services, pension and profit-sharing services, and corporate

---

1. Board of Governors, Federal Reserve System, *Flow of Funds Accounts: Assets and Liabilities Outstanding, December 31, 1978* (Federal Reserve Systeem, Washington, D.C., 1979).

trust services pertaining to shareholder records and payment of dividends. The bank, in short, thinks in terms of a total customer relationship, not just a loan.

Essential ingredients for a successful lending relationship from the bank's standpoint are, first and foremost, honesty and integrity, followed by managerial competence and a willingness to communicate frankly. In connection with a loan request, a bank is likely to seek general information about the firm and its business and about the background, experience, and reputation of its principal officers.

The bank also will want detailed information regarding the nature of the financing requirement, the amounts and timing of the need, the uses to which the funds will be put, and when and how the bank will be repaid. Here is where the financial plan, developed along lines that we discussed in Chapter 5, comes in. A comprehensive plan, including a pro forma income statement and balance sheet and perhaps a cash budget, will prove very valuable to any firm's management when it is negotiating a bank loan. The financial plan not only communicates the information sought by the bank regarding the financing requirement; the mere fact that a plan has been prepared tells the bank that the firm's management is competent and knows its business.

Good communications are also important after the loan is made. Few financial plans are executed exactly as planned. In an uncertain world, we would be surprised if deviations do not occur. When deviations do occur that affect the financing requirement or the firm's overall financial condition, the bank should be informed. Most banks require periodic financial statements from borrowing customers. When problems arise, it is wise for the firm to go beyond merely sending along the statements by calling attention to the problems and outlining the corrective action which is being taken. The firm says, in effect: "These are our problems, and this is what we are doing about them. If you have any suggestions, we would be pleased to have them." By this approach, the firm shares the problems with the bank and gives the bank an opportunity to respond. Banks expect their customers to have problems (banks have problems, too) and usually are pleased to learn that the problems have been recognized and are being acted upon.

Types of Bank Loans

Short-term unsecured bank loans usually take one of three forms: a line of credit, a revolving credit agreement, or a simple single-transaction loan. A *line of credit* is an agreement under which a firm can borrow up to an agreed upon maximum amount at any time during an agreed upon period—often 1 year. Lines of credit are not contractual and are not legally binding upon the bank, but they are nearly always honored. A major advantage of the line of credit is its convenience and administrative simplicity.

A line of credit often is used to finance seasonal working capital requirements or other temporary needs. Banks typically require an annual cleanup of the loan, a period usually of 1 or 2 months during which the loan is completely paid off. If a firm is unable to clean up, the bank will be alerted that the financing requirement may not be entirely seasonal. Lines of credit are renegotiated periodically, often annually, at which time the bank conducts a full review of the customer relationship, the financing requirement, and the firm's plans for the coming year.

A *revolving credit agreement,* unlike the line of credit, involves a contractual and binding commitment by the bank to provide funds. In return for this commitment, the borrower usually pays a fee of $\frac{1}{4}$ to $\frac{1}{2}$ percent per year on the average unused portion of the commitment. The size of the fee depends on credit conditions at the time, that is, the availability of funds in the banking system, and on the relative bargaining power of the bank and the borrower. Like the line of credit, the revolving credit agreement permits the borrower to borrow any amount up to some maximum at any time. Revolving credits often are negotiated for periods longer than a year, and during the period of the contract, are not subject to "clean-up" provisions or to renegotiation or cancellation by the bank because of tight credit conditions.

The line of credit and revolving credit agreement are well suited to firms that need financing frequently and in varying amounts. Where a firm needs financing only occasionally for specific purposes, banks typically treat each request individually.

Interest Rates on Bank Loans

Interest rates on bank loans to firms typically are scaled upward from the so-called *prime rate,* the rate charged to business borrowers with the highest credit rating. Rates for other than prime borrowers may exceed the prime rate by several percentage points. On the other hand, some borrowers may be able to obtain bank loans at below the prevailing prime rate. For example, a survey of short-term commercial and industrial loans made by banks during the week of February 5–10, 1979, when the prime rate was 11¾ percent, showed that the range of rates ran from 10½ percent to 14¼ percent; the weighted average rate of all loans was 12¼ percent.

Interest rates vary from loan to loan and from borrower to borrower for a number of reasons. Slight variations occur from region to region and from state to state, the latter depending to some extent on statutory rate ceilings. Rates vary with the riskiness of the loan, the size of the loan, and often the size of the borrower. The size of the borrower often is related to risk, and the size of the loan is a factor in the bank's administrative costs. For example, it does not take ten times as much work to negotiate and administer a $100,000 loan as a $10,000 loan; in fact, the large loan may even take less work if the borrower is well known and an established customer.

Methods of Computing the Interest Rate

When a lender quotes the nominal or stated interest rate on a loan, we still cannot be sure how much interest we will pay. There are several methods of computing the interest charge; each gives a different *effective* interest rate. Suppose we want to borrow $1,000 for 1 year. The lender quotes a rate of 8 percent. If we pay *interest in arrears on the unpaid balance,* we pay the lender $1,080 in 1 year, $1,000 principal and $80 interest. The effective interest rate is 80/1,000, or 8 percent.

If interest is computed using the *discount* method, the lender advances us $1,000 − 80 = $920, and we repay $1,000 in 1 year. We pay interest of $80 for the use of $920 for 1 year. The effective rate is 80/920, or 8.70 percent.

Suppose now that the loan must be repaid in monthly *installments.* Interest on consumer installment loans often is computed using the *add-on* method. Using this method, 1 year's interest of $80 is added on to the principal, and the result, $1,080, is divided by twelve to get the monthly payment of $90.00. Here, the effective rate is considerably higher than 8 percent, because we are paying off the loan over the year. In effect, over the year we have the use on average of only about half the principal, for which we pay interest of $80. Thus, the effective rate is almost double the stated rate. To compute the effective rate exactly (which in this case is 14.45 percent) requires the use of discounted cash flow techniques, which we will discuss in Part III.

Compensating Balances

In addition to the interest rate, banks often impose other conditions for obtaining a loan. A condition nearly always encountered is that the firm maintain a *compensating balance,* an agreed upon minimum balance to be maintained in the checking account. The minimum balance compensates the bank for clearing checks and other services and for any standby commitment to lend under a line of credit. The amount of the compensating balance usually is determined as a percentage, normally between 10 and 20 percent, of either the amount of the bank's commitment or of the loan outstanding. Under a $1 million line of credit, for example, a firm might be required to maintain a minimum deposit balance of

$150,000 (15 percent) at all times. An additional requirement might be imposed to compensate for other services.

From the bank's standpoint, the compensating balance, if in addition to balances otherwise maintained, has the effect of increasing the rate of return on the loan. By adjusting the compensating balance requirement, banks can vary the price of credit without changing nominal interest rates. This is sometimes an important consideration in the face of interest rate ceilings or political pressures for lower rates. From the firm's standpoint, the compensating balance increases the effective interest rate. If a firm needs $100,000, and must keep 15 percent of the loan on deposit over and above balances otherwise maintained, the firm must borrow a total of $117,647. If the stated interest rate were 9 percent, the firm would pay interest of 0.09 × $117,647 = $10,588 per year, or 10.59 percent on the $100,000 of usable funds.

Effective Cost of Bank Credit

The total cost of bank credit depends on the interest rate, compensating balance requirement, and commitment fees if any. Over the monetary cycle, the effective cost of bank credit varies considerably as interest rates rise and fall and banks adjust nonrate charges. Since bank loan markets are usually less than perfectly price competitive, the total of such costs is likely to vary more widely than short-term market rates in general, such as the United States Treasury Bill rate. During periods of tight money, availability often is more important to a firm than cost. When the Federal Reserve tightens monetary policy, the credit needs of some firms remain unmet. The cost of short-term funds relative to long-term funds over the course of a business cycle is one important consideration in determining the appropriate maturity structure of the firm's liabilities. Although long-term interest rates are higher *on average* than short-term rates, a firm that has long-term sources of funds—for example, via a bond issue—is not exposed to the threat that its funds will be cut off during periods of tight money.

Secured Short-Term Loans

Borrowers and lenders alike would prefer to do business on an unsecured basis. An unsecured loan provides maximum flexibility for the borrower and is less expensive to administer than a secured loan. However, in many situations the risk of default is sufficiently high that lenders are unwilling to lend on an unsecured basis.

A *secured* loan is one against which specific assets are pledged as collateral by the borrower. In the case of short-term loans, lenders usually insist on collateral that is reasonably liquid, that is, that can be sold and thereby converted to cash without great difficulty. Inventory and accounts receivable are most often used. Marketable securities would serve nicely as collateral but seldom are available to firms needing secured loans. Fixed assets, such as equipment and buildings, sometimes are pledged against short-term loans, but more often to obtain long-term funds. Accounts receivable and inventory are usually used as collateral against short-term loans, so these will be discussed in more detail below.

Commercial banks often require collateral under any of the lending arrangements discussed above. In addition to banks, *commercial finance companies* also make secured loans to business firms, with accounts receivable and inventories usually providing the collateral.

The procedure for securing a loan is covered by the Uniform Commercial Code, adopted by all states during the 1960s. An agreement between lender and borrower identifying the collateral is filed in the public records. If the borrower defaults on the terms of the agreement, the lender may seize the collateral and sell it to satisfy the claim. Any excess proceeds are returned to the borrowing firm. If the proceeds are insufficient to satisfy the claim, the lender must share in the remaining assets with unsecured creditors.

It is important to understand the function of collateral from the lender's standpoint. Collateral protects the lender in the event of default, but it does not lead to indifference to the prospect of default. There comes a point on the risk spectrum where lenders refuse the loan even with collateral. Lenders are in business to provide funds, not to liquidate inventories of electronic parts or women's fashion garments or to collect accounts receivable. The real function of collateral is to induce the lender to make a loan that, if unsecured, is too risky in relation to the rate that can be charged and yet still has reasonable prospects of being repaid.

In considering secured financing, we should not lose sight of the effect that pledging a firm's assets has on its other creditors. Trade creditors and other general creditors look to the firm's assets for protection in the event of financial difficulty. If particular assets suddenly are pledged, the position of these unsecured creditors is weakened. Such changes are not likely to go unnoticed and may be taken into account by the affected parties in future transactions.

Loans Against Accounts Receivable

Both banks and commercial finance companies regularly make loans against accounts receivable as collateral. All or part of a firm's receivables may be pledged. Those pledged constitute a *pool* of collateral, with new receivables continuously feeding into the pool and payments by customers reducing it.

Typically, the borrower retains responsibility for credit analysis of its customers and certifies to the lender that customers whose accounts are pledged are solvent. The lender judges the quality of the receivables and often has the option of rejecting any individual accounts. Since the borrower retains title to the receivables, defaults are the borrower's responsibility.

The lender and borrower agree upon a fixed percentage that will be advanced against the receivables. The percentage may vary from 60 to 90 percent, depending on the lender, an evaluation of the riskiness of the receivables, and the administrative costs of the arrangement. Commercial finance companies usually are willing to advance somewhat more than banks.

As the borrowing firm makes sales, the new receivables are assigned to the lender, who advances the agreed upon percentage of the face amount to the borrower. The customers usually are not notified that the account has been assigned and make their payments to the borrowing firm. Many agreements specify that the full amount of payments be sent immediately to the lender to be applied against the loan balance. If the assigned receivables and the loan are in the agreed upon percentage relationship, the lender usually deducts the loan percentage and returns the balance to the borrower.

Loans secured by receivables usually involve high administrative costs to the lender. Charges sometimes are separated into two components, a service charge and an interest rate. The total of these charges vary from a minimum of 2 to 3 percent above the prime rate to figures considerably higher for small or marginal customers, depending on risk and administrative costs.

A major advantage of receivables financing to the borrowing firm is the link between the loan and the assets to be financed. If sales and receivables are seasonal, the loan varies automatically. Besides the relatively high cost, a disadvantage of receivables financing is its administrative complexity.

Factoring

When a firm *factors* its accounts receivable, it sells them to another party, a factor, for cash. Title to the receivables passes to the factor, and the receivables are replaced by cash on the firm's balance sheet. In contrast, when a firm borrows against its receivables as collateral, it retains title, and both receivables and the loan appear on the balance sheet. Many commercial finance companies engage in factoring, along with some commercial banks, who usually conduct their factoring operations as separate subsidiaries of the bank or of a parent holding company.

Sale of the receivables to the factor normally is *without recourse,* meaning that the factor absorbs bad debt losses and cannot look to the seller in the event of default. Occasionally, receivables are sold *with recourse,* in which case uncollectable receivables are returned to the seller, who absorbs the bad debt expense.

The factor normally approves each order and reserves the right to reject individual accounts or orders. Once the order is approved by the factor, the goods are shipped and the customer is notified to remit directly to the factor. Because the customer is notified that the account has been sold to a factor, some firms may be inhibited from using factoring. In industries in which factoring is widely used, notably textiles, shoes, and furniture, there is no stigma attached.

Services performed by the factor include credit analysis, collection, and absorption of bad debts. The fee charged varies with the specific services and ranges between 1 and 3 percent of the face amount of the receivables purchased. If funds are advanced to the seller before the receivables are collected by the factor, an additional interest charge is levied that is normally tied to, and above, the prime rate.

In some situations, factoring offers significant advantages. With a factoring arrangement, a firm avoids the expense of bad debts and also may avoid the necessity of operating a credit department for analysis and collection. Firms that are small or have seasonal sales patterns may realize substantial savings. Costs avoided by the firm are borne by the factor, but because the factor serves many customers, the aggregate cost may be lower. By serving firms with different seasonal patterns, the credit analysis and collection workload may be spread more evenly over the year. By serving a large number of accounts, the factor can realize economics of scale and also can achieve better diversification with respect to default risk. For these reasons, in some industries, a factor can perform the services in question more economically than can firms individually.

To evaluate factoring as a financing arrangement requires a careful analysis of activities and costs and a comparison of the resulting savings with the fee charged by the factor.

Loans Against Inventory

Inventory also often is used as collateral for loans by both banks and commercial finance companies. The nature of the inventory is an important factor in determining the attractiveness of the loan to a lender and the percentage to be advanced. The more readily salable the inventory, the higher the loan percentage is likely to be. A lumber wholesaler's inventory, for example, readily salable as is, likely would justify a higher loan percentage than would an inventory of specialized electronic parts or half-completed electronic instruments. Loan percentages against inventory typically vary from 50 to 90 percent.

The security arrangement is a critical factor in inventory loans and greatly affects the administrative costs. A number of methods are in common use; some leave the inventory in the possession of the borrower, and some place it under the control of a third party.

The simplest arrangement by which a borrower can retain control of the inventory is a *blanket* or *floating lien.* The Uniform Commercial Code includes a provision whereby a borrower may pledge his inventory "in general," without specifying the exact items involved. The floating lien is inexpensive to administer but difficult to police.

Considerably more security is afforded the lender under a *trust receipt loan.* This arrangement often is used to finance automobiles, consumer durable goods, and certain types of equipment. In these applications, it is referred to as *floor planning.* Under such an arrangement, the lender advances the funds to purchase the inventory. The borrower signs a trust receipt, and each item is identified individually by serial number. Usually, title to the goods rests with the lender until sold. After sale, the proceeds belong to the lender and are forwarded immediately by the borrower. As inventory is sold, new inventory is entered into the arrangement; this is controlled individually by serial numbers. Lenders usually audit the inventory periodically to ensure that items that are supposed to be in the inventory, identified by serial number, in fact are there.

With goods in the hands of the borrower, the lender is not protected against fraud or misapplication. To gain complete protection, the goods may be placed under the control of a third party, usually referred to as a warehouseman. The warehouseman is given physical control of the inventory and issues a warehouse receipt assigning the security interest to the lender. The warehouseman releases the inventory to the borrowing firm upon authorization of the lender, which usually requires that some portion of the loan be repaid.

There are two principal types of warehouse arrangements. A *terminal warehouse* is a public warehouse facility to and from which the inventory must be physically transported. Often a more convenient arrangement is the *field warehouse,* operated by the warehouse company on the premises of the borrower. Under this arrangement, a suitable facility is established providing storage under lock and key with direct control by the warehouseman.

Since inventory must be controlled item by item, administrative costs are high under a warehouse arrangement. Floor planning arrangements usually are somewhat less costly, but provide less security and are not suitable for all types of goods. On warehouse loans, interest and service charges usually are listed separately. Interest charges are imposed by the lender and depend on the credit worthiness of the borrower, nature of the inventory, loan percentage, and amount of the loan. Service charges are levied by the warehouse company and depend on the nature of the inventory, handling required, and rate of turnover of the goods under control. Warehouse receipt loans are an expensive method of financing, but in some cases may be the only source available.

The Great Salad Oil Swindle

Warehousing arrangements by no means provide complete security to lenders. The Great Salad Oil Swindle of the early 1960s provides a classic case of what can go wrong if the borrower is determined, ingenious, and dishonest.[2] The case is an extreme one, but worth telling mainly because it is so interesting.

In the late 1950s, a man named Anthony De Angelis established the Allied Crude Oil Vegetable Refining Corporation. Allied was in the business of processing crude vegetable oil, mainly soybean and cottonseed oils, into salad oil.

The oil was stored in large tanks at Bayonne, New Jersey. A number of well-known banks, exporters, and Wall Street investment banking firms lent money to Allied against the oil as collateral. The oil was controlled under a field warehousing arrangement supervised by the American Express Field Warehousing Corporation, a subsidiary of the American Express Company.

The job of the Field Warehousing Company was to supervise the storage of oil and certify that it was indeed on hand in the amounts specified. American Express issued field warehouse receipts, which Allied then used as collateral for loans.

Over the period of 1957–1963, Allied managed to steal hundreds of millions of dollars worth of oil without the Field Warehousing Company's knowledge. The tanks were connected by a complex system of pipes and valves. Allied personnel would pump out the oil in a tank and pump in sea water, leaving a foot or two of oil floating on top of perhaps 40 feet of sea water. Inspectors of the Field Warehousing Company would look into the tank and see only oil. Special devices lowered through ports in the tops of the tanks verified that oil extended to the bottom. Indeed, the oil did extend to the bottom, but only inside special narrow cylindrical chambers installed directly under the ports by Allied personnel. The sea water remained undetected.

When the swindle was finally uncovered, warehouse receipts were outstanding for 1.988 *billion* pounds of oil. Only 134 million pounds were

---

2. N. C. Miller, *The Great Salad Oil Swindle* (Baltimore: Penguin Books, 1965).

actually on hand in the Bayonne tanks. The rest had either disappeared over the period 1957–1963 or never had existed in the first place. The amount of soybean oil certified to be in the Bayonne tanks by the warehouse receipts actually exceeded the total soybean oil stocks in the entire United States as reported by the United States government! The total shortage was 1.854 billion pounds valued at about $175 million.

A total of 51 companies and banks that had lent money to Allied using warehouse receipts as collateral suffered losses totaling $175 million. Two Wall Street investment banking firms went bankrupt, as did the American Express Field Warehousing subsidiary. The list of banks that lost money included nearly every major bank in New York City, as well as major banks in Chicago, on the West Coast, and abroad. The parent American Express Company incurred large losses in making good a portion of the claims.

"Tino" De Angelis eventually went to prison for masterminding the swindle. Little of the $175 million was ever recovered, and just where it all went remains a mystery to this day. The salad oil case remains the classic object lesson in making loans against inventory. All lending officers should study it carefully.

Commercial Paper

Commercial paper is the label given to unsecured short-term promissory notes issued by borrowers to investors. Commercial paper distributed via organized financial markets is known as a *money-market* instrument (along with United States Treasury Bills, bank certificates of deposit, and bankers' acceptances).

Since commercial paper is unsecured, it can be issued only by firms with the highest credit ratings, which usually means only relatively large firms. Although a wide variety of firms use the commercial paper market as a source of funds, the big borrowers are finance companies, financing subsidiaries of large manufacturers such as General Motors Acceptance Corporation and Chrysler Financial Corporation, and commerical banks and bank-holding companies who jointly account for 75 percent of the funds borrowed in this form. Major buyers of commercial paper include nonbank financial institutions such as insurance companies, pension funds and mutual funds, and business firms with temporary excess cash.

Commercial Paper Market[3]

The commercial paper market has grown rapidly since the 1960s, and as of December 31, 1978 some $84 billion was outstanding. The minimum

---

3. For a good discussion of the commercial paper market, see E. M. Hurley "The Commercial Paper Market," *Federal Reserve Bulletin,* June 1977.

denomination is $25,000, although denominations of $100,000 up to several million dollars are much more common. Maturities usually range from 30 to 180 days but may go up to 270 days. Under current regulations, an issue of maturity longer than 270 days would have to be registered with the Securities and Exchange Commission.

The commercial paper market is highly organized, with paper sold both directly and through dealers. Dealers typically charge a commission of $\frac{1}{8}$ to $\frac{1}{4}$ percent. The interest rate on commercial paper usually runs about 1 percent less than the prime lending rate at commercial banks, although in recent years this spread has widened to around $1\frac{1}{2}$ points. For example, from 1976 to 1978 Citibank (First National City Bank of New York) set its prime lending rate so that it was kept approximately equal to the average commercial paper rate for the preceding 3 weeks *plus* $1\frac{1}{2}$ percentage points.[4] The principal buyers of commercial paper are other business corporations who have a temporary surplus of cash.

Commercial Paper as a Source of Funds

We noted above that only large firms with the highest credit ratings have access to the commercial paper market. For such firms, the principal advantage of commercial paper is its lower cost relative to the cost of alternative sources such as the prime bank lending rate. In addition to this saving, the borrowing firm avoids the cost of maintaining compensating balances normally required in connection with bank loans.

Offsetting this cost advantage somewhat is the fact that borrowers in the commercial paper market have to maintain backup lines of credit or revolving credit agreements at commercial banks. When conditions in the money market get tight, these backup lines provide insurance against temporary difficulties in marketing commercial paper. In June 1970, the need for backup bank lines was forcefully demonstrated when the Penn-Central Railroad went bankrupt. Only several weeks prior to the announcement of the bankruptcy petition, Penn-Central's commercial paper had been rated *prime.* After the bankruptcy, the commercial paper market became very "nervous" for several weeks, and some large issuers of commercial paper were unable to market new issues to refinance those that were maturing. The most celebrated case involved Chrysler Financial Corporation, which required an emergency loan from a group of large banks.

For lending agreements to backstop commercial paper, banks typically charge a commitment fee of between $\frac{1}{4}$ and $\frac{1}{2}$ percent. Even with this cost included, commercial paper usually is less expensive than bank

---

4. In January 1979 Citibank changed the base in its formula to the rate on 90-day certificates of deposit.

loans. We would expect this to be true, because the commercial paper market generally is more price-competitive than are bank loan markets. The more competitive the market, the lower the price to the buyer, in this case the buyer of funds.

Besides the cost advantage, some very large issuers of commercial paper find their financing requirements too large to be conveniently served by commercial banks. Banks operate under a limit on the maximum amount that can be lent to any one borrower. A large borrower may need a number of banks to satisfy its total requirement. Such borrowers may find the commercial paper market a more convenient alternative.

Term Loans

Thus far in this chapter, we have discussed sources of short-term funds; these have usually involved maturities of less than 1 year. Let us now consider sources of financing over intermediate periods, usually defined as longer than 1 year but shorter than 8 or 10 years. Loans of such maturity often are referred to as *term loans.*

From the standpoint of the borrower, the key distinctions between short-term and intermediate-term financing concern the uses to which the funds are put and the sources of repayment. As we noted earlier, intermediate-term financing normally is used to finance fixed assets or permanent additions to working capital. Repayment usually must come from profits rather than from liquidation of the assets financed, as in the case of seasonal short-term loans. For this reason, intermediate-term lenders are more concerned with earning power than are short-term lenders. Also for this reason, term loans nearly always are *amortized,* or repaid in installments. The amortization requirement encourages the borrower to earmark a portion of the firm's earnings for debt repayment, and avoids leaving the lender dependent on the borrower's asset structure at the end of the loan's term. Home mortgages are amortized for precisely this same reason.

Why should fixed assets and permanent additions to working capital be financed with intermediate-term or long-term funds? Why not short-term funds, for example, a succession of 6 month loans continually renewed? Matching maturities on the two sides of the balance sheet by financing long-lived assets with long-term funds sounds logical, but does it make economic sense? The answer is that it does, for reasons we will go into in more depth in Part V, where we will discuss the choice between short-term and long-term debt and the relation between maturity structure and liquidity.

We also might raise a second question, namely, why permanent additions to assets should not be financed by long-term funds, equity, or long-term debt, rather than a term loan. Many firms do not have access to the public, long-term capital markets. Long-term debt funds may be available privately from insurance companies, but often not to smaller firms. By financing with a term loan and paying it off in installments, the firm gradually replaces the intermediate-term financing with long-term funds generated internally.

Term loans to business firms are made primarily by banks and insurance companies. These two sources are discussed further below.

Term Loans from Banks

Historically, bankers have preferred short-term seasonal loans, but in recent years, banks have expanded their term lending significantly. Maturities normally range from 3 to 7 years, seldom going beyond 10 years. Banks nearly always require security on term loans; the most often used collateral is equipment or real estate.

Interest rates on term loans usually run $\frac{1}{4}$–1 percent higher than on short-term loans of similar size and riskiness. Because of large shifts in the general level of interest rates during the last 10 years, many banks have moved to a *variable rate* arrangement, whereby the rate on the term loan is tied to the prime rate. Compensating balance requirements raise the effective cost above the nominal rate. Smaller term loans sometimes are handled through the bank's installment loan department, where the effective rate is considerably higher than in the commercial department.

Term loans usually include a greater number of restrictive covenants than do short-term loans. To ensure that the borrower maintains an adequate degree of liquidity, restrictions may be included on minimum net working capital and current ratio. Restrictions also may be placed on the payment of dividends and on the purchase and sale of fixed assets. Pledging assets to others often is prohibited by a *negative pledge clause*. Additional borrowings senior to the term loan in question may also be prohibited. In smaller firms with less depth in management, insurance often is required on the lives of the principal officers. In all cases, periodic financial statements are required of the borrower.

Covenants vary from loan to loan and are a matter of negotiation between borrower and lender. From the borrower's standpoint, covenants such as those discussed above may appear onerous and rigid. Often, however, they are no more restrictive than are the dictates of prudence and sound management. From the lender's standpoint, restrictions are required on term loans that would not be necessary on short-term loans. Over a period of several years, the lender is exposed to risks that cannot be anticipated in advance, such as changes in technology or in the philosophy or quality of management. When trouble appears, the firm is likely to begin to have difficulty meeting all of the restrictions in the loan agreement. The restrictions thus constitute an "early warning" system that alerts the lender to potential problems in time for corrective action to be taken. Here again, we should note the importance of close and frank communications. When trouble begins to develop, the borrower should not wait for the lender to find out. It is better to bring the problem to the lender's attention along with a plan of corrective action.

Term Loans from Insurance Companies

Insurance companies also represent a source of intermediate-term financing to business. To the insurance company, the loan is simply an investment, rather than a part of a larger and continuing customer relationship, as it is to a bank. Insurance companies tend to prefer larger loans and often are unwilling to lend to smaller firms.

Because of the longer maturity of their liabilities, insurance companies prefer maturities of 10 years or longer and often are not interested in those shorter than 7 or 8 years. Prepayment penalties are more common on loans by insurance companies, though other restrictive covenants are similar to those imposed by banks.

Equipment Financing

Loans Against Equipment

Equipment often is pledged as collateral against a term loan from a bank or insurance company. The proceeds of the loan may be used to purchase the equipment itself or for other purposes. Title to the equipment rests with the borrower, whose balance sheet will show both asset and loan. A security interest in the equipment is given to the lender by means of a *chattel mortgage,* which gives the lender the right to seize and sell the equipment in the event of default on the loan by the borrower. Public notice of the lien is filed in the state in which the equipment is located. The word *chattel* literally means *thing* and indicates that the lien is on something other than real property.

Commercial finance companies also represent an important source of equipment financing. Two methods normally are used: conditional sales contracts and leasing.

Conditional Sales Contracts

A *conditional sales contract* is an installment purchase contract under which title to the equipment remains with the lender until all payments are made. Consummation of the contract by passage of title is *conditioned* on the borrower's making all payments. A down payment is nearly always required, and the borrower signs a promissory note for the balance. Under present accounting guidelines, both equipment and loan appear on the borrower's balance sheet. For accounting and tax purposes, the borrower treats the equipment as if he owns it, taking depreciation and deducting only the interest portion of the payment to the lender. The amount of the down payment and the maturity of the contract are set so that the unpaid balance always is below the resale value of the equipment. If the borrower defaults, the lender sells the equipment to satisfy the contract. Maturities usually range between 1 and 4 years.

Leasing

A second method of financing equipment is via a *lease*. A lease is a contractual arrangement under which the *lessee* has the right to use the equipment, and in return makes periodic payments to the owner, the *lessor*. The lessor retains title to the equipment. Accounting and tax treatment of leases is very complex, and the applicable rules have undergone significant change in recent years. Normally, the lessor carries the equipment on his balance sheet as an asset and takes the depreciation on it. The lessee shows nothing on his balance sheet and deducts the full amount of the lease payment as an expense. Thus, the party providing the financing, rather than the user, is treated as the owner for accounting and tax purposes, whereas it is the other way around in the case of the conditional sales contract. To qualify for this treatment, however, certain conditions must be met, and the Internal Revenue Service goes to great lengths to distinguish leases from conditional sales contracts. The accounting profession also is experimenting with new guidelines regarding disclosure of lease contracts in financial statements. In some cases, a lessee is required to capitalize a lease and to show both asset and lease obligation on the balance sheet. Sometimes the accounting treatment may be one way for financial reporting purposes and another way for tax purposes.

Lease contracts to finance equipment usually are written for periods of 1 to 5 years. Commercial banks and finance companies most often act as lessors. On longer-lived assets, such as building and land, lease contracts are written over longer time periods, with insurance companies and pension funds more often acting as lessors. Leases on real estate provide that maintenance, taxes, and insurance expenses are borne by the lessee rather than the lessor as in the case of equipment leases.

Leasing is a very important means of both intermediate-term and long-term financing. It is also complex, and the proper evaluation of leasing as a financing method requires discounted cash flow techniques, which we will not discuss until later.

Government-Sponsored Loan Programs

During the 1950s several programs were established by the federal government to assist small firms in obtaining financing. These programs grew out of a recognition of the financing difficulties encountered by small firms—usually risky and often with no established record on which to base a loan. Private lenders, applying standard economic criteria, often found returns too low to compensate for the risk and administrative expense involved. The difficulties of small firms are especially acute in the case of intermediate-term financing. Recognizing this problem, and feeling that small business is a desirable part of the American system, Congress decided to provide federal assistance. In most cases, assistance takes the form of a goverment guarantee of a loan from a private lender or of special tax treatment, though in some cases the loan is made by the government itself. The principal federal programs are discussed below.[5]

Small Business Administration

In 1953, Congress passed the Small Business Act, establishing the Small Business Administration (SBA). Under the SBA's Business Loan Program, financing assistance is provided to firms that meet its size criteria and are unable to obtain financing through private channels. Manufacturing firms employing less than 250 people, retail firms with sales of less than $1 million, and wholesale firms with sales of less than $5 million are defined as small and are eligible to participate.

Two types of loan arrangements are available. On a *direct* loan, the SBA lends the funds directly. In a *participation* loan, the SBA lends part and a private lending institution, usually a bank, provides the balance. A portion of the funds provided by the private lender are guaranteed by the SBA. In some cases, the private lender provides all the funds under an SBA guarantee. In recent years, most SBA loans have been participating rather than direct. Loans range in amount up to $350,000, with maturities up to 5–7 years. Interest rates on funds advanced by private lenders under SBA guarantee are set by the lender subject to SBA approval.

Most lending under SBA sponsorship has involved intermediate-term credit. Recently, however, the SBA has begun to guarantee short-term revolving credit arrangements. There also is a program under which 15 year mortgages are available.

---

5. A number of programs of assistance to small business exist in addition to those discussed here. Information on these programs can be obtained from the Small Business Administration, Washington, D.C., or from regional SBA offices.

Small Business Investment Companies

The establishment of Small Business Investment Companies (SBIC) was provided for under the Small Business Investment Act of 1958. Unlike the SBA, an SBIC is not a government agency but is licensed by the SBA and operated as a private lending institution, often as a subsidiary of a commercial bank or bank-holding company.

The purpose of an SBIC is to provide risk capital to small businesses, as opposed to intermediate-term financing provided under SBA guarantee. The SBIC operates as a *venture capitalist,* providing "seed" money to new firms during their initial years, when size and risk preclude financing via other sources. The SBIC obtains a part of its own capital from private sources, and part via a loan from the SBA. The SBA loan may be subordinated to loans from private sources.

To qualify for SBIC financing, a firm must meet size criteria set by the SBA. Funds may be provided by sale of common stock or long-term debt to the SBIC. A frequently used device is long-term debt convertible into common stock at the option of the SBIC. If the company is successful, common stock eventually may be sold to the public, and the SBIC will liquidate its interest. Ideally, the SBIC's involvement is limited to a period of a few years during which the fledgling firm grows to the point of attracting private financing.

The mortality rate among firms that obtain SBIC financing usually is high. Unlike SBA loans, SBIC loans are not guaranteed by the government, so the SBIC must earn sufficient returns on its "winners" to offset losses on those not so fortunate. The SBIC has not been as successful as either the individual owners or the Congress had hoped, but since the mid-1960s it has performed an important function on a modest scale.

Finding the Right Source

Some of the financing sources we have discussed are available to all firms, some only to large firms, and some only to small firms. There also are less formal sources that we have not discussed. Suppliers and manufacturers sometimes will aid small firms that are customers or distributors. We discussed conditional sales contracts. Sometimes direct loans and a guarantee or endorsement of a loan from a bank can be negotiated. Friends, relatives, and employees also are potential sources.

Established firms experienced in obtaining outside financing have experts on their payrolls who maintain close contacts with financing sources. For a new firm or a firm using outside financing for the first time, the question often is where to begin. The best answer is to begin with a commercial bank. Almost any firm can benefit from a good banking relationship. A new firm just beginning its existence should first set out to find a bank with which it can work. Banks are in business to provide both money and financial assistance, and often can be helpful in establishing financial management procedures and developing financial plans. The bank's objective is to see that the new firm grows into a customer to which it can lend and provide a variety of other services.

If a bank is unwilling or unable to provide financing, for risk considerations or other reasons, it should be able to suggest other sources. Many banks work with the SBA and are familiar with SBA criteria and application procedures. Banks also have contacts with commercial finance companies that provide financing for accounts receivable, inventories, and equipment, and with SBIC companies and other sources of venture capital.

Summary

To obtain funds, a firm issues claims against its assets and future income. Some are contractual claims (liabilities) and others are ownership claims (equities). Some liabilities (e.g., accounts payable) arise naturally as a consequence of the firm's operations, while others are discretionary, (e.g., bank loans).

The direct suppliers of short- and intermediate-term funds to business firms are other business firms, commercial banks, finance companies, insurance companies, and pension funds. These suppliers are themselves only intermediaries in the chain of finance. Ultimately, the suppliers of all business funds are individuals with funds to save and invest.

Trade credit is credit extended in connection with goods purchased for resale. Nearly all firms rely on trade credit to provide some financing, although the extent of its use varies widely among industries. Although trade credit is interest-free, its use does involve costs. In general, firms should take prompt-payment discounts when offered and otherwise pay within the specified credit period.

Commercial banks are the largest suppliers of unsecured short-term loans to business firms. A comprehensive financial plan is very useful during the process of negotiating bank financing. In addition to the contract interest rate, the effective cost of bank credit includes the cost of compensating balance requirements and any fees that are charged.

A secured loan is one against which specific assets are pledged as collateral by the borrower. Commercial banks and commercial finance companies make the majority of secured loans to business firms. Accounts receivable and inventory are the most commonly used collateral. Factoring, which is the sale of accounts receivable to another party, represents a specialized source of financing.

Commercial paper refers to unsecured short-term promissory notes issued by a borrowing firm directly to a lender. Since it is unsecured and marketable, commercial paper normally can be issued by only the largest and most credit-worthy firms.

Term loans constitute a major source of intermediate-term funds, with maturities ranging from 1 to 7 or 8 years. Most term loans are made by banks and insurance companies and usually are repaid in installments. Term loans often are secured by equipment pledged as collateral. Equipment also is frequently financed via conditional sales contracts and leases. For small businesses, various government-sponsored loan programs are available to provide financial assistance.

Sample Problem

When a firm foregoes cash discounts, it gives up the discount in exchange for the use of the funds for a longer period. We can calculate the effective interest cost on the resulting "loan." Make this calculation in each of the following cases, assuming that the firm pays on the final due date:

1. terms 1/10, net 30
2. terms 3/15, net 40

Solution

Assume the invoice is for $1,000. In case 1 above, if the invoice is paid in 10 days, the firm can take a $10 discount and pay $990. If the discount is foregone, the firm pays $1,000 on day 30. By foregoing the discount, the firm has the use of $990 for 20 days, for which it pays $10. Annualized, the effective interest rate is:

$$\frac{\$10}{\$990} \times \frac{365 \text{ days}}{20 \text{ days}} = 0.184 = 18.4 \text{ percent}$$

In case 2, the firm has the use of $970 for 25 days at a cost of $30. The effective interest rate is:

$$\frac{\$30}{\$970} \times \frac{365 \text{ days}}{25 \text{ days}} = 0.452 = 45.2 \text{ percent}$$

Questions

1. Who are the major suppliers to business firms?
2. What are the costs of using trade credit as a source of funds?
3. How is the financial plan used in arranging bank financing?
4. Describe the major types of short-term unsecured bank loans.

5. What is the purpose of collateral from the lender's standpoint?
6. How might the standards of credit worthiness applied by a bank differ from those applied by a trade creditor?
7. For what reason might a sale of accounts receivable to a factor affect a firm's current ratio differently than would a loan secured by accounts receivable?
8. Why do secured loans often carry higher rates of interest than unsecured loans?
9. What potential advantages do you see in factoring in industries where it is used?
10. Why are intermediate-term lenders more concerned with earning power than are short-term lenders?

Problems   *assume "$1000.- loan"*

1. Calculate the effective annual interest rate that would be lost if the firm paid on the final due date rather than taking the cash discount.
   (a) 2/15, net 45 $\frac{20}{980} \times \frac{365}{30} = \frac{7300}{29,400} = .248 = 24.8\%$
   (b) 3/10, net 30
   (c) 1/15, net 40
   (d) 2/10, net 40

2. Calculate the effective annual interest rate on the following discount loans. (*Hint:* Calculate the interest using the discount method.)
   (a) A $100,000 loan at 7 percent. $= \frac{\$000}{7\%}$ $1000-70 \overset{\$}{=} 930$ $\frac{7000}{93,000} = 7.5\bar{\jmath}$
   (b) A $50,000 loan at 7½ percent. $\frac{7}{7000}$
   (c) A $25,000 loan at 8 percent. $= \frac{25000}{\times 8\%}$ $= 25000 - 2000 = 23000 \frac{2000}{23,000} = 8.7$
       $\frac{}{2000}$

3. Calculate the effective annual interest rate for the following loans.
   (a) The firm needs $10,000, and the lending bank charges 8 percent and requires a 10 percent compensating balance.
   (b) The firm needs $250,000, and the lending bank charges 7½ percent and requires a 15 percent compensating balance.

(b) $\frac{250,000}{85\%} = 294,117.64 -$
$\times 7.5\%$
$\$22,058.82$ (INTEREST)

$\frac{22058.82}{250,000} = \$8.82$ (effective rate)

$\frac{10}{990} \times \frac{365}{10} = \frac{3650}{9900} = .368 = 36.8\%$

4. MSM, Incorporated has been paying its major supplier approximately 20 days after the materials are received. The supplier offers terms of 1/10, net 45 on all open accounts.
   (a) What is the effective annual rate that MSM is giving up by not paying by the tenth day?
   (b) Assuming that a local bank has offered to lend MSM the funds needed to purchase these materials at an effective annual rate of 9½ percent, what strategy do you see as optimal for MSM?

5. Bland Corporation needs an immediate increase in short-term funds and has determined that four sources are available for the required $1,500,000:
   (a) An 8 percent discount loan from the bank with a required compensating balance of 10 percent.

NOTE:
CASH AVAILABLE = LOAN - FEE

INTEREST PD
CASH AVAIL.

$\dfrac{1500000}{\times 8\%}$ $\dfrac{120000}{} + 20^{00} = 140,000$ $\dfrac{140,000}{1,500,000} = 9.33\%$

(b) Commercial paper at 8 percent with a placement fee of $20,000 per year payable at the start of the year.

(c) Foregoing discounts from suppliers at terms of 1/15 net 60.

(d) A bank loan quoted at an effective annual rate of 8 percent but requiring the pledging of accounts receivable.

Calculate the effective annual interest cost of each alternative. Which alternative should Bland choose?

6. DLM Enterprises needs to increase its short-term funds by $2,000,000 and has found two possible loan arrangements:

A) $\dfrac{2,000,000}{\times 11\%}$ $\dfrac{2,000,000}{-220,000}$ $\dfrac{220000}{1,780000} =$
$\dfrac{220,000}{}$ $\dfrac{1,780,000}{}$ 12.3%

Loan *A*: An 11 percent discount loan, with no compensating balance

Loan *B*: An 11 percent nondiscount loan, with a 10 percent compensating balance

B) $2,000,000$ (see 3 B)

Which loan should DLM choose?

7. Refer to Problem 6.

(a) Calculate the nominal interest rate (discount basis) on loan *A* that would make its effective interest rate equal to loan *B*'s interest rate.

10.89%

(b) Calculate the nominal interest rate on loan *B* that would make its effective interest rate equal 12 percent.

10.8%

References

A. B. Abraham, "Factoring—the New Frontier for Commercial Banks," *Journal of Commercial Bank Lending* **53**, 32–43 (April 1971).

N. D. Baxter, *The Commercial Paper Market* (Princeton, N.J.: Princeton University Press, 1964).

"The Commercial Paper Market," *Federal Reserve Bulletin* **63**, 525–536 (June 1977).

D. B. Crane and W. L. White, "Who Benefits from a Floating Prime Rate?," *Harvard Business Review* **50**, 121–129 (Jan.-Feb. 1972).

W. E. Gibson, "Compensating Balance Requirement," *National Banking Review* **2**, 298–311 (Mar. 1965).

D. G. Harris, "Rationing Credit to Business: More Than Just Interest Rates," *Business Review* 3–14 (Aug. 1970).

D. A. Hayes, *Bank Lending Policies: Domestic and International* (Ann Arbor, Mich.: University of Michigan, 1971).

D. R. Hodgman, *Commercial Bank Loan and Investment Policy* (Champaign, Ill.: Bureau of Economic and Business Research, University of Illinois, 1963).

D. M. Jaffee and F. Modigliani, "A Theory and Test of Credit Rationing," *American Economic Review* **59**, 850–872 (Dec. 1969).

M. R. Lazere (ed.), *Commercial Financing* (New York: Ronald Press, 1968).

P. S. Nadler, "Compensating Balances and the Prime at Twilight," *Harvard Business Review* **50**, 112–120 (Jan.-Feb. 1972).

Small Business Administration, *Annual Reports.*

Managing Cash

7

Managing Collections and Disbursements
Determining the Working Cash Balance
Investing Idle Cash

The firm's requirements for working capital and outside financing over the short run are essentially determined by business expectations and its operating plan. Through the use of pro forma analysis, the financial officer can determine, at any point in time, how much cash will be available and how much outside financing will be required. One function of the financial manager is to see that the required amount of financing is obtained at minimum cost to the firm. But the manager is also responsible for evaluating the operating plan itself, especially its intentions and procedures with respect to cash, accounts receivable, and inventory. In this chapter and the next, we will examine the financial officer's contribution to the management of these current assets more closely. We consider cash management in this chapter, and accounts receivable and inventory in the next.

The term *cash* sometimes refers to currency plus checking account balances held at commercial banks, and sometimes also includes *near-cash* assets such as marketable securities or bank time deposits. Earlier, we used the term "liquid assets" to refer to the total of cash plus near-cash. But in this chapter, we will use the term *cash* in its broader sense, that is, as a label for total liquid assets. We will use the term "working" cash balances to refer to the subset currency plus checking accounts. We will not distinguish between the latter two components, since for most firms the checking account is far more important than currency as a working balance.

Firms have two main motives for holding cash, or liquid assets: a *transactions* motive, and a *precautionary* motive. The transactions motive refers to cash balances required in the ordinary course of business—a pool from which the firm makes payments to suppliers, employees, and creditors, and into which it places payments received from customers. These receipts and disbursements constitute a continuous flow through the firm's working cash balance. The precautionary motive refers to cash held for "rainy days," unexpected problems, or opportunities requiring funds on short notice. Precautionary cash balances usually are held in near-cash assets so as to earn interest, since (with some rare exceptions) banks are not permitted to pay interest on checking account balances. In seasonal firms, such as the Neptune Company discussed in Chapter 5, a part of the transaction balance also may be "stored" temporarily in near-cash form during parts of the year.

In order to concentrate on cash management, we will continue to take as given all aspects of the firm's operating plan except those that directly affect its cash position. Inventory levels, for example, will be assumed to be already determined, as will trade credit policy and the level of accounts receivable.

Cash management involves three main questions:

1. How should the storage, collection, and disbursement of working cash balances be managed?
2. Given a total pool of cash, how should the appropriate working balance be determined?
3. How should any temporarily idle funds be invested in interest-bearing assets?

Managing Collections and Disbursements

The Cash Cycle

To size up our problem of cash management, let us examine the flow of cash through a firm's accounts. It is useful to think of the process as a *cycle* in which cash is used to purchase materials, from which are produced goods, which are then sold to customers, who later pay their bills. The firm receives cash from its customers, and the cycle repeats. Diagrammatically, we can represent the cash cycle as in Figure 7-1.

Opportunities to improve efficiency in collecting and disbursing funds center on flows through the current section of the balance sheet, depicted in the bottom part of Figure 7-1. We diagram these flows in more detail in Figure 7-2, which shows the steps along the way as funds flow through the firm's accounts. Let us assume that XYZ Corporation orders raw materials at point *A* and receives them 14 days later at *B*. Terms of 2/10, net 30 are offered, so the firm pays the invoice 10 days later at *C*. However, it takes 2 days for the check to clear, and XYZ's bank account is not charged until point *D*. XYZ turns its inventory six times per year, so 60 days after the materials are received, the product is sold and the customer is billed. The collection period is 30 days, 28 for the customer to pay and 2 for the check to arrive by mail (*G*). XYZ processes the payment and deposits it 2 days later at *H*. Another 2 days elapses while XYZ's bank collects the funds from the customer's bank.

The firm's total financing requirement is affected by the total time lag from point *B* to point *J*. The firm itself can control some factors that determine the various lags, but some it cannot. Some of the lags affect the cash balance, while others affect other components of working capital such as accounts receivable and inventory. In addressing ourselves to cash management, we are concerned with time periods *BCD* and *FGHJ*. Time period *AB* is beyond the firm's control and does not directly affect its financial statements, although it may affect production schedules. Time period *DE* is determined by the firm's production process and inventory policy and affects the total investment in inventory. Time period *EF*

Figure 7-1 The Cash Cycle

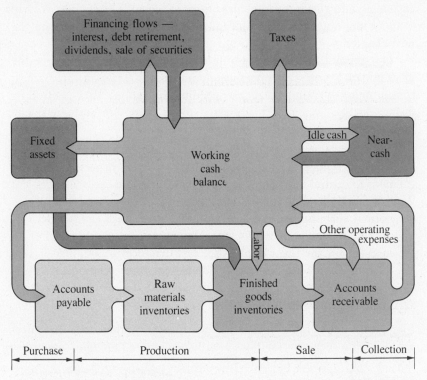

Figure 7-2 Details of the Cash Cycle

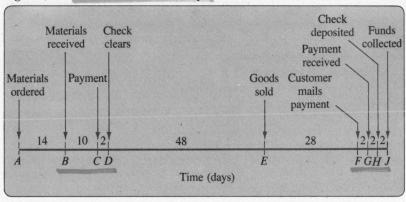

is determined by the firm's credit terms and the payment policies of its customers, and affects the total investment in accounts receivable. We will examine the management of inventory and accounts receivable in the next chapter.

Our present task is to examine what can be done to improve the efficiency of a firm's cash management. We will focus on three areas: concentrating working balances, speeding collections, and controlling disbursements. In a report addressed to its corporate customers, one bank described the problem in these terms:

> The management of cash can be resolved into a few simply stated elements. Quick movement of remittances from dispersed locations to central management prevents lazy or idle cash balances from inflating the total figure required to remain ahead of normal disbursements. As a working asset, cash contributes its best to company profit when temporary surpluses can be invested for the short term. Also, cash balances maintained as deposits contribute positively in bank–borrower relationships.[1]

Concentration Banking

Many firms need only a single checking account. Larger firms that operate over wide geographical areas usually need more than one, sometimes dozens. Where many accounts are needed, *concentration* accounts can be used to minimize the total requirement for working balances. Suppose a company has a number of branch offices, each with a local bank account. Branches collect accounts receivable and make deposits in their local accounts. Each day, funds above a certain predetermined minimum are transferred to a central concentration account, usually at the firm's headquarters. The daily transfer of funds can be made either by a *depository transfer check* or by *wire transfer;* the latter is faster but more expensive.

The funds transferred to the concentration account are available for disbursement for other purposes. As we will see later, the more variable a firm's cash flows, the higher the requirement for working cash balances. By pooling its funds for disbursement in a single account, the aggregate requirement for working balances is lower than it would be if balances were maintained at each branch office. Concentration, in short, permits the firm to "store" its cash more efficiently.

---

1. Victor L. Andrews, "Cash Management: An Overview for the Corporate Treasurer," *The First Report,* First National Bank of Atlanta, Atlanta, Georgia (undated).

Speeding Collections

Another means of conserving cash is to reduce the lag between the time the customer mails the check and the time the funds become collected, that is, from points *F* to *J* in Figure 7-2. Of the 6 day lag in Figure 7-2, 2 days are due to mail time, 2 days are due to processing time within XYZ Corporation, and 2 days are due to collection time within the bank. We will have more to say later about collection within the banking system. Let us now focus on the 4 day lag from *F* to *H*.

Small firms that operate in limited geographical areas can do little to reduce mail time. However, improvements often can be made in processing time within the firm. Suppose XYZ Corporation has credit sales of $5 million per year. With approximately 250 working days per year, XYZ's collections average $20,000 per working day. If XYZ could reduce its processing time from 2 days to 1 day and thereby get the checks to the bank 1 day sooner, its accounts receivable balance would be reduced by $20,000. XYZ's financing requirements would therefore be reduced by $20,000. If XYZ's borrowing cost was 9 percent, savings of about $1,800 per year would be realized. These potential savings could be compared to the cost of faster processing to determine whether the change in processing should be made. We can conclude that internal processing should be speeded up to the point at which the costs of further improvement exceed the savings.

Now let us consider a larger firm that receives remittances from customers over a wide geographical area. Opportunities may exist to reduce both mail time and processing time. One way to reduce mail time is by operating a number of strategically located collection centers to which customer payments are mailed. A concentration banking arrangement along lines described earlier might be used to transfer collected funds to a central account each day.

A second step that may be advantageous is to establish a *lock-box* system, which often can reduce mail and processing time still further. The firm first establishes a number of collection points, taking account of customer locations and mail schedules. At each location, the firm rents a post office box and instructs its customers to remit to the box. The firm's local bank is authorized to pick up mail directly from the box. The bank does so, perhaps several times a day, and deposits the checks in the firm's account. The bank makes a record of names and amounts and other data needed by the firm for internal accounting purposes, and immediately enters the checks for collection.

The lock-box system results in two benefits to the firm: First, the bank performs the clerical tasks of handling the remittances prior to deposit, services which the bank may be able to perform at lower cost. Second, and often more important, the process of collection through the banking system begins immediately upon receipt of the remittance and does not have to wait until the firm completes its processing for internal accounting purposes. In terms of the activities in Figure 7-2, the activity represented by *HJ* now takes place simultaneously with *GH*. The firm processes remittances for internal accounting purposes using data supplied by the bank and can schedule this processing at any time without delaying collection. Using a lock-box system saves as much as 4 days in mailing and processing time. The cost saving to the firm from such a system can be significant. For example, assume Ajax Manufacturing Company handles collections of $10 million a year and has an opportunity to use a bank lock-box system that offers to save 2 days of processing time on each check received. If the company's cost of short-term funds is 10 percent per annum, its *gross* saving would be:

Annual remittances ($10,000,000) × Number of days saved (2 days) × Cost of funds (10 percent a year) × 1/365 = $5,479 a year

The access to the lock-box system is not without cost. The bank will either charge a flat amount for its services or ask that Ajax Company maintain a compensating balance at the bank in exchange for the service. As long as these costs are less than $5,479 a year, the system produces a net gain to the company. Whether the savings will outweigh the costs for a particular company depends mainly on the geographical dispersion of customers, the dollar amount of the average remittance, and the firm's cost of financing.

We see that a major advantage of speeding collections is to free cash and thereby reduce the firm's total financing requirement. There are other advantages as well. By transferring clerical functions to the bank, the firm may reduce its costs, improve internal control, and reduce the possibility of fraud. By getting checks to banks on which they are written sooner, the incidence of checks dishonored for insufficient funds may be reduced.

Collection Time in the Banking System

We have made several references to the time required to collect a check through the banking system (*HJ* in Figure 7-2), but we have made no proposals to shorten it. Let us be more specific about what is involved. Suppose a customer in Chapel Hill, North Carolina, purchases electronics equipment from a firm in Palo Alto, California, and remits with a check drawn on a Chapel Hill bank. The seller deposits the check in a bank in Palo Alto, but the funds are not available for use until the check has been presented physically to the Chapel Hill bank, a process that depends on mail service between the two cities and may take several days. A very extensive clearing network has been established in the United States that involves the commercial banks and the Federal Reserve System. In the majority of cases, clearing times have been reduced to 2 days or less using the facilities of the "Fed" or direct interbank clearings. In the matter of check clearing, the banks are the experts, and firms usually can rely on their banks to minimize the time requirements.

Controlling Disbursements

Just as speeding collections turns accounts receivable into cash and thereby reduces the firm's financing requirements, slowing disbursements does the same. In Chapter 6, we discussed trade credit as a source of funds. There we concluded that the proper policy was to pay within the terms agreed upon, taking cash discounts when offered. We concluded also that there is no point in paying sooner than agreed. By waiting as long as possible, the firm maximizes the extent to which accounts payable are used as a source of funds, a source which requires no interest payment.

Consider the effect of a 1 day change in payment period. The Neptune Company of Chapter 5 planned to purchase about $1.5 million of raw materials in 1980 and followed a policy of paying within credit terms offered by suppliers. Suppose Neptune paid 1 day earlier than necessary. Accounts payable would decline by 1 day's purchases, about $4,100, and financing requirements from other sources would consequently increase by $4,100. At 9 percent, Neptune's interest costs would rise by $370 per year.

Firms with expense-generating activities that cover a wide area often find it advantageous to make disbursements from a single central account. In that way, schedules can be tightly controlled and disbursements can be made on exactly the right day. An alternate arrangement is to disburse from decentralized locations, but to wire transfer the exact amount needed in each local account for all disbursements scheduled that day.

Some firms find it advantageous to exploit the "checkbook float," which is the time between the writing of a check and its presentation for collection, represented by *CD* in Figure 7-2. If this lag can be exploited, it offsets at least partially the lag in the other direction in collecting checks from customers (*HJ*). Because of lag *CD*, a firm's balance on the bank's books is higher than that in its own checkbook. Knowing this, a firm may be able to reduce its working cash requirements. Banks understand checkbook float also, and can be expected to set compensating balances and fees based on balances on their (the banks') books. If a firm exploits checkbook float too far, it increases the likelihood of checks being dishonored for insufficient funds and the accompanying displeasure of both bank and payee.

Integrated Cash Management Systems

Many banks offer integrated cash management systems designed especially for large firms with extensive collection and disbursement activities. Such systems rely heavily on the technology of computers and high-speed data transmission. A system offered by the First National Bank of Atlanta features a system of lock-boxes and remote *zero balance* accounts linked by wire to a centralized master control account where working balances are pooled.[2] The zero balance accounts are used for decentralized collection and disbursement, with funds transferred in and out each day to achieve a zero balance at the day's end. Extensive reports are generated to provide data to the firm for control purposes. Such systems are costly, but provide substantial benefits for firms that can utilize them.

Determining the Appropriate Working Cash Balance

Let us assume the firm now is collecting, storing, and disbursing its cash as efficiently as possible. Given its long-term financial structure—fixed assets, long-term liabilities, and equity—its total cash position at any time is determined by its operating plan. Suppose total cash is more than the firm needs for operating purposes, if disbursements are made according to plan. The Neptune Company, which we discussed earlier, projected a total cash balance as high as $489,000 in November (Table 5-6). Should all these funds be kept in Neptune's checking account? Since checking accounts earn no interest, it is to Neptune's advantage to leave only the amount necessary to operate, and to invest the remainder temporarily in interest-bearing liquid assets until needed.

Our problem, then, is to determine how much cash a firm should maintain in its checking account as a working balance. We will address this question here, and in the next section discuss the investment of amounts above the working balance.

The working balance is maintained for *transaction* purposes—for paying bills and collecting payments on accounts receivable. If the firm maintains too small a working balance, it runs out of cash. It then must

---

2. Victor L. Andrews, "Cash Management: An Overview for the Corporate Treasurer."

liquidate marketable securities if available, or borrow. Liquidating marketable securities and borrowing both involve transaction costs. If, on the other hand, the firm maintains too high a working balance, it foregoes the opportunity to earn interest on marketable securities, that is, it incurs what economists refer to as an *opportunity* cost. Thus, the answer we seek is the *optimal* working balance, rather than the minimum. The optimal working balance occurs when total costs, that is, the sum of the transaction costs and the opportunity cost, are at a minimum. Finding the optimum involves a tradeoff between falling transaction costs against rising opportunity costs. Figure 7-3 depicts the problem graphically. If a firm tries to keep its working balances low, it will find itself selling securities (and later repurchasing securities) more often than if it aims at a higher level of working balances. That is, transaction costs fall as the working balance level rises. Opportunity costs, on the other hand, rise as the level of working balances rises. There is one point, denoted by C^* in Figure 7-3, where the *sum* of the two costs shown as the total cost curve is at a minimum. This is the point efficient management should try to find.

Figure 7-3   The Optimal Working Cash Balance

Compensating Balance Requirements

If a firm uses bank credit as a source of financing, the question of the optimal checking account balance may have a simple answer: It may be dictated by its compensating balance requirements. As we noted in Chapter 6, banks impose minimum balance requirements to compensate for various services such as processing checks and standby commitments to lend.

In some cases, a firm may determine with very little analysis that its optimal working balance is below the bank's compensating balance requirement. In such cases, the latter figure becomes the firm's minimum checking account balance. In other cases, where the answer is not so clear or where compensating balances are not required, we must put pencil to paper to determine the appropriate working balance.

Finding the Optimal Working Balance

Having done all we can to improve our collection and disbursement procedures, let us now take the pattern of receipts and disbursements as given. Over any time period, a firm's beginning and ending cash balances are related as follows:

Ending balance = Beginning balance + Receipts − Disbursements

If receipts and disbursements were constant each day, we would know with certainty what each would be each day and our problem would be simple. Since receipts always would exceed disbursements by the same amount, we could withdraw the ending balance each day and use it for other purposes. In practice, we have two problems: variability and uncertainty. In most firms, receipts and disbursements vary both over the month and over the year. Over a month, receipts and disbursements for current operating expenses are likely to show some variation, perhaps in a regular pattern. In seasonal firms, the amounts also will vary over the year. Less frequent outlays, such as those for capital expenditures, taxes, and dividends, introduce still more variability. Some of this variability may be predictable, but some probably is not. Let us examine these two problems—variability and uncertainty—separately.

Variability

Suppose receipts and disbursements both vary and are not synchronized, but the variations are completely predictable. Determining the appropriate working balance in the face of nonsynchronous but predictable cash flows is a problem of minimizing total costs. If we set the balance too low, we incur high transaction costs; one might say we make too many trips to the bank. If we set the balance too high, we lose too much interest on marketable securities.

The determination of the optimal working balance under conditions of certainty can be viewed as an *inventory problem* in which we balance the costs of too little cash (transaction costs) against the costs of too much cash (opportunity costs).[3] Figure 7-3 views the problem in this way. If

_____

3. Inventory theory was first applied to the cash balance problem by William J. Baumol. "The Transactions Demand for Cash: An Inventory Theoretic Approach," *Quarterly Journal of Economics* **66,** 545–556 (Nov. 1952). The model since has been further developed by other writers.

the cash shortage becomes severe enough, we may begin to forego cash discounts on purchases, adding another element of opportunity cost.

Formal models of the cash balance problem have been developed using inventory theory. Inputs to such a model are the total net cash outflow over the period of time in question, the transaction costs of replenishing the cash balance by selling securities or borrowing, and the interest rate that can be earned on securities. The answer given by the model tells us how often and in what amounts funds should be transferred to the checking account from other sources.

Uncertainty

Receipts and disbursements are very seldom completely predictable. If we go to the opposite extreme and assume receipts and disbursements (or the difference between them) to be completely random, a different kind of model can be developed using the technique of control theory. In addition to information on transaction costs and interest rates on securities, we need a measure of the variability of net cash flows. Using these data, we can determine the optimal maximum and minimum balances in the firm's checking account, denoted by levels X and Y in Figure 7-4.[4]

In Figure 7-4, the firm's working cash balance fluctuates randomly in response to random inflows and outflows. At time t_1, the balance reaches the upper control limit Y. At that point, $(Y - X)$ dollars are transferred out of the cash account and into marketable securities. The balance continues to fluctuate, falling to zero at t_2, at which time X

Figure 7-4 Cash Balance Control Limits

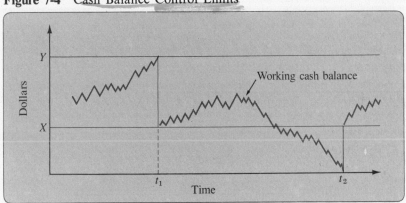

4. The model in Figure 7-4 was taken from Merton H. Miller and Daniel Orr. "A Model of the Demand for Money by Firms." *Quarterly Journal of Economics* **80**, 413–435 (Aug. 1966). Other writers also have applied control limit theory to the cash balance problem.

dollars of marketable securities are sold and the proceeds transferred to the working balance. The control limit model thus gives an answer in terms of maximum and minimum balances and provides a decision rule, rather than a fixed schedule of transfers as did the simple inventory model. One of the important insights of the control limit model is that, where cash flows are uncertain, the greater the variability the higher the minimum balance (X in Figure 7-4).

Using Mathematical Models

Formal mathematical models such as those mentioned above are useful for increasing our understanding of the cash management problem and providing insights and *qualitative* guidance. The models tell us which factors are important and make the tradeoffs explicit. We see, for example, that transaction costs play a central role. If transaction costs were zero, the firm would require no working cash balance at all; it simply would sell securities or borrow to pay every bill.

Are formal mathematical models also useful for *quantitative* applications? In practice, the cash flow patterns of most firms are partly predictable and partly random. Neither the inventory model nor the control limit model is strictly applicable. By combining the insights from formal models with the techniques of cash budgeting and pro forma analysis, many firms can arrive at reasonable answers by experience and experiment. In deciding how far to go in analyzing the problem, we must consider the cost of the analysis. Except in the case of very large firms, quantitative solutions to the cash balance problem using formal mathematical models are likely to be uneconomical. Often, the cost of obtaining the necessary input data and operating the model exceeds the savings over solutions that can be attained by experience and experiment.[5] As always, we must keep an eye on the cost of our analytical techniques as well as on the benefits.

For very small firms, the cash management problem has recently been made much easier by legislation. Firms are allowed to hold savings accounts at commercial banks in amounts up to $150,000. Transfers between these interest-bearing accounts and checking accounts is automatic and virtually costless.

---

5. For a discussion of the usefulness of formal cash management models, see Hans E. Daellenbach, "Are Cash Management Models Worthwhile?," *Journal of Financial and Quantitative Analysis* **9**(4), 607–626 (Sept. 1974). For a description of a cash management model that can be used in practice, see S. F. Maier and J. H. Vander Weide, "A Practical Approach to Short-Run Financial Planning," *Financial Management* **7**, 10–16 (Winter 1978).

Planning Cash Requirements

In most cases, to search for the optimal working cash balance probably overstates our capabilities; we must be content to get reasonably close. Perhaps we should substitute the word "appropriate" for "optimal."

The checking account balance that the firm should maintain is the compensating balance requirement, or the optimal working balance, whichever is greater. Some firms, especially those with seasonal sales patterns, may find that the appropriate working balance varies somewhat over the year. As a firm grows, the appropriate working cash balance also will grow, although probably not proportionally.

Once we have settled on the appropriate balance to be maintained in the checking account, we can integrate cash management into the financial planning process. The projected checking account balance goes into the pro forma balance sheet. Any excess cash over that figure then may be invested in interest-bearing assets.

Investing Idle Cash

Cash in excess of requirements for working balances normally is invested in interest-bearing assets that can be converted readily to cash. A firm might hold excess cash for two principal reasons: First, the firm's working capital requirements may vary over the year, perhaps in a fairly predictable manner if the variation is due to recurring seasonal factors. Variation of this type characterized the Neptune Company discussed in Chapter 5. From the pro forma balance sheet, it was apparent that excess cash would build up during seasonal lows in accounts receivable and inventory, and would be needed later to finance a reexpansion of receivables and inventory during the next seasonal high. We can view the excess cash as a part of the firm's transaction balances. Even though the cash is temporarily idle, there is a predictable requirement for it later.

Second, excess cash may be held to cover unpredictable financing requirements. In a world of uncertainty, cash flows can never be predicted with complete accuracy. Competitors act, technology changes, products fail, strikes occur, and economic conditions vary. On the positive side, attractive investment opportunities may suddenly appear. A firm may choose to hold excess cash to finance such needs if and when they occur. We noted earlier that cash held for such purposes is referred to as a *precautionary* balance and usually is invested in interest-bearing assets until needed.

An alternative exists to the holding of excess cash for either of the two purposes described above. The firm can simply borrow short-term to finance variable requirements as they arise. Under such a policy, the firm would never hold excess cash. A firm's choice between short-term borrowing versus liquid assets as a means of financing variable requirements will depend on policy decisions with respect to the firm's long-term financial structure, particularly the mix of short-term and long-term funds. We will discuss overall financial structure and the relationship between maturity structure and liquidity later, in Part V. Here, we take as given the long-term structure and the amount available for investment in interest-bearing assets.

For many companies, especially larger ones, investing idle cash is a very important matter indeed. Table 7-1 shows the holdings of cash and marketable securities of some major companies during 1977. These numbers are very big. In December 1977, about 175 companies had cash posi-

Table 7-1 Twenty Leading Cash-Rich Companies

Company	Cash and Short-Term Securities (Millions of Dollars) Year-end 1977
IBM	$5,407
Exxon	4,205[a]
Ford	3,371
GM	3,240
GE	1,669[a]
American Express	1,532
AT&T	1,487[b]
Standard Oil (Ind.)	1,401
Standard Oil of Calif.	1,277
Gulf Oil	1,200
Mobil	1,161[a]
Eastman Kodak	958
Boeing	882[a]
Continental Oil	729[a]
Xerox	692
U.S. Steel	685[a]
UAL	679
Westinghouse	640
Phillips Petroleum	614[a]
Texaco	601[a]

Source: Business Week, March 13, 1978.
[a]Third quarter 1977.
[b]2/27/77.

tions of $100 million or more each. Holdings of the 400 largest United States companies combined amounted to more than $60 billion. IBM alone held more than $5 billion, an impressive sum indeed for a single company. On a portfolio of this size, an increase of ½ percentage point in yield adds $27 million to pretax profits! NCR Corporation, with the much more modest sum of $307 million in cash, estimates that careful cash management adds $1 million a year to profits.[6] Clearly, the potential gains from careful cash management can be attractive.

Investment Criteria

A firm might invest excess cash in many types of interest-bearing assets. To choose among the alternatives, we must establish criteria based on our reasons for investing excess cash in the first place. We are investing either temporary transaction balances or precautionary balances or both. When we need the cash, we want to be able to obtain it—all of it—quickly. Given these objectives, we can rule out common stocks and other investments with returns that are not contractual and with prices that often vary widely. Debt securities, with a contractual obligation to pay, are our best candidates. In selecting among debt securities, there are three principal characteristics we should examine: default risk, maturity, and marketability.

Default risk refers to the possibility that interest or principal might not be paid on time and in the amount promised. If the financial markets suddenly perceive a significant risk of default on a particular security, the price of the security is likely to fall substantially, even though default may not actually have occurred. Investors in general are averse to risk, and the possibility of default is sufficient to depress the price. Given our purposes in investing excess cash, we want to steer clear of securities that stand any significant chance of defaulting. In an uncertain world, there is no guarantee that is absolutely certain, except perhaps that of the United States government, with its capacity to create money. However, there are securities available with default risk that is sufficiently low to be almost negligible. In selecting securities, we must keep in mind that risk and return are related, and that low-risk securities provide the lowest returns. We must give up some return in order to purchase safety.

Maturity refers to the time period over which interest and principal payments are to be made. A 20 year bond might promise interest semiannually and prinicpal at the end of the twentieth year. A 6 month bank certificate of deposit would promise interest and principal at the end of the sixth month.

---

6. "Cash Management," *Business Week* 62–68 (March 13, 1978).

When interest rates vary, the prices of fixed-income securities vary. A rise in market rates produces a fall in price, and vice versa. Because of this relationship, debt securities are subject to a second type of risk, *interest rate risk,* in addition to default risk. A United States government bond, though free of default risk, is not immune to interest rate risk. The longer the maturity of a security, the more sensitive its price to interest rate changes and the greater its exposure to interest rate risk. For this reason, short maturities are generally best for investing excess cash.

Marketability refers to the ease with which an asset can be converted to cash. With reference to financial assets, the terms marketability and liquidity often are used synonymously. Marketability has two principal dimensions—price and time—that are interrelated. If an asset can be sold quickly in large amounts at a price that can be determined in advance within narrow limits, the asset is said to be highly marketable or highly liquid. Perhaps the most liquid of all financial assets are United States Treasury Bills (discussed below). On the other hand, if the price that can be realized depends significantly on the time available to sell the asset, the asset is said to be *illiquid.* The more independent the price is of time, the more liquid the asset. A Van Gogh painting appraised at $100,000 likely would fetch far less if the owner were forced to sell it quickly on short notice. Besides price and time, a third attribute of marketability is low transaction costs.

Investment Alternatives

Here we discuss briefly the principal types of interest-bearing assets that meet the criteria of low-default risk, short maturity, and ready marketability. Such securities often are referred to as *money-market* securities.

United States Treasury Bills and Notes are obligations of the United States government. Treasury Bills are one of the most widely used mediums for the temporary investment of excess cash. Bills are issued weekly by the government, are readily marketable, and have maturities at issue ranging from 91 to 360 days. Treasury Notes have initial maturities of 1–5 years. Since Treasury securities are default-free, they have somewhat lower yields than do other marketable securities. Yields are discussed further below.

Federal agency issues are obligations of agencies of the federal government rather than the United States Treasury. Such agencies include the Federal Home Loan Bank, the Federal Land Bank, the Federal National Mortgage Association, and several others. These agencies are closely associated in the minds of investors with the federal government, though their obligations, strictly speaking, are not guaranteed by the government. Yields normally are slightly higher than those on Treasury securities, and maturities range from 1 month to over 10 years.

Bank Certificates of Deposit are fixed-maturity time deposits placed with leading commercial banks. CDs in denominations over $100,000 usually are negotiable, meaning they can be sold in a secondary market prior to maturity. Maturities generally range from 90 to 360 days. CDs of the largest banks generally are considered to be money-market instruments and are marketable. Many banks issue CDs in denominations less than $100,000, although such certificates usually are not negotiable and penalties are imposed if they are not held to maturity. Default risk is quite low, but not zero, as evidenced by the failures of some large banks in 1974. Yields are higher than those on Treasury securities and usually about equal to those on commercial paper (discussed below). The contract rate of interest on CDs smaller than $100,000 is subject to rate ceilings imposed by the Federal Reserve Board, but ceilings are not in effect on CDs of denominations greater than $100,000. These have become the most widely used vehicle for temporarily "storing" idle cash funds.

Commercial paper is the term applied to short-term unsecured promissory notes of large corporations. We discussed commercial paper as a source of funds in Chapter 6. As an investment medium it is the commercial paper of other firms in which we are interested. Commercial paper is regularly issued by major finance companies, banks and bank-holding companies, and some nonfinancial firms. Denominations are usually larger than $100,000 and maturities range up to 270 days. Commercial paper is usually held to maturity, as the secondary market is not well developed.

Besides the principal alternatives discussed above, there are several others that meet our criteria but are less widely used. *Bankers Acceptances* are drafts drawn against deposits in commercial banks. They are used as financing instruments in certain specialized lines of domestic and foreign trade. The draft has a specific payment date, and once accepted by the bank, becomes an obligation of the bank rather than of the initiating firm. By accepting the draft, the bank has guaranteed its payment at maturity. Yields are comparable to those on bank CDs, and maturities are usually less than 180 days.

Repurchase agreements are contracts whereby a firm "lends" by purchasing marketable securities (usually Treasury Bills) from a "borrower" (often a bond dealer), with the agreement that the "borrower" will repurchase the securities at a specified price and time. The price difference represents interest earned by the lender. The arrangement provides great flexibility with respect to maturity, which usually is for periods of a few days to a week. Yields are comparable to those on Treasury Bills.

State and local governments also issue debt securities that often meet our requirements. Income from such securities under present law is not taxable by the federal government. Yields reflect the tax advantage, but often are higher on an after-tax basis than those on taxable securities.

Eurodollar deposits are deposits (CDs of various maturities) denominated in dollars but held at branches of United States banks or other banks located *outside* the United States, principally in London but also in other European financial centers, the Caribbean, and Singapore. These deposits yield rates slightly above domestic United States CD rates, and thus, this market is widely used by multinational corporations as a medium for placing temporarily idle funds. The principal reasons for the higher rate on Eurodollar deposits are that the depository banks are (1) not subject to reserve requirements, (2) not subject to payment of a fee to the Federal Deposit Insurance Corporation (FDIC), and (3) are free from all constraints on the way they allocate funds. In short, their costs are lower, which allows them to offer depositors somewhat higher rates than domestic United States banks can. On the other hand, depositors require a slightly higher rate because the potential risks are also slightly higher. Among these risks are: (1) There is no federal insurance on funds deposited outside the United States. (2) There is no *legal* requirement for a United States parent bank to come to the aid of an overseas branch that may get into trouble. (3) No central bank is obligated to function as a "lender of last resort" should many Eurobanks get into trouble during periods of credit stringency or panic.

Yields

All the characteristics we discussed above—default risk, maturity, and marketability—affect yields. In general, the lower the default risk and the better the marketability, the lower the yield. Securities with these desirable characteristics have higher prices, and since price and yield are inversely related, lower yields.

The relationship between maturity and yield is more complex and changes over time. On an average, short maturities yield less, other factors being equal, because they are subject to less interest rate risk. Rates on short maturities, however, are more volatile than those on longer maturities, and at times exceed the latter.

At any point in time, rates on the major types of money-market securities discussed above are fairly close to one another. For equal maturities, the differentials usually are small and are due to small differences in default risk and marketability.

Over time, the entire structure of short-term rates varies significantly. Such variations are related to the business and monetary cycles, the demand for funds by individuals and firms, and the credit policies of the Federal Reserve, but the single most important factor is the rate of inflation. At the peak of the interest rate cycle that was reached in 1974, money-market rates for business borrowers were close to 12 percent. Thereafter, these rates fell rapidly to just below 5 percent at the end of 1976. Since then, they have risen sharply once more and by mid-1979 surpassed the 10 percent level. The behavior of the federal funds rate and the rate of inflation over recent years is given in Figure 7-5.

Figure 7-5 Inflation and Nominal Interest Rates

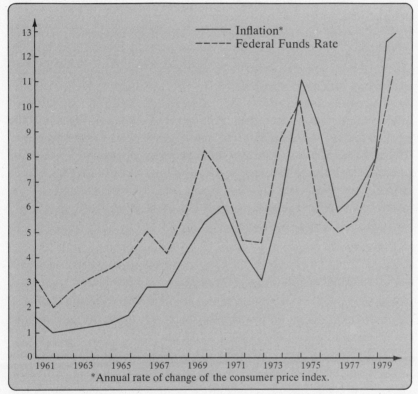

*Annual rate of change of the consumer price index.

Source: Salomon Brothers, *Comments on Credit,* August 17, 1979.

Summary

The term *cash* in this chapter refers to total liquid assets, made up of working cash balance plus interest-bearing securities and deposits. Firms hold cash (liquid assets) for two reasons: to execute financial transactions and for precautionary purposes. The overall problem of cash management comprises three steps: (1) collecting and disbursing funds efficiently, (2) determining the appropriate working cash balance, and (3) investing the remaining excess cash.

Steps to improve the efficiency of collection and disbursement must focus on the cash cycle of the firm. Concentration accounts can be used to reduce the requirement for working balances. Collection time can be reduced by the use of a lock-box system. Disbursements should be made within credit terms but no sooner than required.

A working cash balance is required for transaction purposes. In some cases, bank compensating balance requirements may determine the minimum working balance. Where this is not the case, finding the optimal balance involves a tradeoff between transaction costs (high for low working balances) and opportunity costs (high for high working balances). By combining the qualitative insights from theoretical models with techniques such as cash budgeting and pro forma analysis, most firms can arrive at reasonable answers with some experimentation.

Firms hold liquid assets over and above working-balance requirements for two main reasons: as temporarily idle transaction balances and as precautionary balances. Vehicles for investing such cash reserves should be evaluated on the basis of default risk, maturity, and marketability. Many alternatives exist, including United States Treasury Bills, Federal agency issues, bank certificates of deposit, and commercial paper. Yields on such short-term money-market instruments vary over the business cycle and tend to average slightly less than those of longer-maturity issues.

Sample Problem

The Omark Corporation has a centralized billing system at its headquarters in Chicago to handle average daily collections of $200,000. The collection float for Omark averages 6 days.

1. How much money does Omark have tied up in collection float? $6 \times 201,000$

2. If Omark's opportunity cost on short-term funds is 6 percent, how much does this float cost the company? $\times 6\%$

3. Omark's treasurer is considering a concentration banking system which, she estimates, will reduce float by 2 days. What is the largest total amount of required compensating balances Omark should be willing to accept with the concentration system? (Assume there are no cost savings from the system other than the reduced collection float.)

Solution

1. The total amount of funds tied up in collection float is equal to the firm's average daily collections times the number of days required for collection. For Omark, average daily collections are $200,000, and float is 6 days, so the total amount of funds tied up is:

$$\$200,000 \text{ per day} \times 6 \text{ days} = \$1,200,000$$

2. The cost of float to the firm equals the amount of funds tied up in float

times the opportunity rate at which these funds could be invested. Since Omark can invest the short-term funds to yield 6 percent, the opportunity cost from having $1,200,000 tied up in float is:

$$\$1,200,000 \times 6 \text{ percent} = \$72,000 \text{ per year}$$

3. The concentration banking system would receive Omark's cost by reducing the opportunity cost of float. The system will reduce Omark's float by $200,000/day $\times$ 2 days = $400,000, reducing the Omark's float costs by

$$\$400,000 \times 6 \text{ percent} = \$24,000 \text{ per year}$$

The opportunity cost to Omark of compensating balances equals the required compensating balance times the opportunity cost of short-term funds. The maximum acceptable required compensating balance for Omark is found by equating the opportunity cost of the compensating balance to the savings from the concentration banking system, which we found to be $24,000.

$$\text{Compensating balance} \times 6 \text{ percent} = \$24,000$$

$$\text{Compensating balance} = \frac{\$24,000}{0.06} = \$400,000$$

Questions

1. What are the principal motives for holding cash and liquid assets?
2. From the standpoint of cash management, on what parts of the cash cycle (Figures 7-1 and 7-2) should attention focus?
3. What are the advantages of concentration banking?
4. How can a firm speed the collection of cash?
5. Suppose a firm's cash inflows and outflows are variable but completely predictable. How are the concepts of inventory theory applicable to such a problem?
6. Suppose a firm's cash inflows and outflows are completely random. What approach might a firm use to set its minimum working balance?
7. Why might a firm have idle cash?
8. Discuss the criteria that a firm should use in choosing assets in which to invest idle cash.

Problems

1. The Uptown Supply Company has credit sales of $2 million per year. Collections average $8,000 per day (250 working days per year).

Suppose Uptown could reduce its internal processing time by 1 day. What would be its annual savings, assuming a cost of funds of 9 percent?

2. The Monogram Company is a national retailing concern that sells primarily on a credit basis. Collections from the southern region average $100,000 a day and the total *float* (amount of time it takes from payment mailing to the time when Monogram obtains the use of the funds) is averaging 5 days for customers in this area. The opportunity cost on short-term funds is considered to be 8 percent.

(a) An Atlanta bank has offered to set up a lock-box system which will reduce float by 3 days for a compensating balance of $200,000. Would you recommend that Monogram accept the offer?

(b) The bank also proposes an alternative of a flat annual fee of $10,000. Which option should Monogram prefer?

3. The Celec Company purchases $3 million of raw materials each year on terms of net 30. The purchasing agent currently is paying each invoice 20 working days after its date to make sure that payment is received by suppliers in 30 days. A study shows that payment could be delayed until the 25th working day and still leave enough time for receipt by the 30th day. How much would the company save annually by making this change, assuming a 9 percent cost of funds?

4. The MHF Company currently maintains an account with a Washington, D.C., bank for collections in the southeastern marketing area. The bank handles collections of $500,000 per day in return for a compensating balance of $300,000. The company is considering an alternative of opening two separate accounts in the southeastern area. It has been projected that total processing time could be reduced by 1½ days if accounts are maintained in a Richmond bank and an Atlanta bank, each requiring a $300,000 compensating balance. Would you recommend the two-bank system to MHF Company?

5. The Rice Company currently maintains a centralized billing system at its home office to handle average daily collections of $300,000. The total time for mailing, processing, and clearing has been estimated at 5 days.

(a) If the firm's opportunity cost on short-term funds is 8 percent, how much is this time lag of 5 days costing the company?

(b) If management has designed a system of lock-boxes with regional banks that would reduce float by 2½ days and home office credit department expense by $30,000 annually, what is the largest total amount of required compensating balances that the firm should be willing to accept with the lock-box arrangement?

6. Creative Papers Inc., a nationwide wholesaler of paper supplies, currently has a centralized billing system costing $70,000 annually in

record-keeping expenses with a collection float of 7 days. As the new treasurer of Creative Papers, you have been asked to evaluate two proposed cash management systems. The concentrated banking system would establish five regional banks to handle Creative's accounts and would require a minimum total compensating balance of $2 million. Collection float for this system is estimated to be 5 days. The lock-box system would establish 10 lock-boxes throughout the country with collection float of 3 days. This system would require $3.5 million in compensating balances plus a $0.02 charge per check processed. Your assistant reports the average check from your customers is for $500, and the firm's opportunity costs on short-term funds is 8 percent. All sales are on credit. Assume 250 working days per year.

(a) If average daily collections are $200,000, what is the annual cost of Creative's current system?

(b) What must Creative's average daily collections be for the concentrated system to be preferred to the current system? For the lock-box system to be preferred to the current system?

7. The Flyer Manufacturing Company has an account with a Philadelphia bank for collections in Flyer's northeast sales region. The bank charges the firm a flat annual fee of $20,000 plus a charge of $0.05 per check processed. Presently, annual credit sales are $50 million, and the typical check from customers is for $1,000. Flyer's opportunity cost on short-term funds is 6 percent. The Philadelphia bank has offered to set up a system of four lock-boxes in return for $300,000 in compensating balances plus a charge of $0.03 per check processed. The boxes would be emptied three times daily and would reduce collection float by 2 days.

(a) Would you recommend that Flyer accept the bank's offer? (Assume 250 working days per year.)

(b) What is the largest total amount of required compensating balances that Flyer should be willing to accept for this new arrangement?

8. The Triad Manufacturing Corporation anticipates $1,500,000 in cash outlays during the next year. These outlays are expected to occur uniformly throughout the year. Triad's treasurer reports that the firm can invest in marketable securities yielding 8 percent and that the cost of shifting funds from the marketable securities portfolio to cash is $75 per transaction. Assume that Triad will meet its cash demands by selling its marketable securities. Apply the economic order quantity (EOQ) model described in the appendix to Chapter 8 to answer the following questions.

(a) Determine the optimal size for Triad's transfer of funds from marketable securities to its checking account.

(b) What will be Triad's average cash balance?

(c) How many transfers from marketable securities to cash will be required during the year?

(d) What will be the total cost associated with Triad's cash requirements? (See appendix, Chapter 8.)

(e) How would your answers to (a) and (b) change if transactions costs could be reduced to $50 per transaction? If Triad could invest in marketable securities yielding 10 percent?

References

V. L. Andrews, "Cash Management: An Overview for the Corporate Treasurer," *The First Report* (Atlanta, Ga.: First National Bank of Atlanta, undated).

W. J. Baumol, "The Transactions Demand for Cash: An Inventory Theoretic Approach," *Quarterly Journal of Economics* **66,** 545–556 (Nov. 1952).

H. E. Daellenbach, "Are Cash Management Models Worthwhile?," *Journal of Financial and Quantitative Analysis* **9,** 607–626 (Sept. 1974).

G. Donaldson, *Strategy for Financial Mobility* (Homewood, Ill.: Richard D. Irwin, 1969).

W. E. Donoghue, *The Cash Management Manual* (Holliston, Mass.: Cash Management Institute, 1978).

G. Dufey and I. H. Giddy, *The International Money Market* (Englewood Cliffs, N.J.: Prentice-Hall, 1978).

L. J. Gitman, D. K. Forrester, and J. R. Forrester, "Managing Cash Disbursement Float," *Financial Management* **5,** 15–24 (Summer 1976).

L. J. Gitman, E. A. Moses, and I. T. White, "An Assessment of Corporate Cash Management Practices," *Financial Management* **8,** 32–41 (Spring 1979).

R. H. Jones, "Face to Face with Cash Management: How One Company Does It," *Financial Executive* **37,** 37–39 (Sept. 1969).

S. F. Maier and J. F. Vander Weide, "A Practical Approach to Short-Run Financial Planning," *Financial Management* **7,** 10–16 (Winter 1978).

B. G. Malkiel, *The Term Structure of Interest Rates* (Princeton, N.J.: Princeton University Press, 1966).

D. R. Mehta, *Working Capital Management* (Englewood Cliffs, N.J.: Prentice-Hall, 1974).

M. H. Miller and D. Orr, "A Model of the Demand for Money by Firms," *Quarterly Journal of Economics* **80,** 413–435 (Aug. 1966).

Money Market Instruments (Cleveland, Ohio: Federal Reserve Bank of Cleveland, 1970).

R. M. Nouss and R. E. Markland, "Solving Lock-Box Location Problems," *Financial Management* **8,** 21–31 (Spring 1979).

Y. E. Orgler, *Cash Management* (Belmont, Ca.: Wadsworth, 1970).

F. W. Searby, "Use Your Hidden Cash Resources," *Harvard Business Review* **46,** 74–75 (Mar.–Apr. 1968).

J. C. Van Horne, *The Function and Analysis of Capital Market Rates* (Englewood Cliffs, N.J.: Prentice-Hall, 1970).

% cost for comp bal !   Bal × % = $

Comp one   ① Days ÷ % = %
                  ② Fixed appty cost + % × (our daily collection $)
                  ③   FC
                    − FC
                    ─────
                    (1) FC

                  ④   %
                    − %
                    ─────
                    (1) %

                  ⑤   FC
                      ×(1) %
                     ──────────
                     Ave daily collection

Managing Accounts Receivable and Inventory

8

At the end of 1978, United States nonfinancial corporations, as a group, held over one *trillion* dollars of their assets in the form of current assets (working capital).[1] The two largest components were inventories ($455 billion) and accounts receivable or trade credit extended ($435 billion).

The stock of inventories held by a firm and the amount of trade credit extended by a firm are investments in the sense that each represents a commitment of corporate funds (either of the firm's own capital or of borrowed funds) that the firm can expect to liquidate only at some later point or points in time. These working capital investments differ from a firm's investment in fixed assets such as plant and equipment in only one respect: The average time lag between investment in working capital and its later recoupment is fairly short, that is, a year or less, whereas the corresponding time lag for investment in fixed assets is considerably longer. In spite of this difference, funds committed to working capital assets are investments, and it is therefore the responsibility of financial management to analyze them as carefully as it analyzes longer-term commitments to fixed assets. The "benefits" expected from any proposed increase in working capital assets must be weighed against the "cost" to the firm of holding extra assets, including an allowance for the cost of any additional capital required.

In many situations working capital decisions give rise to a potential conflict between the viewpoint of the financial manager on the one hand and the viewpoint of the operating managers who are in charge of a firm's purchasing, production, and marketing departments on the other. We deal with these potential conflicts in the rest of this chapter. For now, one illustration of the nature of these potential conflicts will suffice.

For example, take a situation in which the marketing manager believes that the level of sales can be increased if the firm's credit policy is loosened, that is, if it would extend credit to a wider range of customers and/or if it would permit an easier collection policy for whatever credit it does extend. Even if the assumption is correct that such a change in credit policy will lead to an increase in sales volume, it does not necessarily follow that the firm should do what the marketing manager believes. For marketing, the maximization of sales volume is a natural and legitimate objective; for the firm, sales maximization is only a "means to an end," and that end, as we saw in Chapter 1, is wealth maximization.

The *loosening* of credit terms may increase sales and thus provide gross benefits to the firm. However, the loosening of credit is not costless. An inevitable consequence of the suggested change in credit policy is that accounts receivable will rise, and this rise imposes several kinds of cost:

---

1. *Federal Reserve Bulletin.* For a description of these data, see "Working Capital of Nonfinancial Corporation," *Fed. Res. Bull.* July 1978.

1. As the firm's credit is extended to a wider group of buyers, the cost of credit analysis will rise, as will the cost of collecting and most likely the "cost" of bad debts (credit that cannot be collected).

2. The increase in accounts receivable has to be financed somehow. If the firm borrows the funds required, there is the out-of-pocket cost of the extra interest payments incurred.

3. If the firm finances the increase in accounts receivable out of its own funds, there is another kind of cost, generally labeled *opportunity costs*, which refers to the fact that if the firm uses funds for this purpose, it cannot also use them in some other possibly lucrative way. Thus, the opportunity cost of using one extra dollar to fund an increase in accounts receivable would be the rate of return that the firm has to forego on the best alternative use available for this dollar.

If it is estimated that the three costs together will exceed the benefits to be derived from increased sales, the suggested change in credit policy would not be a wise move. Of course, the contrary is also true: If benefits promise to exceed costs, the change would increase the firm's net wealth and should be pursued. The important point is that someone within the firm should be there to press the case for the firm's overall objective as opposed to subobjectives such as sales maximization. Usually this is the function of the financial manager. In this particular situation it is his or her duty to see that credit policy and hence that the level of trade credit extended (or the level of accounts receivable) is expanded as long as such an expansion contributes *net benefits* to the firm. It is also his or her duty to see that credit expansion does not proceed beyond this point. In the language of finance, the financial manager's function is to ensure that the firm's investment in accounts receivable is at its optimum level. As we will see later, the same objective holds for the firm's investment in inventories.

We can now summarize our introduction to the more technical discussions that follow. A firm's operating policies and plans with respect to purchasing, production, and marketing are clearly important determinants of its financing requirements for working capital assets. However, the role of the financial manager is by no means a passive one of accommodating financing needs that arise from decisions made elsewhere in the firm. On the contrary, good financial management should play an active role in shaping a firm's policies with respect to accounts receivable and inventory.

Taking the viewpoint of the financial manager, we will analyze changes in the level of accounts receivable and inventory as *investment decisions* using wealth maximization for the firm as a whole as our organizing framework. We will carry this analysis to the point of determing the marginal expected return on investment in receivables and inventory but will defer to a later chapter a discussion of the target or required rate of return.

Investing in Accounts Receivable

We noted above that a firm's policy variables with respect to accounts receivable are credit standards, credit terms, and collection policy. Let us examine these elements in more detail.

Credit Policy

Credit standards are the criteria and guidelines used by a firm to decide which accounts it will and will not extend credit to. The standards are applied to a credit applicant and a decision is made—yes or no.

Credit terms include both the length of the credit period and the discount offered. The *credit period* refers to the period over which credit is granted, usually measured in days from the date of the invoice. Terms of net 30, for example, mean that payment is due 30 days from the date of the invoice. If a *cash discount* is offered, both the amount and the discount period must be specified. Terms of 2/10, net 30 indicate that a 2 percent cash discount may be taken if payment is made within 10 days of the invoice date, otherwise the net (full) amount is due in 30 days.

Collection policy refers to procedures undertaken to collect accounts that have not been paid within the specified period. Included might be letters, telephone calls, personal visits, legal action, and so on. These procedures normally are the province of the credit manager and concern the financial manager only to the extent that they affect the volume of accounts receivable.

We will refer to credit standards, credit terms, and collection policy collectively as the *credit policy* of the firm. We will use the term *loosening* of credit policy to refer to a change toward less rigorous standards in granting credit, more liberal credit terms, and less vigorous collection policies. *Tightening* will refer to changes in the opposite directions.

Credit Policy and Return on Investment

Taken together, the elements of credit policy determine the magnitude of the firm's investment in accounts receivable and the return on that investment. To examine this relationship, consider a firm pursuing a particular credit policy, call it policy *A*. As the policy is applied, certain accounts are accepted and others are rejected. Of those accepted, some will pay regularly on time, some will pay late, and some will default, giving rise to bad debt expense. Of those rejected, some might have been good accounts if credit had been granted. Thus, associated with policy *A* is a particular level of bad debt expense and a particular level of opportunity loss; the latter is the contribution foregone on good accounts that were rejected. Also associated with policy *A* is some level of expense for credit analysis and collection.

Now suppose that credit policy is loosened and a new policy is adopted, call it policy *B*. Some accounts now are granted credit that did not qualify under policy *A*. Because these accounts lie outside previously established guidelines for credit extension, each new extension requires more careful credit analysis. Thus, the new accounts presumably have a higher default rate, so bad debt expense rises, as do expenses of analysis and collection. Lost contribution, however, declines. We can represent the relationships graphically as shown in Figure 8-1. Here, we view credit policy as a continuum, ranging from tight to loose. As policy becomes

Figure 8-1 Credit Policy and Costs

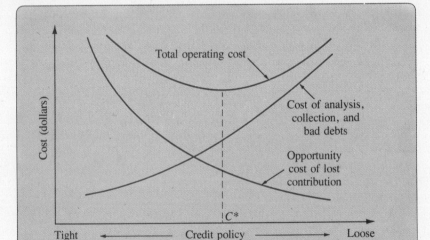

progressively looser, accounts receivable expand. Each increment of new accounts to which credit is granted contains fewer "good" accounts and more "bad" accounts. Expenses of analysis, collection, and bad debts therefore rise at an increasing rate, and lost contribution declines at a decreasing rate. The sum of these costs is the total operating cost of having a particular credit policy and is shown in Figure 8-1 as the U-shaped curve labeled *total operating cost*. A point is reached, C^*, where the sum of total costs is minimized. If the firm loosens credit policy beyond C^*, the additional contribution from the new accounts is less than the additional expense of analysis, collection, and bad debts. Hence, at C^*, *operating profit is maximized.*

Does C^* in Figure 8-1 represent the optimal credit policy? It does not, for two reasons. First, the profits to be earned at C^* are *expected* profits. The figure is subject to uncertainty and may turn out higher or lower than expected. The analysis of Figure 8-1 thus takes us to the point of maximum expected profits, but does not take *risk* into account. Second, at C^*, we maximize expected *operating* profit. We have given no consideration to the *investment* necessary to generate those operating profits and to the return required by those who finance the investment. Suppose, for example, that a firm can increase its operating profit by $1 if it invests $1 million of its own funds to finance an additional million dollars of accounts receivable. Obviously this investment would not be optimal even though it leads to an increase in operating profit! We can remedy both of these difficulties by expanding the analysis to consider *return on investment.* When we do so, we will find that the optimal policy is to the left of C^*, that is, somewhat tighter.

Let us first deal with a potential communications problem. As we noted in Chapter 4, return on investment can be measured in many ways. The measure we will use in this chapter is consistent with that used in our discussion of investment decisions in Part IV. The abbreviation ROI sometimes is used to refer to the *accounting* rate of return, which is useful as a performance measure, but (for reasons discussed in Chapter 11) not as a decision criterion. To avoid confusion with the accounting rate of return and to be consistent with terminology used elsewhere in this book, we will avoid the symbol ROI and use *expected rate of return,* or $E(R)$.

Calculating Expected Return

Let us illustrate the calculation of expected return on investment in accounts receivable with an example. The Delta Electric Company is a large distributor of electrical parts and equipment with facilities in 14 states. In 1979, Delta's sales totaled $46 million and after-tax profits slightly over $1 million.

Delta's profit margins had declined over the last 2 years, and the credit manager felt that one of the reasons was that credit policy was too loose. The manager identified a group of accounts that may have been considered marginal prospects and recommended that policy be tightened to eliminate them. Sales to this group of accounts amounted to about 10 percent of Delta's total sales.

The financial manager decided to calculate the return on investment in these accounts. The first step was to examine the behavior of Delta's costs if the accounts were to be eliminated entirely, in order to get a clear comparison between an ultratight credit policy and existing policies. Using historical data on costs and past knowledge of the business, the financial manager developed the data in Table 8-1.

Table 8-1 Delta Electric Company: Fixed and Variable Costs (Percent of Sales)

	Total	Fixed	Variable
Cost of goods sold	87.0	—	87.0
Warehousing	5.1	2.9	2.2
Selling	4.4	0.3	4.1
Administration	1.1	1.0	0.1
Bad debts	0.13	—	0.13
Collection	0.04	—	0.04
Total costs	97.77	4.2	93.57
Operating profit	2.23	—	—

The financial manager believed that if some of the marginal accounts were eliminated, the fixed costs of the program would remain unchanged and hence that only the costs identifiable as variable would decline. He believed further that bad debt and collection expense were almost entirely attributable to the marginal accounts. Using this information, the manager allocated Delta's income and expense between marginal accounts and "good" accounts as shown in Table 8-2.

Table 8-2 Delta Electric Company: Profit on Marginal Accounts, 1979 (Thousands of Dollars)

	All Accounts	Good Accounts	Marginal Accounts
Sales	$46,000	$41,400	$4,600
Cost of goods sold (0.87)	40,020	36,018	4,002
Gross profit	5,980	5,382	598
Warehousing, fixed (0.029)	1,334	1,334	—
variable (0.022)	1,012	911	101
Selling, fixed (0.003)	138	138	—
variable (0.041)	1,886	1,697	189
Administration, fixed (0.01)	460	460	—
variable (0.001)	46	41	5
Bad debts (0.0013)	60	—	60
Collection (0.0004)	20	—	20
Total operating expense	4,956	4,581	375
Operating profit	$ 1,024	$ 801	$ 223

Assuming that the allocations shown in Table 8-2 are approximately correct, what conclusions should the financial manager draw from these figures? The "good" accounts produced an operating profit of $801,000 on a sales volume of $41,400,000, or a margin of 1.935 percent. The "marginal" accounts added $4,600,000 to sales but $223,000 to operating profit, a margin of 4.85 percent. In other words, the marginal clients accounted for only 10 percent of sales, but they provided 22 percent of total operating profit. Since most of Delta's credit management costs had to be there anyway in order to service the "good" accounts, the *incremental* profits contributed by the "marginal" accounts provided a significant addition to the company's total operating profits.

In order to complete the preliminary analysis, it is necessary to estimate the level of additional investment the firm had to make to sell and service the so-called marginal accounts. Delta's credit files indicated that the receivables balance on marginal accounts averaged $567,000 during 1979. However, this figure overstates the additional amount the firm had to invest in accounts receivable in order to achieve its sales to the marginal accounts. The reason for the overstatement is that the $567,000 figure includes a profit margin on sales (which is not a prior investment) and all fixed costs (which by definition are "fixed" and would be there whether the marginal sales are made or not made). In short, only the *variable cost* component of accounts receivable on the marginal accounts represents an investment. From Table 8-1 we see that this variable component is approximately 93.6 percent of sales and hence only 93.6 percent of $567,000 (i.e., $531,000) represents the average amount the firm had to risk in order to sell to its marginal accounts. The $223,000 a year that these accounts contributed to operating profit amounts to an operating rate of return, before taxes, of nearly 42 percent per annum.

Refining the Analysis

The preliminary analysis outlined above clearly indicates that the financial manager should seriously consider a move to loosen credit policy still further rather than a move to tighten policy. Before making a final decision, further refinements of the analysis are possible, and in many situations such refinements are necessary. These refinements are:

1. Thus far, our calculation of the investment required included only accounts receivable. In practice, expanding the level of sales to include the marginal accounts would probably require some increase in the level of inventories held as well as some increase in operating cash balances, and these increases are also relevant elements in estimating the

total investment required. Of course, any increase in accounts payable or other accruals would provide an offset.

2. We have also assumed that the fixed costs shown in Table 8-1 would, in fact, remain fixed even if sales to marginal accounts are expanded. (Recall that the manager had determined that they were fixed with respect to a decline in sales, but he had not explicitly considered an increase in sales).

3. Refining our estimates to include the considerations listed above would probably give us a figure somewhat below 42 percent per annum for the expected pretax operating rate of return from our incremental sales to more marginal accounts. Our final step would be to ask a critical question with which all of finance is concerned: Given the riskiness of the marginal accounts, is the prospective pretax return good enough to justify the investment? After all, 42 percent (or whatever the adjusted rate might be) is the expected, or most likely, return, but it is not guaranteed. This final issue leads us directly to the central question: How should the proper goal of credit policy be defined?

Goal of Credit Policy

We noted earlier that expenses of analysis, collection, and bad debts rise at an increasing rate as credit policy is loosened. If Delta were to loosen its policy, these expenses would rise relative to the new sales generated, and the expected rate of return, $E(R)$, would fall. Thus, in general, $E(R)$ declines as credit policy is loosened, as shown in Figure 8-2.

How far should credit policy be pushed? At this point, we can give only a qualitative answer: Credit policy should be set at the point where the marginal expected return on additional investment in receivables just equals the return required by those who supply the firm's funds, lenders and investors. At that point, the value of the firm is maximized. We will come back to the question of the required rate of return later in this chapter.

Credit policy often is viewed as a marketing tool with the purpose of expanding sales. Let us be clear about the objective of credit policy. The objective of credit policy is to maximize the value of the firm. Clearly, the goal is not to maximize sales, and just as clearly it is not to minimize bad debt expense. To maximize sales, the firm would sell to anyone on credit; to minimize bad debt expense, it would sell to no one. Nor does the optimum occur at the point where expected operating profits are maximized, point C^* in Figure 8-1. Figure 8-2 shows that when policy is loosened, operating profits increase continuously up to a point as new

Figure 8-2 Credit Policy and Expected Rate of Return

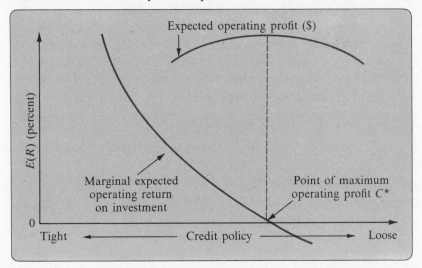

accounts are added. Before the point of maximum profit is reached, the incremental profit, though still positive, has fallen below that necessary to compensate those who finance the additional investment. In other words, expected return falls below the required rate at a point to the left of C^* both in Figure 8-1 and in Figure 8-2. At the point of maximum operating profit, the marginal expected operating rate of return is zero. We will return later to the question of the appropriate required return.

To use a rate of return approach to establish credit policy, we must be able to define specific policy alternatives. We then must identify specific accounts or categories of accounts that would be sold under one policy but not under another. Costs must be separated into fixed and variable components. Incremental earnings and investment under various policy alternatives then can be calculated.

Implementing Credit Policy

Once credit policy has been formulated, it must be translated into operational guidelines for use by the sales and credit departments. Of particular importance are credit standards for selecting individual accounts, because it is through individual decisions, account by account, that policy is implemented.

Selecting Individual Accounts

In principle, the correct approach to selecting accounts is to calculate expected return on each and make a judgment as to whether this expected return is above the required rate. Calculating $E(R)$ on an individual account follows the same general procedure as that discussed above for groups of accounts. Expected earnings are estimated over some convenient period, usually a year, and the investment necessary to generate those earnings is determined. Here again, it is the out-of-pocket investment that is relevant, the cash investment which the firm actually will have at risk at any point in time.

Calculating $E(R)$ on individual accounts is expensive and often cannot be justified on every account. If groups of accounts with similar characteristics can be identified in terms of the product mix sold to the accounts and rate of sales, shortcuts may be possible. For example, it may be found that in a particular group of accounts, the only major difference among accounts is in probability of default. It might be possible to calculate a target default probability at which point the $E(R)$ falls below the required rate. Accounts then would be analyzed only to estimate default probability, with those above the target rejected and those below accepted.

Other more sophisticated techniques are available. *Discriminant analysis* is a technique for discriminating between good and bad accounts based on certain readily available financial data such as firm size, acid test ratio, or accounts payable payment period. The development of a model based on discriminant analysis involves complex statistical techniques, but may be worthwhile for large firms that can justify the development expense.[2]

A similar technique, known as *credit scoring,* has been employed with some success in consumer credit. In this approach, selection criteria are developed by relating past default experience to certain characteristics of the applicant such as age, marital status, income, net worth, house ownership, and so on. New applicants then are scored and a decision is made based on a predetermined cutoff point. Like discriminant analysis, the objective of credit scoring is to reduce the expense of selecting accounts that have a high likelihood of meeting the return criterion.[3]

Monitoring Payment Patterns

Payment patterns by customers affect both the investment in accounts receivable and the return on that investment. It is therefore necessary

---

2. For an application of discriminant analysis to account selection, see William F. Massy, "Statistical Analysis of Relations between Variables," in R. E. Frank, A. A. Keuhn, and W. F. Massy (eds.), *Quantitative Techniques in Marketing Analysis* (Homewood, Ill.: Richard D. Irwin, 1962).
3. See J. H. Myers and E. W. Forgy. "Development of Numerical Credit Scoring Systems," *Journal of the American Statistical Association* **58**, 799–806 (Sept. 1963). Several articles on credit scoring appear in Kalman J. Cohen and Frederick S. Hammer, *Analytical Methods in Banking* (Homewood, Ill.: Richard D. Irwin, 1966).

to monitor payment patterns closely to detect any changes that might be occurring due to a recession or to a change in the application of credit policy or to other reasons.

In Chapter 4, we discussed two techniques for evaluating a firm's collection of receivables. One was *days sales outstanding* (DSO) and the other was the accounts receivable *aging schedule.* These two approaches are widely used and are perfectly adequate in many situations, but in some they are not.

Days sales outstanding is calculated by dividing the accounts receivable balance at any point in time by credit sales per day. The DSO figure thus depends on three main factors: sales rate, averaging period (whether the most recent month, quarter, or year), and underlying pattern of payment by customers. It is the latter that we wish to monitor, but changes in the sales rate or averaging period can produce widely varying DSO figures even when the underlying payment pattern remains stable.[4] In a firm with a seasonal sales pattern, for example, DSO figures will vary over the year even when the payment pattern remains unchanged.

The aging schedule suffers from the same difficulty. For example, the percentage of accounts less than, say, 30 days old will increase during periods when the sales rate rises, and decrease when the sales rate declines. An aging schedule in a seasonal firm thus will be different at different times during the year, even when payment patterns are stable.

In many applications, DSO and the aging schedule are adequate. Where a more refined technique is needed, a useful approach is to identify receivables as to the month of origination, that is, the month in which the sale was made. In this way, the proportion of receivables arising from each prior month can be monitored. One way to organize the data is shown in Table 8-3.[5] The left-hand side of the table represents the month in which the original sales were made, and the column heads indicate the calendar month in which the receivables remain outstanding. Thus, for example, the figure 19 percent in the bottom of the January column tells us that 19 percent of the sales made in November (2 months before January) were still outstanding and uncollected at the end of January. An increase in the fraction of receivables outstanding implies a corresponding *decrease* in payments received. These data indicate that Delta's customers

---

4. For a good discussion of this problem, see Wilber G. Lewellen and Robert W. Johnson, "Better Way to Monitor Accounts Receivable," *Harvard Business Review* **50**(3), 101–109 May–June, 1972).

5. The approach discussed here is that recommended by Lewellen and Johnson, ibid. See also B. K. Stone, "The Payments Approach to the Forecasting and Control of Accounts Receivable," *Financial Management* **5**, 65–82 (Autumn 1976). Stone provides a good discussion of the relationship between the receivables balance fraction outstanding (as in Table 8-3) and the payment proportion—the fraction of an account paid in each month following a sale.

Table 8-3   Delta Electric Company: Receivables as a Percent of Original Sales

Receivables Outstanding as Percent of Sales of	As of Month End				
	Jan.	Feb.	Mar.	Apr. · · ·	Dec.
Same month	89	91	93	90	90
1 month before	62	65	67	61	63
2 months before	19	23	27	22	21

slowed their payments somewhat in February and March and then accelerated again in April. By identifying receivables balances to month of origination, changes in payment pattern can be detected.

Credit Department Procedures

Credit department procedures are the province of the credit manager, but since the credit function often is under the overall supervision of the financial manager, we will touch briefly on these procedures.

Activities of the credit department fall into two main categories: credit analysis and collection. Analysis is concerned with the selection of accounts, that is, the decision of whether to grant credit. In establishing procedures, a benefit/cost point of view must be maintained. Analysis is expensive, and care must be taken to see that the costs of the analysis and selection procedure do not exceed the potential earnings. The extent of the effort devoted to individual accounts must be related to the size of the account or the order and to its riskiness, although the latter cannot be determined until some analysis is performed. Ideally, we would like to devote little effort to accounts of very low and very high risk, and concentrate on those in the middle. The performance measures discussed in Chapter 4 often are useful for making preliminary judgments as to whether further analysis is justified. Where detailed analysis is appropriate, the approaches discussed earlier in this chapter are applicable.

Analysis must begin with information, and the starting point usually is the applicant's own financial statements. Also very useful are specialized sources such as Dun and Bradstreet, who provide a *credit reference book* containing basic data on line of business, net worth, and credit rating for a large number of firms. Dun and Bradstreet *credit reports* then provide much more detailed data on individual firms. Other sources of credit information include local credit bureaus, banks, and other firms.

Collection procedures also are an important area of concern to the credit manager. Collection normally becomes an issue only after an account is past due. A basic question, therefore, is how long an account should be allowed to go past due before collection procedures are initiated. Many techniques then can be applied, including letters, telephone calls, personal visits, and finally, a collection agency or legal action. The guiding principle in deciding how far to go to collect an account is benefits versus costs. Collection is expensive, and we do not want to spend $200 to collect a $100 account.

Evaluating the Credit Function

Evaluating the credit function in a firm is an important responsibility of the financial manager. The responsibility includes both the evaluation of credit policy and the performance of the credit department itself in executing the policy.

From our earlier discussion, it is apparent that neither sales nor bad debt expense can be used as a guide in evaluating credit policy. The proper criterion is expected return on investment, and the firm's investment in receivables must be analyzed periodically to ensure that $E(R)$ guidelines are being met. In evaluating rate of return, the costs of the credit department itself must be taken into account.

Investing in Inventory

Inventories represent another important use of a firm's funds and are therefore an important concern of the financial manager. At any point in time, a firm has a given investment in inventory. For example, if a merchandising firm purchases $1,000,000 of goods for later resale at a profit, that holding should be viewed as an investment, that is, a commitment of funds now in the expectation of subsequent recoupment. As in the case of accounts receivable, we will view a decision to expand inventories as an investment decision. Again, we will use valuation as our basic conceptual framework and will define the financial manager's responsibility as seeing to it that inventories are set at the level that maximizes the value of the firm. As with receivables, we will find that the marginal expected return on investment in inventory declines as inventory is increased, and that the optimum lies at the point at which marginal $E(R)$ equals the rate required by suppliers of funds.

Functions of Inventory

Inventories of manufacturing firms can usefully be classified in three categories: raw materials, work in process, and finished goods. *Raw materials* are materials, parts, and subassemblies that are purchased from others and that become a part of the final product. Usually excluded from raw materials are supplies such as pencils and paper clips that are consumed, but not in the manufacturing process. *Work in process* includes goods in various stages of production. *Finished goods* includes completed products awaiting sale.

The inventory of a wholesaler or retailer, as opposed to a manufacturer, normally would consist of only a single category, goods purchased from others for resale. Among manufacturers, the mix of the three types of inventory varies with the nature of the business. Proximity of raw material supplies, length of the manufacturing process, and durability or perishability of the final product are all determinants. Manufacturers of machine tools or aircraft produced to customer order have large work-in-process inventories and relatively small finished goods inventories. Manufacturers of off-the-shelf hardware items such as hammers and screwdrivers, with short production times and low perishability and obsolescence, are likely to maintain larger finished goods inventories.

Each of the three types of inventory performs a different function. Work in process (WIP) inventory is necessary because production processes are not instantaneous. The total WIP inventory that a firm carries depends on the technology of the business and the firm's efficiency of production. A manufacturer of wire nails or flat washers likely would have a small WIP inventory because only a few steps are required in the production process. A whiskey distiller has a large WIP inventory because of the length of the production process. Subject to the constraints of technology, WIP inventories can be reduced by improving the efficiency of the production process to shorten production time.

Raw material and finished goods inventories perform a different function, namely to act as *buffers* to *decouple* the various activities of the firm so that all do not have to proceed at exactly the same rate. Raw material inventories serve to decouple purchasing and production. If no raw material stocks were maintained, purchases would have to be made continuously at exactly the rate of usage in production. Not only would ordering costs be quite high under such a system, but the firm would be unable to take advantage of cash discounts on purchases.

Finished goods inventories serve to decouple production and sales. Often the most efficient production rate is faster than the sales rate. In such cases, it is advantageous to produce for a period of time, letting finished goods inventories build, and then shut down production for a time. A firm with a seasonal sales pattern may find level production advantageous. In such cases, the sales rate rises above the production rate during parts of the year and falls below at other times, with finished goods inventories alternately rising and falling. The Neptune Company of Chapter 5 is a good example of a firm that follows such a policy. Finished goods inventories also constitute a buffer to absorb unexpected changes in either sales or production rates due to recession, unexpected demand, strikes, or production delays.

We noted above that WIP inventory is necessary because production takes time. In a multistage production process, WIP inventories may serve a second purpose, to decouple the various stages of the production process so that all do not have to proceed at the same rate. Stages involving high setup costs may be most efficiently performed in batches, with WIP inventories accumulated during a production run.

Friction and Uncertainty

We see that raw material and finished goods inventories, and in some cases certain components of WIP, serve as buffers to decouple the various stages from purchasing to final sale. The need for such buffers arises from two characteristics of the world: *friction* and *uncertainty*.

In a world of no friction, no transaction costs would exist. A firm could order any quantity of raw materials as often as it wished without incurring ordering costs. In such a world, there would be no incentive to hold an inventory of raw materials. If production involved no setup costs, a form of friction, and if sales were not uncertain, there would be no incentive to maintain finished goods inventories.

When friction exists in the form of ordering and setup costs, holding inventories become advantageous, even in a world of certainty. When we add uncertainty, the optimal level of inventory increases. Again and again in many areas of decision-making within the firm, and not just in areas related to financial management, we find that these two characteristics of the world—friction and uncertainty—are of central importance.

Costs of Holding Inventories

In discussing the functions of inventories, we have identified the major benefits of holding them. What about costs? It is useful to classify inventory costs into two categories: those that rise with the level of inventory and those that fall.

Rising costs often are referred to as *carrying* costs. Included are costs of storage, servicing, and risk of loss in value. Storage costs include depreciation and/or rent on facilities and equipment, property taxes, insurance, and utilities. Servicing costs include labor for handling the inventory, clerical and accounting costs for record-keeping, and taxes on the inventory itself. Decline in value may take place due to pilferage, fire, deterioration, technological obsolescence, style obsolescence, or price decline. Some of these risks can be insured, in which case the cost of insurance becomes a component of carrying cost. Not all these costs will be incurred by every firm in every situation, and the total cost of carrying inventory varies widely from one situation to another.

Costs that *decline* with the level of inventory include ordering costs, unit purchase costs, production costs, and opportunity costs of lost sales. Ordering costs often are a fixed amount per order placed, without regard to the amount ordered. By ordering less frequently in larger quantities, total ordering costs are reduced, but average inventories are larger. Unit costs of materials purchased may be reduced if quantity discounts can be obtained by purchasing in larger quantities. With larger stocks of raw materials and work in process, longer production runs can be made with less frequent setup, lower total setup costs, and fewer delays. Finally, larger finished goods inventories will reduce stockouts and lost contribution due to sales foregone. This latter cost is an opportunity cost, but an important element in determining the optimal inventory level.

All the costs described above are *operating* costs. As in our analysis of accounts receivable, we will take account of financing costs by comparing the expected return on investment in inventories to the return required by those supplying the funds to finance it.

Inventory Decision Models

The use of inventories as buffer stocks has been studied extensively and a large body of inventory theory has been developed. Inventory theory has been found useful for studying a broad class of problems in addition to the problems of stocking raw materials and finished goods in a firm. Cash and liquidity, for example, can be viewed as inventories and analyzed using inventory theory.[6]

Inventory theory addresses two questions:

1. *How much* should be ordered?
2. *When* should it be ordered?

The first question, how much, arises because of friction, the existence of ordering costs, setup costs, and the like. The second question, when to order, arises because the world is uncertain.

The Economic Order Quantity

Let us take these questions one at a time. We will deal with friction first and assume for the moment that no uncertainty exists with respect to the future. Inventory models deal with the question of how much to order by defining an *economic order quantity* (EOQ). The EOQ involves a tradeoff

6. See William J. Baumol, "The Transactions Demand for Cash—An Inventory-Theoretic Approach," *Quarterly Journal of Economics* **65,** 545–556 (Nov. 1952); Merton H. Miller and Daniel Orr, "A Model of the Demand for Money by Firms," *Quarterly Journal of Economics* **80,** 413–435 (Aug. 1966); and Yair E. Orgler, *Cash Management* (Belmont Ca.: Wadsworth, 1970).

between ordering costs (or setup costs) and carrying costs. A larger order quantity reduces the frequency of ordering and therefore total ordering costs, but increases the average inventory level and therefore carrying costs. The optimal order quantity, the EOQ, is given by

$$EOQ = \sqrt{\frac{2RO}{C}} \qquad (1)$$

where R is the usage per period in units, O is the ordering cost per order, and C is the carrying cost per unit per period. See the Appendix at the end of this chapter for the derivation of expression (1).[7]

To illustrate the use of the EOQ formula, consider an item that is used at the rate of 1,000 units per year. Ordering costs are $25 per order and carrying costs are $20 per unit per year. The EOQ then is

$$EOQ = \sqrt{\frac{2(1,000)(25)}{20}} = 50 \text{ units}$$

Assuming that the usage rate is uniform, we can illustrate the ordering and usage process as in Figure 8-3. At time t_0, 50 units are received and consumed over the period $t_0 - t_1$. At t_1, another 50 units are ordered. We can see that the average inventory level is 25, so that total carrying costs for the year are $25 \times 20 = \$500$. We must place a total of $1,000/50 = 20$ orders per year, so total ordering costs also are $500 per year. The

Figure 8-3 The Economic Order Quantity Model

sum of ordering and carrying costs is $1,000 per year. With a little arithmetic, we can verify that total costs are higher at any order quantity other than 50.

The EOQ formula is widely used in inventory control to determine optimal order quantities. To use the EOQ formula in quantitative applications, the cost of financing must be included as a component of carrying cost. Often, this cost is approximated using the interest cost of debt. However, investment in inventory is not riskless, so the interest rate may understate the real cost of financing, which is the return required by lenders and investors. The use of the interest rate may be a satisfactory approximation for the production manager in calculating order quantities for individual items. When the financial manager views inventory as an investment decision, he must take account of risk and require a return higher than the interest rate.

In addition to its usefulness in quantitative applications, the EOQ model yields several useful qualitative insights. We see the importance of friction costs; if ordering costs were zero, the EOQ would be zero. The firm would order continuously at the usage rate, holding no inventory at all. We see also that the EOQ and therefore the average inventory level varies with the square root of usage. Thus, a doubling of usage does not double the optimal inventory level, but increases it by $\sqrt{2}$, or about 1.4 times.

The basic EOQ model discussed above assumes that delivery is instantaneous when an order is placed. If delivery lead time is known with certainty, the EOQ is unchanged. We simply place the order earlier by the number of days required for delivery. We will discuss the effects of uncertain delivery times in the next section. The availability of quantity discounts does alter the EOQ and can be handled by modifying the analysis. However, quantity discounts are of secondary importance to our discussion here, and we will not deal with them.[8]

Safety Stocks

Now let us reintroduce uncertainty. In practice, uncertainty is likely to exist with respect to delivery times, production rates, and sales rates. Strikes occur, suppliers fail to deliver, and unexpected surges in demand appear. When delivery is delayed or usage unexpectedly increases, a *stockout* is likely to occur. To reduce the likelihood of stockouts, firms hold *safety stocks*, additional inventory over and above that prescribed by the EOQ formula.

---

8. For a treatment of the quantity discount in EOQ models, see Richard I. Levin and Charles A. Kirkpatrick, *Quantitative Approaches to Management*, 3d ed. (New York: McGraw-Hill, 1975), Chap. 7.

Finding the optimal level of safety stock involves a tradeoff between stockout costs and carrying costs. When a stockout occurs, several kinds of costs may be incurred, some out-of-pocket and some opportunity costs. A stockout in raw materials may cause production delays or stoppages and higher costs of scheduling and setup. In continuous-process industries such as paper or synthetic fibers, a production stoppage would be very costly indeed. A stockout in finished goods likely means that sales were lost or, at a minimum, customers inconvenienced. The relationship between on-time delivery and inventory level is not linear, and in most cases resembles the graph in Figure 8-4. The lower the level of inventories held, the larger the volume of delayed deliveries on orders received.

Figure 8-4   Inventories and On-Time Deliveries

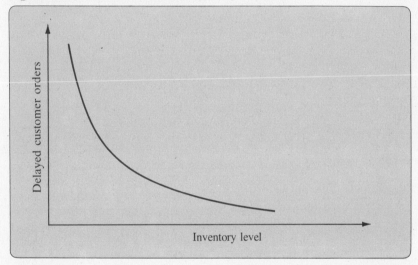

The cost of stockouts includes lost contribution as well as damage to the firm's reputation. Calculating stockout costs is a difficult problem and one about which not much can be said of a general nature. In each situation, it is necessary to identify out-of-pocket and opportunity costs incurred because of the stockout.

The optimal size of the safety stock depends on stockout costs, carrying costs, and the probability that stockouts will occur. The optimal level thus varies directly with

1. stockout costs, either in lost contribution or production inefficiency,
2. uncertainty of usage or sales rates, and
3. uncertainty of delivery times.

The optimum varies inversely with

4. inventory carrying costs.

Analytically, the safety stock is determined by calculating the appropriate *reorder point.*[9] We can diagram the model as in Figure 8-5.

Quantitative models for calculating reorder points and safety stocks are widely used in inventory control systems. It is important to note that having a safety stock still does not eliminate the possibility of a stockout. The safety stock is intended to give a *known probability* of a stockout such that the expected cost of a stockout (cost times probability) is balanced against the inventory carrying cost. The quantitative models show us the important effect of uncertainty—the greater the uncertainty, the higher the optimal level of inventory.

Figure 8-5   Reorder Points and Safety Stocks

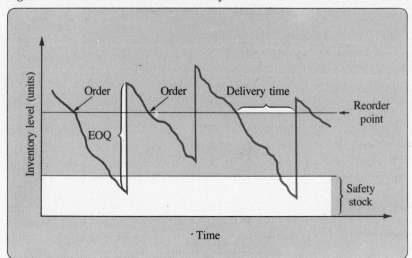

Total Inventory Costs

If we apply inventory theory as described above, in theory we will be led to minimize the total costs of inventory, including opportunity costs of stockouts. Diagrammatically, we can view the relationships as in Figure 8-6. At inventory level I^*, the total out-of-pocket and opportunity costs of inventory are minimized. If another increment of inventory is added, carrying costs exceed the ordering and stockout costs that are saved. Thus, at point I^*, *operating profit* is maximized.

The profit we have maximized in Figure 8-6 is *expected* profit. Although carrying and ordering costs can be estimated fairly accurately,

---

9. For an excellent discussion of inventory models under uncertainty, see Richard I. Levin and Charles A. Kirkpatrick, *Quantitative Approaches to Management,* 3d ed. (New York: McGraw-Hill, 1975), Chap. 8.

Figure 8-6 Minimizing Inventory Costs

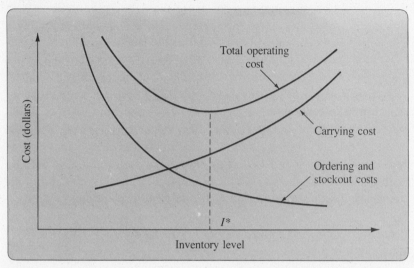

stockout costs may be subject to considerable uncertainty. Thus, we have not yet taken risk into account. Also, we have given no consideration to financing costs, that is, the return required by those who supply funds to the firm. As in the case of accounts receivable, to take account of these factors we must evaluate *expected return on investment*.

Calculating Expected Return

As in the case of accounts receivable, we will illustrate the calculation of expected return on inventory investment with an example. Southeastern Motors, Inc., is a manufacturer of fractional horsepower electric motors used in hand tools, electric fans, appliances, and other similar applications. The product line includes about 60 different models. All models are produced for stock according to a schedule jointly planned by the sales and production departments.

Southeastern's sales totaled $7.8 million in 1979. In the past, inventories had been tightly controlled and were dictated to a considerable extent by production considerations. Inventory turnover in 1979 was 6.3 times, a figure considered quite good by industry standards. However, Southeastern management had become increasingly concerned over sales lost due to stockouts of finished goods inventories. At year-end 1979, total inventories were $800,000, of which $200,000 was in finished goods.

Motivated by the problem of stockouts, management initiated a study to determine whether finished goods inventories should be increased. From historical records of orders received and filled, management estimated that, at the present inventory level, lost sales due to stockouts were running at an annual rate of $625,000. Recall from an earlier discussion that contribution to operating profits is equal to sales *less* variable costs. In this case, since variable costs totaled about 60 percent of sales, or $375,000, lost contribution amounted to $625,000 *less* $375,000, or about $250,000.

The magnitude of the lost contribution figure convinced management that further study was necessary. Lost sales were estimated at four alternative levels of finished goods inventories, each of which represented an incremental increase over current levels. The results are listed in Table 8-4. The analysis showed that if finished goods inventories were increased from the current level of $200,000 to $278,000, lost sales would decline from $625,000 to $475,000 and an additional contribution of $60,000 (last column in Table 8-4) would be realized. Similarly, the additional contribution at inventory levels *B*, *C*, and *D* also was determined.

Table 8-4 Southeastern Motors, Inc.: Lost Sales (Thousands of Dollars)

Policy	Inventory Level[a]	Lost Sales	Lost Contribution[b]	Incremental Contribution
Current	200	625	250	—
A	278	475	190	60
B	414	303	121	69
C	620	153	61	60
D	868	63	25	36

[a]Finished goods inventory only.
[b]Variable costs equal 60 percent of sales.

The next step in the analysis was to determine carrying costs at each inventory level. Carrying costs included warehousing, servicing, taxes, insurance, and record-keeping, and amounted to about 5 percent of the value of the inventory. This figure excluded financing costs. Incremental operating profit was estimated as shown in Table 8-5. By moving to level *A*, carrying costs would increase by $4,000. Subtracting this figure from incremental contribution of $60,000 gives a pretax increase in operating profit of $56,000, or $28,000 after taxes.

From the data in Tables 8-4 and 8-5, expected return on investment was calculated as in Table 8-6.

To move from the current policy to level *A*, Southeastern must invest an additional $78,000 in finished goods inventory. This additional investment is expected to generate additional operating profit of $28,000 per year after taxes, yielding an expected return on investment of 35.9 percent after taxes. Each successive increment of inventory then yields a lower $E(R)$. In interpreting analyses of this sort, let us keep in mind the critical

Table 8-5 Southeastern Motors, Inc.: Incremental Operating Profit (Thousands of Dollars)

Policy	Inventory Level	Carrying Cost[a]	Incremental Carrying Cost	Incremental Contribution[b]	Incremental Operating Profit Before Tax	After Tax[c]
Current	200	10	—	—	—	—
A	278	14	4	60	56	28
B	414	21	7	69	62	31
C	620	31	10	60	50	25
D	868	43	12	36	24	12

[a]5 percent of inventory level.
[b]From Table 8-4.
[c]Taxes at 50 percent.

Table 8-6 Southeastern Motors, Inc.:
Expected Return on Investment in Additional Inventory

Policy	Inventory Level (Thousands)	Incremental Investment[a] (Thousands)	Incremental Operating Profit, After Tax[b] (Thousands)	Incremental $E(R)$ on Investment, After Tax (Percent)
Current	$200	$ —	$ —	—
A	278	78	28	35.9
B	414	136	31	22.8
C	620	206	25	12.1
D	868	248	12	4.8

[a]Out-of-pocket outlay.
[b]From Table 8-5.

assumption that we are making with respect to the behavior of costs. We have identified the costs that vary and those that remain fixed as sales expand due to recovery of lost sales. The validity of the analysis depends on our ability correctly to identify fixed and variable costs in the range of sales in question.

We see in Table 8-6 that the incremental or *marginal E(R)* declines. As finished goods inventories are increased, each successive increment recaptures less lost sales and therefore less lost contribution. At levels *A* and *B*, $E(R)$ appears to be quite attractive. Policy *D*, returning only 4.8 percent after taxes, does not seem attractive. Which policy should Southeastern adopt? The answer depends on the target or required rate of return on investment in inventories. We will return to this topic in the final section in this chapter.

An important feature of the analysis above is that it examines the *incremental* return on successive *increments* of inventory. To move from the current policy to level D would require a total investment of $668,000. This investment would generate additional operating profit of $96,000, an $E(R)$ of 14.4 percent. However, the $E(R)$ on the last increment, from level C to level D, is only 4.8 percent. By looking at several increments, we can better determine the point at which marginal $E(R)$ falls below the required rate. Within increments, the figures in Table 8-6 represent averages. The marginal $E(R)$ on the last dollar of investment in increment B is quite a bit lower than the average $E(R)$, 22.8 percent, on increment B as a whole.

Inventory Policy in Seasonal Firms

Inventory policy in a firm with a pronounced seasonal sales pattern usually involves some additional complicating factors. A major policy question in manufacturing firms with seasonal sales is whether to adopt a level or a seasonal production policy. Where level production is adopted, as in the case of the Neptune Company of Chapter 5, inventory levels vary over the year.

In such situations, production and inventory policy must be considered jointly. Level production results in savings in costs of setup, hiring, training, morale, productivity and related factors. Savings in these areas must be traded off against higher carrying costs due to the higher average inventory level under level production. In some situations, risk of obsolescence or deterioration may represent an important component of total carrying costs.

The return on investment approach is applicable to inventory decisions in seasonal firms, but the analysis is more complex. The general approach is to analyze production and inventory costs under each policy alternative. Annual $E(R)$ then is computed using the average investment in inventory over the year.

Inventory Management

Establishing the appropriate overall level of inventory investment usually is the primary responsibility of the financial manager. Day to day management of inventory usually is the responsibility of the production manager. Included in the production manager's responsibility is the determination of economic order quantities, safety stocks, and reorder points for every individual item stocked. In the case of finished goods, the sales department is likely to take a strong interest in levels of safety stocks. The production manager also is responsible for ordering, receiving, handling, storing, protecting, and issuing inventory. In most firms, inventory management comprises an important set of responsibilities indeed and is a topic on which volumes have been written.[10]

The term *inventory control* is used to describe the responsibilities of the production manager with respect to inventories. Over the past two decades the application of computers has brought major advances to inventory management. Sophisticated automated inventory control systems are now available that integrate many of the necessary functions including determination of EOQs and reorder points, automatic preparation of orders, generation of accounting entries, and compilation of management information.

In most firms, policy formulation and inventory management involve an iterative process that goes on in a more or less continuous manner. Application of EOQ and order-point models item by item is not likely the first time around to lead to aggregate inventory levels that are optimal. Close cooperation is necessary between the financial manager and the production and sales managers. The financial manager's responsibility is a continuing one to evaluate and reevaluate the firm's aggregate investment in inventory to ensure that, at the margin, expected return on investment in inventory is acceptable.

The Required Return on Investment in Receivables and Inventory

From the perspective of the financial manager, our approach to the management of accounts receivable and inventory has centered on calculating expected return on investment at the margin. In each case, we identified policy alternatives, determined incremental investment and operating earnings, and calculated the marginal expected rate of return.

An important feature of our analysis was that we excluded financing costs. We considered only *operating* cash flows; hence, our result was the expected *operating* return. We found in the case of both receivables and inventory that, as the level of investment increases, marginal operating $E(R)$ declines. In each case, we were left with the question of how far to expand. We noted that the optimum, that is, the point at which the value of the firm is maximized, lies at the point where marginal operating $E(R)$ falls below the return necessary to compensate those who supply the funds for investment. This latter rate we referred to as the *required rate of return.*

What is the required rate of return? Is it the rate at which the firm can borrow? It is not, for the borrowing rate is determined by the lenders

---

10. See Richard I. Levin and Charles A. Kirkpatrick, *Quantitative Approaches to Management,* 3d ed. (New York: McGraw-Hill, 1975). Chaps. 7 and 8, and the references cited therein.

to cover the risk of the firm *as a whole* and not the component uses to which the borrowed funds may be put. Each individual investment, for example, marketable securities, accounts receivable and inventory, has a different risk. The higher the risk, the higher should be the "required" return on that specific use of funds. Thus, the overall borrowing rate may not adequately account for the risk of investment in receivables and inventory. In the case of receivables, accounts obtained by loosening credit policy become progressively more risky. Starting with a very tight policy, the cash flows associated with the first increments of expansion of receivables may be subject to little uncertainty, because only the very best customers are granted credit. As policy becomes progressively looser, accounts become subject to an increasing probability of default. By the same token, cash flows associated with expansion of inventory also are uncertain. Recapture of lost sales is not guaranteed, and as inventory is expanded, the degree of uncertainty regarding such recapture increases. We can conclude that, at the margin, the cash flows and therefore the expected return attributable to additional investment in receivables and inventory may be subject to considerable uncertainty.

How is the required rate of return related to risk? This is a question we will examine in depth in Part IV. There, we will find that lenders and investors are risk-averse and require compensation for both time and risk. The more risky the investment opportunity, the higher the return demanded by suppliers of funds. In other words, as risk increases, the required rate of return increases.

As the investment in accounts receivable and inventory is increased, two things happen. First, marginal $E(R)$ falls. Second, risk increases, so the required rate of return increases. We can diagram the relationships as in Figure 8-7. Determination of the marginal $E(R)$ and the required rate of return (RRR) must be done for accounts receivable and inventory separately. Each will have its own marginal $E(R)$ and RRR schedules and its own optimum as diagrammed in Figure 8-7. In each case, the optimum lies at a level of investment below that which maximizes operating profit. In Figure 8-7, operating profit is maximum at the point at which operating $E(R)$ is zero.

In practice, determining the required rate of return is not easy. We know that it slopes upward from the rate on riskless investment, usually taken to be the rate on United States Treasury obligations. One workable approach to determining the required rate is to categorize investments into risk classes. In the case of receivables, accounts might be classified as low, medium, and high risk, and a different required rate established for each. Similarly, estimates of risk might be made for different increments of investment in inventory. In Part IV, we will discuss risk and the determination of the required rate of return in depth.

Figure 8-7 Optimal Investment in Receivables and Inventory

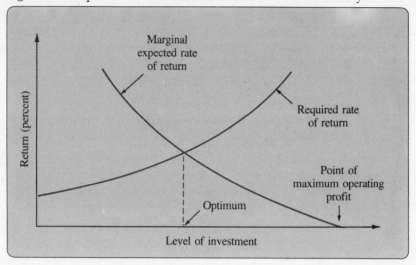

Summary

The financial manager should view the expansion of accounts receivable and inventories as *investment decisions,* using value-maximization as the conceptual framework. Receivables and inventories should be expanded to the point where the marginal expected return on additional investment equals the return required by suppliers of funds.

A firm's credit policy includes credit standards, credit terms, and collection procedures. Taken together, the three elements of credit policy determine the size of the firm's investment in accounts receivable and the return on that investment. As credit policy is loosened, accounts receivable expand. Costs of analysis, collection, and bad debts rise, while opportunity costs of lost sales decline. Where the sum of the costs is minimized, operating profit is maximized. The optimal credit policy, however, is more restrictive because it must consider return on investment rather than operating profits alone. The expected return on incremental investment in accounts receivable can be calculated using data on costs of servicing different categories of accounts.

Once overall credit policy has been formulated using a return on investment approach, the policy must be implemented via decisions on individual accounts. A return on investment approach can be utilized, but often is too expensive for individual accounts. Analytical techniques such as discriminant analysis and credit scoring may be useful. Payment patterns must be monitored to detect changes requiring management attention.

As in the case of receivables, the financial manager should be concerned with the return on investment in inventories. Inventories serve as buffers to decouple the purchasing, production, and sales activities of the firm so that all do not have to proceed at the same rate and so that unexpected events are not disruptive. Such buffers are necessary because of transaction costs (friction losses) and uncertainty. As inventories are expanded, some costs rise and others decline. Rising costs (or carrying costs) include storage costs, servicing costs, and risk of loss in value. Declining costs include costs of ordering, production, and lost sales.

Inventory theory provides a framework for analyzing inventory costs. The economic order quantity (EOQ) model deals with the tradeoff between carrying costs and ordering costs. The control limit model deals with the tradeoff between carrying costs and the cost of being out of required stocks. Minimizing the sum of all inventory costs leads to the point of maximum operating profit. As in the case of accounts receivable, the optimal inventory policy must consider not operating profit alone, but return on investment. The expected return on incremental investment in inventory can be calculated by identifying the various elements of cost associated with different inventory levels, calculating incremental operating profit, and dividing by the required incremental investment.

The objective of both credit policy and inventory policy is to maximize the value of the firm. In both cases, the policy that accomplishes this objective lies at the point where marginal expected operating return falls below the return necessary to compensate suppliers of funds.

Sample Problem

Tampa Building Company sells 5,000 three speed drills a year. The cost of holding inventory is $20 per drill per year and ordering costs are $80 per order.

1. Determine Tampa's economic order quantity for three speed drills, ignoring any potential stockout costs.
2. Determine the total annual inventory costs associated with this economic order quantity.

Solution

1. The economic order quantity (EOQ) can be found by the formula:

$$EOQ = \sqrt{\frac{2RO}{C}}$$

where R is the usage rate per period in units, O is the ordering costs per order, and C is the carrying (holding) costs per unit per period. For Tampa, R is 5,000 drills per year, O is $80 per order, and C is $20 per unit per year.

Substituting into the formula:

$$EOQ = \sqrt{\frac{2 \times 5,000 \times 80}{20}} = 200 \text{ drills}$$

2. The total inventory costs are composed of ordering and carrying costs. The total ordering cost is equal to the number of orders placed times the cost per order. The total carrying cost is equal to the average number of units in inventory times the carrying cost per unit.

For Tampa:

$$\text{Number of orders placed} = \frac{5,000 \text{ drills}}{200 \text{ drills per order}} = 25 \text{ orders}$$

Total ordering costs = 25 orders × $80 per order = $2,000

$$\text{Average inventory} = \frac{200}{2} = 100 \text{ drills}$$

Total carrying costs = 100 drills × $20 per drill = $2,000

Total annual inventory costs = $2,000 + $2,000 = $4,000

Questions

1. With respect to accounts receivable, how might the perspective of the financial manager differ from that of the credit manager?
2. Is the credit policy that maximizes expected operating profit the optimal credit policy? Explain.
3. What is the objective of credit policy?
4. Discuss the problem of monitoring payment patterns in seasonal firms.
5. Suppose that the Delta Electric Company (see text) and a local bank both are considering extending credit to the same customer. Why might Delta and the bank arrive at different decisions?
6. Describe the functions of the three major types of inventory.
7. What are the principal costs of holding inventories?
8. What two questions is inventory theory intended to answer?
9. On what does the optimal size of the safety stock depend?
10. The function of the safety stock is to prevent stockouts. True or false? Explain.

11. Why is the expected return on an investment in accounts receivable subject to uncertainty? In inventory?
12. Considering inventory and receivables separately, the optimal level of investment is the point at which the expected operating profit is maximized. True or false? Explain.

Problems

1. The Candee Corporation is considering liberalizing its credit policies to allow higher-risk customers to buy on credit terms of net 30. The credit department has been informed that variable costs will remain at 80 percent of sales over the new potential sales levels. All new sales will be on credit, and the projected information for each risk class is as shown in the table. The scale of before-tax required returns reflects the increased risk perceived for each risk class of customers. Which, if any, of the risk classes should Candee allow to buy on credit? (Assume a 365 day year.)

Risk Class	Required Return	DSO	New Sales
3	0.24	38	$500,000
4	0.30	45	400,000
5	0.39	58	300,000
6	0.50	70	200,000

2. Assume the credit department for Candee Corporation realized it had failed to include all the relevant costs in Problem 1 and the following additional information is submitted. Which risk classes should Candee allow to buy on credit?

Risk Class	Default Rate (Percent)	Increased Credit Department Expense
3	4	$5,000
4	7	5,000
5	12	5,000
6	20	5,000

3. The CBM Company currently offers credit terms of 1/10, net 30 on annual credit sales of $3,000,000. An average of 50 percent of the current customers take the discount, and the average collection period has consistently remained at 35 days. The percentage default rate has been 1 percent. The company is considering two alternative changes in credit terms as outlined in the table. If sales are projected to remain stable under either alternative and the required before-tax rate of

return on investment in accounts receivable is 0.20, what strategy would you recommend for CBM?

Sales 3,000,000

Credit Terms	Percentage Taking Discount %	DSO	Default Rate (Percent)
2/10, net 30	75	18	0.005
3/10, net 20	98	12	0.001
1/10 Net 30	50	35	.1010

4. Delta Electric Company is considering a request from Bill's Electronics for open account credit in the amount of $1,000 (figured at Delta's selling price). Delta's gross margin on the particular merchandise to be purchased by Bill's is 17 percent. Delta's salesperson expects Bill's to purchase $5,000 of merchandise annually. On all sales, Delta will incur variable expenses of 2 percent for the salesperson's commissions and 1.5 percent for warehousing.

   (a) Calculate the annual expected return on the prospective account with Bill's.

   (b) Suppose Delta establishes 30 percent pretax as the required rate of return on accounts in the risk class in which Bill's falls. Suppose also that there are two possible outcomes: (1) Bill's makes all payments on time, or (2) Bill's defaults immediately and Delta looses its entire investment. What must be the minimum probability of outcome (1) in order to give an expected return of 30 percent pretax?

5. A firm has a $50 per year carrying cost (including costs of financing) on each unit of inventory, an annual usage rate of 10,000 units, and an ordering cost of $100 per order. Ignoring any potential stockout costs:

   (a) Calculate the economic order quantity for the firm.

   (b) What would be the total annual inventory costs of the firm if it orders in this quantity?

6. Assume that the supplier for the firm in Problem 5 offers a quantity discount of 30¢ per unit if the firm orders in lots of 400 units. Should the firm accept the quantity discount?

7. The management of Bland Company is concerned about the seemingly large losses it has been experiencing in lost sales due to frequent stockouts. The company has been carrying a finished goods inventory of $150,000 and has estimated lost sales at $525,000 per year. Variable costs have consistently remained at 75 percent of sales, and carrying costs of inventory (excluding financing costs) are 4 percent annually. Assuming a tax rate of 48 percent, an after-tax required rate of return of 15 percent on investment in inventory, and the projected

figures shown below, determine the optimal level of inventory for the company.

Policy	Inventory Level	Annual Lost Sales
Current	$150,000	$525,000
A	200,000	375,000
B	250,000	250,000
C	300,000	150,000
D	350,000	75,000
E	400,000	25,000
F	450,000	0

8. The Broyhill Finishing Company uses 1,000 gallons of dye #704 per day. The dye can be purchased in drums containing 100 gallons for $50 per drum or in 1,000 gallon drums for $450 per drum. Ordering costs are $10 per order. The company's accountant has estimated the following costs associated with carrying inventory:

   Required rate of return for funds invested in inventory: 15 percent.

   Depreciation and property tax on warehouse space occupied: $100 per month (there is no alternative use for this warehouse space at the present time).

   Insurance on inventory: 5 percent of cost per year.

   (a) What is the economic order quantity assuming that only 100 gallon drums can be ordered? Assume 250 working days per year.
   (b) What is the economic order quantity assuming that only 1,000 gallon drums can be ordered?
   (c) Assuming that the firm must order one size or the other and not mix them, which drum size and ordering policy would you recommend?

9. Jackson Manufacturing Company uses inventory turnover as one performance measure to evaluate its production manager. Currently, Jackson's inventory turnover (CGS/inventory) is ten times per year compared with an industry average of four. Average sales are $450,000 per year. Variable costs have consistently remained at 70 percent of sales with fixed costs of $10,000. Carrying costs of inventory (excluding financing costs) are 5 percent annually. Jackson's sales force has complained that low inventory levels are resulting in lost sales due to stock-

outs. The sales manager has made the following estimates, based on stockout reports:

Inventory Policy	Inventory Turnover	Sales
Current	10	$450,000
A	8	$500,000
B	6	$540,000
C	4	$565,000

     On the basis of these estimates, assuming a 50 percent tax rate and an after-tax required rate of return of 15 percent on investment in inventory, what inventory policy would you recommend?

10. The financial officers of MVB Inc. are concerned that the firm's current credit policy of 75 day terms may be too loose when compared with MVB's competitors' 30 day credit terms. MVB's annual average sales are $1.2 million. Variable costs are 75 percent of sales with fixed costs of $100,000. MVB is considering several alternative credit policies as shown below. Assuming a pretax required rate of return on investment in accounts receivable of 20 percent, which policy would you recommend? (Assume a 360 day year and that all sales are on credit with the average collection period equal to the terms given.)

Policy	Terms	Sales
Current	75 days	$1,200,000
A	60 days	$1,130,000
B	45 days	$1,050,000
C	30 days	$ 950,000

References

E. S. Buffa, *Production-Inventories System: Planning and Control* (Homewood, Ill.: Richard D. Irwin, 1968).

N. C. Hill and K. D. Riener, "Determining the Cash Discount in the Firm's Credit Policy," *Financial Management* **8**, 68–73 (Spring 1979).

R. I. Levin and C. A. Kirkpatrick, *Quantitative Approaches to Management,* 3d ed. (New York: McGraw-Hill, 1975).

K. J. Cohen and F. S. Hammer, *Analytical Methods in Banking* (Homewood, Ill.: Richard D. Irwin, 1966).

W. G. Lewellen, "Finance Subsidiaries and Corporate Borrowing Capacity," *Financial Management* **1**, 21–32 (Spring 1972).

W. G. Lewellen and R. W. Johnson, "Better Way to Monitor Accounts Receivable," *Harvard Business Review* **50**, 21–32 (May–June 1972).

J. F. Magee, "Guides to Inventory Policy, I–III," *Harvard Business Review* **34,** 49–60 (Jan.–Feb. 1956); 103–116 (Mar.–Apr. 1956); 57–70 (May–June 1956).

G. L. Marrah, "Managing Receivables," *Financial Executive* **38,** 4–44 (July 1970).

W. F. Massy, "Statistical Analysis of Relations Between Variables," in R. E. Frank, A. A. Kuehn, and W. F. Massy (eds.), *Quantitative Techniques in Marketing Analysis* (Homewood, Ill.: Richard D. Irwin, 1962).

D. R. Mehta, *Working Capital Management* (Englewood Cliffs, N. J.: Prentice-Hall, 1974).

J. H. Myers and E. W. Forgy, "The Development of Numerical Credit Evaluation Systems," *Journal of the American Statistical Association* **58,** 799–806 (Sept. 1963).

H. R. Patterson, "New Life in the Management of Corporate Receivables," *Credit and Financial Management* **72,** 15–18 (Feb. 1970).

M. Schiff, "Credit and Inventory Management," *Financial Executive* **40,** 28–33 (Nov. 1972).

A. Shapiro, "Optimal Inventory and Credit Granting Strategies Under Inflation and Devaluation," *Journal of Financial and Quantitative Analysis* **8,** 37–46 (Jan. 1973).

A. Snyder, "Principles of Inventory Management," *Financial Executive* **32,** 12–21 (Apr. 1964).

R. S. Stockton, *Basic Inventory Systems: Concepts and Analysis* (Boston: Allyn and Bacon, 1965).

B. K. Stone, "The Payments-Pattern Approach to the Forecasting and Control of Accounts Receivable," *Financial Management* **5,** 65–82 (Autumn 1976).

D. W. Wrightsman, "Optimal Credit Terms for Accounts Receivable," *Quarterly Review of Economics and Business* **9,** 59–66 (Summer 1969).

Appendix: Derivation of the Economic Order Quantity

The economic order quantity (EOQ) involves a tradeoff between ordering (or setup) costs and carrying costs. A larger order quantity reduces the frequency of ordering and therefore total ordering costs, but increases the average inventory and therefore carrying costs. Let

Q = Order quantity
R = Usage per period
O = Order cost per order
C = Carrying cost per period

Assuming usage to be constant over each period, the average inventory is $Q/2$. Total carrying cost per period then is the average number of units times carrying cost per unit, or $(Q/2)C$.

The number of orders placed per period is total usage divided by units per order, or R/Q. Total ordering cost per period then is orders placed times cost per order, or $(R/Q)O$.

Total cost per period then is

$$T = \frac{CQ}{2} + \frac{RO}{Q} \tag{A1}$$

The optimal order size, Q^* (the EOQ), is that which minimizes total cost, T. To determine Q^*, we differentiate expression (A1) with respect to Q, set the result equal to zero, and solve for Q:

$$\frac{dT}{dQ} = \frac{C}{2} - \frac{RO}{Q^2} \tag{A2}$$

Setting (A2) equal to zero and solving for Q, we get

$$\frac{C}{2} - \frac{RO}{Q^2} = 0 \tag{A3}$$

$$Q^2 = \frac{2RO}{C} \tag{A4}$$

$$Q^* = \text{EOQ} = \sqrt{\frac{2RO}{C}} \tag{A5}$$

TIME, RISK, AND VALUE III

Introduction

In order to conduct its business, a firm has to acquire and hold assets. In order to expand, it generally has to acquire and hold even more assets. As of the end of 1978, American Telephone and Telegraph Company (AT&T), the world's largest private corporation, held over $103 *billion* of assets, up from $86 *billion* just 2 years earlier. General Motors Corporation (GM), the largest manufacturing company, held $30.6 billion of assets at year-end 1978 (up from $24.4 billion 2 years earlier). Collectively, United States businesses invested $225 billion dollars in 1978 alone to acquire new plants and equipment *plus* $75 billion to expand the stock of inventories held.

The specific motives underlying these huge outlays vary from one firm to another and within each individual firm. Some investments are made to replace worn-out plants or equipment; some are made to increase production capacity to serve growing markets; some reduce production costs; some develop new products and new markets. But in a market economy, all investments are made with one *overall* motive in common—to produce net economic benefits for the firm, its owners, and and society in general.

The wisdom or lack of wisdom with which investment decisions are made profoundly affects the fortunes of a firm and its stockholders. For example, in 1929 U.S. Steel was the largest industrial company in the country with almost exactly twice the assets held by third-ranked GM. By 1978 GM was nearly three times the size of U.S. Steel in terms of assets, and these assets were generating a net income of $3.5 billion a year against U.S. Steel's $242 million! Clearly, GM must have been making bigger and better investment decisions. In 1945 General Electric (GE) had assets of $858 million, which produced net income of $85 million that year; IBM was much smaller with assets of $134 million and net income of $11 million. By 1978 IBM's assets had grown to $20.7 billion compared to GE's $15 billion, and these assets were generating $3.1 billion in annual net income to IBM shareholders compared to GE's $1.2 billion.

The Role of Financial Management

Financial management plays two important roles in connection with a firm's decision to acquire and hold assets.

1. Its first, and most critical, role is to develop and implement financial criteria against which all outlays of funds for asset acquisitions can be screened in order to select the "good" projects from the "bad."

2. Its second role is to plan the financing for the investments that a firm makes.

The two chapters of Part III deal with the first of the two responsibilities listed above. How can we translate the general idea of evaluating complex investment proposals into operational terms? How can we develop a single, numerical criterion that will give us as correct an answer as possible to the question: Should this particular investment proposal be accepted?

One simple, but quite inadequate, financial criterion would be to ask if an investment promises to make a profit and to accept those that do. It is inadequate and thus misleading because it ignores two very relevant factors: *timing* and *risk*.

Timing. The timing of a benefit is frequently as important as its size. An investment of $100 that promises a profit of $40 5 years hence may not be as good as one that promises a profit of $20 1 year hence. Furthermore, the *time shape* of the expected flow can vary widely from one investment to another. The techniques for dealing with the time element are discussed in Chapter 9.

Risk. Knowing that an investment will yield a profit is not a sufficient basis for accepting it. We have to ask an additional question: Is the promised level of profit sufficient (relative, of course, to the size of the investment outlay)? Benefits promised by even a guaranteed investment must surpass the going rate of return available in the market in order to be acceptable. Investments that offer *less certain* benefits must surpass an even higher rate in order to be acceptable. How should the minimum acceptable rate for risky investment be set? Chapter 10 lays the groundwork for dealing with this difficult question.

In summary, expected *profit* in itself does not provide an adequate basis for making decisions to invest in assets. The size of expected profit is only one dimension of the decision. The expected *timing* of profits, as well as the *quality* of profits (the degree of certainty or uncertainty with which the expectations are held) are two other dimensions that must be taken into account. Yet another dimension of relevance to a decision is the rate of return available in the market at the time the investment is being made.

What we are attempting to do in Chapters 9 and 10 is to find a conceptual basis for reducing *all* of these relevant dimensions into a *single measure* that will tell us whether any given investment outlay is acceptable or not. Later, in Part IV we will discuss the more applied issue of how firms make or should make investment decisions in practice.

Fundamentals of
Discounted Cash Flow

9

In 1938 an economist named J. B. Williams stated that the current value of any asset is the present value of all the future benefits that the asset will deliver.[1] What Williams did was to put in precise terms the age-old concept that the value of an asset depends not on its cost or its past usefulness but on its future usefulness. This concept underlies the modern theory of value.

Value and profits are two measures of economic performance. Consider a business that makes and sells a product, let us say a sandwich shop that produces lunches for students. If the shop's revenues exceed its expenses, we say it is making a profit. This profit is evidence that the output of the business (sandwiches) is more valuable to society than the input it uses (bread, mayonnaise, meat, labor, rent, electricity, and so on). This is what society expects firms to do—to produce outputs more valuable than the resources consumed in their production. If the sandwich shop is showing a loss instead of a profit, society is sending a message to the operator either to become more efficient or to find another line of business.

To make decisions useful to their owners and to society, firms must be able to estimate prospective future performance as well as to measure past performance. Someone contemplating opening a sandwhich shop must be able to estimate what the profits are likely to be. He or she must be able to estimate the value of both the input and the output. The standard way to do this is to estimate revenues from sales and subtract all expenses:

Sales	$1,000
Expenses	900
Profit	$100

Now we come to a big problem in practice. Suppose output occurs much later in time than input. Consider a firm that is contemplating going into business to produce bicycles. A plant costing $500,000 must be constructed and equipped. The firm expects to build 4,000 bicycles a year and to sell them for $100 each. Expenses of production and sale will total $300,000 per year. The plant is expected to last for 8 years. Table 9-1 shows a schedule of prospective profits.

Inputs (the plant) occur now and outputs (bicycles) are spread over the next 8 years. Are the outputs more valuable than the inputs? The first step is to adjust the value of each outflow and inflow to a common point of time. For convenience, the point of time generally used for this pur-

---

1. J. B. Williams, *The Theory of Investment Value* (Cambridge, Mass.: Harvard University Press, 1938).

Table 9-1   Schedule of Prospective Profits for
Bicycle Manufacturer (Thousands of Dollars)

	Present	Year 1	2	3 · · ·	8
Plant	($500)				
Sales		$400	$400	$400 · · ·	$400
Expenses		300	300	300 · · ·	300
Profit		$100	$100	$100 · · ·	$100

pose is the *present,* frequently referred to as time zero or t_0. But, how do we measure the present value of future outputs? Can we simply add up the profits for 8 years ($800,000) and compare this figure to the cost of the plant? We cannot, for money has *time value.* Even if we ignore inflation, $1 received 1 year from today is not worth as much as $1 received today. Let us explore the notion of time value in more depth.

The Time Value of Money

The notion that money has time value is one of the basic concepts of finance. It is also one of the basic complications we must deal with in analyzing capital expenditure decisions.

Imagine a world in which the expected cash inflows and outflows associated with a business decision all take place at the same moment in time and with the same degree of certainty. Analyzing such a decision would be a simple matter of comparing the two flows. Any decision offering a net inflow would be acceptable. If two or more alternative decisions are available, selecting the best one would also be simple: Pick the alternative that offers the largest net inflow.

In the real world, capital expenditure decisions are not that simple. The probable outlays and subsequent inflows expectable from a given project occur at different points in time—sometimes many years apart. Likewise, two alternative projects may involve quite different time patterns of cash flows. To analyze such real-world projects in order to arrive at a decision, we need techniques that allow us to adjust for the difference in timing between outflows and inflows.

In a world of complete certainty, the rate of interest or time value of money represents the standard *rate of exchange* between having access to a sum of money now and having definite access to it at a later point in time. Thus, the rate of interest provides the tool we need for adjusting the value of all cash flows, whenever they are expected to occur, to a single common point of time.

Compound Interest

Let us begin our discussion of the time value of money and the time adjustment process with the subject of compound interest. We know that the rate of interest is the rate at which an individual or firm will be compensated for exchanging money now for money later. We will refer to the original amount as the *principal* amount. The word *compound* refers to the periodic addition of interest earned to the principal amount. After interest is earned over one period, it is added to the account, and then during the next period, interest is earned on the prior period's interest as well as on the principal.

Let us consider an example. Assume that the market rate of interest on savings is 6 percent per year and that the principal amount is $100. Let us also assume that interest is *compounded annually*, that is, added to the principal balance at the end of each year. Then at the end of the first year we would have

Principal	$100.00
Interest for 1 year at 6 percent	6.00
Balance at end of year	$106.00

If the first year's interest is allowed to remain, at the end of the second year we would have

Balance at beginning of second year	$106.00
Interest for second year at 6 percent	6.36
Balance at end of second year	$112.36

Letting W_0 stand for the original principal balance, W_1 for the balance at the end of the first year, and i for the interest rate,[2] we have, in more general terms,

$$W_1 = W_0 + iW_0 = W_0(1 + i)$$

and, where W_2 is the balance at the end of the second year,

$$W_2 = W_1 + iW_1 = W_1(1 + i)$$

so that

---

2. For computational purposes, i is expressed in decimal notation. Thus, at 6 percent, we would have $i = 0.06$ and $(1 + i) = 1.06$.

$$W_2 = W_0(1 + i)(1 + i) = W_0(1 + i)^2$$

Generalizing still further, we can write

$$W_{t+n} = W_t(1 + i)^n \qquad (1)$$

where W_t is the amount at any time t, W_{t+n} is the amount n periods later, n is the number of periods, and i is the rate per period. For example, if $W_t = \$1{,}000$ is the amount invested in 1980 at 6 percent per annum, compounded annually for $n = 10$ years, it will grow to W_{t+10} dollars by 1990, where $W_{t+10} = \$1{,}000\,(1.06)^{10}$. Using a hand calculator or a standard compound interest table, we will find that $\$1{,}000\,(1.06)^{10}$ is equal to $\$1{,}791$.

Frequency of Compounding

In expression (1) above, we have carefully defined n as the number of *periods* and i as the rate per period. We can define the period any way we wish, as a year, a quarter, a month, or even a day. Sometimes we will find situations in which interest is compounded over a period shorter than 1 year.

Let us consider an example. In practice, interest rates are expressed in terms of percent per year. Consider a savings and loan association that offers interest at the rate of 6 percent per year, compounded *semiannually*. If we deposit $\$100$, how much will we have at the end of a year? Applying expression (1), we get

$$W_1 = \$100 \left(1 + \frac{0.06}{2}\right)^2 = \$106.09$$

Note that the rate per period, i, is 6 percent divided by 2, or 3 percent, and the number of periods, n, is 2. If interest were compounded *quarterly*, we would have

$$W_1 = \$100 \left(1 + \frac{0.06}{4}\right)^4 = \$106.14$$

Here, the number of periods is 4 and the rate per period is 6 percent divided by 4, or 1.5 percent.

In the case of 6 percent per year compounded semiannually, the *effective rate* of interest is 6.09 percent. In other words, 6 percent per year compounded semiannually is the equivalent of 6.09 percent per year compounded annually. Likewise, 6 percent per year compounded quarterly is equivalent to 6.14 percent compounded annually. At the mathematical limit, 6 percent a year compounded *continuously* or instantaneously, is equivalent to 6.18 percent compounded annually.

It is apparent that the *frequency of compounding* affects the effective rate of interest. Frequency of compounding is discussed in more depth in Appendix B at the end of this chapter. In some cases, such as the rates offered on savings deposits in banks or savings and loan associations, the frequency of compounding is an important consideration. In many other cases, it is not so important. Unless otherwise noted, we will express interest rates in terms of percent per year and assume annual compounding.

Future Value

Given a sum of money, if we know the rate of interest, we can calculate the sum to which the present sum would grow by any future date. We will refer to that future sum as the *future value* of the present sum. From expression (1) we can see that

$$\text{Future value (FV)} = \text{Present value} \times (1 + i)^n \qquad (2)$$

Let us construct a table of future values for an interest rate of 6 percent. Suppose we start with $1.00 and assume annual compounding. After 1 year, we would have $1.00 + 0.06 = 1.06. After 2 years, we would have

$$\text{FV} = \$1.00 \times (1.06)^2$$

$$= \$1.124$$

Table 9-2 shows a table of values for 6 percent interest.

Table 9-2 Future Values @ 6 Percent

Years Hence	Future Value
1	$1.060
2	1.124
3	1.191
4	1.262
5	1.338
10	1.791
15	2.397
20	3.207
25	4.292
50	18.420

Tables of future values are given at the end of the book.

The Power of Compound Interest

Over long periods, compound interest is very powerful. Adding 6 percent each year does not sound like much, but after 25 years, $1.00 will have grown by a factor of four, and in 50 years, by a factor of eighteen. One thousand dollars set aside when you are born and invested at 6 percent a year would become *$59,000* by the time you retired at age 70. Over longer periods, the results are even more interesting, as Figure 9-1 shows.

Figure 9-1   Compound Growth of $1 @ 6 Percent Interest

Where time periods are very long, the results are spectacular! However, the rate of increase in value is very sensitive to the interest rate. Table 9-3 compares 6 percent to 3 percent. There is quite a difference between 3 percent and 6 percent. One cannot help being impressed with the results at the higher rate. In an inflationary world, however, we must interpret such results cautiously. Suppose the rate of inflation were 3 percent per year. Over a 50 year period, $1.00 would grow to $18.42 at 6 percent, but the cost of living would go up by a factor of 4.384. So the *u*

growth in *purchasing power* would be only $18.42 ÷ 4.384 = $4.202, a much more modest number.

Table 9-3 Future Values

| Years | Future Value of $1 | |
Hence	@ 3 Percent	@ 6 Percent
1	$1.030	$1.060
5	1.159	1.338
10	1.344	1.791
25	2.094	4.292
50	4.384	18.420
75	9.179	79.057
100	19.219	339.302
200	369.356	115,125.904

Length of Time to Double

Sometimes it is useful to know how long it will take something to double in value. Table 9-4 shows selected rates. A rough rule of thumb for calculating time to double is to divide the interest rate into 70. We get 70 years at 1 percent, 35 years at 2 percent, 17.5 years at 4 percent, and so on. We can see from Table 9-4 that the approximation is fairly close at low interest rates but not so good at rates above 10 percent.

Table 9-4 Time to Double

Interest Rate (percent)	Years to Double
1	69.7
2	35.0
4	17.7
6	11.9
8	9.0
10	7.3
15	5.0
20	3.8

70%

Present Value

If we go back to equation (2), which relates future value to present value, we can see that *present value* is simply the inverse of future value. If we have an opportunity to receive a given sum in the future, and we know the appropriate interest rate, we can calculate its value today:

$$\text{Present value} = \frac{\text{Future value}}{(1 + i)^n} \tag{3}$$

More formally, by rewriting (1), we get

$$W_t = \frac{W_{t+n}}{(1 + i)^n} \tag{4}$$

with W, i, t, and n defined as before.

Let us consider an example. Suppose we have an opportunity to receive $100 a year from now. What is its value today if the interest rate is 6 percent? Applying (4), we have

$$W_0 = \frac{\$100}{(1.06)^1} = \$94.34$$

Likewise, the value today of $100 to be received 2 years in the future would be given by

$$W_0 = \frac{\$100}{(1.06)^2} = \$89.00$$

Whereas we spoke of *compounding* cash flows *forward* in time, we speak of *discounting back* in time. In calculating a present value, the interest rate often is referred to as the *discount rate*.

In the above examples, we are calculating the present value of a future sum. If 6 percent represents the rate at which we can earn on savings, we are saying that we would pay no more than $94.34 for an opportunity to receive $100 a year from now, and $89.00 to receive the $100 in 2 years. In other words, $100 a year from now is *equivalent* to $94.34 today; we would be indifferent between the two sums. The same can be said of $89.00 now versus $100.00 in 2 years; we would as soon have one sum as the other. Note that we are assuming that 6 percent correctly expresses our time preference, that is, the rate at which we are willing to exchange present for future sums and vice versa.

Present Value Tables

For use in calculating present values, tables have been constructed for various commonly encountered discount rates and time periods. For convenience, these tables are reproduced at the end of the book. Table I gives the present value of $1 received n years in the future at an interest rate of i percent per year. Values for Table I are calculated using expression (4). To illustrate, the present value (PV) of $1 received 4 years from now, at a discount rate of 6 percent is

$$PV = \frac{\$1}{(1.06)^4} = \$0.792$$

From Table I, we can see that 0.792 is the *present value factor* in the 6 percent column opposite 4 years. Other values in Table I are calculated similarly using expression (4). The values in Table I assume that the $1 payment is received at the end of year n, with interest compounded annually.

To illustrate the use of the present value tables, let us calculate the present value of $100 in 4 years at a discount rate of 6 percent:

$$PV = \$100 \times 0.792 = \$79.20$$

The general expression is

$$PV = \text{Future value} \times \text{Present value factor}$$

This is, of course, equivalent to using expression (4), but use of the present value tables normally is easier.

Present Value of Level Stream of Payments: Annuities

In the examples above, we calculated the present value of a single sum to be received in the future. How do we calculate the present value of a series or *stream* of payments to be received at different dates in the future? The answer is that we simply calculate the present value of each payment separately and add the results. Thus, the present value of $100 to be received at the end of 1 year and $100 at the end of 2 years, at a discount rate of 6 percent, is

$$PV = \frac{\$100}{(1.06)^1} + \frac{\$100}{(1.06)^2}$$

$$= \$94.34 + \$89.00 = \$183.34$$

Using the symbol Σ to indicate summation, we can generalize the above to get

general
DCF
Valuation
model

$$PV = \sum_{t=1}^{n} \frac{C_t}{(1 + i)^t} \qquad (5)$$

where C_t is the amount to be received in period t, and n and i are defined as before.

A stream of level payments is called an *annuity.* Applying expression (5), we can calculate the present value of an annuity as

annuities

$$PV \text{ (Annuity)} = \sum_{t=1}^{n} \frac{A}{(1 + i)^t}$$

$$= A \sum_{t=1}^{n} \frac{1}{(1 + i)^t} \qquad (6)$$

where A is the amount of each annual payment.

To illustrate, the present value of $1 per year for 3 years at 6 percent is

$$PV = \frac{\$1}{1.06} + \frac{\$1}{(1.06)^2} + \frac{\$1}{(1.06)^3}$$

$$= \$2.673$$

and for 4 years it is

$$PV = \$3.465$$

Note

In practice there is little need to use either the formula or the calculations because we can simply look up the answer in special tables that exist. Thus, Table II at the end of this book gives the present value of $1 per year for n years at various rates. These values are *present value factors* for an annuity. Note that in the 6 percent column opposite 3 years we see 2.673, and opposite 4 years, 3.465. The remaining factors in Table II likewise were calculated using expression (6) with $A = \$1$. The values assume annual compounding, with the $1 payment received at the end of each year.

To illustrate the use of Table II, suppose we want to find the present value of $15,000 per year for 4 years at 10 percent. In the 10 percent column opposite 4 years, we find a PV factor of 3.170. So

$$PV = \$15,000 \times 3.170$$

$$= \$47,550$$

Note that this is equivalent to

$$PV = \frac{\$15,000}{(1.10)^1} + \frac{\$15,000}{(1.10)^2} + \frac{\$15,000}{(1.10)^3} + \frac{\$15,000}{(1.10)^4}$$

$$= \$47.550$$

The general expression for using Table II is

$$PV = \text{Payment} \times \text{PV factor} \qquad (7)$$

or

In Table II, as in Table I, we assume that payments are made or received at the end of the year in question.

Solving Annuity Problems

Suppose someone aged 70 wanted to be assured of a given income for the rest of his life, let us say $10,000 per year. He would go to a life insurance company. Life insurance companies sell annuity contracts, a special form of which is called a *lifetime annuity*. Insurance companies estimate average life expectancy for persons of all ages. Persons 70 years old might have a life expectancy of, say, 15 more years. Some 70 year olds will live longer, some not so long, and the average will be 15.

An insurance company would base the annuity contract's purchase price on a 15 year life expectancy and a particular rate of interest based on what it could expect to earn over the following 15 years. Let us assume that this rate is 6 percent for purposes of illustration. What would the purchase price be? Ignoring commissions and other expenses, the purchase price would be the present value of $10,000 per year for 15 years at 6 percent:

$$PV = \sum_{t=1}^{15} \frac{\$10,000}{(1.06)^t}$$

Using Table II at the back of the book, in the 6 percent column opposite 15 years we find a PV factor of 9.712. So the purchase price of the annuity would be

$$PV = \$10,000 \times 9.712$$

$$= \$97,120$$

Suppose our 70 year old retiree does not have $97,000 because he had saved only $50,000. How large an annual annuity could he purchase?

The answer is as follows:

$$PV = \text{Annual payment} \times \text{PV factor of an annuity}$$

$$\therefore \text{Annual payment} = \frac{PV}{\text{PV factor}}$$

$$= \frac{\$50,000}{9.712}$$

$$= \$5,148.27$$

We find that $50,000 would purchase a lifetime annuity of $5,148.27 per year for a 70 year old person with a life expectancy of 15 years.

Future Value of an Annuity

Suppose you plan to work hard over the next 4 years and anticipate saving $1,000 each year. You plan to put your savings in the bank at 6 percent interest. If your plan is to deposit $1,000 at the end of each of the next 4 years, how much would you have at the end of the fourth year? We can calculate the final sum by applying expression (2) to each of the $1,000 deposits individually:

$$FV = \$1,000 \times (1.06)^3 + \$1,000 \times (1.06)^2 + \$1,000 \times (1.06) + \$1,000$$

$$= \$4,374.62$$

Table IV at the end of the book gives future value factors for annuities. As an exercise, work out the answer to the above problem using the tables. The approach is analogous to that used in the case of present value:

$$FV = \text{Payment} \times \text{FV factor}$$

The tables can also be used to calculate the amount that would have to be deposited each period to provide a given sum at the end of some future period.

The future value of an annuity is discussed in more depth in Appendix A at the end of this chapter.

Perpetuities

An annuity that goes on forever is called a *perpetuity*. The present value of a perpetuity of $A per year is

$$\text{PV (Perpetuity)} = \frac{A}{1+i} + \frac{A}{(1+i)^2} + \cdots + \frac{A}{(1+i)^\infty}$$

$$= \sum_{t=1}^{\infty} \frac{A}{(1+i)^t}$$

$$= A \sum_{t=1}^{\infty} \frac{1}{(1+i)^t} \qquad (8)$$

By resorting to some advanced mathematics, we can determine that the infinite series in expression (8) adds up to a finite sum:

$$\sum_{t=1}^{\infty} \frac{1}{(1+i)^t} = \frac{1}{i} \qquad (9)$$

Hence,

$$\text{PV (Perpetuity)} = \frac{\$A}{i} \qquad (10)$$

To illustrate, the present value of $5 per year forever at a 6 percent discount rate is

$$\text{PV} = \frac{\$5}{0.06} = \$83.33$$

We will find later that the valuation expression for a perpetuity, (10), is very useful in valuing certain kinds of income streams in practice.

The Present Value of Irregular Flows

Having dealt with the basic arithmetic of present value, let us apply what we have learned in order to calculate the present value of the cash benefits expected from a hypothetical business investment.

A firm is planning to purchase and install some new equipment at a cost of $500,000. It is expected that the equipment will have an economic life of 5 years, after which it will be sold in the second-hand market, bringing in an expected $60,000 in year 5. During the next 5 years, the firm has a fixed-price 5 year contract to manufacture a definite number of artillery shells for the United States Army. The benefit related to the new equipment is an expected cost-saving each year because having the equipment will save the firm material, energy, and labor costs. The engineering and accounting departments estimate that the year-by-year after-tax cash saving in these costs will be as follows:

Year 1	$80,000
Year 2	100,000
Year 3	125,000
Year 4	150,000
Year 5	200,000

The annual benefits rise over time because material costs, energy costs, and labor costs are all expected to rise rapidly.

The firm has set a 15 percent per annum after-tax rate as a target on cost-saving investment. What is the present value of the benefits expected from the equipment?

To answer this question we have to find the present value, at 15 percent a year, of the stream of cost-savings as estimated. In addition, we must remember that the used equipment is to be sold for an estimated $60,000 at the end of year 5.

The calculation is shown in Table 9-5. Column 1 shows the stream of benefits (including the sale value of the used equipment in year 5). Column 2, drawn from present value Table I at the end of this book, shows the present value factor at a 15 percent discount rate. Assuming for computational simplicity that the benefits accrue at the *end* of each year, column 3 shows the present value of each year's total benefit. The sum of those benefits is shown at the footing of column 3. The present value of all the benefits is $442,470. This is *lower* than the cost of the equipment ($500,000), so the proposed investment should be rejected. In Chapter 11 we will discuss the use of the present value for decision-making in more depth.

Table 9-5   Calculating the PV of a Project's Benefits

Year	Expected Benefit (dollars)	PV Factor (@ 15 percent/year)	PV of Benefits (column 1 × column 2)
1	$80,000	0.870	$69,600
2	100,000	0.756	75,600
3	125,000	0.658	82,250
4	150,000	0.572	85,800
5	260,000	0.497	129,220
Total (1–5)			$442,470

Solving for an Unknown Interest Rate

So far we have solved problems in which the interest rate is known, and we calculated either the present value or the future value of the payments. Suppose the problem is to determine the interest rate necessary to provide a given present or future sum. Consider first a simple case in which we have \$100 and want to invest it to produce \$115 at the end of 2 years. Applying expression (3), we get

$$100 = \frac{\$115}{(1 + i)^2}$$

We must solve for *i*. Rearranging, we get

$$(1 + i)^2 = \frac{\$115}{\$100}$$

$$1 + i = \sqrt{\frac{\$115}{\$100}}$$

$$i = \sqrt{\frac{\$115}{\$100}} - 1$$

$$= 1.072 - 1 = 0.072$$

We would have to invest the \$100 at 7.2 percent per year (compounded annually) to produce \$115 by the end of 2 years.

As we will see later, this calculation provides the basis for determining the *rate of return* on an investment. Suppose we have an investment that requires an outlay of \$100 now and promises to pay \$115 in 2 years. What is the rate of return? The answer is 7.2 percent per year, calculated as shown above.

We can also make the rate of return calculation using PV Table I.

$$PV = FV \times PV \text{ factor}$$

$$PV \text{ factor} = \frac{PV}{FV}$$

$$= \frac{\$100}{\$115} = 0.870$$

Looking in Table I on the 2 year line, we see the following: At 7 percent the PV is 0.873; at 8 percent it is 0.857. Therefore, the interest rate corresponding to a PV factor of 0.870 must be between 7 percent and 8 percent. We can find it via interpolation.

$$\text{Rate} = 7 + \frac{0.873 - 0.870}{0.873 - 0.857}$$

$$= 7 + 0.188$$

$$= 7.188 \text{ percent}$$

We can perform the same calculation with an annuity. Suppose an annuity of $1,000 per year for 3 years costs $2,500. What is the implied rate of return? Using Table II, we have:

$$PV = \text{Payment} \times \text{PV factor}$$

$$\$2,500 = \$1,000 \times \text{Factor}$$

$$\text{Factor} = \frac{\$2,500}{\$1,000}$$

$$= 2.500$$

In Table II, we find on the 3 year line

n	At 9 percent	At ?	At 10 percent
.	.	.	.
.	.	.	.
.	.	.	.
3	2.531	2.500	2.487

By interpolation we find the unknown rate

$$\text{Rate} = 9 + \frac{2.531 - 2.500}{2.531 - 2.487}$$

$$= 9 + 0.705$$

$$= 9.705 \text{ percent}$$

If we had an opportunity to invest $2,500 and earn $1,000 per year for 3 years, we would say the investment promises a rate of return of 9.705 percent per year. In a later chapter we will develop this method of calculating return, and we will refer to it as the *internal rate of return* of an investment.

The General Discounted Cash Flow (DCF) Valuation Model

The basic expression for present value, expression (5), is of fundamental importance in the remainder of this book. We will refer to it as the *general DCF valuation model*. Let us restate it here:

$$PV = \sum_{t=1}^{n} \frac{C_t}{(1 + i)^t}$$

This expression says, simply, that the value of an asset is the sum of all the payments that the asset will generate in the future, discounted back to their present value. The DCF valuation model is quite general in its applicability and can be used in any situation in which value is a function of future cash payments. For example, the value of a bond is simply the present value of all interest and principal payments that the holder of the bond expects to receive. The value of a share of stock is the present value of all payments that its holder expects to receive, namely, dividends and the proceeds from sale at some future date. The value of an entire company may be thought of as the present value of all future cash flows that the company will generate. Again and again throughout this book, we will find applications for the DCF valuation model. In Chapter 1, we noted that the general criterion for financial management decisions is value maximization, that is, we do things that increase value and avoid things that decrease it. The DCF valuation model provides the basic conceptual framework for the valuation criterion. In the next chapter, we will discuss the DCF valuation model in more depth.

The Discount Rate

It is apparent from the preceding discussion that the discount rate plays a central role in discounted cash flow analysis. We should be absolutely clear as to just what the function of the discount rate is. It is the *rate of exchange between time periods*. If we know the rate of exchange over time, we can use it to discount a stream of payments to a single present value that is exactly equivalent in value, or to compound the stream forward to a single terminal value that also is equivalent in value. The discount rate thus is the *rate at which we can shift cash flows between time periods without changing their present value*.

Consider the following cash flows:

	Period	
1	2	3
$200	$350	$250

Assuming, for example, that 6 percent represents the rate of exchange over time, we can apply expression (5) to shift the three flows back to period 0 and thereby determine the present value of the stream, which we find to be $710. Receipt of $710 at period 0 is equivalent to receiving the three flows at the dates indicated. Likewise, we can shift the three flows forward in time, finding them equivalent to $846 received at the end of period 3. We can represent the alternative cash flow patterns as shown in Table 9-6.

Table 9-6 Equivalent Cash Flows

	Period			
	0	1	2	3
A	710			
B		200	350	250
C				846

Provided that we have correctly chosen the discount rate, the three cash flow patterns *A, B,* and *C* in Table 9-6 are exactly equivalent; we would as soon receive one as another. This example demonstrates the real utility of discounted cash flow. With proper choice of the discount rate, we can shift cash flows through time while maintaining value equivalence. Complex patterns of cash flows can be reduced to an equivalent single figure, and decisions with respect to those cash flows are made far easier. If, for example, we can obtain pattern *B* in Table 9-6 for an outlay less than $710, we know that we have a good investment.

In practical applications, how do we know what rate to use as the discount rate? This is one of the most difficult questions we face. In the next chapter, we will discuss valuation under uncertainty. Then in Chapter 11 we will discuss the use of DCF techniques for making decisions. There we will see that the choice of the discount rate is equivalent to setting the required rate of return for an investment, a critical element in making investment decisions. The problem is all the more complex because, as noted earlier, the return on an investment must compensate the investor not only for the passage of time but also for uncertainty. The problem of setting the required rate of return in an uncertain world is dealt with in Chapters 13 and 14.

Summary

Because cash flows generated by investment in long-lived assets usually extend over many time periods, special techniques are necessary to analyze capital investment decisions, techniques that take account of the *time value of money.*

The notion that money has time value is a basic concept of finance. The sooner funds are received, the sooner they can be put to work in other new investments. If funds are received later rather than sooner, the recipient foregoes the interest that could have been earned in the meantime. Therefore, to analyze the economic worth of investment opportunities, we must take account of the *timing* of cash flows as well as their amounts.

The rate of interest represents the rate at which present funds can be exchanged for future funds, and vice versa. The interest rate is the rate of exchange over time that provides the tool for adjusting cash flows to account for differences in timing. The concept of *compound interest* provides the basic computational technique.

The future value of a sum of money equals its present value compounded forward through time at the appropriate interest rate. Similarly, the present value of a future sum is its future value discounted back to the present. The present value of a stream of payments is the sum of the present values of its separate elements. In the case of level streams (annuities), the computation of present value can be simplified using present value tables.

The general discounted cash flow (DCF) valuation model expresses the value of an asset as the sum of all payments that the asset will generate, discounted to their present value. The DCF valuation model provides the basic analytical framework for investment decisions. Using DCF, a complex pattern of cash flows extending over many time periods can be reduced to a single figure that is equivalent in value. The present value of a stream of cash inflows can be compared to the outlay required to generate it. Similarly, two or more alternative investments (each of which generates a complex cash flow stream) can be reduced to present values and compared directly. Via DCF, the evaluation of complex cash flow patterns is greatly simplified.

Sample Problem A

Calculate the present value of the cash flows given below assuming:

1. a 5 percent discount rate, compounded annually
2. an 8 percent discount rate, compounded semiannually

End of Year	Cash Flow
1	$1,000
2	2,000

Solution

1. The present value of these cash flows can be found by using either the present value formula or Table 1 at the end of the text.
    Using the present value equation, we find:

$$PV = \frac{\$1,000}{(1.05)^1} + \frac{\$2,000}{(1.05)^2}$$

$$= \$952.38 + \$1,814.06$$

$$= \$2,766.44$$

Using the present value factors given in Table I:

$$PV = \$1,000 \times (PV \text{ factor for } \$1: n = 1, 5 \text{ percent})$$
$$+ \$2,000 \times (PV \text{ factor}: n = 2, 5 \text{ percent})$$

$$= \$1,000 \, (0.952) + \$2,000 \, (0.907)$$

$$= \$952.00 + \$1,814.00$$

$$= \$2,766.00$$

The difference between the two results is due to rounding.

2. With interest compounded semiannually, the interest rate per period becomes $0.08/2 = 4$ percent. We can write the cash flow pattern in the following manner:

	End of			
	6 months	12 months (1 year)	18 months	24 months (2 years)
Cash flow	0	$1,000	0	$2,000

We can substitute these cash flows into the present value equation to find their present value:

$$PV = \frac{\$0}{(1.04)^1} + \frac{\$1,000}{(1.04)^2} + \frac{\$0}{(1.04)^3} + \frac{\$2,000}{(1.04)^4}$$

$$= \$924.56 + \$1,709.61$$

$$= \$2,634.17$$

Using Table I:

$$PV = \$1,000 \times (PV \text{ factor: } n = 2, 4 \text{ percent})$$
$$+ \$2,000 \times (PV \text{ factor: } n = 4, 4 \text{ percent})$$

$$= \$1,000 \ (0.925) + \$2,000 \ (0.855)$$

$$= \$925 + \$1,710$$

$$= \$2,635.00$$

Note that in using the table, our period is now ½ year and the rate per period is 4 percent. Again, the difference in the two results is due to rounding.

Sample Problem B

Calculate the future value of $500 deposited at the end of each year for 5 years in an account offering 5 percent interest, compounded annually.

Solution

In this problem we will have one deposit of $500 in the account earning interest for four periods (the deposit made at the end of year 1), another $500 deposit earning interest for three periods, another for two periods, the fourth deposit for one period, and the final deposit (made at the end of year 5) will not have earned any interest.

Using the future value formula:

$$FV = \$500(1.05)^4 + \$500(1.05)^3 + \$500(1.05)^2 + \$500(1.05)^1 + \$500$$

$$= \$2,762.82$$

Using Table IV, which gives the future value factor for annuities:

$$FV = \$500(FV \text{ factor for annuity: } n = 5, 5 \text{ percent})$$

$$= \$500 \ (5.526)$$

$$= \$2,763.00$$

Questions

1. Why does money have time value?
2. How is the interest rate established, and what does it represent?
3. What happens to the effective rate of interest as the frequency of compounding is increased?
4. What is an annuity? A perpetuity?

5. You have a choice between a savings account that pays 5 percent compounded quarterly and 5 percent compounded daily. Which would you prefer? Why?

Problems

1. $100 today is equivalent in value to how much at the end of 3 years,
   (a) assuming an interest rate of 10 percent?
   (b) assuming an interest rate of 30 percent?
   (c) assuming an interest rate of 0 percent?
2. $100 at the end of 3 years is equivalent in value to how much today,
   (a) assuming an interest rate of 10 percent?
   (b) assuming an interest rate of 30 percent?
   (c) assuming an interest rate of 0 percent?
3. $500 received at the end of each of the next 3 years is equivalent in value to how much today,
   (a) assuming an interest rate of 4 percent?
   (b) assuming an interest rate of 25 percent?
4. $500 received at the end of each of the next 3 years is equivalent in value to how much at the end of the third year,
   (a) assuming an interest rate of 4 percent?
   (b) assuming an interest rate of 25 percent?
5. $100 is to be received at the end of 1 year, $400 at the end of 2 years, and $800 at the end of 3 years. These receipts are equivalent in value to how much today,
   (a) assuming an interest rate of 6 percent?
   (b) assuming an interest rate of 20 percent?
6. $800 is to be received at the end of 1 year, $400 at the end of 2 years, and $100 at the end of 3 years. These receipts are equivalent in value to how much today,
   (a) assuming an interest rate of 6 percent?
   (b) assuming an interest rate of 20 percent?
   (c) Contrast the results with those of Problem 5. Why are the results different?
7. Find the effective rate of interest for the following:
   (a) 8 percent compounded semiannually.
   (b) 8 percent compounded quarterly.
   (c) 8 percent compounded monthly.
8. Calculate (without using tables) the future value of each of the following investments:
   (a) $1,000 invested for 2 years at 4 percent per year, compounded annually.
   (b) $1,000 invested for 1 year at 4 percent per year, compounded semiannually.

(c) $4,000 invested for 6 months at 8 percent per year, compounded quarterly.

(d) $2,000 invested for 10 months at 6 percent per year, compounded monthly.

9. Calculate (without using tables) the present value of the following cash flows:

   (a) $1,000 to be received at the end of 2 years at 6 percent compounded annually.

   (b) $4,000 to be received at the end of 1 year at 4 percent compounded quarterly.

   (c) $1,000 to be received at the end of 6 months at 12 percent compounded monthly.

   (d) $3,000 to be received at the end of 2 years at 8 percent compounded semiannually.

10. Rework Problem 9 using the present value tables.

11. Calculate the present value of the following stream of payments assuming discount rates of 4 percent, 8 percent, and 12 percent.

Period	Cash Flow
1	$300
2	400
3	600
4	100

12. Calculate the present value of the following annuities if the discount rate is 8 percent:

   (a) $1,000 per year for 5 years.

   (b) $3,000 per year for 7 years.

   (c) $1,000 every 6 months for 2 years.

   (d) $500 per quarter for 3 years.

13. Find the present value of the cash flows shown using a discount rate of 8 percent.

Year	Cash Flow
1–4	$100
5	200
6	300
7–15	100
16	400

14. Calculate the price of a 10 year bond paying a 6 percent semiannual coupon on a face value of $1,000 if the yield to maturity is 8 percent.

15. Consider cash flows of $100 at the end of year 1, $300 at the end of year 2, and $200 at the end of year 3. Assuming an interest rate of 10 percent, calculate the single amount that is equivalent in value
    (a) if received today.
    (b) if received at the end of year 1.
    (c) if received at the end of year 2.
    (d) if received at the end of year 3.

16. Consider cash flows of −$200 at the end of year 1, −$100 at the end of year 2, $100 at the end of year 3, and $300 at the end of year 4. Calculate the present value of these cash flows
    (a) at an interest rate of 5 percent.
    (b) at an interest rate of 20 percent.

17. What is the present value of cash flows of $80 per year forever (in perpetuity),
    (a) assuming an interest rate of 8 percent?
    (b) assuming an interest rate of 10 percent?

18. The Canadian Pacific Railroad has outstanding an issue of 4 percent perpetual bonds, that is, bonds that have no maturity and promise to pay $20 semiannually forever. If the market rate of interest is 9 percent per year (compounded annually) for bonds of this risk class, at what price should the Canadian Pacific "Perpetual 4's" sell?

19. As a graduation present, a wealthy relative has given you $5,000 to be put into one of three investment opportunities. The cash flows generated by each investment are given in the table below. If you must invest the entire $5,000 in only one of these alternatives and if all three have the same risk, which alternative offers the highest rate of return? (Assume you cannot sell your rights to these opportunities and that you will hold any investment to its maturity in year 5.)

	Cash Flows Received (end of year)				
Investment	1	2	3	4	5
A	$1,500	$1,500	$1,500	$1,500	$1,500
B	650	650	650	650	5,650
C	0	0	0	0	9,000

20. At a New Year's party, a friend approaches you for some financial advice. Your friend is celebrating his 30th birthday and wants to start saving for his anticipated retirement at age 65. He wants to be able to withdraw $10,000 from his savings account at the end of each year for 10 years following his retirement (the first withdrawal will be at the

end of his 65th year). Your friend is very risk averse and will only invest his money in the local savings bank, which offers 8 percent interest compounded annually. He wants to make equal, annual deposits at the end of each year in a new savings account he will establish for his retirement fund.

(a) If he starts making these deposits at the end of this year and continues to make deposits until he is 65 (the last deposit will be at the end of his 64th year), what amount must he deposit annually to be able to make the desired withdrawals upon retirement?

(b) Suppose your friend has just inherited a large sum of money and has decided to make one lump sum payment at the end of this year to cover his retirement needs rather than making equal annual payments. What amount would he have to deposit?

21. Your bank has offered you a $15,000 loan. The terms of the loan require you to pay back the loan in five equal annual installments of $4,161.00. The first payment will be made a year from today. What is the effective rate of interest on this loan?

22. You have purchased a new $8,000 sailboat and have the option of paying the entire $8,000 now or making equal, annual payments for the next 4 years, the first payment due 1 year from now. If your time value of money is 7 percent, what would be the largest amount for the annual payments that you would be willing to undertake?

23. Suppose you have decided to start saving money to take a long-awaited world cruise, which you estimate will cost you $6,000. You want to take your cruise 5 years from today. The savings account you established for your trip offers 6 percent interest, compounded annually.

(a) How much will you have to deposit each year (at year-end) to have your $6,000 if your first deposit is made 1 year from today and the final deposit is made on the day the cruise departs?

(b) How much will you have to deposit if the final deposit is made 1 year before the cruise departs?

(c) Suppose the cost of living increases 4 percent per year over the next 5 years. What would be the effective purchasing power in year 5 of your deposits calculated in part (a)?

Appendix A: Annuities

We discussed annuities earlier in this chapter. An annuity is simply a level stream of payments. In this appendix we go into more detail.

The basic expression for the present value of an annuity is

$$\text{PV (annuity)} = \sum_{t=1}^{n} \frac{A}{(1+i)^t} \tag{A1}$$

where A is the amount of the annuity each period and i is the interest rate per period. Here we are assuming that the amount A is received at the end of each period. When the payments are received or paid at the end of each period, the annuity is called an *ordinary annuity*. An annuity the payments of which are received or paid at the beginning of each period is called an *annuity due*. We will discuss only ordinary annuities in this appendix.

Expression (A1) can be rearranged to give

$$\text{PV (annuity)} = A \sum_{t=1}^{n} \frac{1}{(1+i)^t} \tag{A2}$$

The summation adds up the present value factors for n years at i percent. As we noted earlier in this chapter, Table II at the end of the book is constructed using expression (A2) with A equal to $1.

Technically, the summation in expression (A2) is a geometric progression that adds up to a finite sum. Expression (A2) can be written as follows:

$$\text{PV (annuity)} = A \left[\frac{1 - (1+i)^{-n}}{i} \right] \tag{A3}$$

When annuity tables (those in Table II at the end of this book) are not available, expression (A3) can be used to solve any type of ordinary annuity problem.

For example, suppose someone wishes to borrow $40,000 via a mortgage loan in order to buy a house. A savings and loan association offers terms of 10.5 percent annual interest and monthly payments over 25 years. What would the monthly payment be? We apply expression (A3) and solve for A. In this case, i will be $10.5 \div 12 = 0.875$ percent per period and n will be $12 \times 25 = 300$ periods.

$$A\text{(payment)} = \frac{40,000}{\left[\dfrac{1 - (1.00875)^{-300}}{0.00875} \right]}$$

$$= \$377.67 \text{ per month}$$

(1)

A/ 100 × 1.331 = $ 133.^{10} ✓ $ 133.^{10}

B/ 100 × 3.648 $\overset{1.331}{}$ = $ 497.^{10} ✗ (Future Value)
(Compound Interest)
Table III

C/ 100 × 0 = $100. — ✓

? 100
1.30
× 3
2,197 × 100 = 219.^{70}
100. —

(2)

A/ 100 × .751 = 75.^{10} ✗ (Table I)

B/ 100 × .37 = 133. ✗

C/ 100 + 0 = 100 ✓

(Present Value of $1.00 from now Table I)

$100
1.30
$\frac{1}{3}$ = 1,455 $\frac{75.^{10}}{45.^{20}}$

100

(3)

A/ 500 × 2,775 = 1387.^{50} ✓ (Cream of Flour) 1387
table II

5/ 100 — 877 — 871 —

(10)

A/ 1000 2yrs @6% = 1000 x .896 = 896 ✓

B/ 9000 14yr C 4% Qtrly = $\left(4\% \div 4 = 1\% \right)$ 9000 x (N= 4-% = 1) = 3844 ✓

C/ 1000 (6mos) @ 12% Monthly = $\left[12\% \div 12 = 1\% \right]$ 6 periods = 246 = 246 ✓

D/ 3000 2yrs @8% Semi = $\left(8\% \div 2 = 4\% \right)$ 3000 x .9... =
Periods 4@ 4% = .855 = 2565 ✓

(11)

Periods	Flow	4%	8%	12%
1	300	.296		
2	400	.926		
3	600	.858		
4	100			
		$1271.00	$1170	$1077

(12)

$3993

/4 @ 3.993

$3993

(14) Annuity
yrs   Cash Flow   PV Factor

6%

1-20 pmts   30   13.59
            60   6.71

1-20

8% (yr 10)
    $1000   .463

$402.60

463.00

$ 828.00

= Bond pays 6% ($60/yr) regardless of what it sells for.

(15)

(16) yr   Cash flow   PV factor 5%   PV

1   -200   .952   -

2   -100   .907   -

3   +100   .864   +

4   +300   .823   +

NPV +$250

-3350 @ 20%

D/

$287

(2% x 12 qtrs = 10.575)

T/R	Flow	PV Factor	P Value
1-4	100	3.31	331
5	200	.691	131.731
6-15	300	.630	189
7-c	100	3.354	323.70
16	400	.299	119.60
			1169.70

Stream 1-16   100
5   100 additional
6   200 additional
16   300 additional

8,560   1-15
5,200   1-7
3,354

4/ A/ 500 × 3.122 = 1561.— ✓ 1561

B/ 500 × 3.122 (2.6)(20)(3) = 3396.⁵⁰ ✗ 1561

✗ 1906

5/ A/ 100 (1 yr)
400 (2 yr)
800 (3 yr) × 6%

× .943 = 94.³⁰ .943 — 943 ✓
× 1.833 = 733.²⁰ 352.⁰⁰
× 2.673 = 2138.⁴⁰ 6.716⁸

3/ 100
400
800 × 20%

× .833
× 1.528
× 2.673 =

.943
.840 = 2965.²⁰ .840
.837

× .943 = 1.528
× .833 = 611.²⁰ .633
× 2.673 = 1665.⁶⁰ = 2380.⁰⁰ .684
.840 .579

1122.³⁰

6/ A/ 800 1
400 2 × 6%
100 3

× .943 = 754.⁴⁰ .943 754.⁴⁰
× 1.833 = 733.²⁰ .840 356.— 84
× 2.673 = 265.³⁰ .837 1194.⁵⁸ ✓

B/ 800 1
400 2 × 20%
100 3

× .833 = 666.⁴⁰ .833 824.⁰⁵
× 1.528 = 611.²⁰ .684
× 2.107 = 210.⁷⁰ = $1488.³⁰ .579
1194.58

Because of higher rent in the first year of concern, money concert.

Future Value of an Annuity

Earlier in this chapter we discussed the *future value* of an annuity. Suppose you might wish to deposit a certain amount each month or each year in a savings account and to determine what the balance will be as of some certain future date. Or at some point in your life you might wish to contract with an insurance company for a qualified *tax-deferred* annuity for retirement purposes. Under such a plan, the payments are deductible for tax purposes, and taxes that would have been due are deferred until some future date.

The future value of any ordinary annuity (payments at the end of the period) can be expressed as

$$FV \text{ (annuity)} = \sum_{t=0}^{n-1} A(1 + i)^t \tag{A4}$$

$$= A \sum_{t=0}^{n-1} (1 + i)^t \tag{A5}$$

Here again, the summation is a geometric progression that adds up to a finite sum:

$$FV \text{ (annuity)} = A\left[\frac{(1 + i)^n - 1}{i}\right] \tag{A6}$$

Suppose you decide to save $1,500 per year for 15 years, under a qualified individual retirement account (IRA) plan and can deposit the money with an insurance company at 8½ percent interest. At the end of 15 years you would have

$$FV \text{ (annuity)} = \$1,500 \left[\frac{(1.085)^{15} - 1}{0.085}\right]$$

$$= \$42,348.40$$

Payment to Produce a Given Sum

Suppose you have a child and you wish to begin immediately saving for his or her college education. You figure that, on the child's 18th birthday, you will need $20,000. You locate an insurance company offering annuity contracts at 8 percent interest. How much would you have to deposit each year (at year-end)? Applying (A6), we find

$$A \text{ (payment)} = \frac{\$20,000}{\left[\dfrac{(1.08)^{18} - 1}{0.08}\right]}$$

$$= \$534.04 \text{ annually}$$

Suppose you wish to make the deposit monthly. Then there are $18 \times 12 = 216$ periods, and the interest rate is $8 \div 12 = 0.667$ percent per period. The monthly payment is

$$A \text{ (payment)} = \frac{\$20,000}{\left[\dfrac{(1.00667)^{216} - 1}{0.00667}\right]}$$

$$= \$41.66 \text{ monthly}$$

Sometimes the payment necessary to produce a given future sum is called a *sinking fund* payment. This term is often used in connection with amounts set aside by corporations to retire a bond at some future date.

Appendix B: Continuous Compounding

Our general expression for future value, expression (1) in the text of this chapter, is

$$W_{t+n} = W_t (1 + i)^n \tag{B1}$$

If we start with \$1, we have at any time n

$$W_n = \$1(1 + i)^n \tag{B2}$$

where n is the number of periods and i is the rate per period. In the text, we considered the cases of semiannual and quarterly compounding. In principle, we can compound as often as we wish, monthly, weekly, daily, hourly, or by the minute! At the limit, we can compound continuously. To explore the effects of increasing the frequency of compounding, let us modify expression (B2) above as follows:

$$W_n = \$1\left(1 + \frac{i}{x}\right)^{xn} \tag{B3}$$

Now we can let i = the rate per year, set $n = 1$ year, and examine the effects of increasing the frequency of compounding. As x increases, we compound more often over shorter invervals. If we let x increase without limit, we find that

$$\lim_{x \to \infty} \left(1 + \frac{i}{x}\right)^{xn} = e^i \tag{B4}$$

where *e* is the constant 2.718.

To illustrate, let us calculate the future value (FV) of $100 at 6 percent per year with interest compounded continuously:

$$FV = \$100 \times e^{0.06} = \$106.18$$

The *effective rate,* if interest is compounded continuously, is 6.18 percent. Compare this figure to effective rates of 6.09 percent if compounded semi-annually and 6.14 percent if compounded quarterly.

In practice, we seldom encounter situations in which interest is compounded continuously, although there have been cases in which savings and loan associations have offered to calculate interest as if it were compounded continuously. There are, however, situations in which an assumption of continuous compounding is useful for analytical purposes. For example, where economic variables grow over time, an assumption of continuous growth is a better model of reality than an assumption of growth in discrete steps. Where a quantity W_0 grows continuously at a rate of *g* percent per period, we can calculate its value *n* periods in the future as

$$W_n = W_0 e^{gn} \tag{B5}$$

For example, $100 growing continuously at 6 percent per year would become, after 4 years,

$$W_4 = \$100 \times e^{0.06 \times 4} = \$127.12$$

For comparison, $100 at 6 percent for 4 years with annual compounding would total $126.25.

It is worth noting that the quantity *e* is the base for the system of natural logarithms, which find wide use in mathematics and engineering as well as in economics. By modifying expression (B4) we can calculate *e* as

$$\lim_{x \to \infty} \left(1 + \frac{1}{x}\right)^x = 2.718281828 = e$$

Valuation in Financial Markets

10

Risk, Return, and Value
Using Market Evidence
Valuation of Equity Securities
The Capital Asset Pricing Model

In Chapter 9 we dealt with the problem of adjusting a stream of future benefits for the *timing* of these benefits. We found that given a *discount* rate that reflects the time value of money, any such stream of benefits, whether level or irregular, can be reduced to a *single* number known as its *present value.* We turn now to the equally important and more difficult matter of how we set the discount rate to be used.

Risk, Return, and Value

Where the benefit stream is predictable with certainty, the discount rate is simply the *time value of money,* generally defined as the rate of interest on a United States government bond that has the same maturity as the maturity of the investment under consideration. But what if the expected benefits from a business investment project cannot be predicted with a high level of certainty? What if there is a potential risk that the level of benefits will be different than the projected level?

Let us take two investments, *A* and *B*, that are available in 1980 and that promise to generate the following benefits 1 year hence in 1981, depending on whether the United States economy is expanding, contracting, or stable in 1981. Table 10-1 shows the range of benefits.

Table 10-1 Range of Benefits

State of Economy	Benefits Promised	
	Investment *A*	Investment *B*
Contracting	$ 90	$ 0
Stable	100	100
Expanding	110	200

Our economic advisors tell us that they think there is an equal one-third chance that *each* of the three conditions will occur in 1981. Which investment is better? Each offers an *average, most likely,* or *expected* benefit of $100. However, the *range* of possible outcomes is far greater for investment *B* than it is for investment *A*.

Now consider the price that investors might be willing to pay for *A* and *B*. A *risk-neutral* investor, indifferent toward risk by definition, would pay the same price for each. A risk-averse investor would pay less for *B* than for *A* because of *B*'s greater uncertainty. Conversely, a risk-preferent investor, someone who likes to gamble, would pay more for *B* than for *A*.

There is convincing evidence that most investors are risk-averse. Some of us occasionally behave *as if* we were risk-preferent; that is, we go to Las Vegas or Atlantic City to gamble. But these excursions are invariably associated with leisure and fun. In our *normal* transactions, we buy insurance by the millions (which is clearly a sign of risk aversion), and we demand higher promised returns from more risky or more uncertain investments. Very clearly, the higher the level of risk and uncertainty of any *future* stream of benefits, the higher the applicable *discount* rate should be in calculating the present value of those future benefits.

The pragmatic question we seek to answer in Chapter 10 is: *How does the financial market place a value on cash flow streams that are uncertain in size? What discount rate does the market apply?*

In a fundamental sense this is *the* central issue in finance. An enormous body of thinking and research has been devoted to finding a good basis for answering this question. What follows explains some of these investigations. The essential logic of this discussion is summarized by the general DCF formula

$$\text{PV} = \sum_{t=1}^{n} \frac{C_t}{(1 + i)^t} \tag{1}$$

Where C_t is the flow of benefits offered by any investment from year 1 to the end of its economic life, year n, i is the percent per annum discount rate, and PV is the present value of the expected benefits. The symbol Σ indicates summation of the terms. As we discovered in Chapter 9, if we have C_t and i, we can calculate PV. Likewise, if we know C_t and PV, we can estimate what i must be. In the case of uncertain benefits, the topic of this chapter, i is no longer simply the rate of interest but is higher to reflect the risk. The market rate of discount for risky flows is the question to which we now turn.

Using Market Evidence

We have little *direct* systematic evidence on what discount rates are applicable to future benefits offered by risky business investments. If every business investment opportunity had a little tag attached to it that told us how risky it is and at what rate its promised benefits should be discounted, the financial manager's life would be simple indeed! But this is not the case. We have to begin elsewhere to find reliable evidence on discount rates.

One place in which we can find a plentiful supply of *indirect* evidence on discount rates is the securities markets. The evidence is indirect because securities markets can provide little or no information on the rates of return required (i.e., discount rates) on individual tangible assets acquired by a firm or an industry. What the market can provide is evidence on rates of return required (i.e., discount rates) on the *securities* that collectively comprise the ownership of a company or an industry. This information does not give us a final answer to our question, but it does provide us with a numerical starting point.

In Chapter 9, we used the general DCF valuation formula to find value (PV) when the benefit stream (C_t) and the discount rate (i) were given. In this chapter, what we try to do is to find the implied discount rate when the benefit stream is known or can be estimated and the value is known. For the securities of a firm. value is the current market price, which in many cases, we can find in the financial pages of a daily newspaper.

The general DCF formulation thus can be used in either of two ways, to find present values or to find the implied discount rate. Let us begin with a simple numerical illustration of the relationships involved.

For example, consider a $1,000, 20 year United States government bond issued in 1977 that carries a coupon rate of 8 percent payable annually.[1] Assume that the "going" rate of interest in 1980 has risen to 9 percent per annum. We can use the DCF formula to tell us what the going prices of the 1977 bond will be in 1980. We would use the formula:

$$V_0 = \sum_{t=1}^{17} \frac{C_t}{(1 + i)^t} + \frac{P_{17}}{(1 + i)^{17}} \tag{2}$$

where V_0 is the present value or market price of the bond now (in 1980); C_t represents the $80 of interest per annum the bond promises to pay each year; and P_{17} is the promised repayment of the $1,000 at maturity 17 years hence. The discount rate, i, is 9 percent a year, that is, 9 percent is the effective yield required in 1980 by the market on a United States government bond. Note again that in the formula, 9 percent must be expressed in decimal form; 9 percent = 0.09.

Using the present value tables given at the end of this book we can see:

1. The present value of a stream of interest of $1 a year for 17 years discounted at 9 percent is $8.544 (Table II, Column 9, Row 17). Therefore the offered stream of $80 a year is worth $80 × 8.544 or $683.52.

---

1. Bonds are typically sold in units of $1,000.

2. The present value of an expected repayment of $1, 17 years hence (when the bond matures) discounted at the required rate of 9 percent a year is $0.231 (Table I, Column 9, Row 17). Therefore, the offered repayment of $1,000, 17 years hence has a present value of $1,000 × 0.231 or $231.

Adding the two present values tells us that the present value of the bond in 1980 is $683.52 + $231 or $914.52.[2] This is the price at which the bond actually would sell in the financial marketplace.

To summarize, the present value (or fair price) of the United States government bond is $914.52 if it offers a *coupon* rate of 8 percent on face value for 17 years in a world that requires a yield of 9 percent.

Alternatively, we can treat the discount rate as the unknown factor. If the bond offers a coupon rate of 8 percent on its face value for 17 years and its price is quoted at $914.52 per thousand dollars of face value, we can use our DCF formula to infer that the required discount rate (or the required effective *yield to maturity* as it is called) must be 9 percent per annum.

Let us outline the arithmetic to make sure that we understand the process involved. The expected cash flow is $80 a year for 17 years plus $1,000 at the end of year 17. The price of the bond (V_0) is $914.52. What is the rate of return the marketplace seems to require on this asset? We have to find this rate either by trial and error or by looking it up in special bond tables (similar to present value tables) prepared for this purpose. In either case, the question is: At what *rate of discount* is the present value of the expected benefits just equal to $914.52? The answer is 9 percent. The proof is as follows:

1. At 9 percent a year, $80 per annum for 17 years has a present value of $683.52.
2. At 9 percent a year, $1,000 17 years hence has a present value of $231.
3. Therefore, at 9 percent a year and only at 9 percent do the total benefits offered by a bond have a present value of $683.52 + $231, or $914.52.
4. Hence, the market required rate must be 9 percent a year.

---

2. In the real world, bond prices are not quoted in decimals, for example, 91.452 per 100 of face value in the example above, but, rather, in fractions of $1/64$ such as $91^{29}/_{64}$ for government bonds and fractions of $1/8$, such as $91^{3}/_{8}$ for corporate bonds. Most, but not all, bonds pay interest on a semiannual basis. Hence, we must use interest tables that are based on semiannual compounding or discounting as opposed to the annual compounding tables shown in the back of this book.

An Extension to Risky Benefits

When we move from the valuation of United States government bonds to the valuation of *less-than-certain* cash flows, the long-term rate of interest (or the risk-free rate of return) is no longer the appropriate discount rate. We have to use a discount rate that takes the higher risk into account. The reason is that investors who are generally risk-averse will demand a higher rate to compensate them for bearing the added risk.

Let us return to the bond used in the example above (which offers $80 a year in interest for 17 years and promises to repay $1,000 in year 17). However, instead of a United States government bond, let us assume that it is a bond issued by a large airline company, which has experienced some financial difficulties in recent years. Also assume that because of the added risk of default, the market requires a rate of 12 percent on the airline bond rather than the 9 percent required on United States government obligations of the same 17 year maturity. We can think of this required rate as consisting of two components: 9 percent, which reflects the pure time value of money; that is, it is the going risk-free rate of interest; the other 3 percent (12 *less* 9) is a premium for the extra riskiness of holding an airline company bond as opposed to a United States government bond. The market is saying, in effect, that it is less than 100 percent certain that the airline will make the promised interest and principal payments on time.

We can find the present value of the price of the airline bond using the same formula as we did before. But instead of using an *i* of 9 percent (the risk-free rate) in the equation, we would use a higher rate *K* or 12 percent (the rate for an investment with the added risk factor). Henceforth, we will use *i* to denote the risk-free rate of interest and *K* to denote rates that also contain a risk premium. Thus, applying the DCF formula, we would get:

$$V_0 = \sum_{t=1}^{17} \frac{C_t}{(1 + K)^t} + \frac{P_{17}}{(1 + K)^{17}} \tag{3}$$

From Table II, the PV of $80 a year for 17 years discounted at a rate of 12 percent is $80 $\times$ 7.120 (Column 12, Row 17) or $569.60 and from Table I, the PV of $1,000 due 17 years hence at 12 percent is $1,000 $\times$ 0.146 (Column 12, Row 17) or $146.00. Thus, the PV of the airline bond (or its market value) will be $569.60 + $146 or $715.60.

Notice that the higher discount rate for a *given* expected stream of benefits produces a lower value. We are now not only discounting for *time* but for the additional burden of *risk-bearing* as well.

Valuation of Equity Securities

We began by applying the DCF valuation formula to find the value (or price) of a riskless stream of finite length, such as that promised by a United States government bond. We then extended the valuation formula to a riskier stream but still of finite length, such as that promised by a bond issued by an airline. We now move one step further to see how the same DCF formulation provides a basis for valuing the stream of benefits associated with owning a firm or a share in that firm. That is what the equity holders of a firm purchase when they acquire common stock. Now we have an even *riskier* stream (unlike a bond, common stock offers no contractual payment) with no *finite* repayment date, (unlike a bond, common stock offers no specified date for repayment of principal).

Does the same general DCF valuation formula apply? It does. It applies to any investment outlay, because all the formula does is allow us to convert a *stream* of expected benefits (or cash flows), whether finite or infinite, riskless or risky, equal or unequal, into a *single* present value. The big difference in using the valuation formula for equity securities is that the future stream of benefits expected on equities is not known and thus has to be *estimated*.

When we are dealing with equity securities (common stock), the process of discounting future benefits to arrive at present value requires us to use a discount rate, K, which reflects both the going rate on riskless investment *plus* an appropriate premium for the extra riskiness of the particular stream we are discounting. This rate, K, is also called the *capitalization* rate, because it allows us to transform a *stream* or *flow* of expected cash flows into a single number called *present value* or simply *value*. In short, in the DCF valuation framework, the *capitalization* rate is simply another term for the *discount* rate.

Perpetual Level Cash Flows: The Earnings Valuation Model

One particular version of the general DCF valuation formula that has been very widely used in connection with equity securities applies to situations in which the expected benefits are estimated in the form of a level stream that flows perpetually. In other words C_t is a level stream and $C_1 = C_2 = C_3 = \cdots = C_n$ for a very long stretch of time in which n is very large (theoretically infinite). The present value of such a stream has the following extremely simple solution:[3]

$$\text{PV} = \frac{C}{K} \qquad (4)$$

3. We discussed the evaluation of perpetuities in Chapter 9. Sample problem 1 at the end of this chapter provides the proof of expression (4).

where C is the size of the annual flow of benefits and K is the discount or capitalization rate. To find the present value of the stream, all we have to do is to divide the expected annual flow by K. For example, if a firm or a security offers to pay us $20 a year forever and we believe it warrants a discount rate of 10 percent (0.10 in decimal notation), the present value of the stream is $20/0.10 or $200. We would pay $200 now to obtain a right to the expected flow of $20 a year forever if our required rate of return (or discount rate or capitalization rate) were 10 percent.

Do such streams exist? Indeed they do. In fact, the stream of earnings E_t generated by a firm's assets is in principle a level perpetual stream. The concept of cash flow C_t used in the original equation includes both a return *of* capital (sometimes called recoupment) and a return *on* capital (also called profit). Unless a sufficient portion of each year's cash flow is reinvested to maintain the future cash-generating power of a firm's assets, C_t must eventually decline. But what if we do set aside just enough from each year's cash flow and reinvest it to maintain *exactly* the original cash-generation power of the firm's assets? We would, by definition, get a steady, level, and perpetual stream. In theory, this is precisely what depreciation accounting is supposed to accomplish. If, in fact, it does so, we will get a level flow. However, after the annual allowance for depreciation (let us call it Z_t) is subtracted from each year's cash flow (C_t), what we have is no longer cash flow in the original sense but, rather, a flow of earnings (E_t), where $E_t = C_t - Z_t$. Hence, the formulation shown in expression (4) is more generally and properly written as

$$PV = \frac{E}{K} \tag{5}$$

Expression (5) is known as the simple *earnings valuation model.* Like all valuation models, it can be used in two ways: (1) If the level earnings stream E_t can be estimated and (2) if K the appropriate discount or capitalization rate can be estimated, expression (5) allows us to estimate the present value of the expected benefit. Alternatively, if the value is known (for example, the market value of a firm's common stock) and the stream of earnings can be estimated, we can find the discount rate at which the market is capitalizing future earnings because[4]

$$K = \frac{E}{PV} \tag{6}$$

---

4. The inverse of the ratio E/PV is widely used for valuation purposes by security analysts in the form of the price-earnings ratio PV/E.

Limitations of the Earnings Valuation Model

Although it is both simple and familiar, the simple earnings model PV = E/K suffers from a serious limitation. It is valid if and only if the stream of expected earnings E_t is level year after year over a very long (theoretically infinite) period of time. If that critical condition does not hold, expressions (5) and (6) do not hold, and their use can lead to results that are seriously misleading.

The conditions under which expected E_t will, in fact, be a level stream are highly restrictive and rarely hold in the real world. These conditions are:

1. *Price stability:* Earnings will not be level unless prices are stable over time, that is, there is no inflation. If inflation is present, two complications occur that will upset the constancy of the earnings stream. First, the nominal level of earnings will rise with inflation. For example, assume that a company is selling 1,000 units of a product. Costs are $1 a unit, and the selling price is $2 a unit. Let *all* prices and costs double. Clearly, earnings will also double from $1,000 a year to $2,000 a year. Actually inflation in the real world affects costs and prices in far more complex ways. In any case, the "constancy of earnings" assumption of the simple earnings model rarely holds. A second complication is that *depreciation* accounting is based on original cost, so with inflation, the principle of setting aside just enough each year to maintain earning power is very difficult to achieve.

2. *Perfect depreciation policy:* Even in the absence of inflation, it is unlikely that depreciation policy can be set so that it exactly maintains a firm's cash generating power as a perfectly level stream. The routine accounting procedures used in practice cannot reflect the complex ways in which the cash-generating power of different assets actually decays over time. In addition, tax and other considerations often influence accounting procedures to a greater extent than does the conceptual objective of achieving a *level* earnings stream.

3. *Retained earnings:* Although, in theory, the entire earnings stream E_t is available to be paid out to shareholders each year as dividends, very few companies do so. The general practice is to retain and reinvest part of earnings each year. So even if the earnings stream from the *original* stock of assets is level, companies are adding to this stock through their retention/reinvestment policy so that all we can observe is a *growing* stream of earnings from a *growing* stock of assets.

It is possible, of course, to adjust and amend the simple earnings valuation model shown in expressions (5) and (6) to allow for the complications listed above, but when we do so, we will no longer have the simple familiar relationships shown in the model. In short, we will end up by abandoning what is known as the "earnings model" anyway.

Growing Cash Flows: The Dividend Model

The virtue of the level, perpetual stream of earnings assumption is the very simple algebraic solutions it allows for both PV and K. A second particular pattern of cash flows for which a simple algebraic solution can be found for PV and K is a stream that grows over time at a regular rate. Let us assume that this growth rate is g percent per year.

Under this assumption, C_t (the cash flow in any period t) may be written as

$$C_t = C_0(1 + g)^t \tag{7}$$

where C_0 is the initial value. If we assume that the stream is to grow at g percent per period forever, we can solve for its present value by substituting expression (7) into expression (1). Thus, we have

$$PV = \sum_{t=1}^{\infty} \frac{C_0(1 + g)^t}{(1 + K)^t} \tag{8}$$

If we solve expression (8), we find that[5]

$$PV = \frac{C_1}{K - g} \tag{9}$$

Note that expression (9) is defined only for $K > g$, that is, only where the discount rate exceeds the growth rate. In such cases, value converges to a finite sum even though we consider an infinite number of periods.

We should note also that expression (9) assumes the cash flow stream grows at a constant rate forever. Forever is a long time, and the situations in which the assumption holds strictly are quite limited. Expression (9) is useful for theoretical insights, and it does provide a better basis for real-world application than the earnings model. But like any simplified model, it too must be used with caution. We turn now to its applicability.

Dividend Valuation Model

Let us now apply the general DCF model to the valuation of a growing firm. The model tells us that value is a function of the future cash flows

---

5. For a proof of this simplification, see sample problem B at the end of this chapter.

to be received. The cash flows that the owner of shares in a firm actually stands to receive are dividends plus the proceeds from the sale of the shares at some future date. The dividend is the only cash payment made by the firm to the shareholder. In most cases, firms pay out a part of their earnings in the form of dividends and retain a part for reinvestment. The value of a share of stock at $t = 0$, denoted by P_0, which we now use instead of PV, thus is given by

$$P_0 = \frac{D_1}{1 + K_e} + \frac{D_2}{(1 + K_e)^2} + \cdot \cdot \cdot + \frac{D_n + P_n}{(1 + K_e)^n}$$

$$= \sum_{t=1}^{n} \frac{D_t}{(1 + K_e)^t} + \frac{P_n}{(1 + K_e)^n} \tag{10}$$

where D_t is the dividend in period t, P_n is the price at which the share is expected to be sold at the end of the final period, and K_e is the rate of return required by the market on the firm's stock. Note that the value of the shares depends only on cash payments that the holder expects to receive.

On what does the value of the share in period n depend? It depends on dividends to be received from that point on to some point further into the future, and proceeds from sale at that (further) point. Value at that further point in turn depends on dividends from that point on. So we can say that the value of a share of stock is simply the present value of all future dividends we expect to be paid on the share, that is,

$$P_0 = \sum_{t=1}^{\infty} \frac{D_t}{(1 + K_e)^t} \tag{11}$$

If we make the assumption that the dividend is going to grow steadily at the constant rate g, we can apply expression (9) to get the solution for the *steady-state* version of the dividend valuation model, namely, we have exactly what we found in expression (9)

$$P_0 = \frac{D_1}{K_e - g} \tag{12}$$

where D_1 is the dividend expected in the first year, P_0 is the present value of the stream, and K_e is the discount rate applicable to the expected stream.

We can rearrange expression (12) to express K_e as the discount or capitalization rate in terms of P_0, D_1, and g. Since $P_0 = D_1/(K_e - g)$, we can say that

$$K_e - g = \frac{D_1}{P_0}$$

$$K_e = \frac{D_1}{P_0} + g \tag{13}$$

That is, the discount rate implied by a given dividend rate, D_1/P_0, and a given growth rate, g, is simply the *sum* of the two.

The Earnings Model and the Dividend Model

It is useful to compare the simple earnings model discussed earlier with the dividend model we have just outlined. Reducing both to common terminology we have in the earnings model

$$P_0 = \frac{E_1}{K_e} \quad \text{and} \quad K_e = \frac{E_1}{P_0}$$

In the dividend model

$$P_0 = \frac{D_1}{K_e - g} \quad \text{and} \quad K_e = \frac{D_1}{P_0} + g$$

The two formulas look strikingly similar, and indeed they are similar as we will discover if we explore the nature of the growth term, g. The basic difference is a difference in *form* rather than in *substance*.

By definition the earnings model assumes no growth; that is, it is critically dependent on an assumed earnings stream that is level ($E_1 = E_2$, etc.). The dividend model assumes that part of E_t is reinvested each year and that this continuous reinvestment causes E_t to be a growing stream. It also assumes a constant growth rate g.

How can g be constant? One way is if a company always reinvests a given fraction of its earnings each year at a given rate of return. If this is done (assuming no inflation), the earnings and dividends will both grow at a *fixed* rate, denoted by g in the formula. Let us take a simple numerical example to see why this conclusion must follow from the assumptions.

Assume a company has a value of $1,000 ($P_0 = 1,000$). If it is earning $100 ($E_1 = 100$) and it pays out *all* of its earnings as dividends each year, it will continue to earn $100 a year. Clearly, K_e is 10 percent (or 0.10 in our required notation) because only at $K_e = 0.10$ will E_t be 100 if P_0 is 1,000 or vice versa. Now switch to the *growth model*. Assume the company pays out only *half* of earnings as dividends and retains half of E_1 or $50. It reinvests this $50 so that it yields 10 percent a year. Next year's earnings will grow by 5 percent from $100 to $100 plus $5 (the $5 is the *new* earnings of 10 percent on the *new* investment of $50). This growth rate is equal to the fraction of earnings retained (50 percent) multiplied by the rate earned on each reinvested dollar (10 percent). In other words, the growth rate g is equal to the fraction retained, (let us call it b) times the reinvestment rate (let us call it r). In symbols we have $g = br$. As retention and reinvestment continue, earnings will keep rising at a steady g percent a year. In our example, b is 0.5 and r is 0.10, so g must be 0.05 or 5 percent. Thus, between year 1 and year 2 earnings rise from \$100 to \$105. Given a constant 50 percent dividend payout policy, dividends also rise 5 percent from \$50 to \$52.50. The following year (year 3) the level of earnings will rise again because \$52.50 (one half of total earnings of \$105) will again be retained and reinvested to yield 10 percent a year, thus increasing earnings by another 5 percent from \$105 to \$110.25 (\$105 plus 10 percent of \$52.50 or \$5.25). When the reinvestment rate, r, is exactly equal to the discount rate, K_e, the two models are in fact *identical.* We can see why by using the numerical example above.

According to the earnings model, when E and K_e are given, the value (P_0) is E/K_e or \$100/0.10 or \$1,000. Also if E and P_0 are given, K_e must be 0.10 or 10 percent. According to the dividend model, if E_1, D_1, g and K_e are given, the value of the firm (P_0) is $D_1/(K_e - g)$ or \$50/(0.10 - 0.05) or \$50/0.05 or \$1,000. Also if E_1, D_1, g, and P_0 are given, K_e must be 0.10 or 10 percent because

$$K_e = \frac{D_1}{P_0} + g$$

$$= \frac{\$50}{\$1,000} + 0.05$$

$$= 0.05 + 0.05$$

$$= 0.10 \text{ or } 10 \text{ percent}$$

Variable-Growth Dividend Models

Like the constant (level) earnings model on which it improves, the constant-growth dividend model is an oversimplified depiction of a more complex world. The insights that these models provide are useful, and, in fact, they are widely used to estimate the rate of return required by the marketplace on equity securities. Nonetheless, no simple model can give us the ultimate truth. There will always be situations in which the assumptions of the model do not hold.

The weakness of the constant growth dividend model is its assumption that the observed past growth rate will persist into the future indefinitely. This assumption can be especially misleading when it is applied to companies that have grown very rapidly.

As an extreme example, consider Wheelabrator-Frye, a New Hampshire manufacturer of industrial equipment. According to the Fortune-500 Directory for 1978, the company's earnings per share grew at a rate of nearly 50 percent per annum between 1968 and 1978. A constant growth model simply cannot handle a growth rate of this magnitude.

1. At any reasonable discount rate, that is, one under 50 percent a year, the calculated value of this company will be infinite. The model is simply not applicable.
2. If we take value as given (by the current market price of the stock), we find that the market must be discounting projected dividends at a rate greater than 50 percent a year. Such a conclusion is mathematically correct. But it does not have much meaning.

In any case, common sense alone tells us that we cannot project an observed 50 percent growth rate very far into the future and certainly not to infinity! At 50 percent growth a year, the company's sales (which were $780 million in 1978) will grow past the $300 trillion mark in 30 years! The total gross national product of the United States in 1980 is around $2.5 trillion.

One way to resolve the issue is to use a variable–growth model. Such a model would assume that rapid growth can continue for only a short period into the future, beyond which growth declines to a more normal level close to the growth of the economy as a whole. The problem with this solution is that there are few objective methods for estimating how long supergrowth will occur.

The Capital Asset Pricing Model

Dissatisfaction with the limitations of the earnings model and the variable-growth dividend model led to a search for a more comprehensive explanation for how market values and discount rates are determined in securities markets. Such an explanation was developed in the 1960s. It is known as the *capital asset pricing model* (CAPM), and it represents one of the major recent developments in modern financial theory. Our present purpose is not to discuss the CAPM in detail but only to outline the important insights that it provides to the questions we seek to answer.[6]

1. How do the financial markets set a value on assets that offer risky or uncertain returns? Specifically, how much "additional" return is required when the riskiness of returns increases?
2. How can we measure the degree of risk in quantitative terms?

The CAPM provides a basis for answering both of these questions. In order to concentrate on the two key variables, *expected return* and *finan-*

---

6. Chapters 14 and 15 cover the CAPM and its application in greater detail.

cial risk, the scholars who developed the model used a set of idealized assumptions that do not fully hold in the actual world. However, this does not diminish the importance of the ultimate and pragmatic insights we get from the CAPM. For now, let us set aside the assumptions of the model, the rigor with which it was developed, and many of the complications it covers. What does its essential logic and its conclusions tell us about the relationship between risk and return?

The Market Line

Let us assume that there are only two securities traded in the financial market. The first is a United States government bond that offers investors a definite rate of return over the succeeding year. Let us call this the risk-free rate i. The rate changes from 1 year to another, but whatever rate is offered is guaranteed for the year ahead. Let us assume that in 1980 $i = 9$ percent.

The second security is a share in an all-equity fund or portfolio that includes all of the stocks contained in the Standard and Poor's 500 stock average and in the same proportion. Let us call this security the *market portfolio.* The rate of return offered by this security, which we will denote as K_m, cannot be predicted with certainty. Let us assume that the mean or average rate *expected* in 1980 (i.e., the most likely rate) is 15 percent, but it is possible that the actual rate could turn out to be much higher or much lower.

What can we say about the risk or uncertainty associated with the two securities? The market portfolio is clearly riskier than the bond, but how can we quantify the difference? For now, there is no need to develop a specific measure of risk. Let us simply denote the risk of the bond as zero units and the risk of the market portfolio as 100 units.

We can now explore the risk/return relationship that exists in the financial market. In Figure 10-1, we can plot two points, A and B.

A portfolio that contains only risk-free bonds offers an expected rate of 9 percent in our example, with zero risk on our scale. Therefore, we show it as point A on the graph. A portfolio that contains only the equity security (the market portfolio) offers an expected rate of 15 percent in our example, with a risk arbitrarily denoted as 100 units. Therefore, we show it as point B on the graph.

Now, think of other possible portfolios that can exist in this market, that is, portfolios containing different mixtures of the two securities—for example, portfolios invested 90 percent in bonds and 10 percent in stocks, 80 percent in bonds and 20 percent in stocks, and so on. Each of these mixed portfolios will offer a different expected rate and a different degree in risk. In each case, the expected rate will be a weighted average of the basic rates, 9 percent and 15 percent, expected from the two component

Figure 10-1 The Market Line

parts of whatever mix is chosen. The overall risk of each selected mix will also be a weighted average of its two components. For example, a portfolio composed of 50 percent bonds and 50 percent stocks will offer an expected rate of (9 percent × 0.50) + (15 percent × 0.50) or 12 percent and involve a risk of (100 × 0.50) + (0 × 0.50) or 50 units on our scale. We show this particular portfolio as point *C* in Figure 10-1.

Arithmetic tells us that the risk/return combination for all the bond-stock mixtures we can possibly hold will lie on a straight line connecting points *A* and *B*. Table 10-2 shows these risk/return relationships for selected mixes. Column 1 of the table shows the selected portfolio mixes. (It indicates the percentage of the portfolio held in bonds, with the rest held in stocks.) Column 2 shows the expected rate of return from each mix. Column 3 shows the risk (in units) associated with each mix. Finally, column 4, which is derived from column 2, shows the premium in the required expected rate (over and above the risk-free rate of 9 percent) as we move from a riskless all-bond mix to an all-stock mix.

Table 10-2 Expected Return and Risk

(1) Portfolio Mix (percent in bonds)	(2) Expected Rate of Return (percent)	(3) Risk (units)	(4) Premium Required (percent)
100	9.0	0	0
90	9.6	10	0.6
80	10.2	20	1.2
70	10.8	30	1.8
60	11.4	40	2.4
50	12.0	50	3.0
40	12.6	60	3.6
30	13.2	70	4.2
20	13.8	80	4.8
10	14.4	90	5.4
0	15.0	100	6.0

The relationship between the premium in the expected rate and the risk involved is clearly a linear one; that is, the ratio of the expected premium to the risk is *constant*. All mixes offer a risk/return combination that must lie on the line connecting points *A* and *B*. This line, which is generally referred to as the *market line,* gives us a quantitative relationship between return and risk even though we have not chosen a specific way of measuring risk itself except in artificial units.[7]

The Market Risk Premium

Let us move to a more generalized description of the CAPM. Assume the following:

1. Investors are risk-averse; not all investors perhaps, but the ones who set prices in financial markets are.
2. Risk-averse investors will undertake risky investments only if they are compensated for the risk they bear.
3. The greater the perceived risk, the higher the expected return must be.
4. The logic of the market line makes the tradeoff between risk and

---

7. When specific risk measures are chosen, the generalized market line of Figure 10-1 becomes either the *capial* market line or the *security* market line, depending on the particular risk measure used. The distinction is not important to our discussion here. For a discussion of these different risk measures and different versions of the market line, see W. F. Sharpe, *Portfolio Theory and Capital Markets* (New York: McGraw-Hill, 1970).

return explicit by providing a measure of just how much additional return is expected for each additional increment of risk.

In general, if i is the risk-free rate of return, K_m is the expected rate of return on the market portfolio of equities, and S_m is the risk of the market portfolio, we can say that the premium π required by the market on the market portfolio relative to the risk-free rate is given by:

$$\pi_m = K_m - i \tag{14}$$

Hence, the premium *per unit* of risk is given by

$$\frac{\pi_m}{S_m} = \frac{K_m - i}{S_m} \tag{15}$$

In the numerical example used earlier, π_m was 6 percentage points, and S_m was arbitrarily denoted as 100 units.

The numerical values of K_m, S_m, π, and i have been measured over long periods of time by many careful studies, some of which are discussed later in Chapter 14. But let us continue now with our conceptual discussion of expression (15).

What the logic of the market line tells us is that in a rational market the premium expected on *any* possible portfolio (generally denoted by the subscript j) is proportional to the riskiness of that portfolio. Thus, in symbols we would write

$$\frac{\pi_j}{S_j} = \frac{K_j - i}{S_j} \tag{16}$$

The logic of the market line also tells us that the premium-to-risk ratio is a constant. In symbols

$$\frac{K_j - i}{S_j} = \frac{K_m - i}{S_m} \tag{17}$$

Expression (17) represents an equilibrium condition that must hold in a rational financial market. In theory, investors would buy or sell securities (thus changing the price and the expected rate on each) until each security or mix of securities offers the same *reward-to-risk* ratio, that is, the same expected premium per unit of risk.

We can rearrange expression (17) to get the following:

$$K_j = i + (K_m - i)\frac{S_j}{S_m} \tag{18}$$

In expression (18), the ratio S_j/S_m measures the risk of the *particular* security or asset denoted by j *relative* to the risk of the market portfolio.

Substituting the symbol B_j for the ratio S_j/S_m, we can say

$$K_j = i + (K_m - i)B_j \qquad (19)$$

In expression (19), B_j is the relative risk ratio of a particular security j and is often referred to as its *beta coefficient*. What expression (19) tells us is that the expected return on any specific security j (and hence on any financial asset) is equal to the prevailing basic risk-free rate plus B_j times the prevailing premium on the market portfolio. The B_j factor in the equation measures the potential variability of the return on security j relative to the market portfolio.

To illustrate, let us go back to our original numerical example. Consider a portfolio mix that consists of 50 percent risk-free bonds and 50 percent equities. Such a portfolio would provide a return perceived to be only one-half as variable as the possible outcomes of a market portfolio (which has 100 percent stocks). In short, $B_j = 0.5$. Expression (19) tells us that the expected return on such a portfolio will be

$$K_j = 9 + (15 - 9) \times 0.5$$

$$= 12 \text{ percent}$$

This is exactly the answer we got earlier for point C in Figure 10-1.

The full CAPM is more complicated than the very simplified version we have just outlined. It requires that the risk factors S_m and S_j be measured in very special ways that take into account not only the *variability* in expected returns but also the statistical correlation between variation of the return on the individual security and the variation in the market portfolio. We do not have to go into these complex refinements at this point.[8]

The basic contribution of the CAPM can be summarized as follows:

1. The values (prices) placed on financial assets are determined in the financial market by the actions of investors, lenders, and borrowers competing against one another.
2. Expected returns and perceived risk are related. The market is dominated by risk-averse investors who demand higher expected returns on riskier investments.
3. The market as a whole functions so that all financial assets are, roughly speaking, "equally good buys," that is, prices are set so the reward-to-risk ratio is the same for all.

---

8. An appendix to this book provides an introduction to probability concepts and correlation, and Chapter 15 discusses the role of covariation in the CAPM.

4. For assets *not* traded, for example, tangible assets companies acquire, evidence available from the CAPM and the financial market provide a basis for evaluating whether the expected return promised by a particular asset is a good, bad, or indifferent "buy."

The CAPM as a Theoretical Framework

Basic microeconomic theory uses *profit maximization* as a criterion for measuring performance, judging efficiency, and making decisions. The theory of finance introduces uncertainty and the multiperiod nature of the world and uses *value* as the criterion. Value-maximization is the counterpart of profit-maximization in an uncertain, multiperiod world. The basic valuation criterion is the following: Firms should do things that increase their value and avoid things that decrease it.

But the value of future uncertain income streams is ultimately determined in the marketplace by investors. So we need a market theory of the way values are determined. The CAPM provides a basis for such a theory and thus permits us to extend the microeconomic theory of the firm to a market context under conditions of uncertainty. Without the CAPM, the normative theory of business finance would be incomplete. This theory tells us to maximize the value of the firm; the CAPM tells us how values are determined.

Summary

The value of any asset depends on the future benefits that its owner expects to receive from its use. These benefits come in the form of a stream of future payments. The value of a stream of future payments depends on the size, timing, and degree of uncertainty of those payments.

In general, investors are risk-averse. Because of this aversion to risk, expected return and risk in the financial markets are related: The greater the risk, the greater the return demanded by investors.

The DCF valuation model can be applied to the valuation of securities. Since cash flows generated by securities are uncertain, the discount rate must take account of both time and risk. Level cash flows and cash flows growing at a constant rate represent two special cases.

Values of firms, specifically the values of their outstanding stocks and bonds, are determined in the financial markets by the actions of investors, lenders, and borrowers competing against one another. The capital asset pricing model (CAPM) provides the most general theory of valuation under uncertainty. The CAPM expresses prices and yields of risky assets in terms of investor preferences with respect to time and risk. The CAPM relies on the concept of market equilibrium to derive relationships between return and risk for financial assets. In equilibrium, the market risk premium *per unit of risk* is the same for all assets. The CAPM thus provides a theory of valuation and permits an extension of the microeconomic theory of the firm to a market context under conditions of uncertainty.

Sample Problem A

Show why the formula for present value in the simple earnings model

$$PV = \frac{E_1}{K}$$

is correct if, and only if, E is a perpetual level stream.

Solution

The general DCF expression for present value is

$$PV = \frac{E_1}{1 + K} + \frac{E_2}{(1 + K)^2} + \cdots + \frac{E_n}{(1 + K)^n} \qquad \text{(S1)}$$

If E is a level, perpetual stream, we have $n = \infty$ and

$$E_1 = E_2 = \cdots = E_\infty$$

Thus, the general expression simplifies to

$$PV = \frac{E_1}{1 + K}\left[1 + \frac{1}{1 + K} + \frac{1}{(1 + K)^2} + \cdots + \frac{1}{(1 + K)^\infty} \right] \qquad \text{(S2)}$$

The term *inside* the brackets is a diminishing geometric progression of the general form $(1 + a + a^2 + \cdots + a^n)$ in which the factor a, which is equal to $1/(1 + K)$, is smaller than 1. Algebra tells us the sum of such a progression is given by $1/(1 - a)$. Since $a = 1/(1 + K)$, the sum

$$\frac{1}{1 - a} = \frac{1}{1 - \dfrac{1}{1 + K}} = \frac{1 + K}{K}$$

Therefore, the PV in expression (S2) is equal to $E_1/(1 + K) \cdot (1 + K)/K = E_1/K$. If E is not a level perpetual stream, the simplification does not hold.

Sample Problem B

Knott Manufacturing Company is expected to pay a dividend of $1 per share in 1981 and future dividends are expected to grow steadily at 7 percent per annum. Given the uncertainty of these projections the market "requires" an expected return of 15 percent a year on investments in the company's common stock. Show that Knott Manufacturing Company shares will sell at $12.50 per share in 1980.

Solution

Given the assumptions, the expected dividend stream is

$$\$1, \$1.07, (\$1.07)^2, \cdots, (\$1.07)^n \tag{S3}$$

The present value of this expected stream, discounted at the required rate of 15 percent a year is

$$\text{PV} = \$\frac{1}{1.15} + \frac{1.07}{(1.15)^2} + \frac{(1.07)^2}{(1.15)^3} + \cdots + \frac{(1.07)^n}{(1.15)^{n+1}} \tag{S4}$$

or

$$\text{PV} = \$\frac{1}{1.15}\left[1 + \frac{1.07}{1.15} + \frac{(1.07)^2}{(1.15)^2} + \cdots + \frac{(1.07)^n}{(1.15)^n}\right] \tag{S5}$$

The term inside the square brackets is a diminishing geometric progression of the form $1 + a + a^2 + \cdots + a^n$, which, when $n = \infty$, has a sum of $1/(1 - a)$.

Since $a = 1.07/1.15$,

$$\frac{1}{1 - a} = \frac{1}{1 - \dfrac{1.07}{1.15}}$$

$$= \frac{1.15}{1.15 - 1.07}$$

$$= \frac{1.15}{0.08}$$

The present value of expression (S5) when $n = \infty$ is equal to

$$\text{PV} = \$\frac{1}{1.15} \times \frac{1.15}{0.08}$$

$$= \frac{1}{0.08}$$

$$= \$12.50$$

Questions

1. What determines the value of an asset?
2. Explain what is meant by *risk aversion, risk neutrality,* and *risk preference.*
3. How does risk-averse behavior by investors affect returns in the financial markets?
4. What is the *dividend valuation model?*
5. Who determines the values of firms? Explain.
6. What is the capital asset pricing model? Why is it important to financial management?

Problems

1. The Dow Jones Industrial Average (DJIA) provides information on stock prices, earnings, and dividends for the 30 companies included in the average. On June 18, 1979, the "price" for the DJIA was $839.40; earnings for 1979 were estimated at $124.10. Use the simple earnings model to calculate what rate of return the market was requiring on the stocks of the DJIA companies.
2. DJIA dividends for 1979 were estimated at $49.48. Thirteen years earlier in 1966 dividends were $30.42. Use the dividend growth model to calculate what rate of return the market was requiring on the stocks of the DJIA companies.
3. Explain why the two valuation models in Problems 1 and 2 give different answers to the same question.
4. According to the judgment of an investment banker, the common stock of Eastman Kodak should sell at 12 times current earnings. Translate this statement into what rate of return he thinks the market should expect from an investment in Eastman Kodak stock.

References

K. J. Arrow and R. Lind, "Uncertainty and the Evaluation of Public Investment Decisions," *American Economic Review* **60,** 364–378 (June 1970).

R. A. Brealey, *An Introduction to Risk and Return from Common Stocks* (Cambridge, Mass.: MIT Press, 1969).

R. A. Brealey, *Security Prices in a Competitive Market* (Cambridge, Mass.: MIT Press, 1971).

T. E. Copeland and J. F. Weston, *Financial Theory and Corporate Policy* (Reading, Mass.: Addison-Wesley, 1979).

T. R. Dyckman, B. H. Downes, and R. P. Magee, *Efficient Capital Markets and Accounting—A Critical Analysis* (Englewood Cliffs, N.J.: Prentice Hall, 1975).

E. F. Fama, "Efficient Capital Markets—A Review of Theory and Empirical Work," *Journal of Finance* **25,** 383–417 (May 1970).

M. C. Jensen, "Capital Markets—Theory and Evidence," *Bell Journal of Economics and Management Science* **3,** 357–398 (Autumn 1972).

M. C. Jensen, "The Performance of Mutual Funds in the Period 1945-64," *Journal of Finance* **23,** 389–416 (May 1968).

O. M. Joy and C. P. Jones, "Earnings Reports and Market Efficiencies—An Analysis of Contrary Evidence," *Journal of Financial Research* **2,** 51–64 (Spring 1979).

A. B. Laffer and R. D. Ranson, "Some Practical Applications of the Efficient Market Concept," *Financial Management* **7,** 63–75 (Summer 1978).

W. G. Lewellen and G. A. Racette, "Convertible Debt Financing," *Journal of Financial and Quantitative Analysis* **8,** 777–792 (Dec. 1973).

J. Lintner, "The Evaluation of Risk Assets and the Selection of Risky Investments in Stock Portfolios and Capital Budgets," *Review of Economics and Statistics* **47,** 13–77 (Feb. 1965).

E. M. Miller, "Risk, Uncertainty and Divergence of Opinion," *Journal of Finance* **32,** 1151–1168 (Sept. 1977).

F. Modigliani and R. A. Cohn, "Inflation and the Stock Market," *Financial Analysts Journal,* 24–44 (Mar.-Apr. 1979).

J. Mossin, "Equilibrium in a Capital Asset Market," *Econometrica* **34**(4), 768–775 (Oct. 1966).

N. C. Nielsen, "The Investment Decision of the Firm Under Uncertainty and the Allocative Efficiency of Capital Markets," *Journal of Finance* **31,** 587–601 (May 1976).

M. Rubinstein, "A Mean-Variance Synthesis of Corporate Financial Theory," *Journal of Finance* **28,** 167–182 (Mar. 1973).

J. H. Scott, Jr., "On the Theory of Conglomerate Mergers," *Journal of Finance* **32,** 1235–1250 (Sept. 1977).

W. F. Sharpe, "Capital Asset Prices: A Theory of Market Equilibrium Under Conditions of Risk," *Journal of Finance* **19**(3), 425–442 (1964).

W. F. Sharpe, *Portfolio Theory and Capital Markets* (New York: McGraw-Hill, 1970).

K. V. Smith and J. F. Weston, "Further Evaluation of Conglomerate Performance," *Journal of Business Research* **5,** 5–14 (Mar. 1977).

ANALYZING INVESTMENT OPPORTUNITIES IV

Criteria for Investment Decisions

11

Each year business firms commit huge sums of money for capital expenditures. Within each firm different projects or proposals compete for the scarce funds required for their financing. Within the business sector as a whole, individual firms compete among themselves for access to financing. The business sector also competes against other major claimants of available resources—individuals who wish to use a larger share of current output for consumption or for residential construction; nonprofit organizations that wish to expand or equip universities or hospitals; governments that want to build roads, sewers, or submarines; other countries that want us to direct a larger share of our output to them through grants, loans, and investments.

The decision to select one way of investing capital rather than another is obviously an important one—both for the individual firm that undertakes the decision and for society as a whole. The growth in per capita standards of living depends crucially on how well capital expenditure decisions are made. Thus, the investment decision process has received increasing attention both in theory and in practice.

The distinction between *operating* expenditures and *capital* expenditures is not one of motive. Firms spend money on labor and materials in the expectation of producing additional net revenue. Similarly, they spend money on additional plants and equipment with the same purpose in mind. The real distinction concerns the much longer time horizon involved in capital expenditure decision. Investment in labor, materials, and accounts receivable affects cash flows over relatively short periods of time, usually a year or less. In contrast, investments in fixed assets (or capital assets) affect revenues over much longer time periods—ranging from 3 to 30 years or more.

As with *working* capital decisions, capital expenditure decisions (also referred to as *investment* decisions or *capital budgeting* decisions) require a comparison of costs against benefits. However, the fact that the stream of costs and benefits associated with capital expenditures extends far into the future requires us to use more complex tools and techniques in order to analyze them correctly. Indeed, a large part of modern financial theory has been developed over the past 2 decades in response to the difficult questions posed by the capital investment decision: How should long-term investment opportunities be analyzed? Which investments represent wise and efficient uses of funds and therefore should be undertaken, and which not? It will take us all six chapters of Part IV to cover the central and important question of how scarce capital (and in modern society, capital is the key scarce resource) is allocated among many alternative potential uses.

This chapter deals with the various ways in which investment decision can be approached and the major merits and demerits of each major approach. It assumes that estimates are available for the costs and benefits associated with individual investment proposals, that is, that estimates of a project's cash outflows and inflows are known. It also assumes that the required rate of return for each project (which varies both with conditions in the financial markets and with the degree of uncertainty of each project) is known. In short, the chapter concentrates on how all this information can be used in arriving at a decision to select or reject given capital expenditure proposal or how to select between two or more competing proposals.

The Payback Period

One simple and much used method for analyzing investments, especially in new equipment, is known as the *payback* approach. It asks the question: How soon will the estimated cash flow benefits expected from a given investment repay the initial outlay required for its implementation? In short, the payback period measures the length of time required to recover the initial investment outlay. Suppose an investment of $1,000 generates after-tax cash flows of $500, $400, and $300 over a 3 year period. The investment would be recovered about one-third of the way through the third year, so the payback period is 2.33 years. Where the annual cash inflows are equal, the payback period is equal to the initial outlay divided by the annual benefits expected from it.

It is often useful to know the length of time necessary to recover the initial outlay in an investment opportunity. In general, the shorter the better. However, as a criterion for judging the acceptability of an investment opportunity or its worth relative to other opportunities, payback period has serious shortcomings.

First of all, the payback period does not take account of differences in the pattern of cash flows. Consider the two investment opportunities *A* and *B* in Table 11-1. Both investments have the same payback period,

Table 11-1 Payback Period

Investment	Outlay	Year		
		1	2	3
A	($1000)	$600	$400	$300
B	($1000)	$400	$600	$300

namely, 2 years. However, most people would prefer *A* because the inflow is larger in the first year. Payback does not accurately reflect the time value of money.

Suppose the cash inflows from investment *B* continue beyond the third year, but those of investment *A* do not. The payback method ignores cash flows beyond the payback period—a second serious shortcoming.

A third shortcoming concerns setting the target payback period, or the maximum payback period that is acceptable. If we are to use payback to make decisions, we must set a *maximum acceptable* payback period. Unfortunately, theory provides no guidance as to where to draw the line, and it is not easy to relate payback to a more general criterion such as profit-maximization or value-maximization.

However, payback has its uses as a coarse screening device since it answers a question that is often relevant: How long will it take to recover the outlay? Firms with serious liquidity problems or firms in unstable or highly unpredictable lines of business may find payback a useful initial measure, but most firms have found it necessary to go beyond the simple payback measure before arriving at final decisions.[1]

Accounting Return on Investment (AROI)

The cash inflows or profits generated by any investment will vary with the size or scale of the investment itself. To get a meaningful measure, it is necessary to measure dollar returns in relation to the size of the investment outlay necessary to generate them. Such measures of annual return per dollar of outlay often are referred to as the *rate* of return and expressed in percentage terms.

However, there are many ways to measure rates of return. The calculation involves relating some measure of return to some measure of investment. Since both return and investment can be measured in many ways, rate of return is an ambiguous concept unless care is taken to define the terms precisely.

One widely used measure of return is called the *accounting rate of return,* or *accounting return on investment* (AROI). Accounting return on investment can be calculated as the ratio of accounting net income to the initial investment. Consider an investment of $10,000 for the acquisition of a machine. Assume that the machine has a life of 5 years and will produce revenues of $3,500 per year. Assuming straight-line depreciation, the income statement for the project is as follows:

---

1. For a good analysis of the payback criterion and some arguments in favor of its use, see J. M. Blatt, "Investment Evaluation Under Uncertainty," *Financial Management,* **8,** 66–81 (Summer 1979).

Revenue	$3,500
Cash expenses	500
Depreciation ($10,000 ÷ 5)	2,000
Profit before taxes	1,000
Tax @ 48 percent	480
Profit after taxes	$ 520

Using the $10,000 outlay as the investment, the AROI is 10 percent per year before ·taxes and 5.2 percent after taxes.

One could argue that as cash inflows are received, part of the investment is recovered, and that *average* net investment tied up in the machine is a better measure for calculating the AROI than is the initial outlay. If the machine has no salvage value, it could be said that the average investment, that is, the average amount of unrecouped capital, is not $10,000 but $5,000. Using this figure, the AROI would be 20 percent before taxes and 10.4 percent after taxes. Different depreciation methods, for example, declining balance or sum-of-the years digits, will give different results for profit after tax and average investment, and hence different measures of the AROI.

With some ingenuity, we could devise other ways to measure the AROI in addition to those described above. It is clear that many alternatives exist for measuring both the numerator and the denominator. Simply to label something the "accounting return on investment" is not enough; there is no single correct or standard way to calculate the AROI, so to make it meaningful, we must specify its method of calculation.

To use the AROI for decision-making, we must compare it to some target, or minimum acceptable return. If the project's AROI is above the target, we undertake it; if below, we reject it. Since there are many ways to define the AROI, setting the target represents essentially an arbitrary judgment for which theory provides little guidance. As in the case of payback, the target AROI cannot be related to a more general criterion such as profit-maximization or value-maximization.

A second shortcoming of the AROI concerns the multiperiod nature of most investment decisions. Where, as usually is the case, an investment generates returns over more than one accounting period, the AROI is likely to vary period to period. Which AROI do we compare to the target? Suppose the AROI is above the target in one period and below in another. Which AROI do we go by? If we go to an average AROI over the life of the project, we are ignoring the pattern of returns and the time value of money. This problem represents a major shortcoming of all accounting-based measures; where the returns occur in more than one period, we must choose between ambiguity and ignoring the time value of money. It is for this reason that discounted cash flow techniques have replaced accounting ratios for most of the major capital expenditure decisions being made today.

In view of its shortcomings, what are the uses of the AROI? What questions does it answer? It gives us a measure of accounting profits per dollar of investment. It is appropriate at this point to distinguish between decision criteria and performance measures.

Decision Criteria versus Performance Measures

Performance measures address the question: How well did we do? They are usually past oriented. Decision criteria address the question: What *should* we do? They are *future* oriented.

Accounting measures are very useful for purposes of performance measurement and management control. How much did we earn last year? Were last year's earnings above or below the prior year's earnings? Were they above or below our profit plan? What has been the trend in earnings? What has been the trend in AROI? Are our investments becoming more profitable or less in terms of profit per dollar of outlay? Accounting measures such as profit after tax, earnings per share, and return on investment are essential for answering such questions.

Consider now a different set of questions. Is this investment acceptable? Is investment *A* more desirable than *B* or less? Which investment should we undertake? Accounting-based measures often are not useful for answering questions such as these, especially where the investment affects cash flows in more than one accounting period. From our earlier discussion, we see that the major shortcomings of accounting-based measures as decision criteria are

1. accounting measures often are ambiguous as to method of computation;
2. they cannot be related to a more general theoretical criterion of profit-maximization or value-maximization; and
3. most important of all, they ignore the time value of money.

In order to overcome these difficulties, and especially the last one, financial thinking has shifted more and more to the use of discounted cash flow techniques for measuring expected profitability. A recent survey showed that 86 percent of major United States firms use some form of discounted cash flow for evaluating investment opportunities.[2]

_____

2. See L. D. Schall, G. L. Sundem, and W. R. Geijsbeek, "Survey and Analysis of Capital Budgeting Methods," *Journal of Finance* **33**, 281–287 (March 1978).

Internal Rate of Return (IRR)

The most common discounted cash flow (DCF) measure for rate of return is known as the internal rate of return[3] of an investment. This is the rate that discounts all the cash inflows to exactly equal the outlay.

Consider an investment of $100 that is expected to yield cash inflows of $40, $50, and $30 in 1, 2, and 3 years. We set up the problem as follows:

$$\$100 = \frac{\$40}{1 + R} + \frac{\$50}{(1 + R)^2} + \frac{\$30}{(1 + R)^3} \tag{1}$$

The rate, R, that solves the above equation (discounts the inflows to exactly $100) is the *internal rate of return* (IRR) of the investment.

Let us compare the above procedure to the one we used for calculating present value in Chapter 9. To calculate present value, we start with a given discount rate and solve for the present value of the cash inflows. To calculate the IRR, we do the opposite. We set present value equal to the outlay and solve for the discount rate. The general expression for the case considered above is

$$I = \sum_{t=1}^{n} \frac{C_t}{(1 + R)^t} \tag{2}$$

where I is the outlay and C_t is the cash inflow in each period. The IRR is the rate R that solves (2).

How do we calculate the IRR in practice? In most cases, by trial and error! Equation (2), getting a bit technical, is a polynomial of degree n. Where n is 2 or less, the equation can be solved analytically without great difficulty. Where n is 3 or more (and this usually will be the case, since most investments produce cash flows for a number of years), solving the equation analytically becomes increasingly difficult. Indeed, a direct solution is not possible where n is 5 or larger. So we resort to trial and error using the present value tables.

Let us illustrate the method using the problem in expression (1) above. First, we simply guess at the correct rate. Let us try 12 percent. From the present value tables, we get the results listed in Table 11-2.

---

3. The internal rate of return is also known by several other names, such as DCF rate of return, the investor's method rate, true yield, true yield to maturity, the marginal efficiency of investment and the exact method.

Table 11-2 Finding the IRR—First Try

Year	Cash Flow	Present Value Factor @ 12 Percent	Present Value
1	$40	0.893	$35.71
2	50	0.797	39.86
3	30	0.712	21.35
		Total	$96.92

Since our total is less than $100, we know that we have set the rate too high and thereby discounted (reduced) the inflows too much. If we try 8 percent, we get results listed in Table 11-3.

Table 11-3 Finding the IRR—Second Try

Year	Cash Flow	Present Value Factor @ 8 Percent	Present Value
1	$40	0.926	$37.04
2	50	0.857	42.85
3	30	0.794	23.82
		Total	$103.71

The result is now above $100, indicating that 8 percent is too low. If we try 10 percent, we get a present value of $100.19. At 11 percent, we get $98.57. Hence, the IRR lies between 10 and 11 percent. In many cases, it is sufficient to state that the IRR is "about 10 percent," or "between 10 percent and 11 percent." Where greater accuracy is needed, we can interpolate using the present value tables. The procedure is as follows:

Rate (percent)	Present Value
10	100.19
x	100.00
11	98.57

$$\frac{x - 10}{100.19 - 100} = \frac{11 - 10}{100.19 - 98.57}$$

Solving for x gives 10.12 percent. At that discount rate, PV is $100.

Where the annual cash inflows are all equal (a special case sometimes encountered), we can solve for the IRR directly using the tables for the present value of an annuity. Where the inflows are all equal, we can factor C_t out of expression (2) to get

$$I = C \sum_{t=1}^{n} \frac{1}{(1 + R)^t} \tag{3}$$

$$\frac{I}{C} = \sum_{t=1}^{n} \frac{1}{(1 + R)^t} \tag{4}$$

The right-hand side of (4) is the present value of $1 per year for n years at a rate R. Values for R are tabulated in present value Table II at the end of this book.

Let us illustrate the procedure using an investment of $100 that yields inflows of $38.80 per year for 3 years. Dividing I ($100) by C ($38.80), we get 2.577. Looking in the present value Table II opposite 3 years, we find 2.577 in the 8 percent column. Hence, the IRR of the investment is 8 percent.

Sometimes we encounter investments that have outflows in more than 1 year. How then do we define the outlay, I, in order to apply expression (2)? Let us now define the IRR more generally: *The IRR is the rate that discounts all the cash flows to exactly zero.* Mathematically,

$$0 = \sum_{t=0}^{n} \frac{C_t}{(1 + R)^t} \tag{5}$$

The IRR is the rate R that solves the above expression. Note that we are summing from 0 to n in this case; hence, we include the outlay as well. We can see that expressions (5) and (2) amount to the same thing, but now it is not necessary to define certain cash flows as the outlay. Expression (5) and the definition just preceding it, represent the general definition of the IRR applicable to any situation.

The IRR is a time-adjusted rate of return. Its virtue is its absolute precision as to method of calculation. Its definition is standard and there is no ambiguity as to what is being measured, as was true with the AROI. However, while it is precise as to computation, the IRR has some shortcomings as a decision criterion, as we will see shortly.

Bond Yields

Before discussing the IRR as a decision criterion, we will digress for a moment to discuss an important application of the IRR—calculating the yield to maturity (YTM) of a bond. The yield to maturity of a bond is defined as

$$\text{Price} = \frac{C_1}{1 + y} + \frac{C_2}{(1 + y)^2} + \cdots + \frac{C_n}{(1 + y)^n} + \frac{P_n}{(1 + y)^n} \qquad (6)$$

where $C_1, C_2, \ldots, C_n$ are the interest payments to be received on the bond, P_n is the principal amount to be received at the end of period n, and n is the years to maturity. The YTM is the rate y that solves the above equation, and is simply the IRR on an investment in the bond at its current market price. Bond tables are available that permit calculation of the YTM directly, given the current price, coupon interest rate (the annual interest promised on the bond), and the time to maturity. Indeed, the financial world has been using the IRR to measure the exact yield offered by a bond for at least a century, whereas its use as a measure of the yield offered by business capital investments did not begin until the 1950s.

The reason for briefly discussing bond yields here is to note that YTM is an important application of the concept of IRR and to lay the groundwork for later using the IRR in a different way—in determining the *cost of financing*. The yield to the investor in a bond is the cost to the issuer, or borrower. As we will see later, we can use the concept of the IRR to calculate the cost of any type of financing arrangement—bonds, loans, leases, or stock. The DCF cost is the rate that discounts all the payments that the borrower (or issuer) must make to equal the amount borrowed or financed. We will return to this idea in Part V.

Let us turn to the theory and use of DCF decision criteria for capital expenditure decisions.

Discounted Cash Flow (DCF) Decision Criteria

Required Rate of Return

To make capital expenditure decisions using any quantitative criterion, we must first settle on the minimum acceptable, or required, rate of return (RRR). We will deal with the problem of determining the RRR in subsequent chapters, where we will see that the RRR, or minimum acceptable return, is an *opportunity rate*, that is, it depends on what the investor could earn elsewhere on investments having similar risks. For the present, we will take the RRR as given and will use the symbol K to represent it.

Net Present Value

In Chapter 9 we learned how to calculate the present value of a stream of expected future cash flows. The concept of present value is tailor-made for analyzing capital investment decisions. Most capital investment projects involve an initial outlay of funds followed by a stream of future inflows. The *net* present value (NPV) of the investment is simply the present value of the inflows less (net of) the required outlay.

Consider a prospective investment of $100 that is expected to yield cash flows of $30, $50, and $40 over the next 3 years. Suppose the RRR is 15 percent. We calculate the NPV as in Table 11-4.

Table 11-4 Calculating NPV

Inflows	Present Value Factor @ 15 Percent	Present Value
$30	0.870	$ 26.10
50	0.756	37.80
40	0.658	26.32
		90.22
	Less outlay	−$100.00
	Net present value	−$ 9.78

Let us now formulate a general definition of net present value. NPV is defined as the present value of *all* cash flows associated with the investment, including the outlay. In symbols

$$NPV = \sum_{t=0}^{n} \frac{C_t}{(1 + K)^t} \qquad (7)$$

where C_t is the cash flow in period t and K is the RRR. Note that we sum from $t = 0$ and thereby include the initial outlay. It is apparent that NPV equals the present value of the inflows generated by the investment less the present value of the necessary outlays.

To apply expression (7) to our earlier example, we would set the problem up as shown in Table 11-5.

Table 11-5 Calculating NPV

Period	Cash Flow	Present Value Factor @ 15 Percent	Present Value
0	−$100	1.000	−$100.00
1	30	0.870	26.10
2	50	0.756	37.80
3	40	0.658	26.32
		NPV	−$ 9.78

The NPV Investment Criterion

As applied to capital investment decisions, the NPV rule is simple: *Accept any investment the net present value of which is greater than zero when evaluated at the appropriate RRR.* The investment opportunity in Table 11-5 has a negative NPV and therefore is unacceptable.

As we will see later, the NPV rule is consistent with the general criterion for financial management decisions, that is, maximize the value of the firm. Any project with a positive NPV increases the value of the firm and should be undertaken, and vice versa.

Internal Rate of Return Investment Criterion

The internal rate of return investment criterion, or the IRR rule, is equally simple: *Undertake any project the internal rate of return of which exceeds the required rate.*

Consider the investment in the preceding section. By trial and error, we can calculate its IRR. At a discount rate of 8 percent, its NPV is $2.40, and at 10 percent, it is −$1.35. The project's IRR thus is between 8 percent and 10 percent and, since the required rate is 15 percent, the project is unacceptable.

Terminal Value Investment Criterion

There is a third DCF criterion called the *terminal value criterion* that is less often used than NPV and IRR, but worth a brief mention. The terminal value (TV) criterion involves reinvesting all the project's cash inflows as they are received at an assumed reinvestment rate and calculating the terminal value of the inflows at the end of the final period. We compound the cash inflows forward, rather than discounting them back as in the NPV method. We then compound the outlay forward to the end of the final period, using the same assumed reinvestment rate. If the cash inflows have a higher terminal value than the terminal value of the outlay, we should accept the project. The TV rule, then, is: *Accept any project with a positive terminal value when all cash flows, including the initial outlay, are compounded forward at the reinvestment rate.*

What is the appropriate reinvestment rate? It is the rate at which the investor has alternative opportunities to invest at equivalent risk. As we will see in a later chapter, these alternative opportunities also establish the RRR. Hence, the reinvestment rate for applying the TV rule is the same as the discount rate for applying the NPV rule. When the same rates are used, the TV and NPV rules give identical signals in all types of investment decisions. For this reason, we will not discuss the TV rule further. There are, however, complex situations in which a familiarity with the concept of TV is useful.

Comparison of DCF Decision Criteria

As we can see from the foregoing discussion, DCF techniques find their main application in connection with multiperiod decisions—decisions that affect cash flows in more than one period. By providing a mechanism for transferring cash flows through time, discounting and compounding permit us to transform complex cash flow patterns into single dollar or rate figures that then can be compared to a target. As we will see, the two basic DCF approaches of NPV and IRR give equivalent results in some situations but not in others, so an understanding of the limitations of the two approaches is important.

Accept/Reject Decisions

The simplest type of investment decision is whether to *accept* or *reject* a given investment opportunity. Should we undertake it? Yes or no? The NPV and IRR rules always give identical signals in the case of accept/reject decisions.

To see that this is so, let us consider an investment of $100 that yields cash inflows of $50, $60, and $40 over a 3 year period. If we calculate the NPV of this investment opportunity (call it project A) at different discount rates, we find the NPV profile illustrated in Figure 11-1. From the figure, we can see that the IRR of project A is 25 percent, because that is the discount rate at which NPV = 0.

Figure 11-1 NPV versus Discount Rate

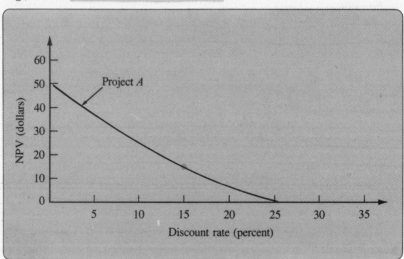

Now, suppose the required rate of return (RRR) is 15 percent. Clearly, NPV is greater than zero at RRR = 15 percent, so the NPV rule signals us to accept the project. The IRR rule also signals accept, because the IRR (25 percent) exceeds the RRR (15 percent).

By looking at Figure 11-1, we can see that NPV > 0 for any discount rate less than 25 percent, which is project *A*'s IRR. We can therefore formulate the following general propositions:

> *If* IRR = RRR, *then* NPV = 0.
> *If* IRR > RRR, *then* NPV > 0.
> *If* IRR < RRR, *then* NPV < 0.

As we will see shortly, certain cash flow patterns have more than one IRR, so the above general propositions hold true only when there is a unique (single) solution to the IRR. Such is the case for normal cash flow patterns, that is, a single outlay followed by a stream of inflows. We will have more to say about multiple solutions to the IRR shortly. For the moment, we can conclude that for normal cash flow patterns (and, as we will see later, for most other patterns encountered in practice as well), the NPV and IRR rules give identical signals in accept/reject decisions.

In passing, let us emphasize an important distinction between the IRR of an investment and the RRR of investors. The IRR depends only on the cash flow pattern of the investment and not at all on the investors; the RRR depends on the preferences of investors with respect to time and risk.

Ranking Decisions

Unfortunately, not all investment decisions involve a simple decision to accept or reject. Often, it is necessary to *rank* investment opportunities, that is, to judge not only whether an opportunity is acceptable, but also whether it is more or less desirable than an alternative opportunity. Ranking is necessary under either of two circumstances:

1. Where capital is *rationed*, that is, there is a limit on funds available for investment.
2. Where two or more investment opportunities are *mutually exclusive*, that is, only one of the opportunities can be undertaken.

We will discuss *capital rationing* in more depth later, when we will see that, in practice, it is quite common to limit the total funds allocated to capital expenditures. We will see also that capital rationing is undesirable on theoretical grounds but necessary under certain circumstances in practice. When funds are limited and when the total required for all acceptable projects (those with a positive NPV) exceeds that limit, it is apparent that projects must be ranked so that the most desirable projects can be undertaken.

There also are circumstances under which two or more projects are *mutually exclusive*, for example, if two or more machines to do the same job are being compared but only one is to be purchased. The same is true of two plants to produce the same product or two alternatives for accomplishing any objective. When investment opportunities are mutually exclusive, we must rank them in order to choose the best.

Where cash flow patterns of alternatives to be ranked are similar, ranking causes no great difficulty. Where patterns depart from the normal pattern of a single outflow followed by a series of inflows, or where the outlays differ, or where the useful lives of the projects differ, complications arise. Let us explore these complications via an illustration.

Earlier we considered a project *A* involving an outlay of $100 followed by inflows of $50, $60, and $40. Let us now consider an alternative, project *B*, involving an outlay of $100 that generates inflows of $20, $30, $45, and $70 over a 4 year period. Let us calculate the NPV of project *B* at different discount rates and plot its profile in Figure 11-2 as we did with project *A* in Figure 11-1. Now, if the RRR = 15 percent, the IRR rule tells us that project *A* is superior to project *B*, because *A*'s IRR is 25 percent and *B*'s is about 19 percent. At the same RRR, that is, 15 percent, the NPV rule tells us the same thing: *A* is superior, because *A*'s NPV at 15 percent is greater than *B*'s.

Suppose, however, that the RRR is not 15 but 8 percent. The IRR rule still tells us that *A* is superior. But now the NPV rule tells us that *B*

Figure 11-2   Comparison of NPV Profiles

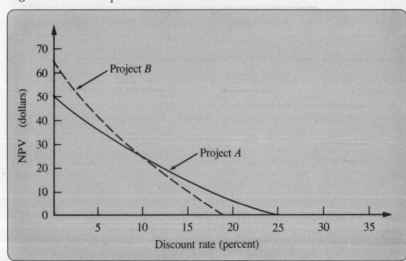

is superior, because it has an NPV of $31.41 at 8 percent versus A's of $29.49. At any RRR less than approximately 10 percent, the point at which the NPV of A and B are approximately equal, the IRR and NPV rules give conflicting signals.

Why is this so? Because the time patterns of the cash flow streams are different. The cash inflows for B total more than those for A ($165 versus $150), but the larger inflows occur later in time. At low discount rates, B is superior; while at high discount rates, B's heavy inflows occurring late in time become less valuable, so that B's NPV falls below A's.

Which rule gives the correct signal? Where there is a conflict, the NPV rule gives the correct ranking. Where the IRR of a project differs significantly from the RRR, the IRR rule can give misleading ranking signals.

The problem has to do with the *reinvestment of intermediate cash flows*. By definition, the RRR is the rate at which we assume that we have opportunities to reinvest. To see the problem more clearly, consider project A again: an outlay of $100, followed by inflows of $50, $60, and $40. Project A's IRR is approximately 25 percent (Figure 11-2). An investor who undertakes project A trades $100 now for the right to receive $50, $60, and $40 over the next 3 years. The IRR of 25 percent appears to say that the investor earns 25 percent per year on the investment. Is the investment equivalent to investing $100 at 25 percent per year for 3 years? If so, then the investor should be as well off at the end of 3 years as he or she would be if $100 were invested at 25 percent per year for 3 years. The answer is that the investment is equivalent to investing $100 at 25 percent per year *only* if the intermediate cash flows of $50, $60, and $40 can themselves be reinvested at 25 percent per year as they are received. Where the cash inflows cannot be reinvested at 25 percent, project A is not equivalent to investing $100 at 25 percent per year. Where the reinvestment rate differs from the IRR, as usually is the case, the IRR can give a misleading signal regarding the worth of one project relative to another.

In our comparison of projects A and B in Figure 11-2, this was the situation, and we found that at reinvestment rates (RRRs) less than 10 percent, the IRR rule did indeed give an incorrect signal. Project B's cash inflows are greater in total than project A's, but they occur later in time. At low reinvestment rates, the greater total outweighs later receipts, and project B is the more desirable project. If, on the other hand, the investor has opportunities to reinvest cash flows at high rates, project A is better because it delivers the cash flows sooner. So, the relative desirability of project A versus project B depends in part on the rate at which cash inflows can be reinvested. In Figure 11-2, we see that project B is better at low discount rates, while project A is better at high rates.

In using the NPV rule, we are forced to deal explicitly with the rate at which cash inflows can be reinvested. We do so by using the assumed reinvestment rate as the discount rate. The IRR rule, on the other hand, makes no assumption at all regarding reinvestment of cash inflows; the IRR of each investment is completely determined by the cash flows of the investment without regard to any reinvestment rate. Since it does not consider opportunities to reinvest cash inflows, the IRR rule can give misleading signals as to the relative worth of investment opportunities whose cash flows have different time patterns. The greater the difference between the IRR and the reinvestment rate, and the greater the difference in time pattern of cash flows, the greater the likelihood of a ranking error.

Unequal Lives

How do we rank two or more mutually exclusive investments that have unequal lives? Project *A* described above had a life of 3 years, while *B* had a life of 4 years. Can the projects be directly compared? It depends.

If the useful life of the projects equals the time horizon over which they are being evaluated, we can compare them directly using the NPV rule, provided, of course, that we use the assumed reinvestment rate to discount the cash flows of both projects. We evaluate both projects over a 4 year horizon, and simply assume that project *A* generates an inflow of $0 in the fourth year.

Problems with unequal lives arise when we analyze activities that are *ongoing*, that is, that are expected to continue beyond the time horizon of the analysis. Cash flows may be expected to continue indefinitely, but for reasons of practicality we have to cut off our analysis at some point. If we are comparing two machines to do the same job, and the machines have unequal useful lives, then one alternative will require an additional outflow for replacement before the other.

One way to handle such problems is to analyze both alternatives over a period equal to the shorter of the useful lives. The longer-lived project will still have some value remaining at that point. That remaining value should be estimated and treated as a cash inflow in the final period of the analysis. The problem of selecting the appropriate time horizon over which to analyze a project is discussed in more depth in a later chapter.

Multiple Solutions

There is a technical difficulty with the IRR rule that deserves brief mention. Certain types of cash flow patterns may have more than one positive discount rate that produces a zero NPV, that is, more than one IRR. It turns out that the number of solutions may be as great as the number of sign reversals in the cash flow stream. A stream with a pattern of $-$, $+$, $+$, $+$, $+$ has only one sign reversal and therefore no more than one positive IRR. A pattern of $-$, $+$, $-$, $+$, $+$, $+$, may have as many as three positive solutions.

Where multiple solutions occur, which solution is correct? The answer is that none is correct. Each "solution" discounts the cash flows to zero, but none is a meaningful measure of project return. In practice, cash flow patterns that yield multiple IRRs are rare. Even patterns with more than one minor sign reversal usually have only one IRR, because it takes extreme cases to produce multiple solutions. Thus, usually the possibility of multiple solutions can be ignored, except for one important group of investments known as *acceleration projects*.

An acceleration project is one in which a petroleum or mining company invests funds in order to *accelerate* the recovery of a given body of oil or minerals. In these situations, the typical cash flow associated with the investment always involves a major reversal of cash flows with the pattern $-$, $+$, $-$, that is, outlays now produce incremental positive flows in the near future (as recovery is accelerated relative to the status quo) followed by negative incremental flows (as the reserves are exhausted earlier than they would have been if the acceleration investment had not been made). The attempt to measure the IRR for such projects frequently yields multiple and hence meaningless solutions.

Superiority of Net Present Value (NPV) in a Complex World

In a simple world where capital is not rationed, projects are independent (i.e., no mutually exclusive projects), and cash flow patterns are normal, we face only accept/reject decisions. In such cases, we can use either the NPV or the IRR rule. In a complex world, where ranking is required, the IRR rule can give erroneous signals. Therefore, the general conclusion today is that on conceptual and theoretical grounds, the NPV rule is superior. If we set the discount rate correctly (no easy task itself), the NPV rule always will give signals that are consistent with the general criterion of maximizing the value of the firm.

The IRR, however, has its uses. Individuals not familiar with DCF techniques often find the concept of present value intuitively unappealing. Some people find rate of return more intuitively understandable than present value. The IRR can be useful for communicating information in such cases. Where IRR is used in connection with investment decisions, its limitations should be kept in mind. Although IRR can give erroneous rankings, in practice IRR and NPV rankings often will be the same.

A useful procedure is to use NPV to double-check any signals given by IRR in ranking decisions.

Strengths and Weaknesses of DCF Methods

In principle, DCF approaches will produce investment decisions that best serve the interests of shareholders. Because they take account of benefits over many future periods, DCF criteria encourage managers to take a long view. The NPV rule, consistently applied over the long run, will produce a higher dollar return to shareholders than any other criterion. Net present value also is consistent with society's goal of efficient utilization of scarce resources.

Discounted cash flow approaches have a shortcoming, however, that sometimes can be important: *They do not consider the impact of an investment on accounting profits.* It is not unusual for an investment to generate low, or even negative, net cash flows in early years, with high cash flows later. In such cases, near-term accounting profits of the firm can be adversely affected. Because great importance often is attached to accounting profits by investors and the stock market, an adverse impact on near-term profits can lead to a reluctance to undertake an investment that may be very desirable in the long run.

There is no denying the potential difficulties that can occur if investors misinterpret the negative effect of a project on near-term profits. However, professional managers are paid to take a long view, and most investors would not be critical of a drop in profits if they knew that large benefits lay in the future. In some cases, the problem can be handled by careful communication of relevant information to investors, although this is not always possible.

Making Decisions versus Measuring Performance

The use of DCF techniques for decision-making sometimes can conflict with performance appraisal based on accounting measures. Consider a firm that uses DCF for making investment decisions and measures executive performance using AROI. Discounted cash flow encourages a long view; AROI, a short view. For example, an investment opportunity that requires a large initial outlay but produces low near-term accounting profits will depress AROI in early years. A manager whose performance is measured using AROI may be reluctant to recommend such an investment no matter how attractive it is in DCF terms. In designing management systems, it is clear that the interaction between decision-making and performance appraisal must be considered carefully.

Properly used, the advantages of DCF far outweigh the disadvantages. Many firms that use DCF as the primary criterion for decisions also use payback and accounting rate of return as supplementary measures. While using DCF to make the decision, these firms find it useful also to know the impact of the decision on accounting measures.[4]

Summary

This chapter deals with the first step in the analysis of investment decisions: selecting a decision criterion. Criteria for investment decisions can be separated into two broad classes: those that are based on discounted cash flow (DCF), and those that are not.

Two widely used non-DCF measures are the *payback* period and the accounting return on investment (AROI). Both answer questions that often are relevant, but both are deficient as measures of the economic worth of investment opportunities, most importantly because they do not take into account the time value of money. In contrast to AROI, the internal rate of return (IRR) of an investment does take into account the timing of cash flows. The IRR is the rate that discounts all of the cash flows of an investment, including the outlay, to zero.

For making investment decisions, decision criteria based on DCF have several important advantages over non-DCF criteria. First and foremost, they take account of time value. Second, they are unambiguous as to computation and so ultimately simpler than accounting measures. Third, they can be related to the general criterion of value-maximization. The two most widely used DCF criteria are the net present value (NPV) rule and the internal rate of return (IRR) rule. Both rules require that a minimum acceptable (or *required*) rate of return be established, a topic discussed in later chapters. The NPV rule is to accept any investment whose NPV is greater than zero when evaluated at the required rate. The IRR rule is to accept any investment whose IRR exceeds the required rate.

The NPV and IRR rules give identical signals in the case of *accept/ reject* decisions. Where alternative opportunities must be *ranked*, the two rules sometimes can give conflicting rankings. Where there is such a conflict, NPV gives the correct ranking. NPV also is superior in situations involving unequal lives or unusual cash flow patterns. In general, the NPV rule is the safest to use because it always gives signals that are consistent with value-maximization, provided that the cash flows are correctly estimated and the correct discount rate is used.

DCF criteria encourage managers to take a long view and to make decisions that are best over the long run. A shortcoming of DCF is that it ignores the impact of a decision on near-term accounting profits. A

---

4. See Schall, Sundem, and Geijsbeek, "Survey and Analysis of Capital Budgeting Methods."

potential conflict therefore exists when DCF is used for decision-making while performance is appraised via accounting measures such as AROI.

Sample Problem

An investment requiring an initial $15,000 cash outlay will return $8,000 in year 1, $7,000 in year 2, and $5,000 in year 3. Calculate the following for this investment:

1. the IRR
2. the payback period
3. the NPV using a 10 percent discount rate

Solution

1. Solving for the IRR involves a trial-and-error process. We want to find the rate, R, that will solve the equation.

$$\$15,000 = \frac{\$8,000}{(1 + R)^1} + \frac{\$7,000}{(1 + R)^2} + \frac{\$5,000}{(1 + R)^3}$$

Using the present value factors from Table I, we can try a rate of 15 percent:

$\$8,000\ (0.870) + 7,000\ (0.756) + 5,000\ (0.658) = \$15,542$

With a 15 percent rate, the present value of the future cash streams exceeds the initial outlay of $15,000 by $542 (the IRR is the rate that equates these two), so we know that the 15 percent rate is too low. We can try higher discount rates, constructing the following table:

Discount Rate (percent)	Net Present Value
15	$542
17	77
18	−153

From this table we know that the IRR is between 17 and 18 percent. If we interpolate, we can solve for a closer approximation of IRR.

$$IRR = 17 + \frac{77 - 0}{77 - (-153)} = 17.33 \text{ percent}$$

IRR $15,000

①

@ 15%

1	8000	.820	6960
2	7000	.756	5292
3	5000	.658	3290
			15542

@ 20%

1		.833	6664
2		.694	4858
3		.579	2895
			14417

17%

1		.855	6840
2		.731	5110
3		.624	3120
			15070

17.33

②

Cash 15000

7000

	0	1	2	3
	15000	8000	7000	5000	?
cum	15000	(7000)	(—)	(+5000)

Year 2

(total payments rcvd = the outlay)

③

NPV

			−15,000
1	8000	.909	7272
2	7000	.826	5782
3	5000	.751	3755
			16809
			−15000
			+1809

2. The payback period can be found by constructing the following table:

	Year			
	0	1	2	3
Cash flow	(15,000)	8,000	7,000	5,000
Cumulative cash flow	(15,000)	(7,000)	0	5,000

The payback period is 2 years. At that point, total payments received equal the outlay.

3. The NPV using a 10 percent discount rate can be found by using the present value factors given in Table I:

NPV = −$15,000 + $8,000 (0.909) + $7,000 (0.826) + $5,000 (0.751)

    = −$15,000 + $16,809

    = $1,809

Questions

1. What are the shortcomings of payback period as an investment criterion?
2. What is the correct method for measuring accounting return on investment?
3. Distinguish between decision criteria and performance measures.
4. What is the definition of the internal rate of return of an investment opportunity?
5. Why is it sometimes necessary to rank investment opportunities?
6. Why do the net present value and internal rate of return rules sometimes give conflicting ranking signals?
7. What important shortcoming do you see in discounted cash flow techniques as applied to investment decisions?

Problems

1. Consider an investment of $5,000 that generates after-tax cash flows of $2,000 per year and net income of $1,000 per year over a 5 year life. Calculate the payback period and the AROI for the investment.

2. A company is trying to decide which of two machines to purchase for a new plant. Each machine requires an investment of $15,000. The after-tax cash flows and the net income figures are listed in the table.

	Machine *A*			Machine *B*	
Year	Cash Flow	Net Income		Cash Flow	Net Income
1	$3,000	$1,000		$6,000	$2,000
2	4,000	2,000		7,000	3,000
3	5,000	3,000		8,000	4,000
4	6,000	4,000			
5	7,000	5,000			
6	8,000	6,000			

(a) Calculate the payback period for each investment.

(b) Calculate the AROI for each investment.

(c) If machine *B* also had an after-tax cash flow of $5,000 in each of the last 3 years, would the payback period change? Why?

3. Calculate the IRR for investment projects *X* and *Y*. Project *X* requires an initial outlay of $12,000 and project *Y* requires an outlay of $16,500.

	Cash Flows	
Year	Project *X*	Project *Y*
1	$1,000	$4,000
2	1,500	6,000
3	4,000	6,000
4	4,000	5,000
5	6,000	5,000

4. Calculate the IRR for the following investments:

   (a) An investment of $27,000 promising a return of $4,000 per year for 13 years.

   (b) An investment of $27,000 promising a return of $3,000 per year for 16 years.

   (c) An investment of $7,070 promising a return of $1,400 per year for 16 years.

5. Calculate the NPV for each of the two investments in Problem 3 if the required rate of return is 10 percent. Which of the two projects would you accept?

6. Calculate the NPV for each of the three investments in Problem 4 if the required rate of return is 12 percent. Which of the three investments would you accept?

7. Two mutually exclusive projects each involve an initial outlay of $800. Project *A* has cash inflows of $200 a year for 8 years, while project *B* has cash inflows of $325 per year for 4 years.

   (a) Calculate the NPV of each project at required rates of return of 0 percent, 7 percent, 14 percent, and 21 percent.

(b) Calculate the IRR of each project.

(c) Construct a plot of each project's NPV similar to the one shown in Figure 11-2.

(d) Which project would you select? Why?

8. Consider the following proposed investments with the indicated cash flows:

		Year-End Cash Inflows		
Investment	Initial Outlay	Year 1	Year 2	Year 3
A	$200	$200	$ 0	$ 0
B	200	100	100	100
C	200	20	100	300
D	200	200	20	20
E	200	140	60	100
F	200	160	160	80

(a) Can you say (by inspection, without computation) that any of these investments are superior to any other?

(b) Rank these investments using the following criteria: payback period; accounting return on investment (treat cash flows as income); internal rate of return; net present value, assuming a required rate of return of 4 percent; net present value, assuming a required rate of return of 50 percent.

(c) What conclusion can you draw from this problem? Why do the rankings differ?

9. An investment requires an initial outlay of $1,000 and an additional outlay of $500 at the end of year 1. The investment generates cash inflows of $600, $800, and $800 at the end of years 2, 3, and 4, respectively.

(a) Calculate the net present value of the investment at a discount rate of 10 percent.

(b) Calculate the internal rate of return.

10. A bank lends $10,000 to a company to purchase a piece of equipment and requires the borrower to repay $2,637.97 per year (at year-end) for 5 years.

(a) Viewing the transaction as an investment decision from the standpoint of the bank, what is the internal rate of return to the bank?

(b) Viewing the transaction from the standpoint of the borrower, calculate the effective interest cost of the loan.

$$\frac{1000}{402.09} = 2.487$$
$$@ 3 \, yrs = 10\%$$

$1259.45 \times ? = 1000$

$? = 1000$

$? = .794$

$8\% = .794$
$@ 3 \, yrs$

11. You have arranged to borrow $1,000 from a bank. The bank offers two repayment plans: $402.09 per year for 3 years (payable at year-end) or a single lump sum repayment of $1,259.45 at the end of the third year.
    (a) Calculate the effective interest cost of each alternative (rate that discounts cash flows to zero).
    (b) Which alternative would you prefer? Why?

12. An investment of $1,000 generates cash inflows of $301.93 per year for 4 years.
    (a) Calculate the payback period of the investment.
    (b) Calculate the net present value of the investment at a discount rate of 8 percent.
    (c) Note that the payback period and the present value factor (from Table II) used in part b are equal. Suggest a way to interpret the present value factors in Table II as payback periods.

13. Calculate the terminal value of the cash flow (by compounding the cash flows forward to the end of year 3) for each of the six investments in Problem 8.
    (a) at an interest rate of 4 percent.
    (b) at an interest rate of 50 percent.
    (c) Rank the investments on the basis of terminal values and compare the rankings with those obtained in Problem 8. What conclusions do you draw?

guess %

$40 \times (?) + 1000 (?) = 912$

12 periods

OR

$80 \times (?) + 1000 (?) = 912$

6 periods ÷ 2

FAC. ¥

$2000 \times ? = 15000$

$? = 15000$
$? = 7.50$
$@ 10 \, yrs \quad 15.16 \, yrs$

14. You have an opportunity to purchase for $912 a bond promising to pay $40 semiannually for 6 years and $1,000 at maturity. What is the bond's yield to maturity? 5%

15. An equipment manufacturer has marketed a new machine that promises to provide your company cash savings of $2,000 after taxes for each year the machine is operated. The useful life of this machine is not known with certainty. The machine will cost your firm $15,000.
    (a) If your firm's required rate of return on such investments is 10 percent, what is the minimum number of full years of life the machine must operate to make this investment acceptable? Ignore any tax effects that may result from the purchase or sale. Table II
    (b) What would be the payback period for the machine? 7.5 yrs
    (c) Suppose your firm requires a payback period of 10 years for new equipment, and your production manager estimates this machine's useful life to be 12 years. Would you recommend purchasing the machine? "No" it takes 15 yrs to get RRR

16. The Walters Company is considering three mutually exclusive investments shown in the table.

Investment	Period			
	0	1	2	3
A	($10,000)	$6,000	$4,000	$3,000
B	($5,000)	($2,000)	$5,000	$6,000
C	($15,000)	$7,120	$7,120	$7,120

(a) Calculate the payback period and IRR for each investment.

(b) If the firm's required rate of return is 10 percent, which investment would you recommend, using NPV analysis? If the firm selected the investment with the highest IRR, would it choose the investment you recommended using NPV as your decision criterion?

17. A building contractor has estimated that using a higher grade of insulating material in your new home could save you $650 a year in heating costs over the next 10 years. If your required rate of return on such investments is 8 percent, what is the maximum amount you would be willing to pay for the higher grade material? (Ignore any possible tax credits, assume that after 10 years the savings differential between grades disappears, and assume that the contractor's estimates are accurate.)

References

H. Bierman, Jr., and S. Smidt, *The Capital Budgeting Decision,* 4th ed. (New York: Macmillan, 1975).

J. M. Blatt, "Investment Evaluation Under Uncertainty," *Financial Management,* **8,** 66–81 (Summer 1979).

H. R. Fogler, "Ranking Techniques and Capital Rationing," *Accounting Review* **47,** 134–143 (Jan. 1972).

L. J. Gitman and J. R. Forrester, Jr., "A Survey of Capital Budgeting Techniques Used by Major U.S. Firms," *Financial Management* **6,** 66–71 (Fall 1977).

R. W. Johnson, *Capital Budgeting* (Belmont, Ca.: Wadsworth, 1970).

J. H. Lorie and L. J. Savage, "Three Problems in Rationing Capital," *Journal of Business* **28,** 229–239 (Oct. 1955).

G. Quirin, *The Capital Expenditures Decision* (Homewood, Ill.: Richard D. Irwin, 1967).

U. E. Reinhardt, "Breakeven Analysis for a Lockheed's TriStar—An Application of Financial Theory," *Journal of Finance* **28,** 821–838 (Sept. 1973).

M. Sarnat and H. Levy, "The Relationship of Rules of Thumb to the Internal Rate of Return: A Restatement and Generalization," *Journal of Finance* **24,** 479–490 (June 1969).

L. D. Schall, G. L. Sundem, and W. R. Geijsbeek, "Survey and Analysis of Capital Budgeting Methods," *Journal of Finance* **33,** 281–287 (Mar. 1978).

B. Schwab and P. Lusztig, "A Comparative Analysis of the Net Present Value and Benefit–Cost Ratios as Measures of Economic Desirability of Investments," *Journal of Finance* **24,** 507–516 (June 1969).

F. W. Searby, "Return to Return on Investment," *Harvard Business Review* **53,** 113–119 (Mar.-Apr. 1975).

E. Solomon, "Alternative Rate of Return Concepts and Their Implications for Utility Regulation," *Bell Journal of Economics and Management Science* **1,** 65–81 (Spring 1970).

E. Solomon, "The Arithmetic of Capital Budgeting Decisions," *Journal of Business* **29,** 124–129 (Apr. 1956).

E. Solomon, *The Theory of Financial Management* (New York: Columbia University Press, 1963).

Appendix: Alternative DCF Return Measures

We discussed the internal rate of return (IRR) in this chapter. We found that the IRR requires no assumption as to the rate at which cash inflows can be reinvested, and for this reason it may give a misleading indication of the relative worth (i.e., rank) of two or more investment opportunities. An investment I with an IRR of R percent is equivalent to investing $\$I$ at R percent per year over the entire time horizon of a project only if the intermediate cash flows can be reinvested at R percent per year. In this appendix, we discuss two other DCF return measures that, unlike the IRR, require an explicit assumption regarding reinvestment of cash inflows. We also will discuss a third measure called the *Profitability Index*. All three measures are useful only in connection with investments with a single outlay at time $t = 0$, followed by a series of inflows (in contrast to NPV and IRR, which can be applied to any cash flow pattern).

Overall Rate of Return

Let us assume that all cash inflows from an investment are reinvested at the opportunity rate, K. At the end of the final period (n), the terminal value (TV) of the cash flows (C) would be

$$TV = C_1(1 + K)^{n-1} + C_2(1 + K)^{n-2} + \cdots + C_n$$

$$= \sum_{t=1}^{n} C_t(1 + K)^{n-t} = \sum_{t=1}^{n} C_t(1 + K)^{-t}(1 + K)^n$$

$$= (1 + K)^n \sum_{t=1}^{n} \frac{C_t}{(1 + K)^t} \qquad (A1)$$

The summation in the last line of the equation is the present value (not the net present value) of the inflows. So $TV = PV(1 + K)^n$.

If we divide the terminal value by the outlay and take the nth root of the quotient, we have a measure of return that we will call the *overall rate of return* (ORR). Mathematically,

$$1 + ORR = \left[\frac{PV(1 + K)^n}{I} \right]^{1/n}$$

$$= (1 + K) \left(\frac{PV}{I} \right)^{1/n}$$

So

$$ORR = (1 + K) \left(\frac{PV}{I} \right)^{1/n} - 1 \qquad (A2)$$

The ORR is the rate that will compound the outlay, I, forward to produce the same terminal value as we would have if the cash inflows produced by the project are reinvested each period at K percent. Mathematically [rearranging expression (A2)],

$$I(1 + \text{ORR})^n = \text{PV}(1 + K)^n$$
$$= \text{Terminal value of inflows} \qquad (A3)$$

So, if we reinvest all cash inflows from an investment at K percent per year, the investment is equivalent to investing the outlay, I, over the same time period at a rate equal to the ORR.

True Rate of Profit

The ORR assumes that cash inflows are entirely reinvested at K. Another measure, which has been called the *true rate of profit* (TRP),[5] assumes that only a portion of the cash inflows are reinvested; the other portion is paid out to owners or is consumed. The TRP is the proportion of the original investment that can be consumed each period while still leaving an amount equal to the outlay at the end of the final period. The TRP thus gives a measure of what is known as *economic income,* the amount that can be consumed each period while leaving the investor exactly as well off at the end of n periods as at the beginning. The TRP is calculated as follows:

$$\text{TRP} = \frac{\text{NPV}}{I} \left\{ \frac{1}{\sum_{t=1}^{n} [1/(1 + K)^t]} \right\} + K \qquad (A4)$$

The summation term is the present value of \$1 per period for n periods at K percent (see Table II at the end of the book).

Profitability Index

The ORR and TRP are rate measures, stated in terms of percent per period. A third DCF measure, known as the Profitability Index (PI) is calculated as follows:

$$\text{PI} = \frac{\text{Present value of inflows}}{\text{Outlay}} = \frac{\text{PV}}{I}$$

$$= \frac{\text{NPV} + I}{I} = \frac{\text{NPV}}{I} + 1 \qquad (A5)$$

---

5. First proposed by Michael Adler, "The True Rate of Return and the Reinvestment Rate," *Engineering Economist* **15** (3) (Spring 1970).

The PI gives a measure of the present value of the cash inflows *per dollar of investment.*

Comparison of Overall Rate of Return, True Rate of Profit, and Profitability Index

By analyzing expressions (A2), (A4), and (A5), we can determine that when a project has NPV > 0, then ORR > K, TRP > K, and PI > 1.0. We know also that when NPV > 0, then IRR > K. Hence, if K is the required rate of return, NPV, IRR, ORR, TRP, and PI all give the same *accept/reject* signal for a given investment.

The same is not true for *ranking* decisions. By analyzing expressions (A2), (A4), and (A5), we can determine that ORR, TRP, and PI all will rank investments in the same order. This ranking will agree with a ranking by NPV if the outlays of all investments being ranked are equal. Where the outlays are not equal, a ranking by ORR, TRP, or PI may differ from a ranking by NPV. From our discussion earlier in this chapter, we know also that a ranking by IRR may differ from a ranking by NPV.

Thus, we see that all five measures give identical accept/reject signals, but only NPV gives ranking signals that always are consistent with our general criterion of value-maximization.

Identifying
Relevant Cash Flows

12

Cash Flows versus Accounting Profits
Incremental Cash Flows
Dealing with Uncertainty
The Decision Horizon
The Objective: Cash Flows after Taxes
Some Special Considerations

In the preceding chapter, we settled on discounted cash flow (DCF) techniques and especially on net present value as providing the best criterion for investment decisions. To what do we apply our DCF techniques? As the term DCF suggests, we are interested in *cash flows* and nothing else. After all, it is *cash* that can be used for consumption or reinvestment.

Cash Flows versus Accounting Profits

It is necessary to draw a clear distinction between *cash flow* and *accounting profit*. Accounting data that are quite useful as performance measures often are less useful as decision criteria. Accounting profits and accounting return on investment are good examples.

As we will see, we are interested in all cash flows affected by the decision under evaluation, no matter how those cash flows are classified for accounting purposes, whether as expenditures or expenses, receipts or income. Noncash items, such as depreciation, are important only if they affect cash flow—for example, by affecting tax payments.

Importance of Good Information

The really difficult tasks in analyzing investment opportunities are deciding what to discount and at what rate. In an uncertain world, estimating cash flows expected in the future often is an exceedingly difficult task. In fact, of the steps in analyzing investments, estimating cash flows probably is the most subject to error. Frequently, investments must be analyzed where no historical analog exists. Even where the opportunity is similar to others undertaken in the past, the world changes rapidly and events take place that often were completely unanticipated.

Not only is estimating future cash flows difficult; it is also important. A good job of analyzing bad information still produces bad results. A careful job of estimating cash flows justifies the expenditure of considerable time and effort. It should be noted also that making cash flow estimates is not a routine clerical task but one that requires the attention of experts in accounting, economics, engineering, cost analysis, and perhaps other fields. Organizational responsibilities in the capital budgeting process are discussed further in a later chapter.

Incremental Cash Flows

Each investment opportunity analyzed by a firm or individual or nonprofit organization is likely to be different. It is impossible to develop a checklist of factors that would cover every situation, but we can develop a general rule that will cover all situations. We then will discuss some of the kinds of cash flows typically encountered in investment analysis.

Incremental Cash Flow Rule

In deciding whether to do something, or whether to pick alternative *A* or alternative *B,* it is *differences* in outcomes that are of interest. What changes as a result of the decision? If *A* is picked rather than *B,* what will be different? Those things that do not change as a result of the decision, or that are the same under either alternative *A* or alternative *B,* can be disregarded. For purposes of estimating cash flows in the analysis of investments, we will call our general rule the *incremental cash flow rule* and state it as follows: The cash flows relevant to the analysis of an investment opportunity are those cash flows and only those cash flows *directly attributable to the investment.*

The concept of *incremental analysis* has wide applicability in decision-making; it is as important a concept as the time value of money, opportunity costs, and optimization. The notion of incremental analysis applies not just to investment decisions, or just to financial management decisions, but to all decisions faced by individuals and firms. Only *differences due to the decision* need be considered. Other factors may be important, but not to the decision at hand.

In analyzing investment opportunities, proper application of the incremental cash flow rule always leads to correct discrimination between cash flows relevant to the decision and those that can be disregarded. While the rule correctly determines relevance, it does not guarantee a correct estimate of magnitude!

The incremental cash flow rule is simple in concept but not always easy to apply. Let us consider some of the cash flows typically encountered in investment analysis. As noted earlier, the following discussion is by no means exhaustive and should not be considered a checklist. The best procedure is to apply the incremental cash flow rule to every investment opportunity individually.

Initial Investment

Often, it is useful to separate the *outlay* required to implement an investment from the benefits that it will produce. Benefits may take the form of increases in revenues or decreases in expenses or both. The terms *initial outlay* or *initial investment* usually are applied to those one-time cash outflows necessary to acquire capital items such as land, buildings, and equipment. Freight, site preparation, and other expenditures necessary to implement a project should be included. Any necessary increase in working capital (discussed below) also might be included under the heading of initial investment, as might other expenditures of a one-time nature such as those for training or research and development. Cash flows classified as part of the initial investment usually occur near the outset of a project but may be spread over more than 1 year. Note also that some items included in initial investment may be capital items that must be depreciated (e.g., equipment), whereas others may be items that can be expensed (e.g., research and development, training).

An initial investment spread over more than 1 year poses no problems in calculating either NPV or IRR. Suppose a firm is considering building a new plant. Construction will take 2 years, and net cash inflows will start in the second year. Projected cash flows are shown in Table 12-1 (we will ignore taxes for purposes of simplicity).

Table 12-1 Outlay Over More Than 1 Year
(Thousands of Dollars)

	Year					
	0	1	2	3	. . .	8
Outlay	(100)	(150)	(50)			
Operating cash inflow	—	—	100	200	. . .	200
Net cash flow	(100)	(150)	50	200	. . .	200

To calculate NPV, we simply discount the cash flows in the last line of Table 12-1 at the appropriate rate. To determine the IRR, we find the rate that gives zero NPV.

There is no strict definition of the term *initial investment,* and in many cases it is not necessary to classify cash flows in this way. Where the term is used, it most often includes cash flows that occur early in the project and are nonrecurring in nature.

Revenues and Expenses

Investments normally are made either to increase revenues or to reduce costs or both. A reduction in costs is just as beneficial as is an increase in revenues—"a penny saved is a penny earned!" Investments aimed at increasing revenues, for example, introduction of a new product or expansion of manufacturing facilities for an existing product, often involve increases in expenses as well as in revenues.

Expenses usually are easier to estimate than are revenues. The incremental cash flow rule tells us to identify all items of expense that change because the investment is made.

Revenues are more difficult to estimate because they often are subject to a greater degree of uncertainty. Revenues involve estimates of the size of the market for a product and the expected share of that market. Both estimates depend on a variety of factors, including price, advertising and promotion, and sales effort. Adding to the uncertainties are the possibilities of shifts in consumer preferences, actions of competitors, technological developments, and changes in the general economic or political environment.

As an illustration of the problem of uncertainty, consider the case of the oil price increases that took place during 1973 and 1974. In the spring of 1973, very few people anticipated that the price of crude oil would increase by a factor of five over the ensuing 18 months, yet the price increase had a profound effect on the United States economy and on the fortunes of many firms. Here we have a case of unexpected changes in expenses rather than revenues. The oil price increase is related to the general problem of dealing with inflation in investment decision-making, which we will discuss later in this chapter.

Working Capital

If working capital is expected to change because of the project being evaluated, the change is relevant and should be included. If an investment is expected to increase sales, it is likely that an increase will be required in accounts receivable, inventory, and perhaps cash. Part of the increase may be offset by increases in accounts payable and miscellaneous accruals. The part that is not offset, the net change in working capital, should be treated as a cash outflow attributable to the project. Working capital increases often represent a significant part of total investment in a project.

A net one-time increase in working capital that occurs early in the project may be viewed as part of the initial investment. Continuing increases in working capital as sales expand in subsequent periods should be included, but normally would not be classified under initial investment. If a project has a definite life span and is terminated at some point, working capital *recaptured* in the final period should be treated as a cash inflow.

To illustrate the treatment of working capital, consider a project that involves the cash flows listed in Table 12-2. In the table, inventories and receivables increase in years 1, 2, and 3, and decrease in years 4 and 5. Increases in inventories and receivables represent cash outflows, and

Table 12-2 Incremental Cash Flows (Thousands of Dollars)

			Year			
	0	1	2	3	4	5
Initial investment	$1,000					
Sales		$ 500	$1,000	$4,000	$2,000	0
Expenses		1,000	1,200	1,600	1,200	$1,000
Change in inventory		200	200	600	(400)	(600)
Change in receivables		100	100	300	(200)	(300)
Change in payables		125	125	425	(325)	(425)

an increase in payables represents a cash inflow. The change in net working capital for each year is given in Table 12-3. In a DCF analysis of the investment, the increases in net working capital in years 1, 2, and 3 represent cash outflows, and the decreases in years 4 and 5 represent cash inflows as net working capital is recaptured.

Table 12-3   Change in Net Working Capital (Thousands of Dollars)

		Year				
	0	1	2	3	4	5
Inventory (increase = outflow)		$200	$200	$600	($400)	($600)
Receivables (increase = outflow)		100	100	300	(200)	(300)
Payables (increase = inflow)		125	125	425	(325)	(425)
Increase in NWC (increase = outflow)		$175	$175	$475	($275)	($475)

Depreciation and Other Noncash Charges

Depreciation is the process of allocating the cost of a long-lived asset to the time periods in which it is used up. A machine that costs $100,000 may have a useful life of 10 years. It makes sense to allocate the $100,000 cost over the 10 years, either via straight-line depreciation ($10,000 per year) or accelerated methods such as declining balance or sum-of-the-years digits. The latter methods allocate more of the asset's cost to early years, when it presumably is more productive, and less to later years. The choice of depreciation method does not affect the total depreciation charged over the 10 years, only the time pattern.

Does depreciation represent a cash flow? Clearly, it does not. The cash flow took place at the time the asset was purchased, and the depreciation in subsequent accounting periods represents a noncash charge.

If depreciation is not a cash flow, is it irrelevant to investment analysis? No, because depreciation affects *taxes*, which *are* cash flows. Every dollar of depreciation reduces taxes by T dollars, where T is the marginal tax rate. To illustrate, consider the $100,000 machine mentioned above and assume that it will be depreciated over a 10 year period at $10,000 per year. If the marginal tax rate were 48 percent[1], the depreciation charge would reduce the firm's taxes (assuming it is making profits!) by $4,800 per year. The tax effect of depreciation often is referred to as the *depreciation tax shield*. Thus, the cash flows directly associated with the purchase of the machine are a $100,000 outflow at the time of purchase and a $4,800 incremental inflow, in the form of reduction in tax payments, each

---

1. For fiscal years beginning after January 1, 1979, the maximum federal tax rate on corporate income was reduced to 46 percent. However, many state and some local governments also tax corporate incomes. For uniformity, we use a total tax rate of 48 percent.

year for 10 years. Note that, in accordance with the incremental cash flow rule, we are interested in *differences*—in this case, the difference between tax payments *with* the machine versus tax payments *without* the machine.

The choice of depreciation method does not affect total taxes paid, only the timing of the payments. The more rapid the depreciation, that is, the higher the depreciation charges in early years, the more are taxes deferred to later years. The United States Treasury Department sets rules as to the allowable method of depreciation, depending on the type and age of the asset.

Since money has time value, deferring taxes is advantageous. On economic grounds, therefore, a case exists for the most rapid depreciation method allowable. However, while producing a higher after-tax cash flow, higher depreciation produces lower accounting profits.

Thus, depreciation is relevant in a DCF analysis only because it affects tax payments, which *are* cash flows. If taxes did not exist or if the tax rate were zero, as it is for certain tax-exempt organizations, depreciation would not be relevant.

Other noncash items, such as amortization of patents or goodwill, allocations of prepaid expenses or deferred income, and the like, should be treated in the same way as depreciation. If it affects another cash item, such as taxes, the effect is relevant. It is cash that counts.

Tax Effects

Taxes are relevant to almost every financial decision that a firm or individual makes, unless, of course, the firm or individual is not subject to taxation. The incremental cash flow rule tells us that if the decision being evaluated affects tax payments, those effects should be considered. It is the *incremental* taxes attributable to the decision that are relevant.

Assuming a federal plus state income tax rate of 48 percent, tax effects are very important to corporations. A dollar's worth of revenue becomes 52¢, and a dollar's worth of depreciation saves 48¢ in taxes. Tax effects are equally as important to individuals, and some individuals pay income taxes at marginal rates higher than the corporate rate. Capital gains, or profits on the sale of capital assets, are taxed by the federal government and many state governments at rates lower than those applied to ordinary income.

When considering an investment opportunity, the net after-tax cash flows expected are the figures that count. Tax payments to governments are just as relevant as are payments to anyone else, and usually are quite large in relation to other cash flows. This brings us to another important general rule: We are interested in *net cash flow after taxes.* This conclusion is, of course, true for individuals as well as for firms.

There are at least two ways to deal with tax effects in analyzing investments. One is to put the cash flows in income statement format. Consider
an investment of $100,000 that produces the cash flows shown in Table
12-4 in the first year. Cash inflow is $15,000. Cash outflows include $3,000
for expenses, $960 for taxes, and $500 for working capital. This gives a
net cash inflow of $10,540.

Table 12-4   Cash Flow After Taxes

	Year 1	
Sales	$15,000[a]	*INFLOW*
Cash expenses	(3,000)[a]	*OUTFLOW*
Depreciation	10,000	
Profit before taxes	2,000	
Tax at 48 percent	(960)[a]	*OUTFLOW*
Profit after taxes (PAT)	1,040	
Increase in working capital	(500)[a]	*OUTFLOW*
Net cash flow after taxes	$10,540	*NET INFLOW*

[a]Cash flow item.

The most direct way to calculate after-tax cash flow is to identify the
cash flow items and subtract the cash outflows from the cash inflows, as
in Table 12-5.

Table 12-5   Cash Flow Items

Sales	$15,000
Less cash expenses	(3,000)
Less taxes	(960)
Cash flow from operations	11,040
Less increase in W/C	(500)
Net cash flow after taxes	$10,540

We can calculate cash flow from operations a simpler way, by taking
profit after tax and adding back depreciation, which is a *noncash* charge.
We get $11,040 for cash flow from operations, as before. Adding deprecia-
tion back to PAT is a handy shortcut to get cash flow from operations, but
it is important to see why it gives the correct answer. We can see why it
does by comparing Tables 12-4, 12-5, and 12-6.

Table 12-6   Adding Depreciation to PAT

Profit after taxes (from Table 12-4)	$ 1,040
Add depreciation	10,000
Cash flow from operations	11,040
Less increase in W/C	(500)
Net cash flow after taxes	$10,540

A second method of dealing with taxes, and probably the simplest method after one becomes accustomed to it, is to convert each cash flow to its *after-tax equivalent*. Applying this method to the above example, we get Table 12-7. Note that we get the same result as before. With respect to sales revenue, we receive $15,000, but taxes increase by $7,200, leaving $7,800 net after taxes. We pay $3,000 in expenses, but as a result, our tax bill declines by $1,440, for a net after-tax expense of $1,560. The depreciation charge of $10,000 provides a depreciation tax shield, that is, a reduction in taxes, of $4,800. The working capital increase has no effect on

Table 12-7   Calculating After-Tax Equivalents

	Pretax		Tax Effect	After-Tax Equivalent
Sales	$15,000	×	(1 − 0.48)	$ 7,800
Cash expenses	(3,000)	×	(1 − 0.48)	(1,560)
Depreciation tax shield	10,000	×	(0.48)	4,800
Working capital	(500)		—	(500)
			Net cash flow after taxes	$10,540

taxes. From the preceding example we derive the general rules in Table 12-8. In this table, T is the tax rate applicable to the cash flow in question. Remember that changes in items such as working capital do not affect taxes. Remember also that noncash expenses reduce taxes, so the tax shield is an *inflow,* not an outflow.

Table 12-8   After-Tax Equivalent Method

Type of Item	Calculation
For cash items—sales, cash expenses, etc.	Pretax amount × (1 − T) = After-tax equivalent
For noncash items—depreciation, etc.	Pretax amount × T = Tax shield

It is important to keep in mind that tax effects may be quite different if the firm is losing money at the time and therefore paying no taxes. Negative taxes are not paid to the firm by the goverment! Tax laws permit carrying losses forward to be applied against future income, and sometimes back against prior years' income. So, when a firm is losing money, tax consequences still may be very important, but the actual cash flows due to tax effects may take place in years other than the current one.

Relevant Cash Flows—An Example

Camino Industries is considering replacing an old machine with a newer model having lower maintenance expense. The old machine has a current book value of $2,000, depreciation charge of $500 per year, and remaining life of 4 years, at which time it will have no salvage value. If the machine were sold today, proceeds would be $1,500. Annual maintenance expense is $1,500. The new machine has a purchase price of $6,000, a life of 4 years, a salvage value at the end of 4 years of $2,000, and annual maintenance expense of $200. Assuming a tax rate of 48 percent, let us construct a table presenting the incremental cash flows of the replacement decision: The result is shown in Table 12-9.

Table 12-9   Cash Flows—Replacement Decision

	Existing	Replacement	Incremental
Depreciation $\times$ T	$240	$480	$240
Maintenance $\times$ $(1 - T)$	(780)	(104)	676
Total annual			$916

	Year				
	0	1	2	3	4
Purchase of new machine	$(6,000)				
Salvage	1,500				$2,000
Salvage, tax shield[a]	240				
Annual net flow		$916	$916	$916	$916
	$(4,260)	$916	$916	$916	$2,916

[a]Current book value of old machine is $2,000. Thus, selling it today for $1,500 yields a book loss of $500 and a tax shield of $500 $\times$ 0.48 = $240. Salvage value of new machine is assumed to be book value so that no tax shield is generated in year 4.

Project Dependence

If an investment opportunity is unaffected by other investment opportunities, and itself does not affect the magnitude of the cash flows of other investments or the likelihood of other investments being undertaken, the investment opportunity is said to be *economically independent*. A project that is economically independent can be evaluated in isolation. A project that is not independent, that is, one that affects another project in some way, must take those effects into account. The incremental cash flow rule tells us to identify the cash flows that will change as a result of undertaking the project being evaluated.

To illustrate, consider a firm contemplating the introduction of a new product. If the new product competes with existing products in the firm's product line, as very often is the case, then the expected reduction in cash flows related to such other products should be taken into account. The cash flows of other products change because the new product is introduced, so they are relevant.

A clear distinction should be drawn between *economic* dependence and *statistical* dependence. Cash flows of two projects may be correlated even though the two projects are economically independent according to the definition above. In fact, cash flows of most investments of a firm or even in a whole economy are correlated to some extent because of the business cycle. Statistical correlation between cash flows of different investments, and its implications for investment decision-making, will be discussed in Chapter 15.

Sequential Decisions

Sometimes an investment opportunity may involve a sequence of decisions over time. For example, consider a decision to introduce a new product. Many new products are test marketed before a commitment to full-scale production. Consider the project outlined in Table 12-10. Test

Table 12-10   New Product Introduction

	Year (Amounts in Thousands of Dollars)				
	1	2	3	4	5
Test Market					
Pilot plant	(100)				
Advertising	(50)				
Other expense	(200)				
Revenue	100				
Net	(250)				
Production Phase					
Plant	—	(1,000)			
Revenue	—	700	900	1,100	1,500
Expense	—	(500)	(600)	(700)	(800)
Net	—	(800)	300	400	700

market expenditures are expected to total $350,000, offset by $100,000 in sales revenue, for a net cash outflow of $250,000. Let us assume that at the end of the test market, the firm will decide on the basis of the test results whether to make the commitment to full-scale production, which requires an additional investment outlay of $1 million in the second year.

An analytical technique useful in analyzing sequential decisions is the *decision tree.* In Figure 12-1 we apply the decision tree to the test market problem. Since a decision to produce will not be made until the test is completed, the cash flows related to production are uncertain. If test results are unfavorable, the project will be terminated and the cash flows related to production will not take place.

Figure 12-1 Decision Tree for New Product Introduction

There are two points of decision with respect to this investment opportunity. The first occurs before the test market. At that point, cash flows related to both the test and to production must be considered, that is, all the expected cash flows as shown in Table 12-10. After the test, another decision must be made. At this point, the cash flows related to the market test are *sunk costs* and are irrelevant to the decision to be made. At this second point, the decision to be made cannot affect the cash flows already made in connection with the market test. Hence, according to the incremental cash flow rule, they are not relevant. The only relevant flows are those related to the production phase.

As a second illustration, suppose a firm installs a piece of machinery that costs $50,000 to do a certain job. Six months later, a new machine that costs $60,000 becomes available; it can do the same job with considerably less labor input, promising savings of $15,000 per year after taxes for the life of the equipment, which is estimated at about 7 years. A net present value analysis shows the installation of the new machine to be highly beneficial. However, someone argues that "It is absurd to spend $60,000 for a new machine when we just finished installing a machine for $50,000. We cannot afford to waste the $50,000." The decision to be made is whether to replace the 6 month old machine with the new model. Is the cost of the 6 month old machine relevant? No. The $50,000 is a sunk cost, which is not affected in any way by the decision being evaluated. The incremental cash flow rule tells us to ignore it.

Abandonment

The possibility of terminating or *abandoning* a project deserves further discussion. In the illustration concerning the new product introduction in Table 12-10 and Figure 12-1, cash flows related to a decision to abandon are assumed to be zero. In fact, there often would be cash flows associated with abandonment that should be considered.

One possibility is that there would be *tax effects* if the project were terminated. Equipment that could not be used elsewhere could be *written off*. That is, if equipment used in the pilot production line originally were set up to be depreciated over several years, there would be some book value remaining after the first year. If the equipment could not be used elsewhere, current tax regulations permit the remaining book value to be deducted as an expense. Suppose the pilot plant equipment had a remaining book value at the end of the first year of $60,000, and the tax rate were 48 percent. The $60,000 represents the portion of original cost not yet deducted from cash flow via depreciation. Deducting the $60,000 reduces taxes by $60,000 × 0.48 = $28,800. Hence, the undepreciated equipment provides a *tax shield* of $28,800.

Suppose, upon termination of the project, the pilot plant equipment could be sold. Revenue from the sale clearly is relevant, and along with tax effects, which now are different, should be considered. If the project is terminated at the end of the first year, the cash flows would be those listed in Table 12-11. Sale of the equipment thus produces $10,000 cash revenue and saves $24,000 in taxes, for a total cash inflow of $34,000.

Table 12-11   Abandoning a Project

	End of First Year
Revenue from sale of equipment	$10,000
Book value of pilot plant	60,000
Loss	50,000
Tax shield @ 48 percent	24,000
Total cash inflow	$34,000

Allocated Costs

Some costs that cannot be directly identified with activities are *allocated* to those activities for accounting purposes. Allocation sometimes is done on the basis of number of workers involved in the activity, floor space used, sales revenue, or some similar common factor. Costs that are allocated in this way often include the president's salary, the cost of operating the company cafeteria, and expenses of various staff departments, including the accounting department.

Consider a firm that allocates overhead on the basis of number of direct labor employees. An investment opportunity involving a certain number of employees could have an overhead charge allocated to it. In considering whether to undertake the investment, should overhead be taken into account? Yes, if overhead expense changes as a result of the investment. If overhead will not change as a result of the decision, it is not relevant, regardless of whether the project later would be subject to an overhead allocation for accounting purposes. The incremental cash flow rule tells us that it is only *incremental overhead* that is relevant.

Is overhead likely to change as a result of a particular investment? Sometimes this is a very difficult question to answer. Consider the addition of a new machine to add to production capacity. It is possible that no discernible changes will occur in supervision, cafeteria expenses, and accounting department expenses. But suppose, after the addition of several new machines, the company finds that it must add an additional foreman, expand the cafeteria, and add a person in the accounting department. The cumulative effect of many decisions eventually causes an increase in overhead expenses.

Overhead expenses have to be paid, and a failure to take them into account can lead to serious mistakes. In the long run, all costs are variable! The incremental cash flow rule gives the right answer, but in the case of overhead it is difficult to apply, for often it is not easy to identify the overhead expenses that really will change, and when the changes will occur.

Consider another example in which a firm allocates overhead on the basis of floor space used. Suppose the firm is evaluating a new machine to replace an existing machine. If the new machine requires less floor space, is the reduction in overhead relevant to the decision? Ordinarily it is not, for there is no change in cash flow. However, if there is an alternative use for the floor space, any cash flows that could be generated through its use would be relevant.

Use of Existing Facilities

Consider another case in which a proposed new investment would use half of an existing building that had been constructed earlier for another purpose. In deciding whether to undertake the new investment, should one-half of the cost of the building be included in the DCF analysis? It depends. If there is *no alternative use* for the building, its cost should be ignored as sunk and not relevant to the decision at hand. If there is an alternative use for the building, then it is relevant. If it is used for the prospective investment, an expenditure will be necessary at some point, perhaps later in time, to replace it for other purposes. That expenditure is attributable to the decision being evaluated and therefore is relevant.

The *alternative use rule* is a corollary of the incremental cash flow rule. If there is an alternative use for the floor space or the building, then there likely will be incremental cash flows that are relevant to the decision being considered. Any time a decision involves the use of existing facilities, the alternative use rule should be applied.

Dealing with Uncertainty

In practice, identifying the cash flows an investment is expected to generate often is the most difficult part of the analysis. A major reason for this is that future cash flows are nearly always uncertain. Thus far in this chapter, we have treated future cash flows as single-valued estimates. Let us not lose sight of the fact that the "best guess" of cash flow in some future year is merely a point within a range of possible outcomes.

Suppose a firm is considering building a plant to manufacture a new product. To focus attention of the problem of uncertainty, let us keep the cash flow pattern simple: an outlay for construction of the plant, followed by a series of inflows as the new product is marketed. The cash flows are given in Table 12-12.

Table 12-12 Most Likely Outcomes
(Thousands of Dollars)

	Year				
	0	1	2	. . .	n
Outlay	($1,000)				
Projected cash flow		$100	$200	. . .	$300
Maximum		130	250	. . .	360
Most likely		100	200	. . .	300
Minimum		70	150	. . .	240

Consider the $100,000 inflow anticipated in year 1. This figure is an estimate of the *most likely* outcome in year 1. The actual outcome may range from, say, $70,000 to $130,000. Likewise, $200,000 is an estimate of the most likely outcome in year 2, with a possible range of $150,000 to $250,000. Technically, the estimate we use is the *expected value* of the distribution of possible outcomes (see the appendix at the end of this book). As a practical matter, we can think of the estimate as the most likely outcome.

How do we take the uncertainty of the cash flows into account? We do it via the *target rate of return* that we set for the project. The greater the uncertainty or risk of the cash flows, the higher the target rate of return. In calculating NPV, we discount the most likely cash flows at a rate that reflects the uncertainty of the flows, or we accomplish the same result by comparing the project's internal rate of return to the target. We will go into the matter of setting return targets in depth in our next two chapters.

Sensitivity Analysis

The actual cash flow generated by an investment in any given year is likely to depend on what happens to each of a large number of underlying variables, such as prices, sales volume, advertising effectiveness, counter-moves by competitors, raw material costs, manufacturing costs, energy costs, and so on. Each of these in turn depends on other uncertain variables such as the state of the economy and the rate of inflation.

The final set of cash flows from which investment analysis calculates a project's expected rate of return is based on a single or point estimate of the key underlying factors. But, as we noted above, each of these is itself uncertain and may turn out higher or lower than anticipated.

No amount of analysis can anticipate all developments in a dynamic and uncertain world. Consider, for example, the announcement of a price freeze by the Nixon administration in August 1971, the quintupling of crude oil prices in 1973–1974, the sharp recession of 1975, and the imposition of wage–price guidelines by the Carter administration in late 1978.

However, a technique known as *sensitivity analysis* gives us important insights into how the final outcome of an investment decision is likely to be affected by possible variations in the underlying factors.[2] Via sensitivity analysis, the project's expected return, or its NPV, can be analyzed for different values of key factors. For example, expected return could be calculated for several different assumptions regarding price and manufacturing costs. The results might be displayed as shown in Table 12-13.

If price and manufacturing cost turn out as expected, the project will return 15 percent. If price is 5 percent lower than anticipated, return will be 10 percent, and if price is 10 percent lower, return will be only

Table 12-13 Sensitivity Analysis of Price and Manufacturing Cost

	Project's Expected Return (Percent)
Price	
10 percent lower	5
5 percent lower	10
Most likely	15
5 percent higher	20
10 percent higher	25
Manufacturing Cost	
6 percent lower	20
3 percent lower	17
Most likely	15
5 percent higher	12
10 percent higher	9

2. For a good discussion of sources of error in making investment decisions and the use of sensitivity analysis in practice, see K. Larry Hastie, "One Businessman's View of Capital Budgeting," *Financial Management* 36–44 (Winter 1974).

5 percent. If manufacturing costs turn out to be 10 percent higher than expected, return will be 9 percent rather than 15 percent.

Sensitivity data also can be displayed graphically, as shown in Figure 12-2.

Figure 12-2 Sensitivity Analysis

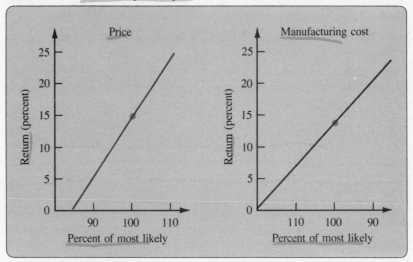

Sensitivity analysis can improve decision-making in a number of ways. First, it indicates which variables and assumptions are most critical and tells management where to focus its analytical efforts. Second, it encourages explicit consideration of uncertainties and risks by managers at different levels. And finally, it identifies areas on which managerial attention should be focused after approval of the project and during implementation.

The Decision Horizon

Over what time period should an investment opportunity be analyzed? The answer depends on the nature of the decision, the decision-maker, the size and importance of the decision, the time and effort that justifiably can be devoted to the analysis, and the time period over which incremental cash flows will be generated.

Some investments involve projects that have well-defined terminal dates, after which cash flows cease. If the period is not too long, it may be well to analyze such projects over their entire lifetimes.

Other investments may involve ongoing activities that are expected to continue indefinitely. An example would be a new plant to produce a product that is expected to have a continuing market. As buildings and equipment wear out, there is a presumption that they will be replaced on a continuing basis.

In the case of ongoing projects, it is clearly necessary to cut off the analysis at some point. The appropriate point, as noted above, depends on the importance of the decision, time available for analysis, and other factors. In general, the longer the horizon the better, although a point of diminishing returns is eventually reached beyond which the increase in accuracy is not sufficient to justify the additional analysis. If an analysis of an ongoing activity is simply cut off at the end of, say, the tenth year, there is an implicit assumption that the remaining value of the project at that point is zero. Often, that is not the case. Where significant, an estimate of the *terminal value* of the project should be made and treated as a cash inflow at the end of the final period of the analysis.

In the case of an ongoing project, the relevant terminal value is the discounted value of all cash flows expected subsequent to that date. But enumeration of those cash flows is what we are trying to avoid! A workable approach often is to estimate the market value of the assets involved in the activity and to treat that value as a cash inflow. Tax effects, for example, taxes on the assumed sale of the assets, should be included as an outflow. Recapture of working capital should be treated as an inflow.

Terminal values far in the future often are subject to a high degree of uncertainty. Even so, terminal values should be considered; if we ignore them, we imply that the best estimate of terminal value is zero. Sometimes an estimate of zero terminal value is justified on grounds of conservatism, but the estimate should be made consciously and not by default. Even if zero appears to be the best estimate of the terminal value of assets, there may be tax effects large enough to warrant consideration.

The Objective: Cash Flows after Taxes

The end point of the analysis, and the objective of our efforts, is *net operating cash flow after taxes*. We then discount these cash flows at a rate appropriate for after-tax flows, that is, the *after-tax required rate of return*.

The reason for carrying out the analysis in after-tax terms is simply that it is after-tax cash flows that investors receive. In some situations, one may encounter analyses carried out on a pretax basis, that is, with pretax cash flows and a pretax required rate of return. Usually, it is possible to perform the analysis in pretax terms, but it becomes difficult to account properly for the effects of depreciation and other noncash charges. In general, there is much less likelihood of error if the analysis is carried out on an after-tax basis.

We have discussed in this chapter some procedures for dealing with tax effects. Suppose tax laws change. Would the procedure discussed above still be applicable? Perhaps not. A change in tax rates would not change the approach, but a change in the method of taxation might. Suppose corporate income were taxed only on the tax returns of the owners, as is done with partnerships and proprietorships. Or suppose the United States changed to a value-added tax, as is used in Europe, rather than an income tax. Some rewriting of finance books would indeed be required. The incremental cash flow rule, however, would live on, and we could turn to it for guidance with respect to any changes in tax laws. It is the incremental cash flows directly attributable to the decision, taxes included, that are relevant.

Some Special Considerations

Keeping Operating and Financing Flows Separate

Sometimes projects arise in which financing arrangements are an integral part of the investment opportunity itself. A good example is a real estate investment in which a mortgage loan on the assets provides a major part of the funds. This situation is less often encountered in firms, other than those involved in real estate investment, because individual investments usually are not identified with specific sources of financing.

Where financing sources are closely related to the investment, there may be the temptation to include interest and principal payments on mortgages or other loans among the cash flows to be discounted. The temptation should be resisted! Mixing the financing flows with the operating flows greatly complicates the problem of determining the appropriate required rate of return at which to discount the net cash flows. When interest and principal are subtracted from operating flows, the remaining cash flows are more variable, that is, more uncertain, than the operating flows themselves.[3] Unless one is very careful, there is a tendency to undercompensate for this increase in variability and to apply a discount rate to the net cash flows (after financing flows are deducted) that is too low. The result can be acceptance of projects that should be rejected.

A safer procedure is to discount the *operating* cash flows of the project, that is, all flows other than interest, principal, and dividend payments. Operating cash flows are defined as those attributable to the project without regard to sources of funds, including cash flows of the sort discussed earlier in this chapter. Where debt, such as a mortgage loan, is used to finance part of an investment, the fact that interest payments are tax-deductible can affect the desirability of the investment. The effect of financing arrangements on investment decisions is discussed in a later chapter.

---

3. Subtracting interest and principal, which are fixed in amount, does not alter the variability in dollar terms of the remainder. However, the variability in percentage terms, per dollar of outlay, increases. The percentage variability is the basis for judging risk.

The Effects of Inflation

Prior to the mid-1960s, the general price indexes increased at only about 1.5–2.0 percent per year on an average. Although important to other decisions, inflation at such relatively low rates usually did not seriously distort the investment decisions of firms and individuals. An exception was decisions that involved investment or financing across international boundaries, when inflation rates in different countries might differ.

The high rates of inflation we have encountered in the United States and elsewhere in the 1970s are a different matter. Inflation has a seriously adverse impact on returns to capital investment because of our current tax laws and rules for treating depreciation.

Suppose a firm is considering an investment of $300,000 that generates the cash flows shown in Table 12-14.[4] The investment has a useful life of 5 years and generates net cash receipts (after cash expenses) of $100,000. Assume a tax rate of 50 percent. As indicated in Table 12-14, the internal rate of return of the investment is 10.4 percent (the rate that discounts $80,000 per year for 5 years back to equal the outlay of $300,000).

Table 12-14 Return on a Hypothetical Investment with Zero Inflation

	1	2	3	4
End of Year	Net Cash Receipts	Cash Receipts Not Taxed Due to Depreciation Charges	Taxes Paid	After-Tax Cash Flow
1	$100,000	$60,000	$20,000	$80,000
2	100,000	60,000	20,000	80,000
3	100,000	60,000	20,000	80,000
4	100,000	60,000	20,000	80,000
5	100,000	60,000	20,000	80,000
IRR = 10.4 percent				

Now consider the impact of inflation of, say, 5 percent per year. Suppose revenues and expenses are affected equally so that net cash receipts grow 5 percent per year. Depreciation is based on historical cost and does not change, so taxable income is higher and taxes are higher. After-tax cash flow also is higher, and the nominal return, calculated by discounting

---

4. This example is from J. A. Tatom and J. E. Turley, "Inflation and Taxes: Disincentives for Capital Formation," *Monthly Review,* Federal Reserve Bank of St. Louis, Jan. 1978. See also C. R. Nelson, "Inflation and Capital Budgeting," *Journal of Finance* **31**, 923–931 (June 1976).

the cash flows in column 4 of Table 12-15, rises to 14.0 percent. But the *real* return, adjusted for inflation (column 5) falls to 8.5 percent.

Table 12-15   Return on a Hypothetical Investment with a 5 Percent Inflation Rate

	1	2	3	4	5
End of Year	Net Cash Receipts	Cash Receipts Not Taxed Due to Depreciation Charges	Taxes Paid	After-Tax Cash Flow	Purchasing Power of After-Tax Cash Flow
1	$105,000	$60,000	$22,500	$82,500	$78,571
2	110,250	60,000	25,125	85,125	77,211
3	115,763	60,000	27,882	87,881	75,915
4	121,501	60,000	30,776	90,775	74,681
5	127,628	60,000	33,814	93,814	73,506

IRR = 14.0 percent nominal, 8.5 percent real

A part of the higher returns under inflation is necessary to compensate lenders and investors for the decline in the purchasing power of the dollar. This *inflation premium* is really a principal payment the purpose of which is to maintain the real (inflation-adjusted) value of the investors' claim. It is not income, but our current tax system treats it as if it were. One purpose of depreciation is to protect the principal from taxation. But the depreciation charge is fixed and does not provide complete protection in an inflationary environment.

The net effect is that inflation causes the government's share of the real returns to rise and the investors' share to fall. Many experts in taxation are very concerned about the implications of this result for capital formation in our economy. Some projects that may have produced adequate returns under low rates of inflation produce returns considered inadequate by investors when inflation rises.[5]

There is little that financial managers can do to remedy the adverse impact of our current tax laws on investment returns. Such remedies are the province of the taxing authorities. However, financial managers can, and must, take inflation into account in analyzing investment opportunities. Here we can state some general rules, but application of these rules in specific situations may not be easy.

---

5. See Tatom and Turley, "Inflation and Taxes," and M. S. Feldstein and J. Slemrod, "How Inflation Distorts the Taxation of Capital Gains," *Harvard Business Review* **56**, 20–22 (Sept.–Oct. 1978).

Inflation has to be recognized both in estimates of cash flows and in target rates of return. The best approach is to project cash flows in nominal (inflated) dollars and then to discount those flows at a rate that also includes an inflation premium. We will return to the matter of how inflation is included in return targets in Chapter 14.

Unhappily, simply adjusting cash flow estimates for the expected rate of change in the *general* price indexes, for example, the Consumer Price Index, often will not do. Inflation affects various industries and firms in different ways. Within a given firm, inflation may affect different elements of the cash flow stream in different ways. Sales revenues may be affected differently from labor costs, and still differently from energy costs. Each situation must be handled separately. About the best that can be said as a general rule is to state expected cash flows in *nominal,* that is, inflated, values, taking into account as well as possible the differential inflation effects on various categories of cash flow. As is always true, the analyst should suit the approach to the task and keep in mind the costs of the analysis itself in terms of time and effort expended in relation to benefits to be gained.

Mergers and Acquisitions

Special problems sometimes arise in identifying relevant cash flows in connection with mergers of two firms or acquisition of one firm by another. Let us assume that firm A is considering the acquisition of firm B and plans to use DCF analysis in deciding whether to make the acquisition. The problem at hand is to determine the cash flows that should be discounted.

When one firm acquires another, there often is a presumption that some operating economies can be achieved. Product lines may be complementary, savings may be possible in production or marketing, or technologies may be mutually reinforcing. Such savings often are referred to as providing *synergy,* or the "two plus two equals five effect." The effects of synergy often are important and should be taken into account in estimating cash flows.

Let us get back to firms A and B. Suppose firm B is a separate corporation and is expected to generate the cash flows listed in Table 12-16, with prosepctive synergy taken into account. Are the cash flows on the bottom line of the table the ones that should be discounted? Usually they are not. The cash flows that should be discounted are those that are available to the investor(s) for reinvestment elsewhere. In a going concern, internal reinvestment is necessary to replace equipment and facilities that are continuously wearing out and thereby to maintain the firm's earning power. Investment over and above replacement requirements is necessary if the firm is to grow. Thus, of the cash flows in Table 12-16, it is likely that a significant part is required for reinvestment for both replacement and growth.

Table 12-16   Evaluating an Acquisition

	Year (Amounts in Thousands of Dollars)					
	1	2	3	4	. . .	10
Expected earnings after taxes	100	110	117	125		160
Depreciation	20	22	24	26		36
Total cash flow after taxes	120	132	141	151		196

At the terminal point of the DCF analysis, firm *B* presumably has some value. The cash flows reinvested during years prior to the terminal date contribute to that terminal value. Hence, if we discount flows that are reinvested and also the terminal value to which they contribute, we will be double counting the effects of the reinvested flows.

In any DCF analysis, the correct procedure is to discount the *net* cash flows available to the investor(s) for investment elsewhere. When we value a share of stock, we discount dividends expected to be received plus expected price at the terminal point of the analysis. When valuing firm *B* above, or any potential acquisition, we should do the same thing: discount the net, or *free,* cash flow available for payment of dividends plus the value of the firm at the terminal point of the analysis. To apply this approach to firm *B,* we would need additional data, namely, the expected level of capital investment in each period. Using these data along with the figures in Table 12-16, we can then calculate the free cash flow available for dividends.

We will consider mergers and acquisitions in more detail in Chapter 24.

Summary

This chapter deals with the second major step in analyzing an investment opportunity, identifying the cash flows that it is expected to generate. In using DCF decision criteria, it is *cash* that matters, rather than accounting profit. Careful cash flow estimates are essential for good decisions.

The *incremental cash flow rule* states that the cash flows that should be considered in analyzing any investment are those cash flows directly attributable to the investment. Although the incremental cash flow rule determines relevance, it does not tell us the correct magnitude. Cash flows that typically must be considered include the initial outlay, revenues, cash expenses, and taxes. The effect of depreciation on taxes must

Sample Problem

①   peel

dep = $800 × 48% = $384

	INCREMENTAL		
	Life	New	
OPERATING SAVINGS	1600 × 48% = $768	= $384	
			780
TOTAL ANNUAL CASH FLOW (AFTER-TAX)	—	—	$1164

CASH FLOWS

	1	2	YEAR 3	4	5
PURCHASE NEW	(8000)				
SALVAGE OLD	1000				
SALVAGE - TAX	1440				
SHIELD DUE TO LOSS	—	✓	1164	1164	1164
ANNUAL CASH FLOW		1164			

Net Cash Flow ⟨5560⟩ $1164 $1164 $1164 $1164

② (RRR 10%)

$$NPU = ⟨5560⟩ + 1.164 \ (PV FACTOR ; N = 5, 10 percent)$$

$$⟨5560⟩ + 1.164 \ (3.791)$$

$$= (5560) + 4412$$

$$= (1147)$$

$$≈ NO''$$

be considered. Changes in net working capital attributable to the investment also are relevant. Investment opportunities that are economically independent can be analyzed individually, whereas projects that are dependent cannot. Projects involving sequential decisions require special techniques such as decision trees. Sunk costs, that is, costs already incurred and unaffected by the decision under evaluation, are irrelevant. Allocated costs, such as overhead, are relevant only if the total of such costs actually changes because of the prospective investment. The use of preexisting facilities by an investment opportunity must be analyzed carefully and some assessment of cost must be made unless there is no alternative use for the existing facilities. The time period over which the analysis is to be made should be selected to balance the need for accuracy against the cost of the analysis.

The end objective of the analysis is cash flow *after taxes*. Treatment of tax effects is a complex and important part of the analysis. In all cases, it is the *operating* cash flows of the investment that are to be evaluated. Financial flows (interest and principal) should be kept separate. The impact of financing arrangements on investment decisions is considered in a later chapter.

Inflation presents a special problem. The best procedure, usually, is to estimate cash flows in nominal (inflated) terms and then to evaluate those flows using required rates of return that also include inflation effects.

Sample Problem

Your firm is considering replacing an existing machine with a newer piece of equipment. The existing machine has a book value of $4,000, annual depreciation charges of $800, and a remaining useful life of 5 years with an expected zero salvage value. The machine could be sold today for $1,000. The new machine would cost $8,000, and it has an expected life of 5 years with a zero salvage value. This new machine is expected to save $1,500 annually in operating expenses. The machine will be depreciated on a straight-line basis.

1. Assuming a tax rate of 48 percent, construct a table of the relevant incremental cash flows for the replacement decision.
2. If the firm's required rate of return on such investments is 10 percent, would you recommend replacement of the existing machine by the newer one?

Solution

1. There are several approaches to finding the incremental cash flows. One method is to convert the cash flows to their after-tax equivalents

as shown in Table 12-8 of the text. Using this method, we can construct the following tables.

	Existing Machine	New Machine	Incremental
Depreciation × Tax rate	$384	$768	$ 384
Operating savings × (1 − Tax rate)	—	—	780
Total annual cash flow (after-tax)			$1,164

Cash Flows		Year				
		1	2	3	4	5
Purchase, new machine	($8,000)					
Salvage, old machine	1,000					
Salvage tax shield due to loss	1,440					
Annual cash flow	—	$1,164	$1,164	$1,164	$1,164	$1,164
Net cash flow	($5,560)	$1,164	$1,164	$1,164	$1,164	$1,164

In the above table, we calculate the depreciation tax shield on the existing machine as $800 × 0.48 = $384. Likewise, the depreciation tax shield on the new machine is $1,600 × 0.48 = $768. The after-tax equivalent of the operating savings is $1,500 (1 − 0.48) = $780.

If we sell the old machine, we show a book loss of $3,000 on the machine. This provides a tax shield of $3,000 × 0.48 = $1,440. Our taxes are reduced by this amount, so it represents a cash inflow. In year 0, we will have a net outflow of cash: $8,000 outflow for the new machine less the inflow of cash from the sale of the old machine and subsequent tax shield. The net cash outflow in year 0 is $5,560.

2. Using NPV as our decision criterion, we would purchase the new machine if the NPV of the decision is greater than zero. The table constructed in part (1) gives us the relevant cash flows. Since the cash flows in years 1–5 are equal, we can use the present value factors given in Table II at the end of the book to discount the cash flows.

$$\text{NPV} = (\$5,560) + \$1,164 \text{ (PV factor: } n = 5, 10 \text{ percent)}$$

$$= (\$5,560) + \$1,164 \text{ (3.791)}$$

$$= (\$1,147)$$

Since the incremental NPV is less than zero, we would not recommend purchase of the machine.

Questions

1. State the incremental cash flow rule.
2. In some cases, investment opportunities involve outlays over several time periods. In such cases, what procedures should be followed to identify the "initial investment"?
3. How should working capital be treated in analyzing investment opportunities?
4. A nonprofit organization not subject to income tax is considering an investment opportunity involving a labor-saving machine. How should depreciation be treated in the analysis?
5. How should sunk costs be taken into account in analyzing investment opportunities?
6. How should allocated expenses such as overhead be treated in analyzing investment opportunities?
7. When an investment opportunity makes use of the existing facilities, how should costs associated with these existing facilities be treated in the analysis?
8. Many investment opportunities give rise to ongoing activities and to cash flow streams that have no well-defined termination points. Over what time period should such investment opportunities be analyzed?
9. In identifying relevant cash flows, the object normally is to determine after-tax cash flows rather than pretax cash flows. Why is it best to deal with after-tax rather than pretax cash flows?
10. Why is it best to evaluate the after-tax operating cash flows of an investment, with financing flows kept separate?
11. How should inflation be taken into account in estimating cash flows?

Problems

1. A firm is considering the following two competing proposals for the purchase of new equipment:

	A	B
Net cash outlay	$10,000	$7,500
Salvage value	0	0
Estimated life	5 years	5 years
Net cash savings before depreciation and taxes		
Years 1–3	$3,000	$2,000
Years 4–5	$2,500	$2,000

Assume straight-line depreciation and a tax rate of 40 percent.

(a) Calculate the net present value of each alternative at a discount rate of 10 percent.

(b) If 10 percent is the required rate of return, which alternative should be selected? Why?

2. Suppose that machine *B* in Problem 1 is expected to have a salvage value of $1,000 at the end of year 5.
   (a) Determine the effect on the NPV (at 10 percent) of alternative *B*.
   (b) Does this change the decision reached in Problem 1, part b? Why, or why not?

3. Determine the internal rate of return of the replacement opportunity described in Table 12-9 of the text.

4. Your firm is considering an expansion project that will increase sales by $1 million per year. Aside from the usual project cash flows, you also recognize that working capital will have to be increased in order to support the new sales volume. Given the balance sheet breakdown shown, expressed as a percentage of sales, and assuming that these percentages are expected to remain constant at the new sales level, what cash flow would you budget for the net increase in working capital? In what period would this outflow occur?

Assets (Percent of Sales)		Liabilities (Percent of Sales)	
Cash	3.0	Accounts payable	12.0
Receivables	15.0	Accrued taxes	2.0
Inventories	22.0	Bonds	21.0
Fixed assets (net)	35.0	Common stock	20.0
		Retained earnings	20.0

5. International Company is considering replacing an old stamping machine with a newer and more efficient model. The old machine had an accounting book value of $12,000 and a projected life of 20 years when it was purchased 10 years ago. The projected salvage value was $2,000 at the time of purchase. The machine has recently begun causing problems with breakdowns and is costing the company $1,000 per year in maintenance expenses. The company has been offered $5,000 for the old machine as a trade-in on a newer model which has a delivered price (before allowance for trade-in) of $11,000. It has a projected life of 10 years and a projected salvage value of $1,000. The new machine will require installation modifications of $2,000 to existing facilities, but it is projected to have a cost savings in production materials of $4,000 per year. Maintenance costs are included in the purchase contract and are borne by the machine manufacturer. Assuming a marginal tax rate of 40 percent and all depreciation via the straight-line method, construct a summary table of relevant cash flows.

6. Chatham Manufacturing Corporation purchased an old building in Washington, D.C., 2 days ago and immediately contracted for $50,000 in exterior renovation. The building has a projected life of 30 years with a zero salvage value, and it cost Chatham $3,610,000. Annual upkeep on the building is estimated at $25,000 and annual property taxes are $50,000. Chatham is considering using the building as a warehousing outlet to reduce current annual storage expenses by $400,000 per year. Alternatively, another firm has offered to lease the building for 30 years at $300,000 per year and assume all required maintenance expense. Assuming a marginal tax rate of 40 percent and all depreciation via the straight-line method, construct a summary table of relevant cash flows. Do you have enough information to be able to recommend what Chatham should do? If not, what additional information do you need?

7. Orange Manufacturing Company has an opportunity to replace an existing piece of equipment with a new machine that performs a particular manufacturing operation more efficiently. The purchase price of the new machine is $16,500. Shipping charges will be $900 and installation $600. Because of a high rate of technological obsolescence, the machine is expected to have a life of only 3 years and to have no salvage value. Direct savings from use of the new machine are expected to be $9,600 in the first year and $8,400 in each of the next 2 years. The old machine has a remaining book value of $2,100 and is being depreciated at a rate of $700 per year. Its remaining useful life is 3 years, at the end of which time it will have no salvage value. If sold now, it will bring $3,000. The applicable tax rate is 48 percent on both income and on gains on sales of equipment. The company uses straight-line depreciation.

   (a) Calculate the net present value of the investment opportunity at a discount rate of 10 percent. Calculate the internal rate of return. If 10 percent is the minimum acceptable rate of return on the investment opportunity, should the old machine be replaced?

   (b) Suppose that the new machine has an estimated salvage value of $3,000 at the end of the third year, and that straight-line depreciation is calculated on this assumption. If all other assumptions are as in part a, what are the NPV at 10 percent and the internal rate of return?

   (c) Suppose that use of the new machine required an immediate investment in additional inventory of $2,500, and that this extra inventory can be liquidated at the end of year 3. If all other assumptions are those of part a, what is the internal rate of return?

8. The Downtown Development Corporation plans to sell a vacant lot and receives two offers: the first, an offer of $800,000 cash; the second,

an offer of $900,000 with $225,000 to be paid immediately and the balance in equal installments over 5 years (at year-end). Which offer should be accepted? Assume that opportunities exist to invest in riskless United States government bonds returning 6 percent.

9. The Allen Company, a manufacturer of inexpensive perfumes and toiletries, is considering an investment in a new perfume, Jasper. The company has spent $75,000 in developing and testing the new fragrance, and the final chemical formula and marketing plans have been decided upon. If Jasper is introduced, it will replace the Rosalyn product line, which has experienced declining sales over the past few years. Jasper can be manufactured and bottled using the same equipment and labor force currently used for Rosalyn without any adjustments or modifications. The equipment being used has a remaining book value of $160,000 and is being depreciated at a rate of $20,000 per year. An additional packaging machine will be required for the Jasper line to accommodate the product's more sophisticated package design. The machine required will cost $50,000 (delivered and installed) and has a projected life of 5 years with no salvage value. The machine is fully automated and will not require any additional personnel for operation. It is expected that this machine will increase overhead maintenance and power expenses by $1,000 per year. The raw material costs for Jasper are expected to be 15¢ per bottle compared to Rosalyn's cost of 10¢ per bottle. Labeling and packaging costs for Jasper are expected to be 20¢ per bottle compared to Rosalyn's 10¢ per bottle. The marketing department has provided projected sales levels and marketing expenses for the Jasper and Rosalyn lines for the next 5 years, which are shown in the table. These forecasts assume that if Jasper is not introduced, Rosalyn will stay on the market, and if Jasper is introduced, Rosalyn will be taken off the

Market Forecasts

	Year				
Jasper Line	1	2	3	4	5
Sales, number of bottles	100,000	100,000	75,000	60,000	30,000
Price per bottle	$ 5.00	$ 5.00	$ 5.00	$ 4.00	$ 4.00
Marketing expenses (assume all are cash outlays)	$200,000	$200,000	$120,000	$50,000	$20,000
Rosalyn Line					
Sales, number of bottles	75,000	75,000	50,000	30,000	20,000
Price per bottle	$ 4.00	$ 4.00	$ 3.50	$ 3.50	$ 3.00
Marketing Expenses	$ 50,000	$ 40,000	$ 40,000	$ 0	$ 0

market. At the end of 5 years it is expected that either product will have exhausted its sales potential and will be taken off the market. No increases in working capital are expected to be needed to support the Jasper line.

(a) Assuming a 50 percent tax rate and straight-line depreciation, construct a summary table of the relevant cash flows for making the decision of introducing Jasper or keeping Rosalyn.

(b) If Allen's required rate of return is 20 percent, what is the incremental NPV of introducing Jasper? (For simplicity, assume all cash flows occur at the end of the year.)

10. Benson Enterprises, Inc., is evaluating alternative uses for a three story manufacturing and warehousing building that had been purchased for $225,000. The company could continue to rent the building to the present occupants for $12,000 per year. The present occupants have indicated an interest in staying in the building for at least another 15 years. Alternatively, the company could modify the existing structure to use for its own manufacturing and warehousing needs. Benson's production engineer feels the building could be adapted to handle one of two new product lines. The cost and revenue data for the two product alternatives are given below:

	Product *A*	Product *B*
Initial cash outlay for building modifications	$ 36,000	$ 54,000
Initial cash outlay for equipment	144,000	162,000
Annual pretax cash revenues (generated for 15 years)	105,000	127,500
Annual pretax cash expenditures (generated for 15 years)	60,000	75,000

The building will be used only for 15 years for either product *A* or *B*. After 15 years, the building will be too small for efficient production of either product line, and Benson plans to rent the building to firms similar to the current occupants. To rent the building again, Benson will have to restore the building to its present layout. The estimated cash cost of restoring the building if product *A* has been undertaken is $3,750; if product *B* has been produced, the cash cost will be $28,125. Benson will depreciate the original building shell (purchased for $225,000) over a 30 year life to zero salvage value regardless of which alternative is chosen. The building modifications and equipment purchases for either product are estimated to have a 15 year life and zero salvage value. All depreciation is done on a straight-line basis. The firm's tax rate is 50 percent, and its required rate of return on such investments is 12 percent, after taxes. Which use of the building for the next 15 years would you recommend to management? For simplicity, assume all cash flows for a given year occur at the end of the year, that the initial outlays for modifications and equipment will occur at $t = 0$, and the restoration outlays will occur at the end of year 15.

11. The Cartwright Company is considering replacing one of its existing machines with a new, more automated and efficient machine. The existing machine was purchased for $93,800 (installed) 4 years ago and is being depreciated on a straight-line basis over a 14 year life to a zero salvage value. The machine could be sold today for $20,000. The new machine could be purchased for $95,000. Installation costs would be an additional $3,000. It is estimated that the new machine could increase output by 10 percent, increasing sales revenue by $15,000 per year. In addition, the machine is expected to reduce operating costs by $18,000 annually. The machine has an expected 10 year life with a $13,000 salvage value and will be depreciated on a straight-line basis. Cartwright's required rate of return on such investments is 10 percent, and the firm's tax rate is 48 percent.

(a) Should Cartwright purchase the new machine?

(b) If the new machine did not reduce any costs but only increased output, what would be your recommendation?

(c) What would the purchase price have to be to change your recommendation?

12. National Foods is considering producing a new gelatin dessert. Tasty, of which management believes consumers will buy 5,000,000 packages each year for 10 years at $0.40 per package. Equipment to produce Tasty will cost National $400,000, and $200,000 of additional net working capital will be required to support Tasty sales. National expects production costs to average 60 percent of net revenues from Tasty, with overhead and sales expenses totaling $500,000 per year. The equipment has a life of 10 years, at which time it will have no salvage value. Working capital is assumed to be fully recovered in year 10. Depreciation is straight-line, and National's tax rate is 48 percent.

(a) Determine the after-tax operating cash flows the Tasty project is expected to generate over its 10 year life.

(b) Find the net present value of the operating cash flows at a required rate of return of 16 percent.

(c) Calculate the internal rate of return of the Tasty project.

(d) Consider the effect on cash flows, net present value, and the internal rate of return if unit demand for Tasty were to fall 10 percent below management's expectations.

(e) Consider the effect on cash flows, net present value, and the internal rate of return if unit demand were to be at the expected level but production costs were to average 70 percent of net revenues.

(f) What conclusions do you draw from the sensitivity analysis?

References

J. S. Ang, J. H. Chua, and R. Sellers, "Generating Cash Flow Estimates: An Actual Study Using the Delphi Technique," *Financial Management* **8,** 64–67, (Spring 1979).

A. D. Bailey and D. L. Jensen, "General Price Level Adjustments in the Capital Budgeting Decision," *Financial Management* **6,** 26–32 (Spring 1977).

P. L. Cooley, R. L. Roenfeldt, and I. Chew, "Capital Budgeting Procedures Under Inflation," *Financial Management* **4,** 18–27 (Winter 1975).

M. S. Feldstein and J. Slemrod, "How Inflation Distorts the Taxation of Capital Gains," *Harvard Business Review* **56,** 20–21 (Sept.–Oct. 1978).

D. B. Hertz, "Investment Policies that Pay Off," *Harvard Business Review* **46,** 96–108 (Jan.–Feb. 1968).

R. K. Jaedicke and R. T. Sprouse, *Accounting Flows: Income, Funds and Cash* (Englewood Cliffs, N.J.: Prentice-Hall, 1965).

R. W. Johnson, *Capital Budgeting* (Belmont, Ca.: Wadsworth, 1970).

C. R. Nelson, "Inflation and Capital Budgeting," *Journal of Finance* **31,** 923–931 (June 1976).

A. C. Shapiro, "Capital Budgeting for the Multinational Corporation," *Financial Management* **7,** 7–16 (Spring 1978).

J. A. Tatom and J. E. Turley, "Inflation and Taxes: Disincentives for Capital Formation," *Monthly Review,* Federal Reserve Bank of St. Louis, Jan. 1978.

J. C. Van Horne, "A Note on Biases in Capital Budgeting Introduced by Inflation," *Journal of Financial and Quantitative Analysis* **6,** 653–658 (Jan. 1971).

The Required
Rate of Return

13

Opportunity Rates
Risk and Risk-Aversion
Role of Markets
Required Rate of Return
Cost of Capital

We now turn to the difficult problem of setting the financial standard for investment decisions: How do we determine the appropriate rate at which to discount the cash flows? No matter what selection criterion we choose, whether a DCF criterion or an accounting-based criterion, we still face the questions: What is the minimum rate we should accept? How much is enough? Had we chosen the simple payback approach, we still would face the question of choosing a maximum acceptable payback period. With a DCF approach, the question is: What is the minimum acceptable rate of return on the project? Henceforth, we will refer to the minimum acceptable return as the *required rate of return* (RRR) for the project, or the *required return* for short.

Opportunity Rates

Opportunity Costs

When an investment is to be made, the investor, whether an individual or a manager acting on behalf of shareholders, always has alternative opportunities to invest funds. If not, there is no decision to be made. Simply leaving funds on deposit in a checking account, or under the mattress, represents an opportunity—with a zero return. There nearly always exists the opportunity to place funds in an instrument or account that promises some positive rate of return.

Let us consider the problem of an investor analyzing an investment opportunity, call it project *X*. Project *X* requires an outlay now and promises a cash return at some point in the future. If the investor undertakes project *X*, he or she foregoes the opportunity to do something else with that money. Hence, by undertaking project *X*, the investor incurs an *opportunity cost*, namely, whatever could have been earned on an alternative investment.

The concept of opportunity cost is a general and useful one. The true economic cost of any action includes all that one must give up in order to undertake the action. Where a cash outlay is involved, as in the purchase of a bicycle for $100, for example, the cost usually is referred to as an *out-of-pocket* cost. Here the cash outlay measures the extent of the lost opportunity to purchase something else.

Some actions involve an opportunity cost only. Consider, for example, an offer of $5 to a schoolboy for mowing the lawn. If he passes up the opportunity, he is $5 poorer. There is an opportunity cost, but no out-of-pocket cost. The term *opportunity cost* usually refers to actions involving an opportunity cost but no out-of-pocket cost.

Required Rate of Return: An Opportunity Rate

Let us return to our investor considering project X. If the investment is made, the investor incurs an opportunity cost equal to what could have been earned on an alternative investment that involves risks similar to those of the project being contemplated. If the investor has an alternative opportunity returning R percent, he or she foregoes R percent by undertaking project X. Hence, the investor should require that project X return at least R percent before deeming it acceptable. The *required rate of return* on project X is R percent. Thus, we can formulate a general definition of the required rate of return on any investment project: *It is the rate foregone on the next best alternative investment opportunity.* As we will see later, we must measure the investment against another of comparable risk. For now, the important point to establish is that the required return on an investment project is an *opportunity rate.*

When we use DCF techniques for evaluating an investment, the required return becomes our target. In a present value analysis, the RRR is the assumed reinvestment rate, the rate at which investors are assumed to be able to reinvest the cash flows generated by the investment. To calculate NPV, the RRR is used as the discount rate. If NPV is positive, the project should be undertaken. Alternately and equivalently, if the internal rate of return of the project exceeds the required rate, the project should be undertaken.

Whose Required Rate of Return?

For an individual, it is clear that the required return on a prospective investment should be set in relation to other opportunities available. What about the case of a professionally managed firm? Whose required return is appropriate? Management's? The shareholders'? The answer depends on whose interests are to be served by making the investment.

Management as Agent of Shareholders

In Chapter 1, we noted that this is a *normative* book; we are presenting a framework describing the way things should be done if certain objectives are to be achieved. We adopted the criterion of maximizing the value of the firm, a criterion based on the more general objective of maximizing shareholder utility. As noted in Chapter 1, maximizing shareholder utility is consistent with the concept of consumer sovereignty, which forms the basis for much of microeconomic theory, and also with efficient allocation of resources within the economy. Our whole approach to financial management in this book thus is based on the principle of optimizing with respect to shareholder interests.

If we are to maximize the value of the firm to the shareholders, then in analyzing an investment project it is the value of the project to the shareholders that is relevant. Since value lies in the eye of the beholder, we must value a cash flow stream using a discount rate that correctly reflects the preferences of those to whom the value accrues. To determine value to shareholders, we must use the *shareholders'* required rate of return.

To see that this is so, consider a firm with a single owner who also is its manager. In evaluating investment opportunities, the owner-manager would use his or her own required rates of return, which would depend on opportunities to invest outside the company. As we will see shortly, these required rates of return would vary with the riskiness of the investment opportunity. Now let us assume that the owner hires someone else to manage the company. The owner tells the new manager: "In analyzing investment opportunities, apply these targets as required rates of return. These are the rates that I can earn outside the company. If you cannot equal or exceed these returns, then pay the money out to me and I will invest it elsewhere."

Now suppose that the owner sells a part of the company to others. We can see that the principle remains the same whether the firm has few shareholders or many. The shareholders say to the management, "Use these rates as targets. If you cannot do at least this well, pay the money out to us and we will invest it elsewhere." The management uses the shareholders' required rates of return in evaluating investment opportunities. Hence, the RRR that management should use is the rate on the next best opportunity foregone by the shareholders, rather than by the firm itself.

Fundamental to our whole approach to the financial management of firms is the concept of *management acting as the agent of the shareholders.* This concept provides an answer to the question: Whose required rate of return? If management is acting to maximize shareholder interests, as it should, then management should evaluate investment opportunities using the shareholders' required rate of return, that is, *the rate the shareholders would use if they were performing the evaluation themselves.* Just how we establish this rate presents many difficulties, such as what to do when the firm has hundreds or thousands of shareholders. The existence of organized financial markets provides an answer to this question. As we will see, the RRR is a *market-determined* rate, established in the financial markets by the collective actions of investors competing against one another.

Risk and Risk-Aversion

An important factor taken into account by investors in setting required rates of return is the riskiness of investment opportunities. To properly account for risk, we must draw a clear distinction between the risk of an investment opportunity and the attitude toward risk of the investor.

Risk

What is risk? A simple and workable definition for our purposes is that risk is the *degree of uncertainty about an outcome.* In statistical terms, the risk of an investment can be measured in an approximate way by the dispersion of the probability distribution about its expected value. One such measure of dispersion is the standard deviation. The standard deviation is only an approximate measure because it captures only a part of those characteristics of a return distribution that may be important to investors in evaluating risk.

Risk is a characteristic of the investment opportunity and has nothing to do with the attitudes of investors. Consider two investments, *A* and *B*, that have the possible payoffs listed in Table 13-1, depending on the

Table 13-1   Uncertain Outcomes

State of Economy	Investment Return	
	A	*B*
Recession	$ 90	$ 0
Normal	100	100
Boom	110	200

state of the economy. Assuming that the three states of the economy are equally likely, the average expected return from both investments is $100. But the return from investment *A* will be between $90 and $110, whereas that from *B* may vary between $0 and $200. There is considerably more uncertainty about the return from *B*, but we have said nothing yet about whether the investor cares about the greater uncertainty.

Risk-Aversion

In general, investors and individuals do care about uncertainty. Suppose you were offered an opportunity to choose one of the two investments, *A* or *B* above. If your choice is *A,* you are *risk-averse* with respect to this decision. If your choice is *B,* you are *risk-preferent.* If you are indifferent between *A* and *B,* you are *risk-neutral* with respect to this decision.

Consider another illustration. Suppose you are offered an opportunity to undertake investment *B* in return for cash payment. The *expected value* of investment *B* is $100, as calculated in Table 13-2. What is the maximum you would be willing to pay for an opportunity to invest in *B*? If less than $100, you are exhibiting risk-averse behavior with respect to this investment opportunity. If more than $100, you are exhibiting

Table 13-2 Expected Value

Payoff	Probability	Weighted Outcome
$ 0	.333	$ 0
100	.333	33.33
200	.333	66.67
	Expected value	$100.00

risk-preference. If exactly $100, you are exhibiting risk-neutrality. In general, an unwillingness to pay an amount as great as the expected value of an uncertain investment opportunity indicates risk-averse behavior; a willingness to pay exactly the expected value indicates risk-neutrality; and a willingness to pay more indicates risk-preference.

It is important to note that a single individual may exhibit risk-averse behavior toward some decisions and risk-preferent behavior toward others. An individual who plays roulette at Las Vegas, an example of risk-preferent behavior, also may own fire insurance on a house, an example of risk-averse behavior. The size of the gamble also may be a factor. The same individual may be risk-preferent toward small gambles, such as flipping coins for nickels, and risk-averse toward large gambles, such as flipping coins for $1,000 a flip.

There is nothing inconsistent or irrational about the behavior of an individual who exhibits risk-aversion toward some gambles and risk-preference toward others. In the case of an individual who is risk-averse toward most financial decisions but who also occasionally exhibits risk-preferent behavior, it is likely that the risk-preferent behavior contains elements of entertainment, for example, gambling at Las Vegas.

Where matters of income and wealth are concerned, as distinct from entertainment, we can safely assume risk-aversion to be characteristic of nearly all individuals. An individual making an investment decision affecting only him- or herself can determine his or her own attitude toward risk. With respect to investors in general, studies of the securities markets provide convincing evidence that the majority of investors in stocks and bonds are risk-averse. This suggests that they are unwilling to pay an amount equal to the expected value of an investment opportunity, that is, they demand a premium for *bearing risk*.[1]

Required Return as a Function of Project Risk

Risk-aversion, risk-neutrality, and risk-preference are statements about an investor's attitude toward risk. Risk-aversion implies that an investor

---

1. For evidence of risk aversion, see I. Friend and M. Blume, "The Demand for Risky Assets," *American Economic Review* **55,** 900–922 (Dec. 1975).

requires compensation for bearing risk. Risk-preference implies that the investor will pay for the opportunity to gamble. Risk-neutrality implies indifference toward risk, that is, that no compensation is required for bearing risk.

The investor's attitude toward risk is an important factor in determining the required rate of return of an investment opportunity. The greater the risk, the greater the compensation required. Thus, risk-aversion, a behavioral characteristic of investors, leads directly to the important proposition that *the required return on an investment opportunity depends on the riskiness of the investment.* We can speak of a *risk/return tradeoff,* as illustrated in Figure 13-1. The greater the risk of the investment opportunity, the more the return required by the investor. The line in Figure 13-1 symbolizes the terms of the risk/return tradeoff.

Figure 13-1   The Risk/Return Tradeoff

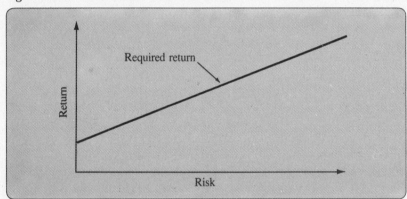

It is important to note that risk-aversion does not imply complete avoidance of risk. It merely implies that compensation is required, and that the greater the risk, the greater the compensation must be. A risk-averse person will undertake a risky investment, even an investment of very high risk, provided that the compensation is sufficiently high.

The concept of risk-aversion has very important implications for investment decisions. For individual investors, the implication is clear that a higher return is required for greater risk. For professionally managed firms, the implication is exactly the same. If shareholders are risk-averse (in general, they are), and if management is to act as agent of those shareholders (it should), then investments of differing risk must be evaluated using different required rates of return if shareholder interests are to be served. Where the net present value method is used, the discount rate used must vary with the riskiness of the investment opportunity, which is determined by the degree of uncertainty surrounding the stream of cash flows that the investment generates.

Compensation for Both Time and Risk

As indicated in Figure 13-1, for an investment of zero risk the required return is not zero. Investors still require compensation for the *passage of time*, because risk-free alternatives are available which offer such a return. Thus, the required return compensates the investor for two things: the passage of time and risk. In symbolic terms, the required return can be represented as

$$RRR = i + \pi$$

where RRR is the required rate of return, i is the risk-free rate of interest, and π is the *risk premium*. Both i and π are established in the financial markets. We will discuss the measurement of i and π in the next chapter.

Role of Markets

We found above that management should use the required return that the shareholders would use if they, the shareholders, were performing the evaluation themselves. Suppose there are thousands of shareholders. Would each shareholder expect management to use a different rate? The existence of organized financial markets provides a way out of this dilemma by establishing a single *market required rate of return* for each degree of risk.

A major function of a market is to establish prices. In a market for goods or services, trading takes place until a price is established that *clears the market,* that is, that equates supply with demand. Figure 13-2 illustrates the typical supply and demand curves of microeconomic theory. As a result of buying and selling decisions by market participants,

Figure 13-2   The Equilibrium Price

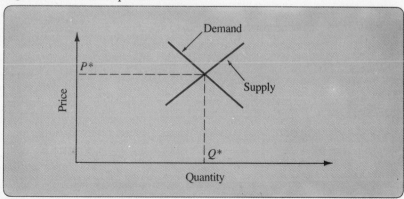

an equilibrium price of P^* is established. At a price of P^*, exactly Q^* units are demanded, and suppliers are willing to produce Q^* units. A lower price leaves some demand unsatisfied, so the price is bid back up. A higher price brings forth excess supply, causing the price to fall. Thus, the equilibrium price of P^* equates supply and demand.

Market Required Rate of Return

A major function of financial markets also is to establish prices. Here, prices are expressed as rates of return on securities. Given risk-averse investors, different rates are established for different degrees of risk. In effect, investments of differing risk are different commodities, each having a different price, that is, a different required rate of return. In principle, a different rate is established by the market for each degree of risk, thus resulting in a *market risk / return schedule,* as illustrated in Figure 13-3.

Figure 13-3   The Market Risk/Return Schedule

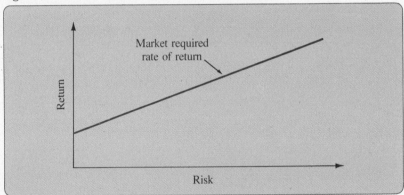

Opportunities to invest exist for all assets for which there are organized and public markets. Such markets exist for a wide variety of financial and real (physical) assets. Considering financial assets, at the low end of the risk spectrum there are savings accounts and, for those with sufficient funds, United States government securities. Of slightly greater, but still low, risk are corporate and municipal bonds. Then come common stocks, varying widely as to risk. There are also commodity futures, usually considered to be of high risk. Markets for all these assets are public and highly organized; information is readily available to participants and costs of entering and transacting are relatively low. Other markets for investment assets, such as real estate, present additional opportunities for some investors but are less highly organized.

Returns in organized and public markets, being available at low cost and little effort, represent the mainimum that an investor should accept on any investment opportunity. Hence, organized markets establish, for every degree of risk, the required rate of return. Since everyone faces essentially the same set of opportunities in the markets, the opportunity rate for any given degree of risk is the *same for every investor.* Hence, given organized markets, we need not worry about a different rate for each shareholder; for an investment opportunity of a given degree of risk, there is a single rate that the market establishes for everyone: that is the rate management should use as the required rate of return. The market risk/return schedule may, and usually does, shift over time in response to changes in economic conditions and investor preferences. But at any point in time, there exists in principle a single market risk/return schedule that establishes the minimum acceptable rates of return for investment projects. Just how we quantify this schedule is a problem that we will discuss in Chapter 14.

Suppose an individual investor or a firm faces an investment opportunity that is more risky than any alternative opportunity generally available to investors in the market. Should the RRR for the investment be set at the level of the most risky alternative market opportunity? In general, no, because the rate appropriate for the less risky alternative would not compensate for the higher risk of the particular opportunity being considered. A premium for the additional risk should be added. The size of the premium may be determined as a matter of subjective judgment or, if the situation warrants, by more objective methods that are discussed in Chapter 14.

Required Rate of Return: Firm versus Project

Required rates of return on risky assets are established in the financial markets by the actions of investors competing against one another. They are opportunity rates—rates investors can earn elsewhere in the financial markets. Let us now extend our discussion to the case of the individual firm.

Required Return on the Firm's Outstanding Securities

Consider a firm that has financed its assets in part by issuing common stock. Given the firm's history, the investments it has undertaken in the past, and its commercial strategy, the market will have a set of expectations regarding the magnitude and riskiness of the firm's future earnings. The market will require a return on the firm's common stock commensurate with the perceived risk.

The riskiness of the return to stockholders depends partly on the firm's operating risk and partly on the degree of financial leverage in its capital structure. Operating risk depends on the uncertainty surrounding the cash flows generated by the firm's investments. Financial leverage is introduced by the use of debt in the capital structure. Debt represents a prior contractual claim against the firm's income and assets. Equity represents a residual ownership claim. The agreed upon interest and principal payments on debt must be made before equity holders are entitled to any return. Equity holders thus receive what's left after debt holders are paid. In good times, when operating returns are high, equity holders receive high returns. When times are bad, equity holders receive low returns, or even no return at all. Since debt holders have a prior claim, equity holders bear the major portion of the firm's operating risk.

As financial leverage is introduced, the firm's operating return goes partly to debt holders and partly to equity holders, with the government also getting a share in the form of tax payments. Since debt represents a fixed prior claim, the variability of the firm's operating cash flows is magnified by leverage, and the return to equity becomes more risky as leverage increases. As risk increases, equity holders demand a higher rate of return.

Let us examine these relationships in symbolic form. Throughout this book, we will use the symbol K to represent the required rate of return. Then K_e will represent the return required by equity holders when debt is present in the firm's capital structure, that is, the return required on *levered* equity. And K_o will represent the return required on unlevered equity, that is, with no debt present in the capital structure. The subscript o stands for "operating" and recognizes the fact that, with no debt in the capital structure, the return required by equity holders depends only on the firm's operating risk. K_e and K_o also are referred to as *capitalization rates*, the rates at which the market *capitalizes* the firm's future cash flows.

With no leverage in the firm's capital structure, the market would require a return on its outstanding shares of K_o. With leverage, it would be K_e. Since financial leverage increases risk, it follows that $K_e > K_o$. We will go into the relationship between K_e and K_o in more depth in Chapter 18.

We will label the interest rate required by holders of the firm's debt K_d. Since the debt represents a prior claim on operating cash flow, the debt of a given firm is always less risky than its equity. Hence, K_d is always less than both K_e and K_o. Even though they are senior to equity, payments to debt holders still are subject to some degree of uncertainty, so in general K_d exceeds the risk-free rate, i. The value of K_d varies from firm to firm, with more risky firms required to pay higher rates of interest than less risky firms.

We now can say something about how these various required rates of return are related. For any given firm, we can see from the discussion above that $K_e \geq K_o > K_d > i$. The values of K_e and K_d are the returns required by holders of the firm's outstanding securities, equity and debt. Most firms invest in projects covering a broad spectrum of risk, from relatively secure cost-reduction projects to much more risky projects involving expansion or new products. The riskiness of a firm's operating cash flow represents a composite of the riskiness of a large number of individual investments, and K_o, K_e, and K_d represent the returns required to compensate investors for the firm's overall or average level of risk.

Required Return on New Investments

What is the required rate of return on a new investment opportunity? Is it the same as K_o? It is not, unless by chance the new investment happens to be equal in riskiness to the firm average. In most cases, firms face investment opportunities that vary widely in riskiness. To undertake new investment, management acts as an agent in committing capital that ultimately belongs to creditors and investors. Those creditors and investors are risk-averse and demand returns that are commensurate with the risk of the investment opportunity to be undertaken. Hence, in general, every investment opportunity has a unique required rate of return that depends on its degree of risk.

Thus, we draw a clear distinction between the return required on the firm's outstanding securities and the return required on specific new investment opportunities not yet undertaken. We will take up this topic in the next chapter and there discuss ways to determine the RRR on an individual investment opportunity.

Cost of Capital

At this point, it is appropriate that we discuss a term that is widely used in the literature of finance—the *cost of capital.* The cost of capital is simply another label for the required rate of return. Because of its wide usage, we define the term and show its relationship to the terminology used in this book.

The cost of capital is the rate of return required by those who supply the capital. It thus is defined in the same way as the cost of any economic good or service. If 40¢ is the price of a cup of coffee, then 40¢ is the amount required by the restauranteur in exchange for the coffee. Similarly, if 15 percent per year is the cost of capital to a firm, those with the capital require 15 percent per year in exchange for the use of the capital. They make this requirement because 15 percent presumably is the rate they can earn elsewhere on other investments of similar risk in the financial markets. The cost of capital and the required rate of return thus are one and the same.

The term *cost of capital* is used in different ways. The phrase *company's cost of capital* or *firm's cost of capital* refers to the market required rate of return, or capitalization rate, on the firm's outstanding securities, that is, the K_e and K_d rates that we discussed above. Used in this sense, the *cost of equity capital* refers to K_e and the *cost of debt capital* to K_d. Sometimes the phrase *cost of capital* may refer to a weighted average of K_e and K_d, the so-called *weighted average cost of capital*. We will come back to the weighted average cost of capital in Chapter 15.

When used to refer to the capitalization rates on outstanding securities (K_e or an average of K_e and K_d), the cost of capital is interpreted as a single figure. For a particular firm, K_e might be, say 15 percent, and a weighted average of K_e and K_d might be, say, 11 percent. The market capitalization rates for individual firms vary according to their riskiness.

In general, the market capitalization rates K_e or an average of K_e and K_d cannot be used to evaluate individual investment opportunities. We found above that the required return of an investment opportunity depends on its riskiness. The relationship between project risk and required return follows directly from risk-aversion on the part of investors, a general behavioral characteristic the validity of which is well-established. Given risk-aversion, the cost of capital thus depends on the way the capital is to be employed, that is, on the riskiness of the investments it is to finance. Management acts as agent of the shareholders to evaluate risk and to determine the appropriate rate that should be *charged* on behalf of the shareholders for the use of the capital. In effect, each investment opportunity has its own individual cost of capital depending on its risk. So for purposes of evaluating investment opportunities, the *cost of capital* must be interpreted as a set of market-determined opportunity rates that vary with risk, that is, as an upward sloping line that is the same for all firms. In short, the *cost of capital* for specific investment opportunities and the *market required rate of return* are one and the same, simply two different labels for the same thing.

Figure 13-4 The Cost of Capital for Specific Investments

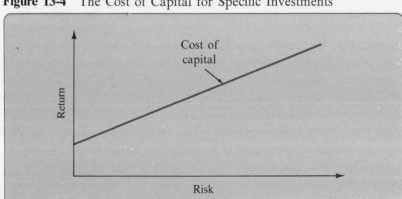

The term *cost of capital* thus can be used in different ways, sometimes to refer to capitalization rates of a firm's securities, other times to the RRR for evaluating investment opportunities. Confusion can arise as to which meaning is intended. Another difficulty with the term *cost of capital* is that it may imply to the unwary that there is some rate (cost) at which capital can be obtained and that this rate is independent of the way in which the capital is to be employed. Such a view is incorrect. The capital being employed is provided by lenders and investors who expect management, acting as agent in their behalf, to take account of their opportunities to invest that capital elsewhere at rates that vary with risk. While there is nothing wrong with the term *cost of capital* if properly interpreted, it has great potential for confusion. To avoid this confusion and to emphasize the relationship between required return and investment risk, we have used the term *required rate of return* throughout most of this book.

Summary

The third major step in making investment decisions, after selecting a criterion and identifying relevant cash flows, is to determine the minimum acceptable rate of return, the *required rate of return* (RRR). The RRR of an investment opportunity is an *opportunity rate,* the rate foregone on the best alternative investment opportunity of comparable risk. In evaluating investment opportunities, management acts as the agent of the shareholders, using the *shareholders'* RRR.

A central factor in determining the RRR is *risk*. In general, risk refers to the degree of uncertainty about an outcome. In the case of investment decisions, risk refers to the uncertainty of future cash flows. Risk is a characteristic of the investment opportunity and has nothing to do with attitudes of investors.

Risk-aversion refers to investor attitudes toward risk. In general, investors are risk-averse and therefore require compensation for bearing risk. Risk-aversion does not imply avoidance of risk, merely that compensation is required for bearing it. The greater the risk, the greater the required compensation. Hence, the RRR of an investment opportunity depends on its riskiness. The RRR compensates the investor for both time and risk and can be expressed as the sum of two components, the risk-free rate of interest and a risk premium.

Required rates of return are *market-determined* by the actions of investors competing against one another. For any given level of risk, there exists a maximum rate that can be earned on investments in the financial markets. The higher the risk, the higher the return. These market rates represent opportunities available to investors outside the firm and, hence, the minimum acceptable on investments inside the firm. Given organized financial markets, required rates of return are the same for all investors and can be represented as an upward-sloping market risk/return schedule.

At any point in time, the market requires a return on a firm's outstanding stock that is commensurate with the perceived level of risk. With no debt present in the firm's capital structure, the required return (K_o) depends only on the firm's operating risk. With leverage, risk to equity holders is greater and they demand a return (K_e) greater than K_o. The return required by holders of the firm's debt (K_d) is the market rate of interest that the firm must pay. For any given firm, it is always true that $K_e \geq K_o > K_d > i$, where i is the risk-free rate of interest. The required rate of return on a prospective new investment depends on its riskiness and therefore will equal the average required rate on the firm's existing operating assets (K_o) only if the risk of the prospective investment equals the average risk of the firm as a whole.

Questions

1. Why can the required rate of return be viewed as an opportunity rate?
2. To what extent should a management's own preferences enter into the establishment of required rates of return?
3. The required rate of return of any investment opportunity is the rate that could be earned on the next best investment opportunity that must be foregone by the firm. Is this true or false? Explain.
4. Distinguish between risk and risk-aversion.
5. Provide examples of risk-averse and risk-preferent behavior. Can a single individual be both risk-averse and risk-preferent?
6. Why does the required return of an investment opportunity depend on its riskiness?
7. What role is played by the financial markets in establishing required rates of return?
8. In practice, required rates of return in any given company should be established by management as a matter of management policy. Is this true or false? Explain.
9. Under what circumstances would the required return on a new investment opportunity equal the rate of return required by the market on a firm's outstanding common stock (assuming no debt in its capital structure)?

Problems

1. You own rights to a lottery with the probabilities and payoffs shown in the table at the top of the facing page.
   Someone has offered to buy your rights to the above lottery for cash. What is the minimum amount you would accept?

Lottery 1 Payoff	Probability	Weighted Outcome
$400	.5	$
600	.5	_____
	Expected value	$_____

2. Repeat Problem 1 for each of the following lotteries:

Lottery	Payoff (Dollars)	Probabilities	Expected Value	Sale Price
2	0/1,000	.5/.5	$	$
3	−1,000/2,000	.5/.5	$	$
4	−25,000/26,000	.5/.5	$	$

Based on your results, what can you say about your own attitude toward risk?

3. In 1738, Daniel Bernoulli presented before the Imperial Academy of Sciences in Petersburg a classic paper on probability[2] in which he discussed the following problem (known as the *Petersburg Paradox*): "Peter tosses a coin and continues to do so until it should land 'heads.' He agrees to give Paul one ducat if he gets heads on the first toss, two ducats if he gets heads on the second, four if on the third, eight if on the fourth, and so on, so that with each additional toss the number of ducats that Peter must pay is doubled."
   (a) What is the expected value of the above gamble (to Paul)?
   (b) What is the maximum amount you would pay to Peter for a chance to play?
   (c) If you were Peter (offering the gamble), what is the minimum entrance fee you would charge?

4. Consider the investment opportunities in the table at the top of the following page, each of which requires the same outlay.
   (a) Rank the four investments in order of riskiness.
   (b) Rank the four investments in descending order of value, assuming that a risk-averse investor is valuing them.
   (c) Repeat part (b) assuming that a risk-neutral investor is valuing the investments.

2. Daniel Bernoulli, "Exposition of a New Theory on the Measurement of Risk," reprinted in S. H. Archer and C. D'Ambrosio (eds.), *The Theory of Business Finance*, 2d ed. (New York: Macmillan, 1976).

Opportunity	Anticipated Cash Inflow	Probability
	$ 0	.333
A	500	.333
	1,000	.333
	0	.05
B	500	.90
	1,000	.05
	0	.15
C	500	.70
	1,000	.15
	0	.0
D	500	1.0
	1,000	.0

References

D. Bernoulli, "Exposition of a New Theory on the Measurement of Risk," reprinted in S. H. Archer and C. D'Ambrosio (eds.), *The Theory of Business Finance,* 2d ed. (New York: Macmillan, 1976).

I. Friend and M. Blume, "The Demand for Risky Assets," *American Economic Review* **55,** 900–922 (Dec. 1975).

C. W. Haley and L. D. Schall, *The Theory of Financial Decisions* (New York: McGraw-Hill, 1973).

J. Hirshleifer. "Risk, The Discount Rate, and Investment Decisions," reprinted in S. H. Archer and C. D'Ambrosio (eds.), *The Theory of Business Finance* 2d ed. (New York: Macmillan, 1976).

D. L. Tuttle and R. H. Litzenberger, "Leverage, Diversification, and Capital Market Effects on a Risk Adjusted Capital Budgeting Framework," reprinted in S. H. Archer and C. D'Ambrosio (eds.), *The Theory of Business Finance,* 2d ed. (New York: Macmillan, 1976).

Setting Return Targets

14

Earning the Market Return
Estimating the Risk Premium
Risk Differences Among Projects
Grouping Investments by Risk Category
The Effects of Inflation
Using Return Targets

When a firm invests, it uses capital funds supplied by others, namely, lenders and investors. It follows that investments undertaken by a firm must earn a return sufficient to compensate suppliers of capital. This proposition is basic to the operation of a private market economy and obvious on its face, yet it is not always applied in practice. Firms sometimes find themselves pressed to put too much emphasis on profits and earnings per share (EPS), to the neglect of long-run return on investment. Such preoccupation with EPS can lead to failure to earn an adequate return on invested capital.[1]

Earning the Market Return

Systematic failure to earn the market required rate of return over an extended period can lead only to serious financial difficulty. Symptoms of such a sustained shortfall in return are a decline in stock price below book value and constrained access to the equity markets, often followed by excessive reliance on debt to obtain needed funds. Managers sometimes lay the blame on the capital markets, when, in fact, the markets are performing exactly as they should in disciplining firms that fail to earn the required rate.

Lockheed's decision to build the L-1011 TriStar provides an interesting case in point. The TriStar is a three-engine wide-bodied jet aircraft capable of carrying up to about 300 passengers. A good deal of data about the TriStar became public during the 1971 Congressional hearings on a $250 million loan guarantee made to Lockheed by the federal government. Using these data, U. E. Reinhardt analyzed the TriStar decision and concluded that at the time Lockheed management committed the company to build TriStar, the plane needed roughly 35 to 40 percent of the then-estimated market for wide-bodied jet aircraft to break even, that is, to earn a zero percent return on invested capital, and more than 100 percent of the market to earn a return of 15 percent.[2] Even granting that some pertinent data may not have been available publicly, it is difficult to conclude after reading Reinhardt's analysis that the TriStar ever had a reasonable prospect of earning a return adequate to compensate suppliers of funds. Lockheed's subsequent financial difficulties with TriStar have been well documented in the press.

Impact on Decisions

No management can ever be sure that any given investment will earn the

---

1. For a discussion of the potential conflicts between earnings per share and return on investment, see Frederick W. Searby, "Return to Return on Investment," *Harvard Business Review* **53**, 113–119 (Mar.–Apr. 1975).
2. U. E. Reinhardt, "Break-Even Analysis of the Lockheed TriStar—An Application of Financial Theory," *Journal of Finance* **28**, 821–838 (Sept. 1973).

required rate of return until time passes and previously uncertain outcomes become known. But to maximize the chances of success, return
targets must be set properly in the first place. Inadequate attention to
return targets can lead a firm to undertake projects that ought to be
rejected and also to the opposite error of rejecting projects that ought to be
undertaken. As an example of this second type of problem, consider the
case of a multidivisional chemical company during the 1960s that used a
single return-on-investment target of 12 percent for evaluating all investment opportunities. At the time, the rate on long-term government bonds
was between 4 and 5 percent.

One project the firm considered was a proposal to build a chlorine
plant. The technology was proven, and the plant was expected to remain
productive for at least 25 years. The plant would supply only part of the
company's total chlorine requirement. Since the plant therefore had a
captive market, the savings from producing the chlorine rather than
purchasing it outside were relatively certain. Although the anticipated
return of 8 to 10 percent was below the 12 percent target, it was well above
returns that shareholders could have earned outside the firm at comparable risk. The firm turned down the project.

The chlorine plant was one of many low-risk cost reduction projects
with returns in the 7 to 10 percent range that were being screened out by
the company's 12 percent cutoff rate. Because these projects were not
undertaken, the company experienced over a period of years a drop in its
rate of capital investment and a decline in its earnings growth.

Proper evaluation of investment opportunities involves many considerations, some qualitative and some quantitative. The specific purpose of
return targets is to impose an economic test to ensure that investments
attractive on strategic or competitive grounds also represent wise and
efficient uses of shareholder capital funds.

Although the use of improper return targets alone would be unlikely
to change the outcome in all or even a majority of the investment decisions
a firm makes, systematic use of inappropriate targets over long periods will
bias decisions in the wrong directions, alter the balance of the investment
mix, and depress profits and growth.

Setting Return Targets: The Company's "Cost of Capital" Approach

Although there is no disagreement that prospective investments should be
expected to earn at least the market required rate of return, putting the
concept to practical use has proved difficult. The problem lies in determining just what the market required return is for any particular investment opportunity.

In the 1950s economists who studied the subject proposed that each firm determine its overall cost of capital, the label given to the average market required rate of return on the firm's equity and long-term debt together, and that this figure be used as the minimum acceptable return on all new investments. This approach had the appeal of consistency with economic theory, and it represented an improvement over approaches, such as the payback period, that ignore both the timing of cash flows and shareholder opportunities to invest outside the firm. In Chapter 13 we discussed the firm's overall cost of capital and its relation to the market RRR for investment opportunities.

The cost of capital approach was first developed for use in regulated industries such as electric and gas utilities and telephone companies. In setting the rates (prices) such companies would be allowed to charge the public for services, the regulatory authorities are required by law to allow the company to cover its operating costs *plus* a fair rate of return on its invested capital. Although the original legislation was not explicit about how a "fair" rate should be defined, especially for equity capital, judicial decisions and regulatory practice provided some guidance. A fair rate should be commensurate with rates earned in those unregulated sectors of the economy that have risks commensurate with the regulated utility, and it should be high enough to attract sufficient new capital in a competitive market for the utility to provide the volume of services required by the public.

In the context of utility regulation, the companywide cost of capital approach to setting the required rate of return makes a great deal of sense. Most utility companies are franchised monopolies that are given an exclusive right to provide needed services in a given area. The objective of regulation is to ensure that the company *as a whole* be allowed to earn a rate of return just sufficient to compensate investors who provide the necessary capital. Furthermore, since most (though not all) utility companies provide a single service, their own investments all have similar risk characteristics. Both reasons justify the use of a single companywide required rate of return based on the company's cost of capital.

The extension of the use of a single required rate of return standard (based on a company's overall cost of capital) to firms operating in the private unregulated sector runs into a large obstacle. The typical firm's investments are not "homogeneous"; indeed they may differ quite widely as far as their risk characteristics are concerned. Therefore, a single yardstick for all investments can be misleading. We discussed this point in Chapter 13.

Let us take an example to show why a single standard can be misleading. Montgomery Ward, a retailing company, acquired Container Corporation, a manufacturer of metal and paper-based containers. The merged firm was called MARCOR. Assume that the retailing company's cost of capital was *x* percent; that is, it should expect an *average* rate of return of *x* percent on new investments in retailing facilities. Assume that Container Corporation's cost of capital was *y* percent. Should the merged firm, MARCOR, set a required rate on all new investments of *x* percent, *y* percent, or some average of *x* and *y*? What if Container had acquired Montgomery Ward, rather than the other way around? Clearly, the idea of using a single companywide cost of capital as the required rate of return on investment is not an adequate answer in this case. To confuse the issue further, Mobil Oil Corp, an integrated oil company, later acquired MARCOR. Should Mobil use the same required rate of return to assay *all* its future investments? In retailing? In containers? In producing oil off the China coast? In United States refineries? In gas stations? In charge accounts owed by motorists? Obviously not.

In short, the companywide cost of capital concept proved difficult to use because it ignored large differences in riskiness among investment projects of different types. Even for most firms that have remained in a single industry, the difference in risk between its various investments is large: investments of funds in marketable securities, in accounts receivable, in inventories, in cost-reduction projects, in new products all entail different levels of risk and therefore "require" different promised rates of return. The companywide cost of capital is simply the *average* overall rate of return required by all of those investments taken collectively. It is not a useful guide to the rate of return required for *each individual* investment decision. Thus, many companies, like the chemical company mentioned earlier, became dissatisfied with the use of a single cost of capital figure as a basis for setting the required rate of return on its various investment projects.

Specific Rates for Specific Investments

What we need is a way of setting a specific required rate of return on each investment (or group of investments) that will explicitly reflect its own specific riskiness. Although the conceptual answer is simple, the practical problem is difficult. We have a lot of evidence from the bond and stock markets on what rate of return the market requires on a company *as a whole* (which allows us to estimate the company's overall cost of capital) but very little evidence on rates of return required on specific types of assets or on investments in such assets.

The dilemma was resolved during the 1960s through the development of a body of theory that directly related the market RRR to the level of risk involved. This theory—the capital asset pricing model (CAPM) which we discussed earlier in Chapter 10—addressed two central questions: How much *additional* return does the market require on each *additional* increment of risk? How should risk be measured in order to translate theory into operational terms?

The new theory showed three things about the required rate of return on projects within a single company: that the RRR is a *line* and not a single figure, that the line slopes upward with increasing risk, and that for projects of a given risk the required rate of return is the same for all firms regardless of each firm's average cost of capital. In short, the CAPM theory showed that each investment opportunity has its own individual cost of capital depending on its risk. We discussed this new interpretation of the cost of capital and its relation to the market RRR at the end of Chapter 13. There we concluded that the cost of capital for specific investment projects and the market RRR are one and the same (see Figure 13-4). From this point on in this chapter we will use the label RRR to refer to return targets for investments. In Chapter 15 we will return to the topic of the firm's cost of capital and discuss it in more technical terms. There we will also discuss the CAPM as a theoretical framework for setting return targets.

The Market Standard

The setting of return targets need not involve complex mathematical formulas. The proper approach stems directly from the fundamental premise that management's job is to act as agent of shareholders in investing shareholder funds. In effect, suppliers of funds say to the management of any firm: "These are the rates we can expect to earn outside the firm. If you cannot equal or exceed these rates, pay the funds out to us as dividends, and we will invest elsewhere."

Market opportunities outside the firm thus set the minimum standards for investment inside the firm. Required rates of return are not set by management, nor are they set by negotiation between management and suppliers of funds. Rather, they are set impersonally in the financial markets by the actions of investors and lenders competing against one another. Management's job is to determine what they are and to use them as standards for evaluating investment opportunities.

Since all investors face essentially the same set of market opportunities, required rates are the same for all investors, individuals and owners of small proprietorships as well as shareholders of large corporations. Because investors are risk-averse, required rates of return depend on risk. The market RRR is the same upward-sloping line for all firms. These are the rates management should use as return targets.

The Risk Premium

One way for management to approach the task of determining required rates of return is to begin with the known rate of return available on riskless investments, such as a savings account or United States government bonds. This rate becomes the investor's minimum required return on any *riskless* opportunity to invest funds, and it should be used to discount the cash flows of equally riskless opportunities in applying the net present value (NPV) investment criterion. As of mid-1979, the rate on long-term United States government bonds was about 9 percent.

The required return for a risky investment then is scaled up from this base rate. Thus, we can think of the required return on any investment as being made up of two components.

$$RRR = i + \pi$$

where i is the long-term, risk-free rate of interest, and π is a premium for risk. We can represent these relationships graphically, as shown in Figure 14-1, in terms of the market risk/return schedule discussed in Chapter 13.

Figure 14-1   The Market Risk/Return Schedule

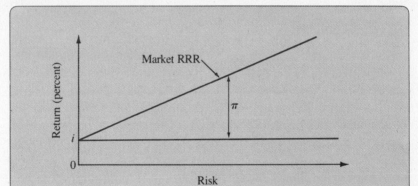

The greater the risk of an investment opportunity, the greater is π and the higher is the RRR. But after defining the general nature of the relationship in terms of i and π, many questions remain unanswered. How is the risk of an investment project to be measured? What is the slope of the line? That is, how much greater is π for each additional increment of risk? How do we actually pick a number to use as the discount rate (the RRR) in calculating NPV? These are the questions to which we now turn.

Estimating the Risk Premium

Since the rates we seek are established in the financial markets by investors themselves, why not ask the investors what those rates are, not directly, but by examining market data on observed relationships between risk and return? The securities markets have been widely studied in recent years and much data has been collected. Although this is the correct approach, many difficulties exist in using market data. One problem is the divergence between the return expected by investors (which is what we want to measure) and the return they actually received (which is all we can actually observe). In spite of such difficulties, market data, averaged over many time periods, represent the best available source of information regarding returns required by investors.

Let us consider first the simplest possible case: a typical firm evaluating a typical investment opportunity, or project. A typical firm is one that lies at about the middle of the risk spectrum. It engages in activities that are neither especially high nor especially low in risk. Thus, by *typical* we mean a firm of average risk. As a further simplification, we will assume for the moment that our typical firm is financed entirely with equity funds and has no long-term debt in its capital structure. The effects of financing arrangements on project evaluation are discussed in Chapter 15.

As do all firms, our typical firm invests in projects that cover a wide spectrum of risk, ranging from cost-reduction projects to projects which invest in the production and marketing of new products. For the moment, however, we will restrict our attention to the *typical project,* which we will define as an investment opportunity of average risk.

Using Market Data

Our task then is to estimate the risk premium, π, for a typical project undertaken by a typical firm. We know that π is determined by the market and that it depends both on the perceived riskiness of the project and on the degree of risk-aversion in the minds of investors. Investors' perceptions of risk and their degree of risk-aversion may well vary from one time period to another. In the spring of 1970, for example, and again in the summer of 1974, investors seemed especially cautious about economic prospects and may have increased the premiums they were demanding for bearing risk. However, at any point in time, looking ahead, we have no way to measure risk perceptions and risk-aversion. Our best approach, therefore, is to use normal data on market risk premiums that have been derived from averages over long periods of time and encompass many cycles.

The fact that the market RRR is the same for all firms makes our job much easier. We can use aggregate data for all firms together rather than gathering data for many firms individually. Several careful studies have been made of market rates of return (i.e., achieved rates of return in the market) for portfolios of common stocks, high-grade bonds and short-

Table 14-1   Rates of Return and Risk Premiums, Selected Periods 1902–1978 (Percent)

	1902–1971 (Friend)	1926–1978 (Ibbotson)
Arithmetic Mean of Annual Returns		
(1) On composite stocks[a]	10.7	11.2
(2) On industrial stocks[a]	12.8	–
(3) On high-grade corporate bonds	4.0	4.1
(4) On long-term United States government bonds	–	3.4
(5) Short-term risk-free rate	3.5	2.5
Risk Premiums Relative to Risk-Free Rate		
(6) Composite stocks	7.2	8.7
(7) Industrial stocks	9.3	–
(8) High-grade corporate bonds	0.5	1.6
Risk Premium on Composite Stocks Relative to		
(9) Corporate bonds	6.7	7.1
(10) Government bonds	–	7.8

Source: Based upon data in Irwin Friend and Marshall Blume, "The Demand for Risky Assets," *American Economic Review* (Dec. 1975) and Roger Ibbotson and Rex Sinquefield, *Stocks, Bonds, Bills and Inflation: Historical Returns (1926–1978)* (Charlottesville, Va.: Financial Analysts Research Foundation, 1979).

[a]The Friend sample included all stocks listed on the New York Stock Exchange. Ibbotson used the Standard & Poor's industrial and composite stock indexes.

term investments.[3] Table 14-1 shows the highlights of two recent studies that cover long time spans and measure returns for different classes of securities. The first study, referred to in the table as Friend, is by Irwin Friend and Marshall Blume, "The Demand for Risky Assets," *American Economic Review* (Dec. 1975). The second study, referred to in the table as Ibbotson, is by Roger Ibbotson and Rex Sinquefield, *Stocks, Bonds, Bills and Inflation: Historical Returns (1926–1978)* (Financial Analysts Research Foundation, 1979).

The table is arranged in two columns. The first column shows the average results obtained in the Friend study for the 70 year period 1902–1971. The second column shows the results obtained by the Ibbotson study and covers the period 1926–1978.

The first five rows of the table give us the arithmetic mean of the annual returns achieved over the various periods. The rates on common stock include dividends plus market appreciation or depreciation.

Let us begin with the truly risk-free rate of return shown in row 5.

3. The first comprehensive study of market rates of return on common stock was by Lawrence Fisher and James H. Lorie, "Rates of Return on Investments in Common Stock," *Journal of Business* 1–21 (Jan. 1964). In 1968, they extended their study to include yearly holding-period returns from 1926 to 1965. See Lawrence Fisher and James H. Lorie, "Rates of Return on Investments in Common Stock: The Year by Year Record 1926–1965," *Journal of Business* 291–316 (July 1968).

Friend defines this as the rate on corporate bonds with 1 year to maturity; Ibbotson defines it as the rate on United States Treasury Bills. The rate on long-term government bonds, that is, the long-term or multiperiod risk-free rate, is higher on average than the short-term, risk-free rate. This is because the price of long-term instruments falls more sharply than the price of short-term instruments when the rate of interest rises. Therefore, even long-term government bonds involve some degree of risk. But for our present purposes, this is the rate we define as the risk-free rate.

The rate on long-term, high-grade corporate bonds is higher than the rate on high-grade bonds—which reflects the far higher risk the market attaches to these instruments.

Portfolios of common stock show rates of return much higher than the rate on high-grade bonds—which reflects the far higher risk the market attaches to these instruments.

Rows 6, 7, and 8 of the table show the average rate of return differentials between the various assets and the short-term, risk-free rate, that is, the *risk premium* which the market received for holding those risky assets as opposed to United States Treasury Bills or other riskless short-term assets. Finally, rows 9 and 10 show the risk premium on common stocks relative to long-term bonds.

What do these data on historical risk premiums tell us? They tell us that, on average, the market requires a higher rate of return on equity than it does on bonds. And they tell us how large that premium has been. For stocks in general (composite stocks in Table 14-1), the premium was between 6.7 and 7.1 percent relative to high-grade corporate bonds (row 9). Relative to United States government bonds, our standard for riskless investment, the premium was about 8 percentage points (row 10).

Looking Ahead

The returns in Table 14-1 and the risk premiums discussed above are *historical* returns realized by investors in the past. Can we use these data to determine risk premiums expected by investors in the future? We can. Since market prices are free to change, we can assume that the average premiums actually earned over very long periods in the past represent a good measure of the normal premium expected. The absolute return on bonds and on equities varies sharply from year to year as inflation and other economic factors change, and so does the difference between bond yield and stock yield. However, the long-run average difference between the two should not change significantly. Therefore, we can assume that in the future, the normal premium will be the same as in the past. In short, the use of long-run historical averages of the required premium as a basis for future projections of this premium is the best approach available, and hence we can assume that 8 percent will represent the normal risk premium required by the market on a portfolio of equity securities relative to government bonds in the future, as it has in the past.

Before we can use these data to evaluate investment opportunities, we have one more adjustment to make. The returns in Table 14-1 are *levered*; debt is present in the capital structures of the firms studied. What we need in order to evaluate operating investments is the return that would be required by the market in the absence of financial leverage. We then can use this RRR as a target for evaluating the operating cash flows of a prospective investment.

If 8 percent was the risk premium on average-risk firms *with* financial leverage, what was the risk premium on an average-risk firm *without* financial leverage, that is, with no debt in its capital structure? We can infer the answer from the data on levered returns in Table 14-1. Since financial leverage increases risk, it also increases the risk premium. So the unlevered risk premium is lower than the levered. The size of the needed downward adjustment depends on two factors, the amount of debt used by firms over the period of the market studies and the effects of taxes and tax-deductibility of interest.

Over the time period covered by our data, there were variations both in the leverage ratios of firms and in tax rates, so we cannot be too precise in our calculations. It seems reasonable to make our calculations using average leverage ratios and average tax rates prevailing over the period 1926–1978. Starting with the levered risk premium relative to government bonds of 8 percent, the necessary adjustments suggest an unlevered risk premium between 5 and 6 percent, the exact answer depending on some complex technical issues that have not yet been resolved.[4] Based on the

---

4. Unlevered risk premiums can be inferred from levered risk premiums using the model of F. Modigliani and M. H. Miller, "Corporate Income Taxes and the Cost of Capital: A Correction," *American Economic Review* **53**, 433–443 (June 1963). Starting with a levered risk premium of 8.1 percent and using average leverage ratios and tax rates during 1926–1976, the Modigliani and Miller (1963) model implies an unlevered risk premium between 6 and 7 percent. The Modigliani and Miller (1963) model takes account of corporate taxes but ignores personal taxes paid by investors. An alternative model, one that does consider personal taxes, is that of M. H. Miller, "Debt and Taxes," *Journal of Finance* **32**, 261–275 (May 1977). The unlevered risk premium inferred from the Miller model lies between 5 and 6 percent. The extent to which personal taxes affect the valuation of securities presently is an unresolved empirical issue. It seems safe to speculate that personal taxes do have some influence and that the unlevered risk premium lies somewhere between the Modigliani and Miller (1963) figure and the Miller (1977) figure. Another important factor to be taken into account is the length of the holding period. The data in Table 14-1 are arithmetic averages of annual holding period returns. Strictly speaking, returns on investment projects ought to be compared to return targets calculated over multiyear periods of comparable length. Assuming a multiyear period reduces the risk premium (see Ibbotson and Sinquefield, *Stocks, Bonds, Bills, and Inflation*). Giving some weight to personal taxes and to the question of holding period, the unlevered risk premium seems likely to lie at the low end of the range suggested by the Miller (1977) model, or about 5 percent.

nature of these issues, the correct answer seems likely to be closer to 5 percentage points than to 6. Therefore, let us accept a certain lack of precision for the moment and round off to the lower figure.

This figure of 5 percent, then, is our estimate of the normal market risk premium (over and above the long-term United States government bond rate) on operating assets of average risk. It applies to *operating* assets because we have eliminated the effects of financial leverage. It applies to investments of *average risk* because it was derived from data for a large number of firms representing a cross section of the United States economy.

To see how the 5 percent figure can be used, consider a firm that is deciding whether to expand a plant that manufactures an established product. Suppose the investment opportunity is judged to be of average risk. Our analysis above indicates that the market requires a return on the investment 5 percent above the long-term government bond rate, which in mid-1979 was roughly 9 percent. Therefore, in evaluating the expansion opportunity, management should use a target of 14 percent as the minimum acceptable return on that investment.

Risk Differences Among Projects

The 5 percent risk premium calculated above is appropriate for typical projects of average risk. In practice, investment opportunities of most firms vary widely in riskiness, even when the firm operates in only a single industry.

In the case of straightforward cost reduction projects, savings often can be estimated with reasonable accuracy, so risk is low. For example, assume that a large aluminum-producing company, which uses natural gas in its smelting operations, holds long-term contracts to purchase gas at 31 cents per million British thermal units (BTU). This price is equivalent to a contract to buy crude oil at a price of about $1.80 per barrel as far as heating value is concerned. The contract expires in 1980, by which time the price of available new gas or oil have both jumped tenfold to $18.00 per barrel, with expectations that even this high price will escalate in the future. If it installs a new set of expensive controls in its producing process, the company knows for certain that it can reduce its energy use by a predictable amount, let us say the equivalent of 1 million barrels a year. This saving is clearly equal to a benefit of $18 million a year at the 1980 price of oil and predictably more if oil prices keep rising. But the saving of at least $18 million a year is virtually certain and definite. The investment required to achieve this expected flow of benefits should therefore be assayed against an RRR only slightly above the United States government bond rate of about 9 percent.

In contrast to cost-saving investments, outlays that are made to produce and market new products inevitably involve larger uncertainties such as acceptance by consumers, countermoves by competitors, advertising effectiveness, untried manufacturing technology, and a host of others. For these reasons, cash flows promised by new products typically are subject to far greater risk than are those of cost reduction projects. Such investment proposals should be assayed against a higher-than-average RRR.

Since investors are risk-averse, managers investing in their behalf are obliged to take account of such risk differences among projects. Investors supplying capital funds expect managers to set high targets for high-risk projects and vice versa. The RRR varies with risk, as indicated earlier in Figure 14-1. Knowing that 5 percent is the market risk premium for investments of average risk, we can redraw Figure 14-1 as shown in Figure 14-2.

Figure 14-2 The Market Risk Premium

We now have two points on the market RRR line. We know i, for it is the long-term government bond rate, and we know that for average-risk investments, the risk premium π is 5 percent above i.

Now we can draw the market RRR line in Figure 14-2. But to determine the RRR for a particular investment opportunity, we must be able to measure its specific risk, a difficult task indeed. We know that π lies between 0 and 5 percent for investments of below-average risk and above 5 percent for investments of above-average risk. To specify π for any particular project requires a quantitative measure of its risk. Quantitative risk estimates in principle can be obtained by applying the concepts of probability theory. Where projects are large and complex, computer-based simulation techniques such as risk analysis can be used. However, these analytical techniques are costly, and even when they are performed carefully, the degree of uncertainty regarding future events often is so great that the precision gained via sophisticated computational techniques can be illusory or even misleading.[5]

Relative Risk Measurement

What is needed, then, is a practical system of risk assessment. One approach is to use a system of *relative* risk measurement, a technique used successfully in managing portfolios of securities.[6]

In such a system, a typical project of average risk serves as a benchmark against which both risk and return are measured.[7] Taking 5 percent as the market required risk premium and 9 percent as the government bond rate (roughly its level as of mid-1979) gives us a target return of 14 percent for the average-risk benchmark project. The target for projects of below-average risk then lies between 9 percent and 14 percent, and for those of above-average risk, above 14 percent.

It is at this point that individual project risk estimates can be used. Where sophisticated computational techniques cannot be justified, informed judgment based on experience usually is adequate. What is needed is an estimate of the risk of the project under evaluation *relative* to the average-risk benchmark project.

Suppose the government bond rate now is 9 percent. The computations we would make for project *A*, judged half as risky as the average project, are:

$$\text{Risk premium} = \frac{1}{2} \times 5 = 2.5 \text{ percent}$$

$$\text{RRR} = i + 2.5 \text{ percent}$$
$$= 9 + 2.5 \text{ percent}$$
$$= 11.5 \text{ percent}$$

5. For a discussion of risk analysis, see David B. Hertz, "Risk Analysis in Capital Investment," *Harvard Business Review* **42,** 95–106 (Jan.–Feb. 1964); and "Investment Policies that Pay Off," *Harvard Business Review* **46,** 96–108 (Jan.–Feb. 1968). A criticism of risk analysis is that its benefits often do not justify its costs. See K. Larry Hastie, "One Businessman's View of Capital Budgeting," *Financial Management* **4,** 36–44 (Winter 1974); and E. Eugene Carter, "What Are the Risks in Risk Analysis?" *Harvard Business Review* **50,** 72–76 (July 1972).
6. In connection with securities, the relative risk ratio is called the beta coefficient, a measure of the volatility of the return of a stock or portfolio relative to the market average. A beta coefficient of 1.0 indicates average volatility and therefore average risk; a beta above 1.0 indicates above-average risk and below 1.0, below-average risk.
7. Measuring risk in this way was first suggested by R. S. Bower and D. L. Lessard, "An Operational Approach to Risk Screening," *Journal of Finance* **28,** 321–328 (May 1973).

For project B, which is judged to be twice as risky, the computations are:

$$\text{Risk premium} = 2 \times 5 = 10 \text{ percent}$$
$$\text{RRR} = i + 10 \text{ percent}$$
$$= 9 + 10 \text{ percent}$$
$$= 19 \text{ percent}$$

Our *general expressions* for the risk premium and RRR for *any project* are:

$$\text{Project risk premium } (\pi) = (5 \text{ percent} \times \text{Project risk ratio})$$

$$\text{Project RRR} = i + \pi$$

The approach we have developed measures risk relative to a typical or average-risk project. One can reasonably ask: Average compared to what? The 5 percent risk premium derived earlier is appropriate for projects that are average in risk for all corporations in the United States economy. Some managers may find it easier to define average or typical within their own firms rather than for the whole economy. Using such an approach, the benchmark project for firm A would be an average-risk project for firm A rather than an average-risk project for the entire economy. Chapter 15 discusses an approach along these lines and discusses more fully the CAPM as the theoretical basis for the simplified approach described above.

Diversification Effects

Thus far, we have viewed investment opportunities in isolation. When a firm invests in a variety of projects, as most firms do, the combination can be viewed as a *portfolio*. In general, a portfolio of investments is less risky than the average of the individual investments considered alone. Hence, when evaluating an investment opportunity, we should take account of the diversifying effect of the investment on the firm's portfolio of investments.

It is important to recognize that neither here nor elsewhere in this book do we address the question of *whether* the firm should diversify. The question of whether to consider investments of a particular type, for example, in a particular industry, involves issues of commercial strategy that go beyond the scope of this book. Resolution of such questions in part determines the nature of the firm's business and hence constitutes the highest level of policy-making within the firm. Policy criteria at this level normally are qualitative and mission-oriented rather than quantitative. Our concern here is with the question of how to evaluate and whether to undertake investments that already have passed the higher-level policy test of consistency with the firm's commercial strategy.

By combining risky securities into a portfolio, an investor normally can achieve a reward/risk combination significantly better than that of any of the individual securities. Hence, for any given level of expected return, a well diversified portfolio is much less risky than a single security.

The same principle applies to the investments of a firm. The variability of a firm's cash flow can be reduced by diversification. The extent to which such a reduction in the variability of a firm's cash flows actually benefits investors depends on the degree of financial frictions present in the markets and on the extent to which investors diversify their portfolios.

A reduction in the variability of a firm's cash flow also reduces the likelihood of encountering *financial distress.* Financial distress comes in many forms, ranging from mild liquidity problems or cash shortages at one extreme to bankruptcy at the other. We can conclude that, other factors being equal, diversification reduces the risk of financial distress and bankruptcy.

In evaluating investment opportunities, diversification effects can be taken into account formally by defining the risk of an individual investment project in terms of its contribution to the riskiness of a larger portfolio of assets. We will discuss the measurement of risk in this way and the treatment of diversification effects in Chapter 15. In the approach discussed above, by measuring risk relative to a typical project, we account for diversification effects in an approximate way. We will see why this is so in Chapter 15.

Grouping Investments by Risk Category

We now have an analytical framework that permits us to deal with investment opportunities of differing risk. Let us apply that framework to the kinds of investments normally encountered in practice.

Investment Opportunity Schedule

Sometimes it is useful to think of the investment opportunities facing a firm in terms of a downward sloping schedule, as shown in Figure 14-3. The downward slope implies that the firm does not have unlimited opportunities to invest. As it expands its rate of investment, it must accept less attractive projects with lower expected rates of return.

Categorizing Investment Projects

In principle, investment opportunities of a given firm will vary in risk over a wide spectrum. In practice, it is infeasible to calculate a separate RRR for each investment opportunity to be evaluated. One practical

Figure 14-3   The Investment Opportunity Schedule

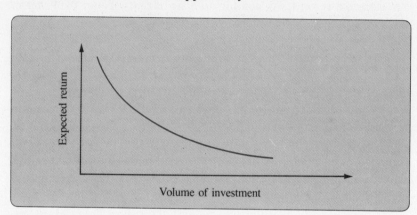

solution to this problem is to group investment opportunities into risk categories. Three possible categories are cost-reduction projects, expansion projects, and new products.

Cost reduction might cover a variety of investment opportunities, usually involving the substitution of equipment for people; substituting a new machine for an older, less efficient one; or substituting a completely new manufacturing facility for an old, outmoded one. Cash flows attributable to such projects often, but not always, can be estimated with reasonable accuracy at least during their first several years.

A second project category might include expansion of existing product lines. Such projects might include expansion of existing facilities or addition of new facilities to manufacture existing products. Since expansion projects involve additional sales revenue, cash flows attributable to such projects usually are more uncertain, and hence more risky, than those of cost-reduction projects.

A third and still more risky project category involves the introduction of new products. Such projects may involve new technology for manufacturing, packaging, or marketing. Judgments may be required of the firm's ability in the future to solve complex engineering and manufacturing problems. The effects of inflation may be very uncertain. The possibility of shifts in consumer preferences, countermoves by competitors, and technological obsolescence must be taken into account. Because of these and other considerations, both the sales revenues and costs associated with new products usually are subject to considerably greater uncertainty than are those associated with the expansion of existing products. Within the new products category, there may be considerable variations in uncertainty.

As a practical approach to capital budgeting, a firm might establish investment categories along the above lines. Required rates of return then could be set by category rather than for each new project individually. Any number of risk categories might be established. For each category, a measure of risk would have to be estimated. Availability of data to make these estimates might be a consideration in defining categories. After estimating risk, the approach described above then could be used to estimate the required rate of return for the category.

If expansion projects, for example, were considered to be of average risk, then the RRR for expansion projects would be approximately equal to $i + 5$ percent. Cost-reduction projects likely would be less risky, and projects involving new products would be more risky. The relationships might be diagrammed as in Figure 14-4, where K symbolizes the RRR.

Figure 14-4 Required Return by Risk Category

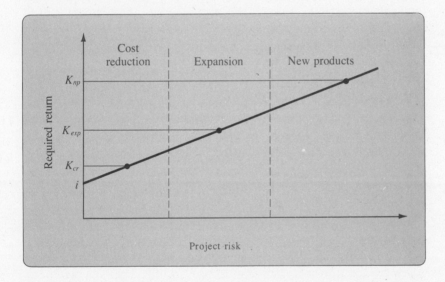

The figure is drawn to indicate that the RRR of a cost-reduction project might be as low as the risk-free rate, i. Most cost-reduction projects involve elements of expansion as well. A new machine or a new plant may simultaneously lower costs and increase capacity. Cash flows generated by such projects involve both inflows and outflows and are subject to some uncertainty; hence, the RRR for cost-reduction projects, denoted by K_{cr} typically lies above i. Occasionally, a cost-reduction project may involve only a reduction of costs and may not affect revenues at all. If the savings are relatively certain, the project should be evaluated at a rate close to the risk-free rate.[8]

Grouping investment projects by risk category represents a further compromise with theory in order to increase the theory's usability. The use of risk categories avoids the necessity of estimating risk for each investment project individually. It is necessary only to make a judgment as to which risk category the project belongs. In a decentralized firm, required rates of return for each risk category might be established by a central group, perhaps with different rates for different organizational units, and the results disseminated to operating units for their use.

Take the case of a national food processor considering the introduction of a new product, a packaged dessert. The project required a pilot manufacturing operation to produce enough product for a 9 month test market. If test results were favorable, full production was to begin. The product was considerably different from leading desserts on the market at the time, and consumer acceptance was uncertain. In addition, some of the production technology was new. For these reasons, the company judged the project to be considerably more risky than average. A system of return targets by risk category suggested a minimum acceptable return in the 18 to 20 percent range.

Use of a Single Discount Rate

Sometimes it is argued that a firm should use a single discount rate for evaluating all projects. Typically, it is suggested that this rate should be equal to the weighted average required return on the firm's outstanding securities, usually labeled the *firm's cost of capital*, which we discussed earlier in this chapter and will return to in Chapter 15. Under such an approach all investment opportunities are evaluated using this single rate.

Such an approach is appropriate and useful when, but only when, all of the firm's prospective investments are of the same risk and approximately equal in risk to the overall risk of the firm. When investments are not all of the same risk, as usually is the case, such an approach is not

---

8. If savings are absolutely certain, the correct rate for a pure cost reduction project is the risk-free rate, *i*. If savings are uncertain, the correct rate depends, in part, on the degree of correlation with the firm's remaining cash flows. If positively correlated, as would be true for most cost reduction projects, the correct rate would lie above the risk-free rate, *i*. See W. G. Lewellen, "Some Observations on Risk-Adjusted Discount Rates," *Journal of Finance* **32**, 1331–1338 (Sept. 1977). Lewellen provides a good discussion of the general problem of discounting cash outflows. He points out that all cash flows, outflows as well as inflows, should be evaluated in a portfolio context, taking proper account of correlation with other returns accruing to the investor.

Figure 14-5 Single versus Multiple Required Rates

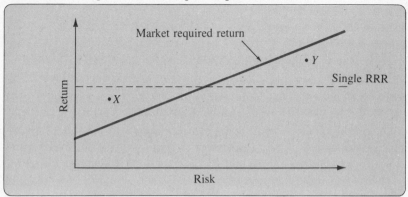

appropriate and will lead to errors in decision-making. To see the consequences of using a single required return for all investments, consider Figure 14-5, in which the points *X* and *Y* represent the risk and return estimated for two investment projects of differing risk. In the figure, use of the single rate (dashed line) reflecting the average risk of the two projects would cause rejection of the low-risk project *X* and acceptance of the high-risk project *Y*, which is exactly the opposite of what the shareholders would wish management to do. If shareholders were performing the evaluation themselves, they would accept project *X* and reject project *Y*. Hence, it is not acceptable to follow an approach of using a single discount rate under the assumption that high- or low-risk projects will average out. Such an approach likely will lead to acceptance of some projects that should be rejected, and rejection of some that should be accepted. A single rate also can lead to errors when ranking is required. Projects must be evaluated individually, using required returns appropriate to their risk.

Those who propose the use of a single required rate argue that, over time, high- and low-risk projects may indeed average out so that the firm's overall risk remains more or less unchanged, and that shareholders may expect management to invest in a mix of projects that brings about this result. However, the use of a single required rate in such a situation is likely to keep rejecting lower-risk projects, so that the firm's overall risk rises over time. The chlorine plant described earlier in this chapter was an example of just this kind of situation.

Low-risk projects, such as *X* in Figure 14-5, may have an expected rate of return lower than that of the average for the firm. The fact that project *X* lowers the firm's expected rate of return may seem bothersome. However, it also lowers firm risk, and the reduction in risk more than offsets the reduction in expected rate of return, so that the value of the firm rises. Although the expected rate of return falls, the total dollar value of the firm to shareholders rises if project X is undertaken. Shareholders are better off.

If a firm's management wishes to maintain a more or less stable overall operating risk, it can offset changes in risk due to investment projects by making changes in working capital policy. For example, the effects of a highly risky investment can be offset by increasing the level of low-risk liquid assets held by the firm. In this way, a firm might undertake an attractive yet risky investment opportunity without changing its overall operating risk.

In practice, firms should and do supplement quantitative analyses of investments by applying qualitative criteria related to their commercial strategies, the risk preferences of their shareholders, and capital and manpower constraints. With respect to any given investment opportunity, the use of an inappropriate discount rate may not change the decision. However, over a long period of time, the use of a single rate to evaluate all investments will bias a firm's decision-making in the wrong directions. The cumulative effect of such bias over many decisions is likely to affect the firm's growth and long-run profitability.

The Effects of Inflation

Inflation must be taken into account in two ways in analyzing investment opportunities. First, we must incorporate the anticipated effects of inflation in estimating cash flows. We discussed this problem in Chapter 12. Inflation also is reflected in the RRR. In the early and middle 1960s, inflation ran at rates of 1–2 percent per year and usually could be ignored without serious error. With the much higher inflation experience of the 1970s, anybody making decisions in the 1980s must pay attention to it!

In an inflationary environment, lenders and suppliers of capital require additional compensation to offset the loss of purchasing power of the dollars with which they will be repaid. The cost of inflation is passed on to the borrower who passes it along to the next party.

Let us consider an example. Suppose the rate of inflation is expected to be zero over the foreseeable future. Suppose further that a lender evaluates an opportunity to lend and decides to charge the borrower 4 percent for a 1 year loan. The lender expects a return of 4 percent. Suppose, however, that prices unexpectedly begin to rise after the loan is made, and they rise by a total of 3 percent over the ensuing year. With prices 3 percent higher, the *real* return to the lender over the year is 1 percent, although the *nominal* return is 4 percent.

If the lender had anticipated the 3 percent inflation, he or she likely would have charged 7 percent for the loan in order to ensure a 4 percent real return—the required rate. In establishing a nominal RRR, the lender adds the expected rate of inflation to his or her required return in real terms. The borrower, anticipating being able to repay in cheaper dollars, is willing to pay the higher rate. Just as the real return to the lender is 7 percent minus 3 percent, or 4 percent, so the real cost to the borrower also is 4 percent.

Because of the reactions of suppliers and users of capital in the above manner, anticipated inflation gradually becomes reflected in all market-determined rates of return. Bond yields rise to include anticipated inflation. Banks, savings and loan associations, and other institutional lenders add an inflation premium to their loan rates. Holders of common stocks revise upward their required rates of return. It is important to note that it is the rate of inflation expected in the future that is incorporated into market rates.

We can conclude that the nominal RRR on any investment (loan, bond, stock, or investment within a firm) should be viewed as the sum of the required real rate of return plus a premium for expected inflation. We should note, however, that all market rates may not always reflect this relationship. When the Federal Reserve follows a restrictive monetary policy, short-term rates may rise above levels that appear to reflect expected inflation. When monetary policy is expansive, short-term rates may fall below those levels. Such deviations may last for periods up to several months. We can conclude that short-term market rates tend to oscillate about a level that reflects the required real rate plus expected inflation. Long-term rates oscillate much less.

Since investors increase their required rates of return to reflect expected inflation, in analyzing investment opportunities, management, acting as the agent of the shareholders, should recognize that the nominal RRR of every investment opportunity also rises during periods of inflation. For example, if the required rate of an investment opportunity in the absence of inflation had been 10 percent, and inflation of 4 percent now is generally expected, the RRR used to evaluate the opportunity rises to about 14 percent. Since the RRR is expressed in nominal terms (including an inflation premium), it should be applied to investment cash flows that also are stated in nominal (inflated) terms.

How do we implement this approach? Fortunately, the necessary adjustments are not difficult. For practical purposes, the job is done automatically by the financial markets by virtue of the premium for anticipated inflation that is reflected in all market rates of return, including the government bond rate.[9]

In the absence of inflation, statistical estimation suggests that the market RRR on long-term United States government bonds would be about 2.5 percent. As of mid-1979, the government bond rate was about 9 percent, reflecting an inflation premium of about 6.5 percent. This premium reflects the market's consensus forecast of average annual inflation over the life of the bonds in question. By using the current government bond rate as our base for setting return targets (i in Figure 14-4), the market's required inflation premium is included automatically.

Some people, including experienced executives, are surprised at the suggestion that the minimum acceptable return on average-risk investments currently is around 14 percent.[10] In the absence of inflation, the RRR on such investments would be close to 7.5 percent (5 percent over the "real" government bond rate of 2.5 percent). With anticipated inflation of 6 to 7 percent per year, all investors demand an additional 6 to 7 percent annual return. This "inflated" return target then is used to evaluate cash flow estimates that also are stated in nominal terms, including the effects of inflation (see Chapter 12).

Using Return Targets

Let us now tie our discussion back to that of earlier Chapters (11 and 12) by asking ourselves what we do with the answer, the return target for a prospective investment, once we have it. We can use it in one of two ways, as the discount rate in calculating the NPV of the project or as the hurdle or cutoff rate against which the project's internal rate of return (IRR) is compared. To use the NPV approach, we apply the relationship (from Chapter 11)

$$\text{NPV} = \sum_{t=0}^{n} \frac{C_t}{(1 + K)^t} \tag{1}$$

In expression (1), C_t is the project's expected after-tax operating cash flow in each period. The word *expected* reminds us that the cash flows we are discounting in each period are not certain; rather, the cash flow figure for

---

9. Just how inflation, especially uncertain inflation, affects risk premiums and perceived risk is not perfectly understood. See J. Lintner, "Inflation and Security Returns," *Journal of Finance* **30**, 259–280 (May 1975); I. Friend, Y. Landskroner, and E. Losq, "The Demand for Risky Assets Under Uncertain Inflation," *Journal of Finance* **31**, 1287–1297 (Dec. 1976); and B. M. Friedman, "Who Puts the Inflation Premium into Nominal Interest Rates?" *Journal of Finance* **33**, 833–845 (June 1978).

10. For a detailed discussion of the impact of inflation on investment decisions, see Samuel L. Hayes, III, "Capital Commitments and the High Cost of Money," *Harvard Business Review* **55**, 155–161 (May–June 1977).

each period is the most likely value (strictly speaking, the expected value). If we use the IRR approach, we calculate the IRR using the *expected* (or most likely) cash flows in each period. We discussed the problem of estimating cash flows, the C_t's in expression (1), in Chapter 12.

In this chapter, we have developed a way to determine what discount rate to use, that is, what to use for K in expression (1). K is our return target, the minimum acceptable return (RRR) for the project.

Now we can see more clearly the link between risk and the RRR. Risk depends on the degree of uncertainty surrounding the cash flow estimates. So the more uncertain the cash flows (C_t), the higher the return target (K) we set for evaluating them. We discount the expected (most likely) cash flows, but the degree of uncertainty surrounding them determines how high we set the target.

Let us consider an example. ABC Corporation is deciding whether to expand its production facilities for manufacturing product Z. Since the project is an expansion of an existing product line, management judges it to be of average risk, so its relative risk ratio is 1.0. The government bond rate currently is 9 percent. So the risk premium π and RRR of the project are

$$\pi = 5 \text{ percent} \times 1.0 = 5 \text{ percent}$$
$$\text{RRR} = i + \pi = 9 + 5 = 14 \text{ percent}$$

The project requires an immediate outlay of $150,000. It is expected to generate incremental after-tax operating cash inflows as follows

Year	1	$40,000
	2	60,000
	3	60,000
	4	30,000

After year 4, product Z will be late in its life cycle, and management feels that no additional cash flows will be generated. The NPV calculation is shown in Table 14-2

Table 14-2

Year	After-Tax Cash Flow	Present Value Factor @ 14 percent	Present Value
0	($150,000)	1.000	($150,000)
1	40,000	0.877	35,080
2	60,000	0.769	46,140
3	60,000	0.675	40,500
4	30,000	0.592	17,760
		Net present value	($ 10,520)

The expansion project has a negative NPV; therefore, on economic grounds, it should not be undertaken. Now is an appropriate time to review the rationale behind rate of return targets and the way in which they should be integrated within the larger planning process of the firm.

An Economic Test

The purpose of return targets is to impose an economic test to ensure that prospective investment opportunities constitute wise and efficient uses of shareholder capital funds. Return targets should be integrated within a larger planning system and should be applied as second-level criteria only after prospective investments have passed a higher level policy screen of consistency with the firm's commercial strategy. Its commercial strategy tells the firm where to look for attractive investment opportunities; return targets tell which of those opportunities to select. In addition to these strategic and economic tests, the evaluation process must take account of risk preferences of shareholders and managers, interactions with other parts of the enterprise, opportunities for operating synergy, constraints on managerial and technical manpower, impact on local communities, environmental factors, and other qualitative considerations.

The weight given to economic considerations varies with the type of project and other circumstances. For a cost reduction project, the economic test likely will be the primary criterion. A decision to introduce a new product, on the other hand, may turn primarily on strategic considerations, with economic criteria playing a secondary, though still important, role.

Although not sufficient by itself, an economic test is wise in nearly all cases, for if a prospective investment cannot earn the market return, suppliers of capital will not wish it undertaken. Lockheed's decision to build the TriStar comes to mind again. No matter how compelling the qualitative arguments, it seems doubtful that Lockheed shareholders would have opted to invest a billion dollars in the project if they had seen the figures themselves.

Comparing Results to Expectations

Suppose a firm sets return targets and faithfully selects investment opportunities according to what the targets dictate. Will the firm actually earn the returns promised by the projects undertaken? The answer is probably not, and the reason involves a phenomenon that economists call "selection bias."

When analysts and managers in a firm calculate expected returns for prospective investments, they will inevitably make errors. They will overestimate returns on some projects and underestimate them on others.

When any group of projects is selected on the basis that the expected return for each is higher than the target return, the process tends to *select* for execution more projects the returns of which have been overestimated and to *reject* more projects the returns of which have been underestimated. The result is that the firm's overall return will turn out to be lower than management thinks it ought to be in view of the investments the firm had selected.

Summary

Required rates of return of investment opportunities are established in the financial markets. The RRR varies with risk and can be expressed as the sum of two components, $i + \pi$, where i is the risk-free rate of interest and π is the risk premium. The greater the risk of an investment opportunity, the greater is the risk premium, π.

Historical data on returns realized by investors over long time periods represent the best source of information on returns required by the market. Recent studies of United States financial markets indicate that 5 percentage points is a reasonable estimate of the normal risk premium required by the market on operating assets of average risk.

For a typical (average-risk) project, the required risk premium equals 5 percent. For projects involving higher or lower risks, the risk premium equals 5 percent times the project's relative risk ratio. The risk premium then is added to the government bond rate, i, to get the RRR.

Investment opportunities of most firms vary widely in riskiness. By classifying investment opportunities into risk categories, required rates of return can be established by category rather than for each project individually. Three categories that would fit many situations are cost reduction, expansion, and new products. Any number of categories can be established to fit a firm's particular circumstances. Where risk categories are used for most projects, very large or otherwise special projects still can be evaluated individually if need be. In nearly all cases, the use of a system of multiple discount rates is preferable to a single rate, which likely will lead to errors in decision making.

Inflation complicates the analysis of investment opportunities, but its effects must be taken into account both in the RRR and in cash flow estimates. Use of the market rate on long-term government bonds as the estimate of the risk-free rate of interest (i) automatically incorporates an inflation premium into the RRR. Cash flow estimates then should be stated in nominal (inflated) terms.

The purpose of return targets is to impose an economic test on prospective investments. Return targets form part of a larger planning system that takes account of the firm's commercial strategy.

Sample Problem

Mr. Park, the financial vice-president of Menlo Corporation, has decided to establish a system for setting return targets for capital investment projects. The company regularly undertakes projects that involve installation of labor-saving machinery. The company operates 12 manufacturing plants located in the United States and frequently receives recommendations from division executives that manufacturing facilities be expanded. Over the past 5 years, the company has built three new plants and marketed a total of eight entirely new products. By gathering data on past investment projects, Mr. Park has determined that most cost reduction projects are about half as risky as expansion projects. New products, on the other hand, are two to three times as risky.

Set up a system of return targets for Menlo Corporation, assuming a United States government bond rate of 8 percent.

Solution

The simplest system for a firm such as Menlo is to establish several risk categories for capital investment projects. In this case, three categories, cost reduction, expansion, and new products, seem to fit the situation. Taking expansion projects to be approximately average in risk, the risk premium for this category would be 5 percent and the return target 5 percent plus the government bond rate, or 13 percent. Cost reduction projects would call for a risk premium of $0.5 \times 5 = 2.5$ percent. Although new products vary somewhat in risk (two to three times as risky as expansion), it would be acceptable as a first approximation to establish a single category for new products with a risk premium of $2.5 \times 5 = 12.5$ percent. The complete system would be as follows:

Category	Risk Premium (percent)	Return Target (percent)
Cost reduction	2.5	10.5
Expansion	5.0	13.0
New products	12.5	20.5

Questions

1. "Required rates of return are set by management based on policies it thinks best for the shareholders." True or false? Explain.
2. What is the best source of information regarding returns required by investors?

3. In determining required rates of return for use by a particular firm, how can market data on the average risk premium for firms in general be used?

4. Measuring project and firm risk is difficult in practice. How can the necessity for this measurement be avoided in determining required rates of return?

5. If a firm operates only in a single industry, is it reasonable to suppose that all of its investment opportunities are of approximately the same degree of risk? Explain.

6. What is the motive for grouping investment opportunities by risk category?

7. If a firm uses a single discount to evaluate projects of widely varying risk characteristics, what is the likely outcome over an extended period of time?

8. How can a firm undertake a high-risk investment opportunity without increasing its overall operating risk?

9. Why are diversification effects relevant in analyzing investment opportunities?

10. What is the effect of inflation on rates of return in the financial markets?

11. Why must inflation be taken into account in evaluating investment opportunities in a firm?

12. The market required rate of return can be viewed as a line that slopes upward to the right (Figure 14-1). What determines the slope of the line?

Problems

1. Gamma Corporation, a firm of average risk, is considering expanding its facilities for manufacturing an established product to meet increasing demand. The product has been marketed for a number of years and is a mainstay of Gamma's line. Incremental cash flows expected to be generated by the new plant have been estimated carefully. A detailed risk analysis indicates that the expected internal rate of return on the investment is 0.20 and that it is approximately average in risk. The current yield to maturity on long-term United States government bonds is 8 percent. Should Gamma undertake the expansion project?

2. Suppose a new competitor enters the market for Gamma Corporation's product (Problem 1) and the uncertainty surrounding the incremental cash flows from the new plant increases. A new study indicates an expected return of 0.15 and a risk approximately 1.5 times that of a typical project. What is the effect on the attractiveness of the opportunity?

3. Gamma Corporation (Problem 1) is considering an investment in labor-saving equipment. The investment is considered to be about half as risky as the typical investment undertaken by Gamma. What should be the required rate of return?

4. The Community Hospital is planning to expand its facilities. Capacity for 50 new beds is needed immediately and another 50 in 5 years. A contractor submits a bid to build the entire 100 bed facility for $500,000. Maintenance and utilities on the 100 bed facility will run $10,000 per year. As an alternative, the contractor is willing to build a 50 bed facility now for $300,000 and to agree to build the remaining 50 bed facility in 5 years for an additional $350,000 under a fixed-price contract. Maintenance and utilities on the 50 bed facility will run $5,000 per year. Assume that the yield to maturity on long-term United States government bonds is 7 percent and that the hospital is not subject to taxation. Which alternative should the hospital elect?

5. The Downtown Municipal Hospital is considering installing an automatic dishwashing facility as a labor-saving measure. The hospital is municipally owned and not subject to taxation. The dishwasher, conveyor system, and other ancillary equipment require an outlay of $45,000 and have an expected life of 8 years, at the end of which time they are expected to have zero salvage value. Electrical power, supplies, and maintenance are expected to cost $1,300 per year. Direct labor savings are expected to be $11,500 annually (two full-time employees). At the time the project is being considered, the yield to maturity on long-term United States government bonds is 7 percent. The rate on an issue of bonds sold recently by the city was 6 percent.
   (a) Can discounted cash flow techniques be used to analyze the decision? If so, what discount rate should be used?
   (b) What decision should the hospital make?

6. The Orion Company has decided to categorize its investment opportunities by degree of risk and to set return targets by risk category. Orion's management has conducted a study of past investment projects to measure their relative risk. A large amount of data was gathered to permit calculation of relative risk ratios. Results of the study are:

Category	Relative Risk
Cost reduction	0.40
Expansion—existing product lines	1.00
New products—existing industries	1.75
New products—new industries	3.00

Develop a system of return targets for Orion. Use a government bond rate of 9 percent.

7. McIntyre Industries is considering a plan to establish return targets for investment decisions in its various divisions. A study of past data indicates that projects in different categories are not uniformly risky from one division to another. For example, cost reduction projects in the Electric Motors Division were found to be generally less risky than cost reduction projects in the Microelectronics Division. These risk differences were due primarily to differences in technology among divisions. Data gathered on relative risk was as shown in the table.

Category	Electric Motors	Electrical Components	Microelectronics
Cost reduction	0.5	0.3	0.8
Expansion	1.0	1.0	1.5
New products	2.0	1.5	3.5

Develop a system of return targets for each division, assuming a government bond rate of 8 percent.

8. Atlantic Leasing Company is considering an investment opportunity involving construction of a plant and then leasing it to a user, the Ajax Manufacturing Corporation. The total outlay for construction would be $1 million. The plant would be leased to Ajax for a period of 10 years. Atlantic would take the depreciation and pay for property taxes and insurance. The net after-tax operating cash inflow to Atlantic during years 1–10, including the lease payment, insurance, and all taxes, would be $115,000 per year. At the end of the 10 years, Atlantic would own the plant. Its market value at that time, net of all taxes, is estimated to be $1 million. Calculate the NPV of the operating cash flows and the terminal value. Assume that, even though the lease payment from Ajax is contractual, it is not riskless because of the possibility, even though small, that Ajax might default. Given this risk, Atlantic has determined the RRR for the operating cash flows (the $115,000 per year) to be 10 percent. The terminal value is subject to greater uncertainty and is to be evaluated using a 14 percent RRR. What decision should Atlantic make?

References

R. S. Bower and J. M. Jenks, "Divisional Screening Rates," *Financial Management* **4**, 42–49 (Autumn 1975).

R. S. Bower and D. R. Lessard, "An Operational Approach to Risk Screening," *Journal of Finance* **28**, 321–328 (May 1973).

R. Brealey, *Security Prices in a Competitive Market* (Cambridge, Mass.: MIT Press, 1971).

E. Brigham, "Hurdle Rates for Screening Capital Expenditure Proposals," *Financial Management* **4,** 17–26 (Autumn 1975).

E. E. Carter, "What Are the Risks in Risk Analysis?" *Harvard Business Review* **50,** 72–76 (July 1972).

P. L. Cooley, R. L. Roenfeldt, and I. Chew, "Capital Budgeting Procedures Under Inflation," *Financial Management* **4,** 18–27 (Winter 1975).

P. L. Cooley, R. L. Roenfeldt, and N. K. Modani, "Interdependence of Market Risk Measures," *Journal of Business* **50,** 356–363 (July 1977).

G. Donaldson, "Strategic Hurdle Rates for Capital Investment," *Harvard Business Review* **50,** 50–55 (Mar.–Apr. 1972).

L. Fisher and J. H. Lorie, "Rates of Return on Investments in Common Stock: The Year by Year Record 1926–1965," *Journal of Business* 291–316 (July 1968).

B. M. Friedman, "Who Put the Inflation Premium into Nominal Interest Rates?" *Journal of Finance* **33,** 833–845 (June 1978).

I. Friend and M. E. Blume, "The Demand for Risky Assets," *American Economic Review* **65,** 900–922 (Dec. 1975).

I. Friend, Y. Landskroner, and E. Losq, "The Demand for Risky Assets under Uncertain Inflation," *Journal of Finance* **31,** 1287–1297 (Dec. 1976).

R. L. Haggerman, "Finance Theory in Rate Hearings," *Financial Management* **5,** 18–21 (Spring 1976).

C. W. Haley and L. D. Schall, *The Theory of Financial Decisions* (New York: McGraw-Hill, 1973).

K. L. Hastie, "One Businessman's View of Capital Budgeting," *Financial Management* **4,** 36–44 (Winter 1974).

S. L. Hayes, III, "Capital Commitments and the High Cost of Money," *Harvard Business Review* **55,** 155–161 (May–June 1977).

D. B. Hertz, "Investment Policies that Pay Off," *Harvard Business Review* **46,** 96–108 (Jan.–Feb. 1968).

R. G. Ibbotson and R. A. Sinquefield, *Stocks, Bonds, Bills and Inflation: The Past (1926–1976) and the Future (1977–2000).* (Charlottesville, Va.: Financial Analysts Research Foundation, 1977).

M. C. Jensen, "Capital Markets: Theory and Evidence," *Bell Journal of Economics and Management Science* **3,** 357–398 (Autumn 1972).

W. G. Lewellen, *The Cost of Capital* (Belmont, Ca.: Wadsworth, 1969).

W. G. Lewellen, "Some Observations on Risk-Adjusted Discount Rates," *Journal of Finance* **32,** 1331–1338 (Sept. 1977).

J. Lintner, "Inflation and Security Returns," *Journal of Finance* **30,** 259–280 (May 1975).

R. H. Litzenberger and A. Budd, "Corporate Investment Criteria and the Evaluation of Risk Assets," *Journal of Financial and Quantitative Analysis* **5,** 395–420 (Dec. 1970).

J. D. Martin and D. F. Scott, "Debt Capacity and the Capital Budgeting Decision," *Financial Management* **5,** 7–14 (Summer 1976).

M. H. Miller, "Debt and Taxes," *Journal of Finance* **32,** 261–275 (May 1977).

F. Modigliani and M. H. Miller, "Corporate Income Taxes and the Cost of Capital: A Correction," *American Economic Review* **53,** 433–443 (June 1963).

C. R. Nelson, "Inflation and Capital Budgeting," *Journal of Finance* **31,** 923–932 (June 1976).

J. J. Pringle, "Using Capital Budgeting Models in Practice," paper presented to Financial Management Association, Montreal, Canada (Oct. 14–16, 1976).

F. Reilly, "Companies and Common Stocks as Inflation Hedges," *The Bulletin* (New York: New York University, 1975).

U. E. Reinhardt, "Break-Even Analysis of Lockheed's TriStar—An Application of Financial Theory," *Journal of Finance* **28,** 821–838 (Sept. 1973).

F. W. Searby, "Return to Return on Investment," *Harvard Business Review* **53,** 113–119 (Mar.-Apr. 1975).

E. Solomon, "Measuring a Company's Cost of Capital," *Journal of Business* **28,** 240–252 (Oct. 1955).

Technical Topics in Investment Analysis

15

A: The Capital Asset Pricing Model

B: The Impact of Financing Mix on Project Evaluation

C: The Weighted Average Cost of Capital

A large body of theory and empirical work underlies the material on capital budgeting covered in Part IV. Some of this underlying work is relatively recent, whereas some dates back to the late 1950s. One of the most important of these theories is the capital asset pricing model, discussed in Section A below. This material provides the theoretical basis for the approach to setting return targets advocated in Chapter 14. Section B deals with the question of how financing arrangements influence project evaluation. Section C discusses the weighted average cost of capital, an alternative approach to the problem of project evaluation. The three sections can be read independently.

A: The Capital Asset Pricing Model

The approach to setting return targets that we discussed in Chapter 14 is based on market data on return and risk. The investment criterion is a simplified version of the criterion derived from a model of the financial markets called the *capital asset pricing model* (CAPM).[1] The CAPM is a theory that describes security prices and yields under equilibrium conditions in an organized financial market. We introduced the basic ideas of the CAPM in Chapter 10. In this section we will go into more detail and adapt the CAPM for use in analyzing investment opportunities.

The CAPM originally was developed under a set of idealized assumptions, with many factors known to exist in practice assumed away in order to concentrate on the more important elements. One of these elements is uncertainty, or risk. The CAPM expresses prices and yields on risky assets in terms of investor preferences with respect to time and risk. The CAPM assumes that individuals are risk-averse and that they attempt to hold *efficient portfolios*; that is, they attempt to maximize the expected return on their portfolios for a given degree of risk. The CAPM also assumes that markets are *perfect*. That is, there are no transaction costs; information is costless and available to all market participants; all participants have equal access to investment opportunities; and financial distress and bankruptcy are costless.

Although originally developed as a theory about the securities markets, the CAPM has important implications for the financial management of firms. The theory of financial management is based on value-maximization as a normative criterion. To complete the conceptual framework, we need a positive or descriptive theory of the way in which

---

1. The CAPM was developed by three principal researchers, William F. Sharpe, "Capital Asset Prices: A Theory of Market Equilibrium under Conditions of Risk," *Journal of Finance* **19**(3), 425–442 (1964); John Lintner, "The Evaluation of Risk Assets and the Selection of Risky Investments in Stock Portfolios and Capital Budgets," *Review of Economics and Statistics* **47**, 13–77 (Feb. 1965); and Jan Mossin, "Equilibrium in a Capital Asset Market," *Econometrics* **34**, 768–755 (Oct. 1966).

values are determined in the marketplace. The CAPM provides such a theory and permits us to extend the microeconomic theory of the firm to a market context under conditions of uncertainty.

Market Equilibrium

As we noted in Chapter 10, the CAPM relies on the concept of *market equilibrium* to derive the return/risk relationship for individual financial assets. In theory, investors would buy and sell individual securities until each offers the same *reward to risk* ratio, that is, the same premium return per unit of risk. Once equilibrium is reached in the market and expected return equals required return, the return/risk ratio for every financial asset would be the same and would equal that for the market as a whole. We can represent this equilibrium symbolically as follows:

$$\frac{K_j - i}{S_j} = \frac{K_m - i}{S_m} \tag{A1}$$

Expression (A1) uses the symbols we discussed earlier in Chapter 10. K_m is the expected return on the *market portfolio*, a representative portfolio of all risky assets that the CAPM uses as its benchmark. S_m is a measure of the riskiness of the market portfolio. Likewise, K_j represents the expected return on any individual risky asset j, and S_j the risk of that asset. As it has throughout this book, i stands for the risk-free rate of interest.

Expression (A1) tells us that in equilibrium the market has adjusted so that all risky assets yield the same risk premium *per unit of risk*. Let us apply this reasoning to the case of firms, specifically to their marketable securities. If we assume that the market treats all firms rationally, and there is no reason to think otherwise, then the risk premium per unit of risk should be the same for all firms. In a well-functioning market, we would expect this to be the case; for if it were not, some firms would be better buys than others and profits could be made by buying the stock of those firms and selling that of others. Such opportunities do not go unnoticed, and we would therefore expect investors to require about the same risk premium per unit of risk for every firm. In equilibrium, the following would be true for every firm:

$$\frac{K_e - i}{S_e} = \frac{K_m - i}{S_m} \tag{A2}$$

where K_e represents the expected value of return on the common stock of any particular firm, and S_e the riskiness of return.

From the discussion above, we can see that the quantity $(K_m - i)/S_m$ is the *market standard* against which all prospective risky investments will be judged. If a firm's stock, or any risky asset in general, is expected to provide a return per unit of risk greater than the market standard, it represents a "good buy," and so its price will be bid upward until the risk-adjusted rate of return it offers is once again in line with other investment opportunities available in the market as a whole.

The CAPM Risk Measure

In expressions (A1) and (A2), we used the symbols S_j, S_e, and S_m to represent risk, without being specific as to how risk ought to be measured. The CAPM requires that risk be measured in a particular way. Where investors hold completely diversified portfolios, as assumed by the CAPM, it is the return and risk of the portfolio as a whole that matters and not the return and risk of the individual securities making up the portfolio. In measuring the risk of an individual security in a portfolio context, it is the contribution of the security to the risk of the portfolio that is important.

As its general measure of risk, the CAPM uses the *standard deviation* of the return. The standard deviation is a measure of dispersion or variability in the probability distribution of a random variable. Here, the random variable is return. In the case of the market portfolio, S_m represents the standard deviation of the return on the market portfolio, and K_m the expected return, or expected value of return. Likewise, S_e represents the standard deviation of the return from an individual security, and K_e the expected return. Portfolio theory tells us that the contribution of an individual security to the risk of the market portfolio is measured by $r_{em}S_e$, where r_{em} is the correlation coefficient of the return of the security with that of the market. Thus, the risk of a security viewed in isolation is S_e, whereas its contribution to the risk of the market portfolio is $r_{em}S_e$. The quantity $r_{em}S_e$ is called the *nondiversifiable* risk of the security, that part of the security's risk that cannot be eliminated by diversification. Likewise, $r_{jm}S_j$ is the nondiversifiable risk of any asset, j.

When we replace our earlier symbols for risk with the specific risk measures required by the CAPM, we obtain the following as our equilibrium relationships:

$$\frac{K_j - i}{r_{jm}S_j} = \frac{K_e - i}{r_{em}S_e} = \frac{K_m - i}{S_m} \tag{A3}$$

In equilibrium, the market risk premium per unit of nondiversifiable risk is the same for all firms and indeed for all risky assets.

The Required Rate of Return

For any asset j, we can arrange (A3) to obtain an expression for K_j:

$$K_j = i + \left(\frac{K_m - i}{S_m} \right) r_{jm} S_j \qquad (A4)$$

In (A4), K_j is the expected rate of return on asset j in equilibrium. It is made up of two components, the risk-free rate of interest, i, plus a risk premium. The risk premium is the product of the market standard $(K_m - i)/S_m$ and the specific risk of asset j, which is $r_{jm} S_j$. We can represent expression (A4) graphically, as in Figure 15-1.

Figure 15-1   The Market Required Rate of Return

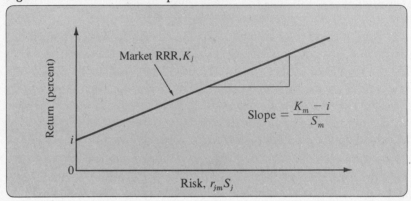

In the figure the intercept i and the slope $(K_m - i)/S_m$ are established in the financial markets by the actions of investors and lenders competing against one another. Risk, $r_{jm} S_j$, is determined by the characteristics of asset j itself.

Similarly, we can express the required rate of return on a firm's stock as

$$K_e = i + \left(\frac{K_m - i}{S_m} \right) r_{em} S_e \qquad (A5)$$

We would graph expression (A5) the way we did (A4) in Figure 15-1. In equilibrium, the expected rates of return of all securities would lie along the upward sloping line. High-risk securities would lie on the upper part of the line, low-risk securities on the lower part.[2]

---

2. Expression (A5) can be rearranged to give $K_e = i + (K_m - i) r_{em} S_e / S_m$. The ratio $r_{em} S_e / S_m$ is the firm's *beta coefficient* mentioned earlier at several points in this book. The beta coefficient is a measure of the volatility of the firm's return relative to the return on the market portfolio. Thus, beta is a measure of relative risk and is widely used in security analysis for this purpose. A beta of 1.0 indicates a firm of average risk. A beta above 1.0 indicates above-average risk, and vice versa. Figure 15-1 could be drawn with beta, B_j, on the horizontal axis and the slope equal to $(K_m - i)$.

The Required Return of an Investment Opportunity

The CAPM provides a standard for investment performance, not just for investments in the financial markets but for investments inside firms as well. The CAPM market standard, $(K_m - i)/S_m$, is the benchmark for *all* risky investment, inside the firm as well as outside. The market thus establishes a standard risk premium per unit of risk available to investors outside the firm and says to the management: "If you can do better than this inside the firm, then invest in our behalf. If you cannot, do not invest. Pay the money (dividends) out to us instead." The market is saying that to be acceptable, an investment must promise a premium return per unit of risk equal to or greater than the market standard.

Just as we did earlier for assets in general and securities of firms, we can rearrange expression (A3) to obtain

$$K_j = i + \left(\frac{K_m - i}{S_m} \right) r_{jm} S_j \qquad \text{(A6)}$$

Expression (A6) is the CAPM capital budgeting criterion. It gives us the RRR (K_j) for any prospective investment opportunity. We can use K_j to discount the after-tax operating cash flows of an investment to determine its net present value, or alternatively, we can use K_j as the "hurdle rate" against which to compare the investment's expected internal rate of return. In Figure 15-1, investment opportunities whose expected returns lie above the upward sloping line are acceptable; those below the line are not.

The Firm as the Benchmark

The CAPM uses the market portfolio as the reference against which the expected return and risk of a prospective investment are measured. The CAPM criterion is theoretically correct in a world in which all investors diversify completely and the financial markets are *frictionless* (meaning that there are no transaction costs of any type, and financial distress and bankruptcy are costless). We noted earlier that in such a frictionless world, investors care only about the return on the portfolio of stocks they own; they do not care about returns of individual firms or projects. In measuring risk in such a world, it is only the contribution of the investment project to the risk of the portfolio that matters. The CAPM measure of project risk, $r_{jm} S_m$, captures this element of risk by using the market portfolio as the benchmark, or reference portfolio, against which risk is measured.

In reality, financial markets are not frictionless, transaction costs do exist, financial distress and bankruptcy are not costless, and investors do not diversify completely. In such circumstances, it is not correct to use the market portfolio as the reference. Another alternative would be to use the firm itself as the reference portfolio.[3] In statistical terms, when a project is small relative to the firm, its contribution to the overall risk of the firm can be measured approximately by $r_{jo}S_j$, where r_{jo} is the coefficient of correlation between the project's cash flows and the firm's cash flows and S_j is the standard deviation of project return. The diversification effect of an individual project could be taken into account formally by using $r_{jo}S_j$ as the measure of project risk rather than $r_{jm}S_j$. The expression for the RRR becomes

$$K_j = i + \left(\frac{K_o - i}{S_o} \right) r_{jo} S_j \tag{A7}$$

where K_o is the RRR on the firm's equity in the absence of leverage and S_o is the riskiness of that return. In (A7), the project's return and risk are measured against a standard, $(K_o - i)/S_o$, that is derived from data on the firm itself, rather than a standard derived from the market as a whole as in (A6).

In the real world of imperfect markets, it is probably true that neither the firm itself nor the market portfolio is a strictly correct standard of reference. Either choice represents a compromise, and the best choice may differ from one firm to another. Practicing managers may find it intuitively more appealing to measure the risk of a prospective investment against a typical project for their own firms rather than against a typical project for the economy as a whole. This advantage would have its price, however, for now an estimate would have to be made of $(K_o - i)$, the market risk premium for the individual firm. The value of $(K_o - i)$ could be estimated from historical data on the firm's outstanding securities, but adjustments would be required for such items as different degrees of leverage in the firm's capital structure relative to all firms. In general, estimates of $(K_o - i)$

---

3. This possibility is discussed by Donald L. Tuttle and Robert H. Litzenberger, "Leverage, Diversification, and Capital Market Effects on a Risk-Adjusted Capital Budgeting Framework," *Journal of Finance* 22, 427–443 (June 1968). In imperfect markets, the issue of which is superior as reference portfolio, market or firm, cannot be resolved on the basis of logical argument. Rather, the issue is an empirical one, the resolution of which depends, in part, on the relative importance to investors of total firm risk as opposed to only the nondiversifiable component. For empirical evidence on this question, see M. C. Findlay, A. E. Gooding, and W. Q. Weaver, "On the Relevant Risk for Determining Capital Expenditure Hurdle Rates," *Financial Management* 5, 9–17 (Winter 1976). They conclude that the case is not proved either way and suggest that practitioners are likely to be more concerned with total firm risk (arguing for the firm as reference) than with nondiversifiable risk alone. Additional evidence that total variability is an important determinant of market values is provided by I. Friend, R. Westerfield, and M. Granito, "New Evidence on the CAPM," *Journal of Finance* 33, 903–916 (June 1978); and I. Friend and R. Westerfield, "Risk and Capital Asset Pricing," working paper, 5–79, The Wharton School, University of Pennsylvania. For a review of various empirical tests of the CAPM, see S. Ross, "The Current Status of the Capital Asset Pricing Model," *Journal of Finance* 33, 885–902 (June 1978).

for individual firms are likely to be less reliable than estimates of $(K_m - i)$ for the market portfolio as a whole.

Problems in Applying the CAPM

The CAPM is one of the most important theoretical developments in finance in many years. It has provided valuable guidance to practicing managers as well as to theoreticians. It has clarified the concept of the required rate of return as a market-determined opportunity rate. It has explicitly defined the market risk premium and established the importance of nondiversifiable risk. Perhaps its greatest contributions are that it specifies the tradeoff between return and risk and makes clear that the cost of capital for all firms is an upward-sloping line and not a single figure.

These are important and valuable *qualitative* insights. When the time comes for *quantitative* applications of the CAPM, for "plugging in numbers," we must become cautious. First of all, the CAPM measures risk as the standard deviation of returns, or more specifically, the product of the standard deviation and a correlation coefficient. However, tests have shown that, with risk measured in this way, the relationship with realized market returns may not be as perfectly linear as the CAPM theory assumes.[4]

It is doubtful that any single measure, such as the standard deviation, can adequately capture all aspects of risk as perceived by investors. For example, there is reason to suppose that skewness is important to investors, yet the standard deviation does not consider skew.[5]

Another problem has to do with time periods. The CAPM is a *single-period* theory; that is, it deals with only a single decision period. In practice, investment opportunities nearly always are multiperiod in character, involving cash flows over a number of time periods. This difficulty can be circumvented to some extent by defining risk measures S_j and S_m over a multiperiod horizon.[6] If this is done, the CAPM appears to be acceptable on theoretical grounds for use in a multiperiod world.[7]

---

4. See Michael C. Jensen, "Capital Markets: Theory and Evidence," *Bell Journal of Economics and Management Science* **3**, 357–398 (Autumn 1972); E. Fama and J. McBeth, "Risk, Return and Equilibrium: Empirical Tests," *Journal of Political Economy* **83**, 607–636 (May–June 1973); Friend, Westerfield, and Granito, "New Evidence on the CAPM"; and Ross, "The Current Status of the CAPM."

5. For an extension of the CAPM to incorporate skewness, see A. Kraus and R. H. Litzenberger, "Skewness Preference and the Valuation of Risk Assets," *Journal of Finance* **31**, 1085–1100 (Sept. 1976). Kraus and Litzenberger provide a more complete CAPM, but its implications for decision-making in practice are not yet clear.

6. See R. S. Bower and D. R. Lessard, "An Operational Approach to Risk Screening," *Journal of Finance* **28**, 321–328 (May 1973). As a means of ensuring that project and firm risk are measured in a consistent manner over comparable time periods, Bower and Lessard suggest defining firm risk as the risk of a *typical project* of the firm.

7. See S. C. Myers and S. M. Turnbull, "Capital Budgeting and the Capital Asset Pricing Model—Good News and Bad News," *Journal of Finance* **32**, 321–333 (May 1977). The good news concerns the theoretical acceptability of the CAPM in a multiperiod world, the bad news, the practical problems of obtaining input data.

Even if all theoretical questions could be settled, formidable problems remain in obtaining the information needed to apply the CAPM. For example, the measure of project risk required by the CAPM $(r_{jm}S_j)$ depends on the life of the project, the growth trend in expected project cash flows, the time pattern of those cash flows, and growth opportunities of the firm.[8] Estimates of r_{jm} and S_j can be made by using techniques such as simulation and risk analysis,[9] but in many cases, the underlying input data are so speculative that the results lack any real credibility. As a result, in reality we cannot measure correlation coefficients and standard deviations with the precision required by the CAPM. Nor do we yet know how to account properly for the effects of "financial friction." For these reasons, strict application of the CAPM to capital budgeting decisions in practice is very difficult.

The fact that the CAPM cannot be applied to capital budgeting problems without modification does not mean that it is not a good theory. As with many economic models, absolute realism is not the objective. Rather, the model provides a way of thinking about the problem, in this case the relationship between return and risk. It yields insights, understanding, and guidance to both scholars and business decision-makers.

An Approximation

Let us now reexamine the simplified approach discussed in Chapter 14. First, let us rearrange expression (A6) as follows:

$$K_j = i + (K_m - i)\frac{r_{jm}S_j}{S_m} \qquad \text{(A8)}$$

In Chapter 14, we estimated $(K_m - i)$ to be about 5 percent with the effects of financial leverage eliminated. We then assumed that the decision-maker could make an "informed judgment" about the risk of a prospective investment opportunity relative to the risk of a typical project of average risk. This amounted to making an estimate of the value of the ratio $r_{jm}S_j/S_m$ without actually estimating each element separately. The numerator, $r_{jm}S_j$, represents the nondiversifiable risk of the project under evaluation. The denominator, S_m, is the risk of the market portfolio. But the nondiversifiable risk of a typical project is equal to S_m. So when we

8. Ibid.
9. For a discussion of risk analysis, see David B. Hertz, "Risk Analysis in Capital Investment," *Harvard Business Review* **42,** 95–106 (Jan.–Feb. 1964); and "Investment Policies that Pay Off," *Harvard Business Review* **46,** 96–108 (Jan.–Feb. 1968). A criticism of risk analysis is that its benefits often do not justify its costs. See K. Larry Hastie, "One Businessman's View of Capital Budgeting," *Financial Management* **4,** 36–44 (Winter 1974); and E. Eugene Carter, "What Are the Risks in Risk Analysis?" *Harvard Business Review* **50,** 72–76 (July 1972).

make an estimate of the risk of a prospective project relative to the risk of a typical project of average risk, we are, in effect, estimating the value of the ratio $r_{jm}S_j/S_m$.[10]

So the simplified approach in Chapter 14 is a straightforward application of the theory of the CAPM, with some gross simplifications in estimating input data. Whether the simple approach of Chapter 14 is any less "accurate" or usable than strict application of the CAPM is a debatable question. For in applying the CAPM as specified, in the final analysis, informed judgments will have to be made in order to estimate the inputs r_{jm} and S_j, and those estimates may be no more accurate than the relative risk estimate suggested in Chapter 14.

B: The Impact of Financing Mix on Project Evaluation

Our discussion of investment decisions, thus far, has not considered the matter of *financing*, that is, the mix of equity and debt funds that the firm uses to finance its operating assets. The issue is straightforward: Should financing arrangements be taken into account in evaluating an investment opportunity, and if so, how?

Financing decisions are clearly an important part of the financial manager's task, and we devote six full chapters to their analysis in Part V, in which we consider the characteristics of debt and equity securities, the impact of financial leverage on the firm's returns, how firms should choose the amount and kind of debt to use, and a number of related issues. The issue that is relevant to our present discussion of investment opportunities is not *how* a firm does its financing but whether the firm's methods of financing should be taken into account in analyzing an investment opportunity. Many have argued that they should, but as we will see, the answer, in most cases, turns out to be no.

The Tax Benefits of Debt

Why might *financing* arrangements be relevant to *investment* decisions? The answer involves *taxes*. If firms and individuals were not taxed by

---

10. With $(K_m - i)$ defined as the unlevered market risk premium, S_m also must be unlevered; that is, S_m must measure market operating risk. This can be done by defining S_m as the risk of a typical project. Defining risk in this way represents an adaptation of the approach suggested by Bower and Lessard, "An Operational Approach to Risk Screening," of measuring firm risk as the risk of a typical project of the firm. Here we are measuring market risk as the risk of a typical project for the economy as a whole. The nondiversifiable risk of a typical project, $r_{xm}S_x$, would equal market risk, S_m, provided S_m is defined as operating risk with the effects of financial leverage eliminated. As Bower and Lessard point out, defining risk in this way avoids some difficult problems of measurement. It was pointed out in Chapter 14 that by measuring project risk against a typical project as a benchmark, diversification effects are taken into account. This is so when the risk of both the project under evaluation and the benchmark project are properly defined as nondiversifiable risk.

governments, financing arrangements would have no bearing on investment decisions, absolutely none. Financing decisions still would be
important but not for the analysis of investment opportunities.

The reason taxes are important to our discussion arises from the fact
that interest paid on debt is tax deductible to the firm. Use of debt
financing in lieu of equity therefore reduces a firm's tax liability. This
reduction in taxes due to interest deductibility often is called the *interest
tax shield*. Money thus saved in lower taxes goes instead to shareholders,
increasing the firm's after-tax cash flows available to those shareholders.
So the question arises: If a prospective investment opportunity can be
financed partly by debt funds, should the project be given credit for the
potential tax savings due to deductibility of the interest on that debt? The
answer would seem to be yes.

But corporate taxes are not the whole story. Investors, namely,
bondholders and stockholders, pay taxes also. Recent theories suggest
that, when debt is used by a firm, corporate taxes saved by the firm may be
offset by the additional taxes eventually paid by investors.[11] To analyze
these issues, we need a conceptual framework for valuing tax benefits.

The Adjusted Present Value Approach[12]

Throughout Part IV we have emphasized the importance of analyzing the
firm's operating cash flows separately from its financing flows. In Chapter
12, we focused on operating flows, and in Chapter 14 we set a return target
to be used to discount those operating flows in order to calculate their
present value. Financing flows—interest, principal payments on debt, and
dividends—were kept out of the discussion entirely.

Let us now bring in those financing flows. If the prospective project is
to be financed partly by debt, the tax shield on that debt ought to be
considered. A complete statement of the *adjusted present value* (APV) of
the project is as follows:[13]

$$APV = NPVO + PVT \tag{B1}$$

In equation (B1), NPVO is the net present value of the project's after-tax
operating cash flows, calculated following the approaches of Chapters 10
through 14, without regard to the way the project is to be financed. PVT is
the present value of the tax shield on the debt financing to be used. Our
problem now is to calculate PVT. As noted above, both corporate and

---

11. See M. H. Miller, "Debt and Taxes," *Journal of Finance* **32,** 261–275 (May 1977).
12. The APV approach described in this section is that of S. C. Myers, "Interactions of
Corporate Financing and Investment Decisions: Implications for Capital Budgeting,"
Journal of Finance **29,** 1–25 (Mar. 1974).
13. Ibid.

personal taxes must be considered. Let us consider these two kinds of taxes one at a time.

Corporate Taxes

If a corporation pays interest of I_t in period t, its taxes are reduced in that period by an amount $I_t T_c$, where T_c is the corporate tax rate. In other words, $I_t T_c$ is the interest tax shield due to corporate taxes. We can discount that tax shield to obtain its present value as follows:

$$\text{PVT}_c = \sum_{t=1}^{n} \frac{I_t T_c}{(1 + K_d)^t} \tag{B2}$$

where PVT_c is the present value of the corporate tax shield and K_d is the rate of return required by debtholders.

How do we define I_t, the interest payment? The amount clearly depends on how much debt is to be used to finance the project. In some cases, the financing associated with an investment can be directly identified, as in the case of a mortgage loan to finance a real estate project. In such cases, the interest payment in each period is easily determined.

In the context of a company, identifying the amount of debt to be associated with a specific investment opportunity is not so easy. Firms normally undertake investments continuously over time, while raising the necessary funds in large blocks rather than for each project individually. Usually it is not possible to determine just where the dollars for a particular project come from. It would be possible to define the financing (debt/equity) mix for any project as equal to the firm's overall financing mix and therefore the same for all projects. Such a definition is incorrect, however, because it ignores the impact of individual projects on a firm's capacity to expand its borrowing, sometimes referred to as the firm's "debt capacity."

In theory, the debt attributable to a particular project should be defined as the project's contribution to the firm's debt capacity.[14] High-risk projects contribute less to a firm's debt capacity than do low-risk projects. Although determining debt attributable to a project in this way is difficult in practice, let us assume for the moment that we can do so and symbolize it by D_j.[15] To keep things simple, let us also assume for the moment that our project is *ongoing* and that its contribution to the firm's debt capacity is permanent and constant, so that D_j does not vary with time. In this case,

---

14. Ibid. Myers gives a theoretical discussion of this issue.
15. For a discussion of techniques for determining project debt in practice, see J. D. Martin and D. F. Scott, Jr., "Debt Capacity and the Capital Budgeting Decision," *Financial Management* **5,** 7–14 (Summer 1976).

$$\text{PVT}_c = \sum_{t=1}^{\infty} \frac{rD_j T_c}{(1 + K_d)^t} \tag{B3}$$

where r is the interest rate the firm pays on debt and D_j is the amount of debt to be used to finance the project. Since we are discounting a perpetuity, we can simplify (B3) to get

$$\text{PVT}_c = \frac{rD_j T_c}{K_d} \tag{B4}$$

When we are considering only corporate taxes and ignoring personal taxes, it is appropriate to discount the tax shield at the rate the firm pays on debt, that is, $K_d = r$. In this case, (B4) reduces to

$$\text{PVT}_c = D_j T_c \tag{B5}$$

Personal Taxes

The above analysis of PVT considers only corporate taxes. What of taxes paid by bondholders on interest that *they* receive? And taxes paid by shareholders on dividends and capital gains? The extent to which personal taxes affect market valuation is complex. It is still an unsettled and controversial issue at present.[16] To explore this question, we need some new symbols. Let T_b represent the tax rate paid by bondholders on the interest income they receive. If the firm pays interest to bondholders equal to rD_j, the bondholders retain after taxes the amount $rD_j(1 - T_b)$. The payment of rD_j to bondholders reduces the amount available to stockholders by a like amount. But the payment is deductible for tax purposes, so the firm's earnings are decreased by only $rD_j(1 - T_c)$, where T_c is the corporate tax rate. Finally, we must account for the fact that stockholders themselves pay personal taxes. Taking these taxes into account, we find that the stockholders net after-tax earnings are decreased by $rD_j(1 - T_c) \cdot (1 - T_s)$, where T_s is the stockholders marginal tax rate.

Let us summarize the effects of the above transaction. When the firm pays interest of rD_j, after all tax effects are taken into account, bondholders receive $rD_j(1 - T_b)$ and stockholders in effect pay $rD_j(1 - T_c) \cdot (1 - T_s)$. The tax effects are as follows:

Bondholders pay tax of	$rD_j T_b$	(B6)
Stockholders save tax of	$rD_j[T_c + T_s(1 - T_c)]$	(B7)

---

16. See Miller, "Debt and Taxes."

Let us now return to the calculation of PVT, the present value of the interest tax shield on debt. Expression (B4) gives PVT taking account of corporate taxes only. When we include personal taxes, we get

$$\text{PVT} = \frac{rD_j[T_c + T_s(1 - T_c) - T_b]}{K_b}$$

$$= \frac{rD_j[(1 - T_b) - (1 - T_s)(1 - T_c)]}{K_b} \qquad \text{(B8)}$$

In (B8), as in (B4), we are assuming that D_j is constant over time so that all tax effects are perpetuities. The discount rate, K_b is the bondholders' after-tax required rate of return, that is, after personal taxes. In practice, this rate would be close to the market rate of interest on tax-exempt municipal bonds. It also could be approximated by $K_b = r(1 - T_b)$. So we could rewrite (B8) as

$$\text{PVT} = \frac{rD_j[(1 - T_b) - (1 - T_s)(1 - T_c)]}{r(1 - T_b)}$$

$$= D_j\left[1 - \frac{(1 - T_s)(1 - T_c)}{(1 - T_b)}\right] \qquad \text{(B9)}$$

An analysis that ignores personal taxes in effect assumes that $T_s = T_b = 0$. In that case, (B9) reduces to (B5). In fact, if T_s is simply assumed equal to T_b, but not necessarily zero, we get the same result.

In practice, personal taxes are not zero, and T_s is not equal to T_b, so (B9) is a more complete expression for the PVT than is (B5). When personal taxes are included in the analysis, some interesting insights emerge. Some financial theorists argue that financial markets adjust in a way that completely eliminates *all* tax effects.[17] According to this view, when markets have reached equilibrium, interest rates and the quantity of bonds issued have adjusted in a way that causes the quantity $(1 - T_b)$ to exactly equal the quantity $(1 - T_s)(1 - T_c)$. With a bit of algebra, one can demonstrate that in this situation, taxes paid by bondholders (B6) *exactly* offset taxes saved by the firm and stockholders (B7). If this is true, then the use of debt does not reduce the total tax liability at all, and PVT = 0, as shown by (B9). This argument leads to the conclusion that *financing considerations can be ignored in making investment decisions*. If this view is correct, then when analyzing a prospective investment opportunity, a firm determines the NPV of the after-tax operating cash flows of the investment without worrying about how the investment is to be financed.

---

17. Miller, "Debt and Taxes," is the leading advocate of this view.

Not all financial theorists agree that life really is this simple. Those in this camp argue that markets do not adjust completely to taxes. If so, then PVT is likely to be greater than zero. Just where the truth lies in this debate is a major unsettled question in finance at present.[18] It seems safe to speculate that personal taxes do have some effect, and PVT is therefore less than suggested by (B5), which considers only corporate taxes. It seems just as safe to speculate that markets do not adjust perfectly and that PVT is greater than zero.

A Practical Solution

Not knowing the answer to the tax question may not be as troublesome as it first appears. Our choice of a "model" of the financial markets enters the capital budgeting process at two points.[19] The first point at which we must choose a model is when we analyze market data to determine the market risk premium for average-risk investment, which we did in Chapter 14. We then must choose a model again when we calculate PVT.

In choosing our models, we should be consistent; that is, we should use the same model both places. For example, we could assume here that tax effects net out to zero and PVT = 0. The same assumption back in Chapter 14 would imply a particular estimate of π, the market risk premium. An assumption that all tax effects net to zero implies a lower π than alternative models that consider corporate taxes but not personal taxes.

Suppose we assume that tax effects net to zero, when in fact they do not. Our estimate of π, the risk premium, would be too low. This would result in our using too low a discount rate in calculating NPVO in expression (B1), thus overstating NPVO. We then would assume PVT to be zero, when in fact it was positive. Thus, we would overstate NPVO and understate PVT.

The happy outcome is that our two errors offset one another. Under some conditions, the two errors offset exactly.[20] In most cases, the offset is not exact, but the resulting error is not large in relation to the other errors inherent in the capital budgeting process, for example, in the estimation of future cash flows.

---

18. For empirical evidence on this issue, see E. H. Kim, W. G. Lewellen, and J. J. McConnell, "Financial Leverage Clienteles; Theory and Evidence," *Journal of Financial Economics*, forthcoming.

19. Currently there are two classes of such models. The first class comprises models based on the work of F. Modigliani and M. H. Miller, "Corporate Income Taxes and the Cost of Capital: A Correction," *American Economic Review* **53**, 433–443 (June 1963). Models in this class consider corporate taxes but ignore personal taxes. The second class of models are those based on Miller's 1977 article "Debt and Taxes" in the *Journal of Finance*. These models consider both corporate and personal taxes.

20. For discussion of this point, see R. S. Harris and J. J. Pringle, "A Note on the Implications of Miller's Argument for Capital Budgeting," working paper, University of North Carolina at Chapel Hill, June 1979.

Ignoring Financing Considerations

Thus, we arrive at an important conclusion: In analyzing investment opportunities of firms using the APV approach, we can ignore financing considerations entirely, provided we use consistent assumptions in estimating the market risk premium used in calculating NPVO. High-risk projects contribute little to a firm's debt capacity in the first place. Potential errors will be greatest in the case of low-risk projects with substantial debt capacity. Even here, the net error is not likely to be large for reasons noted above. It is possible that such an error could cause a firm to forego a project that should have been undertaken, for example, in a situation in which NPVO is slightly negative but a positive PVT more than offsets it to produce a positive APV. If financing were ignored, the negative NPVO would lead to rejecting the project, when, in fact, APV was positive. However, if a project is unacceptable considering only its operating cash flows, the addition of the tax subsidy on debt in most cases would not provide a comfortable basis for reversing the decision.[21]

Exceptions

The preceding analysis applies to the general case of firms that raise funds in public financial markets and whose shareholders are typical of shareholders in general. One implication of the word *typical* is that the marginal tax rates T_s and T_c applicable to the firm in question are approximately the same as the T_s and T_c for firms in general. In particular situations in which investor and firm tax rates differ from those in general, PVT could well be significant.

One such possibility is in the case of real estate projects. Here a significant part of the return to equity investors may be taxed as ordinary income. Furthermore, real estate projects often use a high proportion of debt financing. The result could be that PVT is relevant and significant in evaluating such projects.

We can use expression (B8) to analyze PVT in a real estate project, with one modification. In such projects the debt level and therefore the interest payment typically varies over time. We can modify (B8) to deal with this situation as follows:

$$\text{PVT} = \sum_{t=1}^{n} \frac{I_t[T_c + T_s(1 - T_c) - T_b]}{(1 + K_b)^t} \tag{B10}$$

---

21. A factor not considered in this analysis is the potential costs of financial distress and/or bankruptcy. For a discussion, see H. Hong and A. Rappaport, "Debt Capacity, Optimal Capital Structure, and Capital Budgeting Analysis," *Financial Management* **7**, 7–11 (Autumn 1978). They argue that the present value of potential bankruptcy costs should be deducted from PVT. Their argument strengthens the case for ignoring PVT in analyzing investment opportunities.

In (B10), I_t is the interest payment each period, T_c is the corporate tax rate (applicable only if a corporation undertakes the project), T_b is the marginal tax rate of the mortgage lender, T_s is the tax rate of the equity investor(s) in the project, and K_b is the market rate on tax-exempt municipal bonds.

C: The Weighted Average Cost of Capital

The approach to investment decisions adopted in this book breaks the process into two steps: first, evaluation of operating cash flows and second, evaluation of the effects of financing arrangements. This approach is generally referred to as the adjusted present value (APV) approach.[22] In discussing the APV approach in the preceding section, we found that in most cases involving investment decisions in firms, step two, evaluation of financing, can be omitted. However, where debt provides a large proportion of the needed financing and where equity investors are subject to relatively high tax rates, as may be true in real estate projects, financing arrangements may well be important.

There exists an alternative approach, called the *weighted average cost of capital* (WACC) approach, which has been widely recognized in the literature of finance and in other textbooks. Whereas the APV approach evaluates operating risk and financing in two separate steps, the WACC approach does it in one step. This is accomplished by using a discount rate that includes the effects of operating risk as well as financing risk and tax effects. We discussed the WACC briefly in Chapter 14. Let us now explore the theory and application of the WACC in more depth.

Theory

Assume that a firm has debt in its capital in amount D and that it pays interest to debtholders at rate K_d, the market required rate of return on the firm's debt. Assume further that the firm has equity outstanding with total market value E and that the market RRR on this equity is K_e. K_e often is called the firm's cost of equity capital, and K_d the cost of debt capital. As we have observed elsewhere, RRR and cost of capital are simply two different labels for the same thing.

For the moment, we will consider corporate taxes but not personal taxes. Since interest is tax-deductible to the firm, the after-tax equivalent of the market RRR on debt is $K_d(1 - T_c)$, where T_c is the firm's marginal tax rate. $K_d(1 - T_c)$ is the after-tax cost of debt capital. If the after-tax cost of debt is $K_d(1 - T_c)$ and the cost of equity is K_e, we can calculate a *weighted average* of the two as follows:

---

22. See Myers, "Interactions of Corporate Financing and Investment Decisions."

$$\text{WACC} = K_w = \frac{D}{D + E} K_d (1 - T_c) + \frac{E}{D + E} K_e \qquad \text{(C1)}$$

The cost of debt $K_d(1 - T_c)$ is weighted by its proportion, $D/(D + E)$, in the firm's capital structure. Likewise, K_e is weighted by the proportion of equity, $E/(D + E)$.

For reasons that we will go into shortly, the WACC is appropriate only for evaluating a project of average risk, that is, a project the risk of which equals that of the firm overall. The WACC is not appropriate for projects above or below average in risk. Let us assume for the moment that we are evaluating an average-risk project. In this case "average" is measured relative to the firm itself and not against an average for the entire economy. We would use K_w to discount the after-tax operating cash flows of the project, the same flows we would discount in step one of the APV method [i.e., in calculating NPVO in expression (B1)].

Note that K_w takes account of three important factors simultaneously: (1) the operating risk of the project, which enters via K_e and K_d; (2) the mix of debt and equity used to finance the project, brought in via the weighting terms $D/(D + E)$ and $E/(D + E)$; and (3) tax effects, which enter via $(1 - T_c)$. The presumption is that the project is to be financed by the same proportion of debt and equity as the firm overall. This is appropriate for projects of the same risk as the firm overall, and it is only average-risk projects that should be evaluated using the WACC. If an average-risk project has an operating return exactly equal to K_w, all suppliers of capital will be compensated at exactly their required rates of return. Debtholders would receive K_d and equityholders, K_e. If the operating return of the project exceeds K_w, then equityholders receive more than K_e, since the debtholders' return is fixed at K_d.

Calculating the WACC

Let us calculate the WACC for a typical firm. Suppose the interest rate on the firm's debt is 9.5 percent. From Table 14-1 in Chapter 14, we know that the risk premium on the common stock of a typical firm averages about 7.4 percent above the corporate bond rate. So let us assume that K_e is $9.5 + 7.4 = 16.9$ percent.[23] Suppose the firm's capital structure is 30 percent debt and 70 percent equity and its tax rate is 46 percent. The firm's WACC then is

$$\begin{aligned} K_w &= 0.3(9.5)(1 - 0.46) + 0.7(16.9) \\ &= 13.369 \end{aligned}$$

---

23. K_e for any firm can be calculated from the relationship $(K_e - i) = B_e(K_m - i)$, where B_e is the firm's beta coefficient, discussed in footnote 2 above. Beta coefficients for a large number of United States firms are regularly computed by investment advisory services such as the *Value Line Investment Survey*. Beta is estimated via regression analysis from historical data on firm and market returns.

We would use the rate 13.369 percent to discount a prospective project's after-tax operating cash flows. If the project happened to return exactly 13.369 percent, then equityholders would receive exactly 16.9 percent, and debtholders 9.5 percent.

Comparison of WACC and APV[24]

In theory, the WACC and APV approaches should produce the same result in the case of an average-risk project (average relative to the firm itself). For this happy result to come about would require that we estimate accurately the market risk premium π for average risk investments (which we need in order to use APV) and K_e and K_d, which we need for estimating the WACC. Making these estimates in practice is difficult, and given the likelihood of errors in measurement, a practical comparison of APV and WACC likely would yield estimates of NPV that were close but not identical.

Aside from the problem of measurement error, there is the issue of our understanding of the way financial markets work, especially with respect to the effects of taxation. We raised some of these issues in Chapter 14 and again in Section B of this chapter. In order to estimate π and K_e so as to compare APV and WACC, we need a clear understanding of tax effects and a model of how financial markets work.[25] Since many of these issues are still controversial and unsettled, a quantitative comparison of the two approaches is difficult.[26]

Let us now consider the matter of personal taxes, that is, taxes on bondholders and stockholders. In Section B we discussed a recent theory that holds that personal taxes offset the effects of corporate taxes in financing decisions and that there is therefore no tax advantage to the use of debt.[27] If this position is correct, then firms using the APV approach can ignore financing arrangements in making decisions about investment opportunities. Using the terminology of Section B, the present value of the tax shield on debt, PVT, is zero. The APV of a project thus equals NPVO, the net present value of its operating cash flows.

What does this argument regarding personal taxes imply for the WACC? That is, suppose the effects of corporate and personal taxes do net to zero and debt offers no net tax advantage. It turns out that we still calculate the WACC the same way, using expression (C1). However, the

---

24. For a thorough discussion and comparison of the WACC and APV approaches, see Myers, "Interactions of Corporate Financing and Investment Decisions."

25. As noted in Section B, there are two major competing models, that of Modigliani and Miller (1963), "Corporate Income Taxes and the Cost of Capital," and that of Miller (1977), "Debt and Taxes."

26. As noted above, Myers "Interactions of Corporate Financing and Investment Decisions," provides a thorough theoretical comparison.

27. See Miller (1977), "Debt and Taxes."

answer we get is a bit surprising, for it turns out that K_w equals K_o, the market RRR on the firm's equity in the absence of leverage.[28] If markets adjust completely to eliminate all tax effects, the values for K_e and K_d that we substitute in (C1) always yield the same figure for K_w. That figure is K_o, the firm's unlevered equity capitalization rate. Note that K_o is the rate that we would use in calculating NPVO in the APV approach. Since, in this case of offsetting tax effects, PVT = 0, it follows that APV = NPVO = NPV calculated using the WACC. Thus, in the case of offsetting tax effects, the APV and WACC approaches lead to identical estimates of NPV for an average-risk project. As noted above, the two approaches theoretically give identical estimates in all cases involving average-risk projects, but the equivalence can be more easily demonstrated in this special case.

Regardless of the effects of taxes on market values, (C1) is the correct expression for the WACC. Given accurate estimates of K_d and K_e, (C1) yields an estmate of K_w that is correct for evaluating an average-risk project. If personal and corporate taxes are completely offsetting, we get an estimate of K_w that equals K_o and does not change with leverage. If taxes do not have exactly this effect, we still get an estimate of K_w that accounts for those tax effects properly. The key to achieving this result is to begin with accurate estimates of K_d and K_e.

Applied properly, the APV and WACC approaches both account fully for all taxes, corporate and personal. Both rely on estimates of required rates of return that are inferred from relationships between firm cash flows and market values. Since market values include the effects of personal taxes, when market RRR's are used to calculate project net present values, those net present values likewise include the effects of personal taxes.

Problems with the WACC

Both the WACC and the APV approaches are subject to criticism on a number of theoretical grounds.[29] Some necessary assumptions may not hold in practice, and a number of approximations and compromises are necessary in using either approach. As is true with most theories, a good deal must be "swept under the rug." We do this when what remains is worth having.

---

28. Ibid. Miller shows that, if markets adjust to eliminate tax effects, the value of the firm is invariant with leverage and equal to the value of the unlevered firm. It follows that K_w must be invariant with leverage and equal to K_o, the unlevered equity capitalization rate.

29. See Myers, "Interactions of Corporate Financing and Investment Decisions," for a thorough critique of both approaches. Myers shows that the WACC is valid only under quite restrictive assumptions and argues that APV is superior both theoretically and practically. Another critique of the WACC is given in C. W. Haley and L. D. Schall, "Problems with the Concept of the Cost of Capital," *Journal of Financial and Quantitative Analysis* **13**, 847–871 (Dec. 1978).

One problem with the WACC that cannot be swept under the rug has to do with risk. The WACC is calculated for the firm as a whole and therefore, as noted earlier, is applicable only to projects of average risk. Using the WACC to evaluate all investment opportunities of a particular firm thus makes sense only if all those projects are equally risky. This might be true in regulated utilities, where the idea of the WACC was first used. It is not so in the great majority of firms, for reasons we discussed in Chapter 14.

For projects of average risk, the WACC and APV approaches give the same accept/reject signal. This is not so for projects of differing risk. For some low-risk projects, the WACC would signal reject, whereas the APV approach might signal accept. Conversely, for some high-risk projects, WACC might counsel accept and APV reject. In cases of such conflict, APV provides the correct signal, and WACC is incorrect. The problem is that with risk-averse investors, the market RRR varies with the risk of the investment, whereas the WACC uses a fixed rate for all projects regardless of risk. We discussed this point in detail in Chapter 14 (see Figure 14-5).

How might one use the WACC when projects differ in riskiness? One way would be to start with the WACC for average-risk projects and then add or subtract a risk premium for projects of higher or lower risk. Some firms do it this way. A problem with this approach is that the theory and calculations needed to deal simultaneously with operating risk and financing effects, which the WACC attempts to do, are very complex. The APV method permits adding and subtracting risk premiums in a simpler and more straightforward manner by dealing with operating characteristics and financing in separate steps.

The WACC is widely discussed in the literature of finance and for many years represented the standard approach to setting return targets. Development of the capital asset pricing model (CAPM) provided theoretical guidance for determining risk permiums for projects of any degree of risk. The APV approach permits us to take advantage of the CAPM more easily than does the WACC approach.

Because a companywide WACC cannot be used to evaluate projects of differing risks, the concept of a specific WACC for each project has been put forward. The idea is relatively simple: Depending on the level of project risk involved, it is possible to assign a separate mix of debt and equity to each individual project. Very high risk projects would be assigned no debt at all, average-risk projects would be assigned the same debt ratio the company as a whole uses, low-risk projects would be assigned higher levels of debt utilization. Thus, in a sense, we develop a WACC for each project.

An approach along these lines would begin, not with the firm's WACC, but with the all-equity RRR for the project, K_j, the same K_j used in calculating NPVO in the APV approach of section B. From K_j can be calculated the weighted average return required on the mix of equity and debt to be used in financing the project.[30] This calculation must take account of the effects of both corporate and personal taxes, just as was necessary in calculating PVT in the APV approach. Like the APV approach, this approach of calculating a weighted average required return begins with the all-equity RRR, K_j, and breaks the process into two steps, dealing with operating risk and financing in two separate steps. In many situations, the two approaches are essentially equivalent.

Problems

1. Suppose K_m, the expected return on the market portfolio, is 17 percent; the United States government bond rate (i) is 9 percent; and S_m, the standard deviation of return on the market portfolio, is 0.22. Calculate and interpret the implied "market standard."

2. Draw the market risk/return schedule implied by the data in Problem 1.

3. An analyst calculates the beta coefficient for XYZ Corporation to be 1.3. Suppose $K_m = 0.17$ and $i = 0.09$. Suppose further that the analyst calculates the expected return on XYZ's shares to be 22 percent. Is XYZ a good buy?

4. The data in Problem 1 assume an inflation rate of 6.5 percent per year. Redo Problem 1 assuming an inflation rate of zero.

5. ABC Corporation's stock has a beta coefficient of 1.2. Assume that $K_m = 0.17$ and $i = 0.09$. Calculate the market RRR on ABC's stock, K_e.

6. ABC Corporation (Problem 5) has 35 percent of its capital funds supplied by debt, on which the company pays interest of 10 percent per year and the remainder supplied by equity. Calculate ABC's weighted average cost of capital (WACC), assuming a tax rate of 46 percent.

7. Section A discusses a variant of the CAPM that uses the firm as the reference rather than the market portfolio. Suppose Omega Corporation is evaluating a project of average risk relative to the firm itself. Explain how the "firm reference" model could be used to evaluate the project. Contrast this approach with the use of the WACC to evaluate the project.

References

R. S. Bower and D. R. Lessard, "An Operational Approach to Risk Screening," *Journal of Finance* **28**, 321–328 (May 1973).

---

30. For a description of this approach, see T. E. Copeland and J. F. Weston, *Financial Theory and Corporate Policy* (Reading, Mass.: Addison-Wesley, 1979), Chap. 11.

R. Brealey, *Security Prices in a Competitive Market* (Cambridge, Mass.: MIT Press, 1971).

E. Brigham, "Hurdle Rates for Screening Capital Expenditure Proposals," *Financial Management* **4,** 17–26 (Autumn 1975).

E. Brigham, "Portfolio Theory," reprinted in E. Brigham (ed.), *Readings in Managerial Finance* (New York: Holt Rinehart and Winston, 1971).

E. Brigham and R. L. Crum, "On the Use of the CAPM in Public Utility Rate Cases," *Financial Management* **6,** 7–15 (Summer 1977).

E. E. Carter, "What Are the Risks in Risk Analysis?" *Harvard Business Review* **50,** 72–76 (July 1972).

T. E. Copeland and J. F. Weston, *Financial Theory and Corporate Policy* (Reading, Mass.: Addison-Wesley, 1979).

G. Donaldson, "Strategic Hurdle Rates for Capital Investment," *Harvard Business Review* **50,** 50–55 (Mar.–Apr. 1972).

E. F. Fama and J. D. McBeth, "Risk, Return and Equilibrium: Empirical Tests," *Journal of Political Economy*, **83,** 607–636 (May–June 1973).

M. C. Findlay, A. E. Gooding, and W. Q. Weaver, "On the Relevant Risk for Determining Capital Expenditure Hurdle Rates," *Financial Management* **5,** 9–17 (Winter 1976).

I. Friend and M. E. Blume, "The Demand for Risky Assets," *American Economic Review* **65,** 900–922 (Dec. 1975).

I. Friend and R. Westerfield, "Risk and Capital Asset Pricing," working paper 5–79, The Wharton School, University of Pennsylvania.

I. Friend, R. Westerfield, and M. Granito, "New Evidence on the CAPM," *Journal of Finance*, **33,** 903–916 (June 1978).

C. W. Haley and L. D. Schall, "Problems with the Concept of the Cost of Capital," *Journal of Financial and Quantitative Analysis* **13,** 847–871 (Dec. 1978).

C. W. Haley and L. D. Schall, *The Theory of Financial Decisions* (New York: McGraw-Hill, 1973).

R. S. Harris and J. J. Pringle, "A Note on the Implications of Miller's Argument for Capital Budgeting," working paper, University of North Carolina at Chapel Hill, June 1979.

K. L. Hastie, "One Businessman's View of Capital Budgeting," *Financial Management* **4,** 36–44 (Winter 1974).

D. B. Hertz, "Investment Policies that Pay Off," *Harvard Business Review* **46,** 96–108 (Jan.–Feb. 1968).

D. B. Hertz, "Risk Analysis in Capital Investment," *Harvard Business Review* **42,** 95–106 (Jan.–Feb. 1964).

H. Hong and A. Rappaport, "Debt Capacity, Optimal Capital Structure, and Capital Budgeting Analysis," *Financial Management* **7,** 7–11 (Autumn 1978).

R. Ibbotson and R. Sinquefield, "Stocks, Bonds, Bills and Inflation: Year-by-Year Historical Returns (1926–74)," *Journal of Business* **49,** 11–47 (Jan. 1976).

M. C. Jensen, "Capital Markets: Theory and Evidence," *Bell Journal of Economics and Management Science* **3,** 357–398 (Autumn 1972).

E. H. Kim, W. G. Lewellen, and J. J. McConnell, "Financial Leverage Clienteles: Theory and Evidence," *Journal of Financial Economics*, forthcoming.

A. Kraus and R. H. Litzenberger, "Skewness Preference and the Valuation of Risk Assets," *Journal of Finance* **31,** 1085–1100 (Sept. 1976).

W. G. Lewellen, *The Cost of Capital* (Belmont, Ca.: Wadsworth, 1969).

J. Lintner, "The Evaluation of Risk Assets and the Selection of Risky Investments in Stock Portfolios and Capital Budgets," *Review of Economics and Statistics* **47,** 13–77 (Feb. 1965).

J. Lintner, "Inflation and Security Returns," *Journal of Finance* **30,** 259–280 (May 1975).

R. H. Litzenberger and A. Budd, "Corporate Investment Criteria and the Evaluation of Risk Assets," *Journal of Financial and Quantitative Analysis* **5,** 395–420 (Dec. 1970).

J. D. Martin and D. F. Scott, Jr., "Debt Capacity and the Capital Budgeting Decision," *Financial Management* **5,** 7–14 (Summer 1976).

M. H. Miller, "Debt and Taxes," *Journal of Finance* **32,** 261–275 (May 1977).

F. Modigliani and M. H. Miller, "Corporate Income Taxes and the Cost of Capital: A Correction," *American Economic Review* **53,** 433–443 (June 1963).

J. Mossin, "Equilibrium in a Capital Asset Market," *Econometrica* **34**(4), 768–775 (Oct. 1966).

S. C. Myers, "Interaction of Corporate Financing and Investment Decisions— Implications for Capital Budgeting," *Journal of Finance* **29,** 1–25 (Mar. 1974).

S. C. Myers and S. M. Turnbull, "Capital Budgeting and the Capital Asset Pricing Model—Good News and Bad News," *Journal of Finance* **32,** 321–333 (May 1977).

J. J. Pringle, "Using Capital Budgeting Models in Practice," paper presented to Financial Management Association, Montreal, Canada (Oct. 14–16, 1976).

F. Reilly, "Companies and Common Stocks as Inflation Hedges," *The Bulletin* (New York: New York University, 1975).

S. Ross, "The Current Status of the Capital Asset Pricing Model," *Journal of Finance* **33,** 885–902 (June 1978).

M. Rubinstein, "A Mean-Variance Synthesis of Corporate Financial Theory," *Journal of Finance* **28,** 167–182 (Mar. 1973).

W. F. Sharpe, "Capital Asset Prices: A Theory of Market Equilibrium Under Conditions of Risk," *Journal of Finance* **19**(3), 425–442 (1964).

E. Solomon, "Measuring a Company's Cost of Capital," *Journal of Business* **28,** 240–252 (Oct. 1955).

D. L. Tuttle and R. H. Litzenberger, "Leverage, Diversification, and Capital Market Effects on a Risk-Adjusted Capital Budgeting Framework," *Journal of Finance* **22,** 427–443 (June 1968).

J. F. Weston, "Investment Decisions Using the Capital Asset Pricing Model," *Financial Management* **2,** 25–33 (Spring 1973).

Making Investment Decisions in Practice

16

Valuation as a Decision Criterion
Net Present Value Rule and Society's Goals
Managerial Considerations
Financial Management and Corporate Strategy

Thus far, Part IV has had a singleminded thrust: How *should* a firm make decisions on where it invests capital funds? The overall criterion we have put forward is that capital expenditures should be selected so as to maximize the firm's net present value (NPV). Taking this criterion as given, we have tried to outline the large volume of serious thinking devoted to the questions of how it is best implemented and why some approaches are superior to others. Because there now is a considerable body of theory on the issue, the treatment has been necessarily theoretical, sometimes severely so.

In this final chapter of Part IV we turn to an altogether different range of issues relevant to investment decisions and to judgments about required rates of return. Why is maximum NPV relevant to investors? Why is NPV relevant for society as a whole? How does maximizing NPV relate to the goals of those who actually make these decisions? How does it fit into our present world of welfare, taxation, and regulation?

As we found with respect to our initial questions on *how* to invest, there are no easy, unequivocal answers to these broader questions. All we can do is to provide a framework for thinking about difficult issues and a guide to why some answers are better than others.

Valuation as a Decision Criterion

The function of firms in a market economy is to produce goods and services. When a firm invests, it employs scarce resources to produce goods and services to be sold to consumers. The present value of the net cash flows generated by an investment gives us a measure of the value attached to the output by consumers. The *net* present value gives a measure of the value of the output over and above what it costs to produce it, that is, of *new value created.* In the case of an investment with a positive NPV, the firm is using scarce resources to produce goods and services having a present value higher than the cost to produce them. *Value has been created.*

When value is created, society as a whole is better off. Who, exactly, are the beneficiaries? Let us defer this question until after we see how the value of the firm is affected.

The Net Present Value Rule and the Value of the Firm

Suppose that a firm is considering an investment opportunity with NPV $= \$Y$. What happens to the value of the firm if the investment is undertaken? At the time the investment is being considered, let us define the value of the firm as

$$\text{PV} = I + \sum_{t=1}^{\infty} \frac{C_t}{(1 + K_e)^t} \qquad (1)$$

where PV is the value of the firm before the investment, I is the amount of uncommitted funds available for investment, C_t are cash flows expected from existing investments, and K_e is the required return on the firm's shares given its existing investments. The total value of the firm thus is the present value of cash flows expected from existing investments plus uncommitted funds.

Let us assume that the investment under consideration requires an outlay of $\$I$. The NPV of the project then is

$$\text{NPV of project} = \sum_{t=1}^{n} \frac{P_t}{(1 + K_j)^t} - I \qquad (2)$$

where P_t are the incremental cash flows expected from the project and K_j is the required rate of return of the project.

When the firm undertakes the project, it exchanges $\$I$ for the cash flows the project is expected to generate. The present value of those cash flows over and above the outlay is the NPV of the project. *Hence, the value of the firm changes by the NPV of the project undertaken.*

The Net Present Value Rule and Returns to Shareholders

How does the change in the value of the firm affect shareholders? Shareholders receive their return via dividends and capital gains (or losses!) due to changes in the market price of their shares. In mathematical terms, the *holding period return* (R_t) on a share of stock during period t is

$$R_t = D_t + (P_t - P_{t-1}) \qquad (3)$$

where D_t is the dividend received during period t, P_t is the price at the end of period t, and P_{t-1} is the price at the end of the prior period. The term $(P_t - P_{t-1})$ thus is the *price change* during period t.

We saw in the preceding section that, upon acceptance of an investment, the value of the firm changes by the NPV of the investment. The discount rate used to evaluate the investment is the rate of return required by the market. Hence, acceptance of the investment changes the value of the firm to investors. A critical question is whether this increase in value will be reflected in market price. The answer is yes if investors have the same information as management regarding the cash flows expected from the investment and if management has used the market required rate of return in evaluating those cash flows. Under such circumstances, the market would immediately revalue the firm's shares to reflect the NPV of the new investment.

Obviously, the real world is more complex than the model suggests. Investors seldom have access to the information necessary to evaluate investment opportunities of a firm; indeed, one reason professional managers are hired is to perform this function on behalf of shareholders. The NPV rule can lead to acceptance of investments whose major benefits lie several years into the future, with little, or even adverse, impact on near-term accounting profits. Since, for want of better indicators, current accounting profits often are used by investors as an indicator of longer-run prospects, a project with adverse impact on near-term profits could lead to a decline in stock price rather than to an increase.

However, distant benefits eventually have an effect. When complete information ultimately unfolds into the market, share price will adjust and shareholders will reap the anticipated rewards. We can conclude that, *consistently applied over the long run, the NPV rule will provide a higher total dollar return to shareholders than any other criterion.*

Pursuing this argument just a bit farther, we should note that if a firm undertakes an investment with NPV of $ Y, shareholders are wealthier by $ Y, recognizing that the increase may not be reflected immediately in market price. Alternately, if a firm foregoes an investment with NPV of $ Y, the shareholders are poorer by $ Y. It is an opportunity loss, to be sure, but opportunity losses are just as real as out-of-pocket losses in terms of their impact on welfare. Hence, we can say that the NPV rule, when consistently applied, will leave shareholders better off at any future date than will alternative decision criteria.

The NPV rule is the operational form of the more general criterion of value-maximization. This criterion sometimes is criticized on grounds that stock prices are an unreliable guide to managerial action. Sometimes it is argued that the stock market is irrational and that stock prices depend more on psychological factors than on economics. J. M. Keynes, the great economist of the 1930s, appears to have agreed, referring to the market as ". . . a game of Snap, of Old Maid, of Musical Chairs," with the players all aware that ". . . it is the Old Maid which is circulating, or that when the music stops some of the players may find themselves unseated."[1] If it really is just a game of musical chairs, how can financial managers use market value as a guide to action?

The viability of value-maximization as a normative decision criterion depends on whether managerial actions are reflected in stock prices. Clearly, they are, although there are factors other than managerial actions that also affect stock prices. In the short run, these other factors—general economic conditions, government action, investor psychology—may have a pronounced effect. In the long run, stock prices are a function of the underlying economic variables, earning power and cash flows, and

---

1. J. M. Keynes, *The General Theory of Employment, Interest, and Money* (New York: Harcourt, Brace and World, 1965), pp. 155–156.

these are factors that managerial actions control. We can assume that market price ultimately adjusts to reflect value, or that, in the long run, true value will out.

Rate of Return to Shareholders

Expression (3) measures return to shareholders in dollar terms. While we are on the subject, let us briefly examine ways of measuring return in *rate,* or percentage, terms.

One approach is to calculate the internal rate of return (IRR) on an investment in the firm's shares. First, we must make estimates of dividends that we expect to receive on the shares and of the expected proceeds from sale of the shares at the end of the period over which the evaluation is to be made. Knowing the price at which shares can be bought, we can calculate the IRR. In mathematical terms, the IRR is the discount rate (R) that satisfies the following equation:

$$P_0 = \frac{D_1}{1 + R} + \frac{D_2}{(1 + R)^2} + \cdots + \frac{D_n + P_n}{(1 + R)^n} \qquad (4)$$

where $D_1, D_2, \ldots, D_n$ are anticipated dividends, P_n is anticipated terminal price, and P_0 is present price. Using expression (4), we can say that, if dividends and terminal price are as expected, the IRR will be equal to R. We also can apply expression (4) to historical data and calculate the IRR on an investment in the shares over any prior period.

If we anticipate that earnings, dividends, and price all will grow at more or less the same rate, we can approximate the rate of return to shareholders using a trend approach. From expression (3), we know that dollar return in any period is

$$\text{Dollar return} = D + \Delta P \qquad (5)$$

where D is the dividend received and ΔP is the change in stock price. Dividing both sides by price gives return per dollar invested:

$$\text{Return per dollar} = \frac{D}{P} + \frac{\Delta P}{P} \qquad (6)$$

The quantity D/P is the *dividend yield* on the shares, and $\Delta P/P$ approximates the expected rate of *growth* in share price. Putting (6) in percentage terms gives

$$\text{Return (percent)} = \text{Yield (percent)} + \text{Growth rate (percent)} \qquad (7)$$

Expression (7) often provides a useful way to obtain an estimate of the *trend* value of the return expected on an investment in a stock, recognizing that dividends and price themselves may be variable about trend lines and that return in any particular period may differ from the trend value.

The Net Present Value Rule and Society's Goals

Having satisfied ourselves that the NPV rule best serves the interests of shareholders, let us briefly examine how the rule serves the interests of other segments of society. There are two questions involved in such an examination:

1. If each business firm follows the NPV rule in allocating corporate capital, does it follow that social welfare will also be maximized?
2. What happens to the wealth or NPV which a firm creates through correct capital investment policies? How is it shared?

The answer to both questions depends in part on the economic and industrial organization which prevails in a society. In general, if the prices and costs used in the NPV analysis *correctly* reflect economic values, the NPV rule will lead to the maximization of the total economic welfare of society as a whole. To the extent that prices and costs fail to reflect values, the conclusion will not follow.

Let us look at the four major reasons for a discrepancy between economic value on the one hand and apparent prices and costs on the other.

Lack of Competition

If prices and wages are set in a competitive environment, the observable market prices will better reflect true economic values than if competition does not prevail. Take the extreme case of a monopoly in which a firm, by restraining output and supply, sets prices (presumably) at a level above those which would prevail under competitive conditions. In this situation, decisions that maximize its own NPV will not be consistent with maximizing society's welfare. Likewise, serious restraint of entry into particular labor markets that raises the wage rate for these groups leads to a situation in which a policy of NPV maximization by the individual firm may not lead to the social maximum. Exactly the same conclusion holds if it is the government itself that forces prices or wage rates to levels above or below the levels which would prevail in a freely competitive system.

Externalities

Externalities refers to costs and benefits which the private firm ignores in making its NPV analysis (i.e., costs and benefits which are external to the firm but internal for society). There are dozens of examples, but two will suffice.

Assume that a steel mill to be built at a given location will pollute the air and water around it. However, the mill will be allowed to discharge these pollutants freely into the environment, that is, nobody imposes a fine or fee for pollution. In selecting a discharge system, the steel company therefore assumes there are no costs for environmental preservation, makes its calculations accordingly, and decides to build the mill.

Nonetheless, there are real costs to society as a result of the pollution which occurs. Because the kind of company-oriented NPV analysis we have been discussing ignores these costs, it follows that NPV maximization for the firm may not maximize society's welfare.

Take an alternative situation. The labor costs relevant to a firm are slightly lower in Georgia than in New York. So in making a new investment decision, following the NPV rule, the firm elects to build its new factory in the south and to close the one in New York. What about the possibly high costs to society for supporting the labor which is unemployed in New York as a result of such action? These costs are external to the firm, but are internal to society. Here again maximization of the firm's NPV may not lead to an increase in society's economic welfare.

Social Goods

There is a broad class of goods, such as education, culture, peace, safety, health, and basic scientific research, on which society places a high value, but which for one reason or another consistently fail to command a market price commensurate with this underlying value. If the NPV rule were the sole guide to investments in these areas, society would probably underinvest in them—to its eventual detriment. Thus, in order to move society toward a higher economic maximum, the NPV rule itself has to be supplemented or waived in two ways: The public sector should make major investments in these areas on the basis of other criteria, and private firms should devote a part of their managerial talent and funds toward these objectives without regard to the narrower question of the firm's NPV. (A hard-headed libertarian might argue that neither is necessary. Prices of such social goods should be allowed to rise sufficiently to attract private investment, and so long as they do not, private firms should refrain from using the shareholder's money for these purposes.)

Taxes

A final and extremely troublesome factor is the existence of taxes. In maximizing NPV, firms naturally think in terms of after-tax cash flows. In most cases, maximizing NPV on an after-tax basis will lead to the same decision as we would have if we maximized NPV on a before-tax basis. But sometimes there could be a conflict—the after-tax NPV rule leads to a different course of action than we would get if we followed a before-tax NPV rule. The latter rule selects the alternative that has a larger benefit to society as a whole, whereas the after-tax NPV rule selects the action that maximizes the benefit to the firm. We thus have another case of a clear possibility that the after-tax NPV rule we have advocated will not consistently maximize social welfare.

All of the four sources of inconsistency between the NPV investment rule and the social-maximization objective exist in modern market economies. The real question is what can be done about the situation. Should the NPV rule be abandoned as an investment criterion for private firms? If so, what do we use in place of it? The correct answer is that the rule works better than any alternative for most private investment decisions and should be preserved. Most of the time, maximizing the firm's NPV also maximizes social NPV, because it is the only rule which dictates that a crucial scarce resource, namely, capital, is used as efficiently as possible.

Where the rule leads to a potential conflict between the company's objectives and total social objectives, society should take steps to reduce or eliminate the source which creates the conflict. It should enforce workable competition and conditions of free entry in the market for goods, capital, and labor. It should create conditions in which the more important externalities become internalities, either through a system of regulations or fines or tax inducements. It should itself avoid actions which cause observable prices to depart from market values. It should develop a tax system which least perverts private decisions. For example, a far simpler tax system than we now have would almost never lead to a conflict between the after-tax NPV maximization rule and a before-tax NPV maximization rule.

In short, our conclusion is that the NPV maximization criterion for financial management decisions does a better job of consistently maximizing society's economic welfare than any other workable criterion. It is therefore a necessary condition for maximizing social economic welfare. But it is not in itself a sufficient condition. Society itself can do (and undo) much in order to create conditions in which the application of the rule will lead to even higher levels of total welfare. One solution which will not work is to allow or encourage managers to allocate resources based entirely on their private judgments about what is good for society.

The Distribution of Gains

When a firm invests funds wisely, it creates NPV for itself, for its share-holders, as well as for society as a whole. How are these gains distributed? They are eventually distributed in several ways.

1. If the investment leads to new products, the consumer benefits from their availability. If the investments lead to production efficiencies, then the relative price of the output will decline (assuming a workably competitive system) and this also benefits the consumer.
2. More efficient ways of production also release previously used resources, either for producing more output or for producing other outputs (assuming the system as a whole is flexible enough to maintain reasonably full employment).
3. Efficiency brought about by wise investment also raises the productivity of labor and thus their real wages per hour of work. Thus, labor shares in the gain sooner or later.
4. Part of the increased cash flow from wise investments is paid out in taxes and thus becomes available to society as a whole (assuming the government uses it wisely).
5. Part of the after-tax cash flow is reinvested in more investments and thus the original benefit is multiplied over time.
6. Finally, part of the increased after-tax cash flow is available to pay increased dividends to shareholders and this in turn raises the market value of their holdings (other things being equal).

Clearly, the NPV created by good investment decisions provides widespread benefits to society as a whole. The more NPV that is created after allowing for all costs, the better off society will be. In short, the optimal rule for the financial manager who is analyzing investment alternatives is to maximize NPV.

Managerial Considerations

We have examined the NPV maximization rule from the point of view of shareholders and of society as a whole. We turn now to look at the problem of applying the rule from the point of view of management itself.

Organizational Issues

We begin with a brief look at organizational issues: How are capital investment decisions made in practice and where might potential conflicts arise between the NPV rule on the one hand and other managerial considerations on the other?

The capital investment process as a whole falls into four steps: the creative search for investment opportunities; the gathering of data and forecasts; the analysis; and finally, the decision itself.

In a small firm, all these activities may be carried out by one or a few individuals. In a large firm, many individuals and organizational units may be involved.

In a large organization, project proposals often are initiated by line (operating) units. Data regarding cash flows may be collected by these units or by a central unit such as the corporate controller. Determination of required rates of return usually is centralized under the direction of a chief financial officer or corporate planning officer. Required rates may be established for the firm as a whole or by division. Analysis of investments, including calculation of NPV or other criteria, may be either centralized or decentralized. Final decisions usually are made by top management, either the chief executive officer or a committee. Often, the entire board of directors is involved in approving major projects. A common practice is for the board to delegate to top management discretion for all smaller projects, up to a certain dollar maximum each quarter or year, and to reserve approval of all larger projects for itself. Where final decision-making is centralized, the operating unit sponsoring a proposal often argues its merits.

The issue of centralization versus decentralization is an important one in establishing capital budgeting procedures. Some parts of the process are relatively easy to decentralize, such as identification of relevant cash flows. Other parts, such as selecting decision criteria, establishing required rates of return, and final decision-making, are not easy to decentralize if any degree of uniformity throughout the organization is desired. The approach to capital budgeting should be consistent with the overall organizational philosophy of the firm. We will soon see that in a decentralized firm, the need to centralize certain aspects of capital budgeting creates a potential for conflict.

Decentralization itself can take many forms. Here, we will consider primarily the single firm with a divisionalized structure. Firms with separately incorporated subsidiaries raise still other questions that go beyond the scope of the discussion below.

The basic problem in designing management systems in decentralized firms is ensuring that division goals are consistent with overall firm goals. Capital budgeting in a divisionalized firm raises questions on several major fronts, each of which deserves at least a brief discussion.

Decision-Making and Performance Appraisal

In a decentralized organization, top management must develop a sound method for periodic measurement and evaluation of divisional or plant performance. Such measurements are clearly needed for purposes of overall control. They are also necessary in connection with salary, bonus, and promotion decisions.

One of the major drawbacks of the NPV maximization criterion for decisions is that, in the short run (i.e., a year to year basis) there is no way in which we can directly measure results in these terms: *NPV for a division or plant is not an observable number.*

As a result, alternative performance yardsticks have to be used. These can be wholly objective or partly subjective. Some comparisons give a great deal of weight to a simple yardstick; others use multiple evaluation standards. Examples are:

> Sales (or trend in sales)
>
> Profit contribution (or growth in profit contribution)
>
> Efficiency in terms of cost or trends in costs
>
> Return on investment (ROI)
>
> Personnel relations (or trends in personnel relations)
>
> General condition of plant and facilities

Beyond these measurable quantities, top management's evaluation may include largely subjective impressions, for example, does the division or plant maintain good community relations?

It is natural to expect that the managers who are evaluated by these yardsticks begin to respond by making their decisions as if the yardsticks are the proper criteria to be maximized. The potential conflict between these alternative criteria and the NPV maximization rule can be quite large.

Take sales-maximization or market share-maximization: What if a manager perceives these to be primary objectives, which he then pursues, but at the expense of profits? Or take current operating costs: What if a plant manager does succeed in reducing labor and material costs, but only by expending large sums for more up-to-date equipment? Similar contradictions are apparent for each of the other criteria mentioned above. It is easy enough to keep a plant looking good or to improve plant safety or industrial relations if one is allowed to spend sufficient funds or to incur sufficient costs to bring about these specific results. Clearly, in each of the cases cited, it is also necessary to weigh the beneficial results against the costs of achieving them. Therefore, many companies have shifted to a more compound yardstick, such as ROI, which takes into account results as well as costs, including capital.

Reconciling Division Goals and Corporate Objectives

Return on investment itself, though widely used, is an unsatisfactory measure, because it too can lead to poor decisions—decisions which maximize ROI but fail to maximize NPV. Let us look at a specific example where such a conflict arises. To keep the example simple, we will ignore the existence of income taxes; we assume they are zero.

A building for a plant is leased, but the equipment is owned. The plant is producing 500 units a year of a specialized attachment for a commercial airplane. The sales volume is guaranteed for 5 years, 1980–1984, and so is the price, $1,000 per unit. The estimated annual operating costs (rent, labor, materials, and power) for the 500 units is $400,000 per year for the next 5 years. The operation is highly profitable. It produces operating profits of $100,000 per year before depreciation.

The book value of fixed capital employed is $200,000, which is being depreciated on a straight-line basis at $40,000 a year. Again, to keep things simple, we will assume that net working capital is zero. If it runs well, the plant will enjoy an ROI (and note that we are talking about *accounting* ROI) as shown in Table 16-1.

Table 16-1 Accounting Return on Investment (Existing Plant)[a]

Year	Net Capital (Beginning of Year)	Expected Book Profit	Accounting ROI (Percent)
1977	$200,000	$60,000	30.0
1978	160,000	60,000	37.5
1979	120,000	60,000	50.0
1980	80,000	60,000	75.0
1981	40,000	60,000	150.0
Average	$120,000	$60,000	50.0

[a]Note that income tax rates and working capital are both assumed to be zero.

The plant manager faces a decision. By adding new production equipment to the existing plant at a total installed cost of $320,000, he can achieve an annual savings in operating cost of $100,000, that is, the annual bill for rent, labor, materials, and power is expected, with a high degree of certainty, to decline from $400,000 per year to $300,000 per year.

The aircraft for which the specialized attachment is being manufactured will not be produced after 1984. The contract expires, and hence both the existing equipment and the proposed additional equipment can be assumed to have a zero salvage value at the end of 1984.

How should the plant manager make the decision about acquiring the additional equipment that is available to him? It depends, of course, on the required rate of return (RRR) for new investments in cost-saving equipment. Let us assume that it is a DCF rate of 12 percent per year.

On a DCF basis, the expected rate of return from the incremental investment of $320,000 would be 17 percent a year; that is, at 17 percent, the expected flow of benefits ($100,000 per year for 5 years) has a present value just equal to the $320,000 of incremental investment. The investment therefore is a good one, because it has an expected rate of return higher than the required rate of return. Alternatively, we can say that the project has a positive NPV of about $40,000 (the PV of incremental benefits at the 12 percent RRR is just over $360,000 and the incremental outlay is $320,000).

However, if the plant manager knows that he is going to be evaluated largely on the basis of accounting ROI, he will reject the project, because if he accepts the additional equipment, his ROI scorecard will look less good than it would with the old equipment! This is shown in Table 16-2.

Table 16-2 Accounting Return on Investment (Including New Equipment)

Year	Net Capital (Beginning of Year)	Expected Book Profit	Accounting ROI (Percent)
1977	$520,000	$96,000	18.5
1978	416,000	96,000	23.1
1979	312,000	96,000	30.8
1980	208,000	96,000	46.2
1981	104,000	96,000	92.3
Average	$312,000	$96,000	30.8

If the manager tries to maximize the plant's ROI, he will fail to maximize NPV. The reason for the conflict between the maximize ROI rule and the maximize NPV rule is simple enough. If he installs the new equipment, the plant does not actually lose the high ROI (of 50 percent per year on average book investment) it has been making on existing equipment. It still keeps that. But a new and profitable investment is added to its portfolios. The new investment provides a ROI of 18.75 percent per year (on average book investment). The NPV rule tells us the new investment is a good one. But because ROI is lower than the ROI previously achieved, the average ROI of the two taken together falls.

Clearly, a decision to reject the investment opportunity just because it reduces overall ROI would be a mistake. Yet there is a high danger that most managers who are rated on the basis of their observable ROIs would lean toward a *reject* decision in such a case. The basic cause of the trouble is that the performance standard used by the company to evaluate managers is inconsistent with the company's own best interests.

Some corporations have tried to get around the difficulty by evaluating managers on a combination of two factors, the division's ROI and its growth rate. Several methods are available for defining such a compound standard of performance. One in particular has received increasing attention—the *profit contribution* standard (PC).

Profit contribution may be defined as book profits (P) less a capital charge (CK), which is itself defined as the capital employed (C) multiplied by a required rate of return (K). Thus, we have

$$PC = P - CK \tag{8}$$

By using expression (8) in the example above, we see that the PC of the manager would rise if he accepts the additional investment. With the old equipment and assuming that the required rate of return K is 12 percent, his average 5 year PC would be

$$\$60,000 - (\$120,000 \times 0.12) = \$45,600$$

With the addition of the new equipment, it would be

$$\$96,000 - (\$312,000 \times 0.12) = \$58,560$$

He would be led to the correct decision—to accept the investment—and thus would serve the best interests of his company as well as his own self-interest. He can use NPV to make the decision comfortable in the knowledge that, if his performance later is measured using the PC standard, he will look good.

It is useful to notice a strong analogy behind the problem of reconciling the manager's self-interest with the interest of the corporation as a whole and the earlier problem we discussed—reconciling a corporation's self-interest with that of society as a whole. In each situation, it is up to the larger organization to make rules such that its constituent parts, acting in their own self-interest, will do what serves the larger interest as well.

Other Sources of Conflict in Capital Management

Performance yardsticks are not the only potential source of difficulty in any partly decentralized capital management system. Individual decision centers frequently do not take account of the fact that a proposed project might offer companywide benefits that are larger than the accounting benefits which accrue to the division itself. For example, facilities available from a projected investment might be useful to other divisions. Likewise, a sales force or technology which is developed for one division could save funds in other parts of the company. It is also possible sometimes for other parts of a company to incur costs because of one division's decision—costs which the particular division would tend to ignore because they are external to its set of accounts. Again, the problem is analogous to the externalities problem which exists between the corporation as a whole and society.

Measuring project risk also presents special problems. Some of these concern project size. Consider a project that is very large relative to the size of the division that is to implement it. Failure of the project might so adversely affect overall division performance that the division manager would try to oppose its adoption, even though, from the standpoint of the firm as a whole, the project might be very desirable.

The relationship of project returns in one division to those of other divisions also may affect perceived risk. As we saw in Chapter 14, diversification effects due to interproject correlation may be important to the firm. The top management of a firm may perceive and attach value to such diversifying effects from the standpoint of the firm as a whole, whereas a division manager may not.

Determining the required rate of return presents additional problems. The required return directly affects the projects that will be adopted. If divisions really are decentralized, and division managers are accountable for performance, should they be allowed to establish required rates of return themselves? Or should required returns be determined centrally? There are arguments on both sides of the issue.

One approach mentioned in Chapter 14 is to categorize projects for the company. For example, projects could be divided into cost-reduction projects, expansion projects, and projects involving new products. Top management then might determine required rates for each category for each division. Establishment of required rates by top management should take account of companywide effects as well as of correlation between returns of projects of different divisions in arriving at an appropriate measure of project risk.

The degree of decentralization of capital budgeting then might vary by project category and perhaps by division. It might be appropriate, for example, to decentralize decision-making completely on cost-reduction projects, with top management involved only in determining the required rate of return. Expansion projects might be decentralized below some dollar limit on the outlay. Projects involving an outlay above that limit would be submitted to top management for approval. On new products, approval by top management might be required regardless of size, on grounds that new products involve strategic considerations.

No matter what procedures are adopted, capital budgeting in a decentralized firm will likely involve compromises. Great care should be taken to ensure that the system gives signals to subordinate managers that induce them to behave in ways consistent with the overall goals of the firm, without doing excessive violence to the decentralized organizational philosophy.

Financial Management and Corporate Strategy

At the top management level, capital management is part of a bigger process. While the proper function of top management is to maximize shareholders' wealth, modern management must, in the very interest of the long-run position of shareholders, concern itself with many constituencies other than its owners. These include employees, customers, suppliers, creditors, the government, and the public at large. All these parties have a common interest in economic efficiency. But in addition to efficiency, management must concern itself with ethics, social responsibility, relationships with local communities, and many other factors that are difficult to quantify. Where these concerns conflict with pure economic efficiency, the conflict must be resolved by compromise.

A firm can serve many constituencies and pursue many objectives and still use value-maximization of the firm as its basic criterion for making efficient investment choices. Many of the other requirements for maximizing social welfare—such as a high degree of price competition, the absence of distorting institutional constraints, and the problem of dealing adequately with externalities—are the concern of governmental policy rather than of financial management. If these requirements are met, competition itself will produce an efficient allocation of economic resources and a fair distribution of the value created by good investment decisions.

Goals, Commercial Strategy, and Decision Criteria

The principal function of business firms in a market economy is to produce the goods and services desired by society. Given that role, top management conceives its highest-level policy goal—its reason for being—in qualitative, mission-oriented terms. For example, a firm might think of its goal as that of providing communications services, providing personal transportation, or manufacturing scientific instruments.

Around such a basic statement of purpose a firm develops its commercial strategy, which defines the markets it will serve, the products it will produce, and its production technology. Given the commercial strategy, supporting policies then are defined in research and development, marketing, production, financial management, accounting, and personnel.

In the long run, a firm's commercial strategy is likely to be the principal determinant of whether it really excels or is an "also-ran." Sound policies in marketing, production, finance, and so on, are necessary for real success, but they are not sufficient, and certainly not overriding. Commercial strategy is the end, and supporting policies are the means. Good decision criteria are part of the means toward the broader objectives.

In order to execute its commercial strategy, the firm must acquire certain operating assets. To judge the economic acceptability of investment opportunities, the firm applies value-maximization as a decision criterion, using the NPV rule. By applying the criterion to investment opportunities that already have passed a higher-level policy screen, the firm ensures that its investment decisions support its commercial strategy and represent wise and efficient uses of capital funds. In short, its commercial strategy tells the firm where to look for attractive investment opportunities, and the NPV rule tells it which of those opportunities to select. In addition to the strategic and economic tests, the evaluation process must take account of the risk preferences of shareholders and managers, interactions with other parts of the enterprise, opportunities for operating synergy, constraints on managerial and technical manpower, and other qualitative considerations.

Our concern as financial managers thus is how to evaluate and whether to undertake investments that already have passed a higher-level policy screen of consistency with the firm's commercial strategy. Value-maximization and the NPV rule are *decision criteria* for choosing between alternative courses of action; they are not in themselves the overriding goals.

In this same sense, profit is a measure of economic performance rather than a firm's "reason for being." Firms that conceive sound strategies and execute them well make high profits. High profits indicate that a firm is doing an effective job of producing goods and services desired by society, and thus constitute a reward for a job well done. One executive summed it up this way: "The first responsibility of a company is to serve its customers and serve them well. If you do that, you will make a profit. But the profit is the *result* of the game plan, not the objective."

Evaluating Investment Policy

A firm's commercial strategy must compensate fairly all the parties involved, including employees, suppliers, creditors, and the government,

Figure 16-1

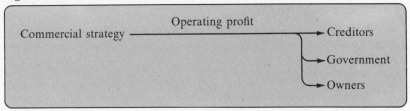

as well as owners. Figure 16-1 represents this requirement schematically.

If the return generated by a firm's commercial strategy is inadequate, one or more of the claimants must subsidize the strategy by accepting an inadequate return. Managers and employees might be underpaid, trade credit stretched, bank loans not repaid on time, or returns to owners too low. Profits are likely to be anemic and, in the case of publicly owned firms, stock price is likely to fall below book value. Such situations are unlikely to be viable for long.

The adequacy of a firm's overall return can be tested by examining its operating return, net of taxes, per dollar of operating assets. The resulting percentage return should equal or exceed the market RRR for investments of similar risk. Return targets for the firm as a whole can be set following the general approach outlined in Chapter 14. The appropriate target for the firm as a whole depends on its overall risk.

By focusing on *operating* return, before interest charges, a judgment can be made as to whether the commercial strategy is generating a satisfactory return. Profit after taxes (after interest charges) per dollar of invested capital or per dollar of equity (often called *return on equity*) is not as useful for this purpose because it combines the effects of both commercial strategy and financing policy. An inadequate operating return can be made to look satisfactory by using high financial leverage.

If the commercial strategy generates an adequate operating return, it is *financeable*, and an appropriate financing plan can be devised. If the return is not adequate, the strategy is not financeable and management would be well advised to correct it. If the problems lie in execution, they may be correctable by improving the efficiency of the firm's operations. If the strategy itself is faulty, it must be altered.

Capital Rationing

A study of corporate behavior provides clear examples of how the use of the NPV rule as an investment criterion might have to give way at least temporarily to larger goals.

In principle, the NPV rule tells us that a firm should undertake all investments or disinvestments that are attractive, that is, which meet the test of increasing the firm's NPV. In practice, top management for other policy reasons might want to restrain the growth (or decline) of the firm's assets to a different rate than the rate which would occur if the NPV rule is followed. One device which is frequently used to achieve orderly growth (or orderly withdrawal from uneconomic activities) is to ration capital. Under a capital rationing system, the top management of the firm decides on the size of the annual capital expenditure budget. This might be based on the volume of funds available to it for investment (without recourse to further long-term stock issues or borrowing) or it might be based on other considerations. In either case, the approach is different from that suggested by the NPV rule—namely, that we should begin with the opportunities available, add up the total funds requirements of all those which will increase the firm's NPV, and arrange for all these requirements to be financed in whatever way seems best.

Under a capital rationing system, it is no longer feasible to make simple accept or reject decisions for each project individually. The firm has to rank the available projects and select the most attractive set of projects which can be financed within the predetermined budget. To do this, it should still use a variant of the broader NPV rule—namely, that individual projects should be ranked by their contribution to NPV and selected accordingly. The required rate of return (RRR) which should be used in calculating project NPVs is the same under capital rationing as it is in the general case where capital is not rationed.

The preceding approach assumes that all projects are known at the time decisions must be made under a capital rationing system. Suppose this is not so. In practice, investment opportunities often unfold more or less continuously through time. If a particular project is undertaken when it arises, it may preclude an even better project next quarter. Such is life, and there is no good solution to this problem. Sometimes it may be feasible to postpone decisions and save up a list of projects for consideration all at once. This approach is often used in practice, but it can delay projects where time might be an important factor for competitive or other reasons.

In many small firms and especially young firms, the need to ration capital arises sometimes not from overriding policy considerations, but simply from the nonavailability of funds. A small, young firm with good investment opportunities may have low current cash inflows, no access to the regular capital markets, and, at the same time, be reluctant to bring in outsiders as equity partners. In such cases, the only sources of outside funds are commercial banks, finance companies, and other sources discussed in Chapter 6. Such sources offer debt funds only, and with no access to outside equity funds, there is a definite limit on total external financing. Where the firm has more investment opportunities than it can accommodate within the financing limit, it must ration capital and rank its projects. The cost of doing so, in terms of opportunities foregone, should be recognized.

Summary

To be viable, any approach to investment decisions must support the overall goals of the firm and must serve the economic interests of society as well as those of shareholders. The general criterion for financial management decisions is to maximize the value of the firm, with value measured in discounted cash flow (DCF) terms. When firms invest wisely, new value is created and society is better off. The increment in value is shared by customers, taxpayers, and shareholders, with the shares to each depending on many complex factors, especially the degree of competition in the markets for goods and services.

When a firm undertakes an investment with a positive net present value (NPV), the value of the firm increases by an amount equal to the NPV of the investment. The NPV rule selects projects that increase returns to shareholders and, over the long run, will provide a higher total dollar return to shareholders than any other criterion. From society's viewpoint, the NPV rule induces firms to make efficient economic choices and to undertake investments that increase total wealth.

While consistent with the goal of maximum social welfare, the NPV rule by itself is not sufficient. Structural deficiencies in the economic system caused by insufficient competition, externalities, and tax biases should be corrected by legislation. Investments in social goods should be treated as public, rather than private, investment decisions. For the goods and services produced by the private sector of the economy, the NPV rule is the rule that society should wish financial managers to use.

Organizational considerations are important in applying DCF techniques to investment decisions in practice. Especially difficult are questions of centralization versus decentralization. While useful for decision making, DCF measures are difficult to use for appraising performance. Other criteria, when used for performance measurement, can induce behavior that is inconsistent with value-maximization. For example, the use of accounting return on investment to measure performance can conflict directly with the use of DCF for making investment decisions. No matter what approaches are adopted, capital budgeting in a decentralized firm likely will involve compromises.

The NPV rule must be applied within an overall policy context. In the long run, the principal determinant of a firm's success is likely to be the viability of its commercial strategy. The NPV rule is a decision criterion that should be applied to investment opportunities that first pass a strategic test of consistency with the firm's commercial strategy.

In theory, the NPV rule states that all projects with a positive NPV should be undertaken and that necessary financing should be arranged to do so. In practice, constraints on the availability of funds often force firms to depart from the dictates of the NPV rule and to ration capital among competing projects. When capital is rationed, the opportunity costs of doing so should be recognized.

Questions

1. How do the investment decisions of firms create new value in a market economy?
2. How is the value of an individual firm affected by the investment decisions it makes?
3. How is the new value created by an investment opportunity delivered to the firm's owners?
4. What is the effect on shareholder wealth of foregoing an investment opportunity with a positive net present value?
5. How can it be said that a decision rule that promotes maximum wealth of shareholders at the same time is consistent with the economic goals of society as a whole?
6. Distinguish between value-maximization as a goal and value-maximization as a decision criterion. Which interpretation do you think is more appropriate?
7. Under what circumstances should a firm reject an investment opportunity with a positive net present value?
8. What policy does financial theory suggest with respect to capital rationing? What practical constraints exist in implementing this theoretical guidance?
9. When capital must be rationed, how should investment opportunities be selected?
10. Why might a division manager come to different conclusions regarding the riskiness of an investment opportunity than would the chief executive officer?
11. What potential conflict do you see in using discounted cash flow techniques for decision-making on investment opportunities, and accounting-based return on investment to measure performance?

Problem

1. The Capital Budgeting Committee of the Chatham Manufacturing Corporation is meeting to consider the company's 1981 capital investment program. Because of funds limitations, the capital budget for 1981 is limited to $700,000.

(a) Given the following investment opportunities, which should be selected?

Project	Outlay (Thousands)	Net Present Value (Thousands)
A	$400	$90
B	150	15
C	150	35
D	250	50
E	250	55
F	150	25

(b) With the best possible decision in part a, how much would the value of the firm increase? How much would the value of the firm have increased if capital had not been rationed? What has been the opportunity cost to shareholders of the capital rationing constraint?

References

K. J. Arrow and R. Lind, "Uncertainty and the Evaluation of Public Investment Decisions," *American Economic Review* **60,** 364–378 (June 1970).

D. C. Dearborn and R. I. Levin, "Error Visibility as a Factor in Executive Performance," *Southern Journal of Business* **6,** 65–70 (Jan. 1972).

K. L. Hastie, "One Businessman's View of Capital Budgeting," *Financial Management* **3,** 36–44 (Winter 1974).

J. M. Keynes, *The General Theory of Employment, Interest, and Money* (New York: Harcourt, Brace and World, 1965).

B. G. Malkiel, "The Capital Formation Problem in the United States," *Journal of Finance* **34,** 291–306, (May 1979).

N. C. Nielsen, "The Investment Decision of the Firm Under Uncertainty and the Allocative Efficiency of Capital Markets," *Journal of Finance* **31,** 587–601 (May 1976).

U. E. Reinhardt, "Break-Even Analysis for Lockheed's TriStar—An Application of Financial Theory," *Journal of Finance* **28,** 821–838 (Sept. 1973).

M. Rubinstein, "A Mean-Variance Synthesis of Corporate Financial Theory," *Journal of Finance* **28,** 167–182 (Mar. 1973).

J. K. Shank and M. Burnell, "Smooth Your Earnings Growth Rate," *Harvard Business Review* **52,** 136–141 (Jan.–Feb. 1974).

E. Solomon, *The Theory of Financial Management* (New York: Columbia University Press, 1963).

H. M. Weingartner, "Capital Rationing: N Authors in Search of a Plot," *Journal of Finance* **32,** 1403–1432 (Dec. 1977).

PLANNING THE FINANCIAL STRUCTURE V

Sources of Long-Term Financing

17

Corporate Financing
Contractual Claims: Debt
Preferred Claims: Preferred Stock
Residual Claims: Common Stock
Leasing
Convertible Securities

In this part of the book we turn to the third major set of problems with which financial management must deal: the problem of deciding the composition of the firm's long-term financing and the associated problem of determining the sources from which long-term funds are derived.

The six chapters in Part V deal with the key questions that must be answered in planning the firm's financial structure. How does financial leverage affect the firm's earnings? Its value? What is the appropriate level of debt? What is the appropriate mix of short-term and long-term debt? How should specialized financing alternatives such as leasing and convertible securities be used? How should dividend policy be set? These are the questions to which we now turn.

A major theme of any book about managerial decision-making is that managers should give careful attention to the matter of risk. In an uncertain world, adverse things can happen, and probably will. In almost every business decision, there is the opportunity to increase the potential return in exchange for greater uncertainty. The terms of the risk/return tradeoff are simple: more return if things work out well, less if they do not.

Risk ultimately boils down to uncertainty as to what cash flows and earnings will turn out to be. It is useful to separate total risk into two components: operating risk and financing risk. *Operating risk* is a function of the firm's commercial strategy and depends on a number of factors, including the variability of revenues, the variability of expenses, and the degree of operating leverage. In practice, operating risk manifests itself in uncertainty regarding future levels of operating earnings, frequently referred to as EBIT (earnings before interest and taxes).

As we will see, for any given level of EBIT, financial leverage brought about by the use of borrowed funds magnifies the variability of earnings flowing to equity shareholders or EPS. Thus, for any given degree of variability of EBIT, we can increase the variability of earnings and EPS by increasing leverage. This leverage effect on the variability of earnings is called *financing risk*. Since total risk, operating plus financing, is what we ultimately are concerned with, variability of EBIT is an important factor both in determining the appropriate level of debt and in choosing between short-term and long-term debt. Tailoring the use of debt to the degree of operating risk is the first principle involved in planning the financial structure.

While operating risk is perhaps the single most important factor in choosing a debt policy, it is not the only consideration relevant to financing decisions. Choice of debt versus equity in a particular situation may depend strongly on the issue of *control*.

Flexibility is another important consideration. It is important to see that financing policies do not impose constraints on the firm's commercial strategy. It is desirable also to maintain flexibility with respect to future financing options, so that the choice of a financing method now does not automatically dictate the decision with respect to subsequent financing in the future. Maintaining flexibility is especially important where a series of outside financings is in prospect.

Another consideration that may be important is *timing*. Conditions in the financial markets may make one alternative preferable to another or may suggest a time at which issuance is more favorable than another time. Any consideration of timing, however, requires at least some ability to forecast future events in the financial markets, an undertaking that requires a good understanding of the way financial rates change.

In any financing decision, there will be a host of considerations in addition to those mentioned here. Industry debt/equity standards, general economic activity, the size of the firm, its credit standing, its access to the capital markets, and regulatory considerations all might be important. In the case of many of these considerations, it is difficult to provide guidelines that are general enough to fit many situations yet specific enough to be useful. Common sense and hard thinking likely are the best prescription.

Throughout this book we have taken care to place our financial management decisions within an overall policy context. In general, a firm's commercial strategy dictates the nature of the investments that it must make. Once investment policy is determined, the firm then tailors its financing policies to fit. Debt/equity mix and maturity structure are determined in light of the nature of the business and the degree of operating risk inherent in the firm's investment policy. Dividend policy is determined last, given the firm's investment opportunities, planned financial structure, and rate of funds generation.

Corporate Financing

Table 17-1 shows the total financial liabilities of nonfinancial corporations in the United States at the end of 1978, that is, it shows their sources of financing, other than equity.

Of the nearly $1,173 billion total, almost 25 percent was derived from trade credit, taxes accrued, and other miscellaneous liabilities which arise spontaneously from normal business operations. The remaining 75 percent, or $886 billion, had to be derived from the long- and short-term credit market.

Bonds

Bonds provided the largest single source of debt funds, accounting for 38 percent of funds raised through the money and capital markets. The

Table 17-1 All Nonfinancial Corporations: Financial Liabilities, December 31, 1978 (Billions of Dollars)

Total Financial Liabilities		$1,172.9
Credit market instruments	845.7	
Other sources of credit	327.2	
Credit Market Instruments		
Corporate bonds		318.3
Tax-exempt bonds		15.8
Mortgages		
Residential		42.7
Commercial		164.7
Bank loans (other than mortgages)		224.0
Commercial paper		15.5
Bankers' acceptances		5.0
Finance company loans		54.1
United States government loans		5.7
Spontaneous Sources		
Trade credit		262.5
Taxes payable		23.9
Foreign Direct Investments in United States Corporations		40.8

Source: Board of Governors, Federal Reserve System, *Flow of Funds, Assets and Liabilities Outstanding,* 1978.

bond total includes funds raised through public issues and private placements. It also includes $15.8 billion of tax-exempt bonds. For particular socially desirable purposes such as environmental pollution control, the United States tax law allows state and local governments to pass on their tax-exempt status to industrial bonds issued by profit-seeking enterprises.

Mortgages

Mortgages, another major form of long-term borrowing, provided 23.0 percent of debt funds raised by corporations through the credit markets. In recent years, a growing part of corporate mortgage financing has been devoted to the construction and financing of homes, apartments, and residential developments. However, the bulk of mortgage borrowing by nonfinancial companies still goes to finance industrial and commercial properties.

Bank Loans

Commercial bank loans provided the third major source of funds for nonfinancial corporations. According to Table 17-1, banks financed about 25 percent of the total funds raised in the credit markets.

Long-Term Debt versus Short-Term Debt

The categories used in Table 17-1 do not allow us to divide total corporate debt by maturity into the two conceptual categories which are most significant for theory, namely, long-term debt and short-term debt. The reason is that the category labeled "Bank loans" is ambiguous as far as maturity is concerned. Some bank loans are clearly short-term loans. Others, such as term loans and revolving credits, are really long-term. A reasonable estimate can be obtained by assuming that 40 percent of bank loans are long-term and 60 percent are short-term.

Doing this, we get a figure of $625 billion for the total long-term debt of nonfinancial corporations, which is over 70 percent of their credit market borrowing or about 53 percent of their total financial liabilities.

Debt versus Equity

Another ratio which plays a major role in financial theory is the ratio of debt to equity. Table 17-1 does not include equities and therefore tells us little about this ratio. We have excellent statistics on national output, income, and borrowing, but our data on national wealth is still relatively primitive. Reliable annual estimates of the book value of the total equity of nonfinancial corporations are not yet available.

We do, however, have reasonably good market value data for all corporate equities (nonfinancial plus financial corporations). While the comparison between these data and the financial liability data shown in Table 17-1 is imperfect, it is not seriously misleading, and we present it, for recent years, in Table 17-2.

Table 17-2 Corporate Debt versus Corporate Equity (Billions of Dollars)

End of Year	Total Debt Liabilities (Nonfinancial Corporations)	Total Market Value of Equities (All Corporations)
1950	124	146
1955	174	317
1960	237	451
1965	349	749
1970	563	907
1975	852	892
1978	1,173	1,086

Source: Board of Governors, Federal Reserve System, *Flow of Funds, Assets and Liabilities Outstanding, Year-End various years, 1950–1978.*

Clearly, equity values fluctuate a great deal more than debt does. But this expresses the very nature of debt financing—indeed, it is one of the key elements in the total problem of corporate financing strategy to which we now turn.

Characteristics of Financing Instruments

Having discussed recent trends in long-term financing in the aggregate, we turn now to a more detailed discussion of the principal types of claims issued by firms in order to acquire funds.

Financing instruments issued by a firm represent claims against the firm's income and assets. Suppliers of capital exchange their funds for these claims against the firm. The principal types of long-term claims issued by firms are debt, preferred stock, and common stock. In addition, firms may lease real assets, or issue convertible securities. These types of claims differ with respect to a number of important characteristics.

It is useful to begin with the characteristics of financing instruments that are of importance. We then will discuss each of the major types—long-term debt, preferred stock, and common stock—individually. Finally, we will consider some of the factors relevant in the choice of financing instruments and in obtaining funds from the capital markets.

The basic security types—debt, preferred stock, and common stock—differ in a number of important respects. First, they may differ with respect to *maturity*. Maturity refers to the time at which the principal amount of the claim is to be paid. A loan might require payments of interest at the end of each year for 3 years and the principal amount at the end of the third year. Such a loan is said to have a 3 year maturity. In the case of a mortgage loan where equal payments are made over the life of the loan, each payment includes some interest and some principal. Here the term *maturity* is somewhat ambiguous; it might refer to the time span over which payments are made or to the average maturity of the loan. As we will see later, some claims, notably common stock and most preferred stock, have no maturity date—they are *perpetual* claims.

In an uncertain world, there always is a chance that the income and/or assets of the firm will be inadequate to satisfy all claimants. Hence, there must be agreement in advance as to whose claim comes first. In short, the *priority,* or *seniority,* of the claims must be established.

We now come to an especially important distinction: that between *contractual* claims and *residual* claims. Contractual claims are called *debt* and involve an agreement by the obligor, firm or individual, to make certain payments of interest and principal at certain times. The agreement is an enforceable contract; if the obligor fails to make the specified payments, the claim holder can take legal action to enforce the claim. Residual claims, on the other hand, involve no enforceable agreement; rather, they entitle the claimant to what is left after higher-priority contractual claims are paid. Contractual claims are nearly always fixed in amount, and residual claims by their nature are variable. Hence, in any given firm, payments to residual claimants are inherently more uncertain than are payments to contractual claimants.

Priorities also may be established within major categories. Some contractual claims may be junior to others; the latter are often referred to as *subordinated.* Some residual claims may be senior to others; preferred stock is senior to common.

As we have noted, financial claims against firms represent claims against both income and assets. In many cases, the claim is against all income and all assets, subject to the priorities established. In some cases, however, specific assets are pledged as *collateral* to secure specific claims. We will discuss secured and unsecured debt in more detail shortly.

Another important difference in claims of different types is tax treatment. Under present law, interest paid on contractual claims is deductible for income tax purposes to the firm or individual paying it. Payments made on residual claims, normally called *dividends* rather than interest, are not deductible under present law.

Different claims also vary with respect to the return required by the claimants. These differences are due primarily to differences in risk, or uncertainty, as to whether the agreed upon payments will be made. Risk-averse investors require a higher return in exchange for a higher degree of risk. Hence, there is an inverse relationship between seniority and required rate of return.

Often in the literature of finance, it is noted that the return required by claim holders is the cost of the particular source of funds to the firm. We discussed the term *cost of capital* earlier. The cost to the firm of different sources of funds can be calculated. In the case of debt claims, we can calculate both a pretax cost and an after-tax equivalent cost. Throughout this book, we have used the term *required rate of return* rather than *cost of capital.* However, in order to maintain a link with the earlier literature and other textbooks, in this chapter, we will discuss the *cost* to the firm of different sources of funds. Let us keep in mind that required rate of return and cost, properly interpreted, are one and the same.

A final important difference among claims of different types concerns the extent to which claim holders can influence the policies of the firm. We will refer to this influence as the right to a *voice in management.* This right may include the right to choose the firm's board of directors and the right to vote on other matters of importance.

Contractual Claims: Debt

Short-term debt generally refers to debt with a maturity shorter than 1 year. *Intermediate-term debt* has no generally agreed upon definition, but usually refers to maturities between 1 and 5–7 years. *Long-term debt,* usually given the label *bonds,* refers to debt with maturities longer than 5–7 years. Sources of short- and intermediate-term debt funds were discussed in Chapter 6. In this chapter, we consider only long-term debt.

A long-term debt contract involves a loan of a specified principal amount and a promise to make periodic interest payments and to repay the principal according to an agreed upon schedule. Repayment schedules are negotiable and may call for the principal to be repaid in one lump sum, in equal installments, or in amounts such that the sum of the interest and principal payment each period is constant. The latter type of schedule is typical of mortgage loans.

The agreement between lenders and borrowers, called the *indenture,* usually includes a number of provisions in addition to the interest rate and repayment schedule. The provisions typically encountered require the borrower to maintain certain financial standards with respect to liquidity and working capital. Restrictions may be placed on the payment of dividends, capital expenditures, or repurchase of common or preferred stock. Such *protective convenants* are designed to protect the position of the lenders by giving them certain rights (discussed further below) in the event the covenants are violated. In a way, the covenants act as an early warning system to signal trouble. Some covenants are relatively simple; others run into hundreds of pages.

Bondholders are represented by a *trustee* whose function it is to administer the agreement and to see that the borrower lives up to its provisions. In the event of *default* on any provision, the trustee generally is required to report the violation to bondholders. The trustee usually is empowered to take legal action to force compliance. Where the firm is unable to comply, the trustee can force bankruptcy proceedings.

Bondholders normally do not have a direct voice in the affairs of the firm or in the voting for directors. They indirectly may influence policies via the protective covenants in the indenture. In the event of default, bondholders then have a much larger voice through the trustee. In the event of a bankruptcy proceeding, bondholders and other contractual claim holders are in virtually complete control, with common stockholders having little say in the settlement.

Claim against Income

The rate of interest on a bond is fixed by contract and often is referred to as the *coupon* rate. Interest on most bonds is paid semiannually, although different schedules sometimes are encountered. In terms of seniority, bondholders have first claim on the firm's income. Interest always is paid on debt before dividends can be paid on preferred and common stock. Even where income is not sufficient to cover interest, firms go to great lengths to avoid defaulting on an interest payment.

Claim against Assets

In general, if a firm remains a going concern, as all parties usually hope will be the case, it is only the claim against income that is operative. The claim against assets comes into play only if the terms of the agreement are not met.

As in the case of the claim on income, the claim of bondholders against assets is senior to that of preferred and common shareholders. With respect to other contractual claim holders, the seniority of a particular claim depends on the terms of the agreement. Where several debt issues are outstanding, there usually is a clearly specified priority. Junior claims are referred to as *subordinated.*

Seniority also depends on whether the bonds are secured by particular assets. *Mortgage bonds* have specific assets, usually buildings or equipment, pledged as security against default on interest or principal payments. In the event of default, mortgage holders are entitled to liquidate the asset(s) to settle their claim, with any excess returned to settle claims of unsecured creditors. Unsecured bonds, having no particular assets pledged as security, are called *debentures.* In the event of trouble, debenture holders stand in line with other unsecured creditors, such as trade creditors and banks, behind secured creditors but ahead of shareholders. When the claims against a firm include both secured and unsecured creditors (and in the latter category there may be both senior and subordinated creditors), the determination of pro rata shares to be received from liquidation of assets becomes a very complex matter.

As we can see, the type of bond—debenture, mortgage bond, subordinated bond—often is defined in terms of the nature of the claim against assets. Many specialized types exist that are not discussed in detail here. There are, for example, *collateral trust* bonds secured by the stocks and bonds of other firms, and *equipment trust certificates* used to finance certain types of equipment. Discussions of these more specialized financing vehicles may be found in the references at the end of this chapter.

Default Risk

Since debt is a contractual claim, debt obligations of a given firm are less risky than are the preferred or common stock of the same firm. In an uncertain world, however, default can and does occur. From the standpoint of lenders, debt obligations of firms are not riskless. From the firm's standpoint, on the other hand, interest and principal payments on debt can be viewed as certain if the firm is to remain in business.

Default risk refers to the risk that the firm will not make the specified payments at the specified times. Bonds of many large corporations are rated as to default risk by rating services.

The two major bond rating agencies are *Moody's* and *Standard and Poor's* (S&P). The former uses the rating of Aaa for the very best bonds, Aa for the next category, A for the next, and Baa for relatively risky bonds. Bonds rated below Baa are those with severe exposure to possible default. Standard and Poor's uses AAA, AA, A, and BBB for its classifications. It has also introduced a new rating, AA− for some bonds. The two agencies do not always agree with each other, so dozens of bond issues are split-rated, that is, rated differently by the two agencies. Thus, the bonds issued by American Telephone and Telegraph are rated triple A by both agencies, but Pacific Telephone is rated triple A by one and double A by the other on its bonds.

Prior to the onset of high inflation in the 1970s, bond rating was mainly an objective skill. It rested heavily on capital structure analysis, the adequacy of operating income relative to fixed charges (known as the *fixed-charge* coverage), and the general trends and fluctuations in the company's earnings. Over the past 5 years of severe inflation (and the steep rise in the cost of energy), bond rating agencies have had to move to broader measures and more subjective judgment. As a result, the number of split ratings has increased dramatically.

By and large, the yield on bonds is inversely related to their ratings. How much difference does a rating make as far as yield is concerned? Some data are shown in Table 17-3. The table shows three important facts:

1. Long-term bond yields have risen sharply since inflation began in 1965. By 1974 they were twice as high as they had been in 1965. After a moderate decline in 1976, they rose again to reach a secondary peak in 1979, which was even higher than those reached in 1974.
2. There is clearly a spread between bond yields which reflects quality differentials.
3. The spread rises during periods of general financial stress; for example, the spreads rose sharply in 1970, 1974–1975, and again in 1979.

Interest Rate Risk

Obligations of the United States government are considered default-free, because the payments are certain to be made. However, government bonds are not totally riskless, for they are subject to a second type of risk: *interest rate* risk. Interest rate risk refers to the risk of a decline in market price due to a rise in the general level of interest rates. Any time the *holding period* (the period over which the investor holds the bond) is shorter than the maturity of the bond, the holder is subject to interest rate risk.

Table 17-3 Interest Rates and Spreads: Newly Issued Long-Term Utilities Bonds, 1962–1979 (Yields in Percent)

Year	Aaa	Aa	A	Baa
1962	4.36	4.34	4.45	4.75
1963	4.31	4.35	4.41	4.64
1964	4.46	4.46	4.55	4.74
1965	4.57	4.62	4.70	4.95
1966	5.44	5.57	5.76	5.98
1967	5.85	5.98	6.18	6.28
1968	6.57	6.72	6.90	7.11
1969	7.75	7.88	8.07	8.54
1970	8.52	8.74	9.15	9.68
1971	7.58	7.69	7.97	8.31
1972	7.34	7.42	7.56	7.89
1973	7.76	7.82	8.00	8.18
1974	9.16	9.47	9.89	9.14[a]
1975	9.11	9.50	10.24	11.17[a]
1976[b]	7.80	8.00	8.30	8.75
1977[b]	8.50	8.65	8.90	9.25
1978[b]	9.38	9.55	9.85	10.35
1979[b]	11.25	11.90	12.35	12.88

Source: Courtesy of Salomon Brothers.

[a] Distorted because there were few Baa offerings during this period.
[b] Figures for these years are year-end.

Purchasing Power Risk

Still a third type of risk, to which holders of all assets are subject, is *purchasing power* risk. Purchasing power risk results from uncertainty about what the future rate of inflation will be. In the case of a government bond, if we know with certainty that we will hold the bond to maturity, there is no default risk and no interest rate risk. If we are uncertain about the future rate of inflation, as most of us are, then we cannot be certain of the real rate of return on the bond.

Interest Cost to the Borrower

In the case of long-term debt funds raised in competitive financial markets, the rate of return required by lenders is a *market-determined* rate. The RRR depends in part on the riskiness of the bond as perceived by the market. The RRR on a bond at any point in time often is called the *yield to maturity* (YTM), which we discussed in Chapter 11. There we found that the price of a bond can be expressed as

$$P_o = \frac{C_1}{1 + y} + \frac{C_2}{(1 + y)^2} + \cdots + \frac{C_n}{(1 + y)^n} + \frac{P_n}{(1 + y)^n} \qquad (1)$$

where $C_1, C_2, \ldots, C_n$ are coupon (interest) payments, P_n is the principal amount due at maturity n years hence, and y is the YTM. The YTM is the internal rate of return on the bond if bought at P_o and held to maturity.

The rate of return required by lenders, call it K_d, is the pretax cost of the debt funds to the firm. At the time a bond is issued, the cost to the firm (K_d) and the YTM to the lender (y) are equal if we exclude flotation costs. If the bonds are issued at *par,* then the coupon rate (C) will equal K_d. Subsequent to issue, y will vary with the level of market rates, but C is fixed over the life of the bond. It is typical to refer to the coupon rate C as the pretax *cost* of the debt issue to the firm (again, excluding issue costs).

As we noted earlier, current tax laws permit deduction of interest for income tax purposes. The *after-tax equivalent* of the interest cost then is $C(1 - T)$. Deductibility of interest is a very important advantage of debt.

Preferred Claims: Preferred Stock

We now turn to the second of the three major types of claims issued by firms—preferred stock. Preferred shareholders are owners, not creditors. However, their claim differs in important respects from that of the residual claimants, the common shareholders.

Claim on Income and Assets

In terms of seniority, preferred claims stand behind all contractual claims of creditors and ahead of the common shareholders. Payments on preferred stock are usually called *dividends.* Such payments are fixed in amount, usually as a percentage of par value. A 7 percent preferred, for example, would pay a dividend of $7 per year if its par value were $100.

Although fixed in amount, preferred dividends are not contractual. Each time they are due to be paid, they must be declared by the board of directors. If for some reason a preferred dividend is not paid, preferred shareholders have no right to take legal action. The agreement between the firm and the preferred shareholders provides only that dividends will be paid in the agreed amounts prior to any payments to common shareholders. In a sense, preferred stock is hybrid security. Like debt, payments are fixed in amount. Unlike debt, payments are not contractual, and failure to make a payment does not bring insolvency or bankruptcy. Since they are not contractual, preferred dividends are not deductible by the firm for income tax purposes.

Nearly all preferred stock issues are *cumulative* in that dividends passed without payment accumulate and must be cleared completely before any payments can be made to common shareholders. Other protective covenants similar to those found in long-term debt and term loan contracts also are often included. For example, common dividends might be restricted to amounts that will maintain a specified current ratio or working capital position. The claim of preferred shareholders against the assets of the firm, like that of common shareholders, is general rather than specific, with no particular assets set aside to settle preferred claims.

Voting rights of preferred shareholders are specified in the corporate charter. Such rights normally concern payment of common dividends and issuance of other classes of securities of equal or higher seniority. In addition, preferred agreements usually provide for election of a specified number of directors by preferred shareholders in the event that the provisions of the preferred agreement are not met.

Cost of Preferred Stock to the Firm

The dividend rate on preferred stock is the rate of return required by the preferred shareholders to induce them to supply capital to the firm. Like required rates on debt and common stock, it is determined competitively in the market by investors, taking account of their opportunities to invest elsewhere. The return required by the market represents the cost of preferred stock to the firm. As always, the rate of return required by preferred shareholders depends in part on the degree of risk perceived by investors. Risk depends, in turn, on the firm's operating risk and the nature of its business, and also on the extent to which there exist prior contractual claims senior to the preferred. Since dividends are not tax deductible, the dividend rate is the after-tax cost to the firm.

Use of Preferred Stock

It was noted earlier that tax deductibility of interest is a major attraction of long-term debt. Preferred stock does not have this advantage. Relative to debt, an advantage of preferred is its flexibility. If earnings fall below expectations or the firm encounters difficulties for other reasons, the preferred dividend can be omitted without the threat of legal action, including bankruptcy. Contractual claims do not offer such flexibility.

While flexible relative to debt, preferred is less flexible than common. Protective covenants exist on preferred, and omission of a preferred dividend normally is viewed by the financial markets as a more serious matter than is omission of a common dividend. Since preferred offers no advantages relative to common through tax deductibility, and is less flexible, it is a suitable financing vehicle only under special circumstances. Over the 5 year period 1974–1978, new issues of preferred stock by United States corporations averaged only $2.9 billion a year compared to new bond issues (including private placements) of $30.7 billion a year and annual new common stock offerings of $7.3 billion.

Public utilities have been among the major issuers of preferred, at least partly in response to regulatory restrictions on the design of utility capital structures. Another specialized use has been in connection with mergers and acquisitions where tax considerations may make preferred stock advantageous as a vehicle for acquiring another firm. Finally, for some corporations, a combination of two circumstances may give preferred financing an edge over both bond financing and financing through a new issue of common stock. These circumstances are: (1) When the market price of its common stock is depressed relative to past and future expected levels, a new common issue would dilute its per-share earnings, a development most managements would prefer to avoid and can avoid by issuing preferred stock. (2) When a company's tax bracket is significantly below the normal 46 percent rate (as might be the case if it has a large investment tax credit or heavy investment outlays that can be expensed for tax purposes), the fact that bond interest payments are tax deductible may be a less important factor than the greater flexibility associated with preferred stock financing.

We can get a further insight to the use of preferred stock by looking at the *demand* side of the equation: who wants to buy preferred stock and why? As we noted in looking at the supply of this form of security, preferred stock is a hybrid that combines the fixity of return normally associated with a bond and the ownership feature normally associated with common stock, and as such, there is a demand for it only under special circumstances. These are:

1. Some investors want high current yields; preferred stock offers a higher yield than does common stock. Since the majority of preferred issues in recent years have been *convertible* preferreds (i.e., convertible into common stock on specified terms), they offer a chance of capital gains, which most bonds do not.

2. Corporations receiving preferred dividends (other than dividends paid by public utilities) are allowed to exempt 85 percent of such receipts in computing their taxable income. (The exemption on public utility preferred dividends is lower.) This feature increases the after-tax yield on preferreds relative to the yield on bonds. As a consequence, for

many fire and casualty insurance companies, which pay normal corporate tax rates on taxable investment income, preferreds offer a better yield than do bonds.

These specialized and hence competing demands for preferred stocks *as investments* leads to a lowering of the gross yields that preferred stock issuers have to pay when they raise funds through this instrument and so, in turn, tilts them to the use of preferred stock financing as opposed to financing via other alternatives.

A good example of how many of these factors come together to induce the use of preferred financing is a large issue ($130 million) of 7½ percent preferred stock sold by Chase Manhattan Corporation (the parent of Chase Manhattan Bank) in 1977. Chase needed more capital, and preferably equity capital rather than long-term debt. On the other side of the demand-supply equation, several cash-rich Puerto Rican subsidiaries of companies such as G. D. Searle, Abbot Laboratories and Pfizer, needed a United States outlet for their investments because the Tax Reform Act of 1976 had stripped away their liberty to invest excess funds outside the United States, tax free. Preferred dividends offered them the next best thing—an investment that was 85 percent tax free. The result— Chase decided to issue a preferred to a group of these companies on a direct-placement basis and did so at a rate that was *lower* than the rate it would have had to pay on a bond issue. Yet, at the same time, the investors received a higher net yield than they could have obtained by buying bonds. Through such circumstances is the market for preferred stock made.

Residual Claims: Common Stock

In any commercial enterprise, someone or some group must have final responsibility for policy and a residual claim to income and assets. This is the role played by common shareholders who are entitled only to what remains after creditors and preferred owners are compensated. In an uncertain world, the residual claim is inherently uncertain as to amount; sometimes residual returns are greater than anticipated, sometimes less.

Returns to common shareholders have two components: dividends and capital gains (or losses). Capital gains arise through changes in the price of the firm's stock. As a firm reinvests and grows, its value presumably increases, and the increase is reflected in a higher stock price. Dividends are declared by action of the board of directors and are not contractual; shareholders cannot take legal action to force payment. Since they are not contractual, dividends on common stock are not deductible for income tax purposes under present laws.

In the material that follows, we concentrate on the characteristics of common stock and the rights of its holders. We defer a discussion of the problems of issuing common stock to Chapter 21.

Some Definitions

In the United States, common stockholders have limited liability, that is, their liability is limited to the amount of their investment. If the corporation's liabilities exceed its assets, the common stockholders cannot be held liable for the difference, as can a proprietor or a member of a partnership.

Common stock is a perpetual claim; it has no maturity. A shareholder can liquidate an investment in the firm only by selling shares to another investor. The value of a share at any point in time is, in the final analysis, a function of the dividends that investors expect to receive, whether in the immediate or distant future.

A corporation's charter specifies the number of shares of common stock that the directors are *authorized* to issue. The number of authorized shares normally can be changed by a vote of the shareholders. When shares are sold to holders, they become *issued. Outstanding* shares are those held at any point in time by the public. If a firm repurchases previously issued shares, such shares are referred to as *treasury* stock; these are issued but not outstanding.

Stock can be issued with or without *par value;* this term has some historical, legal, and accounting significance, but little economic significance. In many states, shareholders are liable to creditors for the difference between the price at which the stock originally was issued and the par value, if the latter is greater. For that reason, par value normally is set at a figure lower than the price at which the stock is to be issued. To illustrate, consider the sale of 100,000 shares of $1 par value stock at an issue price to the public of $10 per share. The accounting entries, ignoring issue costs, are:

Debit	Credit	
Cash $1,000,000	Common stock $1 par	$100,000
	Paid-in surplus	900,000

The *book value* of the stock per share at any point in time is simply net assets available for common shareholders, after subtracting claims of creditors and preferred shareholders, divided by the number of shares. As noted earlier, *market value* for publicly traded stocks is the price at which transactions are taking place. Stocks are bought and sold on the *stock exchanges* and in the *over-the-counter market,* about which we will have more to say in Chapter 21.

Sometimes a firm will issue more than one *class* of common stock, often referred to as *Class A* and *Class B* stock. One of the classes usually has a larger voice in management and a junior claim to income. The senior class takes on some of the characteristics of preferred stock.

A final term that we will use is *equity*. Roughly speaking, equity means "ownership," so it is correct to use the term *equity* to refer to either *preferred equity* or to *common equity*. Where a firm has no preferred stock outstanding, the equity refers to the entire claim of the common stockholders, including retained earnings. Where preferred stock is involved, we should be clear as to which type of equity we mean.

Rights of Residual Owners

The rights of common shareholders are established by the laws of the state in which the corporation is chartered. Many of these rights are spelled out in the charter itself. Some rights belong to the shareholders as a group, and usually are exercised by vote. Such collective rights normally include amending the corporation's charter, usually with the approval of designated state officials; adopting and amending bylaws; electing directors; entering into mergers with other firms; changing the number of authorized shares; and authorizing the issuance of senior claims, such as preferred stock and long-term debt. In addition, shareholders have a number of rights they may exercise as individuals, including the right to sell their shares to others and the right to inspect the records of the firm.

Shareholders normally exercise their collective rights by voting. Most corporations hold a regular annual meeting of shareholders, at which voting takes place on issues presented to the shareholders by the directors. Special meetings sometimes are held to deal with specific issues, such as obtaining shareholder approval for a merger. A shareholder unable to attend may vote by means of a *proxy,* that is, by giving written authorization to someone to represent him at the meeting. Election of directors is by majority vote in many states, but some states permit an alternative system called *cumulative voting,* which makes it easier for minority interests to gain representaion on the board of directors.

The claim on the income and assets of the firm also is a right. We noted earlier that the residual owners are last in line with respect to both income and assets. Creditors and preferred shareholders must receive their interest and dividends before dividends are paid on common stock. In the event of serious difficulty leading to bankruptcy, claims of common shareholders are settled last. In the unhappy event of dissolution of a firm, common shareholders have claim to whatever assets remain after creditors and preferred shareholders are satisfied in full.

In connection with new issues of common stock, laws of many states give existing shareholders the *preemptive* right to maintain their pro rata share in the income and assets of the firm. Under this provision, existing shareholders must be offered first refusal on any new offering of stock prior to sale to the general public. Each existing shareholder has the preemptive right to purchase new shares in the amount necessary to maintain his pro rata share in the firm. *Rights* offerings are discussed in more detail in Chapter 21.

In principle, common stockholders control the policies of the firm via their rights to establish bylaws and to elect directors to represent them. Directors then appoint the executive officers of the firm, generally referred to as *management*. Management's job therefore is to act as agent of the shareholders and to optimize with respect to shareholder interests. This is a normative statement—it describes the way things should be and the way professional managers should behave. In practice, it would be naive to suppose that all managements always do act only in the interests of shareholders. There are many instances in the affairs of corporations in which the interests of managers and shareholders may diverge. Managerial behavior under such circumstances raises important moral, ethical, and perhaps even legal questions, but these are questions that we do not address in this book. The responsibility of professional managers is clear: Optimize with respect to shareholder interests; the way that responsibility is to be discharged is for each manager to decide for himself.

Cost of Common Stock to the Firm: Required Rate of Return

In the literature of finance, we find repeated references to the cost of capital, the cost of debt, and the cost of common stock. We have stated our preference for the term *required rate of return* and pointed out that, properly interpreted, cost and required rate of return are one and the same. We have used the term RRR almost exclusively in this book, but it seems appropriate periodically to reintroduce the term *cost* in order to maintain the link with other writings on the subject.

Since common stock is a residual claim, its return is subject to greater uncertainty than is the return to preferred shareholders and creditors. Since investors as a group are risk-averse, we would expect common shareholders to require a higher rate of return than preferred shareholders and creditors, and indeed, this is the case. In terms of a probability distribution, the return to common has a higher expected value, but also higher dispersion.

Approaches to the problem of estimating the rate of return required by common stockholders were discussed in Part IV. One way to represent this RRR is to define it as the rate that discounts future expected dividends to equal current market price, that is,

$$P_o = \frac{E(D_1)}{1 + K_e} + \frac{E(D_2)}{(1 + K_e)^2} + \cdots \tag{2}$$

$$= \sum_{t=1}^{\infty} \frac{E(D_t)}{(1 + K_e)^t} \tag{3}$$

The discount rate K_e in the above expressions is the market RRR on the firm's stock. Earlier, in Chapter 13, we noted that K_e also has two other commonly used labels: the *equity capitalization rate* and the *cost of equity capital.* There we also noted that, although the RRR for the firm as a whole is a single figure (K_e), the RRR for new investment opportunities varies with the riskiness of each.

Leasing

Firms obtain funds in order to acquire income-producing assets. In the case of physical (nonfinancial) assets, firms that are in business to produce goods and services usually are more interested in using the asset than in ownership per se. A specialized means of acquiring the use of assets without ownership is by *leasing.* Since it represents an alternative to ownership, leasing can be viewed as a specialized means of obtaining funds—one of a number of financing alternatives open to a firm.

A *lease* is a contractual arrangement under which the owner of an asset, the *lessor,* permits another party, the *lessee,* to use the asset for a specified period of time in return for a specified payment. The lessor retains title to the property. The lease contract sets forth the period covered by the lease, the amount and timing of payments to be made by the lessee, provisions for payment of taxes, insurance, maintenance expenses and the like, and provisions for renewal of the lease or purchase of the asset at expiration.

Leasing grew rapidly in popularity during the 1960s and early 1970s. By 1972, leasing accounted for about 14 percent of total investment in capital equipment by business, and the volume of leasing was expanding by about 20 percent per year.[1] In 1975, the Financial Accounting Standards Board, which sets standards for the accounting profession, estimated that more than $11 billion of new equipment was leased in 1974, and that by the end of 1975 equipment under lease would total $100 billion.[2] During this period of rapid growth, many new firms, including a large number of commercial banks, entered the leasing field as lessors.

---

1. Peter Vanderwicken, "The Powerful Logic of the Leasing Boom," *Fortune* (Nov. 1973).
2. "Accounting Board Proposes New Rules in Controversial Area of Lease Reporting," *Wall Street Journal* (Aug. 29, 1975).

It is clear that leasing has become an important means of asset financing. In exchange for use of the asset, the firm can issue a claim against its future cash flows: long-term debt, equity, or a lease obligation. Viewed in this way, leasing is strictly a financing decision. If leasing is selected, the firm incurs a contractual obligation to make payments of fixed amounts at specified times. The lease therefore is analogous to any other financial claim issued by the firm—the firm agrees to make a series of future payments. In that the payments are fixed and contractual, a lease is the functional equivalent of debt.

Types of Leases

The two most frequently encountered types of leases are the *operating* lease and the *financial* lease. Under an operating lease, sometimes called a *maintenance* or *service* lease, the lessor (owner) typically is responsible for maintenance, insurance, and property taxes. Compensation for providing these services is included in the lease payment. Assets leased under operating leases include computers, office equipment, automobiles, trucks, and a wide variety of other types of equipment. Contracts typically are intermediate- to short-term. Computers, for example, typically are leased for 3–5 years and automobiles for 1–3 years. Other types of equipment may be leased or rented on a daily or even an hourly basis. Contracts covering intermediate periods usually are cancelable. Because they usually cover a period considerably shorter than the usable life of the asset, operating leases normally do not fully amortize the original cost of the asset. Rather, the lessor expects either to lease the asset again or to sell it at the expiration of the original contract. Since contracts are short- to intermediate-term and cancelable, the lessor bears the risk of technological obsolescence of the asset.

Financial leases are noncancelable contracts typically covering intermediate to long terms. Provision often is made for renewal or purchase of the asset at expiration. The lessee (user) normally is responsible for maintenance, insurance, and taxes, and for this reason financial leases often are called *net* leases. Types of assets leased under financial leases include aircraft, rail cars, land, and buildings. Normally, the payments under a financial lease fully amortize the original cost of the asset over the term of the lease, which usually approximates the useful life of the asset. Full amortization and noncancelability are the key features that distinguish financial leases from operating leases. Noncancelability implies that the lessee is legally obligated to make all the lease payments regardless of whether he continues to use the asset, and thus can cancel only by paying off the entire contract. Default by the lessee can lead to bankruptcy, just as in the case of a debt contract.

Lease transactions may take one of two forms: a direct acquisition lease or a sale and leaseback. Under a direct acquisition lease, the lessee may lease directly from a manufacturer, as is often done in the case of computers and office equipment. Alternatively, the asset may be acquired by a third party who then leases it to the user. Lessors entering into such transactions include finance companies, commercial banks, specialized leasing companies, and individuals. Individual lessors usually are high-tax-bracket investors who can benefit from depreciation deductions or the investment tax credit.

Under a sale and leaseback, a firm or individual owning an asset sells it to another party and then leases it back. The seller gives up title to the asset but retains its use. The selling price usually approximates the fair market value of the asset. The lease contract is nearly always written as a financial lease with general provisions as outlined earlier.

Motives for Leasing

Leasing represents a specialized financing method that often can provide advantages to the lessee. The alleged advantages of leasing must be examined critically, however, as some may be illusory.

One often-cited advantage of leasing is that it provides 100 percent financing. Elimination of the requirement for a down payment may indeed be a real advantage to a lessee who has no cash. However, we should not lose sight of the fact that lease payments are contractual, and the lease therefore provides the equivalent of 100 percent *debt* financing.

Operating leases may provide a firm greater flexibility than ownership by shifting the risk of obsolescence to the lessor. The same is not true of financial leases, because they are noncancelable and normally cover the useful life of the asset. Where the risk is shifted, we can expect the lessor to require compensation for bearing it, usually incorporating the compensation directly in the lease payment. Taking such risks into account is central to the leasing business, and in general lessors are likely to be more expert at judging the risks than are lessees. So, while flexibility with respect to obsolescence is indeed an advantage of the operating lease, it is one for which the lessee pays. In effect, the lessee buys insurance against obsolescence.

In bankruptcy or reorganization, whether a lease contract is advantageous as compared to ownership depends on circumstances. Under ownership with a mortgage, in the event of default, the mortgagee (lender) is entitled to seize the asset and sell it to satisfy the debt. Any excess accrues to the firm, and any deficiency usually becomes an unsecured general obligation of the firm. Under a lease, the owner may repossess the asset and file a claim for lost rent against the lessee, with the maximum allowable claim depending on the type of asset and the nature of the proceeding. For example, in the case of real property, a claim for lost rent in bankruptcy is limited to a maximum of 1 year's rent. Whether the lessee is better off leasing or owning in the event of distress thus depends on the relation between the current market value of the asset at the time and the remaining lease or debt obligation, and also on the ability of the lessor to find a new lessee. Since these considerations regarding bankruptcy and reorganization mean nothing as long as the firm remains a going concern, they usually are of secondary importance in leasing decisions.

A major consideration in many leasing decisions concerns the *residual value* of the asset at the end of the lease period. By opting for leasing rather than owning, the lessee gives up any claim to residual value. The lessor, on the other hand, benefits from any residual value. If residual values are correctly taken into account and markets for leasing are reasonably competitive, the anticipated residual value should be reflected in lower lease payments. Where residual values are significant, as in real estate projects, they can significantly affect the return to the lessor and the cost to the lessee. We will deal explicitly with residual values in developing an approach to lease analysis later in Chapter 20.

Accounting Treatment

Other advantages sometimes attributed to leasing concern accounting treatment. For financing a particular investment opportunity, leasing may result in higher accounting profits in early years than the alternative of owning if the latter gives rise to high depreciation and interest charges. Even though near-term accounting profits may be higher under leasing, after-tax cash flows may be lower. The effective cost of the lease measured in discounted cash flow terms therefore may be higher and the lease actually disadvantageous in its true economic impact. Whether the favorable impact of a lease on accounting profits is truly an advantage is a question that must be answered with caution.

Another important accounting issue concerns disclosure of lease obligations in firm financial statements. Beginning in 1964, the accounting profession began to require disclosure of information on leases in financial statements or in footnotes to the statements. The guidelines, however, were vague and inconsistently applied. There were cases, for example, in which a given lease was treated one way in the financial statements of the lessee and another in those of the lessor. In most cases, neither the leased asset nor the contractual liability to make lease payments has appeared on the balance sheet of the lessee.

With the growth of leasing to significant levels, uniform reporting and fuller disclosure became imperative, so in 1975, the Financial Accounting

Standards Board (FASB) moved to standardize accounting treatment on financial statements of lessees and lessors alike. One of the most important decisions was to require capitalization of leases on balance sheets of lessees. With capitalization, the present value of the lease payments, discounted at a rate approximating the firm's interest rate on debt, would appear as a liability, and the value of the leasehold (an identical amount) as an asset. Footnote disclosure of details of lease payments and terms also was required. Under the 1975 FASB guidelines, whether a lease would be capitalized or not would depend on criteria involving the term of the lease relative to the economic life of the asset, the purpose of the asset, value at the end of the lease term, and whether title was to be transferred to the lessee at expiration. Application of the new guidelines has led to the capitalization of a large number of leases that previously had been disclosed only in footnotes, including most financial leases.

The move toward capitalization of leases was resisted by some on grounds that firms would lose the benefits of *off-balance-sheet financing* provided by leasing. Just how great the impact of capitalization would be is open to some question. Clearly, full disclosure of the details of lease contracts is necessary for lenders and investors to properly take them into account in valuing shares and in setting borrowing rates and terms.

Convertible Securities

A final form of long-term financing is the convertible security; one that begins as a debenture or as preferred stock but which can later be *converted* at the holder's option (and at a specified rate) into shares of the issuing company's common stock. The use of convertible securities as a financing device developed for two reasons: It appeals to yet another segment of those who supply funds for corporate investment, and it allows a company to raise funds by offering its common stock at a price above the level prevailing at the time the funds are raised. A more complete discussion of convertibles is included in Chapter 20.

Summary

Part V of the book covers the third major question with which financial management must deal: that of how best to finance a firm's operating investments. A firm undertakes investment opportunities in order to execute its commercial strategy. Once investment policy is determined, financing policies are tailored to fit. A principal determinant of financing policy is the degree of operating risk inherent in the firm's commercial strategy. Other important considerations are flexibility, control, and timing.

Major types of long-term financing available to firms are debt, preferred stock, common stock, leases, and convertible securities. The different financing instruments differ with respect to maturity, seniority, whether contractual or residual, use of collateral, tax treatment, cost, and right to voice in management.

Long-term debt is a contractual claim that normally has a maturity in excess of seven years. Protective covenants in the debt contract are designed primarily to protect lenders. The claim of bondholders against income and assets is senior to that of preferred and common stockholders. In addition to default risk, debt holders are subject to interest-rate risk and purchasing-power risk. Deductibility of interest lowers the effective cost of debt to the borrower.

Preferred stockholders are owners, not creditors. Preferred dividends are fixed in amount but are not contractual and are not deductible by the firm for tax purposes. In seniority, preferred claims come after those of bondholders, but ahead of those of common stockholders.

Common stockholders have final responsibility for policy and a residual claim to income and assets. Common stockholders bear the ultimate risks of commercial enterprise, receiving more return than bondholders and preferred stockholders in good times and less in bad times. The return to common stockholders is made up of two components, dividends and capital gains. Dividends are not deductible for tax purposes under present law. The liability of common stockholders is limited to the amount of their investment.

Firms also can obtain the use of operating assets by leasing. A lease is a contractual agreement to make specified future payments and is similar to debt in its effect on firm risk. Operating and financial leases differ with respect to responsibilities of lessor and lessee. The accounting treatment of leases is complex and new guidelines were promulgated in 1975.

Questions

1. In what important respects do the major types of financial claims issued by firms differ?
2. How is the cost of a particular source of funds to the firm related to the rate of return required by the financial markets?
3. In connection with debt claims, what is meant by the term *contractual?*
4. What is a *residual* claim?
5. What is a *subordinated* claim?
6. What is the purpose of protective covenants in a debt contract?
7. How does a mortgage bond differ from a debenture?

8. In general, a bondholder is exposed to three different types of risk. What are they, and how do they differ?
9. What determines the yield to maturity of a bond?
10. Contrast preferred stock with debt and common stock. What are the similarities and differences?
11. What are the key characteristics of common stock?
12. How do common stockholders receive their financial return?
13. How is book value of common stock related to market value?
14. What is meant by the term *preemptive rights?*

References

H. Bierman and B. Brown, "Why Corporations Should Consider Income Bonds," *Financial Executive* **35,** 74 (Oct. 1967).

E. F. Brigham, "An Analysis of Convertible Debentures: Theory and Some Empirical Evidence," *Journal of Finance* **21,** 35–54 (Mar. 1966).

A. Buse, "Expectations, Prices, Coupons and Yields," *Journal of Finance* **25,** 809–818 (Sept. 1970).

A. B. Cohan, *Yields on Corporate Debt Directly Placed* (New York: National Bureau of Economic Research, 1967).

G. Donaldson, "In Defense of Preferred Stock," *Harvard Business Review* **40,** 123–136 (July–Aug. 1962).

R. M. Duvall and D. V. Austin, "Predicting the Results of Proxy Contests," *Journal of Finance* **20,** 464–471 (Sept. 1965).

H. H. Elsaid, "Non-Convertible Preferred Stock as a Financing Instrument, 1950–1965: Comment," *Journal of Finance* **24,** 939–941 (Dec. 1969).

Financial Accounting Standards Board, *Accounting for Leases,* exposure draft (Stamford, Conn., July 22, 1976).

D. E. Fischer and G. A. Wilt, Jr., "Non-Convertible Preferred Stock as a Financing Instrument, 1950–65," *Journal of Finance* **23,** 611–624 (Sept. 1968).

I. Friend and M. E. Blume, "The Demand for Risky Assets," *American Economic Review* **65,** 900–922 (Dec. 1975).

R. D. Gritta, "The Impact of Lease Capitalization," *Financial Analysts Journal* **30,** 47–52 (Mar.–Apr. 1974).

S. L. Hayes, III, "New Interest in Incentive Financing," *Harvard Business Review* **44,** 99–112 (July–Aug. 1966).

S. L. Hayes, III, and H. B. Reiling, "Sophisticated Financing Tool: The Warrant," *Harvard Business Review* **47,** 137–150 (Jan.–Feb. 1969).

J. S. Katzin, "Financial and Legal Problems in the Use of Convertible Securities," *Business Lawyer* **24,** 359–373 (Jan. 1969).

H. Marsh, Jr., "Are Directors Trustees?," *Business Lawyer* **22,** 35–92 (Nov. 1966).

A. B. Meyer, "Designing a Convertible Preferred Issue," *Financial Executive* **36,** 42 (Apr. 1968).

T. Nelson, "Capitalizing Leases—The Effect on Financial Ratios," *Journal of Accountancy* **116,** 49–58 (July 1963).

Opinions of the Accounting Principles Board, Number 5 (New York: American Institute of Certified Public Accountants, 1964).

G. E. Pinches, "Financing with Convertible Preferred Stock, 1960–67," *Journal of Finance* **25,** 53–64 (Mar. 1970).

T. F. Pogue and R. M. Soldofsky, "What's in a Bond Rating?," *Journal of Financial and Quantitative Analysis* **4,** 201–228 (July 1969).

H. P. Riordan and E. C. Duffy, "Lease Financing," *Business Lawyer* **24,** 763–772 (Apr. 1969).

L. Schachner, "The New Accounting for Leases," *Financial Executive* (Feb. 1978).

W. Schwartz, "Warrants: A Form of Equity Capital," *Financial Analysts Journal* **26,** 87–101 (Sept.–Oct. 1970).

R. F. Vancil, "Lease or Borrow—Steps in Negotiation," *Harvard Business Review* **39,** 138–159 (Nov.–Dec. 1961).

R. F. Vancil, *Leasing of Industrial Equipment* (New York: McGraw-Hill, 1963).

P. Vanderwicken, "The Powerful Logic of the Leasing Boom," *Fortune* **88,** 132–136 (Nov. 1973).

"Venture Capital for Small Business—A Symposium," *Business Lawyer* **24,** 935–966 (Apr. 1969).

G. F. Werner and J. J. Weygandt, "Convertible Debt and Earnings Per Share: Pragmatism vs. Good Theory," *Accounting Review* **40,** 280–289 (Apr. 1970).

R. R. West, "An Alternative Approach to Predicting Corporate Bond Ratings," *Journal of Accounting Research* **8,** 118–125 (Spring 1970).

A. Zises, "Law and Order in Lease Accounting," *Financial Executive* **38,** 46–54 (July 1970).

J. Zwick, *A Handbook of Small Business Finance* (Washington, D.C.: Small Business Administration, 1965).

Financial Leverage: Debt versus Equity

18

Operating Leverage and Financial Leverage
Effect of Financial Leverage on Returns
Criteria for Financing Decisions
Leverage and Firm Value
Motives for Borrowing
Implications for Decision-Makers

Cyclical fluctuations in the level of business activity and sales are accompanied by even wider fluctuations in the level of business profits. For example, between the first quarter of 1975 (when the recession of 1973–1975 reached its trough) and the first quarter of 1976, total corporate sales rose 15 percent but total profits (before taxes) rose 60 percent. The fourfold amplification of the profit increase relative to the sales during the early phase of a cyclical expansion increase can be traced to two separate factors.

1. Because some elements of operating expenses are *fixed*, total operating expenses do not rise as rapidly as sales revenue rises. Therefore, operating profits rise faster than sales. Between the first quarter of 1975 and the first quarter of 1976 the operating earnings of corporations (before interest and taxes) rose 45 percent.
2. In addition, nonoperating expenses, such as interest payments, are also relatively fixed. Hence, net corporate profits (after interest charges) rose even faster than operating profits, that is, by 60 percent.

These two factors are referred to as operating leverage and financial leverage. Like the physical lever, which allows a person to amplify his basic strength, the two leverage factors amplify the effects of the basic business cycle.

Operating Leverage and Financial Leverage

In Chapter 3, we defined *operating leverage* in terms of the relationship between fixed and variable operating expenses. The term *operating* expenses refers to expenses related to the firm's operations, or to its commercial activities, and includes all expenses except interest and taxes.

The higher a firm's ratio of fixed to variable operating costs, the higher its operating leverage. An example of a firm with high operating leverage is an airline. In the short run, few of an airline's costs vary with the level of passenger traffic, perhaps only the cost of meals served in flight. Above its break-even passenger load factor, its operating profits rise very rapidly with increases in the number of passengers. Below break-even, the opposite occurs. Contrast this behavior with that of a wholesaler, the majority of whose operating costs are goods purchased for resale. A wholesaler has a low degree of operating leverage, and operating profits are much less sensitive to changes in revenues, up or down.

The degree of operating leverage of a firm thus has a pronounced effect on the sensitivity of its operating profit to revenue changes. For purposes of the analysis that follows, it is convenient to refer to pretax operating profit as *EBIT* (earnings before interest and taxes).

As contrasted with operating leverage, *financial leverage* refers to the mix of debt and equity used to finance the firm's activities. A firm that uses a lot of debt is said to be *highly levered*. The degree of leverage can be measured in *stock* terms, by using the ratio of debt to equity or debt to total sources of funds on the balance sheet. Alternatively, leverage can be defined in *flow* terms, by using the ratio of interest payments to EBIT.

We can see from the preceding definitions that operating leverage determines the extent to which a change in sales revenue affects EBIT. Financial leverage has no effect on EBIT. In analyzing financial leverage from this point on in this chapter, we will take EBIT as our point of departure.

Effect of Financial Leverage on Returns

Magnitude of Returns

Let us first examine the effects of different degrees of financial leverage at a given level of EBIT. Consider a firm with assets of $1,000 and imagine that this might be financed one of three ways: *A*, entirely by equity (common stock); *B*, 30 percent by debt and 70 percent by equity; and *C*, 60 percent by debt and 40 percent by equity. Assume that debt requires an interest rate of 8 percent and equity has a market price of $10 per share. Assume also that the $1,000 in assets generates EBIT of $240. We then have the figures listed in Table 18-1 for the three levels of leverage.

Table 18-1   Effect of Leverage on Earnings per Share

	Leverage		
	A	*B*	*C*
Assets	$1,000	$1,000	$1,000
Debt	0	$ 300	$ 600
Equity	$1,000	$ 700	$ 400
Leverage ratio (percent of debt)	0	30	60
EBIT	$ 240	$ 240	$ 240
Interest @ 8 percent	0	$ 24	$ 48
Profit before taxes	$ 240	$ 216	$ 192
Tax @ 50 percent	$ 120	$ 108	$ 96
Profit after taxes	$ 120	$ 108	$ 96
Shares	100	70	40
Earnings per share (EPS)	$ 1.20	$ 1.54	$ 2.40
Return on equity (ROE, percent)	12.0	15.4	24.0

From Table 18-1, we see that the effect of leverage is quite significant. When financed 30 percent by debt (case *B*), the firm earns $1.54 per share, 28 percent more than the 1.20 earned with no leverage. Return on equity (ROE) is greater by the same percentage. At 60 percent debt, (case *C*), EPS and ROE are double what they are with no leverage.

The table assumes that the firm earns 24 percent before interest and taxes on its assets ($240 on assets of $1,000). The effects of leverage depend very much on the relationship between the firm's ability to earn, or its rate of return on assets, and the interest cost of debt. In the above example, the firm obtains debt funds at a cost of 8 percent and puts those funds to work to earn 24 percent. The more debt it uses, the more favorable the impact. If, on the other hand, the firm could earn only 8 percent on assets, there would be no advantage to the use of debt. In Table 18-1, if EBIT were $80 (8 percent of $1,000 assets), EPS would be $0.40 no matter how much debt were used, and ROE would be 4 percent. If the firm's return were less than the cost of debt, the effects of leverage would be unfavorable. These observations lead us to the general conclusion that, when the return on assets exceeds the interest cost of debt, leverage has a favorable impact on EPS, and vice versa. The more the return exceeds the cost of debt, the more pronounced the impact.

Do we conclude that, when the return/cost relationship is favorable, the more debt the better? The "no free lunch" rule should make us skeptical. The reason for the favorable leverage effect is that debt represents a fixed, prior claim on income. When times are good, debt is advantageous, but what happens if times are not good? Suppose the return/cost relationship suddenly turns from favorable to unfavorable, and EBIT drops? The fixed claim is a two-edged sword! Let us now see what happens when EBIT varies.

Variability of Returns

Earnings before interest and taxes in any given firm is subject to many influences, some peculiar to the firm, some common to all firms in the industry, and some related to general economic conditions that affect all firms. In an uncertain world, EBIT in any period can turn out to be higher or lower than expected. Uncertainty with respect to EBIT often is referred to as *operating risk*.

One major source of operating risk is the business cycle, that is, the possibility of a recession. Other sources may be due to the possibility of technological obsolescence, actions of competitors, shifts in consumer preferences, changes in supply prices (such as the fivefold increase in oil prices in 1973–1974), and so on. Let us simplify matters by assuming that events of this kind can conspire to produce three possible outcomes: a normal year for EBIT, a good year, or a bad year. In reality, many more than three "states of the world" are possible, but these three will serve to illustrate the effect of leverage when EBIT varies. Let us assume that EBIT will be $240 in a normal year, $60 in a bad year, and $400 in a good year. As in Table 18-1, we examine the results at each of three levels of leverage—zero, 30 percent, and 60 percent debt—in Table 18-2. In Tables 18-3 and 18-4, we then summarize the results in terms of impact on EPS.

In normal and good years, an increase in leverage increases EPS. In a bad year, EPS is lower with debt in the capital structure, and the more debt used, the lower is EPS. The effect of leverage is unfavorable. We see also in Table 18-3 that the greater the leverage, the wider the range over which EPS varies from bad year to good. It is interesting also to look at the results in terms of percentage changes that are listed in Table 18-4.

Table 18-2 Leverage Effect with Variable EBIT

	State of the World		
	Bad	Normal	Good
A, No Leverage			
EBIT	$ 60	$240	$400
Interest @ 8 percent	0	0	0
Profit before taxes	$ 60	$240	$400
Tax @ 50 percent	$ 30	$120	$200
Profit after taxes	$ 30	$120	$200
Shares	100	100	100
Earnings per share (EPS)	$ 0.30	$ 1.20	$ 2.00
Return on equity (ROE, percent)	3.0	12.0	20.0
B, 30 Percent Debt			
EBIT	$ 60	$240	$400
Interest @ 8 percent	$ 24	$ 24	$ 24
Profit before taxes	$ 36	$216	$376
Tax @ 50 percent	$ 18	$108	$188
Profit after taxes	$ 18	$108	$188
Shares	70	70	70
Earnings per share (EPS)	$ 0.26	$ 1.54	$ 2.69
Return on equity (ROE, percent)	2.6	15.4	26.9
C, 60 Percent Debt			
EBIT	$ 60	$240	$400
Interest @ 8 percent	$ 48	$ 48	$ 48
Profit before taxes	$ 12	$192	$352
Tax @ 50 percent	$ 6	$ 96	$176
Profit after taxes	$ 6	$ 96	$176
Shares	40	40	40
Earnings per share (EPS)	$ 0.15	$ 2.40	$ 4.40
Return on equity (ROE, percent)	1.5	24.0	44.0

Table 18-3   Earnings per Share

	State of the World		
	Bad	Normal	Good
No leverage	$0.30	$1.20	$2.00
30 percent debt	0.26	1.54	2.69
60 percent debt	0.15	2.40	4.40

Table 18-4   Percentage Change in Earnings per Share Compared to Normal Year

	State of the World	
	Bad	Good
No leverage	−75	+67
30 percent debt	−83	+75
60 percent debt	−94	+83

From Table 18-4, we see that when leverage is used, EPS rises more in good years and falls more in bad years. When EBIT is rising, the more leverage we use the faster EPS rises. When EBIT is falling, greater leverage causes EPS to fall faster. From this analysis, we arrive at the general proposition that *financial leverage increases the variability of EPS and percentage ROE.* Why is this true? It is true because debt constitutes a fixed, prior claim against earnings. No matter what happens to EBIT, a fixed amount of interest must be paid. When EBIT falls, all the decline is deducted from the portion going to equity. As a result, the greater the use of financial leverage, the more sensitive is EPS to changes in EBIT.

Suppose EBIT declines to a level below that required to pay interest. This can happen—and does. In that case, the firm shows a loss. However, it does not necessarily go bankrupt, because it can make the interest payment by drawing down cash or other liquid assets, by borrowing, or, in extreme cases, by selling off operating assets. Where the shortfall is so great that these options are unavailable or inadequate, the firm faces possible bankruptcy if it defaults on its contract to pay interest. So we see that debt brings blessings when times are good, and dangers when times are bad.[1]

---

1. A good example of the effect of financial leverage on variability returns is provided by the airline industry. See R. D. Gritta, "The Effect of Financial Leverage on Air Carrier Earnings: A Break-Even Analysis," *Financial Management* **8,** 53–60 (Summer 1979).

We conclude that for a given degree of variability of EBIT, the more leverage the firm uses the more variable will be its earnings, both in total and per share. It is clear that variability of earnings stems from two factors: variability of EBIT and the extent to which financial leverage is employed. The degree of variability of EBIT is an important factor in deciding the extent to which leverage should be used. We will return to this conclusion later in this chapter.

Analyzing Leverage Using Probabilities

In the parlance of probability theory, EBIT is a random variable. Many outcomes are possible. In principle, we can assign probabilities to those outcomes. To illustrate the application of probability theory to the leverage decision, let us assume that we estimate the probabilities of bad year, normal year, and good year to be .20, .50, and .30 respectively. We can calculate the expected value and standard deviation of EPS as in Table 18-5. From the table, we see that an increase in leverage increases both the mean, or expected value, of EPS and its standard deviation. Recognizing that many states of the world can occur, rather than only three as in our simplified illustration, we can represent the probability distributions of EPS in continuous form as shown in Figure 18-1 (using only two of the leverage cases to avoid cluttering the diagram). For a given degree of operating risk (variability of EBIT), an increase in financial leverage shifts the distribution of EPS to the right (higher expected value) and at the same time increases its dispersion or variability.

Table 18-5 Distribution of Earnings per Share

	State of the World			Expected Value	Standard Deviation
	Bad	Normal	Good		
EBIT	$60	$240	$400		
Probability	0.20	0.50	0.30		
Earnings per share (EPS)					
No leverage	$ 0.30	$ 1.20	$ 2.00	$1.26	$0.59
30 percent debt	0.26	1.54	2.69	1.63	0.85
60 percent debt	0.15	2.40	4.40	2.55	1.48

Risk/Return Tradeoff

Figure 18-1 gives the same message as do Tables 18-3 and 18-4: There is a *tradeoff* between return and risk. As we increase leverage, we increase

Figure 18-1 Effect of Leverage on Earnings per Share

the probability (likelihood) of high returns, but we also increase the likelihood of low returns. With increased leverage, the expected or most likely return is greater, but a price is paid for this advantage: The firm must expose itself to the possibility of lower returns if EBIT turns out to be low. The firm obtains a higher expected return at the expense of greater risk. In an uncertain world, the possibility of unfavorable outcomes always exists. If EBIT declines far enough, because of a drop in sales or a rise in expenses or some combination of the two, bankruptcy becomes a real possibility. As with investment decisions, again we are face to face with the ever-present risk/return tradeoff. Leverage has costs as well as benefits —there is no free lunch!

Leverage and the RRR

How does financial leverage affect the rate of return required by the market on a firm's shares? As leverage increases, risk also increases, and risk-averse investors demand a higher return as compensation for the higher level of risk. The RRR on the firm's shares rises with leverage, other things being equal.

Let us consider these relationships more explicitly. Following conventions established in earlier chapters, let us define K_o as the return required on the firm's shares with no financial leverage present. Let K_e represent the return required on equity when leverage is used. Now imagine what happens when leverage is increased, with everything else held constant. This would be a little awkward to do in practice, but for purposes of understanding the relationships, we can imagine that it is done by issuing debt and using the proceeds to retire equity.

As leverage increases, risk increases, and investors demand a higher return, so K_e rises. The relationship between K_e and K_o was first worked out in the late 1950s by F. Modigliani and M. Miller.[2] They determined the relationship to be the following:

$$K_e = K_o + \frac{D(1 - T)}{E}(K_o - i) \tag{1}$$

In expression (1), D represents the market value of the firm's debt, E the market value of its equity, T the corporate tax rate, and i the risk-free rate of interest. The term $(1 - T)$ accounts for the fact that interest is tax deductible. Starting with zero leverage ($D = 0$), we see that $K_e = K_o$. As leverage increases, D increases and E decreases, so K_e rises. The second term in expression (1) represents the premium for financial risk required by the market. This financial risk premium is equal to the premium for operating risk, $(K_o - i)$, multiplied by the leverage ratio. These relationships are shown graphically in Figure 18-2.

Figure 18-2 Leverage and the RRR

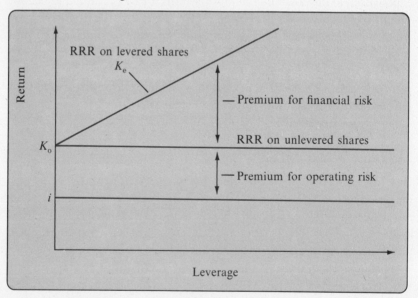

2. The original article was F. Modigliani and M. H. Miller, "The Cost of Capital, Corporation Finance and the Theory of Investment," *American Economic Review* **48,** 261–297 (July 1958). They subsequently clarified some of the tax issues in "Corporate Income Taxes and the Cost of Capital—A Correction," *American Economic Review* **53,** 433–443, (June 1963). Their analysis included corporate taxes but not personal taxes. Personal taxes are included in the more recent work of M. H. Miller, "Debt and Taxes," *Journal of Finance* **32,** 261–276 (May 1977). When personal taxes are included, the relationship between K_e and K_o is altered, but its basic form remains the same, with K_e rising as leverage increases. Miller's argument is discussed in a later section in this chapter.

From our analysis thus far, we can see that financial leverage increases the expected return on the firm's equity but at the expense of increased risk. Because of the increased risk, investors demand a higher return. How do we decide whether the terms of the risk/return tradeoff are favorable, that is, whether to accept increased risk in order to gain increased return? We cannot make this decision simply by examining tables such as 18-5 or graphs such as that in Figure 18-2. These provide insights, but they do not tell us what to do. Let us now consider some criteria for making the debt-equity choice.

Criteria for Financing Decisions

If the future were not uncertain, there would be no risk/return tradeoff. We could ignore risk and consider only return, and financing decisions would be much less difficult. In reality, EBIT is uncertain, and we cannot know which financing alternative is best until we know what the future holds. The best we can do is to say "Given our expectations of what may happen in the future, this plan appears best suited to our needs." To aid in this judgment, we need a decision criterion to use in comparing alternatives. In this section, we discuss several different criteria, some of which we will find useful and some not.

Earnings per Share as a Decision Criterion

In making managerial decisions, firms pay close attention to the impact of decisions on reported EPS. This concern with EPS is quite proper, for EPS is an important measure of the firm's performance and is closely monitored by investors. In earlier chapters, we discussed the importance and usefulness of various accounting measures (EPS included) as *performance measures.* Such measures answer the question "How well did we do, or are we doing?" A *decision criterion,* however, is intended to answer a different question: "What should we do?" For this purpose, EPS has some serious shortcomings.

To see why this is so, let us consider how we would use EPS as a criterion for financing decisions. Since EBIT is uncertain, EPS also is uncertain, so we cannot simply pick the plan with the highest EPS. As the example presented earlier in Table 18-3 indicated, one plan may provide more EPS at one level of EBIT but less at another. One way to formulate an EPS rule would be to pick the plan with the highest EPS at next year's expected (most likely) level of EBIT. In the example of Table 18-3, this rule would lead to selecting a debt level of 60 percent, because under this alternative EPS is highest in a normal year. If the choice were simply that of debt versus equity, debt would be chosen.

Does EPS rule always favor debt? In most cases, it does. Let us see why this is so. If we analyze the behavior of EPS in response to changes in leverage, we will discover an interesting relationship. It turns out that if the firm's after-tax borrowing cost, which we will denote as $K_d(\text{ATX})$, is less than its E/P ratio (current EPS/market price per share), then an increase in leverage, holding EBIT constant, will always increase EPS. A reduction in leverage reduces EPS. If $K_d(\text{ATX}) > E/P$, then the opposite occurs—an increase in leverage reduces EPS. These relationships follow directly from the underlying accounting relationships and they always hold.

To hold EBIT constant while varying its leverage, we could imagine the firm increasing its leverage by issuing bonds and using the proceeds to retire stock, or doing the opposite to reduce leverage. In practice, firms do not often vary their leverage in this way. Usually, the proceeds of new security issues are put to work in earning assets rather than used to retire other securities. But here we are interested in the effect on EPS of a change in leverage while holding everything else, including EBIT, constant.

In practice, what is the relationship likely to be between borrowing costs and the E/P ratio? If the after-tax cost of debt is 4 percent, then E/P is greater for any P/E (price/earnings) ratio of less than 25 and less for P/E ratios above 25.[3] If debt cost is 10 percent pretax and 5 percent after tax, the break-even P/E ratio is 20. Over the past 25 years, the P/E ratios of stocks measured by the Standard and Poor's 500 stock series have ranged between 8 and about 20. The average P/E ratio has gone above 20 on a few occasions, but not very often. During 1974, the level of stock prices dropped sharply and the average P/E fell at one point to 7, the lowest level since 1950. So, for some high-growth, high-P/E, stocks, relationships may be such that $K_d(\text{ATX}) > E/P$. But for most firms most of the time, it is likely that $K_d(\text{ATX}) < E/P$.

What does this fact tell us? That for most firms most of the time, strict application of the EPS rule leads to choosing more debt. When, as usually will be the case, $K_d(\text{ATX}) < E/P$, debt will deliver a higher EPS at the expected level of EBIT. So debt is the indicated choice. If the EPS rule is applied consistently over the long run, the firm is likely to choose debt each time funds are raised, because expected EPS continues to look better with debt.

What is the difficulty with the EPS rule? It ignores risk. It tells us that debt is best because it delivers more EPS at the expected, or most

---

3. For a good discussion of the meaning of P/E ratios and factors influencing them, see W. Beaver and D. Morse, "What Determines Price-Earnings Ratios," *Financial Analysis Journal,* 65–76 (July–Aug. 1978).

likely, level of EBIT. The EPS rule thus considers expected value but not variability about that expected value. Investors are, and should be, concerned with both expected value and variability, and therefore take account of both in valuing a firm's shares. As we will see later in this chapter, if a firm increases its debt beyond some point, it will continue to improve expected EPS, but this could nonetheless result in a decline in the market price of the firm's shares if investors become increasingly concerned about the greater exposure to risk.

Does the EPS rule gives us a warning signal if debt is pushed too far? Unfortunately it does not, and in fact does just the opposite. If debt is pushed too far, there comes a point where stock price begins to fall. Further increases in debt cause expected EPS to rise, the stock price to fall, and the E/P ratio to increase. The E/P ratio rises farther and farther above $K_d(ATX)$, and the signal to choose debt becomes stronger. Hence, once a firm has gone too far in using debt, the EPS rule becomes perverse and treacherous, for it signals the firm to issue still more debt. The ultimate outcome of such a policy is likely to be unpleasant.

Thus, we see that the EPS rule can lead to serious policy errors when applied to financing decisions. Applying it strictly, most firms would be led to use too much debt, since debt is the road to higher expected EPS. A few firms, mainly growth firms with high P/E ratios and hence low E/P ratios, might be led to use too little debt. In fact, the EPS rule counsels firms in the latter group to use no debt at all.

One might wonder at this point why we are going to such lengths to discuss the pitfalls of EPS as a decision criterion. The reason is that, given the great attention paid to EPS by investors, a firm might be led to think that EPS is all that matters, and when faced with a financing decision, to pick the alternative that does the most for EPS. Indeed, a careful reading of the financial press indicates that firms do consider carefully the impact of a financing decision on EPS, and in some cases may view it as controlling. In the case of investment decisions, few would argue that the decision should consider only the effects on first year EPS. The need to consider longer-term effects is clear, and we are therefore led to discounted cash flow techniques and a criterion of value-maximization rather than earnings- or EPS-maximization. With financing decisions, on the other hand, the dangers of using EPS as a criterion often are not so apparent. There often is a tendency to focus on the effects of financing decisions on near-term EPS and the dilution (reduction) of EPS caused by a stock issue relative to a debt issue. Under a strict EPS rule, since more EPS is always better than less, anything that reduces EPS is bound to be bad, and anything that raises EPS is good. This misleading argument loses sight of the fact that EPS is an uncertain quantity, and while EPS may be better under the debt alternative if things turn out as expected, there are circumstances under which the firm would be worse off with debt—in some cases, very much worse off. In short, *looking only at EPS does not deal with the risk/return tradeoff.*

It is important that we be clear with respect to the distinction mentioned earlier between performance measures and decision criteria. Here we are discussing the shortcomings of EPS for the latter purpose. As a performance measure, it is quite useful.

In view of the dangers of relying on EPS in making financing decisions, when faced with such decisions, should the effect on EPS be ignored? It should not, because EPS is an important and closely watched indicator of performance. Investors usually do not have access to projections of future earnings and cash flows, and must rely heavily on historical data. In evaluating financing alternatives, management should analyze carefully the impact of each alternative on EPS and on coverage. Useful techniques for doing so are the EBIT/EPS chart and coverage ratios, which we will discuss in the next chapter. If the alternative to be picked has an adverse impact on near-term EPS, management should communicate carefully and completely to investors the reasons why a plan that adversely affects near-term earnings is nonetheless best in the long run. Management's job is to make decisions that are best for shareholders, considering both short-term and long-term effects. Investors will consider long-run effects if they have the necessary information. Given such information, an adverse impact on EPS in the short run is less likely to be misinterpreted.

Much of the difficulty with EPS stems from the fact that investors seem to pay such close attention to it. They should, for they are using EPS as a measure of the firm's performance, and EPS is useful for this purpose. However, the fact that investors use EPS as a performance measure does not make it useful to management as a decision criterion. By means of careful communication, management can distinguish between the two purposes and reduce chances of misunderstanding. Communication with the market is an important aspect of every financing decision, especially where new issues of securities are contemplated.

Return on Equity

A second criterion that might be applied to financing decisions is return on equity (ROE). Our rule might be to pick the plan that gives the greatest ROE. A moment's reflection reveals that this criterion is subject to essentially the same criticisms as is EPS. Normally, ROE is defined as accounting profit after taxes divided by book equity. The financing plan that produces maximum ROE is nearly always the one that minimizes the use of equity and maximizes the use of debt. Like EPS, ROE is often useful as a performance measure. As a decision criterion, it has the same basic shortcoming as does EPS: It ignores risk.

Cost as a Criterion

Cost is a third criterion. Earlier in Part V we discussed the concept of cost as applied to financing plans along with ways in which the costs of various financing alternatives might be measured. One decision rule might be to pick the alternative with the lowest cost. Such a rule may sound appealing, but it is not.

The cost of any source of funds is the rate of return required by those who supply the funds. Since debt is senior to equity, the debt of a given firm is always less risky than the equity of that same firm. Since investors are risk-averse, holders of a firm's equity always require more return than do holders of its debt. Hence, for any firm, equity costs more than debt—always. Tax-deductibility of interest reduces the cost of debt even further.

In the case of firms to whom both equity and debt are available, debt is always the cheaper of the two. This being so, why use any equity at all? Using cost as our only criterion always would lead to a choice of debt, right up to the point of going bankrupt! Here, as before, using cost as the criterion considers only half of the issue: It ignores risk. Equity costs more, that is, has a higher required rate of return, because it does more: It bears risk. A bicycle costs less than an automobile, and both provide transportation, but to choose the bicycle because it is cheaper ignores some rather obvious differences between the two. Likewise, it is misleading to compare the cost of debt to the cost of equity because, though each is a source of funds, they perform different functions.

Book Value

Sometimes it is argued that a firm should never sell stock below *book value*. Book value usually is defined as tangible net worth per share. Leaving aside inflation effects, book value reflects in a rough way the cost of the firm's assets. Is book value a relevant consideration in making financing decisions?

The market price of a firm's shares reflects the consensus view of investors of the present value of the cash flows that the firm's investments are expected to generate. To say that an investment has a positive net present value (NPV) indicates that the cash flows it is expected to generate have a value greater than the cost of the assets required to generate those flows. If a firm undertakes only investments having a positive NPV, as it should, then in theory its stock price should rise above book value.

If a firm's stock is selling below book value, something has gone wrong. Some of its investments have not worked out as planned, and the market judges the value of future cash flows to be less than the cost of the assets required to generate those cash flows (inflation aside). A market price below book thus represents a bad report for the firm. It may be that the poor performance was due to factors beyond the control of management—general economic conditions, unforeseen cost increases, foreign competition, or any of a number of factors. Sometimes conditions in the world change so rapidly that many firms are adversely affected. In other cases, management error may be the cause.

Sometimes it is argued that a sale of new common stock at a price below book value should be avoided because it *dilutes* the position of existing shareholders. In fact, it does not. The position of existing shareholders has already been diluted by whatever factors caused the market price to fall below book value in the first place. Sale of new stock itself has no effect on value—the firm is worth the same per share the day after the sale as before. Market value may change when a stock issue is announced, but such changes are likely due to information effects—inferences drawn by the market with respect to the firm's investment plans or debt/equity policies. While information effects may have a great impact on market price per share, the act of issuing new securities in and of itself has none.

Suppose a firm decides against selling stock because market price is below book value. If, as a result, it must forego an attractive investment, shareholders are worse off. In this case, their position is diluted by *not* selling stock.

We can conclude that, in general, book value should not be relevant to financing decisions. If funds are needed for attractive investments and equity is the right choice, stock should be sold regardless of the relation between market price and book value. Here again, careful communication to investors of the reasons for the stock issue is very important and may alleviate any fears about dilution. We might recognize here a possibility that management might be reluctant to recommend sale of stock at a price below book value, because to do so draws attention to the price relationship and might require explanations (perhaps perceived as potentially embarrassing) as to why the price fell below book value in the first place. Such reluctance is understandable, but to argue that sale of stock below book value is counter to shareholder interests is a red herring. In such situations it is well to separate the interests of managers from those of shareholders. It is the latter that we should be concerned with.

Market Value

We have looked at four criteria—EPS, ROE, cost, and book value—and found serious shortcomings with each. What about market value? Is our general criterion for financial management decisions—value-maximization —applicable to financing decisons as well as to investment decisions? Indeed it is. We would state the rule as: Pick the financing alternative that gives the highest value for the firm.

In principle, the use of value as our criterion solves our problems with respect to both time and risk. Value takes account of the effects of alternative plans over many future periods rather than only near-term periods. Market value takes account not only of expected value, but also of risk and variability. As a criterion, value deals with the risk/return tradeoff. We say that in principle value does these things, because, while clear in concept, application of value as a criterion is not easy. Earnings per share is much easier to apply, but alas, it is incorrect! To develop valuation as a criterion for financing decisions, we need to know more about the way in which changes in leverage affect value.

Leverage and Firm Value

If we view a firm as a going concern, its value depends on the cash flows it can generate in the future. The firm's pretax operating profit, or EBIT, is divided among three principal claimants, as illustrated in Figure 18-3.

Figure 18-3 Division of EBIT

Debt holders (D) receive their share in the form of interest, the government (G) receives its share in taxes, and equity holders (E) receive what is left. We can think of EBIT as a pie to be divided among the three claimants (Figure 18-4).

Investment decisions determine the size of the EBIT pie, while financing decisions determine the way it is to be sliced. The total value of the firm is its value to owners and creditors together and is determined by the combined slice going to E and D in Figure 18-4. Investment decisions increase the value of the firm by increasing the size of the pie. Financing

Figure 18-4 The EBIT Pie

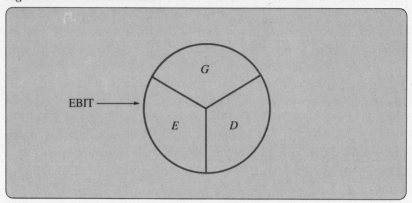

decisions can increase firm value only by reducing the share of the pie going to the government, that is, by reducing the taxes paid by the firm.

Tax Effects

Financing decisions affect the firm's tax liability because interest on debt is tax-deductible.[4] If interest were not deductible, a change in the firm's debt/equity mix would have no effect on taxes. Let us examine the slicing of the EBIT pie with and without deductibility of interest. In Figure 18-5, the firm's EBIT each period is represented by the symbol O. Assume for simplicity that the firm pays interest at a rate, i, on total debt, D. Total interest payments each period are iD. With interest not deductible, the firm pays taxes of OT, where T is the tax rate. As leverage is increased, the share to debt holders increases, the share to equity holders decreases by a like amount, and the share to the government remains unchanged. Thus, the share to debt and equity holders together is fixed at $O(1 - T)$ and does not vary with changes in leverage.

With interest tax-deductible, the government's share each period is lowered by iDT, sometimes called the *tax shield* on interest. The reduction in taxes accrues to equity holders, whose share each period is higher by iDT than it was with interest not deductible. The combined share to debt and equity together also is higher by iDT.

From the analysis in Figure 18-5, we can conclude that interest deductibility is an important benefit of debt financing. With interest not deductible, the use of debt financing in lieu of equity does not make the firm more valuable. The portion of the EBIT pie to be shared by debt and

---

4. For a discussion of the effect of changes in tax laws on the financial policies of firms, see R. H. Litzenberger and J. C. Van Horne, "Elimination of Double Taxation of Dividends and Corporate Financial Policy," *Journal of Finance* **33**, 737–749 (June 1978).

Figure 18-5 Division of EBIT among Claimants

	Share	
	Interest not deductible	Interest deductible
EBIT (O) ──── Debt holders	iD	iD
──── Government	OT	$OT - iDT$
──── Equity holders	$O - iD - OT$	$O - iD - OT + iDT$
Debt and equity together	$O(1 - T)$	$O(1 - T) + iDT$

equity holders, $O(1 - T)$ in Figure 18-5, is fixed in total, and leverage affects only the way the portion is sliced between debt and equity holders. An increase in the size of the slice to one group must come at the expense of the other. Hence, with interest not deductible, leverage cannot increase the combined value of the debt and equity together.

To see this point more clearly, consider a firm whose debt and equity are entirely held by a single individual. With interest not deductible, total payments to debt and equity are fixed, and changes in the split between the two cannot make the holder better or worse off. Given the existence of organized financial markets, the same conclusion holds if there are many holders of the firm's debt and equity.

Although (with interest not deductible) leverage does not increase the total value of the debt and equity, it does affect the cash flow streams going to the two groups. An increase in leverage increases the expected rate of return to equity in percentage terms, but, as we found earlier in this chapter, simultaneously increases the riskiness of that return. As risk increases, risk-averse investors demand a higher return. The increase in risk offsets the increase in expected return, and the value of the equity claim remains unchanged. In other words, while leverage increases the expected return, because of the accompanying increase in risk, the market does not place a higher valuation on that return.

When interest is tax-deductible, the picture changes. An increase in leverage decreases the share of EBIT going to the government, and increases that going to debt and equity. The firm's cash flows increase with leverage because of the *tax subsidy* on the use of debt.

Value of the Tax Subsidy

What value does the market place on this tax subsidy? If the firm had no debt, it would provide to investors a cash flow stream equal to $O(1 - T)$

(Figure 18-5) in each period. This cash flow stream has a value that we will label V_U, where the subscript U signifies unlevered.

With debt present, the stream shared by debt and equity with interest deductible is $O(1 - T) + iDT$. The value of this stream thus is V_U plus the value of the tax shield, iDT. If we assume an infinite valuation horizon, iDT is a perpetuity, and we can determine its present value by discounting. When this problem was first worked out in the early 1960s, it was argued that the tax shield is of approximately the same degree of risk as the interest payments themselves and should be discounted at the same rate, i. Thus, the present value of the tax shield of iDT per period was calculated as $iDT/i = DT$, and the value of the firm with interest deductible as[5]

$$V_L = V_U + DT \qquad (2)$$

where V_L is the value of the levered firm. Graphically, we can represent the relationship as in Figure 18-6.

Figure 18-6 Leverage and Value before Considering Financial Distress

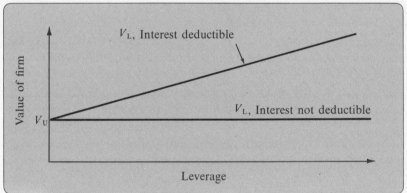

Personal Taxes

The tax benefits considered in Figure 18-6 and expression (2) above take account only of taxes paid by the firm. It is clear that an increase in debt reduces the firm's tax liability and thereby increases total cash flows accruing to debt and equityholders together.

But corporate taxes are not the whole story. Bondholders and stockholders themselves must pay taxes on the returns they receive from the firm. These personal taxes act to offset part of the saving in firm taxes. Some economists argue that the offset is total and that, in general, there is

---

5. Expression (2) was first worked out by Modigliani and Miller, "Corporate Income Taxes and the Cost of Capital—A Correction." This analysis did not consider the effects of personal taxes paid by stockholders and bondholders. Personal taxes are discussed in the next section.

no tax benefit to the use of debt at all.[6] We discussed this argument in Chapter 15 in considering the impact of financing mix on investment decisions.

According to this view, interest rates adjust to reflect the fact that bondholders must pay taxes on the interest that they receive. The interest rate that the firm must pay on debt thus is higher by an amount sufficient to pay the bondholders' tax compared to what it would be if no taxes existed. This extra interest paid by the firm comes out of the stockholders' pockets. The net effect, so this argument goes, is that the taxes saved by shareholders due to deductibility of corporate interest are offset by the taxes paid by bondholders. An increase in debt by a firm would increase its after-tax cash flows, as indicated by Figure 18-5. But this increase is offset by personal taxes paid by bondholders and stockholders (which are not shown in Figure 18-5). In other words, while the *firm's* cash flows are altered by leverage, the net flows to *investors* are not. In the final analysis, when all taxes at all levels are taken into account, the use of debt by a firm provides no net tax benefit to its shareholders. The value of the firm, according to this argument, would be unaffected by changes in leverage, and V_L would always equal V_U.

The extent to which these various tax effects are offsetting is an unsettled question at present.[7] A good deal of additional research is needed to find the answer. We can be reasonably sure, however, that the tax advantage to investors after considering all relevant taxes is less than that suggested if only corporate taxes are taken into account.

To the extent that personal taxes do offset the corporate tax saving, the line in Figure 18-6 would rise less steeply. Since the issue is presently unresolved, it seems best to assume that there is some tax benefit to the use of debt, recognizing that we will not know how much until further studies have been conducted.

Financial Distress

Figure 18-6 implies that the value of the firm continues to rise with leverage no matter how much is used, and therefore that the firm should use as much debt as possible. We have considered the benefits of debt, but not the costs. Since EBIT is uncertain, there is always the possibility that

---

6. The main proponent of this view is M. H. Miller, "Debt and Taxes," *Journal of Finance* **32**, 261–275 (May 1977). Miller's argument recognizes that tax deductibility of interest does provide incentive for firms to issue debt and that some equilibrium level of debt will be issued by firms in the aggregate. The crux of his argument is that once this equilibrium is reached, interest rates and marginal tax rates are such that issuance of debt by an *individual firm* provides no net tax benefits to investors.

7. For a test of the Miller hypothesis, see E. H. Kim, W. G. Lewellen, and J. J. McConnell, "Financial Leverage Clienteles: Theory and Evidence," *Journal of Financial Economics*, forthcoming.

it may drop too low to permit the firm to meet its contractual obligations. An increase in debt thus increases the probability of *financial distress.*

Financial distress usually is a matter of degree, with a declaration of bankruptcy the extreme form. Milder forms of financial distress occur when a firm's cash flows fall below expectations. Liquidity falls and the firm may have difficulty in meeting contractual obligations to its creditors. Costs of such financial distress are those related to modification of investment and financing strategies made necessary by the distress condition. If a firm is forced to forego desirable investments, significant opportunity costs may be incurred. Other costs may be incurred because of the inability of the distressed firm to negotiate effectively with suppliers, to ensure customers of prompt delivery, and to guarantee future availability of parts and service. In a distress situation, creditors may restrict the firm's operations, thereby possibly reducing profitability. Dividend payments to shareholders also may be interrupted. Other kinds of opportunity costs may be incurred due simply to the diversion of management time from operating to financial matters.

Firms often encounter conditions of financial distress, sometimes mild, sometimes not so mild. Bankruptcy involves legal action and occurs much less often. Bankruptcy costs include costs of accountants, lawyers, judges, and lost time of managers in overseeing the bankruptcy proceedings. Even more important may be the opportunity costs of lost output due to underutilization of the firm's labor and physical plant during the bankruptcy proceedings. Losses may be incurred on sale of assets under distress conditions. There also may be psychological costs in the minds of investors, creditors, and managers. There has been little research on the magnitude of costs associated with bankruptcy, but upon reflection it seems reasonable to suppose that they may be significant in relation to the value of the firm. Certainly the consequences of bankruptcy are significant in the minds of the firm's managers.[8]

In addition to costs incurred under conditions of distress, the use of debt may involve other opportunity costs that are more subtle but

---

8. Disagreement exists among financial economists as to the real significance of bankruptcy costs. For a view that bankruptcy costs are relatively small, see J. Warner, "Bankruptcy Costs: Some Evidence," *Journal of Finance* **32,** 337–348 (May 1977). For a good discussion of the distinction between bankruptcy costs and liquidation costs, see R. A. Haugen and L. W. Senbet, "The Insignificance of Bankruptcy Costs to the Theory of Optimal Capital Structure," *Journal of Finance* **33,** 383–394 (May 1978). Their argument that bankruptcy costs are insignificant rests on an assumption that bankruptcy is a matter of concern only to owners and creditors. They argue that bankruptcy is unimportant to all other parties and therefore will have no real effect on relationships between the firm and suppliers, firm and customers, on the morale of managers and employees, and thus no effect at all on the commercial operations of the firm. A contrary view and another discussion of bankruptcy costs can be found in E. H. Kim, "A Mean-Variance Theory of Optimal Financial Structure and Corporate Debt Capacity," *Journal of Finance* **33,** 45–64 (Mar. 1978).

no less important. One of the important conclusions of this analysis is that the optimal amount of debt depends on the firm's operating risk and therefore on the nature of its business. Any use of debt therefore reduces a firm's flexibility to alter its commercial strategy in the direction of higher risk. Consider, for example, a firm contemplating a new venture that promises high returns but also involves high risk. If the firm's preexisting capital structure included a level of debt that would be imprudent if the new venture were undertaken, three options would be available:

1. alter the capital structure,
2. undertake the new venture and operate with too much debt, or
3. forego the new venture.

Each of these options involves costs. Taking account of such costs is difficult because the need to alter the commercial strategy may not be foreseen at the time the debt policy must be set. Nevertheless, the reduction in the firm's commercial flexibility must be counted as a cost of using debt.

Leverage and Value

We conclude that debt has both benefits and costs. The benefits result from the deductibility of interest payments, and the costs result from the possibility of financial distress and reduced commercial flexibility. Choosing the appropriate debt level thus involves a tradeoff. As leverage increases, there comes a point where the expected costs of financial distress and reduced flexibility begin to outweigh the benefits of the tax subsidy. At that point, the value of the firm stops rising with leverage and the optimal debt/equity ratio has been reached. Pushing debt beyond that point would result in a decline in value. We can represent the relationships graphically as in Figure 18-7, with D/E^* representing the optimal debt/equity ratio for the firm.

Another important consideration has to do with the possible loss of tax credits in bankruptcy. If a firm goes bankrupt, tax credits due to losses normally cannot be recovered from the government, unless the firm merges with another firm or manages to carry the tax credits forward after bankruptcy. Thus, higher debt levels reduce the firm's tax liability during periods when profits are earned, but at the same time increase the likelihood of losing tax benefits during other periods if the firm goes bankrupt. These offsetting effects reduce the value of the tax subsidy below the theoretical maximum of DT [expression (2)] and cause the value

Figure 18-7 Leverage and Firm Value

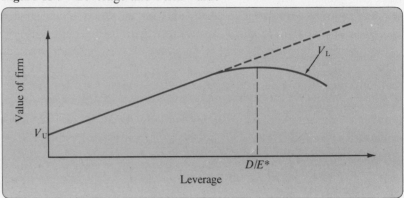

of the firm to decline at high levels of debt, as depicted in Figure 18-7.[9]

From the foregoing discussion, we can conclude that theories explaining the relationship between leverage and firm value are not yet completely developed. A number of factors have been identified that are believed to be important, but their relative importance is not yet perfectly understood. The exact size of the tax subsidy is open to considerable question. Nevertheless, enough is known to suggest that the relationship between leverage and value is more or less as depicted in Figure 18-7. The value of the firm rises with leverage up to a point, and then begins to decline.

Motives for Borrowing

The "tax subsidy" due to deductibility of interest is often cited as a major advantage to the use of debt. However, because of the effects of personal income taxes discussed above, a part of this advantage may be illusory. Rather than accruing entirely to shareholders, the tax subsidy may be shared by other parties. Lenders may get part, if interest rates do indeed

9. For a discussion of these offsetting tax effects, see M. J. Brennan and E. F. Schwartz, "Corporate Income Taxes, Valuation and the Problem of Optimal Capital Structure," *Journal of Business* **51,** 103–114 (Jan. 1978). Factors other than taxes and costs of financial distress also may affect the relationship between financial leverage and firm value. Secured debt (i.e., secured by a pledge of assets) may reduce the firm's liability for future legal damages and therefore affect value differently than unsecured debt. See J. H. Scott, Jr., "Bankruptcy, Secured Debt and Optimal Capital Structure," *Journal of Finance* **32,** 1–20 (Mar. 1977). Also important is the extent to which the firm's value rests on future growth opportunities requiring further discretionary expenditures by the firm. For a discussion of these issues, see S. C. Myers, "The Determinants of Corporate Debt Capacity," *Journal of Financial Economics* **5,** 147–175 (Nov. 1977). Another category of costs that may be important, called *agency costs,* are monitoring and surveillance costs incurred at the insistence of lenders and shareholders to ensure that their interests are protected. For a discussion, see M. Jensen and W. Meckling, "Theory of the Firm: Managerial Behavior, Agency Costs, and Ownership Structure," *Journal of Financial Economics* **2,** 305–360 (October 1976).

adjust to reflect the effects of tax deductibility, as suggested in the preceding section.[10] Customers may share in the subsidy if competition forces the firm to pass part of it along via lower prices. Likewise, part may go to suppliers via higher prices and part to managers and employees via higher salaries and wages.

Just how the tax subsidy on debt gets divided up is very much an unsettled question at present. Until these questions are resolved, financial managers should err on the side of conservatism and assume that the tax advantage to shareholders from the use of debt is probably modest.

Betting on the Future

Firms used debt long before interest was made deductible for tax purposes, so there must be other advantages. Earlier in this chapter, we learned that the effect of financial leverage on returns depends on the relationship between the firm's operating return on assets and the interest cost of debt. If operating return is greater than interest cost, then increasing financial leverage by replacing equity with debt will have a favorable effect on earnings. Earnings and return to equity will be higher with debt than without. Conversely, if operating return is less than interest cost, the firm will be worse off with debt.

So, one motive for using debt is simply to gain the advantage of financial leverage that accrues if things turn out well. A management convinced that the future is bright may want to "lever up" and thereby increase the return to owners. If management's predictions are correct, owners indeed will be better off because of the debt. If the predictions are wrong, the piper must be paid.

Do the financial markets place a higher value on firms that bet on the future by using debt? If there existed managers that could predict the future with certainty, the answer would be yes. But even managers with access to the best information cannot do so, and suppliers of capital in the financial markets know they cannot. Debt can make the owners worse off, perhaps very much worse off, if things do not go well.

Earlier in this chapter, we discussed the effect of debt on the magnitude and variability of returns. We found that, in most cases, debt increases both the expected or *most likely* return and simultaneously increases the variability or *riskiness* of that return. The increase in risk offsets the increase in expected return in the eyes of suppliers of capital, and the current value of the firm is affected only to the extent of tax benefits. We found this to be so in our discussion of the "EBIT pie" and the division of EBIT among its various claimants (Figure 18-5).

10. See Miller, "Debt and Taxes."

The use of debt makes sense only if management is reasonably convinced that operating return on assets in the future will exceed the interest rate on debt. However, even where this is the anticipated outcome, it does not necessarily follow that debt ought to be used. Management must make a judgment that the prospect of higher returns justifies running the risk that returns may turn out to be lower. If the future looks sufficiently bright, management may decide to "bet on the future" via increased use of debt. However, the financial markets are unlikely to place a higher current value on the firm's securities simply because the gamble is being taken. Any immediate effect on firm value results only from tax benefits, which, for reasons discussed earlier, are likely to be modest. In short, the financial markets are likely to give credit for the use of debt only after the returns are all in.

Financing Costs

Another motive for using debt has to do with financing costs. For many firms, and nearly all small firms, debt raised via financial intermediaries is very much cheaper than debt raised via the public financial markets. The main types of financial intermediaries are commercial banks, insurance companies, savings and loan associations, savings banks, and pension funds. We discussed financial intermediaries and their economic role in channeling funds earlier in Chapter 2.

Intermediaries reduce financing costs by reducing the costs of matching up borrowers and lenders. The intermediary acts as "agent" for both borrower and lender in the tasks of gathering funds, credit analysis, record-keeping, and so on. Savers with small amounts can lend much more cheaply and safely by going through a commercial bank than by lending directly to firms. A firm that wants to borrow a million dollars can do so much more cheaply by making one stop at a bank than by gathering small amounts from hundreds or even thousands of individual savers. The net effect is that the entire process of borrowing and lending is much less expensive than it would be if intermediaries did not exist. In technical jargon, financial intermediaries reduce "friction" due to costs of search, acquisition, and information-processing.

Commercial banks are the primary suppliers of funds to small firms. By law, commercial banks deal only in debt contracts. The net result is that debt represents a very economical source of outside funds for many small firms, much more economical than equity capital raised by the public financial markets. For small or little-known firms, raising equity capital via the public financial market is prohibitively expensive because it requires a substantial amount of information-processing and credit analysis by hundreds or even thousands of different individuals. The commercial bank performs this credit analysis and information-processing function on behalf of all of those individuals. Since the commercial bank offers only debt, debt becomes the cheapest source of funds.

Larger firms also often find debt obtained via financial intermediaries an attractive source of funds. Firms with many profitable investment opportunities may find internally generated funds insufficient to satisfy all requirements. Raising the necessary funds by a sale of stock may be considered undesirable because of control considerations or because of the costs and fanfare of a public offering. The alternative of obtaining debt via a loan from a commercial bank or a "private placement" of long-term debt with an insurance company may be quite attractive. By dealing with a financial intermediary, the firm raises the required funds cheaply and conveniently in a single transaction.

We can conclude that there are three main motives for borrowing by firms. One motive is to capture the tax benefits of deductibility of interest. Just how large these benefits are to shareholders after personal taxes is open to some question. Another motive is to exploit the effects of favorable financial leverage. A final motive is to use the cheapest source of funds. Even if there were no tax benefit at all, many firms would borrow for one of the other two reasons. Firms with access to either debt or equity via the public markets might choose to borrow in order to exploit the effects of financial leverage. Firms that cannot raise equity economically choose debt because it is the only economical source of external funds.

Implications for Decision-Makers

Much of the material in this chapter is conceptual and theoretical. What guidance does it provide to decision-makers in practice? Does an understanding of the effects of leverage on returns, risk, and value tell a manager whether to use debt, and if so, how much? The answer is no, for our understanding of many of the key relationships is not sufficiently developed to permit exact quantitative application. The conceptual material does, however, provide a useful way of thinking about the relationships and yields insights and qualitative guidance that is valuable.

One conclusion that emerges is that it is useful to consider debt in terms of its impact on firm value rather than only on earnings. By using value as the framework, we focus on what counts most to shareholders. Shareholders receive their return in the form of dividends and stock price appreciation, not earnings per share. The valuation framework makes clear the fact that excessive use of debt can lower stock price and thereby reduce returns to shareholders, even though expected EPS may increase.

The valuation analysis indicates that the optimal financing mix depends on the risk of bankruptcy and financial distress. The risk of bankruptcy and financial distress depends to an important extent on the *operating risk,* or *business risk,* of the firm. Thus, we draw the important conclusion that the *optimal debt / equity mix depends on the nature of the business and therefore on the kinds of investments that the firm makes.* The more risky the firm's investments, that is, the higher its operating risk, the less debt it should use, and vice versa.[11]

When the firm maintains a more or less stable commercial strategy and remains in the industry in which it historically has operated, it likely will routinely invest in projects covering a wide spectrum of risk. In such cases, high-risk and low-risk projects may average out over time and leave the overall operating risk of the firm, and therefore its optimal debt/equity mix, unchanged. Where a series of investments do have a cumulative effect on the firm's overall operating risk, the optimal debt/equity mix may change enough so that a revision in the actual debt/equity mix may become desirable.

Since the optimal debt/equity mix depends critically on operating risk, it is clear that the optimal mix is not static but is likely to vary over time, perhaps over a wide range. A debt level considered prudent one day may suddenly become too high.

We conclude that market value is the appropriate criterion for financing decisions, as it is for investment decisions. In this chapter, we have used valuation to provide qualitative guidance and a way of thinking about capital structure decisions. We will get down to the difficult task of applying these concepts in the next chapter.

Summary

Financial leverage refers to the mix of debt and equity funds used to finance the firm's activities. Financial leverage affects both the magnitude and the variability of earnings per share (EPS) and return on equity (ROE). For any given level of operating return (EBIT), the effect of an increase in leverage is favorable if the percentage rate of operating return on assets is greater than the interest cost of debt, unfavorable if less. When EBIT varies over time, financial leverage magnifies the variation in EPS and ROE. Variability of EPS and ROE thus stems from two factors: variability of EBIT (operating risk) and the degree of financial leverage employed (financial risk). Thus, in general, the use of financial leverage increases both the expected return to shareholders and the variability of that return, and confronts the financial manager with the fundamental tradeoff between return and risk: more return if things go well, less return if things go poorly.

11. For theoretical development of this point, see Brennan and Schwartz, "Corporate Income Taxes, Valuation and the Problem of Optimal Capital Structure."

To analyze financing alternatives, a decision criterion is needed that takes account of both sides of the risk/return tradeoff. EPS, while very useful as a performance measure, is not usable as a decision criterion because it considers only return and ignores risk. Strict application of the EPS criterion would lead in the majority of cases to the use of too much debt, and in some cases to the use of too little. In no case does the EPS criterion systematically balance return against risk. As decision criteria, ROE and cost suffer from the same shortcoming. Book value is not useful as a criterion because it is largely a reflection of the past rather than the future. The criterion that does deal with the future and with both sides of the risk/return tradeoff is *market value.*

Financial leverage affects the value of the firm in several ways. With interest on debt tax-deductible, an increase in leverage reduces the firm's tax liability and thereby increases the share of EBIT going to equity. At the same time, increased leverage reduces commercial flexibility and increases the probability of financial distress. Choosing the appropriate level of debt involves a tradeoff among these opposing factors. The optimal debt level is that which maximizes the total value of the firm, equity and debt together. A critical determinant of the optimal debt level is the degree of operating risk inherent in the firm's commercial strategy.

The effect of personal taxes may negate some of the benefit of tax deductibility of interest to the firm. Motives for borrowing other than tax benefits include exploiting the favorable effect of financial leverage and reducing total financing costs by using debt supplied by financial intermediaries.

Sample Problem

The Osgood Company has assets of $4 million that are expected to generate $800,000 next year before interest and taxes.

1. Assume that Osgood's assets could be financed in one of three ways:

Policy	Debt (percent)	Equity (percent)
A	0	100
B	20	80
C	50	50

Assume that debt requires an interest rate of 10 percent, that equity has a market price of $20 per share, that market value of equity and book value are equal under each of the alternatives, and that the firm's tax rate is 50 percent. What will be the expected earnings per share and return on equity under each of these plans at next year's expected level of EBIT?

2. In a bad year, Osgood's EBIT may fall as low as $400,000, and in a good year, EBIT may rise to $1,000,000. Calculate the expected earnings per share and return on equity for the high and low EBIT for the financing plans discussed in part 1 above.

Solution

1. This problem can be approached by constructing tables similar to 18-1 and 18-2.

	Policy (Thousands of Dollars)		
	A	B	C
Assets	$4,000	$4,000	$4,000
Debt	0	800	2,000
Equity	4,000	3,200	2,000
Leverage ratio (percent of debt)	0	20	50
EBIT	800	800	800
Interest @ 10 percent	0	80	200
Profit before taxes	800	720	600
Taxes @ 50 percent	400	360	300
Profit after taxes	400	360	300
Shares (thousands)	200	160	100
Earnings per share (EPS)	$ 2.00	$ 2.25	$ 3.00
Return on equity (ROE, percent)	10	11.25	15

Osgood's assets and EBIT are not affected by the choice of a financing plan and will be the same under either plan. Policy *A* is 100 percent equity financed so debt will, of course, equal 0 and equity will equal $4 million. Since there is no debt in Policy *A*, there will be no interest expense associated with Policy *A*. The number of shares of stock outstanding for Policy *A* is 200,000 shares (the amount of equity, $4 million, divided by the market price per share, $20). Note that equity here refers to the initial equity and not additions to equity through retained earnings. EPS under *A* is $2.00 and the return on equity equals 10 percent. Policy *B*, 20 percent debt, has debt of $800,000 ($4 million times 20 percent) and equity of $3,200,000. Interest expense is $80,000, reducing profit before taxes to $720,000. The number of shares outstanding in this plan equals 160,000, resulting in EPS of $2.25 and ROE of 11.25 percent. For Policy *C*, debt and equity equal $2,000,000 each, resulting in $3.00 EPS and ROE of 15 percent.

2. The approach here is the same as in part 1 above, using the different EBIT levels.

	State of the World (Thousands of Dollars)	
	Bad	Good
Policy *A*, 0 percent debt		
EBIT	$ 400	$1,000
Interest @ 10 percent	0	0
Profit before taxes	400	1,000
Taxes @ 50 percent	200	500
Profit after taxes	200	500
Shares (thousands)	200	200
EPS	$1.00	$2.50
ROE (percent)	5	12.5
Policy *B*, 20 percent debt		
EBIT	400	1,000
Interest @ 10 percent	80	80
Profit before taxes	320	920
Taxes @ 50 percent	160	460
Profit after taxes	160	460
Shares (thousands)	160	160
EPS	$1.00	$2.88
ROE (percent)	5	14.4
Policy *C*, 50 percent debt		
EBIT	400	1,000
Interest @ 10 percent	200	200
Profit before taxes	200	800
Taxes @ 50 percent	100	400
Profit after taxes	100	400
Shares (thousands)	100	100
EPS	$1.00	$4.00
ROE (percent)	5	20

Note that if the state of the world is "bad," EPS and ROE are the same under all three financing alternatives. This result occurs because, in state "bad," Osgood's operating earnings are $0.10 per dollar of assets ($400,000 on $4 million assets), exactly the same as the interest rate on debt funds. Since the percentage rate of operating earnings is equal to the rate of interest, the use of leverage does not raise EPS or ROE.

Questions

1. Distinguish financial leverage from operating leverage.
2. How does financial leverage affect earnings after taxes, earnings per share, and percentage return on equity?
3. How does financial leverage affect the variability of return?

4. Why does the presence of financial leverage result in lower earnings per share and return on equity when EBIT falls to low levels?

5. Why is earnings per share unsuitable as a criterion for financing decisions?

6. Why does the use of earnings per share as a criterion for financing decisions result in a bias toward the use of debt?

7. Distinguish between accounting return on equity and return to shareholders. Can you think of an action that increases return on equity but simultaneously reduces return to shareholders?

8. What is the cost of debt funds? Of equity funds? How are the costs of debt and equity funds related for a given firm?

9. Discuss the use of cost as a criterion for financing decisions.

10. In choosing between debt and equity, how should the relationship between the market value and the book value of a firm's stock be taken into account?

11. How does market value as a criterion deal with the risk/return tradeoff in financing decisions?

12. How do financing decisions affect the division of EBIT among its various claimants?

13. What effect does interest deductibility have on the shares of EBIT going to the various claimants?

14. How can the use of debt increase the value of the firm?

15. If interest were not tax-deductible, what advantage would there be in using debt?

16. How is a firm's optimal debt/equity ratio related to its operating risk?

Problems

1. Mr. Steven Lock, President of Lock Enterprises, had recently attended a seminar on the benefits of financial leverage. Lock Enterprises has assets of $2 million financed entirely with 100,000 shares of common stock currently selling at $20 per share. Mr. Lock is considering retiring some of the stock with borrowed funds, which he can obtain at an interest rate of 10 percent. He expects the company to earn $440,000 next year before interest and taxes. The company's tax rate is 50 percent.

   (a) What will be expected earnings per share (EPS) and return on equity (ROE) at next year's expected level of EBIT?

   (b) What would be the effect of increased leverage on expected EPS and ROE? Why?

   (c) Mr. Lock is considering two alternative leverage ratios, 25 percent debt and 50 percent debt (percent debt to total assets). Calculate expected EPS and ROE for each of these debt ratios at next year's expected EBIT.

(d) Mr. Lock thought that, in a bad year, Lock Enterprises' EBIT could fall as low as $100,000, and in a good year could rise as high as $750,000. He wondered what effect this might have at the leverage ratios he was considering. Calculate expected EPS and ROE at the low and high EBIT levels for debt ratios of 0 percent, 25 percent, and 50 percent, and compare the results with those of part c.

2. You have just inherited $10,000 from a relative and are considering the following alternatives for investing it: Bonds at a certain 7 percent return. Stocks at an expected return of 13 percent, with a .50 probability of return of 2 percent and .50 probability of 24 percent. Your brother-in-law's company at an expected return of 20 percent, with a .5 probability of −10 percent and .50 probability of 50 percent.

(a) Calculate the dollar return for each outcome for each alternative.

(b) Calculate the possible dollar returns and the percentage expected return for a combination of one-half bonds and one-half stock.

(c) Calculate the possible dollar returns and the percentage expected return for a combination of one-half bonds and one-half in your brother-in-law's company.

(d) What can you say about the risk/return tradeoff?

3. Assume that a firm is considering expanding assets by $5 million and has determined that it can finance the expansion either through a bond issue carrying a 10 percent interest rate or through a new issue of common stock which can be sold to net the company $20 per share. The firm currently has 400,000 shares of stock outstanding and $6 million of bonds with an 8 percent coupon. The tax rate is 48 percent.

(a) Calculate the EPS for each alternative at EBIT levels of $1 million, $2 million, $3 million, and $4 million.

(b) What can be said from this analysis regarding the choice between bonds and stock?

4. Suppose that in Problem 3 the probabilities of the different EBIT levels are as follows:

EBIT (Millions of Dollars)	Probability
1	.15
2	.35
3	.35
4	.15

(a) Calculate the expected value and standard deviation of earnings per share (EPS) for each of the two alternative financing plans.

(b) What can be said about the risk/return tradeoff?

5. Assume that an individual has $1,000 to invest and is faced with two potential investments. She could invest in a portfolio of common stocks with the three possible outcomes shown below or she could buy risk-free United States Treasury Bills yielding 6 percent. Assuming that interest is tax-deductible, all returns are fully taxable as ordinary income (and all losses result in tax credits of 50 percent), and the marginal tax rate is 50 percent, calculate the terminal value (after 1 year) of the $1,000 investment for three possible investment strategies: Levering the investment through borrowing $500 at 8 percent and investing $1,500 in the stock portfolio. Investing the $1,000 in the stock portfolio. Investing $500 in the stock portfolio and $500 in risk-free United States Treasury Bills.

Possible Portfolio Outcomes	Probability	Return
Good	.25	+25%
Normal	.50	+10%
Bad	.25	− 5%

6. Utilize the information in Problem 5 to calculate the expected value and standard deviation of the terminal value of the portfolio for each of the three degrees of leverage. What can be said about the risk/return tradeoff?

7. Assume that a firm has a market value of $10 million if financed entirely with equity. Calculate the value of the firm if $1 million, $3 million, and $5 million in debt is used to replace an equal amount of equity. Assume a tax rate of 48 percent and ignore the effects of personal taxes. Would the value of the firm continue to increase as more debt is used to replace equity? Why or why not?

8. The A. M. Thomas Corporation is planning to raise $6 million for financing plant additions and working capital. Two alternative financing plans are available to the firm: a new issue of common stock that can be sold to net $30 per share or a bond issue carrying a 7 percent interest rate. Last year's balance sheet and income statements for Thomas Corporation are summarized below. If the economy experiences continued growth next year, the plant addition is expected to increase sales by 20 percent. If the economy slows down, a 15 percent decrease in sales will be experienced. Variable costs are expected to remain at 60 percent of sales and fixed costs are expected to increase by $800,000.

A. M. Thomas Corporation
Balance Sheet
December 31, 1979
(Thousands of Dollars)

Current assets	$ 50,000	Current liabilities	$ 45,000
Net plant and equipment	80,000	Long-term debt	2,000
Other	1,000	Total liabilities	47,000
		Equity:	
		500,000 shares @ $2 par	1,000
		additional paid in capital	42,000
		retained earnings	41,000
Total assets	$131,000	Total liabilities and equity	$131,000

Income Statement
Year-End December 31, 1979
(Thousands of Dollars)

Sales	$20,000
Variable operating expenses	12,000
Fixed operating expenses	5,000
EBIT	3,000
Interest	100
Profit before tax	2,900
Tax @ 50 percent	1,450
Profit after tax	1,450
EPS	$2.90
ROE (percent)	1.73

(a) Calculate the EPS and ROE for each financing alternative at the sales levels expected under continued economic growth and under an economic slowdown. Assume the interest expense on the existing debt will remain at $100,000.

(b) Thomas' staff economist has provided the following forecast for next year's economy:

Outcome	Probability
Continued growth	.75
Slow down	.25

Using this information, calculate the expected value and standard deviation of EPS for each of the two alternative financing plans.

(*Note:* Procedures for calculating expected values and standard deviations can be found in Appendix A at the end of the book.)
9. Suppose that in Problem 8, the Thomas Corporation's variable costs were 40 percent of sales instead of 60 percent and that fixed costs were $9,000,000 instead of $5,000,000 as shown in the income statement below:

A. M. Thomas Corporation	
Income Statement	
Year-End December 31, 1979	
(Thousands of Dollars)	
Sales	$20,000
Variable operating expenses	8,000
Fixed operating expenses	9,000
EBIT	3,000
Interest	100
Profit before tax	2,900
Tax @ 50 percent	1,450
Profit after tax	1,450
EPS	$2.90
ROE (percent)	1.73

What can you say about the degree of operating leverage under this cost structure relative to the cost structure in Problem 8? How does this change in the cost structure affect your answers to part (a) in Problem 8? (Assume that variable costs remain at 40 percent of sales and that fixed costs increase by $800,000 with the plant expansion.) What implications do you see with regard to operating leverage and financing decisions?

References

W. Beaver and D. Morse, "What Determines Price-Earnings Ratios," *Financial Analysts Journal,* 65–76 (July–Aug. 1978).

R. A. Brealey, *Security Prices in a Competitive Market.* (Cambridge, Mass.: MIT Press, 1971).

M. J. Brennan and E. F. Schwartz, "Corporate Income Taxes, Valuation and the Problem of Optimal Capital Structure," *Journal of Business* **51,** 103–114 (Jan. 1978).

D. C. Dearborn and R. I. Levin, "Error Visibility as a Factor in Executive Performance," *Southern Journal of Business* **6,** 65–70 (Jan. 1972).

T. R. Dyckman, D. H. Downes, and Robert D. Magee, *Efficient Markets and Accounting—A Critical Analysis* (Englewood Cliffs, N.J.: Prentice-Hall, 1975).

E. F. Fama, "Efficient Capital Markets: A Review of Theory and Empirical Work," *Journal of Finance* **25,** 383–417 (May 1970).

R. D. Gritta, "The Effect of Financial Leverage on Air Carrier Earnings: A Break-Even Analysis," *Financial Management* **8,** 53–60 (Summer 1979).

C. W. Haley and L. D. Schall, *The Theory of Financial Decisions* (New York: McGraw-Hill, 1973).

R. S. Hamada, "Portfolio Analysis, Market Equilibrium and Corporation Finance," *Journal of Finance* **24,** 13–31 (Mar. 1969).

R. A. Haugen and L. W. Senbet, "The Insignificance of Bankruptcy Costs to the Theory of Optimal Capital Structure," *Journal of Finance* **33,** 383–394 (May 1978).

R. C. Higgins and L. D. Schall, "Corporate Bankruptcy and Conglomerate Merger," *Journal of Finance* **30,** 93–114 (Mar. 1975).

H. Hong, "Inflation and the Market Value of the Firm: Theory and Tests," *Journal of Finance* **32,** 1031–1048 (Sept. 1977).

M. Jensen and W. Meckling, "Theory of the Firm: Managerial Behavior, Agency Costs, and Ownership Structure," *Journal of Financial Economics* **2,** 305–360 (October 1976).

E. H. Kim, "A Mean-Variance Theory of Optimal Financial Structure and Corporate Debt Capacity," *Journal of Finance* **33,** 45–64 (Mar. 1978).

E. H. Kim, W. G. Lewellen, and J. J. McConnell "Financial Leverage Clienteles: Theory and Evidence," *Journal of Financial Economics,* forthcoming.

R. E. Krainer, "Interest Rates, Leverage and Investor Rationality," *Journal of Financial and Quantitative Analysis* **12,** 1–16 (Mar. 1977).

A. Kraus and R. Litzenberger, "A State-Preference Model of Optimal Financial Leverage," *Journal of Finance* **28,** 911–922 (Sept. 1973).

M. H. Miller, "Debt and Taxes," *Journal of Finance* **32,** 261–276 (May 1977).

F. Modigliani and M. H. Miller, "Corporate Income Taxes and the Cost of Capital: A Correction," *American Economic Review* **53,** 433–443 (June 1963).

F. Modigliani and M. H. Miller, "The Cost of Capital, Corporation Finance, and the Theory of Investment," *American Economic Review* **48,** 261–297 (July 1958).

R. C. Moyer, "Forecasting Financial Failure: A Reexamination," *Financial Management* **6,** 9–17 (Spring 1977).

S. C. Myers, "The Determinants of Corporate Debt Capacity," *Journal of Financial Economics* **5,** 147–175 (Nov. 1977).

J. J. Pringle, "Price/Earnings Ratios, Earnings per Share, and Financial Management," *Financial Management* **2,** 34–40 (Spring 1973).

J. H. Scott, Jr., "Bankruptcy, Secured Debt and Optimal Capital Structure," *Journal of Finance* **32,** 1–20 (Mar. 1977).

J. H. Scott, Jr., "A Theory of Optimal Capital Structure," *Bell Journal of Economics* **7,** 33–54 (Spring 1976).

J. H. Scott, Jr., "On the Theory of Conglomerate Mergers," *Journal of Finance* **32,** 1235–1250 (Sept. 1977).

J. E. Stiglitz, "A Re-examination of the Modigliani-Miller Theorem," *American Economic Review* **59,** 784–793 (Dec. 1969).

J. E. Stiglitz, "Some Aspects of the Pure Theory of Corporate Finance: Bankruptcies and Take-overs," *Bell Journal of Economics and Management Science* **3,** 458–482 (Autumn 1972).

G. M. Von Furstenberg and B. G. Malkiel, "Financial Analysis in an Inflationary Environment," *Journal of Finance* **32,** 575–588 (May 1977).

J. Warner, "Bankruptcy Costs: Some Evidence," *Journal of Finance* **32,** 337–348 (May 1977).

Determining the Level of Debt

19

Financial Leverage and Investment Policy
Analyzing Alternative Financing Plans
Defining Debt Capacity
Analyzing Cash Flows
Allowing for Reserve Borrowing Capacity
Choosing the Appropriate Debt Policy

In Chapter 18, we analyzed the effect of financial leverage on return and risk. We concluded that leverage has costs as well as benefits and we therefore found ourselves face to face with the basic question of the tradeoff between risk and return. We turned to valuation as a conceptual framework for resolving the tradeoff question and found that it provided some useful insights and guidance. In particular, we identified certain factors as relevant to the leverage decision and eliminated some that are not. However, the guidance that we found was entirely qualitative, and we did not develop an approach to actually determining how much debt a firm should use.

Now it is time to apply the theory. Our problem is to determine the appropriate mix of debt and equity that the firm should use. Let us keep in mind the motives for using debt. Some firms may find debt advantageous because of its tax benefits. Others may use debt to "lever up" and thereby increase prospective returns to shareholders, recognizing that the price is increased risk. Still others may find debt obtained via financial intermediaries such as banks a less expensive and more convenient way to satisfy investment requirements. Some firms do not have access to equity markets, and, for them, debt is the only available source of outside capital. Whatever the motive, users of debt need a way to decide how much to use.

Financial Leverage and Investment Policy

Optimal Financial Leverage as a Function of Operating Risk

We found in our earlier discussions that a firm's total risk, as measured by variability of earnings, depends partly on its operating risk and partly on the amount of financial leverage used. Operating risk can be measured in terms of variability of earnings before interest and taxes (EBIT). For any given operating risk, an increase in financial leverage increases the variability of net earnings. We were led to the conclusion that the appropriate degree of financial leverage for a firm depends on its operating risk. The higher the operating risk, the less debt the firm should use. The same reasoning applies to individuals: The more variable or uncertain the income, the more risky it is to use debt.

Understanding the relation between leverage and variability still does not tell us how much leverage to use. At what point do the terms of the risk/return tradeoff become unfavorable? To help resolve this question, we turned in Chapter 18 to our general criterion of value-maximization. Since investors are risk-averse, value depends on both expected return and risk. Hence, in principle, we resolve the risk/return tradeoff by pushing leverage to the point where the value of the firm is maximized, but no farther.

We found that the optimal debt ratio involves a tradeoff of the benefits of debt (due to deductibility of interest, lower financing cost, and leverage effects) against the expected costs of financial distress and reduced commercial flexibility. Here we are using the term *financial distress* to include a broad spectrum of problems ranging from relatively minor liquidity shortages all the way to the extreme case, bankruptcy. All these problems are assumed to involve some costs to the firm—the more serious the problem, the higher the cost. Such costs are borne by the shareholders up to the full amount of their investment, and above that point, by creditors. When we refer to the expected cost of financial distress, we mean the magnitude of the cost times the likelihood (probability) of its being incurred.

Using valuation as a framework clarifies the relationship between leverage and operating risk. At zero leverage, we start with some probability of encountering financial distress of one form or another. Increasing leverage increases that probability. There comes a point where the expected costs of financial distress begin to outweigh the benefits. At that point, the debt ratio is optimal. We can see that the extent to which leverage should be used depends on how high the firm's operating risk was to begin with.

The Determinants of Operating Risk

At this point, we should review briefly the determinants of a firm's operating risk. As we noted above, operating risk can be thought of in terms of variability of EBIT. In considering variability of EBIT, it is useful to discuss revenues and expenses separately. Clearly, one major determinant of operating risk is variability of sales revenue. In general, variability of sales depends on the nature of the business, specifically on industry characteristics, effectiveness of marketing efforts, countermoves by competitors, technological developments, shifts in consumer preferences, and similar factors. In addition to industry and company factors, general economic conditions play a part.

Strictly speaking, *predictability* is more important than variability. A manufacturer of garden tools may experience a highly seasonal sales pattern, but a good part of the variability may be predictable. A toy manufacturer also may experience seasonality, but sales may be much more uncertain because of the fadishness of toys. Although individual products may be highly variable, overall sales variability will depend on the degree of diversification of the firm's investments.

Variability of EBIT also depends on variability of operating expenses. One important factor is the firm's degree of *operating leverage*, determined by the ratio of fixed operating expense to variable expense.

A firm with a high proportion of fixed operating expense is said to have a high degree of operating leverage. High operating leverage is good when revenues are rising and bad when they are falling. The degree of operating leverage measures the sensitivity of operating profit to changes in revenues.

Variations in expenses due to factors other than volume changes also contribute to variability of EBIT. Increases in supply prices of materials or labor represent factors of this sort.

A final factor that influences the variability of EBIT is asset structure. We discussed variability of operating revenues above. The firm also may derive revenues from such nonoperating sources as marketable securities held for liquidity purposes. The proportion of total revenues derived from relatively stable nonoperating sources would affect the overall variability of EBIT.

Determining the Appropriate Financial Leverage for a Given Investment Policy

Theory tells us that the optimal debt ratio for a firm depends on its operating risk. This conclusion leads us to an important general proposition—that the appropriate debt ratio for a firm depends on the nature of its business. In other words, *the financing mix should be tailored to the commercial strategy.*

Therefore, in this chapter, we will take the firm's investment policy as given. The question is: Given this set of investments, what is the appropriate mix of debt and equity for financing them? Financial theory talks in terms of an optimum. The theory is precise in concept and gives valuable qualitative guidance, but it is quite difficult to apply quantitatively. To speak of an optimum in practice overstates our capabilities to find it. It seems more realistic to speak of an appropriate debt ratio.

In this chapter, we focus only on the appropriate mix of debt and equity. We defer a discussion of *maturity* structure, that is, the appropriate mix of long-term versus short-term debt, to the next chapter. For now, we will draw no distinction between long-term and short-term debt; in order to determine the appropriate debt ratio, we will view all debt as the same.

Analyzing Alternative Financing Plans

Suppose a firm has decided to raise a given amount of money by issuing either common stock or bonds. How does it make the choice? We know from our earlier discussion that market value is the appropriate decision criterion. However, we also must examine carefully the impact of alternative financing plans on earnings and other key indicators such as interest coverage. Let us begin with an analysis of EPS.

EBIT/EPS Analysis

Given the importance of earnings per share (EPS) as a measure of firm performance, analysis of the impact of financing alternatives on EPS is an important first step. Since earnings before interest and taxes (EBIT) is uncertain, it is useful to examine this impact at different levels of EBIT. One technique for doing so is to construct an EBIT/EPS chart. We developed the basics of EBIT/EPS analysis earlier, in Tables 18-1 through 18-4. Now we will apply the approach to a specific financing alternative.

Consider a firm that has decided to finance a $10 million expansion of its manufacturing facilities by issuing either common stock or bonds. Currently, the firm's stock is selling at $20 per share and it has 2.5 million shares outstanding. Ignoring issue costs, the firm would have to issue 500,000 new shares if it raises the needed funds via a stock issue.

The bond alternative involves a 20 year issue at 8 percent interest. Sinking fund payments of $350,000 are required each year to retire $6.65 million by the end of the nineteenth year, with the final $3.35 million due at the end of the twentieth year.

Let us assume that EBIT in the upcoming year is expected to be $6 million, including the earnings from the expanded facilities. However, EBIT in past years has been highly variable, and could turn out to be considerably above or below the most likely level. Following the procedure in Table 18-1, we can calculate EPS at an EBIT of $6 million as in Table 19-1. In this table, we have introduced a new term, *uncommitted* earnings, that is, earnings remaining after the required sinking fund payment of $350,000. Uncommitted earnings (UEPS) are available for payment of dividends and reinvestment to further expand facilities.

Our objective is a chart that shows the behavior of EPS in response to variations in EBIT. A moment's reflection reveals that EPS is a linear function of EBIT. We have one point on each EBIT/EPS line from Table 19-1. One more is all we need. Often, it is convenient to pick as the second point the intercept of the EPS line and the EBIT axis, or the EBIT level to produce EPS of zero. For the stock plan, EPS of zero requires EBIT = 0. For the bond plan, EBIT of $800,000 is required to cover interest. Now we have two points, and can plot the graphs in Figure 19-1.

From the figure, we see that the break-even EBIT is just under $5 million (we will calculate it exactly below). At that point, EPS is equal under the two plans. If EBIT turns out to be above $5 million, EPS will be higher under the bond plan. If below about $5 million, the stock plan produces higher EPS. The expected EBIT level of $6 million is above the break-even point. Note that break-even for uncommitted EPS is much higher at an EBIT of $9 million. Note also that the lines for the bond

Table 19-1 EPS at the Expected Level of
EBIT (Thousands)

	Stock Plan	Bond Plan
EBIT	$6,000	$6,000
Interest	—	$ 800
Profit before taxes	$6,000	$5,200
Tax @ 50 percent	$3,000	$2,600
Profit after taxes	$3,000	$2,600
Shares	3,000	2,500
EPS	$ 1.00	$ 1.04
Sinking fund	—	$ 350
Uncommitted earnings	$3,000	$2,250
Uncommitted EPS (UEPS)	$ 1.00	$ 0.90

plan carry the notation "first year." Since a sinking fund payment is made each year, interest due will decline slightly each year and the bond line will shift slightly to the left.

Here we see in graphic form the effects of leverage that we found earlier. The slope of the bond line is steeper than that of the stock line, indicating that, with leverage, EPS is more sensitive to changes in EBIT. The steeper slope is advantageous if EBIT rises, and disadvantageous if it falls.

Figure 19-1 EBIT/EPS Chart

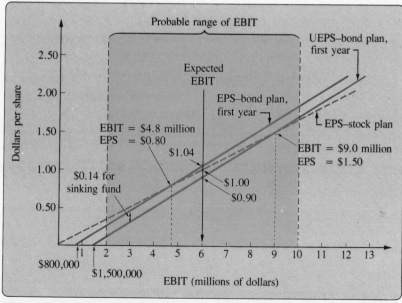

We might ask here which earnings line in Figure 19-1 is the relevant one, the EPS line or the UEPS line? Which should we use in making a decision? Both are relevant, and both should be used, for each answers a different question.

In our example above, we assumed for simplicity that the firm had no other debt outstanding. Often, this is not the case. Where other debt is outstanding, its interest and sinking fund payments, if any, must be included. The old interest and sinking fund payments are added to the new and the total is used to calculate the points necessary to plot the graphs. Note that old interest and sinking fund payments are made under both the stock financing and the bond financing alternatives now under consideration.

We also assumed that the firm had no preferred stock outstanding. The term *earnings per share* is interpreted as *earnings available to common stock* per share. This means that in calculating EPS, we subtract any preferred dividend requirement before dividing by the number of shares.

Calculating Break-Even Points

Sometimes it is useful to calculate EPS and UEPS break-even points algebraically. We know that EPS (or UEPS) is equal under the two plans at break-even. What we need is an expression for EPS under each plan. We set the expressions equal and solve for EBIT, as follows:

EPS Break-Even

$$\underset{EPS\text{–}Bond\ Plan}{\frac{(\text{EBIT} - I)(1 - T)}{N_\text{B}}} = \underset{EPS\text{–}Stock\ Plan}{\frac{\text{EBIT}(1 - T)}{N_\text{S}}} \tag{1}$$

UEPS Break-Even

$$\underset{UEPS\text{–}Bond\ Plan}{\frac{(\text{EBIT} - I)(1 - T) - SF}{N_\text{B}}} = \underset{UEPS\text{–}Stock\ Plan}{\frac{\text{EBIT}(1 - T)}{N_\text{S}}} \tag{2}$$

In the expressions above, N_B and N_S are the numbers of shares of stock outstanding under the bond and stock plans, respectively, SF is the sinking fund payment, I is the interest payment, and T is the tax rate.

For our example, using a 50 percent tax rate, we calculate EPS break-even as

$$\frac{(\text{EBIT} - 800,000)(1 - 0.5)}{2,500,000} = \frac{\text{EBIT}(1 - 0.5)}{3,000,000}$$

Solving for EBIT, we find the break-even point to be at EBIT = $4.8 million. At that point, EPS is $0.80 under both plans.

For UEPS, we have

$$\frac{(\text{EBIT} - 800,000)(1 - 0.5) - 350,000}{2,500,000} = \frac{\text{EBIT}(1 - 0.5)}{3,000,000}$$

Solving, we get EBIT = $9 million, at which point UEPS is $1.50 under both plans.

We should note again that if the firm had had other debt issues outstanding, interest and principal (sinking fund) payments on those issues should be considered in calculating break-even points. In calculating EPS break-even, old interest payments would appear on both sides of expression (1). Likewise, old sinking fund payments would appear on both sides of expression (2). If preferred stock were outstanding, its dividend (and sinking fund, if any) requirements would be subtracted before dividing by N_B and N_S.

Coverage Ratios

Another useful analytical technique for comparing financing alternatives is to calculate *coverage ratios*. The *interest coverage* ratio is the number of times interest payments are covered by EBIT, that is, EBIT divided by pretax interest. We also can calculate the coverage of sinking fund payments. For the bond alternative we have been considering, we calculate coverage as in Table 19-2.

Table 19-2 Coverage Ratios—Bond Plan

Coverage	Pretax Burden	Times Covered at EBIT = $6,000,000
Interest $\dfrac{\text{EBIT}}{I}$	$ 800,000	7.5
Interest plus sinking fund $\dfrac{\text{EBIT}}{I + (SF/0.5)}$	$1,500,000	4.0

Note that to calculate coverage of interest plus sinking fund, the latter must be converted to a pretax basis by dividing by $(1 - T)$. Thus, to make a sinking fund payment of $350,000 requires EBIT of $700,000, which when added to the interest requirement gives a total burden to be covered of $1,500,000. As before, any interest and sinking fund payments on old bonds should be included.

Suppose the firm wished to pay a dividend on its common stock of $0.70 per share. We could calculate a third coverage ratio, the number of times that EBIT covers both debt service and dividend requirements.

On 2.5 million shares, the total dividend would be 2.5 million $\times$ \$0.70 = \$1.75 million, or \$3.5 million on a pretax basis. Added to the \$1.5 million for debt service, we would have a total of \$5 million, which would be covered 1.2 times by EBIT of \$6 million. In a similar manner, we could calculate coverage of preferred dividends if applicable.

What do coverage ratios tell us? They provide a measure of the safety of the interest payment or of whatever specific commitment is being considered. The higher the coverage, the more secure the payment. Thus, an interest coverage ratio of 7.5 tells us that EBIT must fall well short of its expected level of \$6 million before the interest payment is in jeopardy.

The interest coverage ratio simply measures the size of the interest payment relative to EBIT. The reciprocal of this ratio, $I/$EBIT, measures the proportion of EBIT devoted to interest. In this case, we then have \$800,000/\$6,000,000 = 0.13, which tells us that 13 percent of the firm's EBIT must go to interest. Here we have a measure of the firm's debt ratio in flow terms, which may give a more accurate representation of leverage than do debt ratios calculated from balance sheet relationships. One obvious drawback of viewing $I/$EBIT as a measure of leverage is that EBIT often is highly variable, and we get a different leverage ratio for each value of EBIT.

The variability of EBIT points up a major shortcoming of coverage ratios in general. Which EBIT do we use to calculate coverage? In Table 19-2, we calculated coverage at the expected (most likely) level of EBIT. To draw really meaningful conclusions regarding the safety of various payments that the firm is committed to make would require some knowledge of the likelihood of a decline in EBIT to levels at which the payments are threatened. We can calculate coverage at several different levels of EBIT. If we could construct a probability distribution over all possible values of EBIT, we then would have a better feel for the adequacy of various coverage levels.

Setting Debt Policy

Even if we had a probability distribution over all possible EBIT levels, could we say how much coverage is enough? Can we examine the EBIT/EPS chart in Figure 19-1 and decide which plan is best? We cannot, because to say that one plan is "best" requires an unambiguous criterion on which to make the comparison. EBIT/EPS analysis and coverage ratios are very useful in making explicit the impact of leverage on EPS and on the firm's ability to meet its commitments at various levels of EBIT. However, we still face the risk/return tradeoff: Should we accept greater risk in order to gain a higher expected return?

One approach to the problem of setting debt policy is to rely on industry standards. ABC Corporation might calculate the equity or debt ratios for other firms in its industry and set its own ratio equal to the industry average. The logic of the use of industry standards is that debt ratios appropriate for other firms in a similar line of business should be appropriate for ABC Corporation as well. Also, this approach ensures that ABC appears to lenders and investors to be right in line with industry averages.

To illustrate, suppose ABC Corporation were an integrated oil company. ABC management might gather the data listed in Table 19-3. The difficulty with the use of industry standards in this way is that it relies on the judgment of others. Can we be sure that the managements of the other firms in the industry will not err? Also, in many cases, there may be no well-defined industry, that is, no firms whose structure and commercial strategy are similar enough to provide a good comparison. Industry standards, when available, certainly provide a useful benchmark. If a firm is out of line, it should know the reasons why and be satisfied that they are good reasons. But a comparison with industry standards should be the final step, not the beginning point in the analysis.

Table 19-3 Ratio of Equity to Total Assets, Selected Oil Companies, December 31, 1978

	Total Assets (Millions)	Stockholders Equity (Millions)	Equity Ratio (Percent)
Exxon	$41,531	$20,229	48.7
Mobil Oil	22,611	8,910	39.4
Texaco	20,249	9,463	46.7
Standard Oil of California	16,761	8,231	49.1
Gulf Oil	15,036	7,757	51.6
Standard Oil (Indiana)	14,109	7,146	50.6
			Average 47.7

Source: From *Fortune* (May 1979). Reprinted by permission.

Another approach to setting debt policy is to seek the opinion of lenders and investment bankers. ABC Corporation might ask the advice of investment banking firms who regularly participate in marketing debt issues, and of institutional buyers of debt issues such as insurance companies. Commercial banks may provide useful advice. Investment rating services such as Moody's and Standard and Poor's also might be helpful. A firm whose debt already has been rated by such services might be able to draw some inferences from the ratings themselves. If more recent debt issues were rated lower than older issues, indicating a rise in risk, the firm might view this trend as an indication of having pushed its debt far enough.

The opinions of prospective lenders are likely to be very useful, but to rely on them too heavily runs the risk of answering the wrong question. The firm may learn how much the lenders would like to lend, or the maximum that the lenders would be willing to lend. But just because lenders are willing to lend does not mean that the firm should take them up on it. Lenders err also—many firms have encountered serious difficulties because of using too much debt, with once-willing lenders a party to the arrangement. The responsibility for debt policy belongs to management, and the central question is how much debt *should* be used, not how much the lenders are willing to lend.[1]

Besides, the notion that there is some absolute dollar ceiling on the amount that lenders will lend is vague. In practice, such a ceiling may exist. In principle, the amount that lenders will lend should depend on the interest rate that the firm is prepared to pay. By paying a sufficiently high rate, a firm should be able to induce lenders to lend well beyond the debt ratio that is optimal for shareholders.

Defining Debt Capacity

Sometimes it is useful to speak of a firm's *debt capacity*. In view of the discussion above, debt capacity should be defined as the optimal amount of debt from the standpoint of shareholders, which is the amount of debt the firm *should use,* and not as the maximum that lenders will lend. Defining debt capacity as optimal debt provides a useful framework for analyzing policy options. For example, sometimes it is suggested that the use of leases to finance assets increases the firm's total debt capacity because the leases do not appear on the balance sheet. Here debt capacity refers to the willingness of lenders to lend. Even if lenders were fooled by the leases, which is doubtful, should the firm borrow more just because the lenders are willing? In many cases, it should not. If we analyze the leasing decision in the context of the theory of optimal financial leverage, we will conclude that leases are quite similar to debt. Therefore, the use of leases does not increase the optimal debt ratio—the total that the firm should use. Hence, by viewing debt capacity and optimal debt as one and the same, we are able to analyze the leasing decision more effectively.

---

1. For theoretical proof that the optimal debt level for shareholders is less than the maximum amount of debt the financial markets will supply, see E. H. Kim, "A Mean-Variance Theory of Optimal Financial Structure and Corporate Debt Capacity," *Journal of Finance* **33**, 45–64 (Mar. 1978).

How do we determine a firm's debt capacity? To do so requires a method of evaluating the effect of different debt policies on the firm's risk of financial distress. To simplify matters, let us ignore milder financial difficulties for the moment and consider only bankruptcy. The principal factor in avoiding bankruptcy is maintaining the ability to meet contractual interest and principal payments. Hence, it is more useful to view debt capacity in terms of cash flows than in terms of balance sheet ratios of debt to equity. This point becomes all the more clear when we consider that just knowing the principal amount of debt tells us nothing about the repayment schedule and the firm's ability to meet it.

For example, suppose we see that a firm has $1 million in long-term debt outstanding and an equity base of $4 million. The debt/equity ratio is 0.25, not an alarming figure at first glance. But the principal may be due in 2 years, or in 20 years. Clearly, maturity makes a big difference in the firm's ability to meet the payments.

Suppose we find that repayment is to be made over 4 years. We now know a good deal more than before, but not everything we need. Consider the repayment schedules listed in Table 19-4, assuming interest at 8 percent. From this table, we see that even knowing the amount of debt and the maturity does not tell us whether the firm can meet the payments. The firm's ability to do so depends on the total payments required, interest and principal, in relation to the cash flow available to meet them. In Table 19-4, we see only three of an infinite number of possible repayment schedules. It is clear that the cash flow required to service a given amount of debt can cover a wide range. Conversely, a given cash flow can service widely varying principal amounts of debt, depending on the repayment schedule.

Table 19-4 Alternative Repayment Schedules, $1 Million over 4 Years @ 8 Percent (Thousands of Dollars)

Year	A, Principal at Maturity			B, Equal Annual Payments			C, Principal in Equal Installments		
	Interest	Principal	Total	Interest	Principal	Total	Interest	Principal	Total
1	80	—	80	80	222	302	80	250	330
2	80	—	80	62	240	302	60	250	310
3	80	—	80	43	259	302	40	250	290
4	80	1,000	1,080	22	280	302	20	250	270

The repayment schedule on the firm's debt is only half of the picture. We also must examine the firm's ability to meet the schedule. Normally, principal and interest payments are met out of cash flows from operations. During emergencies, however, other sources are available. Marketable securities held for liquidity purposes might be sold and cash drawn down. Other current assets such as inventories and receivables might be reduced, and current liabilities increased. Certain discretionary expenditures might be reduced or postponed, such as those for capital improvements, dividends, or research and development. It is clear that to examine properly the impact of alternate debt policies on the risk of bankruptcy requires a careful analysis of how the firm's cash flows might be affected by adverse developments in the future. The best way to explain how such an analysis works is to examine a specific example of cash flow analysis. Because many variables are involved, cash flow projections can be tedious, but the procedures are essential to good financial planning.

In the following section, the effects of alternative debt policies on the risk of bankruptcy are analyzed in terms of specific numbers. The risk of bankruptcy, however, is not the only consideration in setting debt policy. The optimum also includes a reserve for contingencies and commercial flexibility. We will consider these latter factors in a separate section following the basic cash flow analysis.

Analyzing Cash Flows

To illustrate the approach of using cash flow analysis to determine debt capacity, let us consider a specific situation in detail. The time is late 1979. Omega Manufacturing Corporation is planning its financial structure. The question at issue is the appropriate amount of debt that Omega should use in its capital structure. Currently, Omega's ratio of debt to total capital is 20 percent. Omega management must decide whether to continue the present policy, use more debt, or use less debt.

The objective of the analysis is to determine Omega's debt capacity. During good times, meeting contractual obligations usually is no problem. It is when times are bad that difficulties occur. Thus, what we are interested in is Omega's ability to make contractual payments under adverse conditions. The essence of the approach is to analyze cash flow patterns under conditions of recession.

Omega manufactures a variety of industrial products. Its sales are moderately sensitive to the business cycle. During the mid-1970s, Omega had a very good year in 1973, then suffered a decline in sales in the 1974 recession, and experienced a sharp recovery in 1975. Sales and cash flow data for 1972–1975 are as given in Table 19-5. In this table, a point worth noting is that cash declined by $4.9 million in 1975 even though the firm earned a profit of $6.5 million. A significant factor in explaining the cash decline was the large increase in capital outlays in 1974 and 1975 to establish facilities to manufacture a new product.

Table 19-5 Omega Manufacturing Corporation: Actual Cash Flows, 1972–1975 (Millions)

	1972	1973	1974	1975
Sales	$116.6	$121.1	$112.0	$126.5
Profit after taxes	5.8	7.7	6.7	6.5
Sources of funds				
Operations	21.2	23.1	22.4	22.4
Working capital	3.0	(0.6)	3.1	(1.2)
Total sources	24.2	22.5	25.5	21.2
Uses of funds				
Plant and equipment	(6.8)	(8.2)	(13.2)	(14.5)
Taxes	(3.8)	(3.7)	(3.4)	(3.2)
Lease payments	(1.9)	(2.0)	(2.1)	(2.1)
Interest on debt	(2.0)	(1.8)	(1.7)	(1.6)
Principal on debt	(1.4)	(1.4)	(1.4)	(1.4)
Dividends on common stock	(2.8)	(2.8)	(2.8)	(3.0)
Miscellaneous	(0.1)	(0.2)	(0.7)	(0.3)
Total uses	(18.8)	(20.1)	(25.3)	(26.1)
Change in cash balance	5.4	2.4	0.2	(4.9)

Recession Behavior

Omega management did not consider the behavior of company sales during the 1974 recession to be typical. A study of company data back to 1950 revealed that, in previous recessions, sales volume usually declined for 2 years in a row, then recovered in the third year. Total declines ranged from 12 percent to 16 percent. For purposes of establishing debt capacity, management decided to err on the side of conservatism and to assume that the effect of a recession on sales could last a year longer, with recovery only in the fourth year, and that the total decline could reach 20 percent. Thus, the pattern of sales during future recessions was assumed to be as follows:

	Year of Recession			
Year Prior	1	2	3	4
100 percent	90	80	80	100

In prior recessions, prices of some of Omega's products had fallen somewhat, but the declines had not been significant. However, to be conservative, management decided to assume that prices of products would decline by 3 percent and recover in year 4. Prices of all cost elements were assumed to remain constant.

In some cases, an assumption of constant prices for cost elements during a recession may not be appropriate, because prices in general have continued to rise during recent recessions. The objective should be the best possible estimate of all cash flows, revenues as well as expenses, in nominal terms, with the effects of inflation included.

Omega management was now ready to prepare forecasts of the cash flows under recession conditions. It was decided to group cash flows into three categories: operating cash flows, investment cash flows, and financing flows.

Cash Flows from Operations

Using the relatively pessimistic or adverse assumptions regarding sales volume and price discussed above, operating cash flows over a future recession would be those listed in Table 19-6.

Table 19-6   Omega Manufacturing Corporation: Assumptions Regarding Operating Cash Flows under Future Recession Conditions (Millions)

	Year[a] Prior, 0	Recession Year			
		1	2	3	4
Sales at stable prices	$126.5	$113.9	$101.2	$101.2	$126.5
As percent of year 0 sales	100	90	80	80	100
Sales, 3 percent price decline	$126.5	$110.5	$ 98.2	$ 98.2	$126.5
Cash operating expenses[b]	$101.6	$ 90.7	$ 84.4	$ 82.6	$101.6
Net cash inflow from operations	$ 24.9	$ 19.8	$ 13.8	$ 15.6	$ 24.9

[a]The expected figures for 1979 are used as benchmark figures for the hypothetical year 0.
[b]Excludes nonoperating and financial flows discussed later in Tables 19-7 and 19-8.

Investment Cash Flows

Major investment cash flows include capital outlays for plant and equipment and changes in working capital. These cash flows were projected by Omega management to be those listed in Table 19-7 under recession conditions.

During 1977 and 1978, Omega had made exceptionally large capital outlays, a major part of which were attributable to facilities for a new product. During 1980, outlays of $10 million were planned, which management viewed as approximately the normal level to be expected for about 5 years beyond 1979 if business conditions remained normal. However, in a recession, part of such outlays could be deferred. Nonetheless, management considered some parts of the capital budget to be essential and these therefore had to be given higher priority than maintaining the dividend on common stock. These outlays were estimated to be $3.0 million per year. The remaining $7.0 million was viewed as postponable and of lower priority than the dividend. Management's recession plan for plant and equipment outlays therefore was to cut expenditures as rapidly as possible to the irreducible minimum of $3.0 million, and then to restore the budget to $7.0 million in the year of full sales recovery and to the full amount the following year. However, because of the nature of construction and equipment contracts, it was anticipated that there would be a time lag of at least 1 year in implementing the cuts. The final projected plant and equipment budget appears in Table 19-7.

Table 19-7 Omega Manufacturing Corporation: Forecast of Investment Cash Flows under Recession Conditions (Millions)

	Year Prior, 0	Recession Year			
		1	2	3	4
Plant and equipment expenditures	($10.0)	($10.0)	($5.0)	($3.0)	($ 7.0)
Expenditures for working capital					
Cash	(0.2)	0.3	—	—	(0.4)
Marketable securities	—	0.4	—	—	—
Acccounts receivable	(1.2)	(1.6)	2.4	(1.1)	(3.6)
Inventories	(1.7)	2.6	0.4	(1.2)	(3.4)
Accounts payable	1.6	(2.1)	(2.0)	0.8	1.0
Total working capital expenditures	(1.5)	(0.4)	0.8	(1.5)	(6.4)
Total nonoperating cash outflow	(11.5)	(10.4)	(4.2)	(4.5)	(13.4)

It was anticipated that cash could be drawn down by about $0.3 million during a recession, the reduction coming mainly in compensating balances normally held at commercial banks. Marketable securities worth $0.4 million and held for liquidity purposes would be sold during the first year of the recession. Accounts receivable were expected to rise and require funds during the first year as customers stretched their payments and then to fall with sales and release funds. Inventories were projected to change proportionally with sales.

Financial Flows

Financial flows include lease payments, interest and principal on debt, and dividends on common stock. Lease payments and debt service are contractual and must be maintained, whereas dividends are discretionary. Although discretionary, dividends were viewed as of very high priority by Omega management. Financing flows under Omega's present capital structure were therefore projected as shown in Table 19-8.

Alternative Debt Policies

Omega management was considering two alternative debt policies: one involved a debt ratio of 35 percent (debt to total capital) versus 20 percent at present, and another involved a debt ratio of 50 percent debt. In

Table 19-8   Omega Manufacturing Corporation: Projected Financial Flows under Present Capital Structure (Millions)

	Year Prior, 0	Recession Year			
		1	2	3	4
Lease payments	($ 2.1)	($ 2.1)	($2.1)	($ 2.1)	($ 2.1)
Interest on debt[a]	(1.5)	(1.4)	(1.3)	(1.2)	(1.0)
Principal on debt	(1.4)	(1.4)	(1.4)	(1.4)	(1.4)
Common dividend[b]	(3.0)	(3.0)	(3.0)	(3.0)	(3.0)
Taxes	(3.2)	(2.6)	(2.1)	(2.6)	(3.2)
Total	(11.2)	(10.5)	(9.9)	(10.3)	(10.7)

[a]Principal due was $18.6 million at year-end 1978. Interest rate is 8 percent and interest shown for year 0 is that due in 1979. Sinking fund payments are $1.4 million per year.
[b]Dividend is $2.00 per year on 1.5 million shares outstanding.

Table 19-9, cash flows are presented for each of these alternatives (labeled *A* and *B*) as if they had been implemented. In other words, alternative *A* presents cash flows as if Omega's debt ratio presently were 35 percent, all other factors unchanged. Interest on incremental debt is at 8 percent a year. Dividends on common stock, principal payments, and tax payments are altered commensurately.

Conclusions of the Cash Flow Analysis

Recessions sometimes are difficult to diagnose in their very early stages, and very difficult indeed to forecast. Omega management likely would not have sufficient evidence to implement their recession plan until well into year 1. At that point, sales would be declining and action would be taken to cut back expenses. Action also would be taken to cut back the capital expenditure program in the manner described earlier.

Omega management had established a dividend policy that treats dividends as a long-run residual, and sets the dollar payout so as to be nondecreasing. The dollar payout was set at a level that was thought to give a high probability of avoiding subsequent cuts, although it was recognized that circumstances could arise in which cuts clearly might become necessary. During temporary difficulties, management was willing to postpone, though not to forego, certain types of capital investment projects. Management had decided not to rely on temporary short-term

Table 19-9 Omega Manufacturing Corporation: Alternative Debt Policies (Millions)

	Year Prior, 0	Recession Year 1	2	3	4
Current Capital Structure					
1. Nonfinancial flows (Tables 18-6 and 18-7)	$13.4	$ 9.4	$ 9.6	$11.1	$11.5
2. Financial flows (Table 18-8)	(11.2)	(10.5)	(9.9)	(10.3)	(10.7)
3. Change in cash balance	2.2	(1.1)	(0.3)	0.8	0.8
4. Cumulative change	2.2	1.1	0.8	1.6	2.4
5. Change in cash with dividend eliminated in year 1[a]	2.2	1.9	2.7	3.8	3.8
6. Cumulative change	2.2	4.1	6.8	10.6	14.4
A, 35 Percent Debt					
7. Financial flows	(12.3)	(11.5)	(10.8)	(11.1)	(11.5)
8. Change in cash balance	1.1	(2.1)	(1.2)	—	—
9. Cumulative change	1.1	(1.0)	(2.2)	(2.2)	(2.2)
10. Change in cash with dividend eliminated in year 1[b]	1.1	0.3	1.2	2.4	2.4
11. Cumulative change	1.1	1.4	2.6	5.0	7.4
B, 50 Percent Debt					
12. Financial flows	(13.3)	(12.4)	(11.6)	(11.8)	(12.1)
13. Change in cash balance	0.1	(3.0)	(2.0)	(0.7)	(0.6)
14. Cumulative change	0.1	(2.9)	(4.9)	(5.6)	(6.2)
15. Change in cash with dividend eliminated in year 1[c]	0.1	(1.1)	(0.1)	1.2	1.3
16. Cumulative change	0.1	(1.0)	(1.1)	0.1	1.4

[a]Dividend of $3.0 million per year. Line 5 assumes that the dividend is eliminated completely in year 1 and no dividend at all is paid in years 1–4.
[b]Dividend of $2.4 million per year, with less equity and more debt in capital structure. Same assumption regarding elimination in year 1.
[c]Dividend of $1.9 million per year, with same assumption regarding elimination.

borrowing to maintain either the capital investment program or the dividend during adverse financial circumstances. While management had no objection to such a policy, there was always a possibility that short-term funds would not be available during a recession. Basing policy on an assumption that short-term borrowing would be possible therefore seemed unwise.

The three alternative debt policies then were evaluated in light of these and other policies. With the current capital structure of 20 percent debt, we can see from Table 19-9 (line 3) that Omega runs a cash deficit in years 1 and 2 assuming no cut in the dividend. However, these deficits are financed by the surplus in year 0, the year prior to the onset of the recession. On a cumulative basis (line 4), the analysis indicates that, with the current capital structure, Omega could survive the recession without cutting the dividend on common stock.

If debt were increased to 35 percent, which we refer to as alternative *A*, somewhat larger cash deficits would be run in years 1 and 2 (line 8). In this case, the surplus of $1.1 million in year 0 is not sufficient to finance the subsequent deficits, and a deficit is incurred on a cumulative basis (line 9). If the dividend is cut in year 1, so that the dividend in years 1–4 is zero, the cash deficits are eliminated. We can conclude that under alternative *A*, Omega can survive the recession provided dividends are cut. With a little additional arithmetic, we can see that the dividend could be partially restored in year 2 and fully restored in year 3.

Under alternative *B*, a debt ratio of 50 percent, cash deficits are run in each year of the recession (line 13). With the dividend eliminated, Omega still runs a cash deficit in years 1 and 2, even on a cumulative basis (lines 15 and 16). Thus, policy *B* appears to be unsustainable in a recession, even with a cut in dividends.

What can we conclude from the analysis? Which policies are safe and which not? By asking this question, we can see some of the limitations of financial theory when the practical realities of the world are considered. Policy *A* permits Omega to survive the recession, but with at least some possibility of having to cut the dividend if the recession is severe. Are the additional benefits of policy *A*, compared to the present policy, worth the risk of a dividend cut in a severe recession? Perhaps so, but we can see that the cash flow analysis does not give us a precise answer to the question of the effect of debt policy on bankruptcy risk.

Perhaps it is best to think in terms of a range of debt ratios. In this case, policy *A* appears to exploit the benefits of leverage about as fully as is prudent. We might therefore conclude that, considering only the risk of bankruptcy, Omega could operate safely with a debt ratio of 30–35 percent.

Probabilities

An extension and refinement of the basic cash flow procedure illustrated above can be obtained by introducing probabilities. Probability distributions would be required for revenues and other uncertain cash flows. Probability distributions then could be estimated for the changes in cash balances shown in Table 19-9.

A complete analysis would yield a probability distribution for each cash balance figure in each year. Clearly, such a procedure would greatly increase the complexity of the analysis and the time and effort necessary to carry it out. As a compromise, it would be possible to develop probability distributions for the most promising policy only for the most critical years. Where the additional effort seemed justified, the use of a probability analysis would yield additional insights into the degree of risk that management considered appropriate to assume, for example, with respect to the probability of having to cut the dividend.

Advantages of Cash Flow Analysis

Compared to EBIT/EPS analysis and coverage ratios, cash flow analysis yields a number of additional insights to the crucial task of setting debt policy. First of all, the focus is on the *solvency* of the firm during adverse circumstances rather than on the effects of leverage under normal circumstances. Cash flow analysis also considers *balance sheet changes* and other cash flows that do not appear in the profit and loss statement (such as capital expenditures), whereas EBIT/EPS and coverage do not. Cash flow analysis also gives an *inventory of financial reserves* available in the event of recession. Discretionary cash flows are identified and a *plan of action* is developed in advance. Nothing precludes the development of such a plan in connection with EBIT/EPS analysis, but cash flow analysis yields a plan as an integral part of the procedure. Finally, cash flow analysis views the problem in a dynamic context over time, whereas EBIT/EPS and coverage analysis normally consider only a single year.

We should note also that cash flow analysis is consistent with financial theory. The theory of optimal financial leverage tells us that debt should be used up to the point at which its benefits are outweighed by the expected cost of financial distress and reduced commercial flexibility. Cash flow analysis evaluates the risk of financial distress. We will consider the factors omitted by cash flow analysis in the next section.

Cash flow analysis also has its weaknesses. The analysis may give an illusion of precision that is not justified on the basis of the underlying information. In an uncertain world, the numbers may not capture all the relevant factors. Cash flow analysis, as we have described it here, considers an economic recession as the main source of uncertainty. What about technological developments, or shifts in consumer preferences, or political changes? The cash flow procedure probably can be adapted to include factors of this sort. The main point is that recessions are not the only source of economic unhappiness.

Allowing for Reserve Borrowing Capacity

As noted earlier, the theory developed in Chapter 18 tells us that the optimal debt level includes a reserve for contingencies and commercial flexibility. The cash flow analysis above does not include these factors, mainly because they are very difficult to quantify.

Reserve for Contingencies

The cash flow analysis tells us approximately how much debt a firm can use without running a significant risk of bankruptcy. Should we assume that the risk of bankruptcy is constant through time? We should not. We noted earlier that, in an uncertain world, there are factors in addition to investment policy that can change a firm's operating risk. Therefore, a good case can be made for backing away from the maximum safe debt level indicated by the cash flow analysis. By such a reduction, the firm obtains a margin to allow for error and for changes over time, and a cushion to provide flexibility to deal with problems that cannot be foreseen.

Inflation provides further reason for caution. In the cash flow analysis, cash flows are estimated in nominal terms, with the effects of inflation included. However, considerable uncertainty may exist with respect to what the future rate of inflation will turn out to be. Even though the earlier cash flow estimate is a best guess, uncertainty regarding the rate of inflation suggests that we back away still further from the point of maximum debt indicated by the cash flow analysis.

Maintaining Flexibility for Commercial Strategy

Another reason for operating below the maximum safe debt level is to preserve operating flexibility. A debt policy that might force a firm subsequently to make an undesirable change in its commercial strategy or to forego a desirable change would be costly. An aggressive debt policy might look good at one point, but later, because of changes in technology that make products obsolete or rapid increases in prices of key inputs, that same policy might threaten the firm's existence. Faced with such a situation, a firm might find it necessary to forego investments that it would have made or to alter its strategy in other important ways. Similarly, a firm faced with unexpected and attractive new opportunities might wish to alter its commercial strategy to take advantage of them. If it is unable to do so because of an unwise debt policy adopted earlier, the opportunity cost could be high.

Considerations such as these suggest a cautious approach to debt policy that leaves room for operating flexibility. In the long run, firms succeed primarily because of their commercial strategies rather than because of debt/equity or dividend policies. Management should avoid too much emphasis on the right-hand side of the balance sheet and not lose sight of the fact that successful commercial strategy comes first, and financing policies play a supporting role.

Choosing the Appropriate Debt Policy

How much should the firm back away from the maximum safe debt level because of factors discussed above? We cannot be precise in answering this question. To do so requires far more knowledge of the costs of financial distress and reduced flexibility than we have at present. Our theories provide qualitative guidance, and we can answer some questions with cash flow analysis, but the final decision is a subjective one.

The concept of a reserve for contingencies is especially relevant to firms whose operating risk is especially high, because of size or technology or length of experience. In many such cases, the optimal debt ratio may well be zero.

When a firm uses debt, it takes more risk in hopes of earning higher future returns. Debt has advantages, but to go too far in exploiting them can be costly. The use of debt represents essentially a gamble that the benefits of debt will exceed the costs. Such bets should be placed with caution.

Summary

In planning its financial structure, the first major policy decision facing the firm is that of determining the appropriate level of debt. For some firms, the decision involves a choice between long-term debt and equity. Firms without access to the public equity markets also must decide how much debt they prudently can use.

The choice of an appropriate debt policy involves a tradeoff between benefits and costs of financial leverage. The optimal debt level depends to an important extent on the firm's operating risk. The greater the operating risk, the less debt the firm should use. Therefore, a firm's financing policy should be tailored to its commercial strategy.

Alternative financing plans should be analyzed along several dimensions. EBIT/EPS analysis is useful for evaluating the sensitivity of earnings per share (EPS) and uncommitted earnings per share (UEPS) to changes in EBIT under alternative financing plans. EPS and UEPS break-even points can be calculated to determine the EBIT level at which EPS (or UEPS) is equal under two alternative plans. Coverage ratios provide a measure of the security of interest payments. None of these measures, however, tells the firm how far it should go in using debt. The firm's debt capacity is best defined, not as the maximum amount that lenders are willing to lend, but as the amount of debt the firm *should use,* that is, the shareholder optimum.

A determination of debt capacity requires an analysis of the likelihood of financial distress, which depends on the firm's ability to meet its financial obligations. Cash flow analysis provides the necessary tool. Analysis of cash flows under recession conditions provides information on the effects of alternative financing plans on the risk of insolvency. Cash flow analysis considers balance sheet changes as well as operating flows, and provides an inventory of financial reserves and a plan of action in the event of recession. However, cash flow analysis does not automatically provide a reserve for contingencies and commercial flexibility. In setting debt policy, a firm should allow for these factors by backing away from the maximum safe debt level indicated by cash flow analysis. The appropriate amount of such reserve borrowing capacity is largely a matter of subjective judgment.

Sample Problem

The Franklin Corporation has decided to finance a $4 million improvement program by issuing either common stock or bonds. Currently the firm has 200,000 shares outstanding and no long-term debt. Common stock can be sold to net $40 per share. The bond will be a 25 year issue at 6 percent interest with sinking fund payments starting in year 5. Franklin's tax rate is 50 percent.

1. Assume that Franklin's EBIT next year is expected to be $1.5 million. Calculate the EPS for the two alternative financing plans.
2. Determine the break-even EBIT level.

Solution

1. This type of problem is best attacked by constructing a table similar to the one below, which shows the derivation of EPS for each alternative (thousands except for EPS figures).

	Stock	Debt
EBIT	$1,500	$1,500
Interest	–	240
Profit before tax	1,500	1,260
Tax @ 50 percent	750	630
Profit after tax	750	630
Shares	300	200
EPS	$2.50	$3.15

2. To determine the break-even EBIT levels, we use the formula provided on page 544 of this chapter:

EPS Break-even

$$\underset{N_B}{\underbrace{\frac{(EBIT - I)\,(1 - T)}{N_B}}_{EPS-Bond}} = \underset{N_S}{\underbrace{\frac{EBIT\,(1 - T)}{N_S}}_{EPS-Stock}}$$

where N_B is the number of shares of stock outstanding under bond plan and N_S is the number of shares of stock outstanding under stock plan.

$$\text{Interest } (I) = (0.06)\,(\$4{,}000{,}000) = \$240{,}000$$
$$N_B = 200{,}000 \text{ shares}$$
$$N_S = 200{,}000 + \frac{\$4{,}000{,}000}{\$40/\text{share}} = 200{,}000 + 100{,}000 = 300{,}000 \text{ shares}$$
$$(1 - T) = 0.5$$

Substituting into the formula

$$\frac{(EBIT - \$240{,}000)\,(0.5)}{200{,}000} = \frac{(EBIT)\,(0.5)}{300{,}000}$$

Now we must solve for EBIT. Cross multiplying gives:

$$300{,}000\,[(EBIT - 240{,}000)\,(0.5)] = 200{,}000\,(EBIT)\,(0.5)$$

Expanding:

$$300{,}000\,(0.5\ EBIT - 120{,}000) = 100{,}000\ EBIT$$
$$150{,}000\ EBIT - 36{,}000{,}000{,}000 = 100{,}000\ EBIT$$
$$150{,}000\ EBIT - 100{,}000\ EBIT = 36{,}000{,}000{,}000$$
$$50{,}000\ EBIT = 36{,}000{,}000{,}000$$
$$EBIT = \frac{36{,}000{,}000{,}000}{50{,}000}$$
$$\text{Break-even } EBIT = \$720{,}000$$

Questions

1. What are the principal determinants of a firm's operating risk?
2. Discuss the relationship between the optimal financial structure of a firm and its commercial strategy.
3. Should short-term debt be considered in determining the optimal level of debt?
4. How should a firm's debt capacity be defined?
5. What can be said about a firm's exposure to the risk of financial distress knowing only the total level of debt (principal amount) in its financial structure?
6. What information is provided by a complete analysis of cash flows that normally is not provided by EBIT/EPS and coverage analysis?
7. Should a firm push its debt level right up to the point indicated as safe by a cash flow analysis?

Problems

1. Utilize the information given in Problem 3 in Chapter 18 to construct an EBIT/EPS chart. Which financing alternative would you recommend? Why?
2. Utilize the information given in Problem 3 in Chapter 18 to calculate the EPS break-even point using Equation (1) of this chapter. (*Hint:* Be sure to include old interest payments.)
3. Assume that the firm in Problem 3 in Chapter 18 has a third financing alternative, that of selling 100,000 shares of 11 percent preferred stock to net $50 per share. Beginning in the fifth year after issuance, the firm would make annual sinking fund payments of $500,000 for retirement of the preferred stock over a 10 year period.
   (a) Add to the EBIT/EPS chart in Problem 1 above lines representing the preferred stock alternative in years 1 and 5. (*Note:* Show both EPS and UEPS in year 5.)
   (b) Calculate EPS and UEPS break-even points for the preferred stock plan compared with the common stock plan.
   (c) How attractive is the preferred stock plan? Under what circumstances might the preferred stock plan be attractive?
4. The current balance sheet for Rafferty Corporation shows $10 million of 5 percent bonds and $7.2 million of $4.00 par value common stock. Total current sales of $45.5 million per year are to the United States Navy on a 10 year contract. The United States Air Force has offered a similar 10 year contract for $13.0 million per year. The company has accepted the new contract and now must raise $7.5 million from external sources in order to expand their production facilities. The

financing could be accomplished through a debt issue carrying a 6 percent coupon rate, or by selling shares of common stock to net the company $6.25 per share. EBIT is 3.3 percent of sales and the tax rate is 45 percent.

(a) Calculate the EPS break-even level of EBIT, that is, the level of EBIT at which EPS is equal under the two financing alternatives.

(b) Assuming that a $500,000 per year sinking fund payment would be required on the new debt issue, calculate the UEPS break-even level of EBIT.

(c) Analyze the coverage ratios for Rafferty Corporation under each of the two financing alternatives.

(d) What conclusions can you draw?

5. Omega Manufacturing Corporation, which was described in the text of this chapter, wishes to reevaluate its cash flow forecasts on the assumption of a more severe recession than the one previously considered.

(a) Revise Tables 19-6 and 19-9 in the text assuming the following sales pattern:

	Year of Recession			
Year Prior	1	2	3	4
100%	90%	75%	70%	90%

Assume cash operating expenses to be the same as forecasted in Table 19-6 and the 3 percent price decline to continue through year 4.

(b) What conclusions can be reached from this revised analysis? How do these conclusions compare with those in the text based on a less severe recession?

6. The Bengston Corporation has undertaken a 5 year plant expansion program, which will require $5 million in external capital in year 1 and $6 million in year 2. The company has several alternative financing plans available to it to meet its financing needs:

Plan *A*: Issue $11 million in new common stock in year 1.

Plan *B*: Issue $5 million in new common stock in year 1 and $6 million in 25 year bonds in year 2.

Plan *C*: Issue $5 million in 20 year bonds in year 1 and $6 million in stock in year 2.

Currently the firm has 500,000 shares of stock outstanding and $3 million of 6 percent bonds. Beginning in year 1, sinking fund payments of $300,000 on the existing debt are required to retire the debt in 10 years. The new bond issues in year 1 or year 2 will carry 8 percent interest. If a $5 million bond issue occurs in year 1, annual sinking fund payments of $250,000 will be required starting in year 5. The $6 million bond issue in year 2 will require annual sinking fund payments of $300,000 starting in year 6. Bengston's EBIT this year (year 0) was $3.5 million. Management expects EBIT to grow 10 percent annually over the next 10 years. New common stock can be issued now to net $50 per share.

(a) Calculate the EPS and UEPS at the end of year 2 and at the end of year 6 for each of the financing alternatives. Assume that stock can be issued at the beginning of year 2 to net $50 per share. Assume a 50 percent tax rate.

(b) Calculate the EPS break-even point for plan *A* compared with plan *B* for the end of year 2.

(c) Analyze the coverage ratios under each of the three plans at the end of year 2.

(d) Which alternative would you recommend? What factors do you consider important in making these recommendations?

7. As a new financial analyst for Hill Brothers, Inc., you have been asked to help evaluate the alternative financing plans for the corporation's expansion program. The firm's balance sheet and income statement for the last year are summarized on the facing page.

One alternative financing plan is a new stock issue of $4 million. Stock can be issued to net $25 per share. The other alternative is a 20 year, 9 percent $4 million bond issue with annual sinking fund payments of $200,000 beginning in the first year.

(a) The company has maintained a 50¢ annual dividend in the past and wishes to continue this annual dividend payment regardless of which financing plan is chosen. What level of EBIT would be required in the first year in order to cover interest, sinking funds, and dividend payments?

(b) Calculate EPS break-even points for the bond plan compared with the stock plan for year 1.

(c) Suppose Hill Brothers expects the EBIT level in year 1 to be $1,033,000 with a two-thirds probability that it will be between $833,000 and $1,233,000. Which financing alternative would you recommend, and why?

(d) Calculate the UEPS break-even point for the two plans. Does this change your recommendation in part (c)?

8. Revise Table 19-9 for Omega Corporation using a 30 percent debt alternative.

Hill Brothers
Balance Sheet
December 31, 1979
(Thousands of Dollars)

Current assets	$3,200	Current liabilities	$2,850
Net plant and equipment	5,320	Long-term debt[a]	2,000
Other	480	Total liabilities	4,850
		Equity	
		Common stock—200,000 shares at $1 par	200
		Additional paid in capital	2,800
		Retained earnings	1,150
Total assets	$9,000	Total liabilities and equity	$9,000

[a]Balance of 8 percent 20 year bond issue with annual sinking fund payments of $125,000.

Hill Brothers
Income Statement
for the Year 1979
(Thousands of Dollars)

Sales	$2,030
CGS	1,624
Gross margin	406
Interest[a]	165
Profit before tax	281
Tax @ 48 percent	135
Profit after tax	$ 146

[a]Long-term debt was $2,125,000 at the beginning of 1979. A sinking fund payment of $125,000 was made on June 30, 1979. Interest for the year therefore is $[(\$2,125,000 + 2,000,000) \div 2] \times 0.08 = \$165,000$.

References

G. Donaldson, *Corporate Debt Capacity* (Boston, Mass.: Division of Research, Harvard Business School, 1961).

G. Donaldson, *Strategy for Financial Mobility* (Homewood, Ill.: Richard D. Irwin, 1971).

R. C. Higgins and L. D. Schall, "Corporate Bankruptcy and Conglomerate Merger," *Journal of Finance* **30**, 93–114 (Mar. 1975).

E. H. Kim, "A Mean-Variance Theory of Optimal Financial Structure and Corporate Debt Capacity," *Journal of Finance* **33**, 45–64 (Mar. 1978).

R. E. Krainer, "Interest Rates, Leverage and Investor Rationality," *Journal of Financial and Quantitative Analysis* **12**, 1–16 (Mar. 1977).

R. C. Moyer, "Forecasting Financial Failure: A Reexamination," *Financial Management* **6**, 9–17 (Spring 1977).

J. J. Pringle, "Price/Earnings Ratios, Earnings per Share, and Financial Management, *Financial Management* **2**, 34–40 (Spring 1973).

G. M. Von Furstenberg and B. G. Malkiel, "Financial Analysis in an Inflationary Environment," *Journal of Finance* **32**, 575–588 (May 1977).

Selecting the Form of Debt

20

Short-Term versus Long-Term Debt
Evaluating Financing Costs Using DCF
Leasing
Convertible Securities and Warrants

595

26

Having made a decision as to the appropriate level of debt, we now must decide on the form of debt to be used. A basic decision concerns the choice of short-term versus long-term debt, a choice that determines the maturity structure of the firm's liabilities and its liquidity. Other choices open to the firm include leases, which are a special form of debt, and convertible securities and warrants. Let us consider each of these decisions in turn.

Short-Term versus Long-Term Debt

In structuring the right side of the balance sheet, the firm faces two principal questions: the appropriate mix of equity and debt, and the maturity of the debt, that is, the appropriate mix of short-term versus long-term debt. We considered the debt/equity mix in Chapters 18 and 19. There we were not concerned with the distinction between long-term debt and short-term debt; debt was debt, and we considered only the ratio of total debt to equity.

Now we are concerned with question number two: the maturity of the debt. How much should be long-term and how much short-term? As we will see, maturity is intimately related to the liquidity of the firm, and the liquidity of the firm is not the same as the liquidity of an asset. Much of our discussion of maturity and liquidity will be qualitative and conceptual, intended to provide a way of thinking about the problems. Theoretical models addressing these issues are not yet sufficiently developed to permit us to go very far with quantitative applications.

To clarify the issues, we will take the problem in two steps. First, we will consider the case in which the financing requirement is stable through time. Then we will address the more realistic case in which the firm's operating cash flows and the volume of assets to be financed vary through time.

Stable Financing Requirement

Consider a firm whose earnings are stable from period to period. Let us assume further that the firm reinvests a part of those earnings each year, and that its total assets grow at a steady rate.

Under such circumstances, the total financing requirement, that is, the firm's total liabilities, also will grow at a steady rate. If we assume that the use of at least some debt is appropriate for this firm, we have the option of using either short-term or long-term debt. Graphically, we might represent the situation as in Figure 20-1. In the figure, we represent the two policy alternatives as *A* and *B*. Under *A*, the firm finances a part of the total requirement using long-term liabilities (LTL) and part using short-term liabilities (STL). Under policy *B*, only long-term liabilities are used. Long-term claims might consist of equity or a combination of equity and long-term debt. Short-term claims might consist of bank credit or, if the firm were sufficiently large and well-known, commercial paper sold directly to lenders. In Figure 20-1, we are ignoring short-term

Figure 20-1   Financing a Stable Requirement

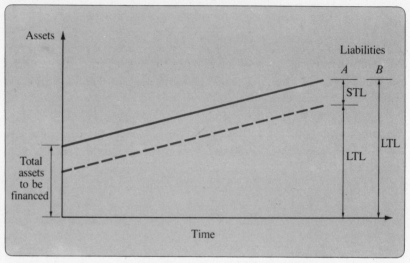

liabilities which arise spontaneously and directly from a firm's operations (such as accounts payable and various accruals). These can be viewed as having been netted out against assets to reduce the total financing requirement. Which policy, *A* or *B*, should the firm pursue? The answer depends on considerations of risk and cost.

Risk Considerations

If the firm pursues policy *A* and finances a part of its permanent assets with short-term funds, those short-term claims must be renewed or re-issued each time they mature. If bank credit is used, the loan must be renewed continually. Suppose upon some maturity date the bank is unwilling or unable to renew the loan? Such a circumstance might arise under conditions of tight money when commercial banks are forced to ration credit. Or the firm's prospects might deteriorate to the point where the bank becomes unwilling to renew. If the firm were using commercial paper, circumstances could arise making it difficult to roll over the paper, or to reissue it upon maturity.

Precisely that happened to Chrysler Financial Corporation, Chrysler Corporation's financing subsidiary, in June 1970. The commercial paper market was panicked by the bankruptcy of the Penn-Central railroad, which had outstanding a large volume of commercial paper. For some weeks following the Penn-Central bankruptcy, many firms, including Chrysler Financial, were unable to roll over their outstanding commercial paper. A group of large banks came to the rescue and provided temporary financing.

If short-term creditors suddenly refused to renew, for whatever reason, the firm likely would have to reduce its operating assets. Those operating assets consist of long-term assets such as plant and equipment and short-term assets such as inventories and accounts receivable. Sale of long-term assets could involve large losses and almost certainly would require the firm to alter its commercial strategy. Reduction of inventories and receivables could be done more easily, but also would require an alteration of marketing and production policies and likely would affect profits. We can conclude that, if short-term creditors suddenly refused to renew, a firm pursuing policy *A* at best would incur opportunity losses due to the necessity to alter its commercial strategy, and at worst could face serious financial difficulty.

Cost of Short-Term versus Long-Term Funds

What about costs? Are there cost differences between long-term and short-term sources? In general, yes. Differences in interest rates due solely to maturity, rather than risk or marketability, often are referred to as the *term structure* of interest rates. Generally, short-term interest rates tend to fluctuate more widely than long-term rates, but the average short-term rate over long periods historically has been lower.

The term structure, however, does not tell the whole story. Short-term rates used in analyzing the term structure normally are market rates on publicly traded issues, usually United States Treasury Bills. When a firm uses bank credit, however, other costs are involved. Banks nearly always impose a *compensating balance* requirement, that is, a requirement that a given amount of funds be left on deposit and not utilized by the firm. Compensating balances increase the effective cost of the loan. For example, if a firm needs $100,000 and must keep 15 percent of the loan on deposit, it must borrow a total of $117,650 to net the $100,000. If the contract rate were 10 percent, the effective rate on the $100,000 actually available to the firm would be 11.76 percent. In addition to compensating balances, banks often impose fees of various sorts. During periods of tight money, these nonrate charges may be increased.

The relative costs of short-term and long-term debt depend to a great extent on the size and reputation of the borrower. As we noted in Chapter 18, small or little-known firms nearly always find debt obtained via a financial intermediary (a commercial bank or an insurance company) less expensive than funds raised directly from the capital markets. For practical purposes, debt via the capital markets is not a realistic alternative. For the smallest firms, commercial bank loans are the best and cheapest source.

For firms with established reputations in the financial markets, the situation is different. It is instructive to think of the cost question with reference to the degree of competition in the different financial markets. In general, bank loan markets are less price competitive than are the national capital markets in which well-known firms raise long-term funds. Where the degree of competition is lower, costs normally are higher. We know that short rates fluctuate more than long rates and, because of maturity considerations alone, actually exceed long rates in some periods. When nonrate costs due to compensating balances and commitment fees are included and differences in competition considered, the effective cost to a firm of short-term bank credit may exceed the cost of long-term debt even on average over long periods.

If more competitive markets provide funds at lower cost, why not raise short-term funds directly in public markets? Some firms do so using commercial paper, as described earlier. When a firm uses commercial paper, it avoids compensating balance requirements and commitment fees, thus obtaining funds at a lower cost than via bank credit. We noted earlier, however, that the commercial paper market is open to relatively few firms. For the great majority, bank credit is the main source of short-term funds.

Even when a firm can borrow in the commercial paper market, some hidden costs usually are involved. We noted earlier the difficult position in which Chrysler Financial Corporation found itself in June 1970, when it was unable to roll over its commercial paper. To guard against such situations, issuers of commercial paper often contract with banks for backup lines of credit to be used in case of difficulties in the commercial paper market. Commitment fees to pay for such backup lines offset to some extent the advantage of commercial paper.

Financing Permanent Requirements with Long-Term Funds

There exists a rule of thumb of long standing that permanent requirements should be financed with long-term funds. In view of risk and cost considerations, this rule seems to be sensible. We must qualify this conclusion with the words "whenever possible," because many firms do not have access to long-term capital markets. Such firms may find it necessary to use short-term debt, mainly bank credit, to finance a part of their permanent requirements.

Variable Financing Requirements

We conclude that, whenever possible, permanent requirements should be financed with long-term funds. But suppose more realistically that the total financing requirement is variable, rather than growing at a steady rate. Such will be the case for nearly all firms in practice. Our reason for analyzing the stable case first, even though it is largely hypothetical, was to clarify the issues.

When a firm's operating cash flows vary through time, the total volume of assets to be financed will vary. Let us separate this variability into two categories: predictable and not predictable. Predictable variations arise mainly from seasonal factors. A toy manufacturer, for example, may have a highly seasonal sales pattern. So too might a manufacturer of sporting equipment such as boats or skis. Many types of retail enterprises are highly seasonal. Much of this variation, however, is due to factors that recur year after year at about the same time. History therefore provides a basis for prediction. In fact, the term seasonal normally refers to those variations that recur and therefore are predictable.

Some firms are subject to seasonal influences, and some are not. Nearly all, however, are also subject to unpredictable variations in cash flows. Factors influencing all firms alike include general economic and monetary conditions. Despite advances in understanding of the economy, recessions still occur and often are unpredictable in advance. Unforeseen spells of inflation also occur which affect a firm's need for funds. Strikes may affect individual firms or entire industries, as may technological developments and shifts in consumer preferences. Along with problems, firms also may face sudden opportunities that affect cash flow, such as new markets to enter. Electronic calculators, for example, created large markets for many firms in a period of only a few years.

Variable cash flows give rise to a financing requirement that varies in total. Much of the variation may be traced to expansion and contraction of accounts receivable and inventories. Fixed asset requirements also may grow in an irregular manner because of the lumpy nature of increments to plant capacity. We can represent this variable requirement as in Figure 20-2. How can the variable component of the requirement in the figure be financed? There are two ways: using *reserve borrowing power* and via holdings of *liquid assets.*

If the firm relies on reserve borrowing power, it simply borrows short-term funds, probably from a bank, as needed. Both sides of the balance sheet expand and contract in step. On the liability side, it is short-term debt that varies. Where the firm has access to both long-term and short-term capital sources, it can finance the fixed portion of its requirement

Figure 20-2 Variable Financing Requirement

with long-term sources and the variable portion with short-term sources. This alternative is represented graphically in Figure 20-3.

If a firm relies on the second alternative, liquid assets, it finances entirely with long-term claims. Sufficient long-term funds are raised to finance both the permanent requirement and the liquid asset buffer. Graphically, we represent this approach in Figure 20-4. Following the policy represented in Figure 20-4, total assets and total liabilities remain constant over time. All the variability is taken up within the current asset section of the balance sheet, with liquid assets expanding and contracting in exact opposition to operating assets, mainly inventories and accounts receivable. When funds are needed for operating assets, liquid assets are sold.

It is not necessary for a firm to rely entirely on one of the alternatives discussed above (Figures 20-3 and 20-4) to the exclusion of the other. Some combination of the two may be preferable. Before pursuing this possibility, let us discuss liquid assets and liquidity.

Liquid Assets

A liquid asset can be sold on short notice at a price about which there is little uncertainty. Perhaps the best examples are marketable short-term securities. Markets for such securities are highly organized, transaction costs of buying and selling are relatively low, price information is readily available, and large quantities of securities normally can be sold without significantly depressing prices. Thus, *liquid* implies both a price and a time dimension—for an asset to be considered liquid, it must be possible to sell it quickly at a price known in advance within narrow limits.

Figure 20-3 Using Short-Term Borrowing to Finance Variable Requirements

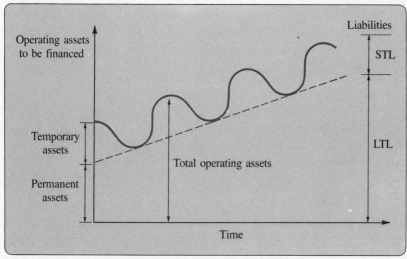

Figure 20-4 Using Liquid Assets to Finance Variable Requirements

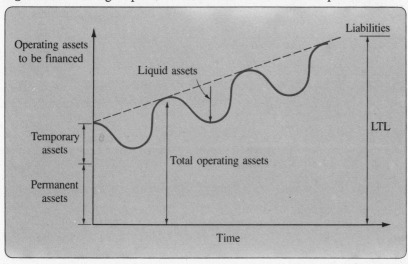

Firms hold liquid assets for a very specific purpose: to convert them quickly to cash when necessary. We already have restricted our definition of liquid assets to marketable securities. Given the purpose of liquid assets, we should restrict ourselves even further and rule out securities whose prices fluctuate or which are subject to default. When the cash is needed, it must be there.

In Chapter 7, we discussed the major types of securities that firms hold as liquid assets. The major candidates are United States Treasury

Bills and notes, federal agency issues, commercial paper of other firms, bank certificates of deposit, and bankers' acceptances. All of these securities are characterized by essentially zero default risk and ready marketability at low transaction costs. Returns on all are more or less comparable, with United States Treasury securities yielding somewhat less than the others.

In addition to default risk, we also must consider price fluctuations due to changes in the level of interest rates. When interest rates rise, bond prices fall. The longer the maturity of the bond, the more sensitive is its price to changes in interest rates. Because of this *interest rate risk,* short maturities are best for liquidity purposes.

Liquidity of the Firm

Suppose a firm with total assets of $10 million holds $1 million in short-term United States Treasury Bills. Is the firm liquid? By looking only at the asset side of the balance sheet, we cannot say. We must look also at the maturity structure of its liabilities. If the firm has a $1 million loan that must be paid the next day, we cannot say that the firm's position is liquid.

Thus, the liquidity of the firm depends not only on its holdings of liquid assets, but also on the maturity structure of its liabilities. Here we see the key relationship between *liquidity and maturity.* This relationship suggests that firm liquidity must be measured in terms of liquid assets net of nonpermanent short-term liabilities.

How does a firm increase its liquidity? If the firm borrows short-term and uses the proceeds to purchase liquid assets of approximately equal maturity, its liquidity has not been increased. If, on the other hand, the firm issues long-term claims and uses the proceeds to acquire liquid assets, liquidity has been increased. Thus, short-term reserve borrowing capacity, while a source of cash, is not a source of liquidity. Liquidity can be purchased only with long-term funds.

The liquidity of the firm thus depends on two factors: its holdings of liquid assets, and the maturity structure of its liabilities. The liquidity of the firm is determined by the *maturity balance* between the two sides of the balance sheet. The shorter the maturity of its assets and the longer the maturity of its liabilities, the higher the firm's liquidity.

Liquidity and Maturity Structure

From the preceding discussion, we can see that when it chooses between short-term and long-term debt, the firm is making an important policy decision with respect to liquidity and maturity structure. We can represent the policy choice as in Figure 20-5. In the more realistic case in which the firm's assets grow over time, the horizontal lines in the figure would slope upward to the right as in Figures 20-2 through 20-4. To keep the analysis simple, we will use the no-growth case illustrated in Figure 20-5.

Figure 20-5 Determining the Level of Liquidity

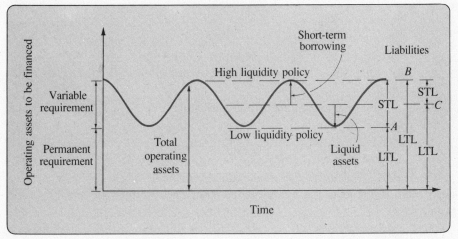

Lines *A* and *B* represent the two policy extremes. If the firm adopts policy *A*, it issues long-term liabilities (LTL) of *A* and finances the entire variable portion by borrowing short-term as needed. If it adopts policy *B*, it finances entirely with LTL, using no short-term borrowing at all and taking up the variations in the liquidity buffer. Policy *A* thus represents a low liquidity policy, and *B* a high liquidity policy.

Policy *C* represents a middle position. When total assets rise above *C*, the peaks are financed with short-term borrowing. During low points, the firm holds excess funds in liquid assets. Note that under policy *C* the firm at any point in time is either holding liquid assets or borrowing short-term, but never both simultaneously.

A low-liquidity policy may expose the firm to opportunity costs. If a firm relies too heavily on short-term borrowing, during periods of tight money, credit may be rationed and the firm may be unable to obtain all the financing it needs. Commercial activities might have to be constrained and attractive opportunities foregone. Flexibility during periods of tight money represents one of the major benefits of liquidity.

An even worse prospect during periods of credit rationing would be an unexpected increase in cash requirements. In an uncertain world, many things can happen that cannot be foreseen. Strikes occur, technology changes, new products fail to meet expectations, foreign oil producers raise prices, and so on. If short-term credit is not available, because of credit rationing or perhaps because creditors do not like the firm's prospects, the firm has no choice but to reduce operating assets. If the period of negative cash flow is prolonged, the potential exists for serious financial difficulty. One of the principal benefits of liquidity is to avoid the costs of such financial distress.

Setting Liquidity Policy

We see from Figure 20-5 that the question of how much liquidity to use is a dynamic, and not a static one. We cannot simply determine the appropriate quantity of liquid assets and assume that we have the answer. A firm following a C type of policy will find its liquid assets varying over time.

The real policy question is "where to draw the line?" In other words, "what is the appropriate total level of long-term financing for the firm?" By answering that question, the firm determines the extent to which it will employ short-term borrowing during peak periods and will hold liquid assets when operating asset requirements decline. An increase in long-term financing reduces short-term borrowing dollar for dollar in every future period in which borrowing occurs, and increases liquid assets during slack periods. Where cash flows are uncertain, as they nearly always are, an increase in long-term financing lowers the probability of having to borrow any given amount of short-term funds.

In practice, a combination policy, represented by C in Figure 20-5, probably is best in most circumstances, and most firms follow such an approach. To make its choice, a firm might project its operating assets and determine the range of variation within some confidence limits, say 5 percent. It could interpret these lower and upper limits as line A and B in Figure 20-5. As noted earlier, in a growing firm, lines A and B would slope up to the right. Having estimated lines A and B, the firm could aim for a point halfway between, or closer to one extreme or the other. The final choice is a judgment call, because our theories of maturity and liquidity are not yet sufficiently developed to permit precise quantitative answers.

What additional qualitative guidance can we gain from our analysis? Where possible, permanent asset requirements should be financed with long-term funds raised in competitive capital markets. In general, the more competitive the market, the lower the cost to the borrower. Many firms with limited access to long-term capital markets will find bank credit the most economical source of funds.

For firms with access to long-term markets, short-term funds should be used to finance unpredictable needs and a portion of seasonal (predictable) requirements. The costs of holding liquid assets often are overestimated, and in terms of the model in Figure 20-5, the optimal policy for most firms is likely to lie closer to policy B (high liquidity) than to A.

In fact, many firms may find it best to finance predictable requirements completely by means of long-term funds in combination with a liquidity buffer, using short-term borrowing only for requirements that cannot be foreseen.

In choosing an appropriate policy, the degree of operating risk of the firm is a key consideration. The higher the operating risk, the more the firm should rely on long-term financing and the more liquid it should be. High-risk firms might find it advisable to increase liquidity to the point where the probability of having to borrow short-term is low.

Timing

A firm's liquidity policy should be set considering long-run factors affecting the firm and its financial environment. However, rate relationships in financial markets sometimes can affect temporarily the choice between short-term and long-term debt. If, for example, the policy choice is long-term debt or equity, but conditions are unfavorable in those markets at the time, the firm may use short-term debt temporarily. An expansionary monetary policy by the Federal Reserve can drive short-term rates below normal levels and make short-term financing unusually attractive.

To profit consistently from swings in interest rates requires an ability to forecast rate changes consistently. Studies of security prices and yields have shown that superior forecasting is very difficult. In fact, consistently superior forecasting is so difficult that, as a matter of general financial policy, most firms should devote more of their energies to determining how much, what kind, and when funds are needed, and less to outguessing the market with respect to timing.

Evaluating Financing Costs Using DCF Techniques

Sometimes it is useful to use DCF techniques to evaluate financing alternatives. A financing plan is, after all, a series of cash flows over time. Analyzing complex cash flow patterns is the job for which DCF techniques are designed.

Suppose a firm faces two financing alternatives, each involving a cash inflow (the proceeds) followed by a series of outflows (the payments). The general cash flow pattern (inflow, then outflows) is opposite that of an investment (outflow, then inflows). The *equivalent interest cost* (EIC) of any financing plan is the rate that discounts all cash flows of the plan to exactly zero. Hence, the EIC is the direct analog of the internal rate of return of an investment and is calculated in exactly the same way. In the case of bonds, the EIC is given the label *yield to maturity.*

In the case of standard loan plans, relevant cash flows are easy to identify and the calculation of the EIC is straightforward. The result is what we would expect: the interest rate on the loan. To illustrate, consider a $1 million loan at 8 percent to be repaid in equal installments of $250,000 over 4 years. The cash flows are listed in Table 20-1, assuming a tax rate of 48 percent.

Table 20-1 Calculating the Equivalent Interest Cost (EIC)

Year	Loan Proceeds	Principal Payment	Interest		Total Cash Flow	
			Pretax	After-Tax	Pretax	After-Tax
0	$1,000,000				$1,000,000	$1,000,000
1		($250,000)	($80,000)	($41,600)	(330,000)	(291,600)
2		(250,000)	(60,000)	(31,200)	(310,000)	(281,200)
3		(250,000)	(40,000)	(20,800)	(290,000)	(270,800)
4		(250,000)	(20,000)	(10,400)	(270,000)	(260,400)
		Rate that discounts cash flows to zero			8.00%	4.16%

As expected, the rate that discounts the pretax cash flows to equal zero is 8.00 percent, the interest rate on the loan. The above procedure verifies that the after-tax EIC is the pretax EIC multiplied by $(1 - T)$, where T is the tax rate. In this case, $8.00 (1 - 0.48) = 4.16$ percent.

One might wonder why we went to such lengths to calculate something whose value we already knew, namely, the interest rate on the loan. We did so to demonstrate the EIC approach in a simple case and to lay the groundwork for applying it to more complex financing plans, such as leases. We will apply the EIC approach to leases in the next section.

Leasing

As we saw in Chapter 17, a lease is a contractual arrangement under which the owner of an asset, the lessor, permits another party, the lessee, to use the asset for a specified period of time in return for a specified payment. Since lease payments are fixed and contractual, a lease is the functional equivalent of debt and has the same effect on firm risk. Thus, a lease can be viewed as a specialized form of debt financing.

To evaluate leasing decisions, we need a way to measure the cost of leasing as a financing alternative. Here we will consider only leases that are noncancellable and therefore equivalent to debt as far as effect on firm risk is concerned. In effect, we restrict our analysis to financial leases. We take the investment decision (the decision to use the asset), as given, and compare leasing to the alternative of owning. The basic approach is to calculate the EIC of the lease, which then can be compared directly to the cost of borrowing.

Equivalent Interest Cost of a Lease[1]

Since leasing provides 100 percent financing, we must compare it to 100 percent debt financing. The most direct way to make this comparison is to calculate the after-tax EIC of the lease and compare it to the after-tax interest rate that the firm would have to pay on long-term debt.

To calculate the EIC, we apply the incremental cash flow rule to identify all cash flows attributable to leasing, that is, those cash flows that will be different if leasing is selected rather than owning. By leasing, the firm avoids the cash outlay required to purchase the asset, incurs an obligation to make lease payments, foregoes the depreciation tax shield, and foregoes the residual (salvage) value of the asset at the expiration of the lease. Costs of operation, maintenance, insurance, property taxes, and the like often are the same under leasing, but if different, the difference represents an incremental cash flow. In the case of all cash flows, associated tax effects must be taken into account.

Some of the incremental cash flows attributable to leasing are inflows (the outlay avoided), and some are outflows (the lease payment, depreciation tax shield foregone, and terminal value foregone). The cash flow pattern thus is analogous to that of a loan—an inflow, followed by a series of outflows. Once the incremental cash flows have been identified, we find the discount rate that causes them to sum to exactly zero. That rate is the after-tax EIC of the lease.

Incremental Cash Flows of Leasing

Our first task is to identify the incremental cash flows attributable to leasing. Generally, five categories of cash flows are involved:

1. acquisition cost of asset,
2. lease payment,
3. depreciation tax shield,
4. operating and maintenance costs, and
5. salvage value

The first item above, the acquisition cost of the asset, is the outlay that will be avoided if the asset is leased rather than purchased. Since it is an outlay avoided, it is treated as a net cash inflow attributable to the lease. The timing of the inflow is the point at which the outlay would have been made.

---

1. The approach described below draws on Rodney L. Roenfeldt and Jerome S. Osteryoung, "Analysis of Financial Leases," *Financial Management* **2**(1), 34–40 (Spring 1973).

The lease payment is the cash payment that will be made to the lessor in each period over the term of the lease, net of taxes. Assuming that the lessee will make a profit in each period, its after-tax lease payment is the pretax payment times one minus the marginal tax rate.

The depreciation tax shield is the tax saving foregone by the lessee due to the fact that depreciation cannot be taken (but is taken by the lessor instead). The tax shield in each period is a cash outflow and is calculated as the depreciation in each period times the marginal tax rate.

In some cases, certain costs of operation, maintenance, insurance, property taxes, or similar items may be different if the asset is leased than if owned. If these costs are greater under leasing, they should be treated as a cash outflow; if less, they should be treated as inflow. Tax effects should be included. If the amounts are uncertain, strictly speaking they should be adjusted for uncertainty. We will ignore this problem in our discussion here.

Residual Value

When an asset is leased rather than purchased, the lessor has title to it at the expiration of the lease. Hence, as compared to owning, the lessee foregoes the benefit of whatever value the asset might have at expiration. This residual value must be treated as a cash outflow attributable to the decision to lease. In many cases, it may be small enough to ignore. In others, notably in connection with leases involving real estate, residual values may be very significant and may have a significant impact on the cost of leasing as compared to owning. The higher the residual value foregone, the higher the cost of leasing relative to owning.

We have two problems to deal with: tax effects and uncertainty regarding the estimate of residual value. Taxes must be taken into account to allow for any tax liability in connection with the residual value. It is the residual value net of taxes that is foregone by leasing. The tax liability is calculated as the estimated residual market value of the asset, less book value at expiration, times the applicable tax rate. The after-tax residual value then is the pretax value less the tax liability. We will illustrate this calculation later.

We now come to a difficult problem: uncertainty. The residual value of the asset is likely to be more uncertain than other elements of the cash flow stream and must be adjusted if the EIC calculation is to give valid results. One method of doing so is to estimate the minimum residual value that reasonably can be anticipated, rather than the most likely. This minimum should be a figure such that there is a low probability of realizing less. We can refer to it as the *risk-adjusted* residual value.[2]

Calculating the Equivalent Interest Cost

Having estimated the incremental cash flows of leasing relative to owning, we now can calculate the EIC of the lease, following the procedure outlined earlier in this chapter. The EIC is the discount rate that sums all the cash flows to zero and is exactly analogous to the internal rate of return (IRR) of an investment. As a measure of cost, the EIC suffers from the same technical shortcoming as does the IRR. It does not take account of the firm's reinvestment rate (see Chapter 11 for a discussion of this problem). For this reason, to be strictly correct, we should refer to the result of this calculation as the *approximate* EIC. In many cases, it is sufficiently accurate. Where it is not, methods exist to calculate the *true* EIC, but we will not consider them here. Let us now illustrate the calculation of the EIC with an example.

We will make the example simple and straightforward in order to illustrate the concepts involved. Suppose a firm has decided that it needs a particular machine. The machine can be purchased for $50,000 or leased from the manufacturer for $11,500 per year under a 5 year noncancellable lease. Lease payments would be due at year-end. If purchased, the firm would receive an investment tax credit of 7 percent. The firm uses straight-line depreciation and Internal Revenue Service regulations permit depreciation of the machine over 5 years. The combined federal and state tax rate is assumed to be 48 percent. The firm's interest rate on long-term debt is 9 percent, before taxes. The lease contract is net, and operating, maintenance, and insurance costs are the same as under ownership.

Let us now determine the incremental cash flows attributable to leasing. By leasing, the firm avoids an immediate outlay of $50,000, but foregoes the tax credit of $3,500, which we will assume to be available immediately. The lease thus provides an inflow of $46,500 in period 0. The annual lease payment net of taxes is $11,500(1 − 0.48) = $5,980 due at the end of years 1–5. Depreciation foregone is $50,000/5 = $10,000 per year, so the tax shield foregone is $10,000(0.48) = $4,800 per year.

---

2. Technically, the appropriate figure to use for the residual value is its *certainty equivalent*. The certainty equivalent is defined as the smallest certain amount that the decision-maker would be just willing to accept in exchange for the uncertain prospect. The decision-maker is indifferent between the uncertain prospect and its certainty equivalent.

The firm's best guess of the market value of the machine at the end of year 5 is $10,000. It is considered highly unlikely that the value will be less than $5,000. Let us therefore use $5,000 as our estimate of the risk-adjusted residual value. Since book value at year 5 will be zero, the firm, if it owns the machine, will have a tax liability against the market value of ($5,000 − 0)(0.48) = $2,400. The adjusted residual value at the end of year 5, net of the tax liability, thus is $2,600. The relevant cash flows are listed in Table 20-2.

Table 20-2 Cash Flows Attributable to Lease

Year	Acquisition Cost	After-Tax Lease Payment	Depreciation Tax Shield	After-Tax Residual Value	Total Cash Flow
0	$46,500	—	—		$ 46,500
1		($5,980)	($4,800)		(10,780)
2		(5,980)	(4,800)		(10,780)
3		(5,980)	(4,800)		(10,780)
4		(5,980)	(4,800)		(10,780)
5		(5,980)	(4,800)	($2,600)	(13,380)

Our task now is to find the rate that discounts the total cash flow stream to zero. Using present value tables, we find that the rate is between 6 and 7 percent. By interpolating, we can determine that it is about 6.5 percent. With a calculator equipped to do discounted cash flow analyses, we can determine it to be exactly 6.65 percent.

How do we interpret the EIC calculated above? What exactly does it tell us? It tells us that the lease is more expensive than borrowing, which the firm can do at an after-tax equivalent rate of 4.68 percent, versus 6.65 percent for the lease.[3]

In practice, leases often turn out to be more expensive than debt, unless the tax advantages to the lessor are sufficient to permit a lease payment which is low enough to reduce the EIC below the borrowing

---

3. For an approach to lease analysis that calculates benefits in dollar terms rather than as a percentage rate, see S. C. Myers, D. A. Dill, and A. J. Bautista, "Valuation of Financial Lease Contracts," *Journal of Finance* **31**, 799–820 (June 1976). The EIC and present value approaches give identical signals where the decision is to accept or reject a given lease, just as the NPV and IRR rules give identical signals in accept or reject capital budgeting decisions. Where the problem is to rank two or more leases, the present value approach to analyzing leases theoretically is superior to the EIC approach for the same reasons that NPV is superior to IRR for ranking investment projects. The present value analysis has the additional advantage of indicating the dollar contribution to firm value of a given lease proposal. EIC, on the other hand, yields a percentage rate that is easy to interpret and can be compared directly to the cost of borrowing.

rate.[4] We will see an example of such a lease in the case of the Anaconda Company, described below. An EIC above the borrowing rate does not necessarily mean that the lease should be rejected. The qualitative advantages of the lease may be worth the additional cost. The EIC tells management just how large a premium it really is paying.

Additional Considerations

We illustrated the calculation of the EIC using a simple example. In practice, leasing decisions often involve a more complex set of cash flows, longer time periods, accelerated depreciation, purchase and renewal options at the expiration of the lease, and so on. Occasionally, situations may be encountered in which an asset can only be leased, that is, it is either leased or it is not used, and no option to purchase exists. In such cases, the investment and financing decisions are made together.

All these complications can be handled using DCF techniques. The computations are more tedious, but the logic is the same.

An Illustration of Leasing—The Anaconda Company

In 1973, the Anaconda Company entered into an agreement to lease a new aluminum reduction mill from a consortium of five banks and one commercial finance company. The mill cost $110.7 million. Anaconda agreed to make 40 semiannual payments over a 20 year period. The first 21 payments were to be $3.985 million each, and the last 19 payments $5.460 million. The lessors were to have title to the mill at the end of the lease in 1993 and also would get the investment tax credit and the depreciation tax shield. Anaconda was to be responsible for all operating cash flows, including maintenance and insurance.

The Anaconda lease illustrates the central importance of taxes in lease financing. The lease turned out to be advantageous to both lessor and lessee at the same time. How can this be? The answer involves taxes. Because the Chilean government had expropriated some of Anaconda's properties in Chile, Anaconda had a large tax loss carry-forward and therefore a very low marginal tax rate for a period several years beyond 1973. If Anaconda had purchased the aluminum reduction mill, it could not have used the depreciation tax shield to full advantage nor the investment tax credit. Via the lease, Anaconda transferred the tax shields that it could not use to the lessors, who could use them. By properly designing the lease terms, Anaconda and the lessors reduced their

---

4. For evidence that most lease contracts have EICs in excess of the cost of debt, see I. W. Sorensen and R. E. Johnson, "Equipment Financial Leasing Practices and Costs: An Empirical Study," *Financial Management* **6**, 33–40 (Spring 1977).

combined tax liability. So, the lease left both Anaconda and the lessors better off, with the tax collector footing the bill.[5]

Convertible Securities and Warrants

We mentioned convertible securities and warrants as sources of funds in Chapter 17. Here we will consider the decision to use these special financing methods.

Convertible Securities

A *convertible* security is one that can be converted at the option of the holder into a security of the same firm but of another type. Both bonds and preferred stock are issued as convertible securities, and in nearly all cases are convertible into shares of common stock. Once converted into common stock, the process cannot be reversed. A holder of a convertible bond thus gives up his position as creditor to become an owner.

The terms of the conversion privilege can be stated in terms of either a conversion price or a conversion ratio. For example, in July 1976, the United States Steel Corporation issued $400 million of 25 year convertible debentures due in the year 2001, and bearing interest at 5¾ percent per year, payable semiannually. The debentures are convertible into the company's common stock at $62.75 a share (i.e., each $1,000 debenture can be exchanged, at the holder's option, into 15.936 shares of common stock). At the time of the issue, United States Steel common stock was selling at $55 a share. Thus, the conversion price had been set about 14 percent above the then market price of the common stock.

Convertible securities nearly always include a *call* feature whereby the issuer, at its option, can call the issue for redemption. However, the purpose of the call feature usually is not to force redemption but to force conversion. When the value of the common shares into which the security is convertible exceeds the call price, holders would opt to convert rather than to redeem. Convertibles usually are issued with the expectation that they will convert. The call feature provides the issuer some control

---

5. For a description of the Anaconda lease, see P. Vanderwicken, "The Powerful Logic of the Leasing Boom," *Fortune* **88**, 132–136 (Nov. 1973). For a detailed financial analysis of the Anaconda lease and a theoretical discussion of lease analysis, see Myers, Dill and Bautista, "Valuation of Financial Lease Contracts," and J. R. Franks and S. C. Hodges, "Valuation of Financial Lease Contracts: A Note," *Journal of Finance* **33**, 657–669 (May 1978). For a theoretical analysis of the tax advantages of leasing, see M. Miller and C. W. Upton, "Leasing, Buying and the Cost of Capital Services," *Journal of Finance* **31**, 761–786 (June 1976). Miller and Upton argue that it is only through tax benefits that leasing can be advantageous to either lessor or lessee. A possible advantage to leasing not considered by Miller and Upton is pointed out by J. H. Scott, Jr., "Bankruptcy, Secured Debt and Optimal Capital Structure," *Journal of Finance* **32**, 1–20 (Mar. 1977). Scott suggests that leases, like secured debt, can reduce the firm's liability for future legal damages.

over the timing of the conversion. We will return to the matter of forced conversion later.

Valuation of Convertible Securities

A convertible security derives value from two sources: its value as a bond or preferred stock, and its potential value as common stock if converted. The same general valuation principles apply in the case of both convertible bonds and convertible preferred stock. In the case of a bond, we can label the two components of value the *bond value* and the *conversion value*. The convertible bond can be thought of as a combination of a bond plus an option to buy the firm's common stock. If the value of the common stock rises, the value of the option and hence that of the convertible bond will rise. If the value of the stock falls, the value of the convertible as a bond provides a floor below which the price of the convertible will not fall. The bond value of a convertible bond can be thought of in the following terms:

$$V_B = \sum_{t=1}^{n} \frac{I}{(1 + K_d)^t} + \frac{P}{(1 + K_d)^n} \qquad (1)$$

where V_B is the value of the convertible bond, I is the annual interest payment, P is the principal amount due at maturity, n is the number of years to maturity, and K_d is the market rate of interest (or yield to maturity) on a nonconvertible bond of the same company or same risk class. Expression (1) represents the standard valuation equation for a bond. For simplicity, the expression assumes annual interest payments rather than the semiannual payments more often encountered in practice.

Consider the United States Steel convertible debenture mentioned earlier. It offered a 5.75 percent interest rate, or $57.50 a year per $1,000 bond at a time when the market interest rate on a straight (nonconvertible) bond for this company would have been around 8.5 percent. Applying expression (1), we find the bond value of such a convertible bond to be

$$V_B = \sum_{t=1}^{25} \frac{\$57.50}{(1.085)^t} + \frac{\$1,000}{(1.085)^{25}}$$

$$= \$588.47 + 130.09$$

$$= \$718.56$$

The conversion value of the bond is the market value of the common stock into which the bond is convertible. The bond described above is convertible into 15.936 shares of common stock and the market price of the stock was $55. The conversion value of each bond was therefore $876.48.

Since the convertible security has value as a bond (or as preferred stock), its market price will not fall below its bond value. Because of the value of this downside protection, a convertible security nearly always sells at a premium over its exact conversion value. The magnitude of this premium depends on the likelihood that conversion value will drop below bond value. The premium therefore is a function of the difference between conversion value and bond value and also of the volatility of the conversion value, which depends on the volatility of the price of the underlying stock.

As noted earlier, the bond value of a convertible bond provides a floor below which its price will not fall. A convertible usually sells at a premium over bond value because of the value of the conversion privilege. Thus, the *conversion premium* of the bond is the amount by which its market price exceeds the higher of its bond value or its conversion value. We can diagram these price relationships as in Figure 20-6.

Figure 20-6   Relationship of Convertible Bond Price to Price of Common Stock

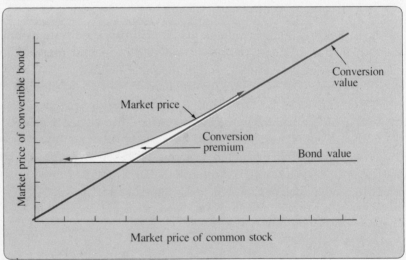

Referring to Figure 20-6, when the conversion value of the bond is below bond value, the conversion premium over bond value can be ascribed to the value of the conversion privilege. When conversion value exceeds bond value, the premium over conversion value can be ascribed to the downside protection of the floor. As the stock price rises, the conversion value rises, and the value of the downside protection declines. Also, the probability of a call of the issue increases, and if called, the bond is worth only its conversion value. On the other side, the farther conversion value falls below bond value, the less the conversion privilege is worth. Consequently, as indicated in Figure 20-6, the conversion premium narrows at both ends of the spectrum of stock prices.

The diagram in Figure 20-6 assumes that the bond value is constant. In fact, the floor provided by the bond value is not fixed, and in practice it may vary because of the same factors that affect stock price. The element K_d in expression (1) represents the rate of return required by the market on a straight debt issue of the firm in question. This RRR may change either in response to a change in the general level of interest rates or to a change in the perceived riskiness of the particular firm's cash flows. For example, an increase in the RRR on the firm's debt from 8.5 to 9.5 percent would cause the bond value in the example cited earlier to drop from $718.56 to $646.09. Thus, a decline in the firm's prospects might give rise to a decline in the bond value of its convertibles just at the time when the bond value is most needed as downside protection against a stock price that is also declining for the same reason. The floor provided by the bond value is not a fixed floor, but one that can vary.

Accounting Treatment

Conversion of a convertible security into common stock affects earnings per share for two reasons: first, the requirement to pay interest (or dividends, in the case of preferred stock) is eliminated, and second, the number of common shares is increased. To take a specific example, assume a company issues $6 million of 7½ percent convertible bonds and that each bond is convertible into 20 shares of stock. Assume further that expected earnings before interest and taxes (EBIT) is $5 million, that the tax rate is 50 percent, and that 500,000 shares of common stock are outstanding before conversion. Earnings per share before and after conversion are shown in Table 20-3.

Table 20-3 Effect of Conversion on Earnings per Share (Thousands)

	Before Conversion	After Conversion
Expected EBIT	$5,000	$5,000
Interest on bonds @ 7.5 percent	450	—
Profit before taxes	4,550	5,000
Taxes @ 50 percent	2,275	2,500
Profit after taxes	2,275	2,500
Common shares outstanding	500	620
Expected earnings per share	$ 4.55	$ 4.03

As indicated, conversion causes the firm's earnings per share to decline. Whether the stock price also will decline depends on circumstances. Conversion reduces expected earnings per share from $4.55 to $4.03 (i.e., by 11.4 percent), but at the same time it also reduces the firm's debt/equity ratio, thereby reducing the riskiness of the EPS. The reduction in risk offsets at least in part the reduction in expected EPS. Applying the theory of financial leverage developed in Chapter 18, the effect on the value of the firm's shares should depend on the effect of the conversion on taxes and bankruptcy risk. If the firm were significantly below its optimal debt ratio, conversion would reduce the total value of the firm by the amount of the net tax benefits foregone, considering both corporate and personal taxes of investors (see discussion in Chapter 18). If the firm were above its optimal debt ratio, conversion theoretically should increase firm value. In the latter case, the reduction in risk would more than offset the reduction in expected EPS.

To assist investors in evaluating the impact of convertible securities, current accounting guidelines require reporting of two EPS figures: primary EPS and fully diluted EPS. The fully diluted figure shows on a pro forma basis what EPS would be if all outstanding convertible securities were converted to common stock.

Financing with Convertibles

Convertible securities usually are issued at a premium over current conversion value. Consider a 7½ percent convertible bond issued by ABC Corporation at $1,000 with a conversion price of $50 (conversion ratio is 20 shares of common stock per bond) and a call price of $1,075. If the market price of the common stock at the time the bonds are issued is $44 per share, the conversion value of the bonds is 20 × $44 = $880. The issue price of $1,000 thus represents a premium of 13.6 percent over the conversion value. The premium also can be calculated by comparing the conversion price, $50, to the market price at the time of issue, $44, a premium of 13.6 percent.

The conversion premium set at time of issue varies from one issue to another, but usually lies between 10 percent and 20 percent. The premium is set by adjusting the conversion ratio. In general, the faster the firm is growing, the higher the premium is set. Most convertible securities are issued with the expectation that they will convert in the not too distant future, say, a period of a few years. A convertible issue thus can be viewed as a deferred common stock issue, with the stock sold for future delivery at a price above current market. Compared to a sale of common stock now, the firm obtains a higher price for the stock, issues fewer shares, and subjects existing shareholders to less earnings dilution. As compared to a straight debt issue, the convertible issue can be sold at a lower interest rate, perhaps 1.5 to 2 percentage points lower. Similarly, convertible preferred stock can be sold at a lower dividend rate than can straight preferred stock.

In order to induce complete conversion, the issue usually must be called by the issuing firm. Calling the issue would force conversion provided the conversion value of the bonds were sufficiently above the call price. If ABC Corporation called its convertible bonds at $1,075 at a time when its stock were selling for $60, holders would be forced to choose between $1,075 in cash or stock worth $1,200. Most, undoubtedly, would convert. Since some reasonable period must be allowed for the transaction to be consummated, firms usually find it wise to wait until conversion value is 10 percent to 20 percent above the call price before calling the issue. Such a margin gives some protection against unexpected drops in the stock price during the conversion period.

When a firm that has issued convertibles does not perform as well as had been expected, its stock price may not rise sufficiently to permit a forced conversion. If this situation persists, the convertible issue is said to be *hung* or *overhanging*. The existence of a hung convertible issue in a firm's capital structure usually is taken as evidence that things have not gone as planned. Often the firm's flexibility with respect to external financing is reduced considerably, since any new issue may be difficult as long as the uncertainty over the convertible issue is unresolved. If the financing constraint causes the firm to alter its commercial strategy, perhaps by foregoing investments that it otherwise would have made, the cost of a hung convertible to the shareholders may be very high. Such potential complications in the event of unfavorable developments constitute an important disadvantage of convertible securities. A firm issuing convertibles therefore must be prepared to see the issue remain as debt or preferred stock for an indefinite period.

A firm may issue convertible securities as a means of obtaining a lower interest rate on debt or a lower dividend on preferred stock than would be possible with a nonconvertible issue. Another motive might arise in a situation in which management felt that its prospects were not being fairly evaluated by the stock market. A convertible offers an opportunity to sell common stock at a premium over current market, assuming that conversion eventually takes place. Rapidly growing firms might find this argument especially appealing.

Convertibles also might be attractive in more specialized financing situations. Consider, for example, a relatively young firm with no track record that is attempting to raise outside capital. In such high-risk situations, investors might wish to participate provided that they share in the firm's good fortunes as equity investors, should the outcome be favorable.

A convertible bond gives them an option on an equity position, but at the same time provides a senior debt claim against assets during the early, more uncertain, period. Other specialized situations in which convertibles might be attractive include mergers and acquisitions. In such cases, tax considerations might make a convertible security attractive to both buyers and sellers.

Warrants

A warrant is an option to purchase a specified number of shares of common stock at a specified price. Warrants typically are issued in connection with bonds and usually are detachable, but not always. If detachable, the warrants can be detached from the bonds and sold separately. Markets exist for detachable warrants and many are listed on the American Stock Exchange, a few on the New York Exchange.

The warrant itself sets forth the terms of the option, which include the number of shares that can be purchased with each warrant, the exercise price, and the time period over which the warrant can be exercised. Most warrants can be exercised over a number of years, and most have a stated expiration date. Sometimes the terms—either the exercise price or the shares per warrant—may change over time. When the warrant is exercised, it is exchanged along with an appropriate sum of money for the specified number of shares of common stock.

Besides providing an option that is detachable, warrants differ from convertible securities in other respects. First, the firm receives additional funds when warrants are exercised, whereas it does not when convertibles convert. Accounting entries in the capital section of the balance sheet differ accordingly. Second, the combination of warrant and bond is more flexible from the holder's standpoint than a convertible bond, because there are two separate claims with different characteristics that both have value. From the firm's standpoint, warrants may provide less control than convertibles, because the firm cannot force holders of warrants to exercise them. Warrants, like convertibles, are taken into account in calculating fully diluted EPS.

The theoretical value of a warrant (W) selling separately in the market is given by

$$W = NP - E \qquad (2)$$

where N is the number of shares of common stock that can be purchased with one warrant, P is the price of the common stock per share, and E is the exercise price of the warrant.

When the market price of the stock is below the exercise price, the theoretical value of the warrant is zero. At expiration, the warrant becomes worthless.

Warrants normally sell at a premium over theoretical value. The magnitude of the premium depends primarily on the time remaining to expiration, the volatility of the common stock, and the opportunity cost of funds to investors.

Like convertibles, warrants provide the holder an option on an equity claim and therefore a chance to share in a firm's good fortunes. Warrants usually are issued in connection with debt securities, sold privately or publicly, but sometimes may be issued by themselves. When issued in connection with debt securities, the motive usually is to "sweeten" the deal and thereby to make the issue easier to sell or salable at a lower rate of interest. In exchange for the option, the buyer accepts the lower rate. A firm with a marginal credit rating faced with an embarrassingly-high interest rate might use warrants to lower the rate. A firm unable to sell a debt issue at any rate, presumably because of risk or the lack of a track record, might find that warrants would make the issue salable. *Venture capitalists* might find warrants an alternative to convertibles as a means of providing funds to a fledgling firm, with the security of a debt claim and also an option on the equity.

Financing in Competitive Markets

From our discussion of the theory of financial leverage in Chapter 18, we know that the total value of the firm to all claimants—creditors, the government, and owners—is entirely a function of its operating cash flows. The firm's operating cash flow can be thought of as a pie to be shared by the three groups. The only way to increase the share going to creditors and owners is to reduce that of the government. Aside from tax effects, financing arrangements merely package the firm's operating cash flow and allocate it among the different classes of claim holders. Unless it reduces the government's share or reduces costs due to "financial friction," a financing arrangement cannot benefit all other classes of claim holders simultaneously. A benefit to one group must come at the expense of another.

The use of convertible securities and warrants does indeed lower the rate of interest (or preferred dividends) to the firm, but at a price. In return for the lower rate, the buyers of convertibles or warrants obtain a claim against the firm's equity. If things turn out favorably, they later will be able to buy the firm's stock at a bargain price. In the case of firms with marginal credit ratings or unproven records, convertible securities and warrants may provide sources of financing not available otherwise. Here again, the firm pays for the accommodation with a claim on its equity.

If a firm issuing convertibles or warrants fully discloses all material information, as it should, we would expect a competitive market to evaluate the firm's prospects in an unbiased manner. The market is likely to value the option on the common stock properly, meaning that overvaluation and undervaluation are about equally likely. In a competitive market, we would expect investors to reduce the dividend or interest rate on the securities by an amount that correctly reflects the value of the option to buy the firm's stock. Thus, the firm pays for the lower interest or dividend rate about what it is worth.[6]

What of the argument that convertibles permit sale of common stock at a premium price at a time when a sale of straight equity may be disadvantageous because of depressed prices? The use of convertibles can offer advantages. However, if the market were placing an unfairly low value on the firm's stock, it likely would place a correspondingly low value on the conversion privilege.

What, then, do we conclude with respect to the use of convertible securities and warrants? For reasons discussed above, convertibles and warrants are unlikely to offer advantages for which the firm does not pay full price. Both are complex securities requiring considerable expertise to market. Convertibles have the additional disadvantage of exposing the firm to potentially serious complications if they do not convert as planned. As noted earlier, a hung convertible issue can constrain a firm's future financing and operating flexibility. The uncertainty regarding future conversion in and of itself may be a drawback. The possibility of complications serious enough to require an alteration of commercial strategy is not a prospect to be taken lightly.

We can conclude that convertible securities and warrants find their main application in specialized financing situations. Besides providing a source of funds to firms unable to use conventional securities, convertibles and warrants also may be useful in mergers and acquisitions and in regulated industries such as utilities. Thus, convertible securities and warrants are specialized securities that provide varying combinations of contractual claims with options on equity. Where the need is specialized, they can be used to advantage.

---

6. For a theoretical development of this argument in the case of convertible debt, see Wilbur G. Lewellen and George A. Racette, "Convertible Debt Financing," *Journal of Financial and Quantitative Analysis* **8**(5), 777–792 (Dec. 1973).

Summary

Once a firm has determined its appropriate level of debt, it then must decide what form the debt should take. The basic decision concerns the choice between short-term and long-term debt. Other choices in more specialized applications include leases, convertible securities, and warrants.

The appropriate mix of short-term and long-term debt depends on the nature of the operating assets to be financed. A firm's total financing requirement for operating assets can be viewed as the sum of two components: a permanent component that may be stable or growing through time, and a variable component that rises and falls over time. In general, the permanent requirement should be financed with long-term funds, equity plus long-term debt. The variable component can be financed either by borrowing short-term as required or by issuing long-term claims and employing a liquid asset buffer that alternately expands and contracts to offset the variations in operating assets.

The liquidity of a firm depends not only on the liquidity of its assets but also on the maturity structure of its liabilities. Hence, when it chooses between short-term and long-term debt, the firm also is setting its liquidity policy. Extensive use of short-term debt to finance variable requirements represents a low liquidity policy. Use of long-term debt (or equity) combined with a liquid asset buffer represents a high liquidity policy. For most firms, the appropriate policy lies between the two extremes. A final choice depends on considerations of risk and cost, with the degree of operating risk of the firm a key factor.

Discounted cash flow techniques can be used to calculate the equivalent interest cost (EIC) of any financing plan. The EIC technique is especially useful in analyzing leases. A noncancellable (financial) lease is the functional equivalent of debt and has the same effect on firm risk. Therefore the EIC of a financial lease can be compared directly to the cost of borrowing.

To calculate the EIC of a lease, the incremental cash flow rule is applied in order to identify the cash flows attributable to the lease. Such cash flows normally include the outlay avoided, the lease payment, the depreciation tax shield, and the residual value of the asset. Given estimates of these cash flows, the EIC of the lease can be calculated to determine whether the lease is more or less expensive than borrowing.

Convertible securities (bonds and preferred stock) and warrants represent additional financing options open to a firm. A convertible security derives its value from two sources, its value as a bond or preferred stock and its value as common stock if converted. Convertible securities normally carry a lower interest or dividend rate than would nonconvertible securities of the same firm, reflecting the value of the option to convert the security into common stock.

Warrants are options to buy common stock at a specified price. Warrants normally are issued in combination with debt securities for the purpose of improving the marketability of the debt and/or obtaining a lower rate of interest. Like convertible securities, warrants find their main application in specialized financing situations.

Sample Problem

The Ozark Printing Company has decided to acquire a new printing press and is trying to decide between leasing and buying the machine. The press can be purchased from the manufacturer for $50,000 (delivered). The machine will be depreciated over a 5 year life, using straight-line depreciation to a zero salvage value. Ozark could lease the machine from the manufacturer for $12,000 per year for 5 years. All operating, maintenance, and insurance costs for the new machine will be borne by Ozark. Ozark has a 48 percent tax rate and a before-tax interest rate on long-term debt of 9 percent.

Which financing alternative do you recommend (assume there is no residual value of the machine in year 5)?

Solution

This problem can be approached by examining the incremental cash flows associated with leasing rather than purchasing. Constructing a table similar to 20-2 is helpful in tracing the cash flow patterns.

Cash Flows Attributable to Lease

Year	Acquisition Cost	After-Tax Lease Payment	Depreciation Tax Shield	After-Tax Residual Value	Total Cash Flow
0	$50,000				$50,000
1		($6,240)	($4,800)		(11,040)
2		(6,240)	(4,800)		(11,040)
3		(6,240)	(4,800)		(11,040)
4		(6,240)	(4,800)		(11,040)
5		(6,240)	(4,800)	0	(11,040)

There are no investment tax credits from purchasing the machine. By leasing rather than purchasing, Ozark saves $50,000, an incremental cash inflow in year 0. The after-tax lease payments equals ($12,000)(1 − 0.48) = $6,240, representing an incremental cash outflow in years 1–5. The depreciation tax shield forgone by leasing equals ($50,000/5)(0.48) = $4,800 per year. We have assumed there is no residual or salvage value. Since we have a series of equal cash outflows, we can solve directly for the EIC:

$50,000 = ($11,040) × (Annuity factor for 5 years, *x* percent)

$$\frac{\$50,000}{\$11,040} = \text{Annuity factor for 5 years, } x \text{ percent}$$

$$= 4.529$$

Looking in Table II at the end of the text, we can find the interest rate that has a factor close to 4.529 for a 5 year period. Our factor, 4.529, lies between the factors for 3 percent and 4 percent. Interpolating:

$$3 \text{ percent} + \frac{4.580 - 4.529}{4.580 - 4.452} = 3 \text{ percent} + 0.398 \approx 3.4 \text{ percent} = \text{EIC}$$

The after-tax equivalent rate for debt equals (1 − 0.48)(0.09) = 0.0468 or 4.68 percent. Comparing the after-tax rate for debt with the EIC for leasing, we see that it is cheaper to lease rather than purchase the machine.

Questions

1. Why is it risky to finance permanent asset requirements with short-term funds?
2. How do the costs of short-term sources of funds compare with those of long-term sources?
3. What are the two major alternative methods of financing asset requirements that vary over time?
4. What is meant by a *liquid* asset?
5. What is *interest rate risk?*
6. How is the liquidity of a firm related to the maturity structure of its assets and liabilities?
7. What risks do you see in adopting a policy of low liquidity?
8. In what way does the decision regarding the level of long-term financing in a firm determine its liquidity policy?
9. How is the appropriate liquidity policy related to the firm's operating risk?
10. How can discounted cash flow techniques be used to evaluate financing alternatives?
11. In what sense can a lease be viewed as a specialized form of debt financing?

12. How can discounted cash flow techniques be used to evaluate leases?
13. What is a convertible security?
14. What is the function of the *call* feature of a convertible security?
15. What is the *conversion premium* of a convertible bond or preferred stock issue?
16. What consequences do you see if a convertible security fails to convert as originally planned?
17. Under what circumstances might warrants be used to advantage in financing?
18. What are the implications of highly competitive financial markets for the use of convertible securities and warrants?

Problems

1. S. E. Company can borrow up to $200,000 from a local bank at 8 percent but is required to maintain a 10 percent compensating balance on all loans.
   (a) How much would S.E. have to borrow if it needs $150,000?
   (b) What is the effective interest cost of the loan?

2. H & L Brock Company has projected their total current assets for each month as shown in the table. Fixed assets will remain constant at $20 million.

Month	Current Assets (Thousands)	Month	Current Assets (Thousands)
January	$ 8,000	July	$ 7,600
February	8,800	August	8,500
March	9,700	September	9,200
April	10,300	October	11,000
May	9,800	November	9,800
June	8,400	December	8,600

   (a) Devise a financing plan for the firm that reflects a moderate liquidity policy by specifying the amount of long-term claims that the firm should issue.
   (b) If payables and accruals average 10 percent of current assets, what is the minimum line of credit that your plan in part a will require?

3. Find the equivalent interest cost of each of the following loans:
   (a) A $1,000 loan repaid in one payment of $1,080 at the end of 1 year.
   (b) A $1,000 loan repaid in four annual payments of $80 each and one final payment of $1,080 at the end of the fifth year.
   (c) A $1,000 loan repaid in five annual payments of $250.44.

(d) A $1,000 loan repaid in five annual payments of $280, $264, $248, $232, and $216.

4. Queens Manufacturing Company has decided to acquire a new pressing machine and is trying to decide between the leasing and buying alternatives. The machine can be purchased from the manufacturer for a delivered price of $85,000. The machine will be depreciated over a 10 year period to a zero salvage value although the firm estimates that it could be sold for a minimum of $5,000 at the end of the 10 years. Alternatively, the manufacturer has offered a financial lease at $11,000 per year for the 10 years with all operating, maintenance, and insurance expense to be borne by the lessee. The firm's before-tax interest rate on long-term debt is 10 percent, all depreciation is straight-line, and the tax rate is 45 percent. Which financing alternative would you recommend?

5. The Mudville public school system plans to install a computer to cut expenses for record-keeping, payroll, and other clerical functions. The manufacturer offers two options: purchase or a noncancellable lease. Outright purchase would require an outlay of $150,000. If purchased, maintenance and insurance would run $1,000 per month. Alternatively, Mudville could lease the computer for an initial term of 4 years at $4,000 per month, maintenance and insurance included. At the end of 4 years, Mudville would have the option of purchasing the computer for $40,000 (the estimated fair market value at that time), leasing for a second 4 year term for $2,500 per month, or terminating the arrangement. At the end of year 8, the computer is expected to have zero salvage value. Lease contracts would be noncancellable in both years 1–4 and 5–8. Operating costs other than maintenance and insurance would be the same under either purchase or lease. The interest rate on long-term United States government bonds is 7 percent, and Mudville's borrowing rate (on tax-free municipal bonds) is 6 percent. How should Mudville finance the computer?

6. Levy Industries has determined that holders of the company's convertible bonds would convert the issue if it were called. The company therefore has decided to force the conversion of the 10,000 outstanding bonds in order to increase their equity base in preparation for future bond issues. The $1,000 par bonds mature in 20 years and carry an 8 percent coupon. Each bond is convertible into 50 shares of common stock. The firm currently has 1.7 million shares of stock outstanding. The tax rate is 48 percent.

(a) Assuming that the market rate of interest on nonconvertible bonds of comparable risk is 9 percent, calculate the bond value of Levy's convertible issue.

(b) Levy's stock currently is selling for $22 per share. Calculate the conversion value of the convertible bonds.

(c) Calculate the effect of conversion on EPS at an expected EBIT of $8 million.

7. The Schlotterbeck Manufacturing Company has decided to acquire a new automated drilling machine for its plant in Portland, Maine. The firm can purhase the machine from the manufacturer for a delivered price of $125,000. If purchased, the machine qualifies for an investment tax credit of 10 percent. The incremental servicing and maintenance costs of the new machine are estimated to be $5,000 annually. These costs would not be incurred if the machine is leased. If purchased, the machine will be depreciated over a 10 year period to a zero salvage value using the straight-line method. Even though depreciation will be based on a zero salvage value, the company anticipates being able to sell the machine for a minimum of $6,000 at the end of the 10 years. Alternatively, Schlotterbeck could lease the machine for an initial term of 5 years at $3,000 per month with the option of purchasing the machine at the end of year 5 for $50,000 (the estimated fair market value at that time) or renew the lease for another 5 year term for $2,000 per month. At the end of year 10, all rights to the machine would revert back to the leasing company and Schlotterbeck would not be given a purchase option. The monthly lease payments include all servicing and maintenance costs for the machine. The firm's tax rate is 48 percent, and its before-tax interest rate on long-term debt is 12 percent.

(a) Which plan would you recommend?

(b) If the firm used the sum of the years' digits rather than straight-line depreciation, how would the cash flow pattern change? (Give a general answer, rather than detailed calculations.)

(c) Suppose this industry is subject to rapid technological changes in production methods, which makes existing equipment obsolete relatively quickly. Would this change your recommendation in part (a)?

8. The Neptune Company, a manufacturer of boats and outboard motors, has a seasonal sales pattern and level production, which results in variable financing requirements. In Chapter 5, pro forma financial statements were developed for the firm's operations in 1980. In constructing the pro forma balance sheet, it was assumed that Neptune would finance its variable requirements through short-term borrowing.

(a) Under the current financing policy reflected in the pro forma balance sheet in Chapter 5 (Table 5-6), what will be Neptune's average borrowing level in 1980? If the bank charges 8.5 percent interest on borrowed funds, what will be Neptune's interest expense for 1980?

(b) Suppose Neptune could issue up to $1.5 million of 20 year bonds carrying a 10 percent interest rate. Devise an alternative financing policy for Neptune that would eliminate the firm's short-term borrowing in 1980. What would be the average level of marketable securities in 1980 under your plan? (Assume a minimum cash balance of $50,000 with excess cash being invested in marketable securities yielding 6 percent.)

(c) Compare the two policies. What factors do you consider important on evaluating and choosing a policy?

9. Two years ago Peterson and Peterson, Inc., sold $5 million in 6 percent, 20 year convertible bonds. The $1,000 par bonds are convertible into 25 shares of common stock each and are callable after 2 years at a price of $1,050. The firm currently has 1.4 million shares of stock outstanding. The stock is currently trading at $45 per share. The marginal tax rate of the firm is 48 percent.

(a) At the time of the bond issue, Peterson stock was selling for $35 a share. What was the initial conversion premium of the convertible issue?

(b) If the interest rate on nonconvertible bonds of comparable risk currently is 8 percent, what is the bond value of Peterson's convertible issue?

(c) What is the current conversion value of Peterson's convertible bonds? What is the minimum price at which you would expect to see the convertible bonds selling? If Peterson's stock price fell to $30 per share, what would be the bonds' minimum price?

References

P. F. Andersen and J. D. Martin, "Lease Versus Purchase Decisions: A Survey of Current Practice," *Financial Management* **6,** 41–47 (Sept. 1977).

P. W. Bacon and E. L. Winn, Jr., "The Impact of Forced Conversion on Stock Prices," *Journal of Finance* **24,** 871–874 (Dec. 1969).

W. J. Baumol, B. G. Malkiel, and R. E. Quandt, "The Evaluation of Convertible Securities," *Quarterly Journal of Economics* **80,** 48–59 (Feb. 1966).

R. S. Bower, "Issues in Lease Financing," *Financial Management* **2,** 25–34 (Winter 1973).

O. D. Bowlin, "The Refunding Decision: Another Special Case in Capital Budgeting," *Journal of Finance* **21,** 55–68 (Mar. 1966).

W. D. Bradford, "Monetary Position, Unanticipated Inflation and Changes in the Value of the Firm," *Quarterly Review of Economics and Business* **16,** 47–53

R. A. Brealey, *Security Prices in a Competitive Market* (Cambridge, Mass.: MIT Press, 1971).

E. F. Brigham, "An Analysis of Convertible Debentures: Theory and Some Empirical Evidence," *Journal of Finance* **21,** 35–54 (Mar. 1966). (Winter 1976).

A. Buse, "Expectations, Coupons, and Yields," *Journal of Finance* **25,** 809–818 (Sept. 1970).

K. Cooper and R. H. Strawser, "Evaluation of Capital Investment Projects Involving Asset Leases," *Financial Management* **4,** 44–49 (Spring 1975).

P. D. Cretein, Jr., "Convertible Premium vs. Stock Prices," *Financial Analysts Journal* **25,** 90–96 (Nov.-Dec. 1969).

J. R. Franks and S. C. Hodges, "Valuation of Financial Lease Contracts: A Note," *Journal of Finance* **33,** 657–669 (May 1978).

R. D. Gritta, "The Impact of Lease Capitalization," *Financial Analysts Journal* **30,** 47–52 (Mar.-Apr. 1974).

F. C. Jen and J. E. Wert, "The Deferred Call Provision and Corporate Bond Yields," *Journal of Financial and Quantitative Analysis* **3,** 157–170 (June 1968).

F. C. Jen and J. E. Wert, "The Effect of Call Risk Upon Corporate Bond Yields," *Journal of Finance* **22,** 637–652 (Dec. 1967).

R. A. Kessel, *The Cyclical Behavior of the Term Structure of Interest Rates* (New York: National Bureau of Economic Research, Occasional Paper #91, 1965).

J. S. Katzin, "Financial and Legal Problems in the Use of Convertible Securities," *Business Lawyer* **24,** 359–373 (Jan. 1969).

W. G. Lewellen and G. A. Racette, "Convertible Debt Financing," *Journal of Financial and Quantitative Analysis* **8,** 777–792 (Dec. 1973).

A. B. Miller, "How to Call Your Convertible," *Harvard Business Review* **49,** 66–70 (May-June 1971).

M. Miller and C. W. Upton, "Leasing, Buying and the Cost of Capital Services," *Journal of Finance* **31,** 761–786 (June 1976).

J. R. Morris, "On Corporate Debt Maturity Strategies," *Journal of Finance* **31,** 29–39 (Mar. 1976).

S. C. Myers, D. A. Dill, and J. A. Bautista, "Valuation of Financial Lease Contracts," *Journal of Finance* **31,** 799–820 (June 1976).

T. J. Nantell, "Equivalence of Leases vs. Buy Analysis," *Financial Management* **2,** 61–65 (Autumn 1973).

G. E. Pinches, "Financing With Convertible Preferred Stock, 1960–1967," *Journal of Finance* **25,** 53–64 (Mar. 1970).

G. Pye, "The Value of Call Deferment on a Bond: Some Empirical Results," *Journal of Finance* **22,** 623–636 (Dec. 1967).

R. L. Roenfeldt and J. S. Osteryoung, "Analysis of Financial Leases," *Financial Management* **2,** 34–40 (Spring 1973).

L. Schachner, "The New Accounting for Leases," *Financial Executive*, Feb. 1978.

J. H. Scott, Jr., "Bankruptcy, Secured Debt and Optimal Capital Structure," *Journal of Finance* **32,** 1–20 (Mar. 1977).

J. P. Shelton, "The Relation of the Price of a Warrant to the Price of Its Associated Stock," *Financial Analysts Journal* **23,** 143–151 (May-June, 1967); 88–99 (July-Aug. 1967).

J. B. Silvers, "Liquidity, Risk and Duration Patterns in Corporate Financing," *Financial Management* **5,** 54–64 (Autumn 1976).

R. M. Soldofsky, "Yield-Risk Performance of Convertible Securities," *Financial Analysts Journal* **39,** 61–65 (Mar.–Apr. 1971).

I. W. Sorensen and R. E. Johnson, "Equipment, Financial Leasing and Costs: An Empirical Study," *Financial Management* **6,** 33–40 (Sept. 1977).

R. A. Stevenson and J. Lavely, "Why a Bond Warrant Issue?," *Financial Executive* **38,** 16–21 (June 1970).

P. Vanderwicken, "The Powerful Logic of the Leasing Boom," *Fortune* **88,** 132–136 (Nov. 1973).

J. C. Van Horne, *The Function and Analysis of Capital Market Rates* (Englewood Cliffs, N.J.: Prentice-Hall, 1970).

J. C. Van Horne, "Warrant Valuation in Relation to Volatility and Opportunity Cost," *Industrial Management Review* **10,** 19–32 (Spring 1969).

R. L. Weil, Jr., J. E. Segall, and D. Greene, Jr., "Premiums on Convertible Bonds," *Journal of Finance* **23,** 445–463 (June 1968).

Issuing and Managing Long-Term Securities

21

Issuing Long-Term Securities
Managing Outstanding Issues
Failure and Reorganization

In this chapter, we discuss the issuance and management of long-term debt and equity securities. We will draw a distinction between *public offerings,* in which securities are sold directly to the investing public, and *private placements,* in which securities are sold to one or a small number of buyers, generally insurance companies. In the first major section below, we consider new issues of debt and equity securities. We then take up the management of outstanding securities after issuance. In the final major section, we discuss business failure and reorganization as a special aspect of relations with creditors and owners.

The material in this chapter, for the most part, is applicable to firms that have reached a stage in their development that permits access to the public capital markets. The financial claims that we shall discuss usually are referred to as *securities.* Firms that are too small or too new to have their securities accepted by the capital markets usually acquire their external funds via *loans,* the label normally given to debt contracts negotiated with financial intermediaries such as commercial banks, finance companies, and insurance companies.

Issuing Long-Term Securities

Firms normally issue debt and equity securities to the public using one of three methods: public offerings through investment bankers, public offerings via privileged subscription, and private placements. We will discuss each of these methods below. We then will discuss government regulation of securities issues, especially requirements for disclosure of information. Finally, we will take up considerations such as issue costs and timing that are pertinent to all types of issues.

Firms that sell securities directly to the public tend to be larger companies. In October, 1975, the American Telephone and Telegraph Company, the world's largest corporation in terms of total assets, sold $552 million of new common stock to the public, in June 1976; it sold a further $690 million, and in November 1977 still another $720 million. Most security offerings are not nearly so large. In fact, the 1977 American Telephone and Telegraph offer was at the time the largest public offering in history. Typical offerings are much smaller, but still run to tens of millions of dollars.

Single buyers, such as insurance companies or banks, usually are unable to supply such large sums, and unwilling to concentrate their investments to such an extent because of risk considerations. Large amounts therefore usually are sold to large numbers of buyers and, accordingly, are labeled *public* offerings. To assist firms in public sales of securities, the specialized institution of investment banking has developed.

Public Offerings through Investment Bankers

Investment bankers are essentially middlemen who bring together the seller of securities, namely the firm, and the buyers, namely the public. The largest investment banking firms are found in New York City, but many regional firms also exist. The specialized function performed by the investment banker is directly analogous to that of the retailer of goods. The investment banker has the expertise and specialized sales organization to do an effective marketing job. Because of this specialization, the investment banker generally can perform the distribution job at lower cost than can the firm itself, which normally would issue securities relatively infrequently.

One of the most important functions of the investment banker is to *underwrite* the issue. The underwriter actually buys the securities from the selling firm and resells them to the public. Thus, a good part of the risk of issuing the securities, for example, adverse reception due to over-pricing or adverse general market fluctuations during the distribution period, is borne by the underwriter. In large issues, a number of under-writers often will join together in a *syndicate* to spread the risk.

A second major function of the investment banker is that of *selling* the securities to investors. The selling and risk-bearing functions are separable, and the investment banker is compensated for both. The total compensation to the investment banker is the difference between the price paid to the issuing firm and the resale price to the public. The total spread usually is divided into an *underwriting profit*, which compensates for risk-bearing, and the *selling concession*, which compensates for the service function of selling.

Not all securities sold through investment bankers are underwritten. Sometimes an issue is sold on a *best efforts* basis, an arrangement under which the investment banker acts as *agent* of the seller and sells as many securities as possible at an agreed upon price. The investment banker has no responsibility for unsold securities and thus bears no risk. Compensation to the investment banker includes only the selling concession.

Another major function of the investment banker is to advise the issuing firm with respect to *pricing* the issue. When the firm has securities of the same class already outstanding, the issue price is likely to be set slightly below the market price of the then outstanding securities. It is in connection with *new issues,* that is, the initial public offering of securities of a given class, that pricing is most critical. For example, when a firm issues common stock for the first time, there is no established market price to serve as a benchmark.

In pricing a new issue, it is in the interests of all parties that the securities be priced fairly, neither too high nor too low. Too high an offering price benefits existing holders at the expense of new holders, whose interests are soon to become a responsibility of the management by virtue of the transaction. Likewise, too low a price damages existing holders. Pricing a new issue is part art and part science, and the judgment of the investment banker, a feel for the market, and experience with similar firms in the past play a key role.

An offering that is underwritten may be sold either on a negotiated or a competitive bid basis. In the former case, the seller and the underwriter mutually agree on the price to be paid for the securities by the underwriter. Under competitive bidding, the seller invites bids from several firms and awards the issue to the highest bidder. Bids are based on the anticipated resale price to the public and the desired spread.

Another important function of the investment banker is to assist the seller and its lawyers in preparing the offering circular or *prospectus* for the securities, which provides important information to potential buyers. We will discuss the prospectus in more detail below in connection with government regulation.

Public Offerings via Privileged Subscription

When new common shares are sold to the general public, the proportionate ownership share of existing shareholders is reduced. For this reason, when new common stock or securities convertible into common stock are to be issued, many firms follow a practice of first offering the new securities to existing shareholders on a *privileged subscription* basis. The right of shareholders to have first chance at purchasing new shares is called a *preemptive* right and is supported by some state laws as well as by the corporate charters of many firms.

When a firm undertakes a *rights offering,* as privileged subscriptions often are called, it mails directly to shareholders one right for each share held. The terms of the offering specify the subscription price and number of rights required to purchase an additional share. For example, if a firm had 1 million shares outstanding and wished to offer 100,000 new shares, it would mail out 1 million rights and require 10 rights to purchase an additional share.

The subscription period during which the rights can be exercised generally runs 20–30 days. During that period, the rights have value because the subscription price is set below the current market price of the stock at the beginning of the subscription period. A shareholder therefore has several options: he can exercise his rights and purchase his pro rata share of the new securities; he can sell his rights; or he can buy additional rights from others not wishing to exercise them and subscribe to more than his pro rata share. One of these alternatives must be selected prior to the end of the subscription period, because at that point the rights become valueless.

When a rights offering is announced, the firm establishes a *date of record.* Owners of the stock on that date will receive rights to subscribe to the new offering. Prior to the record date, the stock sells *rights on,* which means that a purchaser of existing shares in the market prior to the record date will receive rights to the new offering. On the record date, the price of existing shares drops and the stock sells *ex-rights,* meaning that purchasers of the stock after the record date do not receive rights to subscribe to the new offering. By the end of the subscription period, the firm has collected the rights and the subscription proceeds, and any unexercised rights become worthless. Certificates for the new shares are issued at some later date.

Let us explore these price relationships in more detail. Suppose a firm has Y shares of stock outstanding selling at a price of P_o. A rights offering of X new shares is planned. Thus, a total of Y rights will be issued to shareholders, and the number of rights (N) required to purchase one new share is Y/X. The subscription price is set at S, so the shareholder will exchange N rights plus $\$S$ for one new share.

Let us assume that the total value of the firm is unchanged by the announcement of the offering—that there are no *information effects.* When the new shares actually are issued, total value will increase by the amount of new funds obtained, $\$SX$. Total value after the offering is completed thus will be value before plus $\$SX,$ or

$$V_1 = P_o Y + SX \tag{1}$$

Value per share after the offering will be

$$P_1 = \frac{V_1}{Y + X} = \frac{P_o Y + SX}{Y + X} \tag{2}$$

Dividing through by X and noting that $N = Y/X$ shows that

$$P_1 = \frac{P_o N + S}{N + 1} \tag{3}$$

Let us now move back in time to the period after the record date but before the issue date, the period during which the stock sells ex-rights. The act of selling X new shares increases the total value of the firm, but leaves the value per share unchanged. The market price per share does not change on the issue date, and thus is P_1 during the ex-rights period as well.

Continuing back in time, the record date is the date on which the rights take on value independently of the stock. Investors know that on the issue date they will be able to purchase a share of stock for $S + N$ rights. During the subscription period, one right therefore should be worth

$$R = \frac{P_1 - S}{N} \tag{4}$$

While the stock is selling ex-rights, the total value of the firm is the value of the stock plus the value of the rights, or $P_1 Y + RY$. Prior to the record date, total value was $P_0 Y$. Since the total value of the firm remains unchanged on the record date, we see that

$$P_1 Y + RY = P_0 Y \tag{5}$$

or

$$P_1 = P_0 - R \tag{6}$$

The market price of the stock thus drops on the record date by the amount of the value of one right.

Let us illustrate these relationships with an example. ABC Corporation has 100,000 shares outstanding at $50 per share and plans a rights offering of 25,000 shares. The subscription price is set at $40, and 100,000 rights are to be issued. Purchase of one new share thus will require $40 + 4 rights.

Applying expression (3), we find that $P_1 = [(50 \times 4) + 40]/(4 + 1) = \$48$. Applying expression (4), we find $R = (48 - 40)/4 = \$2.00$.

On the record date, the price of ABC stock drops from $50 to $48 and the rights take on an independent value of $2. A holder of a share previously worth $50 now holds a share worth $48 and a right worth $2. On the issue date, 25,000 new shares are issued at $40. The total value of the firm becomes ($50 $\times$ 100,000) + ($40 $\times$ 25,000), or $6 million. With 125,000 shares outstanding, price per share is $48. These various price and value relationships are illustrated in Figure 21-1.

The value given by expression (4) is the theoretical value of one right. In practice, the value of rights during the subscription period may deviate somewhat from the theoretical figure because of transaction costs and speculative pressures. Also, the value of both stock and rights may fluctuate due to changes in investor expectations regarding the firm or the economy.

It is especially important to note that, even though rights have value, the net worth of a shareholder is unchanged by a rights offering. Consider an individual holding four shares of ABC Corporation stock

Figure 21-1 Chronology of Rights Offering

worth $200 plus $40 in cash prior to the offering. If the rights are exercised, the shareholder winds up with five shares worth $48 each, a total of $240. If the four rights are sold, the shareholder winds up with four shares worth $48 each plus $48 in cash, again $240. Note also that to purchase one of the new shares, a nonshareholder must buy four rights at $2 each and put up $40 in addition for a total of $48.

Since the offering itself does not affect shareholder wealth, the subscription price can be set at any figure, provided that it is less than current market. The lower the subscription price, the greater the value of the rights. Thus, setting a lower subscription price does not permit outsiders to buy in at a lower figure, because outsiders must purchase the rights.

To ensure a successful offering, it is important that the market price of the stock not fall below the subscription price. If that were to happen, no one would buy the new shares, because old shares could be bought at a lower price in the open market. Since the subscription price does not affect the net worth of existing shareholders, it can be set low in relation to current market price in order to reduce the likelihood that the rights would not be exercised. The more volatile the market price, the greater the discount should be. It should be noted, however, that the lower the subscription price is set, the greater the number of new shares that must be issued to raise a given amount of money. In deciding this question, the implications for dividend policy must be taken into account.

Some rights offerings are undertaken by the issuing firm without the assistance of an investment banker. The success of such offerings depends in part on factors under the control of management, such as the relation between subscription price and market price and the size of the issue, and also on factors that management cannot control, such as general economic and market developments. To hedge against unfavorable developments that might jeopardize the success of an offering, many firms find it wise to obtain a *standby* commitment from an investment banker, or group of investment bankers, to underwrite any unsubscribed portion of the issue. In this way, the firm ensures that it will receive the funds. For this insurance, the firm pays a fee to the investment banker.

In recent years, the use of rights offerings has fallen off markedly. Many corporations (such as American Telephone and Telegraph) have changed their charters to eliminate the preemptive right previously given to shareholders. They are thus free to go directly to the market.

Dividend Reinvestment Plans

One innovative way of issuing a steady flow of new equity is to allow shareholders to apply their periodic dividend receipts automatically into the purchase of new shares, sometimes at a net price just below the prevailing market price. The American Telephone and Telegraph Company (AT&T), with its huge shareholder group and its perennial appetite for vast quantities of new capital, has been a leader in this financing device, but many other corporations have adopted such a policy, and new issuance of common equity through these programs has grown very rapidly—from an estimated $100 million in 1973 to an estimated $2 billion in 1979.

Direct Sales to the Public

Yet another innovation in recent years is direct sale of securities to the public without the use of an investment banker intermediary. The innovator was Exxon Corporation, which by-passed Wall Street in late 1976 by offering a $50 million issue of new debt securities to the public. In order to bring in small as well as large investors, Exxon used the so-called Dutch auction method. Under this system, prospective investors may submit individual bids (prices) to purchase selected amounts of the issue, but every successful bidder eventually pays the *same price*. This is the lowest price that Exxon had to accept in order to sell the stated $50 million amount of the issue.

Disclosure Requirements

Both the federal and state governments regulate the sale of securities to the public. The principal objective of such regulation is to ensure that adequate information is provided to prospective buyers of the securities and to protect buyers against misinformation and fraud.

The Securities Act of 1933, passed in the aftermath of the Great Depression and in response to stock market abuses of earlier years, sets forth federal regulatory requirements for new security issues. The Securities Exchange Act of 1934 deals with regulation of securities already outstanding. The Securities and Exchange Commission (SEC) administers both sets of requirements.

Under the provisions of the 1933 act, a firm wishing to sell securities to the public must register the issue with the SEC. Issues involving less than $300,000 are subject to considerably less detailed disclosure requirements. Certain specialized types of firms, such as railroads, are exempt from SEC registration requirements, because they are regulated by other government agencies.

The *registration statement* filed with the SEC contains information on the firm's history, its management, financial data, a description of the securities to be offered, uses to which proceeds will be put, and legal and accounting opinions. The firm also must file a *prospectus,* a summary of the information provided in the registration statement. A copy of the first page of the prospectus for an issue of Johns-Manville Corporation common stock is shown in Figure 21-2. The prospectus is the primary vehicle by which information is communicated to prospective investors. It is made available to investors by the investment banker or by the issuing firm if no investment banker is involved.

All parties to a securities offering have an interest in full disclosure of relevant information. The evidence indicates that the securities markets in general do an effective job of processing information and incorporating it into security prices. One of the most important objectives in a new issue is to see that it is priced so that neither new buyers nor existing holders are treated unfairly. Given the evidence regarding market efficiency, a management can rely on the impersonal action of the marketplace to see that the information is evaluated in an unbiased manner. A policy of full disclosure coupled with the market's efficiency is a management's best guarantee that new securities will be issued at fair prices.

Private Placements

Firms often sell securities directly to one or a small group of investors rather than to the public. Such issues are called *private placements.* The great majority of private placements are debt issues; common stock is

Figure 21-2 Example of a Prospectus

PROSPECTUS

2,500,000 Shares

Johns-Manville Corporation

Common Stock

The Company's Common Stock is listed on the New York Stock Exchange. The reported last sale price on such Exchange on May 26, 1976 was $26¾ per share.

THESE SECURITIES HAVE NOT BEEN APPROVED OR DISAPPROVED BY THE SECURITIES AND EXCHANGE COMMISSION NOR HAS THE COMMISSION PASSED UPON THE ACCURACY OR ADEQUACY OF THIS PROSPECTUS. ANY REPRESENTATION TO THE CONTRARY IS A CRIMINAL OFFENSE.

	Price to Public	Underwriting Discounts and Commissions(1)	Proceeds to Company(2)
Per Share	$26.75	$1.15	$25.60
Total	$66,875,000	$2,875,000	$64,000,000

(1) The Company has agreed to indemnify the Underwriters against certain liabilities, including liabilities under the Securities Act of 1933.

(2) Before expenses payable by the Company estimated at $138,000.

These Shares are offered by the Underwriters named herein subject to prior sale, when, as and if issued by the Company and accepted by the Underwriters and subject to the approval of certain legal matters by counsel for the Underwriters. It is expected that certificates for the Shares will be available for delivery on or about June 3, 1976 at the office of Smith Barney, Harris Upham & Co. Incorporated, 20 Broad Street, New York, N. Y. 10005.

Smith Barney, Harris Upham & Co.   Goldman, Sachs & Co.
                    Incorporated

May 26, 1976

Source: Courtesy of Smith Barney, Harris Upham & Co., Inc., and Goldman, Sachs & Co.

placed privately rather infrequently. The data in Table 21-1 indicate that private placements are a very important factor in the corporate debt market. Buyers of private placements are nearly always financial intermediaries such as insurance companies and pension funds.

Table 21-1 Corporate Bond Financing: Public Offerings and Private Placements (Billions of Dollars)[a]

Year	Public	Private	Total	Private (Percent)
1950	2,360	2,560	4,920	52.0
1955	4,119	3,301	7,402	44.5
1960	4,806	3,275	8,081	40.5
1965	5,570	8,150	13,720	59.4
1970	25,385	4,880	30,264	16.1
1975[b]	32,603	10,162	42,766	23.8
1978[b]	19,939	15,239	35,178	43.3

Source: Eli Shapiro and Charles R. Wolf, *The Role of Private Placements in Corporate Finance* (Boston: Graduate School of Business Administration, Harvard University, 1972). Reprinted by permission of Harvard University Press.
[a]Note that components may not add to totals because of rounding.
[b]The 1975 and 1978 data are from *Federal Reserve Bulletin*, A38 (Aug. 1976) and A36 (May 1979).

A firm may opt for a private placement rather than a public offering for any of several reasons. Firms that have not yet reached a sufficient size or established a sufficient track record to permit a public offering may find a private placement feasible. In fact, a major function of the private placement market is to serve as a source of long-term debt financing for smaller, less financially secure firms. In a private placement, a financial intermediary (say, an insurance company) performs the necessary tasks of information gathering and analysis at much less expense than would be the case in a public offering. Smaller amounts of funds, say, in the range of several hundred thousand to several million dollars, can be raised via private placement, whereas such amounts usually would be judged too small for a public offering. Securities and Exchange Commission registration is not required, so private placements generally can be consummated more quickly than can public offerings. Terms can be negotiated directly by lender and borrower without the involvement of an investment banker, although the latter often plays a role both in bringing borrower and lender together and in the negotiations. Since terms are negotiated and the time frame usually is shorter, timing problems due to market fluctuations are less troublesome than in the case of public offerings. Another advantage of a private placement is that the borrower can obtain a forward commitment by the lender to deliver funds in the future at a known rate.

Since registration is not required and no underwriting and selling expenses are involved, the direct expenses of private placements tend to be lower than those of public offerings, thereby reducing effective borrowing costs as much as 1 percentage point for small offerings ($1 million or less) to 0.10 percentage point for large offerings. Interest costs, on the other hand, tend to be slightly higher on private placements. The rate differential depends on the financial strength of the borrower, ranging from essentially no differential for stronger firms to 0.30 percentage point for less secure firms.[1]

The major borrower categories—public utilities, finance companies, and industrial companies—have exhibited quite different patterns of reliance on the private placement market. Public utilities have sold their debt almost entirely in the public markets. Large finance companies have sold a majority of their debt in the public markets. Small finance companies have sold most of their debt in the private markets. During 1953–1970, the 500 largest industrial firms in the United States sold 37 percent of their debt privately, while the remaining smaller industrial firms sold 75 percent privately.[2]

Costs of Issuing Securities

We have discussed two major costs of issuing securities: direct flotation expenses and interest costs. Direct expenses include underwriting commissions, selling expenses, legal fees, printing expenses, and mailing expenses. Another significant expense is related to management time that must be devoted to planning and negotiating an issue. The interest cost of a debt issue represents the return required by lenders. The return required by suppliers of equity funds is paid in the form of dividends and growth in capital values.

Some of these issue costs vary with the size of the issue and some are fixed. Consequently, issue costs as a percentage of funds raised vary inversely with the size of the issue. Raising small amounts of money therefore is uneconomic, and firms generally attempt to limit the frequency of trips to the markets and to finance in *blocks*. This lumpiness imposes short-run constraints on firms' investment policy, as we have noted in earlier chapters.

Timing of Issues

From the standpoint of existing shareholders, it would be desirable to issue long-term securities when stock prices in general are relatively

---

1. See Eli Shapiro and Charles R. Wolf, *The Role of Private Placements in Corporate Finance* (Boston: Graduate School of Business Administration, Harvard University, 1972).
2. Ibid.

high and long-term interest rates are low. Should the financial manager spend significant effort on developing a policy of planned timing for new issues? The answer to the timing question still appears to be controversial. On the one hand, the academic answer is that superior timing is not possible. On the other hand, financial managers behave as if planning can lead to superior timing.

The academic argument runs as follows: Timing requires an ability to forecast future market conditions. But evidence which has led to the modern theory of efficient markets suggests that the prospects for superior forecasting are not encouraging.[3] The theory holds that prices and interest rates reflect all public information in an unbiased manner. Current prices and rates thus reflect a consensus forecast of future prices and rates by the best-informed and best-financed investors. Everyone knows that the consensus forecast could be inaccurate and that the future might well be different from the expectation. But the error is about as likely to be in one direction as the other, and most attempts to outguess the market have only about a 50/50 chance of success.

Given such odds, firms should not attempt to time issues, but rather adopt a general policy of raising funds when needed. Conditions that appear to be depressed as likely as not will turn out, in retrospect, to be not so depressed after all. Deferral of security issues is likely to mean deferral of investment decisions and interference with the firm's commercial strategy. Given the odds of success, a policy of attempting to exploit market movements is unlikely to provide gains that consistently outweigh the costs of interruptions in investment plans. The best policy is thus to let the commercial strategy dictate the timing of external financings, and to rely on full disclosure and market efficiency to ensure fair pricing.

Most practitioners find the academic argument puzzling and they reject its nihilism. They argue that timing, in a broad sense, is possible, and they act as if they believe it. In 1974, when stock prices

3. For discussions of the theory of efficient markets and empirical evidence in its support, see Richard A. Brealey, *An Introduction to Risk and Return from Common Stocks* (Cambridge, Mass.: MIT Press, 1969); and *Security Prices in a Competitive Market* (Cambridge, Mass.: MIT Press, 1971); Eugene F. Fama, "Efficient Capital Markets—A Review of Theory and Empirical Work," *Journal of Finance* **25,** 383–417 (May 1970); Michael C. Jensen, "Capital Markets—Theory and Evidence," *Bell Journal of Economics and Management Science* 3(2), 357–398 (Autumn 1972); and Thomas R. Dyckman, David H. Downes, and Robert P. Magee, *Efficient Capital Markets and Accounting—A Critical Analysis* (Englewood Cliffs, N.J.: Prentice-Hall, 1975). For theoretical arguments and empirical evidence that the market is not perfectly efficient, see E. Miller, "Risk, Uncertainty and Divergence of Opinion," *Journal of Finance* **32,** 1151–1168 (Sept. 1977); H. A. Latané and C. P. Jones, "Standardized Unexpected Earnings—A Progress Report," *Journal of Finance* **32,** 1457–1466 (Dec. 1977); and N. E. Mains, "Risk, the Pricing of Capital Assets, and the Evaluation of Investment Portfolios: Comment," *Journal of Business* **50,** 371-384 (July 1977).

were low and falling, the volume of new stock issues was very much lower than it was in 1972 or 1976 under opposite market conditions. Likewise, the volume of bond issues placed was lower in 1973 and 1974, when long-term interest rates appeared to be high, than in 1975 and 1976, when interest rates were significantly lower.

There are two reasons why the apparent conflict between the two opposing viewpoints is at least partly a false conflict. First, when stock prices are at a low level (such as at the end of 1974) or interest rates are high, it also means that the required rate of return on new capital investments is high, that is, that the investment worth of new capital expenditure proposals is low and hence the pressure to expand capital investment is also low. In other words, the net present value rule suggests that the corporate demand for capital falls when financial market conditions are poor. In a sense, what the academician is saying is "if you have worthwhile investments to make, you should raise the necessary funds by issuing securities, regardless of how you may think security markets are going to change." What the practitioner is saying is that under poor security market conditions, he is willing to postpone capital investments he might be willing to recommend under better security market conditions. Both statements are correct.

Second, when security market conditions are poor, it is very difficult to issue and sell long-term securities even if the company is willing to do so. When the practitioner thinks of timing, he is thinking about this impaired ability to market an issue as well as the price at which it is to be marketed.

What happens in practice is a compromise between the academic idea that superior timing in a forecasting sense is very difficult and the practitioner's idea that there are wrong times and right times to issue long-term securities.

Firms try to develop a flexible financing posture. They draw up a long-range financing plan which indicates the total flow of permanent financing they are likely to need over a 3–5 year period. Within this time span, they go to the long-term securities market when conditions, prices, and rates seem to be more, rather than less, appropriate. In between, they balance their capital needs either through short-term borrowing or by stretching out their capital spending plans.

Other Considerations in Issuing Securities

At this point, it is appropriate to remind ourselves of several other considerations that we have discussed at other points in this book. One such consideration is *control*. Maintenance of control usually is a major consideration in closely held firms when external financing is contemplated. In order to maintain control, a firm may impose restrictions on financing alternatives, which in turn may constrain its investment policy. Control is very important in some situations, but maintaining it is likely to entail costs in terms of reduced access to the financial markets and constraints on commercial strategy.

Another important consideration has to do with *sequencing* of issues when a series of external financings is in prospect. A major objective in planning sequential issues is to maintain flexibility with respect to alternative sources.

Managing Outstanding Issues

Once a firm has issued securities to the public, it incurs some responsibilities for managing the securities after issuance. The discussion in this section pertains primarily to publicly traded issues, although parts of the discussion, such as that pertaining to communication, are pertinent to privately held issues as well.

Trading of Securities after Issuance

If a holder of the bonds or stock of a firm wishes to liquidate his investment, he must sell his securities to someone else. He cannot return them to the issuing firm for redemption. In the case of closely held firms, finding an interested buyer may be difficult. In the case of more widely held firms, *public markets* exist in which shares can be freely bought and sold. Public markets in the United States are of two general types: the organized *stock exchanges* and the *over-the-counter* market.

The best known of the stock exchanges are the New York Stock Exchange and the American Stock Exchange, both located in New York City. There also exist a number of regional exchanges elsewhere in the United States. The exchanges constitute an *auction* market where buyers and sellers state their terms. A *specialist* acts as broker to bring buyers and sellers together, sometimes buying and selling for his own account.

The over-the-counter market is made up of a larger number of investment firms that act as *dealers*. A dealer *makes a market* in the shares of a particular firm by quoting *bid* and *asked* prices at which he stands ready to buy or sell. The dealer is compensated by the spread between the bid and asked prices.

Communication with the Markets

Heading the list of important responsibilities in connection with outstanding issues is *communications*. Earlier in this chapter we discussed

the importance of full disclosure of all pertinent information to prospective buyers of new issues. Here we focus on communication with
holders of existing issues.

Regular Financial Reporting

Since management acts as agent of the owners of the firm, keeping
those owners informed clearly is an important management responsibility. In the case of publicly held firms, SEC regulations require
regular reporting, at least annually, to shareholders. Larger firms also
are required to report to shareholders quarterly. The New York Stock
Exchange requires both annual and quarterly reports by firms whose
stock is traded on the exchange.

The format and content of such published financial reports are
prescribed by the SEC in cooperation with the accounting profession.
Quarterly reports generally are brief and cover the most recent
quarterly and year-to-date information. Annual reports usually are
much more comprehensive; they often include extensive historical
statistical data as well as narrative information on the firm's operations
and plans. Financial statements in annual reports are audited by a certified public accounting firm.

Besides the above published reports, firms also are required to
file certain regular reports directly with the SEC. These reports include standard financial information and also reports of special events
such as changes in directors and principal officers, mergers and acquisitions, lawsuits, large losses, and the like. Information of this sort
also should be reported to shareholders and the investing public, and
most firms follow a policy of doing so.

Firms also are required to hold a general meeting of shareholders
at least annually, at which time directors are elected and other business is conducted. In addition to regularly scheduled communications
via meetings and reports, firms typically communicate a variety of
routine information via press releases.

In addition to reporting historical information, firms should keep
investors fully informed with respect to strategy and policy. Owners
and potential investors are entitled to know what basic goals management has set, the general outline of the commercial strategy, and the
major policies that will be followed. With respect to financial management specifically, investors are entitled to know what management's
target debt/equity ratio is, what policies will be followed with respect
to debt maturity, and what the target dividend payout is. To the extent that competitive considerations permit, future investment opportunities and plans also should be communicated. With respect to all
such policies, the objective is to tell investors what is going on rather

than forcing them to guess. Complete disclosure is good practice not only because owners are entitled to the information, but also because better disclosure promotes fairer pricing of securities. In general, comprehensive disclosure on a regular basis contributes to smaller price fluctuations and avoids surprises.

Regular reporting also lays the groundwork for future securities issues. Where a firm has publicly traded securities, their market price is a major factor in setting the price of a new issue. Hence, the price at which new securities are offered is largely determined by holders of existing securities. For this reason, comprehensive disclosure on an ongoing basis provides the best assurance of fair prices for new issues.

Reporting in Connection with Extraordinary Events

Even with a comprehensive program of disclosure on a regular basis, special effort is required in connection with extraordinary events such as new security offerings or major new investment plans. The factors that determine security prices are future oriented: future cash flows and the riskiness of those cash flows. When only historical information is reported, the market is forced to draw inferences from management actions and whatever data is reported. The announcement of investment, financing, and dividend decisions thus can produce significant and possibly undesirable information effects as the market attempts to draw inferences regarding the future.

For example, announcement of a financing decision may convey information regarding investment opportunities. If the market interprets the announcement of a new financing as a signal that management sees more attractive investment opportunities ahead than previously had been anticipated, the stock price may rise. If the market sees no such ·attractive opportunities, the price may fall. In either case, the market is using the financing decision as the basis for drawing an inference about investment opportunities. Rather than relying on the market to draw the proper inference, it is better to communicate the facts directly.

A similar situation might arise in connection with a change in dividend policy. A cut in dividends, for example, might indicate that management sees attractive investment opportunities ahead and is conserving funds for investment. Alternatively, the market might infer that management sees bad times ahead and is conserving cash for emergency use. The first inference is likely to cause a rise in stock price, the second a fall. To avoid the possibility of incorrect interpretations, management should communicate the reasons for the change carefully and clearly. If the news is bad, owners and prospective investors are entitled to know it.

The preceding examples illustrate situations in which the market draws inferences from management actions. It is clear that straight-forward communication is desirable so that the market bases its actions on facts rather than inferences. A related situation can occur when a management is contemplating an action that is believed to be in the shareholders' interests, but which may be misinterpreted by the market. If funds are needed for investment and the firm is at or near its debt capacity, equity may be the right choice. Will the resulting dilution of earnings per share reduce stock price? Suppose equity is needed at a time when market price is below book value. Will a sale of equity at a price below book value be viewed negatively by the market? A third situation can occur in the case of an invest-ment opportunity with a very high rate of return but low cash flows in early years and therefore adverse implications for near-term ac-counting profits. Fear of misinterpretation and an adverse reception by the market may lead a management to forego actions that in fact are in the shareholders' interests.

Problems of the above sort usually can be minimized by careful communication. Investors are rational and entirely capable of under-standing their own self-interests. If a particular decision is in the interests of shareholders, it is likely that they will agree. If a dividend cut really is needed, it should be made and the reasons carefully communicated. If an investment really does have attractive long-run returns, investors will be quite prepared to ignore an adverse impact on near-term profits. Foregoing such investments does no favors for shareholders. If an equity issue is needed, investors can be persuaded. In fact, firms that issue debt instead of equity for fear of earnings dilution and thereby exceed their debt capacity ultimately will receive a message of disapproval from the market via a low price/earnings ratio.

Communication Policy

From the foregoing discussion of communications, what can we con-clude with respect to appropriate policies? In general, firms should make financial management decisions using value-maximization as a criterion. Insofar as is possible in an uncertain world, a manage-ment can be confident that decisions reached in this way are in the shareholders' interests. Once the appropriate action has been decided, the reasoning behind it should be communicated as completely as possible. Often competitive considerations will make complete disclosure unwise. In such cases, the benefits of disclosure have to be weighed against loss of competitive advantages, with the interests of existing shareholders the guiding criterion. Difficulties with controversial decisions often center on adverse near-term impact on earnings per share. Communications should deal with this problem by explaining long-run implications. Good communication helps management take a long view, which, after all, is management's job.

Listing of Shares

Shares that trade on an exchange, such as the New York or American Stock Exchanges, are said to be *listed* on the exchange. Exchanges have certain requirements with respect to size, years in business, number of shares outstanding, trading volume, market value, and earnings record that must be met before a firm will be accepted for listing. The reporting requirements of the exchanges over and above those already imposed by the SEC are not great in the case of non-financial firms, although there historically have been differences in the case of banks.

Most firms therefore begin their existence as public companies in the over-the-counter market and graduate to an exchange at a later stage in their development. Listed firms make up only a small percentage of the total number of business firms in the United States, but include the great majority of the larger nonfinancial firms. Banks and insurance companies historically have had their shares traded over-the-counter, but recently there has been a strong trend toward listing of bank holding company shares.

Advantages of listing that typically are cited include a better market for shareholders wishing to buy and sell, better accommodation of large transactions, facilitation of future financings, and an improvement in the firm's status. While these indeed may be real advantages, studies of listing have found no evidence that listing itself adds permanently to a firm's value.[4] Thus, listing might be expected to result in somewhat less variability of stock price but not in a higher average price level.

Retiring Outstanding Securities

Long-term debt issues of firms almost without exception[5] have a final maturity date by which the principal must be repaid. Maturities range

---

4. See James C. Van Horne, "New Listings and Their Price Behavior," *Journal of Finance* **25,** 783–794 (Sept. 1970).
5. An exception is the Canadian Pacific 4 percent perpetual bonds, which are consols having no maturity.

from a few years to about 25 years. Maturities beyond about 25 years are rare, because over longer periods the nature of a business and its environment can change radically, and lenders usually want an opportunity to reevaluate the risk from time to time.

Unlike debt, common stock is a perpetual claim with no provision for retirement, although retirement can be accomplished via repurchase. Preferred stock usually carries a provision for retirement but sometimes does not. We will discuss the retirement of each of these basic types of securities below.

Retirement of Long-Term Debt

Long-term debt can be retired in a number of ways. One way is simply to repay the entire principal at maturity. Most issues, however, require periodic repayment via either a *sinking fund* or *serial redemption.* Some bond issues can be called at the option of the issuer. Convertible bonds are retired by conversion into common stock.

Bond issues that provide for periodic repayment may do so via either a sinking fund or serial redemption. Under a *sinking fund* arrangement, the terms of which are set forth in the bond indenture, the firm makes periodic payments, usually annually or semiannually, to the trustee of the bond issue. The trustee uses the funds to retire a specified number of bonds in one of two ways: by open market purchases, or by calling certain bonds at a previously agreed upon price. The trustee will purchase in the open market as long as the market price is less than the call price. When market price is above the call price, the call provision will be exercised. Bonds to be called usually are selected on a lottery basis using their serial numbers to identify them.[6]

The proportion of the total issue to be retired at each sinking fund payment date is set forth in the indenture. The amount of the periodic sinking fund payment usually is fixed so that the same number of bonds is retired each time. Some issues provide for retirement of the entire issue by the final maturity date, whereas others may provide for only partial retirement with a *balloon payment* at maturity.

Sinking fund bonds all have the same maturity date, although a portion of the bonds are retired in advance of maturity under procedures described above. *Serial* bonds, on the other hand, have sequential maturity dates. A $50 million issue, for example, may have $2.5 million in bonds maturing each year for 20 years. Over the life of the issue, bonds are redeemed each year as they mature.

---

6. For a theoretical analysis of callable bonds, see J. E. Ingersoll, "A Contingent Claims Valuation of Convertible Securities," *Journal of Financial Economics* **2,** 289–322 (May 1977).

Under a sinking fund arrangement, the trustee is empowered to call a portion of the bonds each year. Most corporate bond issues also provide for calling the entire issue at the option of the issuer. Some issues permit call at any time, although more typically the call privilege is not effective for 5–10 years after issuance.

Retirement via sinking fund or serial redemption usually is a provision sought by lenders. The option to call the entire issue is a provision sought by the borrower. Call of an entire issue might be advantageous to a firm either to permit changes in capital structure or to permit refunding of the issue at a lower interest rate. The latter reason probably is more often the principal motive for the call provision from the borrower's standpoint. In an uncertain world in which interest rates vary, having the option to retire a bond issue and reborrow at a lower rate clearly is advantageous. The advantage accrues to the shareholders, who would benefit from the reduction in interest costs. To the extent that the call privilege is advantageous to shareholders, it is disadvantageous to holders of the bonds, for in the event that the privilege is exercised, bondholders must give up a security paying an interest rate above the prevailing market. As one would expect in a competitive market, bondholders insist on being compensated for the call privilege. Other factors being equal, the interest rate on a callable issue will be higher. Also, the price at which the bonds are callable is set above par value. In short, the shareholders must pay for the flexibility afforded by the call privilege.

As noted above, the most frequent motive for calling an issue is to *refund* it, that is, to issue a new set of bonds in its place. The usual motive is to refund at a lower interest rate, although sometimes renegotiation of restrictive covenants also is a consideration. Considering only the interest rate motive, the decision of whether to refund can be analyzed using discounted cash flow techniques. To identify the relevant cash flows, we apply the incremental cash flow rule. The firm makes an outlay, essentially the difference between the amount required to call the old issue and the proceeds of the new issue, and receives a stream of inflows consisting mainly of the annual interest savings. Other incremental cash flows include expenses of the transaction and tax effects. Since the interest savings are known with certainty and the expenses and tax effects are subject to little uncertainty, the appropriate discount rate is the after-tax equivalent of the interest rate on the new bonds.

Retirement of Preferred Stock

Although preferred stock has no maturity date and the preferred shareholders' investment is considered permanent, preferred issues nearly always include some provision for retirement. Some issues provide for periodic retirement via a sinking fund, although many do not. Where used, the procedure is essentially the same as that in the case of bond sinking funds.

Nearly all preferred issues include a call privilege. As in the case of callable debt issues, the call price is above par value. Buyers of preferred issues charge for the call privilege by demanding a higher dividend rate. The usual motives for calling a preferred issue are to refinance at a lower dividend rate, to alter the firm's capital structure, or to renegotiate restrictive covenants.

Many preferred issues are convertible into common stock and are subject to retirement in that manner.

Repurchase of Common Stock

Common stock has no maturity and never includes provisions either for periodic retirement or for call. The only means by which common stock can be retired is by repurchase of outstanding shares, either through open market purchases or an *invitation to tender*. In the latter case, a firm invites shareholders to offer or tender their shares to the firm at a specified price. Usually, a minimum and a maximum number of shares that will be repurchased is specified by the firm.

The incidence of repurchasing by firms of their own shares seems to ebb and flow, becoming more prevalent in some periods and then declining again. Several motives may be cited by a firm for repurchasing, one of which is as an alternative to paying dividends. If a firm wishes to distribute a given amount of cash to its shareholders, in lieu of a cash dividend it can simply repurchase an appropriate number of its own shares. Cash received by shareholders upon sale of stock normally would be taxed at capital gain rates, whereas a dividend would have been taxed at the higher ordinary income rate. In effect, repurchase has the potential to transform ordinary income into a capital gain and save the shareholders some taxes. However, the Internal Revenue Service (IRS) has long since noticed the tax advantage to shareholders and has ruled against it. Any repurchase deemed to be in lieu of a dividend is likely to be treated as such by the IRS.

Repurchase, therefore, usually is justified on grounds other than as an alternative to a dividend. Sometimes repurchase is justified as an investment, or a means of improving earnings per share. However, it is improper to view repurchase as an investment under any circumstances. In fact, it is nothing more nor less than a stock issue in reverse. It is true that earnings per share rise, but only in proportion to the reduction in the number of shares. If the shares are repurchased at less than their true value, those shareholders who do not sell realize a gain, but it represents a transfer of wealth from selling shareholders, not new value created, and raises serious questions of ethics.

Sometimes repurchase is justified as a means of accumulating shares for use in future acquisitions or for employee stock options. Here, too, the advantage is illusory, for the purpose is served equally well by issuing new shares.

One motive for repurchase that does make economic sense is to return capital, that is, to achieve a partial liquidation of the firm. If a firm's markets have eroded and a reduction in scale is appropriate, a part of the shareholders' investment can be returned via repurchase. This reason for repurchase is not often used, however, because most managements prefer the alternative of seeking other investments to a partial liquidation.

Another motive for repurchase that is defensible is to effect a change in the firm's debt/equity ratio. If a firm wishes to increase its debt ratio quickly, one way to do so is to issue new debt and use the proceeds to retire common stock. Again, this motive is not often used in practice.

Whatever the motive for repurchase, a management should be especially careful to communicate fully to investors its reasons for the repurchase. Since some shareholders give up all or a part of their interest in the firm, it is especially important as a matter of fairness and ethics that all shareholders have all pertinent information on which to base their decisions, including information regarding the firm's future prospects. As a practical matter, it is essentially impossible for a management to communicate all relevant information. Therefore, being entirely fair to both selling and nonselling shareholders is difficult indeed.

Of the motives usually given for repurchase discussed above, one (repurchase in lieu of a dividend) is not permitted under IRS regulations. Two others (an investment and to obtain shares for other purposes) rest on questionable economic logic. The two that do make economic sense (partial liquidation and increasing the debt ratio) are applicable in situations that do not often occur. In view of the potential ethical questions involved in repurchase, a management contemplating repurchase should consider carefully the benefits and costs and make certain that repurchase is the best vehicle for accomplishing the objectives at hand.

In 1977, International Business Machines (IBM), the world's largest firm in terms of the total market value of shares outstanding, engaged in heavy repurchases of its own stock for motives other than the usual ones cited above. During the stock market boom of the 1960s, the so-called high capitalization growth stocks, such as IBM, Xerox, and Eastman Kodak, were highly favored by the large institutional investors who manage corporate pension fund investments. By 1972, these stocks, and especially IBM, represented a disproportionately large share in most institutional portfolios. After 1972, common stocks performed badly (the level of the market in mid-1979 was some 20 percent below the peak level reached in late 1972) and the previously favored growth stocks fared even worse than stocks in general. Plagued by poor performance, many institutional investors tried to readjust their portfolios to ensure that their own performance would, at minimum, be as good as "the market as a whole." In theory, this required them to sell such stocks as IBM, which were overrepresented in their portfolios. Since most of the institutions were in the same predicament, the notion developed that there was a large net "overhang" of stocks like IBM waiting to be sold, which, in turn, would act as a continuous depressant on the price of these stocks. One reason given for IBM's repurchase decision was to test the validity of the "overhang" thesis. Another reason was that IBM wanted to reduce its huge store of liquid assets, which at this time amounted to some $6.5 billion and that its own stock represented one of the best alternative outlets available. In any case, in February 1977, the company offered to buy up to 5½ million shares at $280 per share. This bid drew offers to sell only 2½ million shares. In July the company renewed its repurchase offer, but on this occasion, the offer was priced "at prevailing market prices" and was aimed directly at large blocks (5,000 shares or more) held by institutional investors.

Failure and Reorganization

Thus far we have discussed issuing and managing securities under more or less normal circumstances. Unhappily, firms are not always as successful as their owners, managers, and creditors had hoped. Many firms encounter financial difficulty of one degree or another during their lives, and some fail. Here we consider failure and reorganization as a special case of managing relationships with suppliers of funds.

The reasons that firms encounter distress are varied. Sometimes external factors are the cause, such as changes in technology or markets. In an uncertain world, even the most capably managed firm is not immune to unexpected difficulty. The case of Bowmar Instruments Corp. is a good recent example of this source of failure. Bowmar, which manufactured handheld calculators, literally boomed in the early 1970s along with the growing market for these glamorous and useful gadgets. Earnings climbed from 3¢ a share in 1970 to $3.75 a share in 1973, and the price of the stock jumped from $3½ to $44⅞. Funds were easy to obtain for an ambitious set of expansion plans. But along came competition. Texas

Instruments and dozens of other companies entered the field. Product prices dropped under the pressure of these competitive entries and rapidly evolving manufacturing technology. By 1974, Bowmar's earnings moved from rapid growth into serious deficits. By early 1975, Bowmar filed for reorganization under Chapter 11 of the bankruptcy laws.

A more frequent reason for serious financial difficulty is poor management. A good example of this is W. T. Grant and Co., a giant retailing chain of over 1,000 stores that went into bankruptcy proceedings in 1975. As the court-appointed trustees explored the reasons for Grant's failure, the evidence clearly pointed to one overriding cause—bad management, exemplified by totally inadequate budgetary, inventory, and credit controls.

In still other cases, financial difficulty may represent a signal that society wishes a reduction in the resources allocated to the activity in question. In a market economy, profits are the ultimate measure of whether resources are being allocated appropriately and managed efficiently.

Financial difficulties vary widely in severity, from relatively minor liquidity problems to complete failure. The number of firms having difficulties severe enough to file bankruptcy petitions is relatively small. The number encountering less severe forms of financial distress is much larger. The more severe the difficulty, the more drastic the remedy required and usually the more formal the procedure for adjustment.

When serious financial difficulties occur, what solutions will best serve the interests of society as a whole? Where the difficulty is due to uncertainty or to management error, rather than the result of a misallocation of resources, it would seem appropriate to maintain the firm as a going concern rather than to terminate its operations. Where misallocation is apparent, orderly procedures are needed for liquidation of the firm and reallocation of remaining resources to other uses. In all cases, the rights of creditors and owners and their claims against the assets and earnings of the firm must be spelled out clearly. To begin our discussion, let us attempt to define business failure more clearly.

Business Failure

Under what conditions should a firm be considered to have failed? We must distinguish between two different situations. In the first, the value of the firm's assets exceeds its liabilities, that is, its net worth is greater than zero, but it is unable to meet its contractual financial obligations. These obligations might include interest and/or principal payments on debt, lease payments, or payments on installment sales contracts. The firm's cash flows are not sufficient to meet the contractual payments. Essentially, the problem is one of *maturity;* the firm's liabilities are maturing faster than its assets.

Such situations involving a shortage of liquidity sometimes are referred to as *technical insolvency.* Where the firm's prospects remain favorable, as implied by a positive net worth, the difficulties often can be resolved by means short of legal bankruptcy. Such adjustments are worked out voluntarily by the firm and its creditors. Where the difficulties are so resolved, the term *failure* probably overstates the case a bit, even though the situation initially involved a default on a financial obligation.

The second type of failure is one in which the firm's liabilities exceed the value of its assets as a going concern, that is, its net worth is zero. Often this type of failure is accompanied by the first type, a liquidity crisis, but the two are separable. In some cases, there may be uncertainty about the eventual value of the assets if the firm is liquidated, and the market price of the firm's stock may not fall entirely to zero. Where it is clear that liabilities exceed the firm's going concern value, the ultimate outcome is likely to be bankruptcy, unless action can be taken to improve the firm's earnings prospects.

Voluntary Adjustments

In a crisis of the first type above, where the difficulty is one of cash flow and liquidity, the firm's value as a going concern exceeds its liabilities. In such situations, creditors usually are better off if they accommodate the firm's short-run difficulties and allow it to remain in operation. In some cases, the firm may be able to adjust its cash flows to meet its financial obligations, with no changes in the terms of the latter. Adjustments of this sort usually involve a sale of assets. For example, accounts receivable or a part of the firm's plant and equipment might be sold. Such sales of assets are likely to be painful, but perhaps less so than the available alternatives.

Where cash flow adjustments are not feasible or inadequate, a second alternative is to adjust the financial obligations to fit the available cash flow. Often such adjustments are worked out between firm and creditors without recourse to the bankruptcy statutes and without the involvement of the courts. One possible adjustment is called an *extension,* whereby the maturity of one or more obligations is extended to give the firm more time to meet it. Another is called a *composition,* under which all creditors agree to accept a partial payment. Where the basic difficulty is due to a liquidity shortage, an extension usually is the appropriate remedy.

Bankruptcy

Where the appropriate remedy cannot be agreed upon informally, relief can be sought by either the firm or its creditors in the courts. Bankruptcies are governed by a federal law, the Chandler Act, often called the Bankruptcy Act, which was passed in 1938. Under the act, a debtor may petition the court for reorganization. Alternatively, under certain circumstances, creditors may petition to have a firm adjudged a bankrupt. Under either case, a basic purpose of the Bankruptcy Act is to maintain the status quo so that no one group of creditors can gain at the expense of another. Time thus is made available to study the situation and determine the appropriate remedy.

When a bankruptcy petition is filed, it usually means that the firm's liabilities exceed its value as a going concern, at least in the eyes of creditors or owners, or both. The question of whether the firm should be reorganized and allowed to continue in operation, or liquidated, still remains.

Most *reorganizations* take place under either Chapter X or Chapter XI of the Bankruptcy Act. The applicable section of the act depends on the nature of the firm's liabilities and whether its securities are publicly or privately held. The objective of the reorganization is to restructure the liabilities so that the firm's anticipated cash flows are sufficient to meet them. Reorganization may involve extension or composition of debt obligations or creation of new classes of securities. During the reorganization, the firm continues to operate, either under its old management or a receiver appointed by the court.

If the liquidation value of the firm is greater than its going concern value, then liquidation of the firm's assets is probably the best remedy. Assets are converted to cash and the proceeds are distributed to claimholders under the *rule of absolute priority,* which states that senior claimants must be paid in full before junior claimants receive anything. Liquidation usually is lengthy and costly.

Summary

Firms have important responsibilities to their suppliers of funds, creditors as well as investors. These responsibilities begin with the issuance of new securities and continue as long as the securities remain outstanding.

Firms normally issue new debt and equity securities to the public using one of three methods: public offerings through investment bankers, public offerings via privileged subscription, and private placements. Investment bankers are middlemen who perform a number of important functions in the issuance of new securities including underwriting, pricing, and selling. Some firms follow a practice of offering new common stock to existing shareholders via a privileged subscription before offering it to the public at large. All public offerings are subject to government regulation, especially with respect to disclosure of pertinent information.

An alternative to a public offering, normally used only for debt issues, is a private placement with one or a small group of investors, usually insurance companies or pension funds. Private placements usually are simpler and quicker than public offerings and represent an important source of long-term financing to smaller, less financially secure firms.

In developing financing plans, the timing of new issues is an important consideration, especially when a sequence of issues is in prospect. Market conditions must be taken into account even though forecasting changes in conditions is very difficult.

One of the most important of the firm's continuing responsibilities after issuance of securities is communication. Comprehensive disclosure of ongoing developments within the firm and of management policies facilitates relations with the financial markets. Especially important is careful communication in connection with extraordinary events or changes in major policies so that investors and creditors can base decisions on facts rather than on inferences.

Long-term debt issues nearly always provide for gradual retirement (repayment) prior to maturity, either via a sinking fund arrangement or serial redemption. Many bond issues also include provision for calling the issue at the option of management. Some preferred stock issues include a sinking fund provision and nearly all include a call privilege. Common stock does not include provision for periodic retirement or for call and can be retired only through repurchase by the firm. Because of the potential for conflict between different groups of shareholders, repurchase should be considered only when it can accomplish clear economic objectives equitably.

The responsibility of a firm to investors and creditors includes provisions for dealing with financial distress. Where the difficulty stems from uncertainty or management error, rather than a misallocation of resources, the interests of creditors and owners as well as society usually are best served by voluntary adjustments or reorganization under the federal Bankruptcy Act, both of which maintain the firm as a going concern. Liquidation of assets is appropriate only if liquidation value exceeds the value of the firm as a going concern.

Questions

1. What are the three principal methods of issuing securities to the public?
2. What are the major functions of investment bankers?
3. What is a *privileged subscription* offering?
4. In a rights offering, how does the subscription price of the offering affect the net worth of shareholders?
5. What is the purpose of federal and state regulation of the securities markets?
6. What is a *private placement* of securities? What are the advantages of private placements?
7. Why do issue costs affect the size and frequency of financing?
8. What responsibilities do firms have to provide information to investors and other participants in the financial markets?
9. Why is it desirable for firms to keep investors informed regarding future plans to the extent possible? How does such information affect the price of the firm's securities?
10. How are long-term debt issues retired?
11. What is a *sinking fund* in connection with bonds or preferred stock?
12. How do *serial bonds* differ from sinking fund bonds?
13. Why do borrowers normally wish to have the option to call a bond issue before maturity?
14. How can common stock be retired?
15. What motives exist for the repurchase by a firm of its own common stock?
16. What potential ethical questions do you see in a decision to repurchase stock?
17. In what way does financial difficulty represent a judgment by society regarding a firm's performance?
18. What is meant by the term *technical insolvency?*
19. What steps are required when a firm encounters financial difficulty?

References

P. W. Bacon, "The Subscription Price in Rights Offerings," *Financial Management* **1**, 59–64 (Summer 1972).

E. Bloch, "Pricing a Corporate Bond Issue: A Look Behind the Scenes," *Essays in Money and Credit* (New York: Federal Reserve Bank of New York, 1964), pp. 72–76.

R. A. Brealey, *Security Prices in a Competitive Market* (Cambridge, Mass.: MIT Press, 1971).

J. M Brown, "Post-Offering Experience of Companies Going Public," *Journal of Business* **43,** 10–18 (Jan. 1970).

A. B. Cohan, *Private Placements and Public Offerings: Market Shares Since 1935* (Chapel Hill, N.C.: School of Business Administration, University of N.C., 1961).

A. B. Cohan, *Yields on Corporate Debt Directly Placed* (New York: National Bureau of Economic Research, 1967).

T. R. Dyckman, D. H. Downes, and R. D. Magee, *Efficient Markets and Accounting—A Critical Analysis* (Englewood Cliffs, N.J.: Prentice-Hall 1975).

E. A. Dyl and M. D. Joehnk, "Competitive versus Negotiated Underwriting of Public Utility Debt," *Bell Journal of Economics* **7,** 680–689 (Autumn 1976).

E. J. Elton and M. J. Gruber, "The Effect of Share Repurchase on the Value of the Firm," *Journal of Finance* **23,** 135–150 (Mar. 1968).

E. F. Fama, "Efficient Capital Markets: A Review of Theory and Empirical Work," *Journal of Finance* **25,** 383–417 (May 1970).

M. Fleuriet, *Public and Private Offerings of Public Debt: Changes in the Yield Spread* (New York: Graduate School of Business Administration, New York University Bulletin 1975-1).

I. Friend, G. W. Hoffman, and W. J. Winn, *The Over-the-Counter Securities Market* (New York: McGraw-Hill, 1958).

I. Friend, *et al., Investment Banking and the New Issues Market* (Cleveland: World, 1967).

S. L. Hayes, III, "Investment Banking: Power Structure in Flux," *Harvard Business Review* **49,** 136–152 (Mar.–Apr. 1971).

J. E. Ingersoll, "A Contingent Claims Valuation of Convertible Securities," *Journal of Financial Economics* **2,** 289–322 (May 1977).

F. C. Jen and J. E. Wert, "The Deferred Call Provision and Corporate Bond Yields," *Journal of Financial and Quantitative Analysis* **3,** 157–170 (June 1968).

F. C. Jen and J. E. Wert, "The Value of the Deferred Call Privilege," *National Banking Review* **3,** 369–378 (Mar. 1966).

M. C. Jensen, "Capital Markets: Theory and Evidence," *The Bell Journal of Economics and Management Science* **3,** 357–398 (Autumn 1972).

K. B. Johnson, T. G. Morton, and M. C. Findlay, III, "An Empirical Analysis of the Flotation Cost of Corporate Securities," *Journal of Finance* **30,** 1129–1134 (Sept. 1975).

A. B. Laffer and R. D. Renson, "Some Practical Applications of the Efficient Market Concept," *Financial Management* **7,** 63–75 (Summer 1978).

H. A. Latané and C. P. Jones, "Standardized Unexpected Earnings—A Progress Report," *Journal of Finance* **32,** 1457–1466 (Dec. 1977).

J. G. McDonald and A. K. Fisher, "New Issue Stock Price Behavior," *Journal of Finance* **27,** 97–102 (Mar. 1972).

N. E. Mains, "Risk, the Pricing of Capital Assets, and the Evaluation of Investment Porfolios: Comment," *Journal of Business* **50,** 371–384 (July 1977).

H. G. Manne (ed.), *Economic Policy and the Regulation of Corporate Securities* (Washington, D.C.: American Enterprise Institute for Public Policy Research, 1969).

K. R. Marks, *The Stock Price Performance of Firms Repurchasing Their Own Shares* (New York: Graduate School of Business Administration, New York University, Bulletin 1976–1).

E. Miller, "Risk, Uncertainty and Divergence of Opinion," *Journal of Finance* **32,** 1151–1168 (Sept. 1977).

G. R. Miller, "Long-Term Small Business Financing from the Underwriter's Point of View," *Journal of Finance* **16,** 280–290 (May 1961).

R. Norgaard and C. Norgaard, "A Critical Examination of Share Repurchase," *Financial Management* **3,** 44–51 (Spring 1974).

G. Pye, "The Value of the Call Deferment on a Bond: Some Empirical Results," *Journal of Finance* **22,** 623–636 (Dec. 1967).

R. I. Robinson and H. J. Bartell, "Uneasy Partnership: SEC/NYSE," *Harvard Business Review* **43,** 76–88 (Jan.–Feb. 1965).

G. A. Sears, "Public Offerings for Smaller Companies," *Harvard Business Review* **46,** 112–120 (Sept.–Oct. 1968).

Securities and Exchange Commission, *Annual Reports* (Washington, D.C.: U.S. Government Printing Office).

E. Shapiro and C. R. Wolf, *The Role of Private Placements in Corporate Finance* (Boston: Graduate School of Business Administration, Harvard University, 1972).

K. G. Stanga, "Disclosure in Published Annual Reports," *Financial Management* **5,** 42–52 (Winter 1976).

S. S. Stewart, "Should a Corporation Repurchase Its Own Stock?" *Journal of Finance* **31,** 911–922 (June 1976).

J. C. Van Horne, "New Listings and Their Price Behavior," *Journal of Finance* **25,** 783–794 (Sept. 1970).

H. M. Weingartner, "Optimal Timing of Bond Refunding," *Management Science* **13,** 511–524 (Mar. 1967).

Dividend Policy

22

Dividends and the Value of the Firm
Information Effects
Interdependence of Decisions
Factors in Setting Dividend Policy
Dividend Policy Goals
Procedural and Legal Considerations
Dividend Policy in Closely Held Firms
Appendix: Stock Dividends and Stock Splits

A major policy decision of the firm involves the basic issue of how the firm's earnings should be divided between retention and payout to residual owners. We are concerned here with dividend policy on common stock, because preferred stock dividends are stipulated.

Most of the material in this chapter pertains to publicly held firms, but dividend policy is also an issue in small or closely held firms, and we will discuss this aspect in a special section later in the chapter. The chapter begins with a brief discussion of the theory of dividend policy in order to provide a basic framework for later analysis. Next we discuss information effects of dividends and the interrelationships between dividend decisions and other financial management decisions. We turn finally to factors that should be considered and goals that should be pursued in setting dividend policy.

Dividends and the Value of the Firm

Throughout this book our basic organizing framework has been *valuation*. We use the value of the firm as the criterion for financial management decisions as well as the yardstick against which we judge those decisions. We found in our earlier discussion that investment decisions affect value; indeed, it is through its investment decisions that a firm creates value and thus benefits both its shareholders and society. We found that financing (debt/equity) decisions also affect value, primarily because of the tax-deductibility of interest payments on debt.

What about dividend decisions? Can a firm be made more valuable by manipulating the proportion of earnings paid out? It is a complex question, so let us attack it by first assuming away many of the complexities in order to understand the underlying relationships. Later, we will add back the complexities.

A World of No Taxes and No Friction

Taxes complicate matters, so we will begin by assuming them away. Financial friction also complicates matters. By *financial friction* we mean things like commissions on the trading of stocks and bonds by investors, flotation (issue) costs on new issues of stocks and bonds by firms, and the time and effort by investors to gather and analyze information necessary to make decisions regarding their investments. At this point, let us also assume that dividend decisions have no *information effects,* that is, that investors draw no inferences from dividend decisions regarding the firm's earning prospects, investment opportunities, or debt/equity policy. We will come back to information effects shortly.

In our simplified world of no taxes, friction, or information effects, shareholders would be indifferent between dividends and capital gains.

Shareholders would wish the firm to undertake all attractive investment opportunities, defined as projects with positive net present values. Such attractive opportunities promise returns greater than those available to investors outside the firm. Hence, the shareholder prefers to forego a dividend now in order to receive a larger dividend in the future, larger by more than enough to compensate for time and risk.

If internal funds were insufficient to finance all attractive projects, the firm would issue new securities, incurring no issue costs in the process. In the opposite case, when internal funds were more than adequate to undertake all attractive projects, the excess would be paid out to shareholders as dividends. In this case, payout would be preferable to retention because the firm, having exhausted all attractive investment opportunities, could invest the remaining funds only at rates below what shareholders themselves could earn outside. Note that under our assumptions, no costs are incurred in paying the dividend. If the firm erred and paid out too much, it would simply issue new securities to get the funds back. It would incur no costs in this process either.

In our simple taxless and frictionless world, the firm treats dividends as a residual. Investment policy is king, for it is through its investment decisions that the firm creates value. Each year, the firm undertakes all attractive investments, issuing new securities if necessary in order to finance them. Where earnings and investment opportunities vary from year to year, as they do in practice, the firm's dividend would also be highly variable from year to year. Such variations would cause no discomfort to investors in our hypothetical world, for they could alter their investment portfolios as often as they wished at no cost to themselves either in time or money. If dissatisfied with a particular firm's dividend payout, they would simply sell its shares and buy those of another firm whose policy is more to their liking.

Thus, in a simplified world with no taxes, no friction, and no information effects, dividend policy has no effect on the value of the firm and thus is a matter of indifference. Dividend policy is simple: pay out what funds are left after making all attractive investments. Errors of calculation make no difference.

In practice, taxes, friction, and information effects do exist. Why, then, do we bother to analyze the problem in the absence of factors known to exist? Because by doing so we isolate these factors as the ones that matter. Now we know where to concentrate our attention.

Before leaving our hypothetical world, let us be explicit on one other point. At the time a dividend is paid, we would expect the price of a share to fall by exactly the amount of the dividend. Hence, when we say that dividend policy does not affect firm value in our hypothetical world, strictly speaking we mean that it does not affect shareholder wealth. We will have more to say later in this chapter about the price behavior of common stock upon payment of a dividend.

Tax Effects

Let us now reintroduce taxes. Here the focus is on *personal* taxes paid by investors, and not on taxes paid by the firm. Investors pay taxes on both dividends and capital gains due to appreciation of market price. If both were taxed at the same rate, personal taxes would introduce no bias. Other factors being equal, shareholders would be indifferent between retention and payout. As in the no-tax case, shareholders would wish management to undertake all attractive investments, and to pay out any funds left over.

In practice, dividends and capital gains are not taxed at the same rates. Under present tax laws, the capital gains tax rate for most individuals is approximately one-half the rate on ordinary income, which is the rate applicable to dividends. This *differential* in tax rates induces a strong bias in favor of retention. In addition, capital gains taxes are paid only upon sale of the stock and thus may be deferred, whereas taxes on dividends accrue in the year that the dividend is received.

Consider, for example, a firm having investment opportunities with expected returns exactly equal to the required rates, that is, equal to shareholders' opportunity rates outside the firm. With no tax differential between capital gains and ordinary income, investors would be indifferent between retention and payout (still assuming no transaction costs). With capital gains taxed at a lower rate, investors would be better off under retention, taking all their return in the form of price appreciation. Those shareholders needing current income simply would sell a portion of their holdings periodically, incurring no transaction costs.

For shareholders who pay taxes, as most individual shareholders do, the tax differential creates a preference for retention when other factors are equal. However, not all shareholders pay taxes. Pension trusts, tax-exempt foundations, and some low-income individuals pay no taxes at all. Present tax laws permit shareholders to exclude from taxation the first $100 in dividends. Corporations, such as insurance companies, pay federal income taxes on only 15 percent of their dividend income. For these firms, there is a tax bias in the opposite direction, for they are taxed on all capital gains.

Individual shareholders outnumber institutional holders, both in numbers and in value of holdings. However, the proportion of total market value owned by institutions has increased markedly in recent years.

Although fewer in number, institutional holders may exert more influence on market prices because they have greater analytical resources and do more trading.

Overall, it is difficult to determine the net effect of the bias due to the differential tax rates on ordinary income and capital gains. The effect likely varies from firm to firm, depending on the makeup of shareholder groups. We can conclude that the tax bias is potentially significant and should be taken into account by a management in setting policy for its firm.

Transaction Costs

Having reintroduced taxes, let us now reintroduce financial friction. One element of friction is caused by commissions on purchases and sales of securities. Such commissions are paid to brokers for executing the transactions and handling related bookkeeping. In percentage terms, commissions vary inversely with the size of the transaction, from 1 percent to 1.5 percent on a transaction of several thousand dollars up to 10 percent or more on transactions of less than $100.

Such commissions tend to exert a bias in favor of payout rather than retention. Shareholders can no longer sell a portion of their holdings costlessly when they need cash. In addition to commissions, the necessity of selling small amounts of stock periodically is inconvenient and involves time and effort. Reevaluation of holdings made necessary by periodic sales also involves effort. Taken together, commissions and these inconvenience costs may be significant on small periodic sales. In such cases, other factors being equal, shareholders needing income would prefer the payment of at least some dividend.

A second type of transaction cost is incurred in the issuance of new securities. Such flotation costs go to compensate investment bankers for assisting in issuing the securities, and they can be significant. Given such costs, a firm no longer can err in calculating funds available for dividends and expect to get the money back later at no cost by selling securities.

Guidance from Theory

Given taxes and friction, we see that a firm's dividend policy does matter, and that shareholders are not likely to be indifferent toward it. The existence of transaction costs to shareholders—commissions as well as inconvenience costs—suggests the desirability of avoiding actions that cause shareholders to have to make transactions that they otherwise could avoid. The existence of flotation costs on new issues suggests avoiding the practice of overpaying in one year and selling securities the next. When friction costs are incurred unnecessarily, shareholder wealth is adversely affected. We will come back to these points again later.

Information Effects

In practice, there is ample evidence that announcements of dividend actions by firms affect the market prices of their shares. Often, the magnitude of the effect goes beyond what can be attributed to friction costs. In the second quarter of 1974, for example, Consolidated Edison, an electric utility serving New York City, omitted its regular quarterly dividend of $0.45 per share. The price of its stock immediately dropped from $18 to about $12, and declined to $8 within 2 weeks. How can we explain this behavior? In terms of information effects, the dividend action sent a message to investors that caused them to revise sharply downward their estimate of the value of Consolidated Edison common stock.

What was the nature of the message? For some time prior to its dividend cut, Consolidated Edison and other electric utilities had been encountering increasing financial difficulties because of the impact of inflation on costs, the reluctance of regulatory officials to grant rate increases, and pressures to take expensive measures to protect the environment. Share prices had been declining as the outlook for utility earnings worsened. The omission of the first-quarter (1974) dividend was taken by investors to mean that the board of directors and management expected things to get even worse. In short, those in the best position to know were saying that things did not look good. The impact on share prices was immediate and dramatic.

Let us consider a different, and this time hypothetical, situation. Consider a firm, ABC Corporation, that historically has paid out a significant portion of earnings, and has increased its dividend payment as earnings have grown. ABC is known to have under development a new family of products that appear quite promising but which will require considerable capital investment. Suddenly ABC's directors announce that, in order to conserve cash, dividends no longer will be increased each quarter, and may even be reduced. What impact might be expected on the firm's stock price? It is possible that investors would interpret the announcement as evidence that investment opportunities did indeed look very attractive. Its stock price might well rise upon the announcement.

Contrast ABC's situation with that of Consolidated Edison. Both firms announced a dividend lower than that previously expected by investors. In both cases conserving cash was the immediate objective. Yet the stock prices in the two cases behaved in exactly the opposite manner. Why? Because of the inference drawn by investors regarding the firms' respective investment opportunities. In Consolidated Edison's case, the dividend action signaled a situation worse than previously envisioned; in ABC's case, a better situation.

Consider another case, that of DEF Corporation. DEF has a history of above-average return on investment and above-average earnings growth, coupled with a very low dividend payout averaging about 5 percent of earnings. Suddenly DEF's board announces that the payout will be increased to approximately 25 percent of earnings. How might the stock price react? It might well fall if investors inferred from the dividend action that DEF's management believed it was running out of high-return investment opportunities.

In each of the cases described above, a common element is that the dividend action was unexpected, that is, the change in policy was a surprise. A change in policy that had been anticipated likely would have had little or no impact on price, because such impact would have already been felt. In all three cases, investors drew an inference from the dividend action about the firm's investment and earnings prospects. As a result, investors revised their estimates of the value of the firm's stock, and stock price moved quickly to a new equilibrium level.

What conclusions can we draw about the information effects of dividend actions? We can say that the magnitude of the information effect can be quite large, but what about the direction? Do dividend increases always lead to an increase in stock price? Not always. In one of the examples above, a dividend increase led to a drop in stock price, and in another case a dividend reduction led to a price increase. We must conclude that we can make no general statement at all regarding the direction of the information effect of a dividend decision. It depends on the inferences drawn by investors, and many different inferences are possible.

Empirical Evidence

The empirical evidence regarding the effects of dividend actions on stock price is mixed. Some studies seem to support the argument that dividends do affect value and therefore should not be treated as a residual, while others seem to support the opposite conclusion. Many of the reasons the evidence is mixed are related to technical difficulties of testing questions of this sort. Many things affect stock prices, and isolating the effect of dividend actions from all other factors is a formidable task. The evidence is mixed also with respect to the significance of information effects; some studies suggest a pronounced effect and others a weak effect. At this point, it seems best to assume that unexpected dividend actions do have the potential for causing significant information effects, especially in the absence of credible communications from management and the board.

Importance of Careful Communications.

A major policy implication of our analysis of information effects concerns the importance of careful communications from management to investors. Given the large potential impact of information effects, management should take great pains to avoid misinterpretation and see that the inferences that the market draws are the correct ones. The more complete the disclosure of important information regarding the firm's prospects and policies, the less investors will rely on inferences and the less the chance for misinterpretation. Management's job is to serve as the agent of the shareholders, and good communication is an important part of that responsibility.

Given the potential information effect of dividends, the question might arise as to whether dividend policy should be used as a communications device. Other methods would seem to be less expensive and less potentially disruptive to shareholders. Rather than using dividends to communicate, the best policy is to communicate the reasons for the dividend policy.

Interdependence of Investment, Financing, and Dividend Decisions

It is apparent from our earlier discussion that dividend, investment, and financing decisions are interdependent. Funds paid out in dividends are unavailable for investment, unless replaced via external financing. We will explore these interdependencies in more depth with an example.

Let us take a firm that has attractive new investment opportunities, defined as opportunities having a positive net present value, requiring an aggregate outlay of 100 (be it dollars, thousands, or millions). These opportunities are in addition to replacement projects, which we will assume exactly equal depreciation charges. The firm has decided that the appropriate debt/equity ratio, given the nature of its business and its operating risk, is 0.30. Historically, it has paid out 60 percent of its earnings in dividends. Its earnings for the period just ended were 120.

The firm thus has three policy variables: the amount of new investment, the debt/equity ratio, and the dividend payout ratio. The data are listed in Table 22-1. In column 1, the firm treats all three decisions as active, that is, it sets each at the desired level. To do so it must raise a total of 52 in new funds by issuing securities, 23 in

Table 22-1 Interdependence of Decisions

	Policies			
		No External Equity		
	(1) No Residual	(2) Investment Residual	(3) Debt/Equity Residual	(4) Dividend Residual
Before external financing				
Debt	300	300	300	300
Equity	1,000	1,000	1,000	1,000
Debt/equity	0.30	0.30	0.30	0.30
Investment opportunities (NPV > 0)[a]	100	62	100	100
Earnings	120	120	120	120
Payout ratio[a]	0.60	0.60	0.60	0.36
Dividends	72	72	72	43
Earnings retained	48	48	48	77
External financing				
Debt	23	14	52	23
Equity	29	0	0	0
After external financing				
Debt	323	314	352	323
Equity	1,077	1,048	1,048	1,077
Debt/equity (optimum = 0.30)[a]	0.30	0.30	0.34	0.30

[a]Policy variables.

debt, and 29 in equity. By doing so, the firm is able to undertake investments totaling 100, pay dividends of 72, and end up at its target debt/equity ratio of 0.30.

What if the firm decides it does not want to sell new stock? It can do so by adopting one of three policies. It can forego some of its investment opportunities (as shown in column 2) and thereby maintain its dividend at 72 and its target debt/equity ratio at 0.30. Alternatively, it can increase its debt ratio to 0.34 (as shown in column 3) and thereby maintain its dividend at 72 and its investment level of 100. Or, finally, it can cut its dividend from 72 to 43 (as shown in column 4) and reduce its payout ratio to 36 percent.

Which should it do? Our theories tell us that foregoing profitable investments is a poor choice. Through its investments, a firm implements its commercial strategy, the pursuit of which is the reason for its existence. To permit financing constraints to hinder that strategy places the cart before the horse. When a firm passes up an investment opportunity having a net present value of $X, shareholders in principle are poorer by $X. Society also sustains an opportunity loss, since such investments increase the wealth of society as a whole.

Suppose we allow the debt/equity mix to be the slack variable. In principle, an optimal debt/equity ratio exists. In practice, finding it is difficult, and operating a few percentage points on either side may not make much difference. However, if the optimal ratio is thought to be 0.30, then operating at a different ratio involves a conscious decision to suboptimize.

If investment and debt/equity decisions both affect firm value, a case exists for treating both as active variables rather than as residuals. In order to do so, we must either cut the dividend or sell stock. Put another way, to avoid cutting the dividend, we must finance a part of it, that is, 29 of the total desired dividend of 72, by selling stock. In effect, we sell stock and use the proceeds to pay dividends. Let us examine this option in more detail.[1]

Financing Dividends via Sale of Stock

Another way to describe this option is to pay a dividend and then sell stock in order to maintain the desired level of investment. Either way, the firm is paying equity money out at the same time it is getting it back.

One argument against this option is that it incurs flotation costs in connection with selling stock. If the dividend were reduced and the stock not sold, the flotation costs would not be incurred.

Another argument involves taxes. Suppose a firm sells common stock to existing shareholders and uses the proceeds to pay dividends to those same shareholders. The shareholders pay income taxes on the dividend, but because of their additional capital contribution, their capital gain tax liability is reduced. If capital gain and ordinary income tax rates were the same, the transaction would not increase the shareholders' total tax liability. However, the timing of the tax payments would differ, because the tax on a dividend would be due in the year paid, whereas the capital gains tax is deferred until the stock is sold.

Since (presently) the capital gains tax rate is lower, shareholders wind up paying more tax if stock is sold and dividends paid than they would if neither action were taken. If dividends are paid first and then stock sold to replace the funds, the effect is the same. Selling the stock to new shareholders also produces the same outcome. In all cases, the dividend/stock sale alternative, as compared to doing neither, leaves existing shareholders worse off by an amount equal to the dividend times the difference between the capital gain and ordinary income tax rates. Note that the firm's investment level is the same under both alternatives, so the tax

---

1. For a good discussion of interdependencies and problems of conflicting management policies regarding growth, capital structure, dividends, and new equity issues, see R. C. Higgins, "How Much Growth Can a Firm Afford?" *Financial Management* **6**, 7–16 (Fall 1977).

and cost issues are the only differences. As noted earlier, many shareholders pay no taxes, and for them, the tax effect does not apply. Others may be in low marginal tax brackets or may be protected by the $100 exclusion. However, to the extent that shareholders do pay taxes, they clearly are hurt by a policy of payout and offsetting sale of stock.

Given the effects of taxes and flotation costs, why would a firm engage in such a policy? Sometimes it may happen because of a change in commercial strategy that calls for a much higher level of investment. The firm may be reluctant to cut its dividend abruptly enough to avoid some sales of stock.

Another class of companies that regularly has engaged in the payout/stock sale policy are the utilities. However, utilities are a special case, because they are regulated monopolies. It may be that the payout/stock sale policy follows from the desire of regulators to have utility managements regularly subjected to the scrutiny and discipline of the financial markets as a way of promoting efficiency. One way to do so is to encourage payout of a substantial portion of earnings and simultaneous financing of new investment via issues of new securities.

Clearly, there are factors that may justify a payout/stock sale policy. In the case of utilities, managements and regulators may feel that the extra costs of taxes and flotation are justified. For other types of firms, the costs and benefits of such a practice should be examined carefully.

Factors to Consider in Setting Dividend Policy

We have laid the groundwork for our analysis of dividend policy with our discussion of theory, information effects, and interdependence. Let us now turn to specific factors that a firm should consider in establishing dividend policy.

Internal Investment Opportunities

From our earlier discussion, it is apparent that opportunities to invest are a major consideration in setting dividend policy. Other considerations aside, when the firm has opportunities to earn returns greater than those available to shareholders outside the firm, retention and reinvestment are appropriate.

Earnings, Cash Flow, and Liquidity

The firm's ability to generate earnings and cash flow also is a factor. When other factors are equal, the more profitable the firm, the more is available for payout. Dividends are paid with cash, so at any given moment a firm's ability to pay a dividend depends on its cash and liquid asset position and/or its capacity to borrow short-term.

External Financing Needs

In a world with taxes, inflation effects, and transaction costs, a firm must plan its program of external financing. For any firm there exists an optimal debt/equity ratio that depends in part on the nature of its business and its operating risk. That ratio should be established as a target. When not at its target debt/equity mix, the firm should take steps to get there. In our example in Table 22-1, we found dividend payout to be interdependent with the target debt/equity ratio, actual debt/equity ratio, and external financing requirements.

Earnings Record and Prospects

Of major importance is the firm's earnings record and prospects for future earnings, and the market's perceptions of those prospects. Both the growth trend and the stability of earnings are also important. The credibility of the dividend policy is important, and to be credible the dividend pattern must be consistent with the earnings pattern. Consider the data for the two firms listed in Table 22-2.

Table 22-2   Credibility of Dividend

	Firm *A*			Firm *B*		
Year	Earnings per Share	Dividend	Payout Ratio	Earnings per Share	Dividend	Payout Ratio
1	$1.38	$0.72	0.52	$1.26	$0.72	0.57
2	1.62	0.72	0.44	1.10	0.72	0.65
3	1.92	0.96	0.50	1.32	0.96	0.73
4	2.08	0.96	0.46	1.12	0.96	0.86
5	2.46	1.20	0.49	1.20	1.20	1.00

Firm *A*'s earnings have shown steady growth, and its dividend policy has been in line with that growth. Investors are likely to feel confident that the historical dividend pattern will be continued, subject, of course, to firm *A*'s ability to continue its growth in earnings. Firm *B*'s earnings, on the other hand, have been erratic around a flat trend, while the dividend has been steadily increased. In view of the earnings record, investors are likely to doubt *B*'s ability to continue the historical pattern of steady dividend increases. Firm *B*'s dividend pattern does not appear to be sustainable. The actual dividend payments in the two cases are identical, but *A*'s pattern is more credible.

Clientele

There is some evidence that different dividend policies attract different types of investors, or different *clienteles*. This argument suggests that firms with high and stable payouts attract investors who prefer a large proportion of their total return in current income. Such investors may well depend on dividends for current consumption and therefore may prefer a dividend that is stable and predictable. On the other hand, because of the differential in tax rates on capital gains and dividends, low payout growth companies might attract investors interested mainly in capital gains. In short, investors attempt to match their own income needs and tax brackets with the magnitude and stability of the firm's payout, with the capital gains tax differential increasing the incentive to do so. The clientele argument is plausible and consistent with most of the available evidence.[2]

Of what significance is the clientele argument? One might argue that if the firm's clientele were used to a particular dividend policy, that policy should not be changed. Most firms for which dividend policy is important are publicly traded. If the firm wished to change its dividend policy, those shareholders not satisfied with the new policy could simply sell their shares and buy those of another firm with a policy suited to their needs. The firm would lose one clientele and attract another.

This argument ignores friction in the system. In making portfolio shifts, shareholders incur transaction costs and also costs in terms of time and effort to gather and analyze information and make decisions. Thus, because of friction in the markets, a change in dividend policy can impose costs on shareholders that are real and potentially significant in magnitude, especially to small shareholders.

Legal and Regulatory Restrictions

Certain institutional investors, in particular insurance companies, are subject to a variety of legal and regulatory restrictions with respect to their investment policies. In some states, laws and/or regulations stipulate that for a firm's stock to qualify for certain institutional portfolios, an uninterrupted dividend record is required over some minimum number of years. Some states prohibit certain institutions, such as savings banks and certain trustees, from holding the bonds of a corporation unless there exists an uninterrupted dividend record on the underlying common stock over some minimum period. Omission of a dividend by a firm thus might result in removal of its stock or bonds or both from the legal list of investments of some institutions. It is difficult to judge the true signifi-

---

2. Evidence of a clientele effect is given by E. J. Elton and M. J. Gruber, "Marginal Stockholder Tax Rates and the Clientele Effect," *Review of Economics and Statistics* **52**, 68–74 (Feb. 1970) and R. R. Pettit, "Taxes, Transactions Costs and the Clientele Effect of Dividends," *Journal of Finance* **5**, 419–436 (Dec. 1977). Much weaker evidence is found by W. G. Lewellen et al., "Some Direct Evidence on the Dividend Clientele Phenomenon," *Journal of Finance* **33**, 1385–1400 (Dec. 1978).

cance of such a development, but it is plausible that institutional interest in a firm's securities may give it a broader, more liquid market and facilitate new issues of securities.

Universities and other endowed educational institutions sometimes are restricted as to their use of capital gains on their securities. Since such institutions are generally not taxed, they might have a preference for stocks with a high payout.

Control

In some cases, control of the firm may be a factor in setting dividend policy. Suppose an individual or group owns a significant interest in a firm, the remainder of the stock being publicly held. The higher the payout, the greater the chance that a subsequent issue of common stock might be required—perhaps because of a change in commercial strategy requiring greater investment. Those in control might prefer to minimize the likelihood of a requirement for new outside capital by opting for low payout and a high liquid asset position.

This argument applies also to firms that, because of size or reputation or other factors, might find their access to public equity markets limited. The lower the payout, the less likely that outside capital would be needed.

Dividend Policy Goals

We now have developed a basic framework of analysis and have discussed the major factors pertinent to setting dividend policy. No two firms are exactly alike, and the policy for a firm must be tailored to its own unique circumstances. However, let us attempt to get down some general policy goals that are applicable to most firms.

A Long-Run Residual

It is apparent that dividend policy depends on many factors that are often confusing and sometimes conflicting. In such situations, we must look to basic principles for guidance. What are those basic principles? First, we know that valuation is the central organizing framework, and that financial management decisions should be analyzed in terms of their effect on the value of the firm rather than on earnings or other yardsticks. Second, we know that it is through its investments that the firm executes its commercial strategy. Investments create value, and when a firm foregoes an attractive investment, shareholders incur an opportunity loss. Third, we know that the debt/equity mix also affects the value of the firm. Fourth, we know that friction exists in the system and that real costs are incurred when the firm issues securities and when shareholders make changes in their holdings.

We know that dividend, investment, and financing decisions are interdependent, and that tradeoffs must be made. We found in our discussion of interdependence earlier in this chapter that the firm must either treat one of the three basic decisions as a residual, or adopt a policy of offsetting dividend payments by selling new common stock. Put another way, the firm cannot actively manage all three policy variables unless it is willing to pay dividends and sell stock simultaneously.

Let us examine these tradeoffs in a long-run setting. As a matter of *long-run policy*, does it make sense for the firm to consciously plan to

1. forego attractive investments?
2. operate at a nonoptimal debt/equity ratio?
3. finance dividend payments by selling stock?

We must conclude that none of these options is sensible as a long-run policy. The only policy that avoids one of the above choices is to treat dividends as a *long-run residual.*

Short-Run Constraints

In the short run, however, the firm faces a number of constraints that make a strictly residual dividend policy infeasible. Since investment requirements and earnings in most firms vary from year to year, treating dividends as a residual each year is likely to lead to a highly variable dividend, probably going to zero in some years. From our earlier discussion, we know that a variable dividend is undesirable. Investors would have a difficult time interpreting the frequent changes in the dividend, and information effects likely would lead to wide fluctuations in stock price. Even if they averaged out over time, such fluctuations would benefit some shareholders at the expense of others who are forced to sell at low points, and therefore it would be a highly unfair policy. In addition, fluctuations in price and dividends would cause shifts in the shareholder group, or clientele, shifts which may impose significant costs on those shareholders who are induced by that policy to alter their holdings. If the residual policy dictated a dividend of zero in any year, the firm's dividend record would be broken and regulatory restrictions might force removal of the firm's securities from approved buy lists of some institutions.

A Long-Run Residual Managed in the Short Run

It is clear that a policy of treating dividends as a residual in the short run is unworkable. A workable compromise is to treat dividends as long-run residual, but to constrain it in the short run in order to avoid undesirable variations in payout.[3] To implement such an approach requires financial planning over a fairly long time horizon—probably 5 years.

First, investment requirements must be estimated, with the estimate providing for all attractive opportunities that the firm expects to face. Next, funds expected to be available internally from earnings and depreciation should be estimated. A target debt/equity ratio then should be set based on the firm's operating risk and other relevant considerations. Given investment requirements, funds from internal sources, and a target debt/equity ratio, the firm can then determine whether, over the planning horizon, residual funds will be available for payout. If so, the ratio of residual funds to total earnings after taxes becomes the firm's *long-run target payout ratio.*

If no residual earnings remain after financing is provided for all attractive investment opportunities, the above approach suggests a policy of no dividend at all. External equity financing would be required to make up any shortfall in internal funds. Where institutional ownership of the firm's securities seems desirable, the firm might wish to compromise by paying a small token dividend with the intention of leaving it fixed over the planning horizon. Where the long-run analysis shows that residual funds will be available, the plan would prescribe dividends and no external equity financing.

The long planning horizon is necessary because the world is uncertain and not frictionless. Investment opportunities cannot be foreseen with complete accuracy each year, nor can earnings be accurately forecast each year. In effect, we plan the long-run dividend payout target based on *trend* values. Needed external financing can be planned in more economical amounts to avoid high issue costs associated with small financings. Also, the long horizon permits time to anticipate changes in commercial strategy or debt/equity policy.

The long-run target is stated in percentage terms, that is, dividends to be paid as a percentage of earnings. The short-run variability that we wish to avoid is variability in the *dollar* payout. Hence, our objective should be to set the dollar payout so as to average out to the target percentage over the planning horizon. As earnings fluctuate from period to period, the percentage payout will fluctuate. In some years, the percentage payout will be below the target and in other years above. In effect, the firm saves during fat years in order to maintain the dividend during lean years.

---

3. The approach suggested here draws on the work of Robert C. Higgins, "The Corporate Dividend-Saving Decision," *Journal of Financial and Quantitative Analysis* **7,** 1527–1542 (Mar. 1972).

Let us illustrate the approach with an example. We assume a 5 year planning horizon over which ABC Corporation foresees investment opportunities requiring net new investment, over and above depreciation charges, of $4 million per year, or $20 million over the 5 years. This investment requirement includes plant and equipment plus additions to working capital. Aggregate earnings after taxes over the period are expected to be $25 million. We will assume that ABC currently is at its target debt/equity ratio of 0.30.

To finance the new investment, retained earnings (RE) plus new debt must equal $20 million, or

$$\text{New debt} + \text{RE} = \$20 \text{ million} \tag{1}$$

To maintain the target debt/equity ratio requires that

$$\text{New debt} = 0.30 \text{ RE} \tag{2}$$

Substituting equation (2) into (1) gives us 1.30 RE = $20 million, which tells us that RE over the 5 years must total $15.40 million. Subtracting this figure from total expected earnings of $25 million indicates that a total of $9.60 million can be paid in dividends over the 5 years, or 38 percent of aggregate earnings. Spread over 5 years, this amounts to $1.92 million per year. New debt of 0.30 × $15.40 = $4.60 million must be raised during the period. We will assume that this is done in year 3.

Table 22-3 Dividends as a Long-Run Residual (Millions of Dollars)

	Year						5 Year Total
	0	1	2	3	4	5	
Earnings	—	7.00	5.00	3.00	6.50	3.50	25.00
Dividends	—	1.92	1.92	1.92	1.92	1.92	9.60
Earnings retained	—	5.08	3.08	1.08	4.58	1.58	15.40
Total equity	200.00	205.08	208.16	209.24	213.82	215.40	—
New debt	—	—	—	4.60	—	—	4.60
Total debt	60.00	60.00	60.00	64.60	64.60	64.60	—
Debt/equity ratio	0.30	0.29	0.29	0.31	0.30	0.30	—
Dividend payout ratio	—	0.27	0.38	0.64	0.30	0.55	0.38
Funds available for investment							
Retained earnings		5.08	3.08	1.08	4.58	1.58	15.40
New debt		—	—	4.60	—	—	4.60
Cumulative total		5.08	8.16	13.84	18.42	20.00	20.00
Cumulative investment							
requirements		4.00	8.00	12.00	16.00	20.00	20.00

Combining the new debt funds of $4.60 million with the RE of $15.40 million gives us the $20 million that we need for new investment. Assuming that earnings vary from year to year as indicated, we have the results listed in Table 22-3 for our 5 year plan.

In this example, we assumed for simplicity that the firm expected a flat earnings trend, with earnings varying each year about that trend. We therefore held the dollar dividend constant each year. If earnings were expected to grow over time, as often would be the case, it would be desirable to modify the approach to permit a gradual increase in the dollar amount of the dividend payout over time. Given information effects, friction, and the existence of a clientele, cuts in the dollar payout are undesirable and should be avoided if at all possible. The best policy therefore would be a dividend that is nondecreasing in dollar terms. As earnings grow, the dividend would be raised in small steps; each step would be taken only when the probability appeared high that the dividend would not have to be cut subsequently.

Communicating the Policy

Whatever specific policy the firm adopts, it is desirable that it be communicated clearly to investors. Investors should not have to guess what policy management intends to follow. Investors then are better prepared to decide whether the policy suits their own preferences and needs. Good communication also reduces the chances of misinterpretation.

Changing the Dividend Policy

Given information effects, friction, and a clientele, consistency in policy is important. Erratic changes are costly and should be avoided. Sometimes, however, a policy change will become necessary, perhaps because of a change in commercial strategy, investment opportunities, or debt/equity policy. Changes in general economic conditions might necessitate a change in policy. Or management simply might find that it had misestimated one or more of the determinants of dividend policy, which in an uncertain world can happen to even the most capable and far-sighted managers.

When a policy change is indicated, management should not shrink from the task. Dividend reductions are painful, but if a reduction is in the shareholders' best interests, it should be made. In such cases, communication becomes all the more important. If the reasons are sensible, investors will understand them. A dividend cut may well lead to a fall in stock price, but careful communications will increase the likelihood that stock price will adjust to the underlying economic realities.[4]

If a lower average payout became necessary, it might be possible to move to the new target gradually. Where a firm's earnings are growing, the dollar payout could be held constant and the average payout ratio allowed to decline over time. Such an approach would avoid a reduction in dollar payout, which could be inconvenient or costly to some shareholders. The policy change and the reasons for it should also be communicated to shareholders.

Procedural and Legal Considerations
Paying Dividends

Each dividend payment must be declared by a vote of the board of directors. Suppose the directors of XYZ Corporation meet on Tuesday, January 21. They declare that the regular first-quarter dividend of $0.25 per share is to be paid on March 12 to all investors who hold the firm's stock on Wednesday, February 12. February 12 becomes the *record date*, and holders on that date become *holders of record.*

To account for the time required to record transfers of ownership, the major stock exchanges subtract four business days from the record date to establish the *ex-dividend* date, in this case it would be Thursday, February 6. Any investor purchasing XYZ stock on or before February 5 would become a holder of record on February 12 and would therefore receive the first-quarter dividend. Investors purchasing on February 6 and thereafter would not receive the dividend. On February 6, the stock thus sells *ex-dividend.* We would expect its price to drop on that date by the amount of the dividend to show that buyers that day will not receive the dividend. Testing this proposition is difficult because of the many factors, other than dividends, that affect prices. Carefully done empirical studies indicate that price does adjust on the ex-dividend date, but by something less than the full amount. The difference is due primarily to the difference in tax rates on dividends and capital gains.

Once declared by the board, dividends become a current liability of the firm. If XYZ had 1 million shares outstanding, the accounting entries on the day of declaration would be a $250,000 credit (increase) in current

---

4. For an analysis of management attitudes about changes in dividend policy, see E. F. Fama and H. Babiak, "Dividend Policy: An Empirical Analysis," *Journal of the American Statistical Association* **63,** 1132–1161 (Dec. 1968). Fama and Babiak conclude that managers generally believe that investors prefer a stable dividend policy. See also R. W. Kolb, "Predicting Dividend Changes," unpublished doctoral dissertation, School of Business Administration, University of North Carolina at Chapel Hill, 1978. Kolb found a marked reluctance among managers to cut dividends. When cuts finally were made, they tended to be large. Increases, on the other hand, tended to be small, the average increase being about 3 percent. This finding supports the notion that managers make dividend increases only that they are reasonably sure can be sustained.

liabilities and a $250,000 debit (decrease) in retained earnings. When the checks are paid, the current liability is eliminated and cash declines by $250,000. The net effect of paying the dividend is a reduction in cash and an offsetting reduction in retained earnings.

Legal Considerations

In many cases, long-term debt indentures and preferred stock agreements contain restrictions on the maximum common stock dividend that can be paid by a firm. Such covenants are designed to protect senior claim holders from excessive withdrawals by residual owners. While frequently encountered, restrictions usually are not troublesome during normal times because they are consistent with what good financial management would require anyway.

In addition to covenants in debt and preferred stock agreements, many state laws place restrictions on dividend payments designed to give further protection to senior claim holders. Many states require that dividends be paid only out of retained earnings. The effect of such a restriction is to permit dividend payments only when retained earnings is a positive figure. The intent of the provision is to permit withdrawal of earnings but not the withdrawal of the original capital contribution. Some states define the original capital contribution as including only the par value of the stock, while others include paid-in capital as well. A few states permit dividends if current earnings, usually over the most recent 12 months, are positive, even though total cumulative retained earnings is negative.

Dividend Policy in Closely Held Firms

The discussion to this point has concentrated on the formulation of dividend policy in publicly held corporations. Much of the discussion does not apply to firms which are not publicly held. In privately held firms, there are no problems with information effects, issue costs, or clientele.

Taxes, however, are a factor, and tax considerations are of major importance in establishing policy in private companies with respect to withdrawals by owners. The form of organization—whether proprietorship, partnership, or corporation—significantly affects the firm's tax status. If certain conditions are met, a corporation having a very small number of shareholders, presently less than ten, may be taxed as a partnership. If the firm is taxed as a corporation, long-range planning of investment and financing needs becomes essential, for if funds are paid out and later returned, taxes would have been paid unnecessarily. The long-range residual approach to planning withdrawals would be appropriate. In many cases, the appropriate policy depends heavily on the income needs and tax brackets of the principals. In some cases, a policy of total retention may be best, but Internal Revenue Service regulations prohibit excessive retention as a means of avoiding income taxes. Given the complexity of the applicable tax laws, expert accounting and legal advice is necessary in most cases.

Summary

In analyzing dividend policy from the standpoint of firm value and shareholder interests, attention should focus on taxes, financial friction, and information effects. Taxes are relevant because of differential tax rates on ordinary income and capital gains. Friction costs include commissions, issue costs, and costs of analysis by investors. Information effects occur when, on the basis of dividend decisions by the firm, investors draw inferences regarding other important events or policies, such as investment opportunities in the future, earnings prospects, or changes in financing policy. Information effects result from unexpected dividend actions and can have a significant impact on stock price in either direction. The potential for undesirable information effects emphasizes the need for careful communication by management to the financial markets.

In setting its dividend policy, a firm must consider many factors in addition to taxes, friction costs, and information effects. It must consider interdependencies among investment, financing, and dividend policies; earnings prospects; liquidity requirements; the makeup of the stockholder group; and legal and regulatory restrictions.

When dividend policy is analyzed in a valuation framework, it becomes clear that, in general, dividends should be treated as a long-run residual. Investment policy comes first, for it is through its investment decisions that a firm executes its commercial strategy. Financing policies then are tailored to fit, with debt/equity policy set first and then dividend policy. Although a residual in the long run, dividends must be managed carefully in the short run to avoid undesirable variations in payout that impose real costs on shareholders. In setting policy, consistency and careful communication are important.

In closely held firms, tax considerations usually are a central factor in determining a payout or withdrawal policy that best serves the interests of owners.

Sample Problem

Rework Table 22-1, assuming the firm had attractive new investment opportunities of 150 rather than 100.

Solution

	(1) No Residual	(2) Investment Residual	(3) Debt/Equity Residual	(4) Dividend Residual
		Policies		
		No External Equity		
Before external financing				
Debt	300	300	300	300
Equity	1,000	1,000	1,000	1,000
Debt/equity	0.30	0.30	0.30	0.30
Investment opportunities	150	62.4	150	150
Earnings	120	120	120	120
Payout ratio	0.60	0.60	0.60	0.038
Dividends	72	72	72	4.6
Earnings retained	48	48	48	115.4
External financing				
Debt	34.6	14.4	102	34.6
Equity	67.4	0	0	0
After external financing				
Debt	334.6	314.4	402	334.6
Equity	1,115.4	1,048	1,048	1,115.4
Debt/equity	0.30	0.30	0.38	0.30

Under policy (1), $102 is required in external financing ($150 − $48). The mix of new financing should result in a final debt/equity ratio = 0.30.

Solving for the amount of new equity:

$$\frac{\text{New debt} + \text{Old debt}}{\text{New equity} + \text{Old equity} + \text{Retained earnings}} = 0.3$$

$$\frac{\text{New debt} + \$300}{\text{New equity} + \$1,048} = 0.3$$

$$\text{New debt} + \$300 = 0.3 \text{ new equity} + \$314.4$$

$$\text{New debt} = 0.3 \text{ new equity} + \$14.4$$

Now, we know that new debt plus new equity must add up to the total $102 needed in external financing. So,

$$\text{New debt} = \$102 - \text{New equity}$$
$$\$102 - \text{New equity} = 0.3 \text{ new equity} + \$14.4$$
$$1.3 \text{ new equity} = \$87.6$$
$$\text{New equity} = \$67.4$$
$$\text{New debt} = \$102 - \$67.4 = \$34.6$$

Under policy (2), only $14.4 can be raised in new debt if no new equity is issued and if the debt/equity and payout ratios are to remain constant. This leaves only $62.4 available for investment ($48 + $14.4). Under policy (3), the entire $102 is raised through new debt, raising the final debt/equity ratio to 0.38. Under policy (4), $34.6 of the required $150 comes from debt, leaving $115.4 to come from retained earnings. This leaves $4.6 for dividends ($120 earnings less $115.4 retained), which represents a 0.038 payout ratio.

Questions

1. In a world of no taxes and no financial friction, a firm cannot be made more valuable by manipulating the dividend payout ratio. True or false? Explain.
2. Discuss the implications of personal income taxes for dividend policy.
3. What types of transaction costs must be considered in setting dividend policy?
4. Describe the information effects that can be induced by dividend actions.
5. Why are investment, financing, and dividend decisions interdependent?
6. What are the principal factors that a firm should consider in setting its dividend policy?
7. Over the long run, which of the three major financial policy variables— investment policy, debt/equity policy, or dividend policy—should be treated as residual?
8. In practice, what constraints operate to prevent a firm from treating dividends as a residual in the short run?
9. Why must dividend policies be planned over a relatively long time horizon?

Problems

1. Rework Table 22-1 in the text for a target dividend payout ratio of 0.65 rather than 0.60. Determine for each of the four policy alternatives the external financing requirements (debt and equity) and the debt and equity levels after external financing is completed.
2. (a) Rework Table 22-3 in the text to provide for an aggregate invest-

ment requirement of $22 million rather than $20 million, timed as follows (numbers are millions of dollars):

	Year					5 Year Total
	1	2	3	4	5	
Investment requirement	4	5	4	5	4	22
Cumulative	4	9	13	18	22	22

(b) Suppose now that the firm currently has a debt/equity ratio of 0.35 (rather than 0.30 as in Table 22-3) and wishes to maintain that ratio. Total equity is $200 million. The investment requirement remains at $22 million. Rework the table a second time.

3. Troxler Manufacturing Company produces components for heavy machine tools. For the past 15 years Troxler has experienced moderate sales and earnings growth. Currently, Troxler is considering expanding its production facilities and product line to include components for sensitive testing equipment. This is a new area of component manufacturing with no dominant firm in the market. Expansion into this line has met Troxler's economic and qualitative criteria for acceptance. The expansion program will require an investment of $30 million in the next year to set up operations. Troxler has 4,000,000 shares of common stock outstanding and has maintained a stable annual dollar dividend of $2.50 per share. Troxler's board of directors is reluctant to have any sudden changes in this dividend level. The firm has a target debt/equity ratio of 0.35. Total earnings after taxes for the past year were $25 million. Earnings are expected to remain constant over the next year. Troxler's balance sheet for the past year indicates the following capital structure (in thousands):

Debt	$14,000
Equity: 4,000,000 common stock @ $1 par	4,000
Additional paid in capital	6,000
Retained earnings	30,000

(a) What is Troxler's current dividend payment ratio?

(b) If Troxler undertakes the new investment and maintains its current dividend payout ratio, how much external financing will be required? To maintain its target debt/equity ratio, how much must be raised in new equity? If new common stock can be issued to net $40 per share, how many new shares must be issued and what will be the effect of this issue on the dollar dividend per share if the current dividend payout ratio is maintained?

(c) Suppose the directors of Troxler are unwilling to undertake a new common stock issue at this time to finance the new investment. What policies could you suggest to the directors so that the new investment can be made? Discuss the advantages and disadvantages of each of your policies.

4. The Wingo Manufacturing Company uses a 5 year time horizon for financial planning. After several months of study and discussion, management has developed the following estimates for the firm's financial performance over the next 5 years:

- Earnings after tax: expected to grow at 5 percent per year for the next 5 years. Wingo's earnings after tax last year were $10 million.
- Investment: total new new investments over the next 5 years are estimated to be $45 million.
- Dividends: stable or growing dollar dividends over the next 5 years. Ms. Howes, Wingo's president, believes the firm's current debt/equity ratio of 0.4 is too high, and she wants this ratio to be lowered to 0.35 during the next 5 years. The firm does not plan to issue any new stock over the next 5 years.

Wingo's balance sheet and other financial data for the past year are summarized below:

Balance Sheet (Millions)

Current assets	$ 56	Current liabilities	$ 49
Net plant and equipment	108	Long-term debt	34
Other	5	Equity	
		5,000,000 shares at $1 par	5
		Additional paid in	25
		Retained earnings	56
Total assets	$169	Total liabilities and equity	$169

Other Financial Data

Profit after tax	$10 million
Shares	5 million
EPS	$ 2.00
Dividend per share	$ .70
Total dividends	$ 3.5 million
Retained earnings	$ 6.5 million

Using the approach outlined in Table 22-3, devise a plan that will enable Wingo to met its projected financial needs and to attain the president's desired dividend and debt/equity levels. What minimum aggregate level of earnings after tax is required over the 5 year period to meet these financial and policy demands?

References

S. Bhattacharya, "Imperfect Information, Dividend Policy, and the Bird-in-the-Hand Fallacy," *Bell Journal of Economics* **10,** 259–270 (Spring 1979).

R. A. Brealey, *Security Prices in a Competitive Market* (Cambridge, Mass.: MIT Press, 1971).

P. C. Eisemann and E. A. Moses, "Stock Dividends: Managements' View, *Financial Analysts Journal,* 77–85 (July–Aug. 1978).

E. J. Elton and M. J. Gruber, "Marginal Stockholder Tax Rates and the Clientele Effect," *Review of Economics and Statistics* **52,** 68–74 (Feb, 1970).

E. F. Fama and H. Babiak, "Dividend Policy: An Empirical Analysis," *Journal of the American Statistical Association* **63,** 1132–1161 (Dec. 1968).

J. E. Finnerty, "Corporate Stock Issue and Repurchase," *Financial Management* **4,** 62–66 (Oct. 1975).

I. Friend and M. Puckett, "Dividends and Stock Prices," *American Economic Review* **54,** 656–682 (Sept. 1964).

R. C. Higgins, "The Corporate Dividend–Saving Decision," *Journal of Financial and Quantitative Analysis* **7,** 1527–1541 (Mar. 1972).

R. C. Higgins, "How Much Growth Can a Firm Afford?" *Financial Management* **6,** 7–16 (Fall 1977).

R. C. Higgins, "Dividend Policy and Increasing Discount Rates: A Clarification," *Journal of Financial and Quantitative Analysis* **7,** 1757–1762 (June 1972).

R. C. Higgins, "Growth, Dividend Policy and Capital Costs in the Electric Utility Industry," *Journal of Finance* **29,** 1189–1202 (Sept. 1974).

R. W. Kolb, "Predicting Dividend Changes," unpublished doctoral dissertation, Graduate School of Business Administration, University of North Carolina at Chapel Hill, 1978.

R. E. Krainer, "A Pedagogic Note on Dividend Policy," *Journal of Financial and Quantitative Analysis* **6,** 1147–1154 (Sept. 1971).

W. G. Lewellen et al., "Some Direct Evidence on the Dividend Clientele Phenomenon," *Journal of Finance* **33,** 1385–1400 (Dec. 1978).

R. H. Litzenberger and J. C. Van Horne, "Elimination of the Double Taxation of Dividends and Corporate Financial Policy," *Journal of Finance* **33,** 737–749 (June 1978).

M. H. Miller and F. Modigliani, "Dividend Policy, Growth, and the Valuation of Shares," *Journal of Business* **34,** 411–433 (Oct. 1961).

R. R. Pettit, "Dividend Announcements. Security Performance, and Market Efficiency," *Journal of Finance* **27,** 993–1007 (Dec. 1972).

R. R. Pettit, "Taxes, Transactions Costs and the Clientele Effect of Dividends," *Journal of Finance* **5,** 419–436 (Dec. 1977).

J. C. Van Horne and J. G. McDonald, "Dividend Policy and New Equity Financing," *Journal of Finance* **26,** 507–519 (May 1971).

J. E. Walter, "Dividend Policy: Its Influence on the Value of Enterprise," *Journal of Finance* **18,** 280–391 (May 1963).

R. Watts, "The Information Content of Dividends," *Journal of Business* **46,** 191–211 (Apr. 1973).

Appendix: Stock Dividends and Stock Splits

This appendix discusses two topics—stock dividends and stock splits—that do not involve a distribution of earnings and therefore are not dividends. Each is more properly considered a recapitalization, or a restructuring, of capital accounts of the firm. We discuss these topics in this chapter because the motives for paying stock dividends are related to those of cash dividends. We include a discussion of stock splits because they are very similar in effect to stock dividends.

Stock Dividends

Some firms pay a *stock dividend* in lieu of, or in combination with, a cash dividend. Stock dividends usually are paid in common stock. Consider a firm whose stock has a par value of $1, was originally sold at $10 per share, and now has a market price of $20. A 10 percent stock dividend is paid. The balance sheet appears in Table 22-4 before and after the stock dividend is paid.

Table 22-4   Stock Dividend

	Before	
Cash $1,000,000	Common stock (1,000,000 shares @ $1 par value)	$ 1,000,000
	Paid-in surplus	9,000,000
	Retained earnings	15,000,000
	Net worth	$25,000,000
	After	
Cash $1,000,000	Common stock (1,100,000 shares @ $1 par value)	$ 1,100,000
	Paid-in surplus	10,900,000
	Retained earnings	13,000,000
	Net worth	$25,000,000

The number of shares outstanding increases by 100,000 (10 percent) to 1,100,000. However, net worth remains the same and no cash has been paid out. The issue of the additional shares has been accompanied by a restructuring—really a relabeling—of accounting entries in the net worth section of the balance sheet. Retained earnings has been reduced by $2,000,000 (100,000 shares times the market price of $20), with $1,900,000 transferred to paid-in surplus and $100,000 to common stock.

Each shareholder now has 10 percent more shares than before. Is the shareholder better off? One firm justified a stock dividend on grounds that it "should enable stockholders to benefit from the improving earnings outlook." However, total earnings are unchanged, so earnings per share decline by 10 percent, and each shareholder's proportional share in earnings is the same as before. To illustrate, consider a shareholder who owned 100 shares before the stock dividend, and assume that total earnings after taxes were $2,000,000, or $2.00 per share before the stock dividend:

	Shares Owned	Earnings per Share	Total Claim on Earnings
Before	100	$2.00	$200
After	110	1.82	200

Since the claim on earnings is unchanged, if the shareholders are better off, it must be because the firm is worth more. Such would be the case if market price per share declined by less than 10 percent. Empirical evidence suggests, however, that prices on average do adjust by the same amount as the stock dividend. A direct analogy is that of two pies, both the same size, with one sliced ten ways and the other, eleven. It seems doubtful that the pie with eleven slices would command a higher price in the market place. Likewise, to argue that a stock dividend can permanently affect the value of a firm requires an assumption of irrationality on the part of investors, not a very comfortable basis for making financial policy. As a final bit of evidence on the true value of stock dividends, we might note that the Internal Revenue Service views them as nontaxable.[5]

With the economic benefits of stock dividends in doubt, what about their cost? The firm incurs costs in connection with issuing the new stock certificates. In addition, owners of small amounts of stock receive fractional shares and must either sell the fractional shares or *round up* by buying more fractional shares to obtain full shares. The cost to the firm of handling these transactions may be significant. There also are costs to shareholders in terms of inconvenience and additional record-keeping.

Occasionally, a firm may use a stock dividend as a mechanism for increasing cash dividend payout. If the dollar dividend per share is held

---

5. For a survey of management attitudes toward stock dividends, see P. C. Eisemann and E. A. Moses, "Stock Dividends: Managements' View," *Financial Analysts Journal,* 77–85 (July–Aug. 1978).

constant, a stock dividend has the effect of increasing the aggregate cash dividend payout by the firm.

Stock Splits

We noted above that a stock dividend is not a distribution of earnings, but a recapitalization of sorts. A closely related type of recapitalization is the *stock split*. A stock split involves different accounting entries from a stock dividend and usually can be accomplished at lower cost because fractional shares can be avoided. Consider the illustration given in Table 22-5 of a two for one split, using the same firm as earlier.

In this case, 1,000,000 new shares are issued and the par value is cut in half. No transfer is made from the retained earnings account. Earnings per share are cut in half. We would expect market price also to be cut in half, and evidence shows that this is what occurs.

Table 22-5   Stock Split

	Before	
Cash $1,000,000	Common stock (1,000,000 shares @ $1 par value)	$ 1,000,000
	Paid-in surplus	9,000,000
	Retained earnings	15,000,000
	Net worth	$25,000,000
	After	
Cash $1,000,000	Common stock (2,000,000 shares @ $0.50 par value)	$ 1,000,000
	Paid-in surplus	9,000,000
	Retained earnings	15,000,000
	Net worth	$25,000,000

One motive for a stock split is to increase the number of shares outstanding and thereby broaden the market for the stock. Another is to reduce the price to a more favorable trading range. The latter argument recognizes that the commission structure on transactions favors trades on a larger number of lower-priced shares. Reducing the price therefore may increase the stock's appeal to investors with small amounts to invest by reducing their costs of transacting. There is no evidence, however, that a broadening of the market, if it does occur, has any lasting impact on the price of the stock. For reasons cited earlier in discussing stock dividends, any such price impact is doubtful.

Special Topics in Financial Management VI

International Aspects of Financial Management

23

The Importance of the Exchange-Rate Problem
Foreign Exchange Exposure
Alternative Translation Methods
Foreign Exchange Market
Dealing with Foreign Exchange Exposure
Multinational Investment Decisions

Thus far, this book has been directed to the problems of financial management within the domestic United States economy. This chapter extends the analysis to the additional problems faced by financial managers of multinational companies, that is, those companies that conduct business or hold investments in two or more countries. Such an extension does not change the validity of the ideas presented in the preceding parts of this book; these ideas are just as applicable to a multinational company or a foreign company operating outside the United States as they are to a purely domestic company. What the extension does require is the introduction of two *new* dimensions to the problems (and opportunities) faced by the financial manager.

The first new dimension is a fairly obvious one. When a company conducts business in another country, it is exposed to that nation's particular set of laws, customs, taxes, and financial institutions; all of these may differ from those prevailing in its own country. Furthermore, in any given year, each individual economy may be in a different phase of the business cycle. Those differences should and do affect the task of the financial manager. Although this *extra* dimension is important, adapting to it involves a knowledge and appreciation of what are essentially *factual* issues: Each nation is different, and the only way to understand these differences is to study each economy and its institutions individually, a task that does not belong in the present chapter.

The second new dimension, which we do cover here, is that multinational financial managers must understand and deal with one extra critical variable—the exchange rate between some other currency and their own. As we will see, the introduction of this variable (the exchange rate and changes in exchange rates) opens up a new and wider range of options and problems for financial managers of multinational companies.

The Importance of the Exchange-Rate Problem

Doing business in more than one country generally requires a firm to own assets, owe liabilities, and make transactions that are denominated in currencies other than its own. The financial results achieved by the parent company are therefore affected not only by the operating results of foreign operations but also by changes in the exchange rates between foreign currencies and its home currency. To take a very simple example, assume that a United States resident (investor X) invested $1,000 in a Mexican venture in December 1976 when the exchange rate was 12.5 Mexican pesos to $1 US. Because the investment is in Mexico, investor X has to convert the initial $1,000 into pesos at the 12.5 pesos/$1 rate and then invest the 12,500 pesos. Assume that investor X gets an operating return of 20 percent a year by December 1977. This means that the 12,500 peso investment will have grown to 15,000 pesos. But meanwhile, the Mexican peso is devalued relative to the United States dollar. When investor X goes to reconvert the 15,000 pesos into dollars in December 1977, the new exchange rate is 22 pesos to $1 US. Thus, in dollars, the investor gets only 15,000/$22 or $682. The *operating* profit was +20 percent a year in pesos, but investor X's *actual* result in dollars was −32 percent a year. In this case, the exchange-rate factor actually overwhelmed the operating results! Generally, the exchange-rate factor is not quite so overwhelming, but it is now large enough to be a critical issue for any multinational financial manager's decision-making.

The emergence of the foreign-exchange "problem" can be traced to the interaction of three major factors:

1. Transactions involving foreign currencies are now a significant and growing segment for many United States companies.
2. The exchange rates of the dollar against other currencies, which were remarkably stable between 1950 and 1970, have been undergoing large changes since 1971.
3. Accounting standards were changed in 1975 to require multinational companies to restate corporate income so as to reflect the effect of the quarterly changes in exchange rates whenever relevant.

In order to understand the background to the extra problems involved in multinational financial management, let us explore these three interacting factors in more detail.

Size and Growth of Multinational Operations

Over the past quarter of a century, the multinational component of United States business firms has grown rapidly. United States exports and imports of goods and services have grown faster than the domestic economy itself. In 1960 the sum of United States exports ($27 billion) and imports ($23 billion) represented less than 10 percent of that year's gross national product (GNP) ($506 billion). By mid-1979 exports and imports had each grown to around $250 billion, and their sum ($500 billion) had risen to over 20 percent of the GNP ($2,400 billion).

The past 25 years have also witnessed a rapid growth in the level of investments held and profits generated by foreign subsidiaries and branches of United States companies. In 1978 the book value of direct investments held by domestic companies outside the United States exceeded $150 billion, and these investments generated a sales volume of around $500 billion a year. During 1979, foreign affiliates of United States firms invested $35 billion in new fixed capital outside the United States or just over 20 percent of the $170 billion their parent companies invested in fixed capital inside the country. For many individual corporations, non–United States earnings now exceed domestic earnings.

Table 23-1, which gives results for 1978, shows the importance of foreign sales and earnings for a dozen well-known United States companies. All of these companies continually face the exchange-rate problem.

Table 23-1 Selected United States Corporations: Share of Foreign Activity to Total Activity 1978 (Percent)

Company	Foreign Share (revenues)	Foreign Share (operating profits)
Exxon (oil)	74	57
Mobil (oil)	59	57
Ford (auto)	35	49
IBM (business machines)	52	51
Citicorp (bank)	68	78
General Electric (Electrical equipment)	22	22
Bank of America (bank)	49	36
Dow Chemical (chemicals)	47	35
Xerox (office equipment)	47	37
Eastman Kodak (cameras)	38	25
Colgate-Palmolive (soaps)	57	62
Pan-Am (airlines)	92	117

Source: Forbes Magazine, June 25, 1979, p. 56.

Floating Exchange Rates

Between 1949 and 1970 exchange rates between the currencies of the major industrial nations and the United States dollar were remarkably stable. In part, this stability was due to the Bretton Woods system, which was established in 1946 as a reaction to chaotic and fluctuating exchange rates that prevailed before World War II. Under the Bretton Woods system, each major nation was required to set a specific *parity rate* for its currency against the United States dollar and to maintain that exchange rate within a very narrow margin above or below the stated parity rate. From time to time, a particular nation had to alter or revalue its parity rate against the dollar. In general, before 1971 such changes were *devaluations*, that is, a reduction of the currency's value relative to United States dollars (one exception was that West Germany *upvalued* its currency, the deutsche mark or DM against the dollar by 5 percent.)

In spite of these shifts, most exchange rates were remarkably stable between 1949, when the Bretton Woods arrangements really took effect, and 1971, when they ended, because the United States dollar itself had to be devalued.

For example, from 1949 to 1971 the exchange rate between the Japanese yen (the currency of the free world's second largest economy) and the dollar was constant at 360 yen to $1 over the entire 22 years. Likewise, the exchange rate between the West German DM (the free world's third largest economy) and the dollar was changed just once, in 1961, and then by only 5 percent. France and the United Kingdom (the fourth and fifth largest economies) had to devalue against the United States dollar, France in 1958 and 1968 and the United Kingdom in 1967; but apart from these changes, exchange rates were virtually constant for many years. The same was true of the Netherlands, Belgium, Switzerland, and most of the Scandinavian countries.

In 1971 the system of *fixed* or *pegged* exchange rates fell apart because the centerpiece of the system itself—the United States dollar—had to be devalued. After a futile attempt to set and maintain a new set of parity rates, the free world moved to a *floating* rate system in 1973. Since 1973 exchange rates between the United States dollar and other major currencies have been changing continuously with large shifts between one calendar quarter and the next. Table 23-2 shows the wide range of movement between the United States dollar and other principal currencies during 1978.

Table 23-2 Selected Foreign Exchange Rates, 1978 (In United States *Cents* per Foreign Currency Unit)

Country	Currency and Symbol	Open (12/30/77)	High	Low	Close (12/29/78)
Canada	Dollar (Can$)	91.4	91.7	84.0	84.3
France	Franc (FF)	21.3	25.2	20.3	24.0
Germany	Deutsche mark (DM)	47.7	58.3	46.4	55.0
Japan[a]	Yen (Y)	41.7[a]	56.8[a]	41.2[a]	51.5[a]
Switzerland	Franc (Sw Fr)	50.2	68.9	48.0	61.7
United Kingdom	Pound (£)	191.7	211.0	180.5	204.2

Source: International Monetary Fund, *International Financial Statistics* (monthly issues) and Harris Bank *Weekly Review of Foreign Exchange Rates.*
[a]United States cents per 100 yen.

Accounting and Reporting Requirements

The growing importance of foreign source income and the marked increase in exchange-rate fluctuations in the 1970s would have forced financial managers of multinational companies to pay much greater attention to the problem of changes in exchange rates. A third development that increased managers' sensitivity to the problem was the promulgation in October 1975 of new accounting regulations for United States companies regarding the treatment and reporting of foreign exchange gains and losses. Then new standards came to be known as FASB #8.[1]

Prior to 1975, multinational firms had been allowed considerable leeway in the accounting methods they used for recognizing and reporting foreign exchange gains or losses. FASB #8 required that a uniform set of accounting procedures be used for all United States companies and that the full effect of exchange gains or losses be carried through a firm's quarterly income statement. In conjunction with the sizable changes in exchange rates between the United States dollar and other currencies, the new accounting requirement led to large fluctuations from one quarter to the next in reported income. As a result, financial managers had to be increasingly concerned with a new task—minimizing losses due to a firm's foreign exchange exposure, a subject to which we now turn.

Foreign Exchange Exposure

It is necessary to distinguish between two quite different types of foreign exchange exposure to which a firm engaged in multinational business is subject. The first, known as *transactions exposure*, exists regardless of how a firm accounts for it. The second, known as *translation exposure* (or accounting exposure), is essentially an accounting issue.

Transactions Exposure

The source of transactions exposure to a United States firm is the existence of relatively short-term contracts or obligations that are denominated in a foreign currency. If the exchange rate changes between the time the contract or obligation is transacted and the time it is settled, the firm will have a foreign exchange loss or gain.

For example, assume a United States publishing firm sells 1,000 books to its Canadian subsidiary on credit for Can$10,000, payment to be made in 90 days. At the time of sale, the exchange rate is Can$1 = $1 US and the United States firm expects to receive $10,000 US. However, it is exposed to the risk that the exchange rate between the Canadian dollar and the United States dollar might change between the time of sale and the time the funds are actually received. In technical parlance, the firm's *exposure* is that it is *long* Can$10,000 for 90 days. If the Canadian dollar falls—for example, to 90¢ US—then the firm will actually receive only $9,000 US, a

---

1. The actual title of the ruling is *Statement of Financial Accounting Standards No. 8, Accounting for the Translation of Foreign Currency Financial Statements* (Financial Accounting Standards Board, Stamford, Connecticut).

decrease of $1,000 relative to its original expectation, and it thus has a foreign exchange transaction loss of $1,000. On the other hand, if the Canadian dollar rises to $1.05 US, it will have a foreign exchange transaction gain of $500 US. The word *exposure* refers to the chance of either a loss or a gain.

The financial management of the United States company can deal with the firm's exposure in several ways:

1. It can do nothing and take the chance of a gain or loss.
2. It can avoid exposure by denominating all of its transactions in the home currency (i.e., United States dollars). But this simply passes the transaction exposure to its Canadian subsidiary.
3. It can shift an equivalent amount of Canadian funds from the Canadian subsidiary to the United States parent at the time the new transaction is entered into. This is tantamount to selling for cash rather than credit.
4. It can "hedge" its exposure by selling the expected Can$10,000 for *forward* delivery 90 days hence. (Hedging operations will be discussed in a subsequent section.)

In a world of fluctuating exchange rates, transactions exposure is a continuous problem that has to be dealt with in one way or another. The decision made can have an important effect on the United States firm's income in that period.

This specific example is simply one illustration of how transactions exposure arises. We can generalize from this example. Foreign exchange transactions exposure exists whenever a firm has short-term assets (such as loans or accounts receivable) or liabilities (such as loans or accounts payable) denominated in a foreign currency that it plans to collect or pay within the current accounting period.

Translation Exposure

When a United States company holds assets and liabilities in other countries, these items are originally measured in currency units other than its own (the United States dollar). In order to prepare a consolidated report covering all of its multinational operations, the company must first *translate* the value of all these foreign assets and liabilities into United States dollars according to generally acceptable rules. Translation exposure (or accounting exposure) measures the impact of a change in exchange rates on the recorded consolidated balance sheet of a multinational company.

The impact of a given change in foreign exchange rates on a parent firm's balance sheet (and/or its income statement) is heavily influenced by the particular set of accounting rules that are used in order to translate foreign denominated items into United States dollars.

Before we discuss alternative accounting approaches to foreign currency translation, it would be useful to illustrate what *translation exposure* means via a simple example.

Let us say that a United States firm has a bank account in Paris of 40,000 French francs (FF) and no other assets and liabilities denominated in francs. On September 30, 19xx, the exchange rate is $1 = 4 FF, and so the item is entered on the company's books as an asset (cash) of $10,000. One quarter later, on December 31, 19xx, the exchange rate of the FF has fallen to $1 = 5 FF. The United States company still holds its 40,000 FF bank account and intends to keep on holding it in Paris. But it would now have to translate this holding on its balance sheet as $8,000. In its fourth quarter report for 19xx, the company would have to record and *report* a loss of $2,000 as far as this asset is concerned. This is a translation loss, and we can say that the company had a translation exposure to such a loss. If, in a subsequent quarter, the FF rises again to the original exchange rate of $1 = 4 FF, the company would record and report a translation gain of $2,000.

Alternative Translation Methods

Accounting professions in different countries have developed different procedures for translating foreign denominated assets and liabilities into the home currency of the parent company. In general, the methods that have been used fall into one of three categories known as:

1. The current/noncurrent method.
2. The monetary/nonmonetary method, also known in the United States as the temporal method.
3. The current-rate method.

The Current/Noncurrent Method

This method was used by United States multinationals prior to the promulgation of FASB #8 in 1975. Under this method all *current* assets and liabilities on the books of foreign subsidiaries or affiliates are translated into dollars (the home currency) at whatever exchange rate is in effect on the closing date of the statement. Balance sheet gains or losses due to shifts in exchange rates are reflected in that period's income statement.

All noncurrent assets and liabilities (i.e., long-term assets and liabilities) are translated at the *original* or *historic* exchange rate, that is, the rate that existed at the time the asset was acquired or the liability incurred. Thus, there are no gains or losses or long-term assets/liabilities (either on the balance sheet or the income statement) until the assets are actually sold or the debts are paid off.

The principal items in the income statement (sales and cash expenses) are translated at the *average* exchange rate for the time period covered by the statement, but items such as *depreciation* expense, which are related to long-term balance sheet assets or liabilities are translated at *historic* rates.

The Monetary/Nonmonetary Method

This method of translating foreign denominated assets/liabilities distinguishes between those items that have a fixed monetary value (in terms of the original currency) and those that do not, in fact, have a fixed monetary value (in terms of the original currency) but that are carried on the books as if they do. This definition sounds complicated but it really is not. Let us illustrate, using the example of a British subsidiary of a United States company.

Items such as cash, accounts receivable, and debts payable are denominated in £ sterling. If the general price level in the United Kingdom doubles or quadruples, it will not change the number of £ held or owed as far as these assets or liabilities are concerned. They are classified as *monetary* items.

On the other hand, other assets such as inventory, plant, property, or equipment are classified as real or nonmonetary assets. Their *value* in £ will rise with British inflation or fall with British deflation. But for *accounting* purposes (assuming original cost or historic account, which is the general rule for United States companies), their values are treated as if they also are fixed in terms of £.

For purposes of translating British assets and liabilities into dollars, the monetary/nonmonetary methods says: Items classified as monetary must be translated at the current exchange rate; items classified as *nonmonetary* must be translated at the original or historic exchange rate, that is, the rate that was in effect when the asset was acquired.

Furthermore, balance sheet gains or losses resulting from the foregoing transactions rule must be carried through to the income statement in the same period as the balance sheet gain or loss occurs.

This translation method is essentially the one adopted by FASB #8. The actual name given to the method by FASB #8 is the *temporal* method. The reason for the change in nomenclature is simple. The temporal method is identical to the monetary/nonmonetary method only when the nonmonetary items in a subsidiary's books are accounted for on the basis of original costs. Since this is virtually universal practice for United States corporate subsidiaries, the FASB #8 definition of the temporal method is the same as our definition of the monetary/non-monetary method.

One important consequence of the FASB #8 ruling has to do with the accounting effect of having long-term debt owed by a United States parent company when the debt is denominated in some foreign currency. For example, assume a United States company borrows the equivalent of $20 million by selling a bond in Switzerland, which is denominated in Swiss francs (Sw Fr). At the time the bonds are sold the exchange rate is $1 = 3 Sw Fr and thus the debt owed is 60 million Sw Fr. Over the past decade the United States dollar has depreciated severely relative to the Swiss franc. Assume in 19xx that the rate goes from $1 = 3 Sw Fr to $1 = 2 Sw Fr. The temporal method will require that the United States company *write up* the debt it owes from the original $20 million (60 million Sw Fr)/3 to $30 million (60 million Sw Fr)/2 and carry a *loss of $10 million to its income statements.*

The Current-Rate Method

The third basic approach to the translation problem is to translate *all* foreign assets, liabilities, and transactions into the home currency at the current rate of exchange, that is, the rate prevailing when the quarterly or annual books are closed. This is the method that most British multinational companies have used and that the British accounting profession has sponsored.

The majority of United States multinational companies would prefer to use the *current-rate method* as opposed to the temporal method imposed on them by FASB #8. As of mid-1979 there was also considerable evidence that the Financial Accounting Standards Board itself was prepared to abandon its original FASB #8 ruling and to move toward some version of the current-rate methodology. Several issues of detail exist that had not been resolved by mid-1979. Should foreign exchange gains or losses be carried through to income statements or should they be reflected only on the balance sheet, where they would be shown as a change in retained earnings, with only a footnote reference to its implications for that period's income? Until these issues are resolved, FASB #8 will remain in force. But the probability is high that FASB #8 will be replaced by the time this book is in print.

In any case, the problem of dealing with transactions exposure and translation exposure will continue to be a serious issue for financial managers as long as exchange rates continue to fluctuate.

Understanding the Foreign Exchange Market

To deal with foreign exchange risk (the exposure to gain or loss on assets or liabilities denominated in some other currency) requires an understanding of how foreign exchange markets work.

The foreign exchange market is now a global network of telephone and cable communications among banks, foreign exchange dealers, and brokers located in the principal financial centers. The ultimate players are multinational companies, exporters, and importers; investors or speculators; and governments—indeed any party that wishes to transfer funds into or from a different currency.

Spot Markets

The term *spot market* refers to transactions for immediate or spot delivery (actually for delivery within 1 or 2 business days). Exchange rates for spot delivery are referred to as *spot rates*.

For example, on July 13, 1979, the spot rate for the United States dollar ($) against the British pound (£) was $2.2255 per £. Against the German deutsche mark (DM), it was $0.5477 per DM. These are *bid* rates in the New York Market, that is, the rate of exchange at which the bank or dealer is willing to purchase the foreign currency for spot delivery from a multinational company. If the multinational wanted to *buy* DM, for example, the rate would be slightly different, $0.5480 per DM in the above illustration. The "spread" represents the bank's profit. In all our examples, we will ignore the bid–ask differential.

Because the spot markets are linked by virtually costless communication and by active dealers, *all* major exchange rates are also linked to one another. For example, using the *bid* quotations for the £/$ exchange rate ($2.2255 per £) and the DM/$ rate ($0.5477 per DM), we can safely say that the £/DM rate must be 2.2255/0.5477 or 4.0634 DM per £.

The market forces that bring about this result are known as *international arbitrage*, a process that means alert dealers and banks have continuous access to exchange rates all over the world and will act to buy any currency that is undervalued and to sell any that is overvalued relative to the total network of exchange values.

In a world of floating rates, spot exchange rates fluctuate continuously in response to the total flow of supply and demand for one currency against another.

Forward Market

In addition to the spot market, there is an established forward market in the major currencies. A forward exchange contract is an agreement between two parties to exchange a specified amount of one currency against a specified amount of another currency at a fixed date in the future; that is, the price or exchange rate is fixed today even though the actual settlement will take place at some predetermined point in the future. Forward rates are typically quoted for delivery 1 month, 3 months, and 6 months hence; however, forward contracts generally can be arranged with most international banks for delivery at any specified date up to 1 year in the future. Contracts running beyond 1 year are also available but require special arrangements.

For example, on July 13, 1979, when the spot rate for the DM was $0.5477 US and the spot rate for the £ was $2.2255 US, the forward rates for the DM and the £ were as follows:

	DM	£
Spot	$0.5477	$2.2255
1 month forward	$0.5502	$2.2190
3 months	$0.5536	$2.2065
6 months	$0.5580	$2.1956
1 year	$0.5651	$2.1758

Notice that the forward DM is more expensive than the spot DM. In technical terms the forward DM sells at a *premium* relative to the spot DM, and the longer the contract, the higher is this premium. In contrast, the forward £ is selling at a *discount* relative to the spot £. As is true of interest rates, it is standard practice to express the premium or discount on forward exchange in percent per annum terms.

The percent premium or discount is calculated as follows. If

S = spot rate
F = forward rate
n = number of months forward
P = forward premium or discount (percent per annum)

We have

$$P = \frac{F - S}{S} \times \frac{12}{n} \times 100 \qquad (1)$$

If the premium is negative, that is, the forward rate is selling at a discount, the symbol D is frequently used instead of a negative sign.

Let us calculate the forward premium for the 6 months forward DM on July 13, 1979, from the data given earlier. It is

$$P = \frac{0.5580 - 0.5477}{0.5477} \times \frac{12}{6} \times 100$$

$$= 3.76 \text{ percent per annum}$$

A similar calculation for the 6 month forward £ would show that P = −2.69 percent per annum. Or we could say for the 6 month forward £, D = 2.69 percent.

The Forward-Spot Differential

Why was the forward DM selling at a premium relative to the spot DM/$ rate and the forward £ at a discount relative to the spot £/$ rate? At first glance, the answer would appear to be that the market was expecting the DM to rise relative to the $ in the future and the £ to fall. This simple answer is only partly true. Forward rates do reflect expectations, but the forward premium or discount is often even more powerfully affected by the difference in interest rates between the two countries. The basic relationship between forward and spot exchange rates and relative interest rates is known as the *interest rate parity theorem*. This theorem is one of the keys to understanding and operating in the foreign exchange markets.

The Interest Rate Parity Theorem

If $i(\$)$, expressed as usual in percent per annum terms, is the 6 month rate of interest on loans or securities denominated in United States dollars, and $i(DM)$ is the corresponding rate for loans on securities of identical risk denominated in deutsche marks, then the interest rate parity theorem says that the following relationship must hold:

$$P = \frac{i(\$) - i(DM)}{1 + i(DM)} \tag{2}$$

That is, the premium on the 6 month forward DM is equal to the difference between the 6 month rate of interest in the two countries divided by one plus the DM rate.[2]

We can check the accuracy of the theorem. On July 13, 1979, the rate of interest on large 6 month certificates of deposit (CDs) denominated in dollars was 10.6875 percent per annum. The corresponding rate on DM denominated 6 month CDs was 7 percent per annum. Applying expression (2) gives 3.45 percent, close to the 6 month premium of 3.76 percent at which the forward DM was trading. The difference can be traced to the fact that we are ignoring the difference between bid/ask prices for spot and forward exchange and other trading costs.

---

2. Where high accuracy is not required, the numerator of expression (2) can be used as an approximation.

The process by which the equality indicated by the interest rate parity theorem is brought about is known as *covered interest arbitrage.*

Let us examine this process. Suppose the theory did not hold. For example, assume that all of the facts given for July 13, 1979, hold but that the dollar interest rate is *not* 10.6875 percent but, rather, that it is 9 percent. Under these assumed conditions, everybody who holds a dollar CD would have a riskless opportunity to gain by (1) cashing it in and using the proceeds to purchase a DM denominated CD, which is paying 7 percent, and (2) at the same time *selling* 6 month DM forward for dollars. Let us illustrate.

Investor *Y* has a $1 million CD paying 9 percent. If he holds the CD, he will have $1,045,000 at the end of 6 months. If he withdraws the $1 million, exchanges it into DM at the spot rate ($0.5477 = 1 DM), he would have 1,825,817 DM. Invested in a 6 month DM CD at 7 percent, this would grow in 6 months to 1,889,721 DM. The investor can contract now to sell this expected sum in the forward exchange market. At the 6 month forward rate of $0.5580 = 1 DM, investor *Y* would receive $1,054,464. This is $9,464 more than the investor would have had by keeping the funds in the dollar instrument. Furthermore, no foreign exchange risk is involved, because the investor has *covered* the transaction through the forward exchange contract and knows from the start just how many dollars he will have at the end of 6 months. Quite naturally he would want to sell the million dollar CD and buy the DM CD. So would holders of other billions of dollars. Thus, the interest rate offered on dollar CDs would have to rise relative to the interest rate on DM or else the forward premium on the DM would have to fall before a new equilibrium could be reached. (An equilibrium position is one in which there are no riskless gains available through arbitrage.) For such an equilibrium to hold, the relationship indicated by the interest rate parity theorem in expression (2) must also hold.

Dealing with Foreign Exchange Exposure

Having taken a very brief excursion into the workings of the foreign exchange market, we can return to the problem that led to the excursion in the first place. How can financial managers deal with the foreign exchange risk to which their firms are exposed because they hold assets or liabilities denominated in another currency?

Hedging

The most commonly used method of removing or reducing foreign exchange risk is to *hedge* the company's foreign exchange exposure through the use of forward exchange contracts whenever these are available. A hedge is simply the general term used for any contract or arrangement that can reduce the risk that arises from the uncertainty of future prices. Here we are interested in a particular "price," the rate of exchange between some foreign currency and the dollar, and hence in a particular form of hedging, the foreign exchange market hedge.

Let us begin by examining how a company can hedge an existing foreign exchange exposure because it holds an asset denominated in a foreign currency. Assume it is now July 13, 1979, and a United States company has £1 million due it in 3 months, through its London subsidiary. The spot exchange rate today is $2.2255 = 1£, and *if* the funds could be transferred today, the £1 million asset (the account receivable) would yield $2,225,500.

But the funds are not available today and will not be available for 3 months. Management is quite uncertain about what the £/$ rate will be in 3 months. If the £ falls relative to the dollar, the company will get less than $2,225,000 in 3 months; if it rises, the company will get more. What should management do?

1. The company can make (or buy) a *forecast* of what the £/$ rate will be in 3 months. If the forecast indicates that the £ is going to rise, management can choose to believe it and do nothing further because the company will gain from the predicted rise. Of course, forecasting exchange rates in a floating rate system is extremely difficult, and the forecast may turn out to be wrong! In any case, the company must accept the uncertainty of not knowing how many dollars it will actually get. What if the forecast is that the £ will fall relative to the dollar?
2. If management does not like bearing uncertainty (whatever the forecast says) or if the forecast is that the £ is going to fall, the company has to act to avoid loss and/or reduce uncertainty. It can do so by converting uncertainty into certainty via selling £1 million now in the forward exchange market for delivery 3 months hence. The 3 month forward rate is known. It is $2.2065 = 1£. Thus, by hedging, the firm can be sure that 3 months hence the London asset will yield exactly $2,206,500.

Hedging Liabilities

Dealing with liabilities denominated in a foreign currency is a little more complicated because it offers a wider range of options. Assume that a United States company has imported some Jaguar automobiles for which it owes the British Leyland Co. £1 million due in 3 months. At the July 13, 1979 rate, the firm owes $2,225,500. But the spot rate 3 months hence when the actual payment is due is uncertain. Again, the firm can try to forecast. If the £ is expected to fall, management can decide to accept the forecast (and the uncertainty) and do nothing. Alternatively, if management dislikes uncertainty or if the forecast suggests that the £ is going to rise, the firm can act by *buying* the 3 month forward £ at the known rate of $2.2065· = 1£, which will lock in the final cost ($2,206,500).

But there is a third option. If the firm's present cash position is strong, it can use $2,206,500 of cash *today* to buy spot £. At the spot rate of $2.2255 = 1£, the firm will get £991,463. If this sum is invested in 3 month £ CDs, which offer an annual rate of 14.125 percent, the firm will earn interest equal to £991,463 × (14.125/4), so the total amount it has in 3 months will be £1,026,474. This will leave a "profit" of £26,474 after the £1 million due British Leyland is paid off.

But is the £26,474 a true profit? It is not. It should not be compared to a *zero* profit on the simple hedging alternative. Rather, it should be compared to the interest *the firm would have earned* had it taken the original $2,206,500 and invested it in 3 month dollar CDs on which the interest rate was 10.6875. In 3 months, such an investment would have grown by $2,206,500 × (10.6875/4), or to $2,265,455. The interest earned is $59,955.

Which is better: £26,474 in three months or $59,955 in three months? The appropriate *rate of exchange* between the two alternatives is today's 3 month forward rate or $2.2065 = 1£. Hence, the £26,474 of interest earned (in £s) is equivalent to $(26,474 × 2.2065) or $58,415. The option of buying spot £s and investing them in London is not as good as the simple option of keeping the cash in dollars and buying the needed £s in the forward market.

Risk Reduction When Formal Hedging Is Not Available

The straightforward approach to risk reduction outlined earlier is possible only when there are organized forward markets for foreign exchange. What if there is no organized forward market for a foreign currency? In order to hedge foreign exchange risks due to exposure in such currencies (for example, Australia or Brazil) the financial manager has to use one of three alternative techniques.

Leading or Lagging. One method is to accelerate conversion and remission of foreign denominated cash assets when the foreign currency is expected to fall in value relative to the dollar. On the other hand, if the currency is expected to rise relative to the dollar, conversion of assets into dollars would be deferred (lagged).

Lending or Borrowing. A second device is to increase short-term local currency borrowing (i.e., borrowing denominated in the foreign currency) whenever the currency is expected to decline relative to the dollar and to reduce borrowing (or increase net lending via trade credit, etc.) when the currency is expected to rise.

Parallel Loans.   A third device is to find another multinational that has the opposite problem to one's own. For example, let us assume that a United States aluminum company has an Australian subsidiary from which it expects to receive $10,000,000 Australian next quarter (the rate of exchange on July 13, 1979, was $1.126 US = $1 Australian). It cannot hedge through the forward market because one does not exist.[3] At the same time a United States automobile manufacturer is planning to remit $10,000,000 US to its Australian subsidiary for an expansion of its automobile manufacturing facilities. Both the aluminum company and the automobile company want to avoid the chance that exchange rates will move against them. With very little effort, arrangements can be made for the aluminum company's subsidiary to *lend* the automobile company's subsidiary the equivalent of $10 million US in Australian dollars at a stated rate of interest, and *at the same time* for the automobile company's parent to lend the aluminum company's parent the same amount of $10 million US at the same stated rate of interest as the Australian loan. In the simplest form of a parallel loan, *both* loans would be settled at some future date by a simple exchange of IOUs. In more complicated forms, the intercompany loan arrangement would specify other adjustments related to future spot rates and relative interest rates in the two countries. In any case, what the two companies have done is to *create* a minimarket in forward exchange where one did not previously exist.

Multinational Investment Decisions

Multinational companies invest funds in long-term assets all over the world. They also invest short-term funds internationally. Finally, they also borrow short-term and long-term funds in foreign markets to finance part or all of their investments. All of these decisions can and should be analyzed using the same basic intellectual framework that is used for analyzing domestic investment and financing decisions, disucssed in the first five parts of this book. However, the framework itself has to be extended in order to incorporate new dimensions.

Long-Run Investments

When a United States firm invests in plant and equipment outside the United States, it has to confront a new variable: *political risk*. The phrase *political risk* covers a wide variety of changes that could occur when funds

---

3. A forward market in Australian dollars is emerging.

are tied up outside the United States. Among the added risks, listed from worst to bad, are:

1. Outright expropriation of assets and property without compensation
2. Expropriation of assets with minimum compensation
3. Nonconvertibility of earnings back into the home currency
4. Taxation
5. Direct controls over prices chargeable, wages and fringe benefits payable to workers, local borrowing ability, rights to remit dividends to parent company, transfer payments to parent company for goods received, and a score of other operating events

One important safeguard available to United States companies operating abroad is the availability of federal insurance against major losses caused by the sovereign action of foreign governments. In 1969 Public Law 91-175 established the *Overseas Private Investment Corporation* (OPIC), which took over federal overseas insurance functions previously located in other agencies. In essence, OPIC *insures* United States owned investments in less-developed countries against three types of risk: (1) expropriation, (2) inconvertibility of foreign earnings, and (3) war, revolution, and insurrection.

The existence of OPIC insurance does not mean that a United States corporation can step into a foreign investment without a great deal of care and planning. However, the same is true—although to a lesser degree—of any large domestic investment. All that is required to extend the analysis of risk to locations outside the United States itself is a sensitivity to the tides of potential political changes in the foreign countries.

Cash Investment Decisions

By definition, investment in cash or cash equivalents, such as liquid short-term investments, are confined to financial markets located in market-oriented economies: the United States and Canada; Western Europe; Japan and smaller growing markets in Singapore, Hong Kong, Bahrein; and the stable Caribbean countries such as Bahamas, Bermuda, and the Cayman Islands.

The cash investment decision is a simple one. How can a company maximize the expected rate of return on its idle cash balance (without increasing risk) by investing in one money market instrument as opposed to another?

To examine this decision, let us go back to July 13, 1979. Assume a multinational treasurer has $1 million that he knows will be "idle" for 6 months. Where should he "place" these funds?

In order to make the decision, the treasurer must make two calculations:

1. How is interest taxed in the various jurisdictions?
2. What is the net *covered* rate of interest he can earn in each of the available markets?

Table 23-3 shows the rates for 6 month investments that prevailed on July 13, 1979.

Table 23-3   Prevailing Rates for 6 Month Investments
(All Rates in Percent per Annum)

	6 Month Rate of Interest (CD rates)	6 Month Forward Premium or Discount
United States ($)	10.6875	
Canada (Canadian $)	10.6875	−0.12
United Kingdom (£)	13.5000	−2.69
France (FF)	12.2500	−1.87
Germany (DM)	7.0000	+3.76
Italy (Lire)	15.0000	−4.94
Netherlands (Florin)	10.0000	+0.66
Switzerland (Sw Fr)	2.1875	+8.60
Japan (Y)	6.1875	+4.43

Where should the treasurer place the $1 million? (For our purposes, we ignore differences in transactions costs and in taxes on interest earned.)

To answer the question, we have to calculate the *covered* interest rate on each investment, that is, the rate we can get in each market *in dollars with exchange rate risk eliminated.*

The approximate answer is provided by simply adding (algebraically)

Table 23-4

	Covered Interest Rate in Dollars (percent)
United States	10.6875
Canada	10.5675
United Kingdom	10.8100
France	10.3800
Germany	10.7600
Italy	10.0600
Netherlands	10.6600
Switzerland	10.7875
Japan	10.6175

the 6 month interest rate in each currency shown in column 1 of Table 23-3 to its forward premium or discount shown in column 2. This gives us Table 23-4.

The 6 month £ CD looks like the best short-term investment. But all the effective *covered* rates cluster very closely. This is exactly what theory suggests should happen in an intelligent market. But at any point in time, there may be differences in expected yields (adjusted for risk). Banks and other professional dealers exploit these differences through arbitrage. Lately, multinational financial managers have also begun to do so. A difference of 0.02 percent may not seem large, but on $1 billion, a correct decision amounts to a net gain of $200,000—more than enough to pay for a 5 minute calculation.

Given the need to minimize foreign exchange exposure risk and to maximize net covered yield on idle cash, it is not surprising that most multinationals now maintain a specialized foreign exchange staff in their treasury departments.

Summary

Doing business in more than one country generally requires a firm to hold assets, owe liabilities, and make transactions that are denominated in currencies other than its own. Therefore, financial managers of such companies must understand and deal with one extra critical variable: the exchange rate between foreign currencies and their own.

The fact that exchange rates now continuously fluctuate much more than they used to exposes a multinational company to the additional risk of losses caused by these exchange-rate fluctuations. A *transactions* gain or loss occurs when the exchange rate changes between the time a contract denominated in another currency is made and the time it is actually settled and recorded. A *translation* gain or loss occurs because United States accounting regulations, known as FASB #8, require a company to recognize the paper gain or loss from any exchange rate change even if the actual settlement date is far in the future.

Multinational companies try to protect themselves from the uncertainty of transactions and translation losses (or gains) stemming from exchange rate fluctuations. One method of protection is to *hedge* potential exposure by making offsetting purchases or sales in the *forward* markets for foreign exchange. To hedge its position, a company that has net monetary assets (assets fixed in value in the foreign currency) will *sell* that currency forward. A company with net monetary liabilities in a foreign currency will *buy* that currency in the forward market. This reduces total exposure and the size of unanticipated gains or losses from future exchange rate changes.

Questions

1. How does the financial manager's task change when the company engages in foreign operations?
2. Describe the difference between a fixed exchange rate system and a floating system.
3. Which of the two systems should a businessperson prefer and why?
4. Refer to Table 23-2 and describe what happened to the exchange rate of the United States dollar during the year 1978. How would you explain what happened?
5. Distinguish between a *transactions* loss on foreign exchange and a *translations* loss.
6. Describe the monetary/nonmonetary method of accounting for a change in a foreign exchange rate.
7. Describe how a corporate treasurer can hedge against the chance of an exchange rate loss on an asset held in French francs.
8. Describe how a corporate treasurer can hedge against the chance of an exchange rate loss on a long-term Swiss franc denominated liability the company has.
9. What is the interest rate parity theorem?
10. What do you understand by the term *covered interest arbitrage*?

Problems

1. Assume that the spot rate for German deutsche marks (DM) in New York is $0.55 per DM.
   (a) What will the spot rate for the United States dollar be in terms of DM on the Frankfurt market?
   (b) If the dollar is quoted at 1.95 DM in Frankfurt, what do you think will happen?
2. On the same day that the spot DM was quoted at $0.55 in New York, the spot Swiss franc was quoted at $0.62.
   (a) What will the spot rate for DM be in the Zurich market?
   (b) If you find that the Zurich quotation for DM is 0.85 Sw Fr = 1 DM, how could you profit from your knowledge?
3. On October 31, 1978, the United States dollar sank to a record low against most foreign currencies. The spot exchange rates on that day (in United States cents per foreign currency unit) are as shown in column 1 in the table on the facing page.
   Three days later, by November 3, 1978, the United States dollar had jumped as shown in column 2.
   (a) Go to the *Wall Street Journal* of that week (or to the financial page of any other daily or weekly paper) and explain what happened to get the dollar to rise so suddenly.

	October 31, 1978	November 3, 1978
Australia	118.1000	115.3000
Canada	85.6800	85.5200
France	24.7831	23.2286
Germany	57.0125	52.8541
Japan (100 yen)	55.7100	52.9100
Switzerland	66.6667	61.6903
United Kingdom	207.0000	198.2500

(b) Go to a recent source of data on spot exchange rates. How do present exchange rates compare with the October 31, 1978, rates?

4. On July 13, 1979, the spot rate for the Swiss franc was 0.6035 US cents. The 3 month forward rate was 0.61805. Express the forward premium on the Swiss franc against the dollar in percent per annum terms.

5. The 12 month CD interest rate on Swiss francs is 2.50 percent. The corresponding interest rate on United States dollars is 10.44 percent. The spot rate for the Swiss franc is 0.6035 cents. The 12 month forward exchange rate is 0.6506. If you had to invest United States dollar funds for 12 months, which instrument would you pick and why?

References

There are several excellent textbooks in the field of International financial management.

G. Dufey and I. H. Giddy, *The International Money Market,* Prentice-Hall Foundations of Finance Series (Englewood Cliffs, N.J.: Prentice-Hall, 1978).

D. K. Eiteman and A. I. Stonehill, *Multinational Business Finance* (Reading, Mass.: Addison-Wesley, 1979).

C. Henning, W. Pigott, and R. H. Scott, *International Financial Management* (New York: McGraw Hill, 1978).

D. R. Lessard, *International Financial Management: Theory and Application* (Boston: Warren, Garham, Lamont, 1979).

D. R. Ricks, *International Dimensions of Corporate Finance,* Prentice-Hall Foundations of Finance Series (Englewood Cliffs, N.J.: Prentice-Hall, 1978).

R. M. Rodriguez and E. E. Carter, *International Financial Management,* 2d ed., (Englewood Cliffs, N.J.: Prentice-Hall, 1979).

Mergers and Acquisitions

24

Varieties of Mergers
Forms of Payment
Motives for Mergers
Conglomerate Mergers of the Late 1960s
The Acquisition Wave of the Late 1970s

A company can expand in two ways, internally or externally. It can grow from within through the normal process of investing funds in new projects; it can also grow by acquiring other ongoing companies and merging their assets and operations into itself. Either route involves an investment decision. Both routes are, or should be, motivated by the same underlying objective: to increase and thus maximize the net present value of the company's stock.

Although the bulk of this book (and especially Parts III and IV), has been directed at *internal* expansion decisions, the logic and analysis also applies to external expansion. However, external growth or the merger and acquisition "game" as it has been called, entails many complex and distinct institutional characteristics that are not present when growth is internal. Hence, it deserves special treatment in a separate chapter.

Varieties of Mergers

Mergers (the combining of two ongoing firms under common ownership) come in a huge and bewildering variety of forms. The motives for merging and the processes through which one is accomplished differ widely from one merger to another. As a result, we do not yet have a single satisfactory basis for classifying mergers, let alone an acceptable theory about why firms seek the merger route in the first place. There is still dispute about whether expansion via the merger route is good, bad, or indifferent as far as our total economic society is concerned!

Merger, Consolidation, and Acquisition

The terms *merger, consolidation,* and *acquisition* are frequently used as if they are synonymous. The differences are slight enough to allow such usage. Technically, a *consolidation* occurs if two existing firms merge into one another to form a new, combined firm that is identified by a new name. For example, firm *A* and firm *B* merge to form a new company called firm *X* or sometimes firm *AB*. An *acquisition* occurs if one firm buys another: if firm *A* buys firm *B* and the result is a bigger (and presumably better) firm *A*.

Congeneric or Conglomerate

Mergers can also be classified by whether they are *congeneric* (two firms in essentially the same or related industries) or *conglomerate* (two firms in quite different industries).

Until the 1960s, most mergers were essentially congeneric. A big wave of mergers occurred around the turn of the century: companies in one industry merged with or were acquired by other companies in the same industry. Steel mills bought or merged with steel mills, and department stores bought or merged with department stores. This type of congeneric merger is referred to as *horizontal integration*.

A second wave of mergers occurred in the 1920s. Unlike the earlier wave, this one involved many mergers between firms where each was active at different *stages of production* within an industry: steel mills acquired coal mines (an essential component of steel) or steel distribution centers (an essential component for selling steel products); automobile manufacturers acquired steel mills (then an essential component of car bodies), and so on. This form of integration is known as *vertical integration*. Today most of our major companies engaged in the production of goods (as opposed to services) are vertically integrated. For example, all of the major aluminum companies own and operate bauxite mining plants (the raw material for aluminum), alumina plants (the intermediate production stage that converts bauxite into aluminum oxide), aluminum reduction plants (which convert alumina into ingots of virtually pure aluminum), and aluminum fabricating plants (which shape aluminum ingots into final usable forms). Likewise, most of the large petroleum companies are "integrated."

Both vertical and horizontal integration are classified as congeneric. In contrast, *conglomerate* mergers involve the combining of two or more companies that operate in unrelated industries. For example, the purchase of Avis, the much-advertised number 2 car rental company, by the International Telephone and Telegraph Company (ITT) would be defined as a conglomerate merger. The large merger wave that occurred in the late 1960s and died out by 1970 was essentially conglomerate in character. The multibillion dollar companies that grew out of this wave, such as Gulf & Western, LTV, Litton Industries, Northwest Industries, and Tenneco are still classified as conglomerates. However, with the changes in conglomerates' fortunes on Wall Street, the word *conglomerate* lost its earlier glamor, and the preferred name for such companies today is *multiindustry* companies.

A fourth merger wave swelled in the late 1970s, and by 1979 it had become large enough to trigger new legislative initiatives designed to bring it under control. Like the wave of the 1960s, it was principally conglomerate in form, but both the motives and the processes were distinctly different. The wave of the late 1970s was essentially a take-over or *acquisition* wave in which one company buys out another with almost no pretense that a "merger" of the two is taking place.

Friendly or Unfriendly

The most recent spate of acquisitions has given rise to the need for yet another basis for classifying mergers: Are they friendly or unfriendly?

In a friendly merger the acquiring company *A,* which plans to acquire another company *B,* approaches *B*'s management discreetly and succeeds in working out a satisfactory offer that will be approved by *B*'s board of directors. Assuming no objection from the government on antitrust grounds, the sale of company *B*'s stock (or sometimes its assets) to company *A* is approved by *B*'s stockholders; the terms of the purchase are approved by *A*'s stockholders and the merger proceeds smoothly.

An unfriendly merger is equivalent to a war between two companies. On hearing that company *A* is about to buy it, company *B*'s management and/or its board of directors put up a large struggle to resist the proposed take-over. The struggle frequently extends into the federal and state courts and generally involves a small army of lawyers, investment bankers, and public relations experts.

One of the more interesting by-products of the acquisition wave of the late 1970s is that it has spawned a colorful new vocabulary to describe the tactics used by the two warring parties in an unfriendly merger proposal—terms such as "Saturday Night Special," "bear hug," "white knight," and "shark repellant," to which we will devote a little space after we cover more prosaic items. In addition to the new vocabulary, the recent take-over wars are likely to spawn some antimerger legislation as well.

Purchase of Assets or Purchase of Stock

An acquisition can take place in one of two ways. The buyer can purchase part or all of the *assets* held by the acquired company, or it can purchase the *common stock* of the acquired company. If the latter method is used, the acquired firm ceases to exist as an independent entity; all of its assets and liabilities are taken over by the buying company.

When only assets are purchased, the selling company will continue to exist, although it is now reduced to a corporate shell. After the sale, its assets consist entirely of the payment received from the buyer, which may be cash or notes or shares of the buyer's stock. It will continue to owe the liabilities outstanding on its books. The selling company can continue to hold the cash or stock it received or invest the cash as it sees fit. Alternatively, it can pay off its liabilities, distribute the cash or stock to its own stockholders as a liquidating dividend, and then dissolve.

The purchase of assets (as opposed to stock) is an easier procedure because it does not require formal approval by the buying company's shareholders, whereas the purchase of stock does. Also, prior to 1950, the purchase of assets was not subject to antitrust objections. However, this has since been changed, which has greatly reduced the procedural advantage of asset as opposed to stock acquisition.

Forms of Payment

One big difference between the mergers that took place in the 1960s and the recent wave of mergers is that in the 1960s the more typical form of payment offered by the acquiring company was its own common stock, whereas in the late 1970s the typical transaction was an outright acquisition of another company's shares for cash or the equivalent of cash.

The form of payment used is a critical distinguishing variable between one merger and another. It has major tax and accounting consequences, and as we will see in a subsequent section, it also reflects the financial motives that underlie the decision to merge.

The Tax Factor

Tax consequences have a powerful influence on economic decisions, and the field of mergers is no exception to this rule. Taxes are sometimes the main reason for a merger. Three examples will show why.

Company *B* has had a series of "losses" (negative taxable income) that are of little use to it individually because it does not expect to make large enough taxable profits over the horizon during which past losses can be used to offset taxes payable on future profits. For company *A*, which is doing well (and therefore paying taxes), company *B*'s tax loss carryover is an attractive "asset." By merging *B* into *A*, those losses can be used in full to offset *A*'s future taxable profits.

An oil company that has large overseas taxes (taxes paid to a foreign government) can use these as a credit against domestic taxes. But if it has insufficient domestic source income, the potential tax credits from overseas operations are of little or no value to it. One way to convert these credits into a valuable resource is to acquire a profitable (taxable) domestic company so that the merged entity can use all of the available foreign tax credit.

Entrepreneur *B*, now aged 60, has built a very successful company of which he is the sole owner and which represents virtually all his wealth. His children are not interested in running the business. He wants to diversify his assets so that the family's wealth is not completely dependent on the single line of activity represented by his company. He could sell the business outright, but that would involve a huge and immediate payment of capital gains taxes. If he merges his company into another larger company *A*, and receives *A*'s common stock in payment, he can achieve both of his objectives. He will hold a less risky asset (*A*'s common stock) and one that is less dependent on his active participation. He will also defer the payment of taxes until such time as he or his heirs *sell* the stock they receive.

Even when taxes, as such, are not the main reason for a merger, the tax implications of a merger are important both for the seller and the buyer.

The tax status of the selling company's owners is determined by the means of payment they receive from the buyer. If the buyer pays cash or the equivalent of cash for their stock, any gain (or loss) the sellers have is taxable in the year payment is received. If the buyer's payment is in the form of shares of its own voting stock, any gain (or loss) the sellers have is not taxable until they sell the shares they receive.

The sellers' point of view can therefore be stated quite simply: Other things being equal, they would prefer to receive payment in a form that allows them to defer taxes payable if a taxable *gain* is involved or alternatively, one that allows immediate recognition of a loss for tax purposes if a taxable *loss* is incurred.

The buying company's point of view with respect to tax implications is more complex. The tax consequences for the buyer depend on how the assets it has acquired are *accounted for* on its books, and this, in turn, is affected by the form of payment used in acquiring the assets.

Accounting Treatment

Accounting principles recognize two methods for incorporating the assets of the acquired company into the acquirer's books. One method is known as a *purchase,* the other as a *pooling of interests.*[1]

Under the purchase method, the acquired assets are carried on the buying company's books at the total price paid for them. (Cash or the market value of stock paid *plus* the debts assumed.)

Under the pooling of interests method, the assets acquired are transferred to the buying company's books at their net book value, that is, exactly as they were valued on the selling company's books prior to the acquisition.

From a buying company's point of view, each of these accounting methods has advantages as well as disadvantages.

If the price paid for the assets is above the original net book value, the purchase method sometimes allows the buying company to "write-up" the depreciable assets and thus to charge a higher depreciation deduction in future years both for book and for tax purposes. Such a "higher" charge reduces future tax liabilities and so increases its future net after-tax cash flows. But this advantage of the purchase method is offset by a further complication. If the total price paid for the acquired assets exceeds their "fair market value" (generally defined as the market price at which the

---

1. Acceptable accounting practice with respect to these methods is laid out in *Opinions of the Accounting Principles Board*, No. 16 (New York: American Institute of Certified Public Accountants, 1970).

individual physical assets could have been sold), then under the purchase method, the buying company can transfer the acquired assets only at their "fair market value"; the excess has to be transferred as "goodwill." The trouble with goodwill is that it *has to be* amortized (i.e., depreciated) over time for reporting purposes, and this will reduce future reported earnings. However, the annual amortization of goodwill is not deductible for tax purposes. In brief, when the goodwill factor exists, the buying company gets the worst of both worlds—higher taxable income and lower reported income! This would lead the buying company to prefer the pooling of interests method of accounting, which eliminates the goodwill problem.

Accounting regulations do not allow a buying company to use the pooling of interests method unless strict conditions are met. The critical condition is that the buying company has to pay the seller in voting stock. This, in turn, has consequences for a seller.

Even at the simple level, the tax and accounting complications have an influence on the way the terms of even a friendly merger are worked out. When the means of payment proposed is neither straight cash nor straight common stock, the complications multiply significantly.

Motives for Mergers

Why do firms choose to grow externally by purchasing other firms that they then merge into their own? There are as many reasons for mergers as there are mergers! But all of them can be summarized under a single purpose: A firm invests in another firm because it believes that the move will increase the net present value of its stock. The same motive underlies the willingness of an acquired firm to be acquired. The expectations are fulfilled if two conditions are met. If $V(A)$ is the market value of the acquiring firm A, $V(B)$ is the market value of the acquired firm B, and $V(A + B)$ is the market value of the combined firm, a successful merger is one in which:

1. $V(A + B) > V(A) + V(B)$.
2. Each firm gets some of the extra value created. (The buzz word for this extra value is *synergy*.)

The pragmatic question is: How can $V(A + B)$ be greater than $V(A) + V(B)$?

We have already seen that tax savings can be one source of the added value for one or both parties. In the long run, market values reflect the net present value of after-tax cash flows; so for any given cash flow if the combined tax liabilities of a merged company can be reduced, this in itself will raise net present value. But there are other factors in addition to taxes. One legitimate factor is referred to as economies of scale.

Economies of Scale

When two firms are combined, some costs can be eliminated and others can be reduced. One chief executive officer (CEO) costs less than two, even if his pay is increased somewhat because of the merger. The merged firm will also need only one chief financial officer, one R & D department, one of any other *overhead* function.

There are also other, less obvious, sources of cost reduction. A larger combined firm will have better and cheaper access to financial markets, whether these be banks or stock and bond flotations. If the acquired firm has unused capacity to incur debt, the combined firm will also enjoy a larger access to financial markets.

Even at the operational level (assuming a congeneric merger), there are the prospects of economies of scale via more efficient data processing systems, more efficient producing facilities, and more efficient distribution networks.

Risk Reduction via Diversification

One reason frequently offered for external expansion is that a company can reduce its overall risk by diversifying into new activities. As we saw earlier, especially in Chapter 14, risk reduction should *reduce* the capitalization rate that the market applies against a firm's cash flow and hence *increase* its net present value.

The real issues are (1) why cannot a company reduce the riskiness of its future cash flow via *inside* growth as opposed to growth via external acquisition, and (2) does external diversification really increase value by reducing risk?

Unlike the tax incentive factor and the economies of scale factor, the risk reduction rationale for external growth via mergers is far harder to justify in terms of *ultimate* results to the owners as opposed to what might be called proximate or *intermediate* results. Many companies defend an acquisition of a company in a business diverse from its own on the grounds that the combined enterprise will have lower joint risks than the risk of the two separately. This may well be true. It may also be true that the most economical way in which the acquiring firm can enter the acquired firm's business is through an acquisition. But does the alleged risk reduction really increase the net present value of its owners? The academic answer is that it probably does not. A combined firm that consists of $\frac{1}{2}A + \frac{1}{2}B$ may well be less risky than A alone or B alone, but it also may not do stockholders any good because they can, on their own, hold a portfolio consisting of $\frac{1}{2}A$ and $\frac{1}{2}B$. Furthermore, they would avoid the out-of-pocket legal and financial costs of the actual merger. In theory at least, the pure risk reduction motive for growth via merger (as opposed to true economies that affect net cash flow) can be justified only in terms of the management's risk. By and large, this conclusion is supported by empirical evidence. But, as usual, there are exceptions to the rule. Some conglomerates, notably the Teledyne Corporation, have succeeded in putting together a combination of diverse companies that jointly seem to command a higher value than the sum of their component parts.

Managerial Motives

The motives that prompt *management* as opposed to *owners* to buy, sell, or not sell companies is far harder to define because managers may or may not fall under our general net present value maximization rule. Frequently, the interest of managers is identical to that of owners. They own shares or options to buy shares at a preset price, and their predominant personal interest is therefore the same as that of any other shareholder. On the other hand, their work and their position in the company may also be an important dimension of their total satisfaction. Sometimes these interests may be in conflict.[2] When such a conflict exists, mergers that should be consummated (because they offer real benefits) may not be consummated and mergers that should not be consummated (because they do not offer real benefits) are, in fact, concluded.

Financial Motives

With mergers, as with many things in life, the "bottom line" is money—or "financial value" as that is sometimes called. Properly interpreted, there is nothing wrong with or crass about the concept of maximizing financial value. Indeed, it generally is the same thing as maximizing net present value or true economic value. However, the objective can be perverted and was frequently perverted during the merger wave of the 1960s. The twist took the following form: *Do those things that increase earnings per share (EPS) because it will increase the market price of a company.* This EPS edict sounds like the one we have been using, that is, *maximizing net present value,* but it is not the same thing. In the 1960s it led a lot of companies and stockholders into trouble.

Conglomerate Mergers of the Late 1960s

The large wave of mergers that took place in the late 1960s had three notable features:

1. It was mainly conglomerate in character.

---

2. For a discussion of this point, see D. Norr, "Management and the Investor," *Financial Analysis Journal,* 45–48 (Mar.–Apr. 1979).

2. Like other previous merger waves, it took place in a setting of high and rising prices for common stocks, especially of the so-called growth stocks that were highly favored by the public.
3. It involved a curious confusion between two quite distinct phenomena—true growth on the one hand and a mere increase in the reported earnings per share (EPS) of many companies that participated in the merger movement.

The third feature is critical to a proper understanding of what occurred.

True growth occurs only if a company has the ability to create and exploit opportunities to invest funds at a higher average rate than the rate of return required by shareholders. Net present value is positive because expected return exceeds required return. Because future earnings for such a company will be higher than current earnings, the market price (P) of such a company will and should be high relative to current earnings (E). In other words, it will command a high P/E ratio relative to other stocks.[3]

When true growth exists, a company's EPS stream will rise over time. However, the reverse is not true. A mere rise in a company's EPS does not necessarily imply true growth!

During the late 1960s, many companies deliberately pursued the objective of increasing EPS through the acquisition route. For a while, the marketplace mistook mere growth in EPS for true growth and priced the shares of these companies accordingly. As we will presently see, such a process cannot go on for too long. When it ended, the illusory values collapsed, and the acquisition game, or "bootstrapping" EPS numbers as it has been called, came to an end.

EPS Growth Through Acquisition

How can a company get its EPS to grow rapidly through the acquisition route? The answer is simple. It can do so by acquiring a company that has a lower P/E ratio than its own.

Let us illustrate the phenomenon. Table 24-1 lists the principal financial characteristics of two companies, *X* and *Y*.

Company *X* enjoyed good growth in the past because it has been reinvesting part of its annual earnings in better-than-average investment opportunities open to it. These opportunities are no longer available, and the company begins to seek growth through external acquisition. It has a P/E ratio of 25, and its stock is selling at $50 per share. Company *Y* is a smaller no-growth company with a P/E ratio of 10. Its stock is selling at $10 per share.

---

3. See the growth valuation models discussed in Chapter 10.

Table 24-1 Principal Financial Data

	Company X	Company Y
Number of shares outstanding	1 million	1 million
Market value per share	$50	$10
Current earnings	$2 million	$1 million
Earnings per share (EPS)	$2	$1
P/E ratio	25x	10x

Company X offers to buy company Y with payment to be made with company X stock at the rate of one share of X for four shares of Y. The offer is equivalent to a market value of $12.50 per share of Y, a 25 percent premium over Y's prevailing market price. Company Y's stockholders accept, and the transaction is consummated.

Let us assume that no genuine economies of scale take place as a result of the merger. The new company would now have the following characteristics:

1. Its earnings would be $3,000,000 ($2 million from X and $1 million from Y).
2. The number of shares outstanding would be 1,250,000 (the original 1 million shares plus the 250,000 issued to purchase Y).
3. EPS would therefore be $2.40.

In brief, company X has just increased its EPS from $2 to $2.40, a jump of 20 percent. No true growth has occurred. Indeed, because company Y is a no-growth company, the combined company is likely to enjoy a lower true growth in the future than company X would have achieved on its own. Nonetheless, the jump in EPS creates the illusion of rapid growth. The high P/E ratio of 25 *seems* to be justified, and the price of its stock rises from $50 to $60 a share.

What does the management of company X do for an encore? It seeks out another target company to acquire. Assume it finds one (company Z) just like the Y it has just bought. It offers the shareholders of the new company Z one share of its stock (worth $60) for five shares of Z—and again, attracted by the 20 percent premium that they believe they are getting over the market price of their stock, Z's stockholders agree to the purchase. After the second merger, the now bigger X will have the following characteristics:

1. Its earnings will be $4 million.
2. Including the 200,000 new shares issued to purchase Z, it will have a total of 1,450,000 shares outstanding.

3. Its EPS will therefore be $2.76, an increase of 15 percent over the $2.40 reported earlier.
4. If the market continues to be fooled by the illusory growth X appears to be achieving, it will continue to price these earnings at the high multiple of 25 times and the price of X's stock will rise to $69 per share.

How long can such a process go on? The answer is, not very long. To obtain the initial 20 percent jump in EPS through acquisition, company X had to buy company Y. But note that the acquisition of company Z produced only a 15 percent jump. To keep up its 20 percent a year track record of "growth," X would have had to purchase *larger* earnings the second time. In others words, to maintain the pace of EPS growth that gives it a P/E ratio of 25 in the market place, it would have to acquire new companies at an accelerating rate. After it has added 10 or 20 companies to itself, the market will begin to recognize the fact that X is not a true growth company at all, but essentially a collection of no-growth companies that warrant a P/E ratio of 10 rather than 25. When this realization dawns, the price of X's stock will drop sharply, and the acquisition game will come to an end. Essentially, that is what happened to many of the conglomerates in the late 1960s.

The Acquisition Wave of the Late 1970s

A new wave of mergers began in the mid-1970s, and by 1979, merger activity in the United States seemed almost frenzied. Over the 5 year period 1971–1975, approximately 40 firms with assets of $100 million or more were merged into acquiring companies. In 1978 alone the number of large mergers rose to 80, and by 1979, the scope and size of total merger activity had matched, if not surpassed, the level of similar activity in the late 1960s.

The recent merger wave differs from earlier merger waves in several significant ways. Indeed, it is more properly described as a take-over wave in which cash-rich companies simply bought other companies as blithely as they would more normally buy a plant or equipment.

Stock Prices

One significant difference was that in previous merger waves the level of stock prices was high and rising. In the late 1970s, stock prices were abnormally low relative to the flow of sales, earnings, and dividends. Allowing for the sharp decline in the purchasing power of the dollar between 1972 and 1980, stock prices in real terms had fallen sharply.

The difference can be stated in very simple terms. During the late 1960s, companies with very high P/E ratios for their stocks looking at other companies with low P/E ratios found them to be a bargain if they could be purchased through an exchange of shares. In 1979 most stock prices were so low relative to everything else, companies that had the cash to buy other companies found them to be a bargain compared to investment in plant and equipment. The reason for this can be documented.

The stocks in the popular Dow Jones industrial average (DJIA) sold at an *average* P/E ratio of 17 times annual earnings during the 9 year period 1962–1971. In the first half of 1979 these stocks sold at a P/E ratio of less than eight times annual earnings. The level of stock prices (again measured by the DJIA) was actually lower in June 1979 than it had been 15 years earlier at the end of 1964. Over those same 15 years, the replacement cost of the real fixed assets underlying industrial companies had just about *tripled*.

The huge disparity we have just described between the price of stocks in the late 1970s and the price of real assets in that period, is one clear reason for the most recent wave of acquisitions. It was a lot cheaper to buy a company, its facilities, and its earning power by buying up its shares than it was to build the equivalent facilities and earning power from scratch.

The low value placed on stocks relative to real assets was a major financial factor driving the large acquisition wave in 1979, but it was not the only factor. Another financial factor that influenced merger decisions was that although nominal interest rates seemed high (e.g., prime corporate bond yields were close to 10 percent) *real after-tax* interest rates were very low; indeed, they were negative. Because interest is a tax-deductible expense, a 10 percent nominal interest rate amounts to only 5 percent for most companies. With an inflation rate in excess of 10 percent a year, this means that a corporation can earn a real rate of only –5 percent by investing its spare cash or alternatively, if it is not cash-rich, the real cost of borrowing is also about –5 percent. It is therefore not surprising that companies started to use their spare cash or their borrowing power to buy other companies.

Size and Premiums in Merger Deals

A second major difference between the most recent merger wave and those that preceded it was the sheer size of the companies that were purchased, as well as the size of the payments made. Between 1976 when General Electric bought Utah International, a natural resource company with assets worth $2 billion and 1979 when National Steel made its bid to buy United Financial Corp. (a California savings and loan company) with assets valued at $2½ billion, an unprecedented number of billion-dollar companies were purchased.

The premiums paid over the market price of stock also reached record proportions in the late 1970s. This was a result of the intense competition for suitable acquisitions. Whereas in the 1960s a premium of 20–40 percent over market value was typical, in the late 1970s premiums in excess of 100 percent over market became fairly common.

Tactical Innovations

A third element of difference that marked the acquisition or take-over movement of the late 1970s was the armory of anti-take-over strategies developed by managements that had no desire to be swallowed by another company. Although many mergers were friendly ones, for most large publicly held companies whose shares were selling at only 3 or 5 times their annual earnings, the threat that some smart but unwelcome outsider might seek control through purchase was ever present.

Developing a protective strategy against a potential take-over by an outsider became a highly specialized profession in the late 1970s. The armory of protective devices included the following:

1. Retain a legal firm to advise the company in the event the expected raid actually occurs.
2. Retain an investment banking firm to advise the company on how much above current market value its stock is really worth.
3. Work on preparatory plans to make a counteroffer to shareholders for the company to repurchase their shares at a higher price than the other party offers.
4. Acquire assets in a smaller company, either in Canada or in a regulated industry. The Canadian government requires any purchaser of a company with Canadian assets to clear with it before a merger deal can be consummated. Likewise, the existence of a regulated division within a company can extend and complicate the hearings that any large merger will require.
5. If it is suspected that a particular company is going to come acquiring, buy a subsidiary that will give the acquirer a lot of antitrust problems.
6. Cram up on state statutes, wherever the company operates, that will allow delay and confusion because many states have the power to enjoin action for 60 or 90 days.
7. Develop a capability to fight a "proxy" battle, that is, to reach and persuade all the stockholders that the merger offer is an inadequate one.

All of the foregoing tactics are purely preparatory ones, and they are known collectively and colorfully as "shark repellants."

The potential acquirer also makes careful preparation for the resistance it suspects it might receive. Careful homework can avert resistance in the first place. The GE–Utah International merger encountered little resistance because the entire offer was very carefully planned. One tactic so commonly used that it is referred to as the "bear hug" is to make it clear to *both* stockholders and senior managers of the firm targeted for acquisition that *their* interests are going to be taken care of even more handsomely than in the past.

On the other hand, the potential acquirer might feel that the coziest of bear hugs will not work. In such a situation the proper tactics would be to take over a company by surprise by springing a public tender offer to buy shares at a stated price. Since federal law (which insists on a minimum period for thought, e.g., 10 days) does not allow complete surprise, the aggressor's tactic is to announce its public tender offer (to buy any or all shares offered to it in the next 10 days at *x* dollars a share) on a Saturday. This minimizes the working time in which the target company can put its strategies to work. Such an offer is now known as a "Saturday Night Special."

One tactic the target company can use when an offer from an unwanted source arrives is to find another, friendlier company that will match or better the offer. According to the vocabulary of the merger wave of the late 1970s, it finds a "white knight" to rescue it from the clutches of the unwanted buyer. This tactic has worked as frequently as it has failed.

Antimerger Legislation

Merger waves tend to induce antimerger legislation. The Sherman Antitrust Act of 1890 was a reaction against the horizontal merger movement. Its purpose was to prevent large firms (trusts) from developing monopoly power. The Clayton Act of 1914 and the establishment of the Federal Trade Commission (FTC) in that same year were also designed to suppress monopolistic behavior on the part of private corporations. The Celler Antimerger Act of 1950 was another piece of legislation designed to prevent acquisitions of assets or companies in which the effect of such acquisition might be "substantially to lessen competition."

The latest wave of acquisitions and mergers has also led in some circles to the cry for increased control by the federal government. This time there are two issues.

1. One issue is *bigness*. Should corporate cash be allowed to buy companies even if competition in the narrow sense is not threatened?

2. A second issue is whether companies in industries like petroleum and steel should be allowed freedom to invest their funds outside their own industry.

On the one hand, the Justice Department and some senior members of the United States Senate have introduced bills that will curb both freedoms. On the other, the opposition to these bills argues that the bills are discriminatory, arbitrary, and ill-advised. The debate itself will not be resolved until the early 1980s. By then the newest acquisition wave might be even stronger or it might be dead. The deciding factor for these two alternatives will be the behavior of inflation and stock prices over the next few years.

Summary

A decision to buy the shares of another company or its assets is essentially a capital budgeting decision, and it should be treated as such for analytical purposes. There are sound reasons for some mergers and some unsound ones for others. The sound reasons rest on the augmentation of net present value. The combined company should have a higher value than the sum of the parts that are combined—a quality referred to as *synergy*. Among the unsound reasons is the notion that merging is one way of increasing the surviving company's EPS.

Mergers in the United States have occurred in waves. The first wave, around the turn of the century, was essentially a wave of *horizontal* mergers—companies joining with other similar companies in similar industries. The wave of the 1920s was essentially a wave of *vertical* integration. A third wave in the late 1960s was essentially a *conglomerate* wave—the systematic acquisition by some firms of firms in totally unrelated industries. The fourth wave, which is still going strong, is essentially a *take-over* wave.

Questions

1. Define a congeneric merger. Give examples of some congeneric mergers.
2. What is a conglomerate merger? Give examples of some conglomerate companies.
3. If you are a stockholder in a company the stock of which is being sold to an acquiring company, would you prefer that the payment be in cash or in the buying company's common stock? Why?

4. What is the major difference between the *purchase* method of accounting for a merger and the *pooling of interests* method?
5. Explain why a rapid increase in a company's per share earnings (EPS) does not necessarily mean that it is a growth company.

Problems

1. Tar Heel Industries and the Palo Alto Manufacturing Corporation have been discussing the possibility of merging. The following information is available:

	Tar Heel	Palo Alto
Earnings available to common (in millions)	$100	$35
Number of common shares outstanding (in millions)	10	5

(a) Calculate the earnings per share (EPS) for each company prior to merger.
(b) If the companies were to merge with an exchange ratio of one to one (one share of Tar Heel stock for one share of Palo Alto stock), what would be the EPS of the merged company, assuming no synergistic effect upon earnings?
(c) What would be the accretion or dilution in EPS for shareholders of each company if the exchange were as described in part b?
(d) Redo parts b and c for an exchange ratio equal to two to one, where two shares of Palo Alto stock are exchanged for one share of Tar Heel stock.

2. Company *A* has proposed an acquisition of company *B* through an exchange of stock, with the exchange ratio based on the market price of the stock of the two firms just prior to merger. The following information on the two companies prior to merger is available:

	A	B
Market price per share	$ 32	$64
Earnings available to common (in millions)	$120	$80
Number of common shares outstanding (in millions)	50	10

(a) Calculate the (EPS) for each firm prior to merger.
(b) Calculate the price/earnings (P/E) ratio for each firm prior to merger.

(c) What is the market value exchange ratio for the proposed exchange (the number of shares of A that B's shareholders would demand)?

(d) Assuming no synergistic effects on earnings, what would be the EPS for the new corporation if the firms were to merge at the exchange ratio calculated in part (c)? How does this compare with your answer to part (a)?

3. National Paper Corporation has made an offer to the shareholders of the Delaware Cup Company of one share of its stock for two shares of the Delaware Cup Company stock. The following information is available just prior to the exchange.

	National	Delaware
Market price per share	$32	$10
Earnings available to common (in millions)	$10	$ 2
Number of common shares outstanding (in millions)	5	2

(a) Calculate the EPS and P/E ratios for each company prior to merger.

(b) Calculate the market price exchange ratio of stock of Delaware Cup for that of National Paper.

(c) If the P/E ratio of the surviving corporation were to remain the same as that of National Paper prior to the exchange, what would be the market price of a share of stock of the merged corporation, assuming no synergistic effects upon earnings?

(d) What would the P/E ratio of the resulting corporation have to be for the market value of the resulting corporation to just equal the sum of market values of the component companies just prior to the merger?

4. Company *C* has acquired company *D* through an exchange of stock based on the market prices of the firms' stocks prior to merger. For accounting purposes, the transaction will be handled as a purchase. The financial information for the companies prior to the merger is available in the tables on the following page.

(a) Calculate the following for each firm prior to merger:
Book value per share
EPS
P/E ratio

(b) What is the market price exchange ratio?

(c) What is the total market value of stock in company *C* exchanged for company *D* stock?

Balance Sheet	C	D
Current assets	$ 500,000	$ 15,000
Fixed assets	2,500,000	285,000
Other assets	200,000	50,000
Total assets	$3,200,000	$350,000
Current liabilities	$ 500,000	$ 75,000
Long-term debt	700,000	25,000
Common stock	800,000	35,000
Capital surplus	400,000	15,000
Retained earnings	800,000	200,000
Total liabilities and equity	$3,200,000	$350,000

Additional information:

Par value of stock	$8	$1
Earnings available to common	$300,000	$100,000
Market price per share	$24	$15

References

W. W. Alberts and J. Segall (eds.), *The Corporate Merger* (Chicago: University of Chicago Press, 1966).

Celler Committee Staff Report, *Investigation of Conglomerate Corporations*, U.S. Government Printing Office, June 1, 1971.

Michael Gort, "An Economic Disturbance Theory of Mergers," *Quarterly Journal of Economics*, 624–642 (Nov. 1969).

K. D. Larson and N. J. Gonedes, "Business Combinations: An Exchange Ratio Determination Model," *Accounting Review* **44**, 720–728 (Oct. 1969).

H. Levy and M. Sarnat, "Diversification, Portfolio Analysis and the Uneasy Case for Conglomerate Mergers," *Journal of Finance* **25**, 795–802 (Sept. 1970).

W. G. Lewellen, "A Pure Financial Rationale for the Conglomerate Merger," *Journal of Finance* **26**, 521–537 (May 1971).

G. Mandelker, "Risk and Return: The Case of Merging Firms," *Journal of Financial Economics*, 303–335 (1974).

R. W. Melicher and D. F. Rush, "Evidence on the Acquisition-Related Performance of Conglomerate Firms," *Journal of Finance*, 141–149 (Mar. 1974).

D. Norr, "Management and the Investor," *Financial Analysts Journal*, 45–48 (Mar.–Apr. 1979).

U. E. Reinhardt, *Mergers and Consolidations: A Corporate Financial Approach* (Morristown, N.J.: General Learning Press, 1972).

Appendix:
Probability Concepts

Probabilities
Expected Value
Measures of Dispersion
Conditional Probabilities
Correlation and Covariance

Nearly all business decisions require us to look into the future and therefore involve uncertainty in one way or another. Dealing with uncertainty is a central problem for financial management. This is especially so for capital expenditure decisions, where our horizon of analysis has to stretch years and sometimes decades into the uncertain future.

Thus far, apart from a few verbal qualifications about risk, we have abstracted from the uncertainty problem. We did so in order to deal with the other problems that arise from the long time horizon of capital expenditure decisions—such as the techniques of time adjustment, the analysis and selection of decision criteria, and the identification of the flows relevant to the decision process. But sooner or later risk and uncertainty must be integrated into the framework of thinking and measurement that we have been developing.

For most of the business and financial variables that concern us, nobody has yet come up with a direct and objective way of measuring risks and uncertainties. Evaluation of individual future events will therefore continue to require a large measure of judgment and even of intuition. But this does not mean that no systematic approaches to the problem of risk are available. For centuries, a large area of human thinking—namely statistics and especially the field of probability statistics—has devoted itself to thinking systematically about risk. Many of the insights developed in these areas can be and have been applied to the problem of analyzing financial risks. This appendix deals with the statistical concepts that are clearly relevant and useful not only for capital expenditure decisions but other financial decisions as well. After a brief review of general probability concepts, we will discuss the following: expected value, measures of dispersion, conditional probabilities, and correlation and covariance.

Probabilities

Chapters 11 and 12 used simple examples to illustrate the calculation of a project's internal rate of return or net present value. Thus, project *A* in Chapter 11 (Figure 11-1) was assumed to require an outlay of $100 in year 0 and to generate cash flows of $50, $60, and $40 in years 1, 2, and 3, respectively. What exactly does such a single estimate for an inflow of $50 in year 1 mean? That $50 is the *only possible outcome?* Obviously not. What the people who make such an estimate have in mind is a *range* of possible outcomes which we summarized as the single number 50.

In practice, we would capture the fullest insight of those who provide the estimate by looking more deeply both at the range of values they had in mind and the *probabilities* they attach to each segment of the range. Such an approach might yield the information listed in Table 1. Let us review what we have in this table and at the same time review some of the terminology used in the field of probability.

Table 1 Probability Distribution of Cash Flow

Cash Inflows in Year 1	Probability (Percent)
$ 5–15	1
$15–25	5
$25–35	10
$35–45	20
$45–55	28
$55–65	20
$65–75	10
$75–85	5
$85–95	1
	100

We have a *range* of possible outcomes for cash flow in year 1 arranged in the form of a *frequency distribution* known as a *probability distribution.* The uncertain outcome, in this case, cash flow in year 1, often is referred to as a *random variable.* If we calculate the rate of return associated with each possible future cash flow, the rate of return would also be a random variable. The *probability* that a particular event will occur is a measure of its likelihood of occurrence. We can speak of the probability of a particular outcome or the probability that a random variable will take on a particular value. Probabilities normally are stated as decimal fractions normalized to 1.0, but they also can be expressed in percentage terms.

To characterize a set of outcomes in terms of probabilities, the outcomes must be *mutually exclusive* (i.e., it must be true that only one of the outcomes described can occur) and *collectively exhaustive* (i.e., the outcomes described must include all possible outcomes). When these two conditions are met, the probabilities will sum to 100 percent, as shown in Table 1, although statisticians generally prefer to express probabilities in decimal notation, that is, 5 percent would be written as .05, in which case the probabilities would add up to 1.0.

Objective probabilities are those that can be determined from prior experience and on which there is general agreement. Examples are probabilities associated with the flip of a coin, the roll of a die, the spin of a roulette wheel, or a hand of poker. *Subjective* probabilities are determined by means of informed judgment based on whatever information is available. In financial management, and business generally, decisions usually have no exact historical analog, and probabilities cannot be calculated from frequency distributions of past outcomes. Therefore, the probabilities we use are nearly always subjective probabilities, because each decision nearly always involves some unique elements. The probabilities associated with our estimates of cash flow are subjective probabilities.

Probability distributions such as the one shown indicate the complete set of probabilities over all possible outcomes of a particular action. Probability distributions are of two general types, discrete and continuous. In *discrete* distributions, the outcomes can be separated and counted individually. Examples are the flip of a coin (two outcomes), roll of a die (six outcomes), and turn of a roulette wheel (38 outcomes). *Continuous* distributions describe events with an infinite number of possible outcomes that cannot be separately counted. Whereas discrete random variables change value in jumps, continuous variables change smoothly. In the case of discrete distributions, we can speak of the probability that a particular outcome will occur. With continuous distributions, to be strictly correct we must speak of the probability that the outcome will lie between two values. Graphically, discrete and continuous probability distributions are represented as shown in Figure 1.

Figure 1   Discrete and Continuous Distributions

usually have no exact historical analog

An example of a discrete distribution that finds wide application in decision-making is the *binomial* distribution. In contrast, the *normal* distribution is continuous and is useful to describe a wide variety of phenomena. The normal distribution occurs very often naturally where a random variable actually represents the sum of a number of other random variables. In finance and economics, many variables such as cash flow, sales, profits, or return on investment are continuous for all practical purposes.

Thus, in our example in Table 1, cash flow is very nearly continuous, that is, cash flow in year 1 could be $5.01, or $5.02, and so on all the way to $95. For practical purposes, the potential outcomes have been grouped in broad *class intervals.*

Expected Value

How can we summarize the information provided in Table 1? In two ways:

1. We can find the *most likely* or *most probable* outcome. In this case, it would be $50, the midpoint of the most probable class interval, which is $45–55.
2. We can calculate the arithmetic *mean* or average of all the potential outcomes with each outcome *weighted* by the probability that it will occur. This number is also known as the *expected value* of the variable. The calculation is shown in Table 2. This time the probabilities are expressed in decimal form.

Table 2   Calculating Expected Value

(1) Midpoint of Frequency Interval	(2) Probability	Column 1 × Column 2
$10	.01	$ 0.10
20	.05	1.00
30	.10	3.00
40	.20	8.00
50	.28	14.00
60	.20	12.00
70	.10	7.00
80	.05	4.00
90	.01	0.90
Total	1.00	$50.00

In our example, the *mean* or *expected value* is also $50, and the same as the *most likely value.* The reason the expected value and the most likely value are equal is that the distribution is *symmetrical.* Where the distributions are nonsymmetrical, or *skewed,* as shown in Figure 2, the expected value will not be equal to the most likely value. In such cases, it is the expected value which more correctly summarizes the value of the variable and hence the one which should be used.

In connection with investment opportunities, positive skew is generally considered desirable, because it indicates that outcomes well above the mean are more likely than outcomes well below the mean. Distributions in finance and economics often are skewed, although taking skew

Figure 2   Skewed Distributions

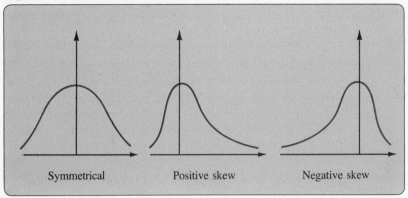

| Symmetrical | Positive skew | Negative skew |

into account mathematically usually is very difficult because of both data limitations and computational problems.

Measures of Dispersion

The expected value gives us one very important piece of information, the weighted average of all possible outcomes. It tells us nothing, however, about the *dispersion* of outcomes around the expected value. Consider the two investment opportunities illustrated in Figure 3. Both *A* and *B* have the same expected value, 1,000, but clearly they are not equivalent. Opportunity *A* has far more dispersion. In connection with investment opportunities, and many other business decisions as well, the dispersion of outcomes provides a measure of the degree of uncertainty, or risk, involved.

There are various ways to measure dispersion statistically. One of the most useful is known as the *standard deviation.* With reference to future events, the standard deviation can be used as a measure of the degree

Figure 3   Differences in Dispersion

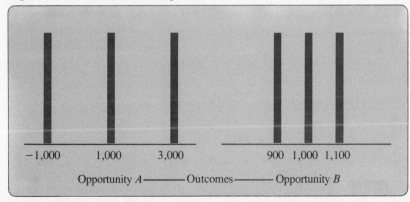

| −1,000 | 1,000 | 3,000 | | 900 | 1,000 | 1,100 |

Opportunity *A* ————Outcomes———— Opportunity *B*

Table 3 Calculating Standard Deviation

(1) Midpoint of Frequency Interval	(2) Deviation (d)	(3) Column 2 Squared (d^2)	(4) Probability (p)	(5) Column 3 × Column 4 (pd^2)
$10	−40	1,600	.01	16
20	−30	900	.05	45
30	−20	400	.10	40
40	−10	100	.20	20
50	0	0	.28	0
60	+10	100	.20	20
70	+20	400	.10	40
80	+30	900	.05	45
90	+40	1,600	.01	16

$$\text{Total } \Sigma pd^2 = \sigma^2 = 242$$
$$\text{Standard deviation } \sigma = \sqrt{242}$$
$$= 15.56$$

of dispersion, or uncertainty, about an expected outcome. Used in this way, the standard deviation is defined as the square root of the mean of the squared deviations, where deviation is the difference between an outcome and the expected value of all outcomes. To calculate the standard deviation, we calculate the expected value of the squared deviations, weighting the square of each deviation by its probability of occurrence. We then take the square root of the result. Table 3 illustrates the calculation of the standard deviation for the probability distribution of cash flow shown in Tables 1 and 2.

We now know that the cash flow in year 1 has an expected value of $50 with a standard deviation of $15.56. In the case of normal distributions, such as the one in our example (as well as many others in the world of financial management), the standard deviation is especially useful in telling us the probability that a variable will lie above or below some particular value. We find this out by using a table of areas under the normal curve. For example, in the illustration we have been using, assume we are critically interested in whether cash flow might fall below $8, because that represents an annual fixed charge we must pay on funds borrowed to finance the initial outlay. Knowledge of the characteristics of the normal curve would tell us that the probability that cash flow will be below $8 is less than 1 percent, that is, the chances are less than 1 in 100 that the adverse development will occur.

The really important question about the standard deviation is whether it provides a reliable proxy or surrogate measure for the degree of *risk* involved. If so, it provides a way in which risk can be quantified and thus incorporated systematically into the analytical framework of finance.

Much empirical work has been done lately on the question of whether *variability* (measured, for example, by the standard deviation) is a good surrogate measure for risk. While the results are not precise, they do indicate that for rates of return in the financial markets, risk and variability are related. Thus, higher levels of risk (as measured by variability) are consistently associated with higher returns in the marketplace. As we will see later, this finding enables us systematically to approach the difficult task of determining the required rate of return for risky investment outlays, which up to now we have simply assumed as given.

Conditional Probabilities

The theory of *conditional* probabilities is not of central importance for most financial decisions, but it does have some useful applications and so warrants our brief attention. For example, the illustration of decision trees we used in Chapter 12 is one potential, and sometimes important, area of application.

Events are said to be *statistically independent* if the occurrence of one event has no effect on the occurrence of another event. Consider two successive flips of a coin. The outcome of the first flip has no effect on the outcome of the second. Similarly, if a single die is rolled twice in succession, the outcome of the first roll has no effect on the second. The outcome of the second roll is said to be independent of the first.

In contrast, the world offers some clear examples of *dependent* events. Consider two urns, *A* and *B*. Urn *A* contains 10 red balls and 20 blue balls. Urn *B* contains 10 green balls and 20 yellow balls. We flip a coin. If heads comes up, we draw from urn *A;* if tails, from urn *B*. Is the probability of drawing a red ball dependent on the outcome of the flip of the coin? Clearly it is.

Consider a plan to introduce a new product that involves first a test market, and then a decision to produce or not based on the results of the test market. The probability of success, that is, achieving a given level of sales, depends on the outcome of the test.

In the example above involving the urns, the probability of drawing a red ball from urn *A* is $\frac{1}{3} = .33$. The probability of an *opportunity* to draw from urn *A* is $\frac{1}{2} = .50$. The *conditional* probability of a red ball, *given* a head, is .33. The conditional probability of a red ball, given a tail, is 0. The *marginal* probability of a red ball is $.50 \times .33 = .165$.

We can express the conditional probability of event *A*, given the occurrence of event *B*, as

$$P(A \mid B) = \frac{P(AB)}{P(B)}$$

where $P(AB)$ is the probability that A and B both will occur and $P(B)$ is the probability of B.

With this concept in mind, let us return to the decision tree illustration we used in Chapter 12. There we were primarily interested in the problem of identifying the correct cash flows. Here we are interested in arriving at a decision using probability concepts.

Let us assume we can subjectively estimate the probability that the test market phase of the project has a .3 (30 percent) chance of failure, in which case we will terminate the project. If the other 70 percent chance of test market success actually transpires, we will continue with the production phase. How should the overall idea of going ahead with the initial test market phase be analyzed?

In Table 4, the CF column under each year summarizes the relevant cash flows. Thus, under year 1 the test market outlay is made, and the net outlay is $250,000. If the project succeeds, the production phase outlay of $800,000 is incurred in year 2. If it fails, we recoup a cash inflow of $34,000 in year 1.

Table 4 A Test Market Decision (Thousands of Dollars)

Activity	Probability	Year 1 CF^a	Year 1 Wtd^b	Year 2 CF	Year 2 Wtd	Year 3 CF	Year 3 Wtd	Year 4 CF	Year 4 Wtd	Year 5 CF	Year 5 Wtd
Test market	1.0	(250)	(250)	0	0	0	0	0	0	0	0
Production	0.7	0	0	(800)	(560)	300	210	400	280	700	490
Terminate	0.3	34	10	0	0	0	0	0	0	0	0
Expected cash flow			(240)		(560)		210		280		490

^{a}CF = cash flow. ^{b}Wtd = weighted.

The column labeled Wtd (weighted) under each year weights the outlays or inflows by the probability of their occurrence. Thus, before the project is launched we have the expected values of cash flows as shown in the last line of Table 4:

Year 1	−$240,000
Year 2	−$560,000
Year 3	+$210,000
Year 4	+$280,000
Year 5	+$490,000

We can then apply the required rate of return for a project of this riskiness in order to decide if it is an acceptable decision. Assume the required rate of return is 15 percent per year. The NPV of the project can be calculated following the approach of Chapter 11. We find NPV to be — $90,350 so the project should be rejected.

Correlation and Covariance

The term *correlation* implies that a relationship exists between two variables. Sales of television sets may be correlated with personal disposable income. Sales of a particular product are likely to be correlated with the level of advertising expenditures for the product.

The notion of correlation is especially important in economics and finance, because many economic and financial variables are related to one another. At the level of the economy as a whole, gross national product (GNP), personal consumption, business sales, personal income, and corporate profits, to name a few, all tend to move together. At the level of the individual firm, sales, expenses, and profits are correlated both among themselves and very likely also with measures of aggregate economic activity such as GNP. The many complex interdependencies in our economy contribute to this moving together and give rise to business and monetary cycles. Projections of sales, cash flow, and costs require an understanding of the relationship between the individual firm's activity and the general economy.

Correlation is also an important concept for capital expenditure decisions. We have assumed thus far that each project is assayed on its own merit. This may not be true. An oil company such as Mobil may deliberately choose to invest funds in a retail firm such as Marcor rather than in more exploratory drilling in order to *diversify* its total cash flow. Diversification analysis rests on the statistical theory of correlation.

Coefficient of Correlation

Intuitively, correlation between two variables implies that they move together. The *coefficient of correlation* gives us a more precise statistical measure. The correlation coefficient ranges from $+1.0$ to -1.0. Perfect positive correlation, a coefficient of $+1.0$, indicates that the two variables move together in perfect *lock step*. Consider the following data:

	Variable	
	A	*B*
	4	7
	3	6
	5	8
	7	10
	6	9
Mean	5	8

Variables A and B have, by design, a correlation coefficient of $+1.0$. In each pair of observations, A and B deviate from their respective means by the same amount. Thus, when A is 7 (2 above its mean), B is 10 (2 above its mean). So A and B move by equal amounts about their respective means.

Now consider these data:

	Variable	
	C	D
	4	11
	7	8
	6	9
	8	7
	5	10
Mean	6	9

Variables C and D are perfectly *negatively* correlated (-1.0). In each pair of observations, C and D deviate from their respective means by the same absolute amount, but in opposite directions. Thus, when C is above its mean by 2, D is below its mean by 2. So C and D move in perfect opposition about their respective means.

Two variables that are completely unrelated to one another would have a correlation coefficient of zero. To illustrate, suppose that we roll two dice a very large number of times; each time we record the outcome of each die separately. Since the outcome of each die is independent of the other, we would expect the numbers representing the pairs of outcomes to be uncorrelated.

Correlation, Dependence, and Causation

Events that are independent are always uncorrelated, that is, they have a correlation coefficient of zero. However, the reverse is not necessarily true. It is possible to conceive of events that are dependent but related in such a way as to have a zero correlation coefficient. Thus, independence implies zero correlation, but zero correlation does not necessarily imply independence. In finance and economics, we do not often encounter variables that are uncorrelated yet dependent.

In interpreting correlation, we must be especially careful in drawing inferences about *causation*. Two variables may be highly correlated even when no causal relationship exists between them. Such statistical relationships often occur when two variables are both related to a third. Consider the hypothetical data given in Table 5.

Table 5 Correlation and Causation

Year	Egg Production (Millions)	Sales of Television Sets (Thousands)
1967	15,750	4,720
1968	15,895	4,910
1969	16,210	4,920
1970	16,350	4,850
1971	16,590	5,040
1972	16,880	5,110
1973	17,050	5,095
1974	17,125	5,020

The coefficient of correlation of egg production and sales of television sets in the above sample is 0.86. Does a causal relationship exist? Probably not. Both, however, probably are related to population growth. Many economic variables that have no causal relationship may grow over time and therefore may exhibit positive correlation. In contrast, suppose we examine data on sales of stereo equipment and personal disposable income and find them to be correlated. Here we probably would conclude that a causal relationship does exist. The moral: Correlation does not imply causation!

Calculating the Correlation Coefficient

The coefficient of correlation between variables X and Y is defined as

$$r_{XY} = \frac{\text{COV}(X, Y)}{\sigma_X \sigma_Y} \tag{1}$$

where $\text{COV}(X, Y)$ is the *covariance* of X and Y, σ_X is the standard deviation of X, and σ_Y is the standard deviation of Y. The covariance is defined as

$$\text{COV}(X, Y) = E[(X - \overline{X})(Y - \overline{Y})] \tag{2}$$

where E is the expected value operator, $\overline{X}$ is the mean of X, and $\overline{Y}$ is the mean of Y. We can rewrite (2) as

$$\text{COV}(X, Y) = \frac{1}{n} \sum_{i=1}^{n} [(X_i - \overline{X})(Y_i - \overline{Y})] \tag{3}$$

In expression (3), the subscript i denotes individual observations of the variables X and Y, and n is the number of pairs of observations. Expression (3) simplifies to

$$\text{COV}(X, Y) = \frac{1}{n} \sum_{i=1}^{n} X_i Y_i - \overline{X}\,\overline{Y} \tag{4}$$

So we have

$$r_{XY} = \frac{\frac{1}{n} \sum_{i=1}^{n} X_i Y_i - \overline{X}\,\overline{Y}}{\sigma_X \sigma_Y} \tag{5}$$

Let us calculate the correlation coefficient for the following data:

X	Y
4	8
2	7
5	11
6	14
8	15

We calculate the means and find $\overline{X} = 5$, $\overline{Y} = 11$. Now we set up Table 6. From the data in the table, we see that

$$\frac{1}{n} \sum_{i=1}^{n} X_i Y_i = \frac{1}{5}(305) = 61.0$$

and

$$\sigma_X = \sqrt{\frac{1}{n} \Sigma(X_i - \overline{X})^2} = \sqrt{\frac{1}{5}(20)} = 2.0$$

$$\sigma_Y = \sqrt{\frac{1}{n} \Sigma(Y_i - \overline{Y})^2} = \sqrt{\frac{1}{5}(50)} = 3.16$$

If we apply expression (5), the coefficient of correlation is

$$r_{XY} = \frac{61.0 - (5)(11)}{(2.0)(3.16)} = 0.95$$

Table 6 Calculating the Correlation Coefficient

X	Y	XY	$X - \overline{X}$	$(X - \overline{X})^2$	$Y - \overline{Y}$	$(Y - \overline{Y})^2$
4	8	32	−1	1	−3	9
2	7	14	−3	9	−4	16
5	11	55	0	0	0	0
6	14	84	1	1	3	9
8	15	120	3	9	4	16
		305		20		50

Summary

Most business decisions must be made in the face of uncertainty. In the case of investment decisions specifically, future cash flows nearly always are subject to some degree of uncertainty. While they cannot reduce uncertainty, various techniques are available for dealing with it analytically. The most important of these techniques for application to financial management decisions are based on probability concepts and sensitivity analysis.

When an outcome is uncertain, it can take on more than one value, usually a range of values. The *probability* that a particular outcome will occur is a measure of its likelihood of occurrence. A *probability distribution* describes the complete set of probabilities over all possible outcomes of a particular action. The weighted average outcome is called the *expected value*. In the case of symmetrical distributions, the expected value is the same as the *most likely* outcome (that with the highest probability of occurrence). In many other cases, the two are approximately equal.

Expected value and most likely value provide measures of central tendency but say nothing about the *dispersion* or range of possible outcomes. A useful measure of disperion is the *standard deviation.* The standard deviation is widely used in finance as a surrogate measure of risk.

Sometimes the probability of one event is *conditional* on the outcome of another event. Conditional probabilities are useful for analyzing sequential decisions.

Two variables are said to be statistically *correlated* when changes in the value of one are related to changes in the value of the other. The *correlation coefficient* provides a measure of the degree of correlation between two variables. Correlation does not necessarily imply causation.

Questions

1. How can probability concepts be used to deal with uncertainty in financial management decisions?
2. Under what circumstances would the expected value of a probability distribution differ from the most likely outcome?
3. The standard deviation is a widely used measure of the degree of dispersion of outcomes in a probability distribution. Can you think of other measures of dispersion?
4. The application of the concept of *conditional probability* to a test market decision is described in the text. Can you think of another example of the application of conditional probability?
5. When two variables are statistically correlated either positively or negatively, what inferences can be drawn about causation, that is, whether a change in one variable causes a change in the other?

6. By combining investments into a portfolio, an investor can reduce risk. What role does correlation between returns of the investments in a portfolio play in reducing the risk of the portfolio?

Problems

1. Knott Enterprises is considering an investment opportunity that will generate cash inflows over a 3 year period. The magnitude of the cash flows is expected to depend on general economic conditions. Cash flow estimates are as follows:

State of Economy	Year		
	1	2	3
Recession	$ 800	$ 950	$1,200
Normal	1,000	1,200	1,500
Boom	1,200	1,450	1,800

The probability of a recession is estimated to be .25, a normal economy .50, and a boom .25. Calculate the expected value and standard deviation of cash flow in each year.

2. The sales of Tarheel Enterprises are sensitive to general economic conditions. The company's sales forecast for the upcoming year indicates sales of $1 million if economic conditions are normal. If the economy enters a recession, sales for the year are expected to fall to $625,000. If a boom occurs, sales are expected to rise to $1.4 million. The probability of a normal economy is .50, a recession .20, and a boom .30. Cost of goods sold amounts to 60 percent of sales. General and administrative expenses (excluding depreciation) will total $250,000 regardless of economic conditions. Depreciation will total $50,000. The company is subject to a tax rate of 50 percent. Calculate the expected value and standard deviation of each of the following: sales, profit after tax, and cash flow from operations after tax. (*Note:* In any situation in which profit before tax is zero or negative, assume that taxes are zero.)

3. You are considering making an investment in the common stock of Gamma Corporation. As is true of stocks in general, the price of Gamma stock is sensitive to general stock market movements. Market experts have estimated that there is a probability of .60 that the stock market will rise next year, and .40 that it will fall. If the market rises,

there is a .70 probability that the price of Gamma stock will rise. If the market falls, the probability that Gamma will rise is only .20. What is the probability that the price of Gamma stock will rise over the next year?

4. Consider the following two investment opportunities:

Investment A (Outlay, $1,000)		Investment B (Outlay, $2,000)	
Return	Probability	Return	Probability
$ 600	.30	$1,500	.30
1,050	.40	2,100	.40
1,500	.30	2,800	.30

Assuming that standard deviation of return is a useful measure of risk, which of the two investments is more risky? In reaching a conclusion, calculate standard deviation of return both in dollar terms and in percentage terms.

5. Niklas Industries is considering an opportunity to drill for oil. The project involves first a seismic test to evaluate the prospects of a successful well, and then a decision on whether to drill or not, based on the results of the test. The seismic test will cost $30,000. Drilling will cost an additional $200,000. Assume that both figures are net of tax effects. Prior experience indicates that the probability of a positive test is .70. If the test is negative, the project will be abandoned and no well will be drilled. If the test is positive, potential payoffs of drilling and probabilities are as follows:

Outcomes of Drilling, Given Positive
Seismic Test

Outcome	Probability	Payoff
Success	.60	$400,000
Break-even	.30	200,000
Dry hole	.10	0

Payoffs in the table are net after-tax cash flows from sale of oil. Assume that drilling and marketing require a total of 1 year's time, so that payoffs are received 1 year after the outlay for drilling.

(a) Calculate the expected value of the payoffs from drilling, given a positive seismic test.

(b) Calculate the expected return and standard deviation of return in percentage terms of a decision to drill, given a positive seismic test.

References

H. Bierman, C. T. Bonini, Jr., and W. H. Houseman, *Quantitative Analysis for Business Decisions,* 4th ed. (Homewood, Ill.: Richard D. Irwin, 1973).

I. N. Draper and W. E. Lawrence, *Probability: An Introductory Course* (Chicago: Markham, 1970).

M. Goldman, *Introduction to Probability and Statistics* (New York: Harcourt Brace Jovanovich, 1970).

R. I. Levin, and C. A. Kirkpatrick, *Quantitative Approaches to Management,* 3d ed. (New York: McGraw-Hill, 1975).

E. W. Martin, Jr., *Mathematics for Decision Making: A Programmed Basic Text* (Homewood, Ill.: Richard D. Irwin, 1969).

J. J. Martin, *Bayesian Decision Problems and Markov Chains* (New York: John Wiley, 1967).

R. Schlaifer, *Analysis of Decision Under Undercertainty* (New York: McGraw-Hill, 1969).

R. Schlaifer, *Introduction to Statistics for Business Decisions* (New York: McGraw-Hill, 1961).

R. Schlaifer, *Probability and Statistics for Business Decisions* (New York: McGraw-Hill, 1959).

H. M. Wagner, *Principles of Management Science, with Applications to Executive Decisions* (Englewood Cliffs, N.J.: Prentice-Hall, 1970).

Table I Present Value of $1 Due at the End of *n* Years

n	1%	2%	3%	4%	5%	6%	7%	8%	9%	10%
1	0.990	0.980	0.970	0.962	0.952	0.943	0.935	0.926	0.917	0.909
2	0.980	0.961	0.943	0.925	0.907	0.890	0.873	0.857	0.842	0.826
3	0.971	0.942	0.915	0.889	0.864	0.840	0.816	0.794	0.772	0.751
4	0.961	0.924	0.888	0.855	0.823	0.792	0.763	0.735	0.708	0.683
5	0.951	0.906	0.863	0.822	0.784	0.747	0.713	0.681	0.650	0.621
6	0.942	0.888	0.837	0.790	0.746	0.705	0.666	0.630	0.596	0.564
7	0.933	0.871	0.813	0.760	0.711	0.665	0.623	0.583	0.547	0.513
8	0.923	0.853	0.789	0.731	0.677	0.627	0.582	0.540	0.502	0.467
9	0.914	0.837	0.766	0.703	0.645	0.592	0.544	0.500	0.460	0.424
10	0.905	0.820	0.744	0.676	0.614	0.558	0.508	0.463	0.422	0.386
11	0.896	0.804	0.722	0.650	0.585	0.527	0.475	0.429	0.388	0.350
12	0.887	0.788	0.701	0.625	0.557	0.497	0.444	0.397	0.356	0.319
13	0.879	0.773	0.681	0.601	0.530	0.469	0.415	0.368	0.326	0.290
14	0.870	0.758	0.661	0.577	0.505	0.442	0.388	0.340	0.299	0.263
15	0.861	0.743	0.642	0.555	0.481	0.417	0.362	0.315	0.275	0.239
16	0.853	0.728	0.623	0.534	0.458	0.394	0.339	0.299	0.252	0.218
17	0.844	0.714	0.605	0.513	0.436	0.371	0.317	0.270	0.231	0.198
18	0.836	0.700	0.587	0.494	0.416	0.350	0.296	0.250	0.212	0.180
19	0.828	0.686	0.570	0.475	0.396	0.331	0.277	0.232	0.194	0.164
20	0.820	0.673	0.554	0.456	0.377	0.312	0.258	0.215	0.178	0.149
21	0.811	0.660	0.538	0.439	0.359	0.294	0.242	0.199	0.164	0.135
22	0.803	0.647	0.522	0.422	0.342	0.278	0.226	0.184	0.150	0.123
23	0.795	0.634	0.507	0.406	0.326	0.262	0.211	0.170	0.138	0.112
24	0.788	0.622	0.492	0.390	0.310	0.247	0.197	0.158	0.126	0.102
25	0.780	0.610	0.478	0.375	0.295	0.233	0.184	0.146	0.116	0.092
30	0.742	0.552	0.412	0.308	0.231	0.174	0.131	0.099	0.075	0.057
35	0.706	0.500	0.355	0.253	0.181	0.130	0.094	0.068	0.049	0.036
40	0.672	0.453	0.307	0.208	0.142	0.097	0.067	0.046	0.032	0.022
45	0.639	0.410	0.264	0.171	0.111	0.073	0.048	0.031	0.021	0.014
50	0.608	0.372	0.228	0.141	0.087	0.054	0.034	0.021	0.013	0.009

Table I *(continued)*

n	11%	12%	13%	14%	15%	16%	17%	18%	19%	20%
1	0.901	0.893	0.885	0.877	0.870	0.862	0.855	0.847	0.840	0.833
2	0.812	0.797	0.783	0.769	0.756	0.743	0.731	0.718	0.706	0.694
3	0.731	0.712	0.693	0.675	0.658	0.641	0.624	0.609	0.593	0.579
4	0.659	0.636	0.613	0.592	0.572	0.552	0.534	0.516	0.499	0.482
5	0.593	0.567	0.543	0.519	0.497	0.476	0.456	0.437	0.419	0.402
6	0.535	0.507	0.480	0.456	0.432	0.410	0.390	0.370	0.352	0.333
7	0.482	0.452	0.425	0.400	0.376	0.354	0.333	0.314	0.296	0.279
8	0.434	0.404	0.376	0.351	0.327	0.305	0.285	0.266	0.249	0.233
9	0.391	0.361	0.333	0.308	0.284	0.263	0.243	0.225	0.209	0.194
10	0.352	0.322	0.295	0.270	0.247	0.227	0.208	0.191	0.176	0.162
11	0.317	0.287	0.261	0.237	0.215	0.195	0.178	0.162	0.148	0.135
12	0.286	0.257	0.231	0.208	0.187	0.168	0.152	0.137	0.124	0.112
13	0.258	0.229	0.204	0.182	0.163	0.145	0.130	0.116	0.104	0.093
14	0.232	0.205	0.181	0.160	0.141	0.125	0.111	0.099	0.088	0.078
15	0.209	0.183	0.160	0.140	0.123	0.108	0.095	0.084	0.074	0.065
16	0.188	0.163	0.142	0.123	0.107	0.093	0.081	0.071	0.062	0.054
17	0.170	0.146	0.125	0.108	0.093	0.080	0.069	0.060	0.052	0.045
18	0.153	0.130	0.111	0.095	0.081	0.069	0.059	0.051	0.044	0.038
19	0.138	0.116	0.098	0.083	0.070	0.060	0.051	0.043	0.037	0.031
20	0.124	0.104	0.087	0.073	0.061	0.051	0.043	0.037	0.031	0.026
21	0.112	0.093	0.077	0.064	0.053	0.044	0.037	0.031	0.026	0.022
22	0.101	0.083	0.068	0.056	0.046	0.038	0.032	0.026	0.022	0.018
23	0.091	0.074	0.060	0.049	0.040	0.033	0.027	0.022	0.018	0.015
24	0.082	0.066	0.053	0.043	0.035	0.028	0.023	0.019	0.015	0.013
25	0.074	0.059	0.047	0.038	0.030	0.024	0.020	0.016	0.013	0.010
30	0.044	0.033	0.026	0.020	0.015	0.012	0.009	0.007	0.005	0.004
35	0.026	0.019	0.014	0.010	0.008	0.006	0.004	0.003	0.002	0.002
40	0.015	0.011	0.008	0.005	0.004	0.003	0.002	0.001	0.001	0.001
45	0.009	0.006	0.004	0.003	0.002	0.001	0.001	0.001		
50	0.005	0.003	0.002	0.001	0.001	0.001				

n	21%	22%	23%	24%	25%	26%	27%	28%	29%	30%
1	0.826	0.820	0.813	0.806	0.800	0.794	0.787	0.781	0.775	0.769
2	0.683	0.672	0.661	0.650	0.640	0.630	0.620	0.610	0.601	0.592
3	0.564	0.551	0.537	0.524	0.512	0.500	0.488	0.477	0.466	0.455
4	0.467	0.451	0.437	0.423	0.410	0.397	0.384	0.373	0.361	0.350
5	0.386	0.370	0.355	0.341	0.328	0.315	0.303	0.291	0.280	0.269
6	0.319	0.303	0.289	0.275	0.262	0.250	0.238	0.227	0.217	0.207
7	0.263	0.249	0.235	0.222	0.210	0.198	0.188	0.178	0.168	0.159
8	0.218	0.204	0.191	0.179	0.168	0.157	0.148	0.139	0.130	0.123
9	0.180	0.167	0.155	0.144	0.134	0.125	0.116	0.108	0.101	0.094
10	0.149	0.137	0.126	0.116	0.107	0.099	0.092	0.085	0.078	0.073
11	0.123	0.112	0.103	0.094	0.086	0.079	0.072	0.066	0.061	0.056
12	0.102	0.092	0.083	0.076	0.069	0.062	0.057	0.052	0.047	0.043
13	0.084	0.075	0.068	0.061	0.055	0.050	0.045	0.040	0.037	0.033
14	0.069	0.062	0.055	0.049	0.044	0.039	0.035	0.032	0.028	0.025
15	0.057	0.051	0.045	0.040	0.035	0.031	0.028	0.025	0.022	0.020
16	0.047	0.042	0.036	0.032	0.028	0.025	0.022	0.019	0.017	0.015
17	0.039	0.034	0.030	0.026	0.023	0.020	0.017	0.015	0.013	0.012
18	0.032	0.028	0.024	0.021	0.018	0.016	0.014	0.012	0.010	0.009
19	0.027	0.023	0.020	0.017	0.014	0.012	0.011	0.009	0.008	0.007
20	0.022	0.019	0.016	0.014	0.012	0.010	0.008	0.007	0.006	0.005
21	0.018	0.015	0.013	0.011	0.009	0.008	0.007	0.006	0.005	0.004
22	0.015	0.013	0.011	0.009	0.007	0.006	0.005	0.004	0.004	0.003
23	0.012	0.010	0.009	0.007	0.006	0.005	0.004	0.003	0.003	0.002
24	0.010	0.008	0.007	0.006	0.005	0.004	0.003	0.003	0.002	0.002
25	0.009	0.007	0.006	0.005	0.004	0.003	0.003	0.002	0.002	0.001
30	0.003	0.003	0.002	0.002	0.001	0.001	0.001	0.001		
35	0.001	0.001	0.001	0.001						
40										
45										
50										

Table I   *(continued)*

n	31%	32%	33%	34%	35%	36%	37%	38%	39%	40%	50%
1	0.763	0.758	0.752	0.746	0.741	0.735	0.730	0.725	0.719	0.714	0.667
2	0.583	0.574	0.565	0.557	0.549	0.541	0.533	0.525	0.518	0.510	0.444
3	0.445	0.435	0.425	0.416	0.406	0.398	0.389	0.381	0.372	0.364	0.296
4	0.340	0.329	0.320	0.310	0.301	0.292	0.284	0.276	0.268	0.260	0.198
5	0.259	0.250	0.240	0.231	0.223	0.215	0.207	0.200	0.193	0.186	0.132
6	0.198	0.189	0.181	0.173	0.165	0.158	0.151	0.145	0.139	0.133	0.088
7	0.151	0.143	0.136	0.129	0.122	0.116	0.110	0.105	0.100	0.095	0.059
8	0.115	0.108	0.102	0.096	0.091	0.085	0.081	0.076	0.072	0.068	0.039
9	0.088	0.082	0.077	0.072	0.067	0.063	0.059	0.055	0.052	0.048	0.026
10	0.067	0.062	0.058	0.054	0.050	0.046	0.043	0.040	0.037	0.035	0.017
11	0.051	0.047	0.043	0.040	0.037	0.034	0.031	0.029	0.027	0.025	0.012
12	0.039	0.036	0.033	0.030	0.027	0.025	0.023	0.021	0.019	0.018	0.008
13	0.030	0.027	0.025	0.022	0.020	0.018	0.017	0.015	0.014	0.013	0.005
14	0.023	0.021	0.018	0.017	0.015	0.014	0.012	0.011	0.010	0.009	0.003
15	0.017	0.016	0.014	0.012	0.011	0.010	0.009	0.008	0.007	0.006	0.002
16	0.013	0.012	0.010	0.009	0.008	0.007	0.006	0.006	0.005	0.005	0.002
17	0.010	0.009	0.008	0.007	0.006	0.005	0.005	0.004	0.004	0.003	0.001
18	0.008	0.007	0.006	0.005	0.005	0.004	0.003	0.003	0.003	0.002	0.001
19	0.006	0.005	0.004	0.004	0.003	0.003	0.003	0.002	0.002	0.002	
20	0.005	0.004	0.003	0.003	0.002	0.002	0.002	0.002	0.002	0.001	
21	0.003	0.003	0.003	0.002	0.002	0.002	0.001	0.001	0.001	0.001	
22	0.003	0.002	0.002	0.002	0.001	0.001	0.001	0.001	0.001	0.001	
23	0.002	0.002	0.001	0.001	0.001	0.001	0.001	0.001	0.001		
24	0.002	0.001	0.001	0.001	0.001	0.001	0.001				
25	0.001	0.001	0.001	0.001	0.001						
30											
35											
40											
45											
50											

STREAM OF FLOWS — when flow is the same a year (summary of common flows)

Table II Present Value of $1 per Year for n Years

n	1%	2%	3%	4%	5%	6%	7%	8%	9%	10%
1	0.990	0.980	0.971	0.962	0.952	0.943	0.935	0.926	0.917	0.909
2	1.970	1.942	1.914	1.886	1.859	1.833	1.808	1.783	1.759	1.736
3	2.941	2.884	2.829	2.775	2.723	2.673	2.624	2.577	2.531	2.487
4	3.902	3.808	3.717	3.630	3.546	3.465	3.387	3.312	3.240	3.170
5	4.854	4.713	4.580	4.452	4.330	4.212	4.100	3.993	3.890	3.791
6	5.796	5.601	5.417	5.242	5.076	4.917	4.767	4.623	4.486	4.355
7	6.728	6.472	6.230	6.002	5.786	5.582	5.389	5.206	5.033	4.868
8	7.652	7.325	7.020	6.733	6.463	6.210	5.971	5.747	5.535	5.335
9	8.566	8.162	7.786	7.435	7.108	6.802	6.515	6.247	5.985	5.759
10	9.471	8.983	8.530	8.111	7.722	7.360	7.024	6.710	6.418	6.145
11	10.368	9.787	9.253	8.760	8.306	7.887	7.499	7.139	6.805	6.495
12	11.255	10.575	9.954	9.385	8.863	8.384	7.943	7.536	7.161	6.814
13	12.134	11.348	10.635	9.986	9.394	8.853	8.358	7.904	7.487	7.103
14	13.004	12.106	11.296	10.563	9.899	9.295	8.745	8.244	7.786	7.367
15	13.865	12.849	11.938	11.118	10.380	9.712	9.108	8.560	8.061	7.606
16	14.718	13.578	12.561	11.652	10.838	10.106	9.447	8.851	8.313	7.824
17	15.562	14.292	13.166	12.166	11.274	10.477	9.763	9.122	8.544	8.022
18	16.398	14.992	13.753	12.659	11.690	10.828	10.059	9.372	8.756	8.201
19	17.226	15.678	14.324	13.134	12.085	11.158	10.336	9.604	8.950	8.365
20	18.046	16.351	14.877	13.590	12.462	11.470	10.594	9.818	9.129	8.514
21	18.857	17.011	15.415	14.029	12.821	11.764	10.836	10.017	9.292	8.649
22	19.661	17.658	15.937	14.451	13.163	12.042	11.061	10.201	9.442	8.772
23	20.456	18.292	16.444	14.857	13.489	12.303	11.272	10.371	9.580	8.883
24	21.244	18.914	16.936	15.247	13.799	12.550	11.469	10.529	9.707	8.985
25	22.023	19.523	17.413	15.622	14.094	12.783	11.654	10.675	9.823	9.077
30	25.808	22.396	19.600	17.292	15.372	13.765	12.409	11.258	10.274	9.427
35	29.409	24.999	21.487	18.665	16.374	14.498	12.948	11.655	10.567	9.644
40	32.835	27.355	23.115	19.793	17.159	15.046	13.332	11.925	10.757	9.779
45	36.095	29.490	24.519	20.720	17.774	15.456	13.606	12.108	10.881	9.863
50	39.196	31.424	25.730	21.482	18.256	15.762	13.801	12.233	10.962	9.915

Table II *(continued)*

n	11%	12%	13%	14%	15%	16%	17%	18%	19%	20%
1	0.901	0.893	0.885	0.377	0.870	0.862	0.855	0.848	0.840	0.833
2	1.713	1.690	1.668	1.647	1.626	1.605	1.585	1.566	1.547	1.528
3	2.444	2.402	2.361	2.322	2.283	2.246	2.210	2.174	2.140	2.107
4	3.102	3.037	2.975	2.914	2.855	2.798	2.743	2.690	2.639	2.589
5	3.696	3.605	3.517	3.433	3.352	3.274	3.199	3.127	3.058	2.991
6	4.231	4.111	3.998	3.889	3.785	3.685	3.589	3.498	3.410	3.326
7	4.712	4.564	4.423	4.288	4.160	4.039	3.922	3.812	3.706	3.605
8	5.146	4.968	4.799	4.639	4.487	4.344	4.207	4.078	3.954	3.837
9	5.537	5.328	5.132	4.946	4.772	4.607	4.451	4.303	4.163	4.031
10	5.889	5.650	5.426	5.216	5.019	4.833	4.659	4.494	4.339	4.193
11	6.207	5.938	5.687	5.453	5.234	5.029	4.836	4.656	4.487	4.327
12	6.492	6.194	5.918	5.660	5.421	5.197	4.988	4.793	4.611	4.439
13	6.750	6.424	6.122	5.842	5.583	5.342	5.118	4.910	4.715	4.533
14	6.982	6.628	6.303	6.002	5.725	5.468	5.229	5.008	4.802	4.611
15	7.191	6.811	6.462	6.142	5.847	5.576	5.324	5.092	4.876	4.676
16	7.379	6.974	6.604	6.265	5.954	5.669	5.405	5.162	4.938	4.730
17	7.549	7.120	6.729	6.373	6.047	5.749	5.475	5.222	4.990	4.775
18	7.702	7.250	6.840	6.467	6.128	5.818	5.534	5.273	5.033	4.812
19	7.839	7.366	6.938	6.550	6.198	5.878	5.585	5.316	5.070	4.844
20	7.963	7.469	7.025	6.623	6.259	5.929	5.628	5.353	5.101	4.870
21	8.075	7.562	7.102	6.687	6.313	5.973	5.665	5.384	5.127	4.891
22	8.176	7.645	7.170	6.743	6.359	6.011	5.696	5.410	5.149	4.909
23	8.266	7.718	7.230	6.792	6.399	6.044	5.723	5.432	5.167	4.925
24	8.348	7.784	7.283	6.835	6.434	6.073	5.747	5.451	5.182	4.937
25	8.422	7.843	7.330	6.873	6.464	6.097	5.766	5.467	5.195	4.948
30	8.694	8.055	7.496	7.003	6.566	6.177	5.829	5.517	5.235	4.979
35	8.855	8.176	7.586	7.070	6.617	6.215	5.858	5.539	5.251	4.992
40	8.951	8.244	7.634	7.105	6.642	6.233	5.871	5.548	5.258	4.997
45	9.008	8.283	7.661	7.123	6.654	6.242	5.877	5.552	5.261	4.999
50	9.042	8.304	7.675	7.133	6.661	6.246	5.880	5.554	5.262	4.999

n	21%	22%	23%	24%	25%	26%	27%	28%	29%	30%
1	0.826	0.820	0.813	0.807	0.800	0.794	0.787	0.781	0.775	0.769
2	1.510	1.492	1.474	1.457	1.440	1.424	1.407	1.392	1.376	1.361
3	2.074	2.042	2.011	1.981	1.952	1.923	1.896	1.868	1.842	1.816
4	2.540	2.494	2.448	2.404	2.362	2.320	2.280	2.241	2.203	2.166
5	2.926	2.864	2.804	2.745	2.689	2.635	2.583	2.532	2.483	2.436
6	3.245	3.167	3.092	3.021	2.951	2.885	2.821	2.759	2.700	2.643
7	3.508	3.416	3.327	3.242	3.161	3.083	3.009	2.937	2.868	2.802
8	3.726	3.619	3.518	3.421	3.329	3.241	3.156	3.076	2.999	2.925
9	3.905	3.786	3.673	3.566	3.463	3.366	3.273	3.184	3.010	3.019
10	4.054	3.923	3.799	3.682	3.571	3.465	3.364	3.269	3.178	3.092
11	4.177	4.035	3.902	3.776	3.656	3.544	3.437	3.335	3.239	3.147
12	4.279	4.127	3.985	3.851	3.725	3.606	3.493	3.387	3.286	3.190
13	4.362	4.203	4.053	3.912	3.780	3.656	3.638	3.427	3.322	3.223
14	4.432	4.265	4.108	3.962	3.824	3.695	3.573	3.459	3.351	3.249
15	4.489	4.315	4.153	4.001	3.859	3.726	3.601	3.483	3.373	3.268
16	4.536	4.357	4.189	4.033	3.887	3.751	3.623	3.503	3.390	3.283
17	4.576	4.391	4.219	4.059	3.910	3.771	3.640	3.518	3.403	3.295
18	4.608	4.419	4.243	4.080	3.928	3.786	3.654	3.529	3.413	3.304
19	4.635	4.442	4.263	4.097	3.942	3.799	3.664	3.539	3.421	3.311
20	4.657	4.460	4.279	4.110	3.954	3.808	3.673	3.546	3.427	3.316
21	4.675	4.476	4.292	4.121	3.963	3.816	3.679	3.551	3.432	3.320
22	4.690	4.488	4.302	4.130	3.971	3.822	3.684	3.556	3.436	3.323
23	4.703	4.499	4.311	4.137	3.976	3.827	3.689	3.559	3.438	3.325
24	4.713	4.507	4.318	4.143	3.981	3.831	3.692	3.562	3.441	3.327
25	4.721	4.514	4.323	4.147	3.985	3.834	3.694	3.564	3.442	3.329
30	4.746	4.534	4.339	4.160	3.995	3.842	3.701	3.569	3.447	3.332
35	4.756	4.541	4.345	4.164	3.998	3.845	3.703	3.571	3.448	3.333
40	4.760	4.544	4.347	4.166	3.999	3.846	3.703	3.571	3.448	3.333
45	4.761	4.545	4.347	4.166	4.000	3.846	3.704	3.571	3.448	3.333
50	4.762	4.545	4.348	4.167	4.000	3.846	3.704	3.571	3.448	3.333

Table II (continued)

n	31%	32%	33%	34%	35%	36%	37%	38%	39%	40%	50%
1	0.763	0.758	0.752	0.746	0.741	0.735	0.730	0.725	0.719	0.714	0.667
2	1.346	1.332	1.317	1.303	1.289	1.276	1.263	1.250	1.237	1.225	1.111
3	1.791	1.766	1.742	1.719	1.696	1.674	1.652	1.630	1.609	1.589	1.407
4	2.131	2.096	2.062	2.029	1.997	1.966	1.936	1.906	1.877	1.849	1.605
5	2.390	2.345	2.302	2.260	2.220	2.181	2.143	2.106	2.070	2.035	1.737
6	2.588	2.534	2.483	2.433	2.386	2.339	2.294	2.251	2.209	2.168	1.824
7	2.739	2.678	2.619	2.562	2.508	2.455	2.404	2.356	2.308	2.263	1.883
8	2.854	2.786	2.721	2.658	2.598	2.540	2.485	2.432	2.380	2.331	1.922
9	2.942	2.868	2.798	2.730	2.665	2.603	2.544	2.487	2.432	2.379	1.948
10	3.009	2.930	2.855	2.784	2.715	2.650	2.587	2.527	2.469	2.414	1.965
11	3.060	2.978	2.899	2.824	2.752	2.683	2.618	2.556	2.496	2.438	1.977
12	3.100	3.013	2.931	2.853	2.779	2.708	2.641	2.576	2.515	2.456	1.985
13	3.129	3.040	2.956	2.876	2.799	2.727	2.658	2.592	2.529	2.469	1.990
14	3.152	3.061	2.974	2.892	2.814	2.740	2.670	2.603	2.539	2.478	1.993
15	3.170	3.076	2.988	2.905	2.826	2.750	2.679	2.611	2.546	2.484	1.995
16	3.183	3.088	2.999	2.914	2.834	2.758	2.685	2.616	2.551	2.489	1.997
17	3.193	3.097	3.007	2.921	2.840	2.763	2.690	2.621	2.555	2.492	1.998
18	3.201	3.104	3.012	2.926	2.844	2.767	2.693	2.624	2.557	2.494	1.999
19	3.207	3.109	3.017	2.930	2.848	2.770	2.696	2.626	2.559	2.496	1.999
20	3.211	3.113	3.020	2.933	2.850	2.772	2.698	2.627	2.561	2.497	1.999
21	3.215	3.116	3.023	2.935	2.852	2.773	2.699	2.629	2.562	2.498	2.000
22	3.217	3.118	3.025	2.937	2.853	2.775	2.700	2.629	2.562	2.499	2.000
23	3.219	3.120	3.026	2.938	2.854	2.775	2.701	2.630	2.563	2.499	2.000
24	3.221	3.121	3.027	2.939	2.855	2.776	2.701	2.630	2.563	2.499	2.000
25	3.222	3.122	3.028	2.939	2.856	2.777	2.702	2.631	2.563	2.499	2.000
30	3.225	3.124	3.030	2.941	2.857	2.778	2.702	2.631	2.564	2.500	2.000
35	3.226	3.125	3.030	2.941	2.857	2.778	2.702	2.632	2.564	2.500	2.000
40	3.226	3.125	3.030	2.941	2.857	2.778	2.702	2.632	2.564	2.500	2.000
45	3.226	3.125	3.030	2.941	2.857	2.778	2.702	2.632	2.564	2.500	2.000
50	3.226	3.125	3.030	2.941	2.857	2.778	2.702	2.632	2.564	2.500	2.000

Table III Future Value of $1 at the End of *n* Years

n	1%	2%	3%	4%	5%	6%	7%	8%	9%	10%
01	1.010	1.020	1.030	1.040	1.050	1.060	1.070	1.080	1.090	1.100
02	1.020	1.040	1.061	1.082	1.103	1.124	1.145	1.166	1.188	1.210
03	1.030	1.061	1.093	1.125	1.158	1.191	1.225	1.260	1.295	1.331
04	1.041	1.082	1.126	1.170	1.216	1.263	1.311	1.361	1.417	1.464
05	1.051	1.104	1.159	1.217	1.276	1.338	1.403	1.469	1.539	1.611
06	1.062	1.126	1.194	1.265	1.340	1.419	1.501	1.587	1.677	1.772
07	1.072	1.149	1.230	1.316	1.407	1.504	1.606	1.714	1.828	1.949
08	1.083	1.172	1.267	1.369	1.478	1.594	1.718	1.851	1.993	2.144
09	1.094	1.195	1.305	1.423	1.551	1.690	1.839	1.999	2.172	2.358
10	1.105	1.219	1.344	1.480	1.629	1.791	1.967	2.159	2.367	2.594
11	1.116	1.243	1.384	1.540	1.710	1.898	2.105	2.332	2.580	2.853
12	1.127	1.268	1.426	1.602	1.796	2.012	2.252	2.518	2.813	3.138
13	1.138	1.294	1.469	1.665	1.886	2.133	2.410	2.720	3.066	3.452
14	1.150	1.320	1.513	1.732	1.980	2.261	2.579	2.937	3.342	3.798
15	1.161	1.346	1.558	1.801	2.079	2.397	2.759	3.172	3.643	4.177
16	1.173	1.373	1.605	1.873	2.183	2.540	2.952	3.426	3.970	4.595
17	1.184	1.400	1.653	1.948	2.292	2.693	3.159	3.700	4.328	5.054
18	1.196	1.428	1.702	2.026	2.407	2.854	3.380	3.996	4.717	5.560
19	1.208	1.457	1.754	2.107	2.527	3.026	3.617	4.316	5.142	6.116
20	1.220	1.486	1.806	2.191	2.653	3.207	3.870	4.661	5.604	6.728
21	1.232	1.516	1.860	2.279	2.786	3.400	4.141	5.034	6.109	7.400
22	1.245	1.546	1.916	2.370	2.925	3.604	4.430	5.437	6.659	8.140
23	1.257	1.577	1.974	2.465	3.072	3.820	4.741	5.871	7.258	8.954
24	1.270	1.608	2.033	2.563	3.225	4.049	5.072	6.341	7.911	9.850
25	1.282	1.641	2.094	2.666	3.386	4.292	5.427	6.849	8.623	10.835

Table III *(continued)*

n	11%	12%	13%	14%	15%	16%	17%	18%	19%	20%
01	1.110	1.120	1.130	1.140	1.150	1.160	1.170	1.180	1.190	1.200
02	1.232	1.254	1.277	1.300	1.323	1.346	1.369	1.392	1.416	1.440
03	1.368	1.405	1.443	1.482	1.521	1.561	1.602	1.643	1.685	1.728
04	1.518	1.574	1.631	1.689	1.749	1.811	1.874	1.939	2.005	2.074
05	1.685	1.762	1.842	1.925	2.011	2.100	2.193	2.288	2.386	2.488
06	1.870	1.974	2.082	2.195	2.313	2.436	2.565	2.700	2.840	2.986
07	2.076	2.211	2.353	2.502	2.660	2.826	3.001	3.186	3.379	3.583
08	2.305	2.476	2.658	2.853	3.059	3.278	3.512	3.759	4.021	4.300
09	2.558	2.773	3.004	3.252	3.518	3.803	4.108	4.436	4.786	5.160
10	2.839	3.106	3.395	3.707	4.046	4.411	4.807	5.234	5.695	6.192
11	3.152	3.479	3.836	4.226	4.652	5.117	5.624	6.176	6.777	7.430
12	3.499	3.896	4.335	4.818	5.350	5.936	6.580	7.288	8.064	8.916
13	3.883	4.364	4.898	5.492	6.153	6.886	7.699	8.599	9.597	10.699
14	4.310	4.887	5.535	6.262	7.076	7.988	9.008	10.147	11.420	12.839
15	4.785	5.474	6.254	7.138	8.137	9.266	10.539	11.974	13.590	15.407
16	5.311	6.130	7.067	8.137	9.358	10.748	12.330	14.129	16.172	18.488
17	5.895	6.866	7.986	9.277	10.761	12.468	14.427	16.672	19.244	22.186
18	6.544	7.690	9.024	10.575	12.376	14.463	16.879	19.673	22.901	26.623
19	7.263	8.613	10.107	12.056	14.232	16.777	19.748	23.214	27.252	31.948
20	8.062	9.646	11.523	13.744	16.367	19.461	23.106	27.393	32.429	38.338
21	8.949	10.804	13.021	15.668	18.822	22.575	27.034	32.324	38.591	46.005
22	9.934	12.100	14.714	17.861	21.645	26.186	31.629	38.142	45.923	55.206
23	11.026	13.552	16.627	20.362	24.892	30.376	37.006	45.008	54.649	66.247
24	12.239	15.179	18.788	23.212	28.625	35.236	43.297	53.109	65.032	79.497
25	13.586	17.000	21.232	26.462	32.919	40.874	50.658	62.669	77.388	95.396

Table IV Future Value of $1 per Year for n Years

n	1%	2%	3%	4%	5%	6%	7%	8%	9%	10%
01	1.000	1.000	1.000	1.000	1.000	1.000	1.000	1.000	1.000	1.000
02	2.010	2.020	2.030	2.040	2.050	2.060	2.070	2.080	2.090	2.100
03	3.030	3.060	3.091	3.122	3.153	3.183	3.214	3.246	3.278	3.310
04	4.060	4.122	4.184	4.246	4.310	4.375	4.440	4.506	4.573	4.641
05	5.101	5.204	5.309	5.416	5.526	5.637	5.718	5.866	5.984	6.105
06	6.152	6.308	6.468	6.633	6.802	6.975	7.153	7.336	7.523	7.716
07	7.214	7.434	7.663	7.898	8.142	8.393	8.654	8.923	9.200	9.487
08	8.286	8.583	8.892	9.214	9.549	9.898	10.260	10.637	11.028	11.436
09	9.369	9.755	10.159	10.583	11.027	11.491	11.978	12.488	13.021	13.579
10	10.462	10.950	11.464	12.006	12.578	13.181	13.816	14.487	15.193	15.937
11	11.567	12.169	12.808	13.486	14.207	14.972	15.784	16.645	17.560	18.531
12	12.683	13.412	14.192	15.026	15.917	16.870	17.888	18.977	20.141	21.384
13	13.809	14.680	15.618	16.627	17.713	18.882	20.141	21.495	22.953	24.523
14	14.947	15.974	17.086	18.292	19.599	21.051	22.550	24.215	26.019	27.975
15	16.097	17.293	18.599	20.024	21.579	23.276	25.129	27.152	29.361	31.772
16	17.258	18.639	20.157	21.825	23.657	25.673	27.888	30.324	33.003	35.950
17	18.430	20.012	21.762	23.698	25.840	28.213	30.840	33.750	30.973	40.545
18	19.615	21.412	23.414	25.645	28.132	30.906	33.999	37.450	41.301	45.599
19	20.811	22.841	25.117	27.671	30.539	33.760	37.379	41.446	46.019	51.159
20	22.019	24.297	26.870	29.778	33.066	36.786	40.995	45.762	51.160	57.275
21	23.239	25.783	28.676	31.969	35.719	39.993	44.865	50.423	56.764	64.002
22	24.472	27.299	30.537	34.248	38.505	42.392	49.006	55.457	62.873	71.403
23	25.716	28.845	32.453	36.618	41.430	46.996	53.436	60.893	69.532	79.543
24	26.973	30.422	34.426	39.083	44.502	50.816	58.177	66.765	76.790	88.497
25	28.243	32.030	36.459	41.646	47.727	54.865	63.249	73.106	84.701	98.347

Table IV *(continued)*

n	11%	12%	13%	14%	15%	16%	17%	18%	19%	20%
01	1.000	1.000	1.000	1.000	1.000	1.000	1.000	1.000	1.000	1.000
02	2.110	2.120	2.130	2.140	2.150	2.160	2.170	2.180	2.190	2.200
03	3.342	3.374	3.401	3.439	3.472	3.501	3.539	3.572	3.606	3.640
04	4.710	4.779	4.850	4.921	4.993	5.067	5.141	5.216	5.290	5.368
05	6.229	6.353	6.480	6.610	6.742	6.877	7.015	7.154	7.297	7.442
06	7.913	8.115	8.323	8.536	8.754	8.978	9.207	9.442	9.683	9.930
07	9.784	10.089	10.405	10.730	11.067	11.414	11.772	12.142	12.523	12.916
08	11.859	12.300	12.757	13.233	13.723	14.240	14.774	15.327	15.902	16.499
09	14.164	14.776	15.415	16.085	16.786	17.518	18.285	19.086	19.924	20.799
10	16.722	17.549	18.420	19.337	20.304	21.321	22.393	23.521	24.709	25.959
11	19.562	20.655	21.815	23.044	24.349	25.733	27.200	28.755	30.404	32.150
12	22.714	24.133	25.650	27.271	29.002	30.850	32.824	34.931	37.180	39.580
13	26.212	28.029	29.985	32.089	34.352	36.786	39.404	42.219	45.245	48.497
14	30.095	32.393	34.883	37.581	40.505	43.672	47.103	50.818	54.842	59.196
15	34.405	37.280	40.418	43.842	47.581	51.659	56.112	60.965	66.263	72.035
16	39.190	42.753	46.672	50.981	55.717	60.925	66.647	72.939	79.853	87.440
17	44.501	48.883	53.739	59.118	65.073	71.675	78.984	87.067	96.021	105.931
18	50.696	55.750	61.725	68.393	75.840	84.144	93.406	103.740	115.266	128.117
19	56.939	63.440	70.054	78.971	88.213	98.606	110.285	123.414	138.166	154.740
20	64.203	72.053	80.946	91.029	102.444	115.380	130.033	146.628	165.418	186.688
21	72.265	81.709	92.469	104.768	118.810	134.841	153.139	174.021	197.847	225.026
22	81.214	92.500	105.491	120.436	137.632	157.415	180.172	206.345	236.438	271.031
23	91.145	104.603	120.205	138.297	159.276	183.601	211.801	244.487	282.362	326.237
24	102.174	118.155	136.831	158.659	184.168	213.978	248.808	289.494	337.010	392.484
25	114.413	133.334	155.620	181.871	212.793	249.214	292.105	342.603	402.042	471.981

Glossary

A

AAA or Aaa (triple A)/Highest-quality rating assigned to corporate bonds by the two major bond-rating agencies; Standard and Poor's uses the AAA designation and Moody's uses Aaa.

Aaa/AA/"Split" rating. In this case, Moody's has assigned a triple A rating and Standard and Poor's a double A rating.

Abandonment value/Amount that can be realized by liquidating an investment before the end of its life.

Accelerated depreciation/Method of depreciation where the cost of an asset is written off at a faster rate than under the straight-line method. Two techniques used are sum-of-the-years digits and double declining balance.

Acceptance/Also called a banker's acceptance. A bill for goods shipped (generally to an importer) for which a commercial bank *accepts* the obligation to pay the amount stated on the face of the bill on the date specified. One of several short-term money-market instruments used in the United States.

Accruals/Expenses incurred but not paid.

Acid test/Ratio of a company's current assets (excluding inventories) to its current liabilities. Used as a supplementary measure of the firm's liquidity; a ratio larger than unity is regarded as excellent.

Acquisition/The purchase of one firm by another, with the acquirer becoming the surviving enterprise.

Aging schedule/Schedule that indicates length of time accounts receivable have been outstanding and gives the percentage of receivables not past due and the percentage past due by specified periods. Also used for accounts payable.

Amortize/Repay in installments.

Annuity/Stream of level payments.

Arbitrage/Process of selling overvalued and buying undervalued assets in related markets which are temporarily out of equilibrium.

Assets/All items owned by a business firm or individual (including property rights) which have a money value. Items listed on the left-hand side of a balance sheet in company accounts in the United States.

Auction/General method used for selling new issues of United States government securities. In a normal auction (sometimes referred to as an "English auction"), individual price and quantity bids by perspective purchasers are accepted at the bid price starting with the highest offer and going down the ladder until all securities are sold. In the so-called "Dutch auction" (used only infrequently), *all* successful bidders pay a uniform price, that is, the lowest price accepted to sell the entire issue.

B

Balance sheet/Statement of assets, liabilities, and capital at the close of business on the date indicated. In the United States, the tradition is to value assets and liabilities on the basis of their *historical* or *original* dollar cost.

Balloon payment/Final large payment that results when a debt is not fully amortized; the preceding payments are smaller.

Banker's acceptance/*See Acceptance.* When purchased by a commercial bank other than the accepting bank, a banker's acceptance is reported and counted as part of commercial and industrial loans.

Bankruptcy/Procedure for formally liquidating or reorganizing a business; carried out under the jurisdiction of the courts.

Basis point/One one-hundredth of a percentage point; used for measuring small changes in interest rates.

Beta coefficient/Measure of the sensitivity of the return on a firm's shares relative to general market movements.

Bond/Long-term debt instrument.

Book value/Tangible net worth per share of common stock as shown in accounting records; net assets available for common stock divided by the number of shares.

Break-even analysis/Analytical technique for studying the relation between profits and sales volume, or between EBIT and EPS.

Break-even point/Volume of sales at which total costs equal total revenues (profits equal zero). In EBIT/EPS analysis, EBIT level at which EPS is equal under two alternative plans.

Budget/Generic term used in various specific ways to describe the process of projecting or forecasting receipts and expenditures over a defined future period. Also used for the document that embodies such projections.

Bylaws/Rules formally adopted by shareholders of a corporation to guide the conduct of its directors and officers. Bylaws may limit, but not extend, the powers conferred by the corporate charter.

C

Call/Option to buy (call) a share of stock at a specified price within a specified period. Also, redeeming a bond or preferred stock issue before its normal maturity, usually at a premium above face value.

Call premium/Amount in excess of par value that must be paid when a security is called.

Call privilege/Provision incorporated in a bond or preferred-stock agreement giving the issuer the right to call (or repurchase) the security at a specified price.

Capital asset/Asset such as plant or machinery with an expected productive life of more than 1 year that is not bought and sold in the ordinary course of business.

Capital asset pricing model (CAPM)/Theory dealing with the structure of security prices and yields under conditions of risk.

Capital expenditure (budgeting) decisions/Decisions concerning expenditures on long-lived assets such as plants and equipment.

Capital gains/Profits on the sale of capital assets held 6 months or more.

Capital losses/Losses on the sale of capital assets.

Capital market/Financial markets for long-term debt issues and stocks.

Capital rationing/Situation in which a firm's total capital expenditure is constrained by a fixed maximum regardless of opportunities.

Capital structure/Permanent long-term financing of the firm, including long-term debt, preferred stock, and net worth; does not include short-term debt or reserve accounts.

Capitalization rate/Rate at which a stream of future cash flows is discounted to find the present value; also called *discount rate.*

Cartel/Agreement among business enterprises (or nations) to limit competition among themselves, especially on price.

Cash budget/Time-phased schedule of cash receipts and disbursements.

Cash cycle/Time between payment for raw materials and collection of accounts receivable.

Cash flow/Total receipts from sales *less* actual cash expenditures required to achieve those sales.

Certificate of deposit (CD)/Evidence of short-term debt issued by a commercial bank (with a specified rate of interest and maturity date) to a depositor of funds. An important money-market instrument widely used by corporate treasurers as a vehicle for placing temporarily idle funds. Large-denomination CD's (i.e., $100,000 or more) are not subject to the interest rate ceilings imposed by Regulation Q on other time and savings accounts at banks.

Chattel mortgage/Mortgage on personal property (not real property), such as equipment.

Circulating capital/Term used by many earlier works in economics to describe *working capital.*

Claim/Entitlement to a given sum of money.

Clears the market/Equates supply and demand.

Coefficient of variation/Standard deviation divided by the mean.

Collateral/Assets used to secure a loan.

Commercial paper/Unsecured, short-term notes issued by large firms to meet seasonal financing needs. Also used as a vehicle for investing short-term corporate funds.

Commitment fee/Fee paid to a lender to ensure access to credit.

Common stock/Share in a firm that entitles the holder to a portion of earnings or assets of the firm after creditors and preferred owners are compensated.

Compensating balance/Required minimum checking account balance that must be maintained by a firm with a commercial bank; generally, 10–15 percent of the amount of loans outstanding. Varies with money-market conditions.

Competitive bidding/Procedure for selling new securities via open bidding by prospective buyers, as opposed to *negotiated* sale

municipalities, and regulated industries such as public utilities and railroads.

Composition/Method of reorganization where creditors voluntarily reduce their claims on the debtor firm.

Compound interest/Interest earned on the initial principal and also on the accumulated interest of prior periods.

Compounding/Process of determining the future value of a payment or series of payments when compound interest is applied.

Conditional sales contract/Method of financing new equipment by paying in installments, during which time the lender retains title to the equipment.

Congeneric merger/The merger of two firms in essentially the same or closely related industries.

Conglomerate merger/The merger of two or more firms in completely different industries.

Consolidated financial statement/Financial statement which combines a parent company's balance sheet and income statement with those of its domestic and financial subsidiaries. The SEC requires consolidation when a corporation owns over 50 percent of another business entity.

Consolidation/The merger of two existing firms to form a new combined firm with a new name.

Consumer sovereignty/Social system in which the consumer, rather than the state, determines what will be produced.

Continuous compounding/Compounding interest continuously rather than in discrete time periods.

Contractual claim/Entitlement to fixed future sums of money secured by a written contract.

Conversion price/Price at which convertible securities can be converted into common stock.

Conversion ratio/Number of shares of common stock that may be obtained by converting one convertible bond or share of convertible preferred stock.

Convertible securities/Bonds or preferred stocks that are exchangeable at the option of the holder for common stock.

Corporation/Entity created by law, empowered to own assets, incur liabilities, and engage in specified activities.

Correlation coefficient/Measure of the relationship between two variables.

Cost benefit analysis/System for evaluating a course of action by comparing the economic costs to the economic benefits expected from that action.

Cost of capital/Rate of return required by the market.

Coupon rate/Annual payment offered by a contractual bond.

Covariance/Correlation between two variables (r_{XY}) multiplied by the standard deviation of each variable $(\sigma_X \sigma_Y)$.

Covenant/Clause in loan agreement . that is designed to protect the lender.

Covered rate of interest/The interest rate that can be earned in investments in foreign currencies with exchange rate risk eliminated.

Credit analysis/Analysis aimed at determining the ability of a firm to meet its short-term obligations. The major sources of data and information are (1) Dun and Bradstreet credit reports and (2) Robert Morris Associates, an association of bank credit managers which provides specialized information for member banks.

Current assets/Assets convertible into cash or generally expected to be converted into cash within the next 12 months. Included are such items as cash, marketable securities, notes and accounts receivable from customers, inventories, and prepaid expenses.

Current liabilities/Items due and payable within 1 year.

Current ratio/Ratio of current assets to current liabilities.

Cut-off rate/Minimum rate of return acceptable on investment opportunities.

D

Debenture/Unsecured bond.

Debt ratio/Total debt divided by total assets.

Default/Failure to fulfill a contract.

Depreciation/Literally, a decrease in value. Methods used by accountants to allocate the original cost of a capital asset to each time period over which the asset is used to produce revenue. Depreciation methods used for purposes of computing taxable income may differ from methods used for computing income reported to shareholders.

Devaluation/Reduction in the value of one country's currency relative to other currencies.

Director/Individual member of board of directors of a corporation which serves collectively as agent of the corporation and is responsible for its governance in the interests of shareholders. In the United States, the board of directors delegates most of its powers to appointed corporate officers who conduct the day-to-day management of the corporation, but the board (through its committees) retains direct operating control and responsibility for major matters such as the external and internal auditing of operations, dividend policy, corporate conduct and ethics, executive compensation, and large capital expenditures.

Discount basis/Conventional method of measuring or quoting annual rate of interest on several short-term financial instruments such as Treasury bills, commercial paper, and banker's acceptances.

Discount rate/Interest rate used in calculating present value.

Discounted cash flow (DCF) technique/Method of analysis that takes account of the time value of money by applying the concepts of compound interest. The value of an asset can be expressed as the sum of all payments that asset will generate, discounted to their present value. Criteria used are internal rate of return (IRR) rule, net present value (NPV) rule, and terminal value (TV) rule.

Disinvestment (divestment)/Selling or abandoning a previous investment.

Dispersion/Scatter of results (actual or expected) around the most likely or expected result.

Diversifiable risk/Risk that can be eliminated by diversification.

Dividend/Payment made on a residual claim, such as to stockholders.

Dividend yield/Ratio of the current dividend to the current price of a share of stock.

DuPont system/System of analysis originally developed by the DuPont Company, designed to show the relationship between return on investment, asset turnover, and profit margin.

E

Earnings before interest and taxes (EBIT)/ Operating profit.

Earnings per share (EPS)/Profit after taxes (PAT) divided by number of shares outstanding.

Economic order quantity (EOQ)/Optimal order quantity as function of usage per period in units, ordering cost per order, and carrying cost per unit per period.

Economies of scale/Economic savings due to increasing size as fixed costs are spread over a larger activities base.

Equipment certificates/Debt obligations issued by railroads and other transportation companies for the purpose of financing equipment purchases. Interest and principal are secured by a lien on specified items of transportation equipment.

Equity/Net worth of a business, including capital stock, capital (paid-in) surplus, earned surplus (retained earnings), and certain net worth reserves. *Common equity* is the part of the total net worth that belongs to common shareholders. *Total equity* includes preferred shareholders.

Ex-dividend date/Date on which the right to the current dividend no longer accompanies a stock; 4 working days before the record date.

Ex-rights/Date on which new offering purchase rights are no longer transferred to the purchaser of the stock.

Exchange rate/Rate at which currency of one country can be exchanged for currency of another country.

Exercise price/Price that must be paid for a share of common stock when it is bought by exercising a warrant.

Expected rate of return, $E(R)$/Rate of return a firm or individual expects to realize from an investment; the mean of the probability distribution of possible returns.

Extension/Method of reorganization in which creditors voluntarily postpone the date of required payment on past-due obligations.

Externalities/Cost or benefits not generally counted within the accepted methods of accounting for any given entity or subentity.

F

Factoring/Method of financing where the firm sells its accounts receivable to another party, a factor, for cash.

Field warehouse/Warehouse on the premises of the borrowing firm, operated by a warehouse company under lock and key.

Financial Accounting Standards Board (FASB)/ A seven member board established in 1973 to promulgate United States financial accounting standards and practices for the profession.

Financial lease/Lease that does not provide for maintenance services by lessor, is not cancellable, and is fully amortized over the life of the lease. (See Operating lease.)

Financial leverage/Ratio of debt to equity, or ratio of fixed financial charges to operating profit before fixed charges.

Financial risk/Portion of total corporate risk that results from using debt (over and above basic business risk).

Financial structure/Composition of the right-hand side of the balance sheet.

First-in first-out (FIFO)/Method of valuing inventories and cost of goods sold. Under inflationary conditions the method overstates ending inventory, understates cost of goods sold, and hence overstates profits. (*See Last-in first-out.*)

Fixed assets/Assets that do not vary with short-run changes in level of a firm's operations, for example, plants and equipment.

Fixed costs/Costs that do not vary with the level of output.

Floating exchange rates/Exchange rates that float up or down with supply and demand in the foreign exchange markets.

Flotation cost/Cost of issuing new securities.

Forward rate/Exchange rate at which a foreign currency can be bought or sold now for delivery at a specified future date. The forward market is used by corporate treasurers to hedge against possible losses from unexpected fluctuations in exchange rates of foreign currencies in which a company has a financial interest.

Future value (FV)/Present value compounded forward through time at an appropriate interest rate.

G

Goodwill/Intangible assets of a firm equal to the excess of the price paid for a going concern over its book value.

Guaranteed stock/Preferred or common stock for which the payment of dividends is guaranteed by another corporation.

H

Hedge/To reduce risks by contracting with another party to bear the risk. Transactions in foreign currencies can be hedged by buying or selling foreign currencies in the forward market.

Horizontal integration/Congeneric mergers involving firms in the same line of business.

Hurdle rate/Minimum acceptable rate of return on a project; if the expected rate of return is below the hurdle rate, the project is not acceptable.

I

Illiquid/Not easily convertible into the sum of money originally invested.

Income bond/Bond that pays interest only if the current interest is earned.

Incremental cash flow/Cash flow directly attributable to an investment project.

Indenture/Agreement between the issuer of a bond and the bondholder.

Insolvency/Inability to meet maturing debt obligations.

Interest rate parity theorem/A theorem relating interest rates in two countries to the current and forward exchange rates of the two countries.

Internal rate of return (IRR)/Rate that discounts all cash flows, including the outlay, to zero. Equivalent to the yield to maturity on a bond.

Investment/1. Commitment of funds for the purpose of future gains.
2. Commitment of funds for acquiring tangible capital goods.

Investment banker/Middleman who underwrites and distributes new investment securities, bringing together the seller of securities (the firm) and the buyer (the public).

Investment tax credit/Specified percentage of the dollar amount of new investments in certain categories of assets that can be deducted from income tax by a business firm.

J

Junior securities/Securities that have a lower-priority claim on the assets and income of the issuer than senior securities.

L

Last-in first-out (LIFO)/Alternative method of valuing inventories and cost of goods sold. A company may switch to the LIFO method for tax purposes only if it also uses LIFO for reporting purposes. (*See First-in first-out.*)

Lease/Contractual agreement under which the owner of an asset (lessor) permits another party (lessee) to use the asset for a specified period of time in return for a specified payment.

Leverage factor/Ratio of debt to equity, or ratio of fixed charges of debt to total earnings before deduction of such charges.

Lien/Lender's claim on assets pledged to secure a loan.

Line of credit/Agreement under which a firm can borrow up to an agreed upon maximum amount during an agreed upon period of time (often 1 year) from a bank or insurance company.

Liquid asset/Asset that can be sold on short notice for a price about which there is little uncertainty.

Liquidity (of firm)/Maturity structure of balance sheet.

Listed securities/Securities traded on an organized security exchange.

Lock-box/Service for speeding up collections and reducing float.

London Money Market/Outside of New York, the largest and best developed of the world's money centers. The vast Euro-dollar market which is widely used by treasurers of multinational companies is largely centered in London.

Long-term debt/Contractual obligations with more than 10 years to maturity at time of issue. The line between intermediate-term and long-term debt is not precise.

M

Marginal cost/Cost of an additional unit.

Marginal revenue/Gross revenue from one additional unit of output.

Market portfolio/Representative portfolio of all risky assets.

Maturity/Period of time over which interest and final principal payments on a loan must be paid.

Merger/Combination of two or more previously existing companies into a single entity.

Money market/Financial markets in which short-term debt instruments such as Treasury bills, commercial paper, and certificates of deposit are traded.

Mortgage/Pledge of designated property as security for a loan.

Municipal bond/Bond issued by a state, city, or other political subdivision on which interest is exempt from federal income tax.

N

Net present value (NPV)/Present value of future returns, discounted at the required rate of return, minus the present value of the cost of the investment.

Net worth/Capital and surplus of a firm; capital stock, capital surplus (paid-in capital), earned surplus (retained earnings), and sometimes certain reserves and preferred stock.

Nominal interest rate/Contract rate of interest. (*See Real rate.*)

Nondiversifiable risk/Risk that cannot be eliminated by diversification.

Normal probability distribution/Symmetrical, bell-shaped curve.

O

Objective probability distributions/Probability distributions determined by statistical procedures based on historical experience.

Operating lease/Lease contract under which lessor provides maintenance and insurance. Operating leases normally are cancellable and normally do not fully amortize the equipment over the life of the lease. (*See Financial lease.*)

Operating leverage/Sensitivity of operating profit to changes in sales; depends on ratio of fixed operating costs to total operating costs.

Operating risk/Risk inherent in a firm's operations. Synonymous with business risk. Contrasted with financial risk.

Opportunity cost/Cost of a course of action measured by benefits foregone on alternative actions.

Opportunity rate/Rate of return foregone on the best alternative investment available.

Ordinary income/Income from the normal operations of a firm; excludes gains or losses from the sale of capital assets or other nonrecurring events.

Organized exchanges/Formal organizations that conduct an auction market in listed investment securities.

Over-the-counter market/Market for securities not listed on organized exchanges.

P

Par value/Nominal or face value of a stock or bond; has some legal and accounting significance but little economic significance.

Partnership/Firm involving two or more partners who are individually and collectively liable for all the firm's debts.

Payback period/Length of time required to recoup the outlay of an investment.

Payout ratio/Percentage of earnings paid out in the form of dividends.

Perpetuity/Stream of level payments (annuity) that continues forever.

Portfolio/Combination or collection of assets.

Portfolio effect/Reduction in variability or risk due to diversification effect.

Portfolio theory/Concerns the selection of portfolios of investments that provide the highest expected return for a specified degree of risk.

Preemptive right/Provision contained in some corporate charters and bylaws that gives common shareholders the right to purchase new issues of common stock (or securities convertible to common stock) on a pro rata basis.

Preferred stock/Share in a firm that entitles the holder to a fixed portion of the earnings or assets of the firm after creditors are compensated and ahead of common shareholders.

Present value (PV)/Discounted value today of a future payment, or stream of payments.

Price/earnings ratio (P/E)/Ratio of market price of stock to earnings; high P/E ratios indicate high expected growth or low risk.

Prime rate/Lowest rate of interest commercial banks charge to business borrowers with the highest credit rating.

Principal/Original amount of an investment or a loan.

Pro forma/"As if." A pro forma financial statement may be prepared to show how the actual statement would look if future or past projections or changes in corporate structure were realized.

Profit center/Unit of a large, decentralized firm established for budgeting or other management control purposes. Permits fixing of responsibility for profits and/or return on investment.

Profit margin/Difference between revenues and total expenses, including taxes, expressed as a percentage of revenues.

Profitability index (PI)/Present value of cash inflows per dollar of investment.

Prospectus/Document describing a new security issue; issued to meet SEC requirements.

Proxy/Document giving one person the authority or power to act for another.

Proxy fight/An attempt to gain control of a company via shareholder voting.

R

Rate of return/Generic term measuring rate of profit per dollar of investment. Can be measured in accounting terms (accounting return on investment, AROI) or in discounted cash flow terms (internal rate of return, IRR).

Real rate/Nominal rate adjusted to remove the effect of a changing price level; rate measured in dollars of constant purchasing power.

Record date/Date established by a firm as the final date that gives a shareholder rights to a current dividend or rights to subscribe to a new offering.

Recourse agreement/When accounts receivable are sold to a factor *with recourse*, if the account receivable cannot be collected, the selling firm must repurchase the account from the factor. When accounts receivable are sold to a factor *without recourse*, the factor must absorb bad debts.

Rediscount rate/Rate of interest at which a commercial member bank may borrow from a Federal Reserve Bank.

Refunding/Replacement of an old debt issue through the sale of a new issue.

Reinvestment rate/Rate of return at which cash flows from an investment can be reinvested. In calculating present value, the assumed reinvestment rate is used as the discount rate (required rate of return).

Reorganization/Financial restructuring of a firm in financial difficulties under the provisions of the federal Bankruptcy Act.

Required rate of return (RRR)/Rate of return that suppliers of capital (the financial markets) expect to receive for the use of the capital. The RRR is a market-determined opportunity rate.

Residual claim/Common stock; a claim entitled to all earnings and assets after prior claims have been fully satisfied.

Residual value/Value of leased property at the end of the lease period.

Retained earnings/Portion of earnings not paid out in dividends.

Return on investment (ROI)/Return per dollar of investment; measure of the efficiency with which capital resources are used. (*See Rate of return.*)

Revenue bonds/Tax-exempt municipal bonds, interest on which is serviced by the revenues from specified facilities rather than by taxes. Recent legislation allows business corporations, working through a political subdivision, to finance their major pollution-control expenditures through the issue of revenue bonds.

Right/Short-term option to buy a specified number of shares of a new issue of securities at a specified subscription price; issued to existing shareholders.

Risk/Degree of uncertainty about an outcome; exposure to chance of loss.

Risk premium/Required rate of return over and above the return on a riskless investment.

S

Safety stocks/Inventory held to reduce the probability of stockouts.

Sale and leaseback/Procedure where a firm sells land, buildings or equipment to another party and, at the same time, makes an agreement to lease the property back for a specified period.

Salvage value/Value of a capital asset at the end of a specified period; (see Residual value).

Senior securities/Claims that must be satisfied before payments can be made to more junior securities.

Sensitivity analysis/Technique for determining the effect of changes in individual underlying variables on the final outcome.

Short-term debt/Obligations with less than 1 year to maturity.

Simple interest/Interest rate applicable when interest is earned only on the initial principal.

Simulation/Technique where probable future events are simulated on a computer.

Sinking fund/Required annual payment over and above interest designed gradually to retire a bond or a preferred stock issue.

Small Business Administration (SBA)/Government agency organized to aid small firms.

Sole Proprietorship/Firm owned by one individual.

Spot rate/The current rate of exchange between two currencies.

Standard deviation/Measure of the variability of a set of observations from its average value.

Stock dividend/Dividend paid in the form of additional shares of stock rather than cash.

Stock split/Accounting transaction to increase the number of shares outstanding.

Stockout/Depletion of inventory.

Subordinated debenture/Bond that has a claim on income and assets only after all obligations to more senior debt have been paid.

Subscription price/Price at which a security may be purchased in a rights offering.

Synergy/The "two plus two equals five effect," where, for example, a merger effects operating savings that increase the joint earnings of two merging companies.

Systematic risk/Risk that cannot be eliminated by diversification. Nondiversifiable risk.

T

Tender offers/Direct offer by a firm to shareholders to purchase stock, either its own or of another firm.

Term loan/Loan obtained for a period of more than 1 year and less than 8–10 years; usually amortized.

Terminal warehouse/Public warehouse used by many firms to store inventory.

Trade credit/Credit extended in connection with goods purchased for resale and recorded as an account payable by the buying firm.

Transactions exposure/The risk of a change in exchange rate between the time a contract is consummated and the time payment is made.

Translation exposure/The exposure to changes in income or net worth in connection with assets held in foreign countries, such exposure resulting from accounting conventions and changes in exchange rates rather than from specific transactions.

Treasury stock/Common stock repurchased by the issuing firm.

Trust receipt/Instrument acknowledging that certain goods are held in trust.

Trustee/Representative of bondholders who sees that the terms of the indenture are met.

Turnover/1. Frequency with which inventories are converted into sales, generally measured by dividing annual cost of goods sold by average inventory.

2. In British and some continental usage, refers to sales volume.

U

Underwrite/To buy new issues of securities from the issuing firm and resell them to the public. Normally a function of investment banking firms.

Underwriting syndicate/Group of investment banking firms formed to purchase and distribute a new issue of securities.

Unlisted securities/Securities traded in the over-the-counter market.

Unsecured loan/Loan against which no specific assets are pledged as collateral.

Usury/The charging of a higher rate of interest on a loan than the ceiling rate set by state laws. Corporate obligations are generally exempt from usury laws.

Utility theory/Theory dealing with the relationships among money income, the utility of money to an individual, and the individual's willingness to accept risk.

Utilities/Generic term used for securities of electric, gas, telephone, water, and other regulated public utilities. Railroads are also regulated public utilities in the legal sense, but their securities are classified separately.

V

Vertical integration/Congeneric mergers involving activities at different stages in a production process; for example, the acquisition of an aluminum fabricating plant by a company involved primarily in aluminum reduction.

W

Warehouse receipt/Receipt acknowledging storage of specified goods frequently used as collateral for short-term bank loans.

Warrant/Option to buy a specified number of shares of common stock at a specified exercise price.

Working capital/Current assets of a firm: cash, marketable securities, accounts receivable, and inventories. *Gross working capital* is total current assets. *Net Working capital* is current assets minus current liabilities.

Write-off/Also write-down. To recognize a loss or an asset on a corporation's books of account.

Y

Yield to maturity (YTM)/Internal rate of return on a long-term bond.

Index